LINGUISTIC ANALYSIS

of the

GREEK NEW TESTAMENT

Studies in Tools, Methods, and Practice

STANLEY E. PORTER

Baker Academic

a division of Baker Publishing Group

Grand Rapids, Michigan

© 2015 by Stanley E. Porter

Published by Baker Academic
a division of Baker Publishing Group
P.O. Box 6287, Grand Rapids, MI 49516-6287
www.bakeracademic.com

Printed and bound by CPI Group (UK) Ltd, Croydon, CR0 4YY

Library of Congress Cataloging-in-Publication Data
Porter, Stanley E., 1956– author.
    Linguistic analysis of the Greek New Testament : studies in tools, methods, and practice / Stanley E. Porter.
        pages cm
    Includes bibliographical references and indexes.
    ISBN 978-0-8010-4998-9 (pbk.)
    1. Greek language, Biblical. 2. Bible. New Testament—Language, style. I. Title.
PA810.P56 2015
487'.4—dc23   2014046440

Unless otherwise indicated, Scripture quotations are the author's translation.

15   16   17   18   19   20   21   7   6   5   4   3   2   1

Dedicated to
Lorraine DeHaan Porter
and
Wendy J. Porter
Two Extraordinary Women of God

Contents

Preface

All of the essays in this volume address matters of the Greek New Testament, especially in its linguistic dimensions, variously conceived and defined. There are some theoretical essays, but most of them are applied to particular problems and texts within the Greek New Testament.

None of the essays in this volume has been published before, although one of them draws on a paper published previously. However, the essays were written for a variety of original purposes. Most of them—somewhere around seventeen of them, if I have remembered and counted correctly—were originally delivered at conferences such as the Society of Biblical Literature or Society for New Testament Studies or as invited papers (sometimes both). I appreciated the responses that I received from those who attended, heard, and discussed the papers further. I am especially appreciative of one student at Westminster Seminary in Korea who took the time to go through one paper in detail and provide written comments. These were very helpful, and I am sure that if I read Korean, I would have benefited even further from additional comments he made. In any case, thank you to all who took these papers seriously and responded to them. I also am thankful for the fervent and continuous debate with my former colleague Professor Arthur Gibson about one of the papers. I deeply miss these discussions, and I wish we had been able to continue them over the years. I am sure I have not convinced you, Arthur, about proper nouns, but I have done my best. I am also thankful for comments made on various papers by several of my students, former students, friends, and colleagues, including (but not inclusively) Gus Konkel, Matthew Brook O'Donnell, Hughson Ong, Francis Pang, Andrew Pitts, Steven Studebaker, Randall Tan, and Cynthia Long Westfall, who have even gone so far as to suggest terms and wordings that I have adopted. I also thank Bryan Fletcher for compiling the indexes.

Getting these papers into publishable shape has required the work of two people in particular. I thank my former student and now colleague Christopher Land for initially editing and setting up most of these files for publication. He offered much editorial help and many useful comments on the various essays, from which I have greatly benefited. I also thank my former student Gregory Fewster for his similar help, especially with a couple of essays that were far from being in the complete form that they needed to be. Both of these colleagues have taken on this project with fervor and made the final product much better than it would have been. They not only paid attention to the many small things but also offered global comments and criticism, to the point of suggesting other words and adding words and sentences (and sometimes more!) here and there (many, if not most, of which I have gladly accepted and incorporated), along with rewriting numerous sections. I am very grateful to both for their excellent work.

These papers were mostly written during my time at two different institutions. The University of Surrey Roehampton (now Roehampton University) and McMaster Divinity College both provided the opportunity to complete the research and writing of these papers. Even though I am president of the latter institution, and that is truly my full-time day (and sometimes also night) job, I have been supported in my off-hours research pursuits.

I also thank my friends at Baker Academic for their help in making this project possible, especially James Ernest.

I conclude with thanks once again to my tremendous wife, Wendy, both for being an academic colleague extraordinaire and, far more importantly, for being the soul and spirit of our lives together.

Abbreviations

General

chap(s).	chapter(s)	SIL	Summer Institute of Linguistics
col(s).	column(s)		
esp.	especially	SFL	systemic functional linguistics
ibid.	in the same source		
p(p).	page(s)	v(v).	verse(s)
rev.	revised		

Ancient Texts, Text Types, and Versions

LXX	Septuagint	*Literature*. University of California, Irvine, 1972–. http://www.tlg.uci.edu/
MT	Masoretic Text	
TLG	*Thesaurus linguae Graecae: A Digital Library of Greek*	

Modern Versions

AV	Authorized Version	LB	The Living Bible
BBE	The Bible in Basic English	NASB	New American Standard Bible
CEB	Common English Bible		
CEV	Contemporary English Version	NEB	New English Bible
		NET	New English Translation (The NET Bible)
ESV	English Standard Version		
GNB	Good News Bible	NIV	New International Version
HCSB	Holman Christian Standard Bible	NJB	New Jerusalem Bible
		NKJV	New King James Version
JB	Jerusalem Bible	NLT	New Living Translation

REB   Revised English Bible   TNIV   Today's New International
RSV   Revised Standard Version   Version

Hebrew Bible / Old Testament

Gen.	Genesis	Song	Song of Songs
Exod.	Exodus	Isa.	Isaiah
Lev.	Leviticus	Jer.	Jeremiah
Num.	Numbers	Lam.	Lamentations
Deut.	Deuteronomy	Ezek.	Ezekiel
Josh.	Joshua	Dan.	Daniel
Judg.	Judges	Hos.	Hosea
Ruth	Ruth	Joel	Joel
1–2 Sam.	1–2 Samuel	Amos	Amos
1–2 Kings	1–2 Kings	Obad.	Obadiah
1–2 Chron.	1–2 Chronicles	Jon.	Jonah
Ezra	Ezra	Mic.	Micah
Neh.	Nehemiah	Nah.	Nahum
Esther	Esther	Hab.	Habakkuk
Job	Job	Zeph.	Zephaniah
Ps./Pss.	Psalms	Hag.	Haggai
Prov.	Proverbs	Zech.	Zechariah
Eccles.	Ecclesiastes	Mal.	Malachi

New Testament

Matt.	Matthew	1–2 Thess.	1–2 Thessalonians
Mark	Mark	1–2 Tim.	1–2 Timothy
Luke	Luke	Titus	Titus
John	John	Philem.	Philemon
Acts	Acts	Heb.	Hebrews
Rom.	Romans	James	James
1–2 Cor.	1–2 Corinthians	1–2 Pet.	1–2 Peter
Gal.	Galatians	1–3 John	1–3 John
Eph.	Ephesians	Jude	Jude
Phil.	Philippians	Rev.	Revelation
Col.	Colossians		

Apocrypha and Septuagint

1–4 Macc.   1–4 Maccabees

Dead Sea Scrolls

4QMMT   *4QHalakhic Letter*

Greek and Latin Works

Aristotle

Rhet.   Rhetorica (Rhetoric)

Dionysius of Halicarnassus

Or.   Oration

Josephus

Ant.   Jewish Antiquities

Longinus

Subl.   De sublimitate (On the Sublime)

Secondary Sources

AAAH   Acta academiae aboensis: Humaniora

AARAS   American Academy of Religion Academy Series

AB   Anchor Bible

AC   Acta classica

ADP   Advances in Discourse Processes

AJP   American Journal of Philology

AL   Archivum linguisticum

ALLS   Applied Linguistics and Language Study

AnBib   Analecta biblica

ASCP   Amsterdam Studies in Classical Philology

ATANT   Abhandlungen zur Theologie des Alten und Neuen Testaments

AUSSGS   Acta Universitatis Stockholmiensis: Studia Graeca Stockholmiensia

AUSTR   American University Studies: Theology and Religion

BAGD   Bauer, W., W. F. Arndt, F. W. Gingrich, and F. W. Danker. Greek-English Lexicon of the New Testament and Other Early Christian Literature. 2nd. ed. Chicago, 1979

BAGL   Biblical and Ancient Greek Linguistics

BASP   Bulletin of the American Society of Papyrologists

BBR   Bulletin for Biblical Research

BCAW   Blackwell Companions to the Ancient World

BCILL   Bibliothèque des Cahiers de l'Institut de Linguistique de Louvain

BDAG   Bauer, W., F. W. Danker, W. F. Arndt, and F. W. Gingrich. Greek-English Lexicon of the New Testament and Other Early Christian Literature. 3rd ed. Chicago, 2000

BDB   Brown, F., S. R. Driver, and C. A. Briggs. A Hebrew and English Lexicon of the Old Testament. Oxford, 1907

BDF   Blass, F., and A. Debrunner. A Greek Grammar of the New Testament and Other Early Christian Literature. Translated by R. W. Funk. Chicago: University of Chicago Press, 1961

BECNT   Baker Exegetical Commentary on the New Testament

BETL   Bibliotheca ephemeridum theologicarum lovaniensium

Bib	*Biblica*	DPLSMi	De proprietatibus litterarum, Series minor
BibSem	Biblical Seminar		
BICS	*Bulletin of the Institute of Classical Studies*	DS	Discourse Studies
		ÉBib	Études bibliques
BILS	Berkeley Insights in Linguistics and Semiotics	ECC	Eerdmans Critical Commentary
BIS	Biblical Interpretation Series	ECHC	Early Christianity in Its Hellenistic Context
BLG	Biblical Languages: Greek	EFN	Estudios de filología neotestamentaria
BLH	Biblical Languages: Hebrew		
		EKK	Evangelisch-katholischer Kommentar zum Neuen Testament
BNTC	Black's New Testament Commentaries		
BSLP	*Bulletin de la Société de Linguistique de Paris*	ELS	English Language Series
		ENT	Estudios de Nuevo Testamento
BT	*The Bible Translator*		
BZNW	Beihefte zur Zeitschrift für die neutestamentliche Wissenschaft	*ETL*	*Ephemerides theologicae lovanienses*
		EvQ	*Evangelical Quarterly*
CAL	Cambridge Approaches to Linguistics	*ExpTim*	*Expository Times*
		FGS	Functional Grammar Series
CBC	Cambridge Bible Commentary		
		FL	*Foundations of Language*
CBQMS	Catholic Biblical Quarterly Monograph Series	*FN*	*Filología neotestamentaria*
		GBSNT	Guides to Biblical Scholarship: New Testament
CBR	*Currents in Research: Biblical Studies*		
		GNC	Good News Commentary
CIP	Cambridge Introductions to Philosophy	GP	Gospel Perspectives
		GSE	Gothenburg Studies in English
CL	Collection linguistique		
ConBNT	Coniectanea biblica: New Testament Series	*GTJ*	*Grace Theological Journal*
		HA	Handbuch der Altertumwissenschaft
CPC	Collection de philologie classique		
		HS	*Historische Sprachforschung*
CQ	*Classical Quarterly*		
CSCC	Comparative Studies in Cultures and Civilizations	*HSCP*	*Harvard Studies in Classical Philology*
		HTB	Histoire du texte biblique
CSL	Cambridge Studies in Linguistics	HUT	Hermeneutische Untersuchungen zur Theologie
CTL	Cambridge Textbooks in Linguistics		
		HvTSt	*Hervormde teologiese studies*
DEL	Describing English Language		

IBC	Interpretation: A Bible Commentary for Teaching and Preaching	*JPrag*	*Journal of Pragmatics*
ICC	International Critical Commentary	*JQL*	*Journal of Quantitative Linguistics*
IF	*Indogermanische Forschungen*	*JSHJ*	*Journal for the Study of the Historical Jesus*
IJAL	*International Journal of American Linguistics*	JSJSup	Supplements to the Journal for the Study of Judaism
Int	*Interpretation*	*JSNT*	*Journal for the Study of the New Testament*
ISBL	Indiana Studies in Biblical Literature	JSNTSup	Journal for the Study of the New Testament: Supplement Series
ITS	International Theological Studies	JSOTSup	Journal for the Study of the Old Testament: Supplement Series
JAAR	*Journal of the American Academy of Religion*	*JSPL*	*Journal for the Study of Paul and His Letters*
JBL	*Journal of Biblical Literature*	JSPSup	Journal for the Study of the Pseudepigrapha: Supplement Series
JBLMS	Journal of Biblical Literature Monograph Series	JOST	Johannine Studies Series
JCP	*Jahrbücher für classische Philologie*	*JTS*	*Journal of Theological Studies*
JD	Jian Dao	KEK	Kritisch-exegetischer Kommentar über das Neue Testament (Meyer-Kommentar)
JETS	*Journal of the Evangelical Theological Society*		
JGRChJ	*Journal of Greco-Roman Christianity and Judaism*	KNT	Kommentar zum Neuen Testament
JIS	*Journal of Indo-European Studies*	LA	Linguistische Arbeiten
JISM	Journal of Indo-European Studies Monographs	LAL	Library of Arabic Linguistics
JLSMa	Janua linguarum, Series maior	LBS	Linguistic Biblical Studies
JLSMi	Janua linguarum, Series minor	LE	Linguistics Edition
JLSP	Janua linguarum, Series practica	LHBOTS	Library of Hebrew Bible and Old Testament Studies
JMALS	*Journal of the Midland Association for Linguistic Studies*	*LHS*	*Linguistics and the Human Sciences*
JÖB	*Jahrbuch der österreichischen Byzantinistik*	*LI*	*Linguistic Inquiry*
		LLC	*Literary and Linguistic Computing*
JPhil	*Journal of Philology*	LLL	Longman Linguistics Library

LN	Linguistique nouvelle	*NTS*	*New Testament Studies*
LNTS	Library of New Testament Studies	NTTS	New Testament Tools and Studies
LPS	Library of Pauline Studies	OLS	Open Linguistics Series
LSJ	Liddell, H. G., R. Scott, and H. S. Jones. *A Greek-English Lexicon*. 9th ed. with rev. supplement. Oxford, 1996	*OPTT*	*Occasional Papers in Translation and Textlinguistics*
		ORP	Oxford Readings in Philosophy
		OSS	Oxford Studies in Sociolinguistics
LSL	Lodz Studies in Language		
LVC	*Language Variation and Change*	OTM	Oxford Theological Monographs
LW	Language Workbooks	*PasJ*	*Pastoral Journal*
MJTM	*McMaster Journal of Theology and Ministry*	PelNTC	Pelican New Testament Commentaries
MNTC	Moffatt New Testament Commentary	PFES	Publications of the Finnish Exegetical Society
MNTS	McMaster New Testament Studies	PilNTC	Pillar New Testament Commentary
NCBC	New Cambridge Bible Commentary	PLB	Papyrologica Lugduno-Batava
NCUC	Nouvelle collection à l'usage des classes	*PR*	*Philosophical Review*
NET	Neutestamentliche Entwürfe zur Theologie	PAST	Pauline Studies
		PV	Papyrologica vindobonensia
NGS	New Gospel Studies	QULPM	Quellen und Untersuchungen zur lateinischen Philologie des Mittelalters
NICNT	New International Commentary on the New Testament		
NIGTC	New International Greek Testament Commentary	*RB*	*Revue biblique*
		RILP	Roehampton Institute London Papers
NLLT	*Natural Language and Linguistic Theory*	*RJ*	*Reformed Journal*
NovT	*Novum Testamentum*	RNT	Regensburger Neues Testament
NovTSup	Novum Testamentum Supplements	RSL	Research Surveys in Linguistics
NTD	Das Neue Testament Deutsch	RSGL	Routledge Studies in Germanic Linguistics
NTG	New Testament Guides		
NTL	New Testament Library	RTT	Research in Text Theory
NTM	New Testament Monographs	SBFA	Studium Biblicum Franciscanum Analecta
NTT	New Testament Theology	SBG	Studies in Biblical Greek

SBLCP	Society of Biblical Literature Centennial Publications	SubBi	Subsidia biblica
SBLDS	Society of Biblical Literature Dissertation Series	*SWPLL*	*Sheffield Working Papers in Language and Linguistics*
SBLMS	Society of Biblical Literature Monograph Series	*TAPA*	*Transactions of the American Philological Association*
SBLRBS	Society of Biblical Literature Resources for Biblical Study	*TDNT*	*Theological Dictionary of the New Testament.* Edited by G. Kittel and G. Friedrich. Translated by G. W. Bromiley. 10 vols. Grand Rapids, 1964–76
SBLSBS	Society of Biblical Literature Sources for Biblical Study	TENT	Texts and Editions for New Testament Study
SBLSymS	Society of Biblical Literature Symposium Series	THNT	Theologischer Handkommentar zum Neuen Testament
SCL	Studies in Christianity and Literature		
SEL	Studies in English Language	*TJ*	*Trinity Journal*
SemSt	Semeia Studies	*TLZ*	*Theologische Literaturzeitung*
SIS	Studies in Interactional Sociolinguistics	TMEA	Travaux et mémoires: Études anciennes
SJT	*Scottish Journal of Theology*	TMO	Travaux de la Maison de l'Orient
SNTG	Studies in New Testament Greek	TNTC	Tyndale New Testament Commentaries
SNTSMS	Society for New Testament Studies Monograph Series	*TPS*	*Transactions of the Philological Society*
SNTW	Studies of the New Testament and Its World	*TSK*	*Theologische Studien und Kritiken*
SP	Sacra pagina	TUGAL	Texte und Untersuchungen zur Geschichte der altchristlichen Literatur
SPap	*Studia papyrologica*		
SPIB	Scripta Pontificii Instituti Biblici		
SSCFL	Studies in the Social and Cultural Foundations of Language	*TWNT*	*Theologisches Wörterbuch zum Neuen Testament.* Edited by G. Kittel and G. Friedrich. 10 vols. Stuttgart, 1932–79
SSEJC	Studies in Scripture in Early Judaism and Christianity	*TynBul*	*Tyndale Bulletin*
START	*Selected Technical Articles Related to Translation*	*TZT*	*Tübingen Zeitschrift für Theologie*
StBL	Studies in Biblical Literature	UBSMS	United Bible Societies Monograph Series

UISK	Untersuchungen zur indo-germanischen Sprach- und Kulturwissenschaft	WUNT	Wissenschaftliche Untersuchungen zum Neuen Testament
USFISFCJ	University of South Florida International Studies in Formative Christianity and Judaism	ZB	Zürcher Bibelkommentare
		ZECNT	Zondervan Exegetical Commentary on the New Testament
VE	*Vox evangelica*	ZNW	*Zeitschrift für die neutestamentliche Wissenschaft und die Kunde der älteren Kirche*
WBC	Word Biblical Commentary		
WLQ	*Wisconsin Lutheran Quarterly*		

Introduction

This volume of essays continues work done on Greek language and linguistics that I have been fortunate to be able to engage in from the very beginning of my academic career. My first published academic article was in the area of Greek language and linguistics, and, although I did not realize it at the time, it helped to set the course for at least one major strand of my subsequent research, writing, and teaching career. In that first article I examined the adjectival attributive genitive in ancient Greek, especially those instances within the less frequent syntactical patterns in the New Testament.[1] Later, what began as a complicated attempt to find a PhD thesis topic, and led to completing a PhD in the fields of both biblical studies and linguistics (systemic functional linguistics in particular), has continued to be a productive area of ever-expanding research. I firmly believe that matters of Greek language and linguistics are essential to understanding the Greek New Testament; in that sense, knowledge of Greek linguistics is a fundamental hermeneutical stance that should be pursued by every serious student of the New Testament.[2] By

1. S. E. Porter, "The Adjectival Attributive Genitive in the New Testament: A Grammatical Study," *TJ* 4 (1983): 3–17.
2. Hermeneutics is a closely related area that I have also pursued in some depth, especially recently. See S. E. Porter, "Hermeneutics, Biblical Interpretation and Theology: Hunch, Holy Spirit or Hard Work?," in *Beyond the Bible: Moving from Scripture to Theology*, by I. H. Marshall, with essays by K. Vanhoozer and S. E. Porter (Grand Rapids: Baker Academic; Milton Keynes: Paternoster, 2004), 97–127; Porter, "What Difference Does Hermeneutics Make? Hermeneutical Theory Applied," *JD* 34 / /*PasJ* 27 (July 2010): 1–50; S. E. Porter and J. C. Robinson, *Hermeneutics: An Introduction to Interpretive Theory* (Grand Rapids: Eerdmans, 2011); Porter, "A Single Horizon Hermeneutics: A Proposal for Interpretive Identification," *MJTM* 13 (2011–12): 45–66; Porter, "What Exactly Is Theological Interpretation of Scripture, and Is It Hermeneutically Robust Enough for the Task to Which It Has Been Appointed?," in *Horizons in Hermeneutics: A Festschrift in Honor of Anthony C. Thiselton*, ed. S. E. Porter and

"knowledge of Greek," I do not mean what some people claim is knowledge on the basis of finishing one or two years of Greek study (especially employing some of the widely used but inadequate pedagogical grammatical tools) or traditional grammar or the invocation of the work of outmoded and outdated reference tools. What I mean is a robust and insightful development of appropriate linguistically based methods for study of the Greek New Testament. Such work is the exception to most of what represents itself under the name of exegesis. It is disconcerting to see many of the latest commentaries and numerous journal articles make statements about the Greek New Testament and yet show absolutely no knowledge of any of the recent discussion of ancient Greek. They sometimes even use such naive and unfounded knowledge as the basis for what can only be called, as a result, highly tenuous exegetical conclusions. This volume is designed to help remedy this situation, at least in part, by providing some insights into various areas of Greek grammar and linguistics along with providing examples of application of linguistics to particular problems in Greek.

My first major work in Greek language and linguistics, a major monograph on verbal aspect theory and the Greek of the New Testament, led to linguistically related work in at least two major areas.[3] The first was in areas more particularly linguistic in nature. Several of my earliest scholarly articles addressed matters of general linguistics, even if they had direct application to the work that I was doing in study of the Greek of the New Testament. This resulted in publications on vagueness and ambiguity,[4] and on tense-form terminology.[5] Another area of general linguistic interest came about first through the basic corpus-based approach of my original research on verbal aspect, and then later in the collaborative work of my then-student and later colleague Matthew Brook O'Donnell on corpus linguistics. The study of ancient languages raises a unique set of corpus problems, some of which we have addressed in our research.[6] Since then, I have also contributed linguistic overviews of the

M. R. Malcolm (Grand Rapids: Eerdmans, 2013), 234–67; Porter, "Biblical Hermeneutics and Theological Responsibility," in *The Future of Biblical Interpretation: Responsible Plurality in Biblical Hermeneutics*, ed. S. E. Porter and M. R. Malcolm (Downers Grove, IL: IVP Academic, 2013), 29–50. See also S. E. Porter and B. M. Stovell, eds., *Biblical Hermeneutics: Five Views* (Downers Grove, IL: IVP Academic, 2012).

3. S. E. Porter, *Verbal Aspect in the Greek of the New Testament, with Reference to Tense and Mood*, SBG 1 (New York: Peter Lang, 1989; 2nd ed., 1993).

4. S. E. Porter and N. J. C. Gotteri (my doctoral supervisor in linguistics), "Ambiguity, Vagueness and the Working Systemic Linguist," *SWPLL* 2 (1985): 105–18.

5. S. E. Porter, "Tense Terminology and Greek Language Study: A Linguistic Re-Evaluation," *SWPLL* 3 (1986): 77–86; revised and reprinted in *Studies in the Greek New Testament: Theory and Practice* by S. E. Porter, SBG 6 (New York: Peter Lang, 1996), 39–48.

6. M. B. O'Donnell, S. E. Porter, and J. T. Reed, "OpenText.org: The Problems and Prospects of Working with Ancient Discourse," in *Proceedings of the Corpus Linguistics 2001 Conference*,

New Testament and Septuagint for a linguistic reference work.[7] I have also attempted to formulate what the distinctives of linguistically based Greek grammatical study look like in relation to more traditional areas of Greek scholarship, such as traditional grammar and classical philology.[8]

Within the field of New Testament Greek language and linguistic studies, my second major area, I have extended my initial studies on verbal aspect into five other major research areas. These lines are discussed in various ways within this fundamental research, though they have often been overlooked because they are overshadowed by the major topic of discussion, verbal aspect. The first area is continued discussion of verbal aspect,[9] as well as tense and mood (the three together often referred to as "TMA," or tense-mood-aspect), and their relationships to things such as temporal reference and even syntax.[10] Verbal aspect is a topic to which I return in several of the chapters in this volume. One of the frequently heard though rarely supported responses to my theory of aspect is that choice of verbal aspect is influenced by the Greek verbal system itself or by lexical choice. In a corpus-based study of the Greek of the New

---

ed. P. Rayson et al. (Lancaster: Lancaster University, 2001), 413–22; printed also in *A Rainbow of Corpora: Corpus Linguistics and the Languages of the World*, ed. A. Wilson, P. Rayson, and T. McEnery, LE 40 (Munich: Lincom, 2003), 109–19; S. E. Porter and M. B. O'Donnell, "Theoretical Issues for Corpus Linguistics and the Study of Ancient Languages," in *Corpus Linguistics by the Lune: A Festschrift for Geoffrey Leech*, ed. A. Wilson, P. Rayson, and T. McEnery, LSL 8 (Frankfurt am Main: Peter Lang, 2003), 119–37.

7. S. E. Porter, "New Testament" and "Septuagint," in *Encyclopedia of Ancient Greek Language and Linguistics*, ed. G. K. Giannakis (Leiden: Brill, 2014), 2:497–500, 3:287–90.

8. S. E. Porter, "Studying Ancient Languages from a Modern Linguistic Perspective: Essential Terms and Terminology," *FN* 2 (1989): 147–72. See also Porter, "Problems in the Language of the Bible: Misunderstandings that Continue to Plague Biblical Interpretation," in *The Nature of Religious Language: A Colloquium*, ed. S. E. Porter, RILP 1 (Sheffield: Sheffield Academic Press, 1996), 20–46, where a number of topics are discussed.

9. S. E. Porter, "In Defence of Verbal Aspect," in *Biblical Greek Language and Linguistics: Open Questions in Current Research*, ed. S. E. Porter and D. A. Carson, JSNTSup 80, SNTG 1 (Sheffield: Sheffield Academic Press, 1993), 26–45; revised and reprinted in Porter, *Studies in the Greek New Testament*, 21–38.

10. S. E. Porter, "Vague Verbs, Periphrastics, and Matthew 16:19," *FN* 1 (1988) 155–73; revised and reprinted in Porter, *Studies in the Greek New Testament*, 103–24; Porter, "Verbal Aspect in NT Greek and Bible Translation: A Review of Research," *TIC Talk* 15 (Spring 1991): 1–3; Porter, "The Date of the Composition of Hebrews and Use of the Present Tense-Form," in *Crossing the Boundaries: Essays on Biblical Interpretation in Honour of Michael D. Goulder*, ed. S. E. Porter, P. Joyce, and D. E. Orton, BIS 8 (Leiden: Brill, 1994), 313–32; Porter, "Time and Order in Participles in Mark and Luke: A Response to Robert Picirilli," *BBR* 17 (2007): 261–67; Porter, "Verbal Aspect and Discourse Function in Mark 16:1–8: Three Significant Instances," in *Studies in the Greek Bible: Essays in Honor of Francis T. Gignac, S.J.*, ed. J. Corley and V. Skemp, CBQMS 44 (Washington, DC: Catholic Biblical Association of America, 2008), 123–37; Porter, "What Can We Learn about Greek Grammar from a Mosaic?," in *The Language of the New Testament: Context, History, and Development*, ed. S. E. Porter and A. W. Pitts, ECHC 3, LBS 6 (Leiden: Brill, 2013), 29–41.

Testament, Matthew O'Donnell and I show, from a probabilistic standpoint, that the aspectual system within the Greek verbal system is for all intents and purposes completely independent.[11] In an article on lexical choice, I also show that lexical influence on verbal aspectual choice is also very limited.[12] Through this work, I (and others) demonstrate, I believe, that such counterclaims are simply not defensible, and that such arguments should be dropped, and with them theories (such as *Aktionsart* or lexical aspect), even of grammatical aspect, that are based upon them. Related to verbal aspect and other areas of Greek usage is the notion of prominence, the means by which language users indicate the salience of various linguistic elements. In an earlier work titled "Prominence: A Theoretical Overview," I attempt to provide a system for determining Greek prominence in relationship to markedness and foregrounding.[13]

The second major strand I have continued to develop is general work on the history and development of the Greek language, where I have attempted to show the appropriate position of the Hellenistic Greek of the New Testament in relation to the varieties of Greek that came before it, and how study of the Greek of the New Testament—widely ignored by students of Classical Greek—has made significant contributions to our understanding of Greek.[14] Related to this is my offering of extended critique of some of the

11. S. E. Porter and M. B. O'Donnell, "The Greek Verbal Network Viewed from a Probabilistic Standpoint: An Exercise in Hallidayan Linguistics," *FN* 14 (2001): 3–41.

12. S. E. Porter, "Aspect Theory and Lexicography," in *Biblical Greek Language and Lexicography: Essays in Honor of Frederick W. Danker*, ed. B. A. Taylor et al. (Grand Rapids: Eerdmans, 2004), 207–22.

13. S. E. Porter, "Prominence: A Theoretical Overview," in *The Linguist as Pedagogue: Trends in the Teaching and Linguistic Analysis of the Greek New Testament*, ed. S. E. Porter and M. B. O'Donnell, NTM 11 (Sheffield: Sheffield Phoenix Press, 2009), 45–74; cf. also Porter, "Verbal Aspect as a Prominence Indicator: A Response to Jody Barnard," in *Greeks, Jews, and Christians: Historical, Religious, and Philological Studies in Honor of Jesús Peláez del Rosal*, ed. L. R. Lanzillotta and I. M. Gallarte (Córdoba: Ediciones el Almendro, 2013), 421–48.

14. S. E. Porter, "The Language of the Apocalypse in Recent Discussion," *NTS* 35 (1989): 582–603; Porter, "Introduction: The Greek of the New Testament as a Disputed Area of Research," in *The Language of the New Testament: Classic Essays*, ed. S. E. Porter, JSNTSup 60 (Sheffield: Sheffield Academic Press, 1991), 11–38; revised and reprinted in Porter, *Studies in the Greek New Testament*, 75–99; Porter, "Is ἀμβιτεύειν Really ἐμβατεύειν (P. Oxy XVII 2110.15)?," *BASP* 27 (1990): 45–47; Porter, "The Greek Language of the New Testament," in *Handbook to Exegesis of the New Testament*, ed. S. E. Porter, NTTS 25 (Leiden: Brill, 1997), 99–130; Porter, "Greek of the New Testament," in *Dictionary of New Testament Background*, ed. C. A. Evans and S. E. Porter (Downers Grove, IL: InterVarsity, 2000), 426–35; Porter, "Greek Language," in vol. 2 of *The New Interpreter's Dictionary of the Bible*, ed. K. D. Sakenfeld (Nashville: Abingdon, 2007), 673–81; Porter, "Languages of the Bible," in *Dictionary of the Bible and Western Culture: A Handbook for Students*, ed. M. A. Beavis and M. J. Gilmour (Sheffield: Sheffield Phoenix Press, 2012), 286–87. My historical interest comes through in A. Wifstrand, *Epochs and Styles: Selected Writings on the New Testament, Greek Language and Greek Culture in the Post-Classical Era*, ed. L. Rydbeck and S. E. Porter, trans. D. Searby, WUNT 179 (Tübingen: Mohr Siebeck, 2005).

tools and approaches used in contemporary Greek study, including grammars and commentaries.[15]

The third area is sociolinguistics, the specific topic of chapter 7 in this volume. Sociolinguistics is a major field of linguistic study, and the several intertwined subareas where I have made a contribution are diglossia, multilingualism, and historical sociolinguistics. Diglossia is related to the area of register study and is concerned with how various language users shift and adjust their linguistic choice within their potential repertoires for various socially and textually determined reasons.[16] The second subarea of sociolinguistics, multilingualism, is directly relevant to the milieu in which the New Testament was written, especially in relation to matters such as style, register, and prestige languages.[17] The Mediterranean world of the first century was multilingual, and this affects issues such as the language of Jesus and the use of language by a variety of New Testament writers, such as Paul, a Diaspora Jew who lived for a time in Palestine but traveled throughout the greater Mediterranean Greco-Roman world.[18] This sociolinguistic work has significance for Greek Egypt as well.[19] Historical sociolinguistics studies the sociolinguistic dynamics of the ancient world on the basis of historical evidence of the varieties of language used by various peoples.[20] Within an SFL (systemic functional linguistics)

15. S. E. Porter and J. T. Reed, "Greek Grammar since BDF: A Retrospective and Prospective Analysis," *FN* 4 (1991): 143–64; Porter, "A Modern Grammar of an Ancient Language: A Critique of the Schmidt Proposal," *Forum* 2 (1999): 201–13; Porter, "Linguistic Criticism," in *Dictionary of Biblical Criticism and Interpretation*, ed. S. E. Porter (London: Routledge, 2007), 199–202; Porter, "The Linguistic Competence of New Testament Commentaries," in *On the Writing of New Testament Commentaries: Festschrift for Grant R. Osborne on the Occasion of His 70th Birthday*, ed. S. E. Porter and E. J. Schnabel, TENT 8 (Leiden: Brill, 2012), 33–56; Porter, "Commentaries on the Book of Romans," in Porter and Schnabel, *New Testament Commentaries*, 365–404.

16. S. E. Porter, "The Functional Distribution of Koine Greek in First-Century Palestine," in *Diglossia and Other Topics in New Testament Linguistics*, ed. S. E. Porter, JSNTSup 193, SNTG 6 (Sheffield: Sheffield Academic Press, 2000), 53–78.

17. S. E. Porter, "The Greek Papyri of the Judaean Desert and the World of the Roman East," in *The Scrolls and the Scriptures: Qumran Fifty Years After*, ed. S. E. Porter and C. A. Evans, RILP 3, JSPSup 26 (Sheffield: Sheffield Academic Press, 1997), 293–316.

18. S. E. Porter, "The Languages That Paul Did Not Speak," in *Paul's World*, ed. S. E. Porter, PAST 4 (Leiden: Brill, 2008), 131–49; Porter, "The Language(s) Jesus Spoke," in *Handbook for the Study of the Historical Jesus*, vol. 3, *The Historical Jesus*, ed. T. Holmén and S. E. Porter (Leiden: Brill, 2011), 2455–71.

19. S. E. Porter, "History of Scholarship on the Language of the Septuagint," in *Handbuch zur Septuaginta*, vol. 4, *Sprache*, ed. E. Bons and J. Joosten (Gütersloh: Gütersloher Verlag, forthcoming).

20. S. E. Porter, "The Greek of the Jews and Early Christians: The Language of the People from a Historical Sociolinguistic Perspective," in *Far from Minimal: Celebrating the Work and Influence of Philip R. Davies*, ed. D. Burns and J. W. Rogerson, LHBOTS 484 (London: T&T Clark, 2012), 350–64.

framework (itself a sociolinguistic theory), the notion of register is important since it provides a means for describing typical instances of language use within the context of situation of a discourse.[21] Register studies continue to be underdeveloped in New Testament research (see chap. 13 in this volume), even though there has been some work that has paved the way in this regard.

The fourth area of continued research is concerned with the language of Jesus (closely related to sociolinguistics above).[22] Within the context of Mediterranean multilingualism, I have examined the languages of Jesus and attempted to develop linguistically based criteria for determining the historical reliability of sayings of Jesus. To that end, I have developed three linguistically based criteria for authenticating the words of Jesus and applied them to various Gospel-recorded instances: Greek language and its context, Greek textual variance, and discourse features.[23]

The fifth and final strand of New Testament linguistic research is discourse analysis.[24] In some ways, discourse analysis has been an overriding concern of my work from the start, as I have tried to position my study of Greek within

21. S. E. Porter, "Dialect and Register in the Greek of the New Testament: Theory," in *Rethinking Contexts, Rereading Texts: Contributions from the Social Sciences to Biblical Interpretation*, ed. M. D. Carroll R., JSOTSup 299 (Sheffield: Sheffield Academic Press, 2000), 190–208; Porter, "Register in the Greek of the New Testament: Application with Reference to Mark's Gospel," in Carroll R., *Rethinking Contexts, Rereading Texts*, 209–29.

22. S. E. Porter, "Did Jesus Ever Teach in Greek?," *TynBul* 44 (1993): 199–235; revised and reprinted in Porter, *Studies in the Greek New Testament*, 139–71; Porter, "Jesus and the Use of Greek in Galilee," in *Studying the Historical Jesus: Evaluations of the State of Current Research*, ed. B. Chilton and C. A. Evans, NTTS 19 (Leiden: Brill, 1994), 123–54; Porter, "Jesus and the Use of Greek: A Response to Maurice Casey," *BBR* 10 (2000): 71–87; Porter, "Language Criticism," in *Encyclopedia of the Historical Jesus*, ed. C. A. Evans (London: Routledge, 2008), 361–65.

23. S. E. Porter, *The Criteria for Authenticity in Historical-Jesus Research: Previous Discussion and New Proposals*, JSNTSup 191 (Sheffield: Sheffield Academic Press, 2000), 126–237; Porter, "Luke 17.11–19 and the Criteria for Authenticity Revisited," *JSHJ* 1 (2003): 201–24; Porter, "The Criterion of Greek Language and Its Context: A Further Response," *JSHJ* 4 (2006): 69–74; Porter, "The Role of Greek Language Criteria in Historical Jesus Research," in *Handbook for the Study of the Historical Jesus*, vol. 1, *How to Study the Historical Jesus*, ed. T. Holmén and S. E. Porter (Leiden: Brill, 2011), 361–404. These criteria were anticipated on the basis of S. E. Porter and M. B. O'Donnell, "The Implications of Textual Variants for Authenticating the Words of Jesus," in *Authenticating the Words of Jesus*, ed. B. Chilton and C. A. Evans, NTTS 28.1 (Leiden: Brill, 1999), 97–133; Porter and O'Donnell, "The Implications of Textual Variants for Authenticating the Activities of Jesus," in *Authenticating the Activities of Jesus*, ed. B. Chilton and C. A. Evans, NTTS 28.2 (Leiden: Brill, 1999), 121–51.

24. S. E. Porter, "Discourse Analysis and New Testament Studies: An Introductory Survey," in *Discourse Analysis and Other Topics in Biblical Greek*, ed. S. E. Porter and D. A. Carson, JSNTSup 113, SNTG 2 (Sheffield: Sheffield Academic Press, 1995), 14–35; Porter, "Rhetorical Analysis and Discourse Analysis of the Pauline Corpus," in *The Rhetorical Analysis of Scripture: Essays from the 1995 London Conference*, ed. S. E. Porter and T. H. Olbricht, JSNTSup 146 (Sheffield: Sheffield Academic Press, 1997), 249–74; Porter, "Is Critical Discourse Analysis Critical? An Evaluation Using Philemon as a Test Case," in *Discourse Analysis and the New Testament:*

larger discourse concerns. This has led to my writing the first grammar of New Testament Greek that utilized discourse principles within a strong linguistic framework,[25] and to my being one of only a few to write on the grammar of the *Gospel of Peter* and the first to write a discourse analysis of that noncanonical gospel.[26] With Jeffrey Reed and Matthew O'Donnell, I have also coauthored an elementary Greek grammar that incorporates a linguistic framework into its presentation and organization.[27]

Besides my work in New Testament Greek language and linguistics study, a second major field where I have undertaken serious research is the area of New Testament lexicography, including semantic-domain theory. My interests here have been both theoretical and practical. I have written one of the only full-scale studies of a Greek lexeme within all of ancient Greek usage, a study of καταλλάσσω ("reconcile") and its cognates from earliest usage to the sixth century AD.[28] This is a further example of corpus-based study, in which I examined all of the contexts in which the lexeme appears and analyzed its major syntactical patterns. I followed this up with several related studies on particular New Testament passages.[29] I also have been concerned with the more theoretical issues of lexicography, where I have become an overt proponent of lexical monosemy rather than the traditional polysemy,[30] and

Approaches and Results, ed. S. E. Porter and J. T. Reed, JSNTSup 170, SNTG 4 (Sheffield: Sheffield Academic Press, 1999), 47–70.

25. S. E. Porter, *Idioms of the Greek New Testament*, BLG 2 (Sheffield: Sheffield Academic Press, 1992; 2nd ed., 1994).

26. S. E. Porter, "The Greek of the Gospel of Peter: Implications for Syntax and Discourse Study," in *Das Evangelium nach Petrus: Text, Kontexte, Intertexte*, ed. T. J. Kraus and T. Nicklas, TUGAL 158 (Berlin: de Gruyter, 2007), 77–90.

27. S. E. Porter, J. T. Reed, and M. B. O'Donnell, *Fundamentals of New Testament Greek* (Grand Rapids: Eerdmans, 2010); S. E. Porter and J. T. Reed, *Fundamentals of New Testament Greek: Workbook* (Grand Rapids: Eerdmans, 2010).

28. S. E. Porter, *Καταλλάσσω in Ancient Greek Literature, with Reference to the Pauline Writings*, EFN 5 (Córdoba: Ediciones el Almendro, 1994).

29. S. E. Porter, "Reconciliation and 2 Cor 5,18–21," in *The Corinthian Correspondence*, ed. R. Bieringer, BETL 125 (Leuven: Leuven University Press, 1996), 693–705; Porter, "Καταλλάσσω in Ancient Greek Literature and Romans 5: A Study of Pauline Usage," in Porter, *Studies in the Greek New Testament*, 195–212. For other lexical studies, see Porter, "How Should κολλώμενος in 1 Corinthians 6:16, 17 Be Translated?," *ETL* 67 (1991): 105–6; S. E. Porter and M. B. O'Donnell, "Semantics and Patterns of Argumentation in the Book of Romans: Definitions, Proposals, Data and Experiments," in Porter, *Diglossia*, 154–204; S. E. Porter, "The Concept of Covenant in Paul," in *The Concept of the Covenant in the Second Temple Period*, ed. S. E. Porter and J. C. R. de Roo, JSJSup 71 (Leiden: Brill, 2003), 269–85; Porter, "Penitence and Repentance in the Epistles," in *Repentance in Christian Theology*, ed. M. J. Boda and G. T. Smith (Collegeville, MN: Liturgical Press, 2006), 127–50.

30. S. E. Porter, "Greek Linguistics and Lexicography," in *Understanding the Times: New Testament Studies in the 21st Century; Essays in Honor of D. A. Carson on the Occasion of His 65th Birthday*, ed. A. J. Köstenberger and R. W. Yarbrough (Wheaton, IL: Crossway, 2011),

have opposed the insidious tendency of New Testament studies toward theological lexicography.[31] In this volume chapters 3 and 4 also figure into this
discussion of lexicography by critiquing two standard lexicons and making
some constructive proposals.[32]

A third area of research and writing not already mentioned above is my
work in translation studies, a field often excluded from discussion of linguistics
"proper" (or improper, I would say). Beginning with my study of the Contemporary English Version and Mark 1:4, an important verse in translation
theorizing,[33] I have extended that research and developed a framework for
examining various types of translations.[34] This framework attempts to move
beyond the usual bifurcation between literal and dynamic equivalence and
to explore a fuller range of interlingual translational options,[35] along with
using discourse analysis as a means of translational analysis and evaluation.[36]

19–61, which also discusses verbal aspect in some detail; Porter, "Matthew and Mark: The
Contribution of Recent Linguistic Thought," in *Mark and Matthew: Comparative Readings*,
part 1, *Understanding the Earliest Gospels in Their First-Century Settings*, ed. E.-M. Becker and
A. Runesson, WUNT 271 (Tübingen: Mohr Siebeck, 2011), 97–119, which also offers a critique
of the use of linguistics in such scholarship; Porter, "Θαυμάζω in Mark 6:6 and Luke 11:38: A
Note on Monosemy," *BAGL* 2 (2013): 75–79.

31. S. E. Porter, "Is *dipsuchos* (James 1:8; 4:8) a 'Christian' Word?," *Bib* 71 (1990): 469–98;
Porter, "Lexicons (Theological)," in Porter, *Dictionary of Biblical Criticism and Interpretation*,
195–96.

32. See also S. E. Porter, "Romans 13:1–7 as Pauline Political Rhetoric," *FN* 3 (6; 1990):
115–39, where New Testament lexicography, though not central, is crucial to my argument.

33. S. E. Porter, "The Contemporary English Version and the Ideology of Translation," in
Translating the Bible: Problems and Prospects, ed. S. E. Porter and R. S. Hess, JSNTSup 173
(Sheffield: Sheffield Academic Press, 1999), 18–45.

34. S. E. Porter, "Mark 1.4, Baptism and Translation," in *Baptism, the New Testament and
the Church: Historical and Contemporary Studies in Honour of R. E. O. White*, ed. S. E. Porter
and A. R. Cross, JSNTSup 171 (Sheffield: Sheffield Academic Press, 1999), 81–98; Porter, "Some
Issues in Modern Translation Theory and Study of the Greek New Testament," *CBR* 9 (2001):
350–82; Porter, "Modern Translations," in *The Oxford Illustrated History of the Bible*, ed.
J. Rogerson (Oxford: Oxford University Press, 2001), 134–61; Porter, "Translations of the Bible
(since the KJV)," in Porter, *Dictionary of Biblical Criticism and Interpretation*, 362–69; Porter,
"Eugene Nida and Translation," *BT* 56 (2005): 8–19; Porter, "Language and Translation of
the New Testament," in *The Oxford Handbook of Biblical Studies*, ed. J. W. Rogerson and
J. M. Lieu (Oxford: Oxford University Press, 2006), 184–210; Porter, "Translation, Exegesis,
and 1 Thessalonians 2:14–15: Could a Comma Have Changed the Course of History?," *BT* 64
(2013): 82–98; S. E. Porter and H. T. Ong, "'Standard of Faith' or 'Measure of a Trusteeship'?
A Study in Romans 12:3—A Response," *JGRChJ* 9 (2013): 97–103.

35. S. E. Porter, "Assessing Translation Theory: Beyond Literal and Dynamic Equivalence,"
in *Translating the New Testament: Text, Translation, Theology*, ed. S. E. Porter and M. J. Boda,
MNTS (Grand Rapids: Eerdmans, 2009), 117–45; Porter, *How We Got the New Testament: Text,
Transmission, Translation* (Grand Rapids: Baker Academic, 2013), esp. 147–210.

36. S. E. Porter and M. B. O'Donnell, "Comparative Discourse Analysis as a Tool in Assessing
Translations Using Luke 16:19–31 as a Test Case," in Porter and Boda, *Translating the New
Testament*, 185–99.

Along the way, I have also written a number of linguistically framed articles on a variety of other topics in study of the Greek New Testament. This is actually the second volume I have published that includes a variety of my linguistic papers. The first one, however, contained mostly (though not only) previously published papers.[37] These papers included an introduction to Greek language and linguistics,[38] a treatment of the Greek verb γίνομαι ("become") as a verb of location,[39] an article on Romans 5 that discusses a number of linguistic matters,[40] and a treatment of Wittgenstein's classes of utterances in Paul with special reference to Galatians 3:28–29,[41] among others that are less linguistic in orientation or that are mentioned elsewhere in this introduction. In individual studies, I have also continued to explore a range of topics in Greek language and linguistics. One of these is the area of linguistic determinism or relativity, what is sometimes known as the Sapir-Whorf hypothesis, in which I critically examine the question of how one's language influences one's thought.[42] Another of these areas is word and constituent order, also a topic that I take up in one of the chapters in this book.[43] I am gratified to see that there has been some recent work on this topic: it remains an understudied area, full of unjustified suppositions. Another topic is the Greek case system, where I have responded to some research differentiating grammatical and semantic case by arguing for the need for a formally based approach.[44] Andrew Pitts and I have also applied case grammar to the issue of πίστις Χριστοῦ ("faith of Christ") and the genitive, and we believe, contrary to much theologizing, that a linguistic analysis can actually solve this enduring linguistic and hence theological problem.[45] I believe that there is too much

37. Porter, *Studies in the Greek New Testament*.

38. S. E. Porter, "Greek Language and Linguistics (Keeping Up with Recent Studies 17)," *ExpTim* 103 (1991–92): 202–8; revised and reprinted in Porter, *Studies in the Greek New Testament*, 7–20.

39. S. E. Porter, "'In the Vicinity of Jericho': Luke 18:35 in the Light of Its Synoptic Parallels," *BBR* 2 (1992): 91–104; revised and reprinted in Porter, *Studies in the Greek New Testament*, 125–38.

40. S. E. Porter, "The Argument of Romans 5: Can a Rhetorical Question Make a Difference?," *JBL* 110 (1991): 655–77; revised and reprinted in Porter, *Studies in the Greek New Testament*, 213–38.

41. S. E. Porter, "Wittgenstein's Classes of Utterances and Pauline Ethical Texts," *JETS* 32 (1989): 85–97; revised and reprinted in Porter, *Studies in the Greek New Testament*, 239–54.

42. S. E. Porter, "Two Myths: Corporate Personality and Language/Mentality Determinism," *SJT* 43 (1990): 289–307; Porter, "An Assessment of Some New Testament-Related Assumptions for Open Theism in the Writings of Clark Pinnock," in *Semper Reformandum: Studies in Honour of Clark H. Pinnock*, ed. S. E. Porter and A. R. Cross (Carlisle: Paternoster, 2003), 160–82.

43. S. E. Porter, "Word Order and Clause Structure in New Testament Greek: An Unexplored Area of Greek Linguistics Using Philippians as a Test Case," *FN* 6 (1993): 177–205.

44. S. E. Porter, "The Case for Case Revisited," *Jian Dao* 6 (1996): 13–28.

45. S. E. Porter and A. W. Pitts, "Πίστις with a Preposition and Genitive Modifier: Lexical, Semantic, and Syntactic Considerations in the πίστις Χριστοῦ Discussion," in *The Faith of Jesus*

invested in the theological issues for some to concede that such a solution is not only available, but also quite possibly correct. I have also written an essay that tackles some of the issues surrounding the notorious problem of the Greek middle voice.[46] Along with Matthew O'Donnell, I have also written on the so-called vocative case, attempting to bring some clarity to a case that stands out in a variety of linguistically definable ways.[47] We have also written on conjunctions, an area that has not been well discussed from a linguistic standpoint because of the failure to see the conjunctive system as just that—a linguistic system, and not comprising a mixed set of discrete elements.[48] A major advancement of discourse-based study of language—Greek included—is examination of units above the clause. One of these units is the paragraph, which I have endeavored to define linguistically.[49] Nevertheless, study of the paragraph (or equivalent) remains woefully underdeveloped. Future research in linguistics, whether ancient or modern, will need, I believe, to move to formalizing analysis of the paragraph. I, along with Matthew O'Donnell, have also applied the kind of linguistically oriented work noted above to the Greek of the documentary papyri.[50] Even though I continue to work within the SFL

Christ: Exegetical, Biblical, and Theological Studies, ed. M. F. Bird and P. M. Sprinkle (Peabody, MA: Hendrickson; Carlisle: Paternoster, 2009), 33–53.

46. S. E. Porter, "Did Paul Baptize Himself? A Problem of the Greek Voice System," in *Dimensions of Baptism*, ed. S. E. Porter and A. R. Cross, JSNTSup 234 (Sheffield: Sheffield Academic Press, 2002), 91–109.

47. S. E. Porter and M. B. O'Donnell, "The Vocative Case in Greek: Addressing the Case at Hand," in *Grammatica intellectio Scripturae: Saggi filologici di Greco biblico in onore di Lino Cignelli OFM*, ed. R. Pierri, SBFA 68 (Jerusalem: Franciscan Printing Press, 2006), 35–48.

48. S. E. Porter and M. B. O'Donnell, "Conjunctions, Clines and Levels of Discourse," *FN* 20 (2007): 3–14.

49. S. E. Porter, "Pericope Markers and the Paragraph: Textual and Linguistic Considerations," in *The Impact of Unit Delimitation on Exegesis*, ed. R. de Hoop, M. C. A. Korpel, and S. E. Porter, Pericope 7 (Leiden: Brill, 2008), 175–95.

50. S. E. Porter, "New Testament Studies and Papyrology: What Can We Learn from Each Other?," in *Akten des 23. Internationalen Papyrologenkongresses, Wien, 22.–28. Juli 2001*, ed. B. Palme, PV 1 (Vienna: Verlag der Österreichischen Akademie der Wissenschaften, 2007), 559–72; Porter, "Prolegomena to a Syntax of the Greek Papyri," in *Proceedings of the 24th International Congress of Papyrology, Helsinki, 1st–7th of August 2004*, ed. J. Frösén, T. Purola and E. Salmenkivi (Helsinki: Societas Scientiarum Fennica, 2007), 921–33; S. E. Porter and M. B. O'Donnell, "Building and Examining Linguistic Phenomena in a Corpus of Representative Papyri," in *The Language of the Papyri*, ed. T. V. Evans and D. D. Obbink (Oxford: Oxford University Press, 2010), 287–311; Porter, "Buried Linguistic Treasure in the Babatha Archive," in *Proceedings of the 25th International Congress of Papyrology, Ann Arbor, July 29–August 4, 2007*, ed. T. Gagos, ASP Special Edition (Ann Arbor: Scholarly Publishing Office, The University of Michigan Library, 2010), 623–32; Porter, "The Babatha Archive, the Egyptian Papyri and Their Implications for Study of the Greek New Testament," in *Early Christian Manuscripts: Examples of Applied Method and Approach*, ed. T. J. Kraus and T. Nicklas, TENT 5 (Leiden: Brill, 2010), 213–37.

framework, I have also explored some other related topics in linguistics and utilized other approaches to linguistics than the SFL approach, for which I am perhaps best known.[51] In the course of my work, and at periodic intervals, I have also offered several critical summaries of some of the major issues or the state of play within Greek grammatical study,[52] as well as preparing the New Testament Greek bibliography for the Oxford On-Line Bibliographies.[53] I have also published a number of other studies that depend upon linguistics, even if linguistics does not figure as prominently as it does in most of the essays noted in this introduction.[54]

This volume continues several of the major lines of scholarly research that I have indicated above and includes a number of papers delivered at a variety of conferences over the years or written for other purposes. Even though some of

51. S. E. Porter, "A Functional Letter Perspective: Towards a Grammar of Epistolary Form," in *Paul and the Ancient Letter Form*, ed. S. E. Porter and S. A. Adams, PAST 6 (Leiden: Brill, 2010), 9–31; Porter, "Why Hasn't Literary Stylistics Caught On in New Testament Studies?," in *Discourse Studies and Biblical Interpretation: A Festschrift in Honor of Stephen H. Levinsohn*, ed. S. E. Runge (Bellingham, WA: Logos Bible Software, 2011), 35–57; Porter, "How Do We Know What We Think We Know? Methodological Reflections on Jesus Research," in *Jesus Research: New Methodologies and Perceptions*, ed. J. H. Charlesworth with B. Rhea in consultation with P. Pokorný (Grand Rapids: Eerdmans, 2014), 82–99.

52. S. E. Porter, "New Perspectives on the Exegesis of the New Testament: Anglo-American Insights," in *Herkunft und Zukunft der neutestamentlichen Wissenschaft*, ed. O. Wischmeyer, NET 6 (Tübingen: Francke, 2003), 63–84; Porter, "Linguistics and Biblical Interpretation," in *Methods of Biblical Interpretation: Excerpted from the Dictionary of Biblical Interpretation* (Nashville: Abingdon, 2004), 35–40; Porter, "Greek Grammar and Syntax," in *The Face of New Testament Studies: A Survey of Recent Research*, ed. S. McKnight and G. R. Osborne (Grand Rapids: Baker Academic, 2004), 76–103; S. E. Porter and A. W. Pitts, "New Testament Greek Language and Linguistics in Recent Research," *CBR* 6 (2008): 214–55; Porter, "Greek Grammar and Lexicography," in Porter, *Dictionary of Biblical Criticism and Interpretation*, 136–39.

53. S. E. Porter, "Greek Language," in *Oxford Bibliographies Online: Biblical Studies*, ed. C. Ferraro (New York: Oxford University Press, 2014).

54. S. E. Porter, "ἴστε γινώσκοντες in Ephesians 5:5: Does Chiasm Solve a Problem?," *ZNW* 81 (1990): 270–76; Porter, "P.Oxy. 744.4 and Colossians 3:9," *Bib* 73 (1992): 565–67; Porter, "Linguistics and Rhetorical Criticism," in *Linguistics and the New Testament: Critical Junctures*, ed. S. E. Porter and D. A. Carson, JSNTSup 168, SNTG 5 (Sheffield: Sheffield Academic Press, 1999), 63–92; Porter, "Latin Language," in Evans and Porter, *Dictionary of New Testament Background*, 630–31; Porter, "The Ending of John's Gospel," in *From Biblical Criticism to Biblical Faith: Essays in Honor of Lee Martin McDonald*, ed. C. A. Evans and W. Brackney (Macon, GA: Mercer University Press, 2007), 55–73; Porter, "Allusions and Echoes," in *As It Is Written: Studying Paul's Use of Scripture*, ed. S. E. Porter and C. D. Stanley, SBLSymS 50 (Atlanta: Scholars Press, 2008), 29–40; Porter, "Did Paul Speak Latin?," in *Paul: Jew, Greek, and Roman*, ed. S. E. Porter, PAST 5 (Leiden: Brill, 2008), 289–308; Porter, "Granville Sharp's Rule: A Response to Dan Wallace, or Why a Critical Book Review Should Be Left Alone," *JETS* 56 (2013): 93–100; S. E. Porter and W. V. Cirafesi, "ὑστερέω and πίστις Χριστοῦ in Romans 3:23: A Response to Steven Enderlein," *JSPL* 3 (2013): 1–9; S. E. Porter, "Not Only That (οὐ μόνον), but It Has Been Said Before: A Response to Verlyn Verbrugge, or Why Reading Previous Scholarship Can Avoid Scholarly Misunderstandings," *JETS* 56 (2013) 577–83.

the papers were written and delivered some time ago, I have not attempted to bring them up to date in every regard (especially by adding bibliography) but have let them stand as statements addressing particular issues. The volume is structured around three major organizational groupings of the essays. The first group comprises the text and tools necessary for linguistic analysis of the Greek New Testament. In this section, I first raise the question of who owns the Greek New Testament. By this, I mean to ask the question of who owns the modern eclectic Greek New Testament that is promoted and widely sold by a number of different people—all apparently purporting it to be the original Greek, or as close as we can come to it (otherwise, why undertake this particular project?). I also tackle some of the computer-related needs of those interested in serious study of the Greek New Testament, finding that, even with the surrounding hyperbole regarding computer technology, we have still not progressed as far as we need to. I close this section with two essays on matters of lexicography, one reviewing the Louw-Nida semantic-domains lexicon and the other the fairly recently revised Bauer lexicon by Frederick Danker. I believe that the Louw-Nida lexicon is an underutilized resource in New Testament studies, while the Bauer type of lexicon is probably best seen as reflecting an earlier day and age in lexicography.

The second part of this volume is concerned with ways to approach analysis—in other words, linguistic orientations to the Greek of the New Testament. Most of these approaches overtly reflect the SFL method that I have found so productive in most of the studies that I have done—although I have not used this method exclusively, as noted above, or simply attempted to impose categories developed for the study of English, a configurational language, on ancient Greek, a nonconfigurational language. This second group of essays includes an introductory exploration of the value of linguistics for biblical interpretation that outlines some of my views on lexicographical study; a discussion of how linguistics within a multidisciplinary orientation can contribute to exegesis; an exploration of some of the topics in sociolinguistics that I have pursued in other venues and that merit further exploration; an overview of discourse analysis applied to the study of the Greek New Testament; and an explanation of the ideational metafunction within a register framework (both metafunctions and register being essential concepts in SFL). The close of this section includes three essays that address criticisms of my approach to verbal aspect. The first is a response to a much earlier essay by K. L. McKay. Some may wonder why I have taken so long to respond to him. I have been asked this on several occasions, and I have asked myself as well. One of the reasons is that in most respects McKay and I agree, and so his article did not seem to warrant a confrontative response. Nevertheless, after further thought and seeing references to his article by others, I include a few words in response here. The next essay responds to comments first made by Buist Fanning at a conference and then in printed form regarding my approach to aspect, especially its relationship to temporality. I tackle his three objections (concerning the augment, the performative present, and the arguments of Daniel Wallace), as well as a further one regarding aspectually vague verbs, a notion that I introduced into Greek language study. I show that there is little to argue for on behalf of Fanning's proposals, and in fact quite a bit to argue against. The final essay tackles an area where I have followed and developed the research of several important grammarians before me, especially J. P. Louw and K. L. McKay, in defining the Greek perfect tense-form as grammatical-izing stative aspect. There are some other Greek grammarians who for various reasons—either a restricted view of binarism or a confused notion of aspect and *Aktionsart*—have hesitated to pursue a definition of the semantics of the perfect tense-form as having its own semantic function. In this essay, I defend my conception of stative aspect.

In the third and final section of this book, I include several essays that il-lustrate linguistically informed biblical analysis being undertaken. The first is a register analysis of Mark 13. I have previously used Mark 13 as an example text when I developed a discourse-features criterion for historical-Jesus study. In this volume, I use the notion of register as user-based variety of language to explicate Mark 13. I follow this essay on Mark with one on Matthew's Gospel, in particular the so-called Great Commission in Matthew 28:19–20. I examine the language of this important passage in order to determine through grammatical analysis the organization of its thought. The next essay explores alterations in verbal aspect in extrabiblical Greek and the Synoptic Gospels, as an attempt to bring aspectual study to bear on the study of Synoptic relations. The fourth essay surveys and critiques recent research in John's Gospel and suggests that a variety of linguistically based means of examining this Gospel might prove more productive in the future than has some previous literary-oriented research. Here I offer examples of three different types of linguistic analysis, including literary stylistics, discourse analysis, and register analysis (all admittedly influenced by SFL). In the next chapter I offer an examination of the opponents in three of Paul's letters—Philemon, Romans, and Colossians—by drawing upon the structuralist and functional model of Karl Bühler, a member of the Prague Linguistics Circle and predecessor of Hallidayan functionalism. This chapter is followed by a short study of the grammar of 1 Timothy 2:8. Then in the next chapter I revisit the state of play in word-order studies in New Testament scholarship, attempting to clear the ground and offer some ways forward in this still understudied and, unfortunately, underconceptualized area.

In the next chapter, going where previous philosophers of language have not dared to go, I explore the notion of a proper noun in Greek—what appears to be a straightforward topic made more difficult by the language itself. I close the volume with an essay that brings the linguistic category of hyponymy to bear on the question of the Trinity—at least on how God/Father, Son, and Holy Spirit are conceptualized lexically in the New Testament.

I realize that much more could be said at virtually every point in these essays. I have not written them to be definitive studies in any regard (certainly not regarding bibliography), but rather as steps forward in what I believe is an essential and developing discussion. As I mentioned above, I am troubled by exegesis that shows no apparent awareness of the complex issues involved in the study of the Greek of the New Testament. I do not in any way wish to minimize the complexity of such interpretive problems or pretend that all of them are easily solved simply by invoking a vague notion of linguistics. However, I believe that much more can and should be done in this field—we can never know its usefulness unless we make the effort. This volume is an attempt to establish some of the theory that might be usefully employed in such linguistic study, and to demonstrate its possibilities in some explorations of the Greek New Testament.

Texts and Tools
for Analysis

1

Who Owns the Greek Text of the New Testament?

Issues That Promote and Hinder Further Study

Introduction

Let me begin by making one point very clearly: I am not a lawyer of any kind, much less a copyright lawyer, nor the son of a lawyer. But I am a scholar who is very interested in the Greek text of the New Testament, and so I am unavoidably interested in the accessibility of that text, as are all of us who have a share in New Testament studies. This interest and concern has prompted my investigation into this issue. I do not pretend that what I have discovered is in any way legally sound, or that anything I say here would stand up in any legal context, such as a courtroom. Please do not take what I write here as in any way offering legal advice. It is not meant as that. What I intend to offer is a preliminary exploration of the issue of copyright and how it relates to the Greek text of the New Testament.

There has been much controversy over the years regarding the issue of who owns an ancient text. One of the most well known of these recent confrontations has concerned the so-called Qumran text 4QMMT.[1] To summarize a

1. My discussion here is based upon the several accounts and documents found in T. H. Lim, H. L. MacQueen, and C. M. Carmichael, eds., *On Scrolls, Artefacts and Intellectual Property*,

complex set of events, let me offer the following précis. Access to many of the Dead Sea Scrolls was limited for a number of years and for a variety of reasons, which need not be discussed in this essay. A number of scholars were concerned about what they perceived to be an inordinate delay in getting the scrolls published, and they were trying in various ways to force those who had access to the scrolls to open up that access. During this time, a number of scholars were purportedly working on various scrolls, or fragments of them, and sometimes their results were discussed at conferences or made available in various ways to other scholars—all without indicating or implying publication. One such text was the so-called 4QMMT. This manuscript, or set of fragments, had originally been assigned to the American scholar John Strugnell, who then had brought in the Israeli scholar Elisha Qimron to work on it with him. It appears that through the course of their working together, the major burden of the work had shifted from Strugnell to Qimron, who had created and made available in limited fashion copies of the text, including an assemblage of the fragments and reconstruction of readings for lacunae. An anonymous copy of this document apparently came into the hands of the editor of a journal in Poland, who proceeded to publish it, but with a disclaimer regarding knowledge of its provenance, or even its authenticity. It seems that, when Qimron found out that this document had been published, through legal means he was able to get the journal to cease distribution, and the editor apologized for promulgating the text without permission or acknowledgment of its editor or editors. Through a subsequent series of fortuitous events, the American publisher Herschel Shanks came into possession of copies of photographs showing the Dead Sea Scrolls. In conjunction with the American scholars Robert Eisenman and James Robinson as editors of the volume, in 1991 Shanks published a facsimile edition of these plates. He also apparently included publication of a photocopy of 120 of the 132 lines of 4QMMT, a copy of the page that had appeared in the Polish journal. As a result, in 1992 Qimron filed suit in an Israeli court for copyright violation, contending that he owned the copyright on this edition of the text of 4QMMT and that the publication by someone else had denied him what was legally his right and resulted in serious financial and other consequences. This court case was heard, and a verdict was rendered in 1993 by an Israeli district court, finding for the plaintiff, Qimron, and assigning damages. This verdict was appealed to the Israeli Supreme Court, which in 2000 issued its verdict upholding the district court's decision.

JSPSup 38 (Sheffield: Sheffield Academic Press, 2001), especially the translation of the ensuing legal case, D. Dorner, "The Judgment," 26–62, and "Appendix: The Supreme Court Judgment," 232–58.

These legal cases raised a series of intriguing questions regarding jurisdiction (the edition was published in the United States, but the suit was filed in Israel), which laws are applicable and on what basis (as I will note below, copyright laws vary from country to country, but in this case the Israeli district court deemed that the laws were considered the same, even though the United States does not appear to recognize *droit moral* [see below] in the same way that Israel does), what type and level of proof are required with regard to matters of copyright, and how damages are decided. But the most important issue that remained central to the case, and that is central to my discussion here, is what constitutes copyrightable material. How does copyright relate to the editor of an edited document, and what is the relation of the editorial task to the handling of ancient texts? One can clearly see that these questions are relevant for those who work with the Greek text of the New Testament. To put the matter more succinctly, the question for New Testament scholars is this: can a modern edited edition of the ancient Greek text of the New Testament be copyrighted? This is the issue I address here. A number of important considerations must be discussed.

What Is the Purpose of Copyright?

As I noted above—and I understand that this is a fairly common legal procedure in such cases—even though the facsimile edition of Shanks was published in the United States, because several copies were sold or distributed in Israel, the Israeli courts decided that they had jurisdiction. In such cases, however, it is not uncommon for a court to also make reference to or introduce the laws of the other jurisdiction. In fact, as I understand it, in many legal systems there is a provision for an understanding that the laws of the respective countries are deemed to be equivalent under "the 'presumption of equal laws' doctrine"[2] and to enshrine the same principles of justice, and that one of the parties would need to show that this is not the case.[3]

I state this because the first question that must be raised concerns the purpose of copyright, and it seems to me that the purpose of copyright is one area where US law is different from that of other countries. In fact, the US legal position on copyright not only appears to be different from that of other countries, but also appears to be different from the popular understanding of it. Most people think of copyright as a means of protecting their work

2. See C. A. Carson, "The Application of American Copyright Law to the Dead Sea Scrolls Controversy," in Lim, MacQueen, and Carmichael, *On Scrolls*, 74–98 (quotation, p. 76).

3. On the issue of jurisdiction, see P. L. C. Torremans, "Choice of Law regarding Copyright and the Dead Sea Scrolls: The Basic Principles," in Lim, MacQueen, and Carmichael, *On Scrolls*, 116–27.

and defending against that work being misappropriated by others. It also appears that this is the understanding of copyright in some other countries, such as Britain. However, the US law on copyright is explicitly designed for a very different purpose: the promotion and dissemination of knowledge. In discussions of copyright in US law, a distinction is made between the facts and the expression of them. What copyright protects is an individual's creative expression, not the facts that are being conveyed. The facts are considered to be in the public domain, and these cannot be copyrighted. This type of positivistic approach to facts versus their interpretation may rankle some, but it seems to be one that US law makes. What is more, even an individual's expression is not copyrightable if that expression is thought to be the only way that something could be expressed; that is, it does not demonstrate the requisite creativity. Thus the names in a phone book cannot be copyrighted, and neither can the choice of putting them in alphabetical order, since this is the most self-evidently logical way to display them. If one were to display them upside down and according to the second letter of the first name, I suppose that would arguably be copyrightable, since it is a unique form of expression.

My experience indicates that many people have a consistent, but perhaps a consistently wrong, idea of what copyright means, at least in the United States. In the light of the emphasis in the United States upon freedom of speech and information, as well as a reticence toward other forms of restraint on expression, it is not surprising to find out that the US copyright law promotes the spread and dissemination of ideas. The goal is for as much information as possible to be made available so that as many people as can make use of it have access without being unduly hindered in their use of this information. In fact, it has been pointed out that this understanding of copyright finds its basis in the US Constitution, which states that copyright is "to promote the progress of science and useful arts, by securing for limited times to authors and inventors the exclusive right to their respective writings and discoveries." European law, and in particular British law, does not have anything equivalent to this. According to H. L. MacQueen, British and European copyright laws are "founded much more on the basis of respect for the personality of the author and its expression in his or her work."[4] However, US copyright provides for a wider dissemination of human knowledge.[5]

4. H. L. MacQueen, "Copyright Law and the Dead Sea Scrolls: A British Perspective," in Lim, MacQueen, and Carmichael, *On Scrolls*, 99–115 (quotation, p. 101). This has also led Britain to adopt the *droit moral*, or moral right of identification as the author of a work, and it is re-flected in a statement often found on the bibliographical information page of published books.

5. Carson, "Application of American Copyright," 89. Carson also says, "Certainly, nowhere is the tension between free access to knowledge and the copyright holder's proprietary interest more at odds than in an academic setting."

What Is Copyrightable?

The second question that must be raised concerns the definition of copyrightable material. What is it that can or cannot be copyrighted? In this area we encounter another fundamental difference of opinion. I will leave aside the issue of Israeli copyright law and will deal in particular—though admittedly in a superficial and nonprofessional way—with copyright law in Britain, Germany, and the United States. On the basis of what I have said above, it is perhaps not surprising that there are differences among the various countries. In Britain, to a large extent copyright law has been governed by a statement made in 1916 by Mr. Justice Peterson to the effect that "what is worth copying is worth protecting."[6] From that statement, as far as what I have read indicates, in England copyrightability is dictated upon the fact that someone has in essence invested skill and labor in whatever task has been undertaken.[7] This provides for a broad definition of what constitutes copyrightability, so that virtually any product of one's efforts becomes copyrightable. Germany and most of the rest of Europe, by contrast, require that the work created be "the author's own personal or intellectual creation" in order to be covered by copyright.[8] Here the emphasis is upon the intellectual component in the creation, rather than simply the author having demonstrated that a certain amount of skill and labor were invested in the task. The US copyright law is the most narrow and restrictive: it grants copyright "only in original works of authorship which have been fixed in a tangible medium of expression."[9] Or, expressed otherwise, "The limited monopoly granted by copyright applies only to the expression of ideas, not the ideas themselves."[10] The emphasis in US copyright law is upon the originality of the works involved.

One can see that there are a number of potential conflicts over what can be copyrighted on the basis of these distinctions. Although most countries are now signatories of a general copyright law (the Berne Convention, signed in 1886), there are still apparent discrepancies. According to what I have read, apparently pressure is being exerted upon Britain to change its law so it is in more general conformity with the laws elsewhere in Europe regarding copyright. This would bring the law into closer relation to the law in the United States, but the US law is still more restrictive.

6. See MacQueen, "Copyright Law," 105.
7. Ibid.
8. Ibid., 100.
9. Carson, "Application of American Copyright Law," 76.
10. Ibid., 84.

Application of Copyright Law to the Task of Editing

Now I wish to raise several questions regarding how what I have said above relates to the task of editing a text. Let me begin by saying a couple of things about what I have summarized above in relation to the Qimron-versus-Shanks case. Again, my opinion is not that of a lawyer, but from what I have read, I get the clear impression that if the case had been tried in Britain, with the law the way that it is now, Qimron may well have had a similar judgment in his favor. It would have been potentially provable, if not admitted by the defendants, that Qimron had invested skill and labor in the editing task. In fact, my reading of the case transcript indicates that the court did accept that Qimron brought unique personal skills in Hebrew philology and halakic law to the task, and that this constituted the basis for his claiming copyright prerogative.

In my reading, I did not come across a clear indication of how the case would have fared in a European court, but I can imagine that the more restrictive definition would have made it more difficult for Qimron to win his case. He would have had to prove that the edited text was his own personal or intellectual creation. In the transcript of the case, one example was given of how Qimron decided between variant readings, and perhaps this would have been enough to constitute the work as his personal or intellectual creation, although I highly doubt it.

I think that it is generally conceded, and has been argued by at least two US experts in copyright law, that in terms of US law, the verdict almost assuredly would have gone against Qimron. The reasons that I gather for this are several. One reason is the clear statement of the US law that copyright only applies to original works. In this sense, the authors of the original scrolls themselves—insofar as the scrolls are original—would have a claim to copyright; yet due to the passage of time, their expressions are now in the public domain. A second reason relates to how the editing task is defined. If the editing task is confined to examining variant readings in order to determine which of them is closest to the original, then the resulting work fails the test of originality since it is an attempt at reconstructing what was written by someone else. The better the editor, by definition the less original is the editor's work, and hence the less copyrightable is the product. This seems to apply whether one actually has the variants to choose from in the fragmentary remains themselves, or whether one or more of the variants is not to be found in the manuscripts but is conjectured by the editor. In both cases, the goal of finding what an original author wrote is the same. A third reason for the opinion that the verdict in the United States would have gone against Qimron is raised by editorial work that requires the piecing together of fragmentary manuscripts. Does such work qualify for copyright? Certainly the compilation of a work from preexisting materials is copyrightable in certain instances and under certain circumstances, such as the work done by an editor who compiles a collection of others' essays, as they were never previously gathered together. Nevertheless, the piecing together of fragments of an ancient text does not appear to be copyrightable, for the very reasons I have just noted. The goal of the piecing together of the fragments is to reconstruct the original text, not create an original work. Although there may be a number of ways in which the fragments could be arranged, only a limited number of possibilities are likely if one is seeking conformity with what the original text said. Even when the editorial process is tedious, involving many fragments, as long as it is trying to reconstruct an earlier original, it probably is not copyrightable under US law.

Copyright Law and the Ancient Greek New Testament Text

Now I turn directly to the ancient Greek text of the New Testament and ask: is the ancient Greek text of the New Testament copyrightable? Clearly, one must first answer another question: copyrightable where?

If we are asking the question in relation to British law as it apparently currently stands, a case can perhaps be made that an edition of the Greek New Testament can be copyrighted. As I have already stated, British law provides a very low standard for qualification and is currently under pressure because too many works (so some say) are being accorded copyright.[11] Yet when we look at the issue in relation to European and US copyright laws, significant obstacles emerge. To understand why this is so, we must carefully consider what the modern Greek New Testament is and what it purports to be. I am referring, of course, to what is today commonly called the Nestle-Aland Greek New Testament.

Eberhard Nestle's text, as most scholars are aware, was originally an edition based upon three previous editions, those of Constantin Tischendorf, B. F. Westcott and F. J. A. Hort, and Richard Weymouth (and later Bernhard Weiss). Nestle adopted readings that appeared in two or more of the three texts. This undoubtedly involved labor, but one may well question the level of skill, since the avowed purpose was simply to make widely available the results of nineteenth-century scholarship.[12] Of course, even if Nestle's text were

11. MacQueen, "Copyright Law," 105, 109.
12. Introduction to the 26th edition of the Nestle-Aland *Novum Testamentum Graece*, 39*. The statement has been changed slightly, though remains in essence the same, in the introduction to the 27th edition of the Nestle-Aland *Novum Testamentum Graece*, 44*. A similar idea

copyrightable by today's standards, the edition itself—no matter how many reprints with varying apparatuses have been made—is public domain since Nestle died in 1913. The same rationale is true for the editions of Westcott and Hort and of Tischendorf.

In order to see if there is any justification for the copyright of the more recent text contained in the 26th edition of the *Novum Testamentum Graece*, by 2012 with some few modifications in the 28th edition, let us consider three comments that have been made regarding that Greek text (the newer editions do not affect the point). In *The Text of the New Testament*, Kurt Aland and Barbara Aland write, "The new text is . . . based . . . on a review of all the evidence that is in any way relevant to establishing the original text, whether Greek manuscripts as early as the second century, or versions, or writings of early Church Fathers in various languages—always examining the original texts while constantly reviewing the external factors which affect the value of their testimony."[13] These remarks are mostly relevant in relation to British copyright law, which is largely predicated on the notion that any investment of skill and labor deserves to be protected.

Since it is unquestionable that effort and even skill have been invested in the text of the *Novum Testamentum Graece*, the text appears to be copyrightable under British law. It can also be granted, on the basis of the above quotation, that the text meets similar requirements imposed in other jurisdictions. German copyright law, for instance, requires (in part) that new editions "represent the result of scientific analysis."[14]

A second important comment appears in the introduction to the 26th edition of the *Novum Testamentum Graece*, which appeared in 1979. The author of the introduction (Kurt and Barbara Aland?) draws attention to insights gained from the Greek papyri and then appeals to these insights as an indication that the 26th edition represents an advance over earlier texts. A contrast is made with Westcott and Hort's work, which was clearly dependent upon the two major codices (Sinaiticus and Vaticanus). The introduction concludes that these codices cannot provide guidance for the text that is used today: "The age of Westcott-Hort and of Tischendorf is definitely over!"[15]

---

stood behind the earlier Cambridge Greek Testament for Schools and Colleges, which created a text based upon Tischendorf and Tregelles.

13. K. Aland and B. Aland, *The Text of the New Testament: An Introduction to the Critical Editions and to the Theory and Practice of Modern Textual Criticism*, 2nd ed., trans. E. F. Rhodes (Grand Rapids: Eerdmans, 1989), 36.

14. MacQueen, "Copyright Law," 111, citing German Copyright Act 1965, s. 70(1).

15. Introduction to the 26th edition of the Nestle-Aland *Novum Testamentum Graece*, 43*.

The thrust of this comment, and the general impression given by the introduction, is that the text of the 26th edition of the *Novum Testamentum Graece* differs significantly from earlier editions of the Greek New Testament because it incorporates new evidence that renders previous editions obsolete. This is important because it would seem to be the primary way one could lay claim to copyright under German law, which applies copyright to editions "if they represent the result of scientific analysis [see above] *and* differ in a significant manner from previously known editions of the works or texts."[16] Remember, however, that the basis of the previous editions of the Nestle(-Aland) Greek Testament is in fact Tischendorf, Westcott and Hort, and a couple of other texts; and the editions up to the 25th, according to the textual scholar Philip Comfort, are virtually identical, varying only in the apparatus. According to Comfort, the Nestle-Aland 26th edition makes only 176 changes from the 25th edition, based upon new evidence from the papyri.[17] The 27th edition apparently was unchanged from the 26th. According to the Nestle-Aland website maintained by the German Bible Society, the 28th edition includes a further 34 changes (in the Catholic Epistles), making a maximum number of 210 changes in the 28th edition from the 25th (assuming none were changed back to match a previous edition). Now if each of these changes involved a variant unit of two words (most probably involve only a single word), that would mean 420 words changed out of a total of 138,100 in the entire New Testament, a change amounting to 0.3 percent. Clearly, if the availability of new evidence has resulted in a change of only 0.3 percent, then the age of Tischendorf and Westcott and Hort is not over. Even though the Nestle-Aland texts represent "the result of scientific analysis," I find it hard to believe that changes to 0.3 percent of a text constitute a "significant" alteration, particularly when the vast majority of those changes involve single words. As one scholar points out, the amount of change necessary for a copyrightable composition cannot be a single letter or even a single word, and a single line is even dubious: although how much change would be sufficient remains unknown, it appears to require a "significant" amount.[18] It is thus questionable whether the Nestle-Aland text

16. MacQueen, "Copyright Law," 111, citing German Copyright Act 1965, s. 70(1) (italics added).

17. P. W. Comfort, *The Quest for the Original Text of the New Testament* (Grand Rapids: Baker, 1992), 123. There may be other changes, but I am not clear what the justification for those would be, apart from correcting incidental errors. Even if they represent individual decisions on the basis of other evidence, presumably they would reflect an attempt to correct readings now deemed less reliable than new readings deemed closer to the original text.

18. D. Nimmer, "Assaying Qimron's Originality," in Lim, MacQueen, and Carmichael, *On Scrolls*, 159–76 (quotation, 163n24). He cites a decision from 1946 in which the judge suggests that only "extraordinarily fanciful lines" should be accorded copyright.

of the Greek New Testament can lay claim to copyright protection in jurisdictions where copyright laws impose a requirement of significant change. The edition may not even qualify under German copyright law.

A third statement by Kurt Aland highlights an even more significant obstacle, however, especially when the issue is looked at in the light of how I understand European and US laws on copyright. Reflecting on the text of the 26th edition, Aland suggests that it can be said to have met the goal of providing an edition of the New Testament "in the original Greek."[19] Even though such a statement is tempered in the introduction to the 27th edition,[20] the goal of the text-critical enterprise remains the same: the original text of the New Testament. In European law, it is required that a copyrightable work be its author's personal or intellectual creation. For US copyright law, the germane issue seems to be the issue of creativity or originality. Yet it appears to me that the Nestle-Aland text fails both standards in three significant regards. First, it fails insofar as the number of changes from previous editions is not sufficient for the work as a whole to warrant the label of being creative or original. To the contrary, the Nestle-Aland text appears to be highly derivative, to the point that 99.7 percent of it reflects earlier texts. Second, and more important, the nature of the changes made from previous editions prevents them from constituting expressions of creativity and originality. Each of the changes, as far as I know, is intended to be a change from the reading in one set of manuscripts to another, or to what the editors think must have been in the original manuscript.[21] In other words, there is no variant that supplies a

19. K. Aland, "Der neue 'Standard-Text' in seinem Verhältnis zu den frühen Papyri und Majuskeln," in *New Testament Textual Criticism: Its Significance for Exegesis; Essays in Honour of Bruce M. Metzger*, ed. E. J. Epp and G. D. Fee (Oxford: Clarendon, 1981), 274–75, cited in E. J. Epp, "Textual Criticism in the Exegesis of the New Testament, with an Excursus on Canon," in *Handbook to Exegesis of the New Testament*, ed. S. E. Porter, NTTS 25 (Leiden: Brill, 1997), 90; compare K. Aland, "The Significance of the Papyri for Progress in New Testament Research," in *The Bible in Modern Scholarship: Papers Read at the 100th Meeting of the Society of Biblical Literature, December 28–30, 1964*, ed. J. P. Hyatt (Nashville: Abingdon, 1965), 325–46, esp. 341. See also, for discussion of the goal of textual criticism of the Greek New Testament, S. E. Porter, *How We Got the New Testament: Text, Transmission, Translation* (Grand Rapids: Baker Academic, 2013), 9–76.

20. The introduction to the 27th edition of the Nestle-Aland *Novum Testamentum Graece* states, "It should naturally be understood that this text is a working text (in the sense of the century-long Nestle tradition): it is not to be considered as definitive, but as a stimulus to further efforts toward defining and verifying the text of the New Testament" (p. 44*). However, it also states immediately following, "For many reasons, however, the present edition has not been deemed an appropriate occasion for introducing textual changes" (it is the same as the 26th edition, which varies in only 176 places from the previous edition, to which Aland refers).

21. The issue has been raised regarding what have been called "zero" or "conjectural" readings in the Nestle-Aland text, but I assume that the editors were, according to their stated intentions, attempting to identify the original reading, even if inadvertently they reconstructed

completely new or original piece of text; each one was written by a previous (ancient) scribe or is meant to reflect what such a scribe should have written. Some of these scribes perhaps could sustain a claim to creativity and originality, but the same cannot be said about the editor who simply selects one particular reading from among others, even if it is a conjectural reading. A work such as this cannot be deemed a personal or intellectual creation when its components are directly attributable to others, presumably as part of a previously existing text. A third obstacle is the fact that the goal for editing the Greek New Testament, by definition as noted above, is reconstruction of the original.[22] Each contemporary decision to change the text of an older edition of the Greek New Testament represents a conscious attempt to come closer to reconstructing the ancient original text.

Now, clearly nobody would attempt to copyright the Greek New Testament if the original manuscripts of its books suddenly materialized, so, in the absence of such an unlikely development, can the (attempted) reconstruction of those manuscripts be deemed a creative process resulting in originality? Copyright law seems to indicate that, even when an original text is not extant, fidelity to the original is the goal of the editorial process, and so failure to have the original does not change the result. The edited text is unoriginal insofar as it purports to be a reconstruction of the original text. The paradox of creating an edition, according to US copyright law, therefore, is that the textual editing task, by definition, creates a product that is not subject to copyright protection. The only kind of edition that would be subject to such protection is one that laid no claim to reconstructing the original but attempted to introduce wantonly variant readings created by the editor. Such an edition would, of course, be unreliable and worthless for scholars of the original text of the Greek New Testament.

This consideration of the evidence forces me to conclude that the text of the ancient Greek New Testament as presented in the Nestle-Aland edition (and by implication the United Bible Societies' *Greek New Testament* also, which claims to be the same word for word) probably is not protectable by copyright under European law, and almost assuredly not protectable by copyright under US law. The latter conclusion is consistent with US copyright law on

---

the text without manuscript support or if intentionally they believed that a nonattested reading was original. See M. A. Robinson, "Rule 9, Isolated Variants, and the 'Test-Tube' Nature of the NA[27]/UBS[4] Text: A Byzantine-Priority Perspective," in *Translating the New Testament: Text, Translation, Theology*, ed. S. E. Porter and M. J. Boda (Grand Rapids: Eerdmans, 2009), 27–61, esp. 60–61.

22. Some might contest this, but if the goal is not reconstruction of the original, it must be reconstruction of some early ancient edition, as long as one wants to have people use this text as an approximation of the ancient Greek New Testament.

the dissemination of information, in which such dissemination is designed to create access to knowledge rather than restrict access and protect information.

Conclusion

As I noted at the outset, I am not a lawyer nor the son of a lawyer, but what information I have discovered seems to point away from the possibility of copyrighting the currently used Greek New Testament, and probably any other edition of the Greek New Testament that purports to reconstruct the original or something reliably similar to it.

My discussion, of course, has not addressed things such as punctuation or the critical apparatus. These are, in fact, two separate issues, as I see it. It may be possible to copyright modern punctuation decisions, since these do not reconstruct what the original documents contained. Even here, however, one must be careful, at least in regard to US copyright law, insofar as the range of punctuation marks is limited. If a sentence demands a period, then I am skeptical whether there is any creative element involved in putting that period in its place, in which case punctuation probably cannot be copyrighted. The critical apparatus, at least the arrangement of it and the format, probably is copyrightable. However, again, it is questionable to me whether the readings from the various manuscripts themselves are copyrightable, since they are all derived from ancient manuscripts and supposed to be facts (errors in the apparatus notwithstanding).

The ancient text of the Greek New Testament itself, especially when considered under European or US law, does not in itself appear to be a text that can be subject to copyright by its editors; after all, those editors are attempting to reconstruct and disseminate an ancient Greek text as it came from the pens of ancient writers, whether the original authors or their close compatriots. This conclusion is consistent with the kind of public access to information that is so important to the world of scholarship. Such public access deserves to be supported and promoted in all of the work that we as scholars do.

2

Analyzing the Computer Needs of New Testament Greek Exegetes

Introduction

Biblical studies scholars are fortunate to have computer-based resources to utilize in their study. For example, among a number of other available resources for studying the text, most are familiar with Accordance, LOGOS, and the BibleWorks programs. There are others, less well known but also valuable for their similar provision of the text of the Greek New Testament in a machine-readable and searchable format.[1]

By comparison, both those scholars primarily engaged in classical studies (the other major discipline involved in the study of ancient Greek texts) and those in New Testament studies have access to the very valuable tool of the *Thesaurus linguae Graecae* (*TLG*), with originally its several CDs of material and now its online version, and the web-based Perseus project. In its current configuration, according to its website, the *TLG* includes more than 105 million words of ancient Greek authors ranging from the eighth century BC to

---

1. Within the ever-changing environment of computer technology, I am not trying to offer an exhaustive survey of the field but am merely attempting to describe my interaction with it to make larger observations.

the fifteenth century AD, as well as including some documentary papyri and inscriptions. New Testament scholars who have availed themselves of the *TLG* are well aware of what valuable resources it provides. One has at one's fingertips the recorded texts of thousands of authors and millions of their words. However, there are also severe limitations to this material when one compares these with what is available through BibleWorks or Accordance. The *TLG* is basically an archive of computer-readable texts, which at least ostensibly purports to facilitate retrieval of individual lexical items, or sets of lexical items within certain ranges of proximity (I will return to this below). In other words, this is essentially a concordance resource.[2] Yet it is often useful for the kinds of studies that classical and biblical scholars wish to perform. For example, traditional word studies are still important for many studies of ancient texts, including those of New Testament scholars. Through the *TLG*, all of the occurrences of a given Greek lexical item can be retrieved, placing the use of this lexical item found in the Greek New Testament within the larger context of all instances of this word in ancient usage.

There are also, however, some noticeable shortcomings of this approach as well. The first is that, as noted already, the *TLG* is essentially a concordance database. I admit that it has made progress in this regard, developing from a heavily morphologically dependent database to one that allows searching of individual lemmata. When I began my work with the *TLG*, it was designed to search not lemmata but individual letter characters. I made one of the earliest attempts at a complete study of a given Greek lexical item using the *TLG*, the word καταλλάσσω in all of ancient Greek literature.[3] To retrieve all of the instances of this word, I had to search several different letter combinations. I could not simply search for the lemma καταλλάσσω/ειν, since the words apparently were tagged by strings of individual letters. So, in order to have all of the occurrences of this word in ancient Greek literature, I had to search for a variety of partial forms of the word, such as καταλλασσ/ττ, κατηλλασσ/ττ, κατηλλαξ, καταλλαξ, κατηλλαχ, καταλλαχ, κατηλλαγ, and καταλλαγ. As a result, however, not only did I get all of the verb forms of καταλλάσσω but I also got the noun forms (since this database did not differentiate parts of speech) and a number of other words that have these letter combinations in

2. For the most comprehensive discussion of corpus linguistics, including types of corpora, in New Testament studies, see M. B. O'Donnell, *Corpus Linguistics and the Greek of the New Testament*, NTM 6 (Sheffield: Sheffield Phoenix Press, 2005), esp. 38–167.

3. S. E. Porter, *Καταλλάσσω in Ancient Greek Literature, with Reference to the Pauline Writings*, EFN 5 (Córdoba: Ediciones el Almendro, 1994). This study was actually completed in 1991, and the searches were done on the mainframe computer housed in the *TLG* offices at the University of California, Irvine.

them as well. The issue has now been remedied, so as to allow for specification of morphological forms of the lemma to be searched. This helps to eliminate one of the major shortcomings of concordance searches: often a search produces a larger number of hits, or more data, than one is requesting or even prepared to handle. Even with the specific constraints that I had set on my search for forms of καταλλάσσω in its different verbal stems, I was unable to limit the search sufficiently to produce that result alone. From the start, the *TLG* had adequate recall, but now it has increased its precision by allowing for searches of individual lemmata. This nevertheless leads to the third shortcoming of the *TLG*: it does not (as far as I can tell) provide for grammatical or syntactical searches of much complexity at all. The so-called complex searches of the online *TLG* are only rough at best. They provide a couple of different combinations of word occurrences in proximity. This is not truly a syntactical search, where one may need to specify not only parts of speech but also inflections and declensions, and ideally even word, word group, or clause relations, if not more. The reason is simply that little to no syntactical information has been included in the annotation of the words of the *TLG* database, so that this information is not directly retrievable. The database has been created with an emphasis on size rather than detail, so it is unlikely that, at least in its current form, this will be altered.

An advantage of the Perseus project is that its database has lexical and morphological tagging and allows for collocational analysis. The types of searches possible certainly are larger than those of the *TLG* and much to be welcomed, but there are limitations also. The number of annotated texts is comparably much smaller, being limited to essentially major classical authors with a few others (papyri are apparently no longer accessible through Perseus). This limits the direct applicability for students of the New Testament, who ideally should be trying to position the Greek of the New Testament within contemporary Greek usage rather than seeing it primarily in relation to the classical authors. Such a mismatch in comparison has until now been one of the major problems, I believe, in coming to terms with the nature of the Greek of the New Testament. The morphological tagging is a step forward, especially since this includes lemmata, but there is still no syntactical annotation beyond collocation. When I have tried to use the program, it seems to work quite slowly even with only this basic information. There have also been a number of discrepancies in the results produced, which leads me to believe that perhaps the annotation has been inconsistent. As an example, a search for καταλλάσσω on the Perseus database found only 37 examples in its corpus of literature, rather than the well over 350 that I found through the *TLG* (though admittedly with cognates included). The results clearly cannot be relied upon as a thorough or comprehensive study of this lexical item in ancient Greek.

Within these limitations, the *TLG* and the Perseus project have, nonetheless, proved invaluable. The range of literature included in the *TLG* allows for meaningful generic studies to be performed, especially because the *TLG* canon of authors provides basic categorizations of its authors, which can be used to limit searches (e.g., philosopher, medical writer, etc.).[4] This generic sensitivity is something that has often hindered New Testament research, with its failure to appreciate the forms of ancient literature. The stretch of time covered by the authors also allows for genuine diachronic study to be performed, so that a trajectory for New Testament and other usage can be established. One of the most beneficial uses has been the expansion of the archive to include the papyri and inscriptions. With these resources available, it has helped papyrologists and other epigraphers immensely in the identification of ancient authors and in the establishment and retrieval of ancient idioms particular to types of ancient texts, such as documentary papyri. In a significant research project, I used the *TLG* to try to trace the identity of the author of a carefully written fragmentary papyrus manuscript that my wife and I were working on. Once we had read enough of the letters on two lines, I performed a search of the three major and significant words in the *TLG*. Even though two of the words were proximate, the search still produced six hits. The last hit proved to be correct, allowing us to identify our papyrus fragment as a text from the sixth-century Christian writer Romanos Melodus, the fourth papyrus or parchment of this author to be discovered (all of his other manuscripts are medieval documents).[5] No doubt because of the resources of the *TLG*, we were able to identify the author and the text with publication of the papyrus—the first time that this has happened with one of the four Romanos Melodus papyri/parchments, no doubt because previous papyrologists had not had the *TLG* available to help them in their search (identification of the author has usually come about later by other scholars).

In the light of my comments on the *TLG* and my use of it, I hope that I have shown myself sufficiently favorably inclined toward the use of computers in New Testament Greek study. I have reported my use of the *TLG* to accomplish what I think is one of the first complete studies of a Greek lexical item from its earliest use through to the sixth century AD. In addition, I have

4. L. Berkowitz and K. A. Squitier, *Thesaurus Linguae Graecae: Canon of Greek Authors and Works* (New York: Oxford University Press, 1990). This has now been supplemented by further authors, accessible through the *TLG* website.

5. See S. E. Porter and W. J. Porter, "P. Vindob. G 26225: A New Romanos Melodus Papyrus in the Vienna Collection," *JÖB* 52 (2002): 135–48.

worked extensively with what was first GRAMCORD and now Accordance throughout most of my academic career. My first published article, in 1983, was based upon the findings from a GRAMCORD search when it was available only on a mainframe computer (then housed at Indiana University). For a long time the GRAMCORD manual (when such things were printed and in existence) referred to my study as an example of how to utilize the resources of the computer program.[6] I used various computer-based resources for my doctoral research on Greek verbal structure,[7] and for numerous articles and chapters since then.[8] I am also one of the principals in the OpenText.org project, which is the single most innovative annotated database for study of the Greek New Testament and has featured in a number of recent computer-related initiatives. Therefore, I hope that any of the comments that I make in this chapter regarding Accordance and BibleWorks (and the like) are taken in the spirit in which they are intended, as comments made by a longtime user of computer technology and someone able to see and appreciate its many benefits (though without being particularly knowledgeable in the intricacies of how computers actually work, which is why I use a Mac).

In thinking about the available computer resources for study of the Greek New Testament, I have repeatedly come back to three areas in which, I think, questions should be raised about how the technology has been developed and what it purports to be doing. Perhaps some of my observations will only reveal my own lack of thorough and detailed knowledge of how to use these resources, but my suspicion is that if these are problems for me, then they may well be problems or at least questions for others as well—or at least should be, since some may not even have probed as far as I have but rather have simply accepted what their computer printouts or displays have told them.

6. S. E. Porter, "The Adjectival Attributive Genitive in the New Testament: A Grammatical Study," *TJ* 4 (1983): 3–17.

7. S. E. Porter, *Verbal Aspect in the Greek of the New Testament, with Reference to Tense and Mood*, SBG 1 (New York: Peter Lang, 1989).

8. For example, S. E. Porter, "Is *dipsuchos* (James 1:8; 4:8) a 'Christian' Word?," *Bib* 71 (1990): 469–98; Porter, "What Does It Mean to Be 'Saved by Childbirth' (1 Timothy 2:15)?," *JSNT* 49 (1993): 87–102; S. E. Porter and M. B. O'Donnell, "The Implications of Textual Variants for Authenticating the Words of Jesus," in *Authenticating the Words of Jesus*, ed. B. Chilton and C. A. Evans, NTTS 28.1 (Leiden: Brill, 1999), 97–133; S. E. Porter, "The Functional Distribution of Koine Greek in First-Century Palestine," and S. E. Porter and M. B. O'Donnell, "Semantics and Patterns of Argumentation in the Book of Romans: Definitions, Proposals, Data and Experiments," both in *Diglossia and Other Topics in New Testament Linguistics*, ed. S. E. Porter, JSNTSup 193, SNTG 6 (Sheffield: Sheffield Academic Press, 2000), 53–78, 154–204; Porter and O'Donnell, "The Greek Verbal Network Viewed from a Probabilistic Standpoint: An Exercise in Hallidayan Linguistics," *FN* 14 (2001): 3–41. It will be obvious from the above that Matthew Brook O'Donnell, my former student and now colleague, and also OpenText.org principal, is a genuine computer aficionado, for which I have long been grateful.

Closing Ranks against the Friendly?

My first criticism of the current computer resources for the study of the New Testament grows directly out of the set of observations that I have made above. Let us say that in dealing with the Greek of the New Testament, a researcher wishes to add a text to that of the New Testament (say, the apocryphal gospel fragments) for the sake of close textual comparison rather than working with the New Testament, the Septuagint, or Josephus (I have some serious questions about why Josephus seems to be in the Christian canon, at least for many scholars, but that is another issue). Or let us say that in the course of retrieving certain information from the data available, the interpreter disagrees with some of the findings, or even finds an error and wishes to correct it. Or let us say that to facilitate the study, the researcher wishes to enhance the current program by adding further searches and means of displaying the results, features still unavailable. In any of these areas, to be quite blunt, there is next to nothing that can be done, except write to the producers of the particular database and search program and request that in a future version they correct or alter such findings, or add new or different search or display capabilities, or get busy on the annotation of further texts. In other words, the user is essentially excluded from altering the database or the search program of the purchased software. The reason for this is simple. The producers of the databases and the programs have restricted outside access to this information so that they can provide the added features and facilities according to their own schedule of updating such things.

I can attest from personal experience, however, that such limitations have both positive and negative sides to them. On the one hand, I do not want to have to become a computer programmer and software developer in order to run my basic search programs (I did that in the eighth grade and disliked it immensely). I want to leave this to those who are interested in such things and far more expert. Furthermore, I am not interested in depriving these people of their livelihoods, especially since they have done so much good for biblical research by making such resources widely available, and through doing so have provided a meaningful and hopefully fulfilling life for themselves. However, such limitations do have their immediate and residual liabilities, and I have had to confront each one of them in the course of my own research and the use of computer-generated research tools.

For example, if there is an error in the database, or even a consistently made but highly contentious annotation, it means that I cannot count on completely accurate information individually or globally in this particular search area for as long as I access this database. It also calls into question the reliability of data retrieved in other areas. One simply does not have time to check every single result to ensure accuracy, so one is beholden to those who have annotated the texts (whether these are the same people who have developed the software or those who have made use of others' databases). In the course of doing my doctoral research, I uncovered a number of at least debatable annotations, if not errors, in the data that I received from such a computer-generated search. I dutifully passed these on to the appropriate people, and I believe that at least some of the changes were incorporated in later versions of the database. But my own results were skewed, so that I had to redo my own calculations based upon these corrected findings. That is supposed to be one of the reasons for the turn to computer-generated searches: more speed and accuracy than manual searches. However, to be fair, due to the diligence of those involved (and perhaps others like me at the earlier stages who scrutinized such results), it is rare that actual errors are now to be found in the databases; although, as further layers of annotation are added, the same problem repeats itself at every level, besides the issue of higher levels of abstraction resulting in a greater probability of ambiguous analyses. In other words, one does not need an error, but simply a disagreement over analysis, to realize a problem.

Nevertheless, there are still places at these lower levels of analysis where I might disagree with the findings of those who have tagged the text in the database. The difference of opinion might not constitute an error, but it could have the same effect on my production of reliable and useful results for my purposes. For example, for a long time one of the differences between Accordance (and then GRAMCORD, when it existed) and BibleWorks was that for middle/passive forms of the present tense-form, one of the programs recorded the form simply as middle/passive, while the other disambiguated the form. In either case, my research has found instances where I have wanted to know whether the form was middle or passive according to various criteria but have often disagreed with the findings when the specification has been made. These forms have now been disambiguated, as far as I can tell, but that adds the further question of whether every analysis of a form as either middle or passive is correct (and do I have the time to investigate each one?).

Furthermore, in some of my research I was working on the Greek apocryphal gospel fragments, trying to find a way to use these documents in New Testament textual criticism but without wishing to have them introduced as textual witnesses on the level of the continuous New Testament manuscripts.[9]

---

9. See S. E. Porter, "Apocryphal Gospels and the Text of the New Testament before AD 200," in *The New Testament Text in Early Christianity: Proceedings of the Lille Colloquium, July 2000 = Le texte du Nouveau Testament au début du christianisme: Actes du colloque de Lille, juillet 2000*, ed. C.-B. Amphoux and J. K. Elliott, HTB 6 (Lausanne: Éditions du Zèbre, 2003), 235–58;

It would have been very useful for my purposes to have had these texts in a machine-readable format and tagged according to Accordance or BibleWorks specifications so that I could have performed the same kinds of searches on these documents. Instead, I had to do my own manual searches of these documents, gathering together and scrutinizing a number of different types and kinds of printed editions. Also, in the course of my work, I have on many different occasions wished to display my results in a variety of ways, including things such as complex bar graphs, line graphs, and a variety of other means that would provide a more graphic way of visualizing the data versus simple graphs of frequency of occurrence and other such basic displays. A major emphasis in my research has been to appreciate the recurring patterns of language usage, against which deviations can be plotted in order to appreciate those instances where marked features are present. A complex graphic display makes it possible to plot such alterations in patterns in a highly visible way. This is not possible unless the search software includes such options.

In other words, my major criticism here is that those who have established and to date controlled the computer-based resources have done so in such a way that the resource is essentially a closed system. Access to the tagged text is closed, access to the various types of searches that can be done is closed, and access to how the results of such searches are displayed is closed. As receptive as the software developers may be to any given individual's ideas, one must wait until the next upgrade to get such improvements, if they are made at all, since the tendency is to include features that will have the widest appeal rather than cater to the desires of a given individual.

A Word May Be What You Say It Is, But What Is a Discourse?

My next set of observations grows out of several comments I made in the section above, comments identifying some limitations in the annotation of texts in the databases. I pointed out that the annotation of the text is a static feature that the user cannot alter, whether the tagging was wrong or, more usually, simply a matter of disagreement. There are a number of instances that one can cite where the annotation used by the databases is problematic. The examples that I will cite fall into the categories of ambiguity, merger, and gradience.[10]

Porter, "Early Apocryphal Gospels and the New Testament Text," in *The Early Text of the New Testament*, ed. C. E. Hill and M. J. Kruger (Oxford: Oxford University Press, 2012), 350–69.

10. See S. Johannson, "Grammatical Tagging and Total Accountability," in *Papers on Language and Literature: Presented to Alvar Ellegård and Erik Frykman*, ed. S. Bäckman and G. Kjellmer, GSE 60 (Göteborg: Acta Universitatis Gothoburgensis, 1998), 208–20.

I begin with instances of ambiguity. For example, as noted above, there is the difficulty of the middle/passive present (and perfect) tense-forms. At an earlier stage, one of the major differences between the GRAMCORD and Friberg texts, I believe, was that one simply left the tag as middle/passive, while the other tried to disambiguate this form, and in doing so provided labels such as middle, passive, middle or passive, deponent middle, deponent passive, and middle or deponent passive. At a later stage, the former tagged text disambiguated these forms as well, labeling them as middle or passive. We can see that there is a problem here, however, besides the fact that the long list of labels does not actually seem to come close to solving the problem.[11] It appears that for both of these databases, the word is the basic unit for parsing, which is a standard theoretical approach probably deeply enshrined since everyone's first-year Greek class. One parses words on the basis of the morphology. According to that criterion, the database with the middle/passive designation was being entirely faithful to the principle, since the individual form, taken simply as an individual word, is indeed genuinely ambiguous; that is, it can be one of two different forms that have the same morphology. However, searches of the database in terms of voice result in some very difficult data to handle. One might search a given book and find a certain number of active-voice verbs, a smaller number of passive-voice verbs, a few middle-voice verbs, and a surprisingly large number of middle/passives. What does one do if trying to understand the semantic category of voice, not merely the range of forms and how they are distributed across a corpus?[12] This kind of difficulty undoubtedly led to both databases eventually offering specific annotations of these forms. However, in order to do so, they had to violate the principle of parsing according to individual word forms: they had to appeal to some other set of criteria, whether this is called collocation, syntax, context, or something else. Whatever it is, it is no longer based upon the word alone, but rather upon some larger linguistic category.

A very clear and obvious further example that one might cite is various instances of the article. For example, the article τῶν can be parsed as masculine, feminine, or neuter genitive plural. Similar examples are to be found with τοῖς, τό, and τά. However, as far as I know, none of the databases has

---

11. This is made more problematic in the light of recent discussion that calls into question the designation "deponent" as an appropriate and meaningful label in Greek. See the arguments to set aside deponency as a semantic category in J. T. Pennington, "Setting Aside 'Deponency': Rediscovering the Greek Middle Voice in New Testament Studies," in *The Linguist as Pedagogue: Trends in the Teaching and Linguistic Analysis of the Greek New Testament*, ed. S. E. Porter and M. B. O'Donnell, NTM 11 (Sheffield: Sheffield Phoenix Press, 2009), 181–203.

12. This is a very real problem, as is seen in Porter and O'Donnell, "Greek Verbal Network."

any trouble in offering a specific parsing of these words in virtually all instances. To do otherwise would seem to invoke chaos for searches, since one would have data that one could not differentiate. Nevertheless, the fact that τῶν is not ambiguously parsed means that appeal has been made to a unit larger than this word, such as the noun with which it is linked: perhaps νόμων, in which the parsing is masculine, or ἐκκλησιῶν, in which case it is feminine.

My point is that the databases currently available for research into New Testament Greek are ostensibly word-based. In many instances this may be possible to maintain, since a given word may only have a single parsing. In the difficult instances, however, one needs the particular help of such a program, and here it is harder if not impossible to maintain the word-based approach. In other words, practical analytical exigencies demand appeal to a rank higher than the word. But what is that level, and how well equipped are the computer resources to handle such a departure from their purported basis? In some instances it is difficult to know. With reference to the articles noted above, the appeal is probably to the word group—that is, the group of words of which a (in this case) noun is the head term, with its preceding and following specifiers, qualifiers, and determiners, such as the article. It is more difficult to know what the rank of determination is when dealing with the middle/passive voice-form, but I suspect that higher ranks or extended passages of discourse are being examined here. For example, categorization of a word as deponent—if the category should be used at all (and I doubt it)—is different from saying that it is middle or passive. There are different categories involved. Deponency is a statement about paradigmatic development and availability, and possibly about some notion of voice-form substitution. It actually says nothing about whether the form is middle or passive when these formal designations are then used semantically. In that sense, if one retains the category of deponency, a form could be both deponent (i.e., there is not a complete voice paradigm) and active, middle, or passive in meaning. In order to decide these variables, one must appeal to several factors that extend beyond the word, and even beyond the word group. For example, to make determinations of voice—that is, to decide whether a form of a verb is middle or passive—one would need to examine syntactical and semantic features such as implied or expressed adjuncts (indicating agency), the use and types of subjects and complements, and primary and secondary agency, among other things. At the least, one needs to appeal to a variety of syntactical and semantic features that extend to the rank of the clause, if not beyond. None of this information, as far as I can tell, is provided in either of the mentioned databases when one searches for or is given parsings for middle or passive forms of the present, or parsings for perfect tense-forms.[13]

Instances of merger and gradience are even more difficult for the databases to handle. Merger involves cases in which there are two possible structural interpretations of a form, but the difference is slight or possibly even nonexistent. A good example of merger is the use of negatives. In most studies of the Greek of the New Testament, the standard distinction in negation is to notice the difference between the forms οὐ and μή. For some of the databases, no distinction is offered even at this level, with the label of negative particle being given to both. It seems to me that negation occurs with at least two ranks of syntactical analysis in Greek, that of the word group and that of the clause (some might say the word or constituent). Negation of the word group would include the use of negative pronouns (e.g., οὐδείς, μηδείς, etc.), or the negation of a participle or infinitive (e.g., Matt. 1:19: "not wanting to stigmatize her," μὴ θέλων αὐτὴν δειγματίσαι), among others. The negating force of the negative particle extends only to that word group, not beyond. In other words, the negation does not carry to other constituents of the clause. Negation of the clause involves instances where a single negative particle carries its force over the entire clause. Thus, for example, in Mark 9:9 ("if not [unless] when the son of man might be raised from the dead," εἰ μὴ ὅταν ὁ υἱὸς τοῦ ἀνθρώπου ἐκ νεκρῶν ἀναστῇ), the negative is part of a conjunction that negates the entire temporal clause. But what of an instance such as Matthew 7:6 ("Don't give a holy thing to dogs, and don't cast your pearls before swine," μὴ δῶτε τὸ ἅγιον τοῖς κυσὶν μηδὲ βάλητε τοὺς μαργαρίτας ὑμῶν ἔμπροσθεν τῶν χοίρων)? The negative force clearly extends over the entire clause, but the particle seems to negate the verb specifically. In this instance of merger there may be a structural difference, but it may be slight or nonexistent. In any case, something as basic as negation is not treated by the databases available to New Testament scholars, apart from a simple morphological tagging. Disambiguation has occurred in voice, appealing to larger units for the extent of negation, even though similar kinds of syntactical implications are clearly present; yet the databases leave the differentiation unspecified (even for the difference between οὐ and μή).

Gradience involves a form that can be placed into two or more linguistic categories. This is the category that perhaps stretches the traditional databases

13. For treatment of some issues concerning voice, see M. B. O'Donnell, "Some New Testament Words for Resurrection and the Company They Keep," in *Resurrection*, ed. S. E. Porter, M. A. Hayes, and D. Tombs, JSNTSup 186; RILP 5 (London: Sheffield Academic Press, 1999), 136–65; S. E. Porter, "Did Paul Baptize Himself? A Problem of the Greek Voice System," in *Dimensions of Baptism*, ed. S. E. Porter and A. R. Cross, JSNTSup 234 (Sheffield: Sheffield Academic Press, 2002), 91–109.

the furthest. Particular difficulties are to be seen with various particles, such as ὡς, which is sometimes labeled a particle (comparative) and sometimes a conjunction (subordinator), often of either a comparative or temporal type, but could also be labeled a preposition if one is labeling according to function. Numerous other particles present similar problems, with the most difficult probably being the so-called conjunctions. We all know that function-words such as conjunctions are particularly difficult to analyze, so it is understandable that those who tag the texts of the New Testament Greek databases have had trouble as well. Yet one might well wonder whether they have made the correct decisions. For example, we know several words can be used in a variety of connective or other ways. One of the most important of these is the apparently simple word καί. If this word were to be parsed simply on its own, one could designate it as a particle (though it is not annotated in this way by at least one database), and perhaps as a conjunction or adverbial particle. Right here we see the potential difficulty, however. In some instances it might be possible to make such a distinction, but in others it is not. Even so, when such a distinction is made, the deciding criteria are already beyond the rank of the word. These criteria may involve syntactical features (e.g., καί as conjunction appears at the beginning of clauses, while adverbial καί is internal to the clause, although we know that this will not always work as a distinction because καί can be used to connect two or more equal items within a clause). More likely, this distinction will involve even larger contextual or discourse factors. It is odd that, in some of the databases, such distinctions are not made, however, with καί being categorized as a coordinating conjunction whether it connects clauses or word groups or whatever else. In this instance, discourse-based judgments have not been made regarding the conjunctions. But I think that a crucial distinction has been missed: a coordinating function between word groups is different from one between clauses. To make such a distinction implies that one has an explicit theory of discourse to rely upon, something that cannot be assumed in the current databases.[14]

Many, if not most, of us probably have come to realize the aforementioned features of the databases that we use. However, there are some implications of such an orientation that we may not all be aware of. For example, do we know in exactly what instances the criteria for annotation of texts have gone beyond the word, or must we discover that on a search-by-search basis? This certainly adds some uncertainty to our work, since we run the serious risk of inadvertently (or perhaps systemically) committing a category mistake; yet it

---

14. For treatment of conjunctions, see S. E. Porter and M. B. O'Donnell, "Conjunctions, Clines and Levels of Discourse," *FN* 20 (2007): 3–14.

also alters the foundation upon which the tagging is based—that is, the word-based approach. One relatively straightforward, yet in some ways provocative, move is to eliminate the word as the basic unit. As self-evident as it seems to be, the word has always been problematic in linguistics. If the word group were used instead as the basic unit of grouping for annotation, it would seem to eliminate a number (but certainly not all) of the basic parsing problems. More important, as far as I am concerned, is to articulate and apply a theory of discourse that can stand behind the annotation of texts. In the case of voice, it appears that those who label it are still dealing with a large senten-tial grammar—that is, discourse as consisting of sentences, as if a discourse were one large sentence and analyzable in these terms. The judgments being made regarding conjunctions seem to be made along different lines, however. There appear to be competing tendencies. On the one hand, there seems to be a maximalist view taken as to the contribution of the individual word when considering voice, but a minimalist view of καί. In each case the tag is affixed to the word alone, with no explicit larger unit invoked. This reinforces the importance of the word. On the other hand, in order to arrive at such a description, one must look at units larger than the clause, at least as large as two clauses in many instances, in order to arrive at such descriptions. In most recent linguistic research into conjunctions, the trend is to take a minimalist view, but one that recognizes function. The minimalist view sees conjunctions contributing a minimum amount of semantic substance to the discourse, with the meaning coming from the concepts being linked by them.[15]

In any case, what is clear is that although the Greek databases purport to be word-based, in various ways they have been forced into tagging their texts on the basis of units larger (or higher) than the word. How large these units are, and how one arrives at a comprehensive theory of discourse, is clearly not evident. In fact, because of the haphazard nature of the venture beyond the word, I strongly doubt whether a concept of discourse is in place at all. Such a concept needs to be articulated, however, if for no other reason than to determine what counts for evidence in the tagging of texts and to ensure that similar criteria are applied in all instances, something that currently does not seem to be in operation. Yet once the gate to larger discourse consider-ations has been opened, like the uncorked bottle, it is hard to get the genie to go back inside. Nor should we necessarily want it to do so, since it is to the various higher ranks of discourse that the analysis to date has pushed us.

15. See S. L. Black, *Sentence Conjunctions in the Gospel of Matthew: καί, δέ, τότε, γάρ, οὖν and Asyndeton in Narrative Discourse*, JSNTSup 216, SNTG 9 (Sheffield: Sheffield Academic Press, 2002).

As noted above, the individual word has come under renewed attack, since such an apparently basic concept has in many ways proved itself unable to bear the weight of a number of fundamental issues needing to be faced in discussing units of grammar in a language. Furthermore, as also recognized above, categories beyond the word have already been invoked in the creation of the databases that we use. This has been done by means of selecting various types of basic relationships, such as indicating an element within a span of a number of words, or followed by or preceded by another element. These are essentially searches of collocations of lexical items. They are not done in an explicit way that shows how linguistic levels relate to each other structurally or semantically. I believe that it is time for us to take the major leap forward of not merely begrudgingly acknowledging this, but positively developing substantial discourse theories that can be transferred into a system for annotating texts.

Recent work that I have been involved in with OpenText.org, the most linguistically sophisticated and highly annotated database, shows that, at least for ancient Greek, morphology is very important, but that the word group is probably the single most important rank for basic text annotation, since it allows for morphemes to be analyzed in fundamental syntactical relations. However, I have also discovered, much to my surprise, that among the kinds of discourse theories that seem to hold out the most promise for textual analysis and transference to annotated texts, syntax is only one feature of the text, not the paramount unit of structure. In too much linguistic work there has been a close relation between the word and syntax—that is, between the individual words making up clauses, with analysis not extending beyond these categories. If recent productive work continues to develop, it looks as though the ranks of structure will proceed from word group to clause to pericope to discourse, and then to context of situation and then culture. If this is right, future work on the Greek of the New Testament will need to discuss the Greek language by using these categories. Rather than being bound to traditional grammatical categories, as effective as they might be for teaching the language, we will need to discuss the language in relation to the major units of structural organization and meaning. The results of such study will need to be included in the information provided in annotated texts, so that others can benefit from the work involved. Besides, the exercise itself of annotating a text compels those involved to make firm decisions on the structure of the language, from the smallest to the largest units, and with regard to their relations. Along with this change in orientation are the greater demands that such annotation places upon any search software to be able to create and display complex searches that extend over a wide range of texts. Each and every one of the categories mentioned above will need to be able to be searched and displayed. For example, if in discourse-analytical terms one is interested in plotting not just the use of particular lexical items but also the semantic domains in which they occur, this requires a sophisticated mapping of the lexical forms with the domain structure. There are also a number of more complex types of linguistic searches that might be expected, including matching of semantic and morphological features at the level of the pericope, to establish such discourse categories as prominence. The results would need to be displayed in ways that enable the interpreter to grasp the discourse implications of such patterns and to present them in a way that is clear for others to examine as well.

The Corpus Lying before You Is Alive and Growing

When the earliest New Testament Greek databases were first developed, they were at the forefront of annotated text development for ancient languages. When these databases were first developed the *TLG* was only in its infancy, and it took a number of years for that tool to gain the size and bulk that it has today. All of these developments are impressive and commendable. However, one cannot help but notice that one of the biggest factors in the fairly recent development of the *TLG* and New Testament databases is simply the expansion in size of the archive or corpus. I refer to the *TLG* as an archive, since there is little premeditated thought to the various parameters that might be set on establishing it as any kind of a representative corpus. It is simply an attempt to encode as many of the ancient Greek texts as possible. The available texts are less a result of selection of representative texts than accidents of history and the scribal tendencies and desires of the Alexandrian librarians and later archivists. On the other hand, the New Testament does qualify, I believe, as a corpus rather than simply as an archive, since there is a conscious process that has differentiated various literary types within the entire corpus. To the New Testament, now other texts, such as the Septuagint and Josephus and apocryphal works, have been added by various developers. Even though the sizes of the corpora are growing, however, the basic orientation has not changed. The search programs for the New Testament are still essentially concordance based, so that they produce more quickly what one in many ways used to be able to find using a traditional concordance—that is, a list of the occurrences of a particular word, or words with particular morphological features (e.g., particular case, tense-form, etc.). As noted above, these search programs are very useful for performing word studies, and with respect to the New Testament for producing basic collocational searches.

What is missing in such work, however, is an appreciation of the corpus implications of such archiving as is being done. Corpus linguistics not only is concerned with building corpora of texts but also strongly endorses the use of such corpora as the basis for making linguistic judgments about how people use language. In several of its manifestations, corpus linguistics has many similarities to the kind of approach exemplified by the *TLG*. Corpus linguistics often emphasizes the compiling of as large a corpus of natural language as is possible, so that searches can be made across a suitable body of material to find quantifiable generalized patterns. In much corpus linguistics, the emphasis is upon lexical searches and the collocations of individual lexical items (usually a key word in context [KWIC]). The advantage of these kinds of corpus-based studies is that they have shown that the larger the amount of data, the easier it is to establish and quantify particular patterns of language usage. However, there are limitations to such an approach, especially when it is applied to an ancient, epigraphic language such as Greek, where the corpus is finite by definition.[16] There is not an endless supply of currently produced natural language to be included, as opposed to the millions of words in an English database, but rather a finite amount of ancient Greek writings, as even the *TLG* project has recognized. Nevertheless, we can learn from corpus linguistics that it is important to try to gain as much information about and access to the language as is possible.

One of the perennial problems in New Testament study is the question of the kind of Greek to be found in it. Many of the criteria used to make such determinations are inadequately based on limited corpora, when what is needed is a larger corpus of Greek to allow for more than simple lexical searches. What in many ways is desirable is a balanced database nearing the size of the *TLG*, but tagged more like the OpenText.org database yet extended to the discourse level. This would allow students of ancient Greek to make substantial generalizations that are valid insofar as the extant corpus of ancient Greek is concerned. A reasonable place to start such a corpus-based study is the creation of a corpus of representative ancient Greek texts—of which the New Testament is a part. I began such a categorization a number of years

16. See, e.g., O'Donnell, *Corpus Linguistics*; S. E. Porter and M. B. O'Donnell, "Theoretical Issues for Corpus Linguistics and the Study of Ancient Languages," in *Corpus Linguistics by the Lune: A Festschrift for Geoffrey Leech*, ed. A. Wilson, P. Rayson, and T. McEnery, LSL 8 (Frankfurt am Main: Peter Lang, 2003), 119–37; M. B. O'Donnell, S. E. Porter, and J. T. Reed, "OpenText.org: The Problems and Prospects of Working with Ancient Discourse," in *A Rainbow of Corpora: Corpus Linguistics and the Languages of the World*, ed. A. Wilson, P. Rayson, and T. McEnery, LE 40 (Munich: Lincom, 2003), 109–29. This work is influenced by neo-Firthian corpus linguistics, on which, see T. McEnery and A. Hardie, *Corpus Linguistics: Method, Theory and Practice*, CTL (Cambridge: Cambridge University Press, 2012), 122–66.

ago, when I differentiated levels of usage not according to genre but according to register type (or style).[17] I differentiated four registers: vulgar, nonliterary, literary, and Atticistic. I would want to make this far more sophisticated and differentiated now, and I have attempted to do so for Paul's register styles.[18] However, having a body of texts classified by levels of language is an important starting point for corpus-based studies of the New Testament.

Conclusion

Without minimizing the contribution of those who have developed the databases and software that are so vital to our discipline, I would like to conclude by drawing attention to a couple of factors. The first is that there are several built-in difficulties with the current databases and software. These difficulties point to some fundamental problems that need to be addressed from a theoretical angle, but that have not yet been fully appreciated. Recognition of them does carry with it the threat of promising to revolutionize the entire way the data are examined and tagged for retrieval. The second factor is that several external initiatives are underway that have promise of helping those who are developing databases and software for use in New Testament study. Some of these have to do with what it means to define and develop a corpus of texts for computer retrieval. Others of these present a radically different orientation to how such computer materials are designed and developed, such as is suggested by the open-source software movement. Much of what I have written above is clearly beyond the abilities or even time of a few people, no matter how dedicated they might be. It will require numerous people simply to be involved in the tagging of texts according to reasoned discourse criteria. This says nothing of those needing to be involved in developing software

17. Porter, *Verbal Aspect*, 153. This has been developed further by M. B. O'Donnell, "Designing and Compiling a Register-Balanced Corpus of Hellenistic Greek for the Purpose of Linguistic Description and Investigation," in Porter, *Diglossia*, 255–97. O'Donnell has proposed a very basic corpus deemed to be generally representative of Hellenistic Greek. Preliminary work in that respect has been done in S. E. Porter and M. B. O'Donnell, "Building and Examining Linguistic Phenomena in a Corpus of Representative Papyri," in *The Language of the Papyri*, ed. T. V. Evans and D. D. Obbink (Oxford: Oxford University Press, 2010), 287–311; S. E. Porter, "Buried Linguistic Treasure in the Babatha Archive," in *Proceedings of the 25th International Congress of Papyrology, Ann Arbor, July 29–August 4, 2007*, ed. T. Gagos, ASP Special Edition (Ann Arbor: Scholarly Publishing Office, The University of Michigan Library, 2010), 623–32; Porter, "The Babatha Archive, the Egyptian Papyri and Their Implications for Study of the Greek New Testament," in *Early Christian Manuscripts: Examples of Applied Method and Approach*, ed. T. J. Kraus and T. Nicklas, TENT 5 (Leiden: Brill, 2010), 213–37.

18. Porter, "Functional Distribution of Koine Greek."

that will allow users to maximize the benefit of having such a large, richly-annotated text available.

This is where the open-source software movement perhaps has a place in New Testament studies. Rather than relying upon one or two companies for these future developments, we probably will require the work of many more people dedicated to seeing such plans come to fruition. Rather than each working independently and in competition with each other, as valuable as the competition can be for pushing forward development, it seems to bode better for progress if all are working together toward a common goal. The open-source software movement has taken a very different approach from that of the closed-source software movement, of which most developers of New Testament Greek software are apparently a part, and to which most of us have become accustomed, due to the way computers and software have traditionally developed. The emphasis in the open-source software movement is to make available the codes, the software, and the data for use by others, with the proviso that they too make it available to yet others, adding any of their contributions to the growing body of data. With open access, users are encouraged not only to use but also to further develop the database and software, so that it is then available for others to search and to use. The larger number of interested people has potential for actually making it possible to have a large corpus of machine-readable texts for New Testament study. This continues to be the goal of the OpenText.org project.

In any case, for most of us New Testament scholars, it appears impossible for us to do our research, and even our teaching, without availing ourselves of computer-aided materials. For the progress that has been made in this area, we are very grateful. However, it seems that now is time for another major leap forward in what we are doing with these resources in order to utilize the research potential of our corpus.

3

"On the Shoulders of Giants"

The Expansion and Application
of the Louw-Nida Lexicon

Introduction

In the past several decades, one of the most significant contributions to New Testament lexicography has been the development and publication of the semantic-domain Greek lexicon developed by J. P. Louw (1932–2013) and Eugene Nida (1914–2011).[1] Both of these men were well-known linguists and contributed

This paper initially took the form of a joint presentation, coauthored with Matthew Brook O'Donnell, made at the annual meeting of the Society of Biblical Literature, Philadelphia, Pennsylvania, November 19–22, 2005. This particular manifestation reflects my own portion of the presentation. His sizable contribution to this discussion can be found in, among other sources, M. B. O'Donnell, *Corpus Linguistics and the Greek of the New Testament*, NTM 6 (Sheffield: Sheffield Phoenix Press, 2005), 314–96.

1. J. P. Louw and E. A. Nida, *Greek-English Lexicon of the New Testament Based on Semantic Domains*, 2 vols. (New York: United Bible Societies, 1988). The principles of the lexicon are found on 1:vi–xx. See also E. A. Nida, *Componential Analysis of Meaning: An Introduction to Semantic Structures* (The Hague: Mouton, 1975); E. A. Nida, J. P. Louw, and R. B. Smith, "Semantic Domains and Componential Analysis of Meaning," in *Current Issues in Linguistic Theory*, ed. R. W. Cole (Bloomington: Indiana University Press, 1977), 139–67; E. A. Nida and J. P. Louw, *Lexical Semantics of the Greek New Testament*, SBLRBS 25 (Atlanta: Scholars Press, 1992).

greatly to biblical and general linguistics, with the lexicon serving as an important culmination of their work. In this brief chapter I wish to provide an overview of the lexicon, expressing its value for New Testament and linguistic scholarship as well as registering some reservations I have about its organization and linguistic theory. The Louw-Nida lexicon employs a polysemous approach to lexical meaning, which creates some difficulties in the organization of the lexicon itself, especially in the placement of words within more than one domain. I alternatively propose that these problems could be avoided by shifting to a monosemous approach to lexical meaning. The benefits of such an approach are briefly articulated with reference to exegesis of Romans 5.

The Structure of the Louw-Nida Lexicon

I begin with some comments on the structure of the lexicon.

The Lexicon Itself

In contrast to traditional lexicons, the Louw-Nida lexicon organizes its entries according to semantic domains (ninety-three of them) rather than alphabetic ordering. Lexemes are grouped together based on their semantic relations (determined by componential analysis) with respect to higher order, abstract categories of meaning. Large domains of meaning consist of still smaller and more specific categories, within which reside a collection of partially synonymous and antonymous words. The benefit of such a presentation is that its grouping more closely resembles the way in which semantic information is stored, accessed, and employed by language users. Besides easy access to synonyms and antonyms, the arrangement of domains into subdomains reveals other semantic relations such as co-hyponyms and other ordinate and superordinate relations. Because of this structural organization, ease of referencing (such as cross-referencing) may be limited in comparison to the traditional alphabetic dictionary. However, a second volume accompanies the lexicon and has an alphabetic index to aid the search for specific lexemes. For those who hold to a polysemous theory of lexical semantics, the index allows the user to grasp the distribution of a lexeme across one or more domains (if this is indeed the case).

Lexical Semantic Theory and the Louw-Nida Lexicon

Once we have understood the nature of the lexicon itself, the question that emerges is this: what constitutes an adequate theory of lexical semantics to evaluate what the lexicon is and how it functions? At least four areas need to be explored in lexical theory.

The first question is the type of dictionary or lexicon the Louw-Nida lexicon represents. The two major types of dictionary are the ordinary dictionary and the semanticist dictionary.[2] Features of the ordinary dictionary include the following: circular, interconnected definitions; precise common-language definitions; definitions in terms of glosses or translational equivalents; and a tendency toward encyclopedic knowledge. A semanticist dictionary is distinguished by the following features: the use of semantic primes in its interconnected definitions; definitions distinct from glosses; distinction between homographs and polysemous words; precise sense relations such as hyponymy, antonymy, synonymy, and meronymy; and attention to logical relations, especially analytic or contradictory relations.

The Louw-Nida lexicon is clearly a hybrid of both an ordinary and a semanticist dictionary. The lexicon has many features of the semanticist dictionary, but it is packaged in such a way that it is usable as an ordinary dictionary. This may be because it was designed for translators rather than for professional linguists.[3] The use of the semantic-domain categories is a means of addressing the issue of semantic primes. If these primes constitute basic components of meaning, or the *Grundbedeutung*,[4] then they constitute the underlying framework for the organization of the lexical stock into its respective domains. This organization follows from Nida's work on componential analysis, in which he established the framework for such a system of analysis for Greek. There have been numerous criticisms of semantic-domain theory, much of it centered around what constitutes the categories, and hence the semantic primes, to be used, and how one quantifies the relations among them.[5] Lexical semantics typically deals more with paradigmatic than with syntagmatic relations, although there is something to be said for lexicons of the future perhaps doing more with collocation or "units," as Louw-Nida describes them.[6]

The Louw-Nida lexicon attempts to provide definitions rather than simply glosses, although it provides the latter as well. These definitions are formulated around distinctive features connected with a particular term. However, these componential or distinctive feature definitions are not included in the lexicon

2. J. R. Hurford, B. Heasley, and M. B. Smith, *Semantics: A Coursebook*, 2nd ed. (Cambridge: Cambridge University Press, 2007), 194–205.

3. See Nida and Louw, *Greek-English Lexicon*, 1:viii. I find this distinction problematic, as the lexicon represents an important step forward in linguistically astute lexicography.

4. Ibid., 1:xviii.

5. S. E. Porter, *Studies in the Greek New Testament: Theory and Practice*, SBG 6 (New York: Peter Lang, 1996), 70–71.

6. Louw and Nida, *Greek-English Lexicon*, see index (vol. 2).

itself, but rather are rewritten in ordinary language. There is thus also no use of technical logical terms to indicate these relations. Logical relations, however, are implied by the organization of the lexicon. Within any domain, there are often a number of subdomains. This use of subdomains tends to indicate a loose attempt at hyponymous relations, with the superordinate term having a number of hyponyms. These are not technically hyponymous, however, since the purported hyponym is often not an entailment of the superordinate term. Other relations are even less formally indicated. Synonymy is indicated by the close proximity of one word to another in the lexicon (what Louw and Nida sometimes call "lumping"), and antonyms are sometimes indicated by being moved away from other terms ("splitting").[7] One of the assumptions to be noted in the lexicon is that Louw and Nida believe that there are "no synonyms." By this, they mean that two words, even if they denote the same thing, are different in their connotations or associative meanings (I will return to this notion below).

Since the lexicon is arranged by semantic domains, rather than simply alphabetically, there is what might at first glance appear to be an easy way to distinguish homographs from polysemous words. Homographs are placed in distinctly different domains; that is, they are two lexemes that are written with the same lettering but are in fact two different lexemes. Polysemous words are those placed in the same or related domains and hence share distinctive features yet differ in one or more other features. Louw and Nida, however, do not appear to make such a distinction. They speak of a single lexeme having different or diverse meanings rather than make the distinction between homographs and polysemous words.[8] Since they do not use explicit displays of semantic components or logical distinctions to distinguish senses, there is no way to tell whether they are talking of homographs or polysemous words, or whether they even entertain this distinction.

The next area of investigation is the difference between sense, reference, and denotation. The standard distinction made in lexical semantics is between sense and reference, with reference being the external relations of words to things, or the capacity of language to refer, and sense the internal relations among words—that is, as thought of in terms of how they occupy semantic space. John Lyons added denotation as a useful category to indicate what is typically regarded as the notion of reference—that is, the relation between a lexeme and an extralinguistic entity.[9] Reference, according to Lyons, is restricted to the relationship between a lexeme and an extralinguistic entity when it is

7. Ibid., 1:ix–xvi.
8. Ibid., 1:ix.
9. J. Lyons, *Semantics*, 2 vols. (Cambridge: Cambridge University Press, 1977), 1:207.

used in a particular instance of use.[10] Louw and Nida are not entirely clear in their definition of such categories. They use the language of reference in the sense of a lexeme and its relation to the extralinguistic world (Lyons's denotation), but they tend to use the distinction between designative or denotative and connotative or associative meanings.[11] The implication is that designative or denotative meaning is fundamental, as associative or connotative meaning is confined to subtle distinctions that are often unnecessary to make explicit.[12] This means that the notion of designative or denotative meaning must indicate that all lexemes are referential, clearly something that can only be the case if reference is extended beyond "things" to everything. It also seems to indicate that denotation or designative meaning must also be made to handle what is often called sense relations in a language. In any case, the distinction is not clear, and denotation seems to have to carry a lot of semantic weight.

Some Hypotheses about Word Senses and Their Implications for Sense Selection and Disambiguation (and Other Mouthfuls)

In this section I explore two different means by which word senses can be disambiguated, and the implications that these proposals would have for restructuring the Louw-Nida lexicon.

Words Are Monosemous

One of the ways in which the senses of words can be disambiguated is if every word is monosemous. One of the distinguishing features of most dictionaries—and the Louw-Nida lexicon is no different in this regard—is that lexemes often have multiple meanings: they are polysemous.[13] As I noted above, this may mean that a given lexeme is placed in several different semantic domains, or at the least that one lexeme is placed in several different categories within a single domain. This notion of polysemy has been called into question.[14] The argument

---

10. Lyons, *Semantics*, 1:174.

11. Louw and Nida, *Greek-English Lexicon*, 1:xv.

12. Ibid., 1:xii.

13. The literature on polysemy is large, especially in works on semantics. For a representative statement, see D. A. Cruse, *Meaning in Language: An Introduction to Semantics and Pragmatics*, 2nd ed. (Oxford: Oxford University Press, 2004). For polysemy in lexicography, see R. H. Robins, "Polysemy and the Lexicographer," in *Studies in Lexicography*, ed. R. Burchfield (Oxford: Clarendon, 1987), 52–75.

14. See C. Ruhl, *On Monosemy: A Study in Linguistic Semantics* (New York: SUNY Press, 1989), which I follow here. For recent work on monosemy in ancient Greek, see S. E. Porter,

is essentially that, rather than an individual lexeme contributing maximalist meaning to a given utterance, the lexeme contributes minimal meaning. What is often thought of and seen as its lexical meaning is the result of the contribution of cotextual or linguistic and contextual or extralinguistic factors. Another way of stating this is to distinguish between the inherent meaning of a lexeme as semantic and its additional or instrumental meaning as pragmatic, or the distinction between the abstract formal meaning of a lexeme and the specific functional meaning of its use in context.[15] As a result, when these cotextual and contextual factors are excluded from the estimation of meaning of a given lexeme, there are essentially two types of lexical meaning: "Some words have a single, highly abstract meaning; other words, referring to highly diverse realities, represent the unity of that diversity."[16] The example that Charles Ruhl uses is the English verb "take": "The thief took the jewels." "The thief took his own jewels." "The jeweler took his jewels." "The jeweler took his hat." "John took his hat." "The king took the jewels."[17] Ruhl shows that in fact there is a common, highly abstract, and almost empty sense of the verb "take," in which the cotext and (hypothetical) context indicate when the distinction is between taking what is legitimately one's own and stealing. Ruhl also uses the example of prepositions, in which there is a highly abstract semantic meaning (often based on a local meaning) of which a given instance is a "pragmatically modulated subspecies."[18] Ruhl's analysis indicates that both intuition and usage are necessary to deal with the data. The lexicon of a language constitutes a closed class of items, arranged in semantic fields. These semantic fields are arranged from closed to open classes, with the closed class of words the basis of open classes of words. The closed class (primary words, such as primary or grammatical words) is more semantic, and the open class (less primary words) is less semantic and more pragmatic in definition. However, on the continuum of syntax-semantics-pragmatics, pragmatics is extralinguistic or contextual.[19]

"Matthew and Mark: The Contribution of Recent Linguistic Thought," in *Mark and Matthew: Comparative Readings*, part 1, *Understanding the Earliest Gospels in Their First-Century Settings*, ed. E.-M. Becker and A. Runesson, WUNT 271 (Tübingen: Mohr Siebeck, 2011), 97–119, esp. 105–9; Porter, "Greek Linguistics and Lexicography," in *Understanding the Times: New Testament Studies in the 21st Century; Essays in Honor of D. A. Carson on the Occasion of His 65th Birthday*, ed. A. J. Köstenberger and R. W. Yarbrough (Wheaton, IL: Crossway, 2011), 19–61, esp. 27–37; G. P. Fewster, *Creation Language in Romans 8: A Study in Monosemy*, LBS 8 (Leiden: Brill, 2013); S. E. Porter, "Θαυμάζω in Mark 6:6 and Luke 11:38: A Note on Monosemy," *BAGL* 2 (2013): 75–79.

15. Ruhl, *On Monosemy*, ix.
16. Ibid., vii.
17. Ibid., 6.
18. Ibid., xiii.
19. Ibid., 234–36.

The implications of such analysis for a restructuring of the Louw-Nida lexicon are significant. There are several ways of examining the lexicon of New Testament Greek. The first is to appreciate what Ruhl calls the monosemic bias and attempt to define the meaning of the words, often by using highly abstract or diversity-encompassing definitions. This may mean that one will simply be able to select one of the definitions already suggested for individual words in the lexicon, or it may mean that a new definition needs to be developed. For example, the word ἔχω is listed under ten different domains in the Louw-Nida lexicon (domains 13, 18, 23, 24, 31, 33, 40, 49, 57, and 90). Even those listed under different domains often have similarities in English gloss, such as "possess," "hold on to," or "hold a view." The meaning of this Greek verb may well be that of "having," with all of the diversity that this verb implies in English. The second consideration is distinguishing between the closed class of primary words, those words that are more semantic, and the more open class of less primary words that are more pragmatic. The Louw-Nida lexicon distinguishes between (1) objects or entities (domains 1–12), (2) events (domains 13–57), and (3) abstracts (domains 58–91).[20] Clearly, abstracts are not the closed class of primary words. It appears that certain types of entities and events would constitute this closed class, such as verbs of being, doing, having, and so on. Thus the lexicon would need to be restructured in two major ways.

One Sense per Genre or Register

A means by which a word can be disambiguated in a given context is if every word has a single sense according to the genre or register.[21] There has been much confusion over the notion of genre, especially in relation to register. Some have linked the two together,[22] while others have distinguished the two.[23] The notion

20. Louw and Nida, *Greek-English Lexicon*, 1:vi.

21. For a recent overview of the issues, though with their own perspective, see D. Biber and S. Conrad, *Register, Genre, and Style*, CTL (Cambridge: Cambridge University Press, 2009). See also M. Ghadessy, ed., *Register Analysis: Theory and Practice* (London: Pinter, 1993); H. Leckie-Tarry, *Language and Context: A Functional Linguistic Theory of Register*, ed. D. Birch (London: Pinter, 1995).

22. See, for example, M. A. K. Halliday, *Language as Social Semiotic: The Social Interpretation of Language and Meaning* (London: Edward Arnold, 1978), 142–45; Halliday, "Text as Semantic Choice in Social Contexts," in *Grammars and Descriptions: Studies in Text Theory and Text Analysis*, ed. T. A. van Dijk and J. S. Petöfi, RTT 1 (Berlin: de Gruyter, 1977), 202–3 (though Halliday sees genre as more of a subcategory involving the mode of discourse); J. T. Reed, *A Discourse Analysis of Philippians: Method and Rhetoric in the Debate over Literary Integrity*, JSNTSup 136 (Sheffield: Sheffield Academic Press, 1997), 53.

23. For example, J. R. Martin, *English Text: System and Structure* (Philadelphia: John Benjamins, 1992); S. E. Porter, "Dialect and Register in the Greek of the New Testament: Theory,"

of genre is sufficiently confusing that a distinction should be made between the two. "Genre" should be reserved as a term for the various conventional literary types that were available within a given context of culture. Thus the notion of genre is temporally and culturally restricted, such that the genres that were available in classical Greece, Constantinian Rome, and twentieth-century America would be distinctly different and in need of definition according to the culture of the day, even if they shared the same name, such as biography, romance, history, drama, poetry, or the like. Register, however, is distinct from genre, and it functions within given genres. Register addresses not the context of culture but rather the context of situation—that is, a reconstruction of the linguistic situation in which a given discourse would or could have been generated. Sometimes a register will be coterminous with a genre, and sometimes a register will not be. Thus a parable within a gospel in the New Testament might constitute its own register of language and thus imply its own context of situation. This might well be distinct from the register of Jesus speaking to a given audience, even if in speaking to that audience he were to use that particular parable. This might also be distinct from the register of the gospel in which Jesus speaks and tells this parable. Within a single genre of the gospel, there may be differentiation of various registers or subregisters, depending upon the units under examination.[24]

The theory of register disambiguating lexical meaning implies that within a given register of usage—the type of language that is used within a given typical unit of discourse—an individual lexical item will have only one meaning. If the theory of monosemous lexical meaning stated above is correct, it follows that this will be true of a given register as well. However, if polysemous lexical meaning is in effect, this theory states that, within a given register, the register of usage is sufficient to ensure that only a single lexical meaning is found for a given lexeme. This would mean that within such a register, the cotextual and situational contextual factors are such that the register prescribes a single meaning. Situational usage, including

in *Rethinking Contexts, Rereading Texts: Contributions from the Social Sciences to Biblical Interpretation*, ed. M. D. Carroll R., JSOTSup 299 (Sheffield: Sheffield Academic Press, 2000), 202–3; M. B. O'Donnell, "Designing and Compiling a Register-Balanced Corpus of Hellenistic Greek for the Purpose of Linguistic Description and Investigation," in *Diglossia and Other Topics in New Testament Linguistics*, ed. S. E. Porter, JSNTSup 193, SNTG 6 (Sheffield: Sheffield Academic Press, 2000), 278–79; J. R. Martin and D. Rose, *Genre Relations: Mapping Culture* (London: Equinox, 2008), 9–20.

24. The question of registers and subregisters is a highly contentious one, for which a category is needed (not style, as per Biber and Conrad, *Register*, 18). On these issues, see R. Hasan, "The Nursery Tale as a Genre," in *Ways of Saying, Ways of Meaning: Selected Papers of Ruqaiya Hasan*, ed. C. Cloran et al. (London: Cassell, 1996), 51–72.

features such as other lexical choice, syntax, and cotext, restrict the sense of the word to one of its possible senses. The standard example often used in lexical semantics is the English word "bank": "I put my money in the bank" and "I fished from the left bank." Words such as "money" and "put" with the word "bank" indicate that here the word "bank" has the sense of "safe place to put money"; words such as "fish" and the directional word "left" with the word "bank" indicate that here the word "bank" is a "side of a river."[25]

The implications of this theory for the Louw-Nida lexicon are that it would need to be restructured along several different lines. The major line of restructuring would be to take into consideration various register types. The first consideration would be that a number of register types would need to be determined in order to restrict the types of meanings pertinent in a given context of situation. Such a development has, to my knowledge, never been done, and seems highly unlikely to be accomplished, because of the very notion of context of situation as I have defined it. Those who equate context of situation and genre are able to arrive at a number of broad context types that could be instrumental in formulating such a hypothesis. Such a limitation may drive one back to redefining the notion of genre and register as synonymous concepts. However, for the reasons stated above, I do not favor such an approach. This would mean that this part of the lexicon could at best be prototypical rather than definitive: it would need to be restructured around prototypical context types that would define limiting factors to be taken into account. The second consideration is that various cotextual factors would need to be defined. This would push the lexicon to develop more so-called units, or collocation-based descriptions. These units would need to be based around usage of individual lexical items in relation to both syntagmatic and paradigmatic factors—that is, the kinds of syntagms in which a given lexeme appears, and the variety of paradigmatic choice to fill such syntagmatic strings. This development is conceivable, although it would require that the lexicon grow in significant length to handle the variety of possibilities.[26] The recent work by Paul Danove on predicate structure (valency) of a select number of verbs in Greek indicates a preliminary attempt at a lexicon of certain words

25. A monosemous understanding of the word "bank" would indicate an abstract sense of secure structure, which might be modulated to indicate a building for placing money or an accumulation of land to establish the course of a river.

26. Some important work on collocation includes: M. Hoey, *Lexical Priming: A New Theory of Words and Language* (London: Routledge, 2005); G. Barnbrook, O. Mason, and R. Krishnamurthy, *Collocation: Applications and Implications* (Basingstoke: Palgrave Macmillan, 2013).

that takes into account their predicate structure.[27] However, Danove's proposal is formal and generative, and thus not contextual.

The Example of Romans 5

In this section I have selected Romans 5 as a unit for analysis. Key lexemes in this chapter will be analyzed with reference to the Louw-Nida lexicon in order to examine its usefulness. These observations will be filtered through a monosemous bias, with suggestions for improvement of the lexicon and lexical theory.

Words Are Monosemous

If we adopt the notion that words are monosemous, one of the first choices that we need to make is what we will select as the monosemous lexical meaning for a given lexeme, or what definition we will create if no single definition is sufficient. Upon examining the usage in Romans 5 in relation to the domains offered, we can see the vast majority of the words for which multiple domains are given as comfortably fitting within the first domain listed (this often departs from numerical order). This seems to imply that the Louw-Nida lexicon has worked from semantic primes to extensions. This movement is clearly seen in a number of words, such as κόσμος. Domain 1, "Geographical objects and features," encompasses glosses such as "universe" and "earth." Other domains, such as 9, "People," and 41, "Behavior and related states," with the gloss "world system," appear to be extensions of the sense of universe or earth—meaning the people or people-systems contained within the earth. Even more extensive are domains 59, "Quantity," and 79, "Features of objects." The same can be said for others of the entries, where there are a number of unnecessary extensions that could be eliminated.

Yet several other instances are more difficult to decide, and there the monosemous disambiguation may not provide the most readily apparent explanation. First are instances where the first domain does not apply and where the most readily pertinent domain does not appear to be an extension. Examples include δόξα (Rom. 5:2), where domain 79, "Features of objects," does not

---

27. P. L. Danove, *Linguistics and Exegesis in the Gospel of Mark: Applications of a Case Frame Analysis*, JSNTSup 218, SNTG 10 (Sheffield: Sheffield Academic Press, 2001). Somewhat similar is the Spanish-Greek dictionary project by J. Mateos and J. Peláez, *Diccionario Griego-Español del Nuevo Testamento*, 5 vols. (Córdoba: Ediciones el Almendro; Fundación Épsilon, 2000–).

seem pertinent, but where the cotext, including the previous verb in domain 33, indicates that this domain, "Communication," may be appropriate. This example, however, may indicate the need for an adjustment in the domains of the lexicon. The reason for this suggestion is that it appears that domain 79 reflects interpretation of this lexeme on the basis of Septuagintal usage, rather than earlier Greek usage, where "opinion" was the primary semantic feature. A second example concerns Χριστός. The two domains listed for this lexeme are 93, "Names of persons and places," and 53, "Religious activities." It appears that if the Gospels were in play (rather than Paul's Letter to the Romans), domain 53 would be the most pertinent domain. However, debate regarding whether Paul is using "Christ" as part of Jesus's name or as a title nudges the meaning toward consideration of domain 93.[28] Again, this may be a difficulty created by the lexicon, in which the meaning of the lexeme is within domain 53, but where the cotextual Pauline usage incorporates this meaning into the name of an individual.

The second set of examples comprises instances where it is difficult to fit all of the usage under a single domain. The major example is with the verb δικαιόω and its cognates. The first domain is 34, "Association," but this does not seem to be appropriate for the way the word is used in Romans 5. A more plausible domain is 56, "Courts and legal procedures." However, there are also several cognate words in Romans 5. One is δικαίωμα (vv. 16, 18) and the other is δικαίωσις (v. 18). Δικαίωσις has only a single domain, 88, "Moral and ethical qualities and related behavior." If cognate words are used as determinative, the lexeme δικαίωσις, belonging to only a single domain, becomes determinative for all usage in Romans 5. In many ways, this pattern is consonant with domain selection for other words, since a number of other words are in domain 88: παράπτωμα (vv. 16, 17, 18), ἁμαρτάνω (vv. 12, 16), ἁμαρτωλός (v. 19), and ἁμαρτία (vv. 12, 20), as well as probably χάρις (vv. 2, 15, 17, 20), as this is the first domain listed. However, χάρισμα (v. 15), which has only a single domain, 57, "Possess, transfer, exchange," seems to indicate that χάρις should be in domain 57 as well (the semantic relation of cognates is evidenced in the use of verbs of motion in v. 12, εἰσῆλθεν and διῆλθεν). Easier to eliminate is domain 88, listed for λαμβάνω, even though two instances appear in this context (vv. 11, 17). However, if domain 88 is the proper one for δικαιόω and its cognates, this cannot be determined at the outset of considering the unit, since domain 34 is the first domain listed for the verb form.

---

28. This issue is opened up again in M. V. Novenson, "Can the Messiahship of Jesus Be Read off Paul's Grammar? Nils Dahl's Criteria 50 Years Later," *NTS* 56 (2010): 396–412.

One Sense per Genre or Register

For the sake of argument here, we will assume that Romans 5 constitutes a single register of usage. Within the argument of the book of Romans, after establishing the cause for God's activity in Jesus Christ, and the importance of righteousness/justification for addressing human sinfulness, Paul in this new section turns to discussion of personal relationship with God, described by means of reconciliation. On the basis of this analysis, one can posit that lexical usage is restricted to a single sense on the basis of this textual unit.

On the one hand, this proposal appears to address a number of the difficulties of other hypotheses regarding disambiguation of lexical meanings. Where there are multiple senses recognized for words, only a single sense needs to be operative in this given register of usage. This seems to be the case for a number of lexical items. These include χάρις (note comments above) (Rom. 5:2, 15, 17, 20), εἰμί (vv. 6, 8, 10, 13, 14), ἀποθνήσκω (vv. 6, 7, 8), πᾶς (vv. 12, 18), πολύς (vv. 9, 15, 16, 17, 19), and ἄνθρωπος (vv. 15, 18, 19), among others. Once the operative domain is determined, the sense seems to fit the context of situation.

On the other hand, the question becomes how one decides among the several differing domains, if one assumes that lexemes may be polysemous and that there may be competing choices of sense. One possible means of disambiguation is by means of clausal structural units—that is, syntagmatic groupings of domains. Simple clauses appear to be too small to be determinative (as some of them consist of only one or two clausal components), but a clause complex of at least two clauses (e.g., primary and embedded) might be more instructive. However, even in these instances there is no simple way to determine how one moves from lexemes with a single domain to those with multiple domains. Another and potentially more functional means by which such judgments can be made is to examine the domain environment—that is, the range of domains operative within a given environment of usage. One of the ways to determine these domains is first with reference to those lexical items for which there is only a single domain. Examples of these domains in Romans 5 are 33, "Communication," 25, "Attitudes and emotions," and 88, "Moral and ethical qualities and related behavior," among others. The use of these domains to establish parameters for other domain selection works in some instances. For example, in verses 4–5, in the chain progression, there are several examples of domain 25 for words such as ὑπομονή, ἐλπίς, and καταισχύνω. The presumption would be that the other words in close proximity share this or a related domain. This seems to be the case, so that δοκιμή is in domain 27, "Learn." This does not seem to work in other instances, however. For example, in verses 1–2 are a number of words in domains such as 31, "Hold a view, believe, trust," such as πίστις; and 33, "Communication," such as προσαγωγή and καυχάομαι. However, this does not mean that all of the words in this environment should be identified as in domains in the 30s, even though these domains are listed as possible domains for the senses of these lexemes. Thus ἔχω probably is best placed not in domain 31, but in domain 18, "Attachment"; δικαιόω is not in domains 34, "Association," 37, "Control, rule," or 36, "Guide, discipline, follow" (but in 88, as noted above); and χάρις is not in domain 33 (but also in 88).

Conclusion

As I have indicated on several occasions, the Louw-Nida lexicon is an important contribution to New Testament lexicography, and its impact has not yet been fully realized by New Testament scholars. However, in spite of its advances, the lexicon is not without shortcomings. In this chapter I have attempted to elucidate some of these, as well as provide what I think are some important ways forward if this type of lexicon is to be developed and expanded upon. A most promising avenue is the adoption of a monosemous approach to lexical meaning, as opposed to Louw and Nida's more traditional polysemy. Monosemy is an elegant lexical semantic theory that avoids many of the theoretical difficulties inherent in a polysemous approach. In my short analysis of Romans 5, I have shown a number of places where a monosemous lexical theory makes good sense of the use of particular lexemes, accounting for the modulation of sense and posing helpful semantic relationships among different lexemes. It is my hope that these observations can be built upon in the development of a new monosemous lexicon that makes a general contribution to the linguistic study of the Greek of the New Testament and also provides a worthwhile tool for exegetes as well as translators and others.

4

The Blessings and Curses
of Producing a Lexicon

Introduction

The huge difficulty involved in producing a bilingual lexicon of an ancient language must be recognized.[1] The late Professor Frederick Danker (1920–2012) has chronicled the evolution of BDAG[2] as the latest in a long line of important lexicographical works for New Testament study.[3] When one notes the kinds of difficulties that have been confronted in producing this work—personal, political, economic, physical, and so on—the development of this lexicon becomes a memorial to the undying and unstinting efforts of a line of important

---

1. J. A. L. Lee, *A History of New Testament Lexicography*, SBG 8 (New York: Peter Lang, 2003).

2. W. Bauer, *A Greek-English Lexicon of the New Testament and Other Early Christian Literature*, ed. F. W. Danker, 3rd ed. (Chicago: University of Chicago Press, 2000).

3. F. W. Danker, "Lexical Evolution and Linguistic Hazard" (paper presented at the annual meeting of the Society of Biblical Literature, Boston, Massachusetts, November 21, 1999). See also G. Kittel, *Lexicographia Sacra: Two Lectures on the Making of the "Theologisches Wörterbuch zum Neuen Testament"* (London: SPCK, 1938); G. Friedrich, "Pre-History of the Theological Dictionary of the New Testament," in vol. 10 of *Theological Dictionary of the New Testament*, ed G. Kittel and G. Friedrich, trans. G. W. Bromiley (Grand Rapids: Eerdmans, 1976), 613–61.

scholars such as Edwin Preuschen, Walter Bauer, Kurt Aland, William Arndt, and Wilbur Gingrich, and certainly not least to Professor Danker himself, who clearly devoted years of concentrated effort to this task. When this lexicon was published in its latest revision, Professor Danker promoted it in a series of open discussions and responses rather than taking more traditional means of promotion and advertisement. He is to be commended for this, since doing so ran the risk of being subjected to various types of criticism. As we all know, it is much easier to sit on the sidelines and critically comment on larger issues and specific points than it is to have undertaken the task itself. That is especially true in this case, where critical comments were being offered even before the volume appeared in print. Probably few of us would have been willing to be involved in such an evolving project for over forty years. In the light of this, like his predecessors, Professor Danker is to be highly commended for seeing this edition through to completion. I was one of those asked to make comments upon the lexicon at the time, not once but twice in public venues. I appreciate Professor Danker's willingness to engage the issues and respond to his critics, this one included. Thus, in the spirit of open critical scholarly discussion, even though Professor Danker is no longer able to respond, I wish to make further comments on BDAG, in the hope that some of the issues of contemporary lexicography can be reopened and further examined.

The Blessings

There are a number of important advances in this new edition of the lexicon. At the time of its publication, Professor Danker himself had already drawn attention to several of these (e.g., making important corrections, including only words that actually exist), and I wish merely to cite those that I think are the most useful in the light of the further comments that I will make. The most obvious advance is that this lexicon attempts to provide meanings and functions, and to distinguish these from translational equivalents or glosses, which were traditionally provided in lexicons. As I will note below, however, BDAG is not the only lexicon to do so, and the basis for such judgments warrants further scrutiny. A further noteworthy advance is the effort to make categorical distinctions evident, which is done most obviously by the use of a clear system for outlining the discussions of the individual entries. A third contribution is the updated bibliography, especially in relevant and available resources for English readers. Professor Danker's attention to many of the classic but often-neglected works of secondary literature is a timely reminder that much is overlooked in the common procedure of simply listing bibliography but not reading it, or only dealing closely with bibliography appearing in the last ten or fifteen years. I believe that it still remains to be seen how several of these noteworthy advances will make their presence felt in scholarly discussion, and what the positive effects they have on exegesis will be, including in the writing of commentaries, where Danker has declared that the lexicon in general still has a major contribution to make.

The Curses

There are also bound to be a number of shortcomings with a project of this sort. I will categorize these under three headings. Some of them are built into this lexicon project as a part of what it is by definition, and I will mention these but not spend significant time on them. Some of the shortcomings are the almost inevitable failings that are specific to the execution of this particular project, and I will mention some examples as emblematic of a larger number of such problems. Finally, and most important, some of the problems are systemic and bring to the fore the kinds of frontier issues that might be considered in contemporary lexicography as a potential branch of linguistics.

The Development of This Lexicon Project

One of the major shortcomings of this project is that this lexicon is, to a large extent, simply the latest English version of a monument to nineteenth-century German scholarship. English-language New Testament scholarship—in fact, English-language ancient studies, including classics—owes a huge and continuing debt to German scholarship of the nineteenth century.[4] We are all immensely indebted to the industry that resulted for the first time in major critical editions of ancient scholars (e.g., the Teubner series), and produced scholars such as Constantin Tischendorf, to name only one among many.[5] Along with the huge production of primary texts, there came the need for basic scholarly tools to aid in the interpretation of those texts, such as grammars and lexicons. English-language New Testament scholarship once utilized the New

4. This point is well illustrated by F. W. Danker in *A Century of Greco-Roman Philology: Featuring the American Philological Association and the Society of Biblical Literature*, SBLCP (Atlanta: Scholars Press, 1988). For example, even though American classicists early on went their own intellectual way, many of them were previously educated in Germany, such as Herbert Weir Smyth, Basil Gildersleeve, and Paul Shorey.
5. See S. E. Porter, *Constantine Tischendorf: The Life and Work of a 19th Century Bible Hunter* (London: Bloomsbury, 2015).

Testament Greek grammar of Georg Winer in various English translations,[6] and now relies heavily, at times almost exclusively, upon the 1961 English translation of Friedrich Blass's 1896 grammar of New Testament Greek, revised and enhanced through the course of the twentieth century, but still distinctly a product of the nineteenth century.[7] It is worth noting, to place Blass's grammar within the development of Greek linguistics of the time, that Blass eschewed the comparative philological method and placed his work within the classical philology of the nineteenth century, despite their convergence at numerous points even in his grammar.[8] Similar in many ways is the case of the Bauer

6. G. B. Winer, *Grammatik des neutestamentlichen Sprachidioms* (Leipzig: Vogel, 1822), which went to seven editions (the last revised by G. Lünemann), with an eighth edition begun but never finished by P. W. Schmiedel (Göttingen: Vandenhoeck & Ruprecht, 1894–98). English translations that have continued to be used are those by E. Masson of the sixth edition of 1855 (*A Grammar of the New Testament Diction* [Edinburgh: T&T Clark, 1859], with several following editions), W. F. Moulton (*A Treatise on the Grammar of New Testament Greek, Regarded as a Sure Basis for New Testament Exegesis* [Edinburgh: T&T Clark, 1870], with three editions), and J. H. Thayer of the seventh edition of 1867 (*A Grammar of the Idiom of the New Testament* [Andover, MA: Draper, 1869]). See also A. Buttmann, *Grammatik des neutestamentlichen Sprachgebrauchs* (Berlin: Ferd. Dümmler, 1859), trans. J. H. Thayer as *A Grammar of the New Testament Greek* (Andover, MA: Draper, 1873).

7. F. Blass, *Grammatik des neutestamentlichen Griechisch* (Göttingen: Vandenhoeck & Ruprecht, 1896). The publishing history of this volume is as follows: 2nd ed. 1902; 3rd ed. 1911; 4th ed. 1913, revised by A. Debrunner (see note below); 5th ed. 1921; 6th ed. 1931; 7th ed., "umgearb. u. vermehrte" by Debrunner (see note below); 8th ed. 1949; 9th ed. 1954; 10th ed. 1959; 11th ed. 1961; 12th ed. 1965, with an appendix by D. Tabachowitz (see note below); 13th ed. 1970; 14th ed. 1975, revised by F. Rehkopf (see note below); 15th ed. 1979; 16th ed. 1984; 17th ed. 1990; 18th ed. 2001.

8. In his dedicatory preface to Professor August Fick, Blass states the following at the outset: "Als Sie mich vor Zeiten in Göttingen die Anfangsgründe des Sanskrit lehrten, mochten Sie vielleicht im Stillen denken, dass ich mich einmal, wenn nicht gerade den indischen Studien, doch der vergleichenden Sprachforschung zuwenden würde. Das ist nicht eingetreten; denn die klassische Philologie, und insonderheit das Griechische, war mir zu sehr ans Herz gewachsen, und die vergleichende Sprachforschung nahm, wie Sie wissen, bald ihren sehr eignen Gang, auf dem ich nicht mitkommen konnte" (*Grammatik*, iii, "Since you previously taught me in Göttingen the rudiments of Sanskrit, you might privately think that sometime I would certainly turn to comparative philology, if not directly to Indo-European studies. That has not happened. Since classical philology, and especially Greek, has been of great interest to me, I have not been able to pursue it, and comparative philology, as you know, has taken its own course"). This part of the preface has not been reproduced in any of the German editions since at least the fourth, and has never in any portion been included in the English versions. In his preface to the fourth edition Albert Debrunner takes these words as an indication that it would be appropriate for revision to be undertaken by a comparative philologist, which revisions he confines mostly to matters of phonology and accidence, leaving syntax relatively untouched. Although in his preface Robert Funk says that "both format and content have been radically transformed since Blass created the work," my perusal of the various editions indicates that the format has indeed changed but that the content is still very much the same, often including the exact same examples. As Funk further states, "The basic principles upon which it is based have remained substantially the same" (xii), a fact borne out by the similar perspectives of classical and comparative philology

lexicon. Bauer's lexicon developed as an enhanced revision of Preuschen's lexicon of 1910,[9] which was the same kind of product of nineteenth-century German scholarly industry, as Danker admits.[10] Without elucidating the points, such results of nineteenth-century industry are bound to, and do, reflect the mind-set and orientation of the nineteenth century. The major theoretical backdrop of this kind of work is its essentially prelinguistic methodology, whether this is expressed as a kind of classical philology that evaluates the Greek of the New Testament against classical norms[11] or is manifested in the kind of linguistic determinism so often found in Germanic thinkers, such as Wilhelm von Humboldt with his linkage of language and thought[12] and the

---

(see S. E. Porter and J. T. Reed, "Greek Grammar since BDF: A Retrospective and Prospective Analysis," *FN* 4 [1991]: 143–64, esp. 145). Most of the supposed editions are merely reprints with a few corrections, with the German editions 1–3, 4–6, 7–8, 9–13, and 14–18 being essentially the same. English translations of Blass and later Blass and Debrunner are by H. St. J. Thackeray (*Grammar of New Testament Greek* [London: Macmillan, 1898; 2nd ed., 1905]) and R. W. Funk (*A Greek Grammar of the New Testament and Other Early Christian Literature* [Chicago: University of Chicago Press, 1961]).

9. E. Preuschen, *Vollständiges griechisch-deutsches Handwörterbuch zu den Schriften des Neuen Testaments und der übrigen urchristlichen Literatur* (Gießen: Töpelmann, 1910).

10. "Although the revision of Preuschen's work marked an advance on that particular work, it is important to recognize that Bauer remained in the mainstream of a long Teutonic lexical tradition" (Danker, "Lexical Evolution," 10). Works that served as predecessors were C. G. Wilke, *Clavis Novi Testamenti Philologica* (Leipzig: Arnold, 1841; 2 vols., 2nd ed., 1851; rev. ed. by C. L. W. Grimm, 1862–68; 2nd ed., 1879; 3rd ed., 1886); H. Cremer, *Biblisch-theologisches Wörterbuch der Neutestamentliche Gräcität* (Gotha: F. A. Berthes, 1866; 11th ed., rev. by J. Kögel, 1923); J. H. Thayer, *A Greek-English Lexicon of the New Testament* (New York: American Book Company, 1886; 2nd ed., 1889), the last of which is dependent upon Wilke and Grimm. See also J. P. Louw, "The Present State of New Testament Lexicography," in *Lexicography and Translation*, ed. J. P. Louw (Roggebaai: Bible Society of South Africa, 1985), 97–117.

11. This was a common attitude of much nineteenth-century and even twentieth-century Greek study. See Porter and Reed, "Greek Grammar since BDF," 145–46, citing, among others, J. H. Moulton (*An Introduction to the Study of New Testament Greek*, 2nd ed. [London: Kelly, 1903], 9), who characterized such a position as engaging in a pedantry of classical learning; and H. St. J. Thackeray (*A Grammar of the Old Testament in Greek: According to the Septuagint* [Cambridge: Cambridge University Press, 1909]), who said that Koine Greek "is not estimated at its true worth when regarded merely as a debased and decadent Greek" (p. 21).

12. See W. von Humboldt, *Über die Verschiedenheit des menschlichen Sprachbaues und ihren Einfluss auf die geistige Entwickelung des Menschengeschlechts* (Berlin: Königlichen Akademie der Wissenschaften, 1836); ET, *On Language: On the Diversity of Human Language Construction and its Influence on the Mental Development of the Human Species*, ed. M. Losonsky, trans. P. Heath (Cambridge: Cambridge University Press, 1999). Von Humboldt's views in more recent times were perpetuated in the so-called Sapir-Whorf hypothesis (see E. Sapir, *Language: An Introduction to the Study of Speech* [New York: Harcourt, Brace, 1921]; B. L. Whorf, *Language, Thought, and Reality: Selected Writings of Benjamin Lee Whorf*, ed. J. B. Carroll [Cambridge, MA: MIT Press, 1952]), evaluated by J. A. Lucy, *Grammatical Categories and Cognition: A Case Study of the Linguistic Relativity Hypothesis*, SSCFL 13 (Cambridge: Cambridge University Press,

New Grammarians with their immutable phonological rules.[13] In lexicography this tendency has resulted in the notion that words are things (i.e., there is an inherent relationship between signifier and signified), the confusion of words and concept, and the idea that reference is a property of words, not of their users. The most obvious lexicographical victim of this theoretical framework is *Theologisches Wörterbuch zum Neuen Testament / Theological Dictionary of the New Testament*,[14] but the Bauer lexicon is a product of this intellectual mind-set as well. Added to this is the fact that the Bauer lexicon in English has always been a translation of the German edition.[15] The latest incarnation is perhaps a further departure from being a direct translation than previous editions, but this seems to be more obvious around the edges than at the core of the work. As Danker observed, sometimes the English version rearranges the entries, restores and enhances bibliography, and adds a few words, but the core of most entries comes from the Bauer lexicon. This is unfortunate, because modern linguistics has produced a great deal of research regarding the concept of meaning, and much of this research is directly relevant to lexicography. I will return to this point below.

Failings of BDAG

Besides evaluating the broad theoretical framework of the lexicon, I also wish to evaluate its own internal consistency—that is, evaluate it on its own terms. This set of observations relates to the kinds of problems that would be encountered by a user who simply picks up the lexicon and attempts to use it as a guide to understanding the words of the Greek New Testament. In surveying the entries of BDAG, I have come across some different kinds of shortcomings that I think are worth noting. These examples are not meant to be exhaustive, but they suggest categories of shortcomings that might be encountered in its use.

1992), and J. J. Gumperz and S. C. Levinson, eds., *Rethinking Linguistic Relativity*, SSCFL 17 (Cambridge: Cambridge University Press, 1996). For further discussion, see chap. 7 in the present volume.

13. See K. R. Jankowsky, *The Neogrammarians*, JLSMi 116 (The Hague: Mouton, 1972).

14. See J. Barr, *The Semantics of Biblical Language* (Oxford: Oxford University Press, 1961).

15. W. Bauer, *Griechisch-Deutsches Wörterbuch zu den Schriften des Neuen Testaments und der übrigen urchristlichen Literatur*, 2nd ed. (Giessen: Töpelmann, 1928); 3rd ed., Berlin: de Gruyter, 1937; 4th ed., 1952; 5th ed., 1958; 6th ed., rev. K. Aland and B. Aland with V. Reichmann, 1988. The history of the English translation, *A Greek-English Lexicon of the New Testament and Other Early Christian Literature* (Chicago: University of Chicago Press), is as follows: based upon the 4th German ed. (trans. W. F. Arndt and F. W. Gingrich; 1957); based upon the 5th German ed. (rev. F. W. Gingrich and F. W. Danker; 2nd ed., 1979); and based upon the 6th German ed. (ed. F. W. Danker; 3rd ed., 2000).

The first, and perhaps most obvious, are instances where simply the wrong meaning has been given. An example of this is the word αὐλός, which is defined as "*flute*." Regarding the lexicon, Danker notes that the meanings and functions are offered in bold, but the glosses or translational equivalents are given in bold italics. In this instance, "*flute*" is given in bold italics as both the meaning and the gloss, and that is all that is said. This seems to me to be unfortunate in several respects. First, it is probably wrong, as both the meaning and the gloss, because the word "flute" in English conveys the wrong sense entirely. As the musicologist Willi Apel says in the *Harvard Dictionary of Music*, αὐλός "is not a flute (as has frequently been stated) but an oboe with double reed."[16] Αὐλός was the Greek title given to a class of wind instruments that used double reeds to produce sound. They usually were depicted as having two pipes and were blown from the end, with the player having a band around the head, probably to aid in sound production. So "double oboe" might well be a better translational equivalent. Second, in this case the new lexicon has violated its own principles by failing to provide a description of the meaning (e.g., "double reed wind instrument probably sounding like an oboe, played in pairs") and has used simply a translational equivalent—and a wrong one at that. This shows that the distinction between meaning and gloss, though useful, is not always easy to use or maintain. This difficulty is further illustrated in some instances where the gloss perhaps overinterprets the word. An example of this is Ἀαρών. Proper names are notoriously difficult in linguistics, since they are used to refer and do not have sense, except perhaps in theological lexicons, or in works that are attempting to tease out the metaphorical literary accretions of lexical usage (see chap. 20, on proper nouns, below). "Aaron" is an example of this: he is described in BDAG as "Embodies the (high) priesthood," an enhanced definition from the previous definition of BAGD ("Represents the priesthood"). On the one hand, this description may reflect a theological definition, in which case it well illustrates that the Bauer lexicon is still maintaining the kind of theological lexicography of a previous era. On the other hand, this sort of definition may be an attempt to reflect the Jewish cultural practice of using Ἀαρών as a metonym (metaphor by association). This still raises questions of whether a lexicon should attempt to capture such metaphorical uses and, if so, how this should be represented.

The second type of example is where unclear meanings and orderings are provided. An example here is the Greek verb γίνομαι, especially with BDAG's seventh meaning being given as "to come into a certain state or possess certain

16. W. Apel, "Aulos," in *Harvard Dictionary of Music*, ed. W. Apel, 2nd ed. (Cambridge, MA: Belknap Press of Harvard University Press, 1969), 63.

characteristics, *to be, prove to be, turn out to be*." A number of observations can be made here. First, there is the question of whether this is the best way to express this meaning in English (I have not checked the German, so I have no idea how close they are). I have my doubts. Second, the entry makes a comparison with εἰμί, which suggests that γίνομαι is a member of the category of verbs of existence. Definition 8, "to be present at a given time, be there," with the added note "hence *exist*," seems to continue this linkage in the form of an impersonal translation for the verb. One must wonder, however, whether the difference between meanings 7 and 8 is that of γίνομαι or of English translation. Third, the relation to the other meanings offered and the way they are arranged both need to be examined, especially if some but not all of the meanings of γίνομαι place it in the category of verbs of existence. At the least, one probably should have two major categories of meaning. However, the arrangement of the meanings is even more complex than this. The first meaning offered for γίνομαι is "to come into being through process of birth or natural production, *be born, be produced*." According to the examples given, this meaning has one of the lowest frequencies of use. The reason for its inclusion first is unclear, since it does not seem to constitute any kind of fundamental meaning. There probably should be some clearer ordering of the meanings, with frequency of use being one of the possible ways of arranging the entries.

The third set of examples is derived from inconsistencies found in the explanatory categories. Words that seem to evidence these inconsistencies are the Greek preposition εἰς and conjunction ἵνα. Of course, such function words are bound to be problematic in lexicography, often circumvented by the provision of a gloss that hides more than it reveals (e.g., "to" or "that," in these instances). In his lexicon, Professor Danker has tried to come to terms with the limitations, but I am not convinced that he has fully succeeded. For εἰς he gives the meaning categories of (1) "extension involving a goal or place, *into, in, toward, to*"; (2) "extension in time, *to, until, on*"; (3) "marker of degree, *up to*"; (4) "marker of goals involving affective/abstract/suitability aspects, *into, to*" (again, one wonders if this is understandable English); (5) "marker of a specific point of reference, *for, to, with respect to, with reference to*"; (6) "marker of a guarantee, *by*"; (7) "distributive marker"; (8) (here is a real oddity, to be discussed further below) "The predicate nom. and the predicate acc. are somet[imes] replaced by εἰς w. acc. under Semitic influence, which has strengthened Gk. tendencies in the same direction"; and then (9) "marker of instrumentality, *by, with*." I will return to the question of bilingualism below, but one can see that there are essentially three categories of meaning expatiated upon here: extension, marker, and Semitic substitute. It seems to me that the various more specific meanings should be offered under these three categories, if they are to be retained at all, but that poses a serious question. What seems to be lacking is any kind of a systematic way of quantifying meaning in this definition (and others). There is no apparent means by which components of meaning are defined and articulated. Instead, I suggest that these nine meanings or even three categories appear to be more categories found to reflect the translational glosses rather than categories based on meaningful elements for which appropriate translations are offered.

The definition of ἵνα provides a different kind of problem. The categories offered are the following: (1) "marker to denote purpose, aim, or goal, *in order that, that*, final sense"; (2) "marker of objective, *that*"; (3) "marker serving as substitute for the inf[initive] of result, *so that*"; and (4) "marker of retroactive emphasis, *that*." The mixed categories being used here are semantic and syntactical ones. The first two indicate relations between clauses, the third indicates substitution for a whole clause based upon the infinitive, and the fourth is simply indicating syntactical placement of the word ἵνα. For each of these two words, there are some lists of functions, but the principles of categorization are not consistent. As a result, I am not sure that one actually gains a firm idea of what it is that these words mean and do.

The fourth set of examples concerns the use of bibliography. Some examples are uneven (e.g., αὐθεντέω, ἀββα), while others fail to distinguish what the bibliography contributes to the entry (e.g., ἵνα). Regarding the uneven bibliography, under αὐθεντέω, there is mention of a couple of fairly recent articles in *New Testament Studies*, but no mention of a number of detailed linguistic studies that add to this debate.[17] Of course, no entry can be complete, but this is a word that recently has been highly debated, and the recent discussion, while being far from solving the complexities involved, has (at least in some instances) added to our knowledge of the Hellenistic language milieu in which this word was used. This raises the further question of whether there is

17. Some of this recent literature includes: C. C. Kroeger, "Ancient Heresies and a Strange Greek Verb," *RJ* 29, no. 3 (1979): 12–15; R. C. Kroeger and C. C. Kroeger, *I Suffer Not a Woman: Rethinking 1 Timothy 2:11–15 in Light of Ancient Evidence* (Grand Rapids: Baker, 1992), esp. 79–104; A. J. Panning, "αὐθέντης—A Word Study," *WLQ* 78 (1981): 185–91; L. E. Wilshire, "1 Timothy 2:12 Revisited: A Reply to Paul W. Barnett and Timothy J. Harris," *EvQ* 65 (1993): 43–55; A. C. Perriman, "What Eve Did, What Women Shouldn't Do: The Meaning of αὐθεντέω in 1 Timothy 2:12," *TynBul* 44 (1993): 129–42; H. S. Baldwin, "A Difficult Word—αὐθεντέω in 1 Timothy 2:12" and "Appendix 2: αὐθεντέω in Ancient Greek Literature," both in *Women in the Church: A Fresh Analysis of 1 Timothy 2:9–15*, ed. A. J. Köstenberger, T. R. Schreiner and H. S. Baldwin (Grand Rapids: Baker Books, 1995), 65–80, 269–305 (the first of Baldwin's articles republished in revised form under the title "An Important Word: Αὐθεντέω in 1 Timothy 2:12," in *Women in the Church: An Analysis and Application of 1 Timothy 2:9–15*, ed. A. J. Köstenberger and T. R. Schreiner, 2nd ed. [Grand Rapids: Baker Academic, 2005], 39–51); A. Wolters, "A Semantic Study of αὐθέντης and Its Derivatives," *JGRChJ* 1 (2000): 145–75.

a correlation between the amount of secondary literature listed in the lexicon entry, the amount published on the word, and the importance or difficulty of the word in recent scholarship. An obvious case where crucial overlooked bibliography influences how a word is best understood is the word ἀββα. Of course, BDAG cites, among other sources, the classic work by Joachim Jeremias,[18] but it does not include the important refutation by James Barr, one that decisively decimates Jeremias's and related theories.[19] Regarding the failure to use the bibliography, a good instance is found under ἵνα, where a reasonably recent article by Ineke Sluiter is cited.[20] The abbreviated title of the article leaves it unclear how this particular article contributes to the debate over ἵνα. The entry says that the use of ἵνα in Mark 4:12 = Luke 8:10 probably is to be taken as final. However, Sluiter's article is evaluating the causal use of ἵνα. She concludes that the causal use is valid, but mostly found in later sources (fourth and fifth century AD, with the phenomenon perhaps going back to the second), and under particular linguistic circumstances; however, she does not endorse a single New Testament example as being causal. Perhaps a means of indicating the way in which the bibliography contributes to the debate would be helpful.

The fifth set of examples is concerned with the appropriateness of the comments included (e.g., bilingualism and εἰς) and the question of how interpretive the lexicon should be (e.g., Ἰουδαῖος). These examples raise serious questions about what the parameters of a lexicon legitimately are, since the first gets into matters that stretch beyond lexicography and into such things as syntax, and even the sociolinguistic category of multilingualism; and the second involves matters of exegesis. For example, when discussing the preposition εἰς (meaning 6 above), the comment is made under "marker of a guarantee, by" that "the sole use of εἰς in a series of datives with ἐν may reflect bilingualism." This seems to be a lexicographical comment not on the meaning or function of the preposition in context, but rather on the larger linguistic milieu in which it is used, and the possible reasons for it. There are not the equivalent kinds of comments made at other places in the lexicon regarding other words. Whereas Semitic influence has been a large topic in New Testament studies,

---

18. J. Jeremias, *Abba: Studien zur neutestamentlichen Theologie und Zeitgeschichte* (Göttingen: Vandenhoeck & Ruprecht, 1966), 21–41; Jeremias, *The Central Message of the New Testament* (London: SCM, 1965), 9–30.

19. J. Barr, "Abba Isn't Daddy," *JTS* 39 (1988): 28–47.

20. I. Sluiter, "Causal ἵνα—Sound Greek," *Glotta* 70 (1992): 39–53. Sluiter defines the context in which causal ἵνα is found: the ἵνα clause precedes the main clause, ἵνα is followed by the aorist subjunctive, and the main verb is in a "past" tense. For recent discussion, but from the perspective of relevance theory, see M. G. Sim, *Marking Thought and Talk in New Testament Greek: New Light from Linguistics on the Particles ἵνα and ὅτι* (Eugene, OR: Pickwick, 2010).

as most New Testament scholars are well aware, it is often treated—as it is here in the lexicon—as an isolated matter, without consideration of the larger linguistic issues. Insofar as meaning and function are concerned, one could well argue that the use in context is the important lexicographical matter, no matter how one accounts for it.

When discussing the word Ἰουδαῖος, Danker includes an extended note that reflects contemporary exegetical discussion on the issue of how the Jews are depicted in the New Testament. This is a very legitimate debate; however, one must wonder whether it is appropriate to include this extended description here in this lexicon, which is supposed to be concerned with the meaning or function of these individual words in their context, especially when similar regard is not given to words such as Ῥωμαῖος and ἔθνος. For Ἰουδαῖος, Danker endorses the loanword "Judean," but this probably is incorrect, not least because it raises as many questions as it answers (e.g., Does it describe those who live in or originated in the area? What are its relations to bloodlines?). Danker claims to wish to avoid the word "Jew" because the term "Judaism" "suggests a monolithic entity that fails to take account of the many varieties of thought and social expression associated with such adherents." Surely the same argument could be made for Ῥωμαῖος or ἔθνος, but it is not. I think that Danker gets closer to his reasons for the use of "Judean" when he says, "Incalculable harm has been caused by simply glossing [Ἰουδαῖος] with 'Jew,' for many readers or auditors of Bible translations do not practice the historical judgment necessary to distinguish between circumstances and events of an ancient time and contemporary ethnic-religious-social realities, with the result that anti-Judaism in the modern sense of the term is needlessly fostered through biblical texts." Danker is undoubtedly correct about there being problems of anti-Judaism, but I do not believe that they have been caused by simple glosses. They have been caused by a complex of reasons, and simply changing an entry in a lexicon will neither address nor resolve them. Unfortunately, here Danker has left lexicography behind and goes beyond even the theological lexicography that we associate with *TWNT/TDNT* to practice a form of lexicography as ethical-moral correction (not evidenced in other entries in the lexicon, such as πορνεία), showing that we have perhaps made far less progress in lexicography than we thought.[21]

---

21. A similar statement could be made on the basis of a recent article by John Lee, in which he uncovers etymological fallacies in three recent "pocket" lexicons of the Greek New Testament. I think that distinction between transparency and etymology might have helped his analysis. See J. A. L. Lee, "Etymological Follies: Three Recent Lexicons of the New Testament," *NovT* 55 (2013): 383–403.

A Future for Lexicography

In the light of the several issues raised above, especially those in which various syntactical and grammatical problems have been inadvertently introduced into the new lexicon, I wish to pursue this matter further by introducing issues that I think should be raised in lexicography that contends to be on the cutting edge of the study of words. Lexicography has long been the poor stepchild of modern linguistics and is often not even included in linguistic study, even though semantics has become an important and productive area.[22] However, recent productive work in a variety of areas of linguistics and lexicography provides a means of making some advances in New Testament lexicography as well. I think it is unfortunate that more of what has been learned in recent linguistic theory, including lexicography, has not been utilized in BDAG. I wish to introduce two areas here for discussion, although this is far from a complete or exhaustive list of the topics or areas that might be introduced.[23]

The first is semantic-domain (or semantic-field) theory. Danker notes that semantic-domain theory has been applied to the study of the New Testament in his commendation of the Louw-Nida lexicon,[24] but in my opinion, the fact that BDAG does not use this approach is more than simply, to use Danker's words, "an exhibition of cultural lag."[25] I do not think that the achievement the Louw-Nida lexicon represents has been fully recognized among New Testament scholars. Yes, the Louw-Nida lexicon has some odd features, such as requiring two volumes because the words are not alphabetical, some of the categories are not self-evident and seem to be based upon English rather than Greek categories, extrabiblical Greek does not figure as prominently as one would like, there is a lack of syntactical information, and few seem to know quite what to do with the fact that a word falls into a particular domain.[26] However, linguists have commended this lexicon as a significant advance in

22. On some of the issues involved in lexicography and linguistics, see S. E. Porter, *Studies in the Greek New Testament: Theory and Practice*, SBG 6 (New York: Peter Lang, 1996), 49–74; Porter, "Greek Linguistics and Lexicography," in *Understanding the Times: New Testament Studies in the 21st Century; Essays in Honor of D. A. Carson on the Occasion of his 65th Birthday*, ed. A. J. Köstenberger and R. W. Yarbrough (Wheaton, IL: Crossway, 2011), 19–61, esp. 21–37.

23. I believe also that lexicography should be approached from a "monosemic bias" (C. Ruhl, *On Monosemy: A Study in Linguistic Semantics* [New York: SUNY Press, 1989]). For defense of such an orientation, see chap. 3 in the present volume.

24. J. P. Louw and E. A. Nida, *Greek-English Lexicon of the New Testament Based on Semantic Domains*, 2 vols. (New York: United Bible Societies, 1988); see also E. A. Nida and J. P. Louw, *Lexical Semantics of the Greek New Testament*, SBLRBS 25 (Atlanta: Scholars Press, 1992).

25. Danker, "Lexical Evolution," 32.

26. See, e.g., J. A. L. Lee, "The United Bible Societies' Lexicon and Its Analysis of Meanings," *FN* 5 (1992): 167–89.

lexicography because it is one of the first and most thoroughgoing attempts to categorize and treat the vocabulary of an entire language by means of identifying how words seem to be handled by the users of the language.[27] Even Danker tacitly recognizes the importance of this feature, as when he says of ἀγαθοποιΐα that it "is part of the semantic field relating to the esteem in which Gr[eco]-Rom[an] persons of exceptional merit were held." However, he does not show the other members of this field or how this field relates to others.

Traditional biblical lexicons, with which we are all too familiar (apart from BDB, and that is one of its major shortcomings), are rigidly alphabetical. But this is simply not the way users of languages seem to organize and to draw upon their language's lexicon. A simple exercise illustrates this. Think of all of the words that you know, and start writing them down in alphabetical order, starting with *A*, and be sure and get all of the words within *A* correctly alphabetical as well. Most people cannot get very far. However, now think of words that are concerned with the human body, or food, or any similarly broad category. One can very easily produce long lists of words that cluster together. A language user's mental lexicon seems to be organized around larger clusters of meaning. Such an approach has potential for arranging and thinking of the lexicon by means of how the users themselves organize it, domains of meaning can be established on the basis of shared and differentiated meanings, and various dimensions and relations of meaning (i.e., a hierarchy of meanings) can be established.[28]

I am convinced that lexicography needs to discuss words by means of how they are semantically related: semantic-domain theory is a major step in this direction; and the Louw-Nida lexicon is a major first step for New Testament scholars. Semantic-domain theory, which is closely linked to componential analysis (the differentiation of components of meaning establishes the domains and the individual meanings, which I will discuss below), has been around for a long time—some would say that it in fact goes back to Wilhelm von Humboldt—and it is not merely a new or recent innovation designed to throw New Testament scholars into a panic over new jargon.[29] There have been major

27. See E. A. Nida, J. P. Louw, and R. B. Smith, "Semantic Domains and Componential Analysis of Meaning," in *Current Issues in Linguistic Theory*, ed. R. W. Cole (Bloomington: Indiana University Press, 1977), 139–67.

28. Nida, Louw, and Smith, "Semantic Domains," 142–43.

29. For a brief history of discussion, see J. Lyons, *Semantics*, 2 vols. (Cambridge: Cambridge University Press, 1977), 1:250–61. Works in English that develop semantic field theory include S. Öhman, "Theories of the Linguistic Field," *Word* 9 (1953): 123–34; S. Ullmann, *The Principles of Semantics*, 2nd ed. (Oxford: Blackwell, 1957), 152–70; A. Lehrer, *Semantic Fields and Lexical Structure* (Amsterdam: North Holland, 1974), esp. 15–45; Nida, Louw, and Smith, "Semantic Domains"; Nida and Louw, *Lexical Semantics*. Applications of semantic field theory to ancient

writings on the subject that date back nearly fifty years, with plenty of theory and practical work that stands behind it. This situation is the reason I am disappointed that BDAG does not make use of semantic-domain theory. I am not necessarily saying that one needs to write an entirely new lexicon the same way Louw and Nida have done in order to appropriate many of its advances, because even by using a traditional alphabetical dictionary, one could create a supplemental set of semantic-domain lists to guide users.[30] Various lists of synonyms and antonyms have been created; but I am speaking of something far more elaborate, in which multidimensional relations are depicted, including synonyms and opposites (including antonyms), but also hyponyms, ranging from broad superordinate categories to more specific ones.[31] As BDAG currently stands, a user has no clear idea of how any given word relates to another in its sense relations, or even frequency of usage. Semantic-domain descriptions could illustrate how words within domains relate to each other in regard to conceptual and distributional categories. This would help exegetes to determine the level and type of vocabulary being used by a given author, and then to be able to note when significant vocabulary is being used and in what way.

One of the shortcomings of the Louw-Nida lexicon is that it does not make explicit the kind of componential analysis that has led them to their semantic domains. There is no doubt that the concept of componential analysis itself is subject to debate (e.g., over such issues as semantic primitives, linguistic universals, etc.), but, as D. A. Cruse has said, "Representing complex meanings in terms of simpler ones is as problem-ridden in theory as it is indispensable in practice."[32] An approach using an explicit componential approach that

---

Greek include J. Lyons, *Structural Semantics: An Analysis of Part of the Vocabulary of Plato* (Oxford: Blackwell, 1963); H. R. Rawlings III, *A Semantic Study of Prophasis to 400 BC* (Wiesbaden: F. Steiner, 1975); see also, in New Testament studies, M. Silva, *Biblical Words and Their Meaning: An Introduction to Lexical Semantics*, rev. ed. (Grand Rapids: Zondervan, 1994), esp. 161–63, 176–77, 185, 188–94; P. Cotterell and M. Turner, *Linguistics and Biblical Interpretation* (London: SPCK, 1989), 154–55, for very rudimentary statements.

30. To some extent fulfilled in T. Muraoka, *A Greek-English Lexicon of the Septuagint: Twelve Prophets* (Louvain: Peeters, 1993), where semantically related terms are listed.

31. See Porter, *Studies in the Greek New Testament*, 71–73.

32. D. A. Cruse, *Lexical Semantics*, CTL (Cambridge: Cambridge University Press, 1986), 22. For an overview of componential analysis, see Lyons, *Semantics*, 1:317–35; Lyons says, "It is probably true to say that the majority of structural semanticists subscribe nowadays to some version or other of componential analysis" (p. 317). Important works in English include U. Weinreich, "On the Semantic Structure of Language," in *Universals of Language*, ed. J. Greenberg, 2nd ed. (Cambridge, MA: MIT Press, 1966), 142–216; E. A. Nida, *Toward a Science of Translating: With Special Reference to the Principles and Procedures Involved in Bible Translating* (Leiden: Brill, 1964), esp. 82–87; Nida, *Componential Analysis of Meaning: An Introduction to Semantic Structures* (The Hague: Mouton, 1975); M. Bierwisch, "Semantics," in *New Horizons in Linguistics*, ed. J. Lyons (Harmondsworth: Penguin, 1970), 166–84; Lehrer,

attempts to be explicit in its analysis has relatively recently begun to appear (five volumes to date), under the editorship of Juan Mateos (though now deceased) and Jesús Peláez, as the *Diccionario Griego-Español del Nuevo Testamento (DGENT)*.[33] The first fascicle, from Ἀαρών to αἱματεκχυσία, utilizes the method of componential analysis developed in previous publications (neither apparently known by Danker),[34] and displays these in a semantic analysis for each sememe, or sense of a given word, excluding personal names. As a result, this dictionary also distinguishes between meaning and translation, offered in terms of a description of the meaning and translational equivalents, but also in terms of denotation and connotation as illustrated by the semantic formula. The semantic formula for each sememe is composed of a specified relation between five major semantic categories (*especies semánticas*): entity (*E = Entidad*); attribute (*A = Atributo*), such as quality, dimension, form; activity (*H = Hecho*), such as state, action, process; relation (*R = Relación*), such as proximity, anteriority, dependence; and determination (*D = Determinación*), such as actualized, situated, or objective.[35] On the basis of these semantic categories, a semic analysis is performed that shows the relations of these categories and the particular semantic features of each and arrives at a sememe, or sense, for a given word. The semantic analysis is displayed within a box to indicate the denotation of the word, and the analysis that leads to or away from this denotation indicates the connotations.

So far, this may sound a bit abstract, but I think theory is important for any exercise of this sort, and I appreciate that the Greek-Spanish lexicon has attempted to be explicit. To test the results, however, it is perhaps worth comparing the treatment of one word in the BDAG and this Greek-Spanish lexicon to get a sense of their differences in application. BDAG defines ἀγαθός as having two major meanings (though with several submeanings): (1) "pert.

Semantic Fields, esp. 46–75; D. Geeraerts, *Theories of Lexical Semantics* (Oxford: Oxford University Press, 2010), esp. 70–80.

33. J. Mateos and J. Peláez, eds., *Diccionario Griego-Español del Nuevo Testamento*, 5 vols. (Córdoba: Ediciones el Almendro; Fundación Épsilon, 2000–). My presentation on this dictionary has benefited from having heard my colleague Jesús Peláez speak about it several times (in presentations and otherwise) and our discussions about it. The example below is from one of his handouts.

34. J. Mateos, *Método de análisis semántico: Aplicado al Griego del Nuevo Testamento*, EFN 1 (Córdoba: Ediciones el Almendro, 1989); J. Peláez, *Metodología del Diccionario Griego-Español del Nuevo Testamento*, EFN 6 (Córdoba: Ediciones el Almendro; Fundación Épsilon, 1996). The method is first explained by Mateos, and expanded and developed by Peláez. Peláez offers a critique of previous lexicons, such as Bauer (pp. 37–43) and especially Louw-Nida (pp. 43–64), spending most of his time on the latter. Although he rightly points to a number of shortcomings of their dictionary, he does commend it as a pioneering effort that has established a new way of doing lexicography (p. 64).

35. See Mateos, *Método*, 11; Peláez, *Metodología*, 68.

to meeting a relatively high standard of quality"; (2) "pert. to meeting a high
standard of worth and merit, good." It is difficult to know how these meanings are being differentiated. Is it that one is only a relatively high standard,
while the other is a genuinely high standard, or is it a distinction of quality
versus merit and worth—that is, objective versus subjective? I am not sure
that one can tell from what is printed. The Greek-Spanish lexicon offers three
senses for ἀγαθός: (1) "'possessing a favourable disposition toward another
or others, manifested in the conduct shown toward them,' good, charitable,
benign, honest, generous"; (2) "'lending itself well to service,' diligent, hard-
working, reliable"; (3) "'being right in itself and/or favourable for humanity,'
good, right." Some may see these descriptions as no clearer than those in
BDAG; what differentiates them is the semantic formula offered for each.
The semantic formula for the first sense offers as the denotation a static, subjective, and favorable attitude or disposition (H) that is manifested (R) in a
dynamic activity (H'). The connotation of the word is that there is a personal
or individual agent ($E1$), and the action terminates in a human individual or
individuals ($E2$). The second semantic formula denotes not an activity as the
meaning of this use of the word, but the determination of its excellent and
efficient quality (D). The connotation is that this quality terminates on the
individual, human subject of the attribution (E) defined by the active, dynamic
service elicited (H). A subdefinition is offered here in which a qualification of
the service is specified (A). The third semantic formula denotes a dynamic and
favorable activity (H) that has correctness (A). The connotation is that there is
a material entity ($E1$) with this quality that terminates on individual humans
with its beneficent effect ($E2$). Consistent with componential analysis, there
are several features that the denotations and connotations have in common,
as well as distinguishing semantic features that give each sememe, or sense, its
distinctive character. It is not my purpose here to fully explain, and much less
to defend, this new Greek-Spanish lexicon. However, I think it is worth noting
that it represents a major step forward over the traditional lexicon, because
it not only has meanings and translations, but also attempts to quantify and
display how these are arrived at and how they differ from each other in terms
of components of meaning.

    As I noted above, there are numerous places in BDAG where syntactical or
grammatical issues are raised. The lexicon as traditionally conceived begins
with the word and then attempts to build from the individual word to larger
structures.[36] Certainly there is some validity in this approach, since we realize
that individual words are useful elements in the construction and expression

---

36. See Porter, Studies in the Greek New Testament, 52–63.

of meaning. However, one may also argue that the emphasis upon the word is one of the reasons there has been serious question of much past exegesis and lexicography. If the word is seen to be the essential and basic element, there can be a tendency to exalt the position of the individual word to the point of creating entire and whole theologies around these individual words, treated almost as if they existed apart from any larger linguistic context, simply as self-contained symbols in their own right. This is one of the major problems with theological lexicography noted above. However, even if one concedes that words do have meanings, they have these meanings as they relate to other words, and this is where syntax and other cotextual features are so important. In fact, one could well argue that much more can and should be made of integrating the lexicon with other grammatical information. This can be realized in several different forms. A reasonably simple and straightforward approach is simply to note in a lexicon much more of the syntactical information regarding the given entries. For example, as noted above regarding some of the function words, this is already done in a lexicon, but it could be extended to include other words as well, including nouns and verbs. For example, one could note how many places or arguments a verb has (subject, complement, etc.), and what types of entities fill these places (related ideas are often discussed in terms of valency). Entire grammars have been written around such principles, such as R. A. Hudson's *Word Grammar*,[37] where he defines the grammar of the language as contained within the information known about how each word functions, with no constituents larger than the word.

A more radical idea is to explore the systemic functional linguistic (SFL) notion that lexis is the most delicate grammar.[38] One stream of SFL thought believes that the grammar of a language is realized in the numerous meaning choices that the user makes, until such a point where this potential for meaning must be realized in linguistic substance, in the words of the language. In this sense, the lexicon is a part of the grammar, and in fact the most delicate

37. R. A. Hudson, *Word Grammar* (Oxford: Blackwell, 1984). Compare the construction grammar of P. L. Danove, "The Theory of Construction Grammar and Its Application to New Testament Greek," in *Biblical Greek Language and Linguistics: Open Questions in Current Research*, ed. S. E. Porter and D. A. Carson, JSNTSup 80, SNTG 1 (Sheffield: JSOT Press, 1993), 119–51.

38. See R. Hasan, "The Grammarian's Dream: Lexis as Most Delicate Grammar," in *New Developments in Systemic Linguistics*, vol. 1, *Theory and Description*, ed. M. A. K. Halliday and R. P. Fawcett (London: Pinter, 1987), 184–211; compare M. A. K. Halliday, "Categories of the Theory of Grammar," *Word* 17 (1961): 241–92, esp. 267; Halliday, "Lexis as a Linguistic Level," in *In Memory of J. R. Firth*, ed. C. E. Bazell et al. (London: Longmans, 1966), 148–62; more recently, M. A. K. Halliday, "Lexicology," in *Lexicology: A Short Introduction*, ed. M. A. K. Halliday and C. Yallop (London: Continuum, 2004), 1–22.

or specific and particular choice to be made in the grammatical system—that point where semantic potential takes actual linguistic shape.[39] Here one can see the relation between semantic field theory and both grammar and lexicon. When one desires to communicate, one makes choices, and these closed choices—regarding assertion or question, positive or negative, emphasis on subject or complement, and so forth—finally result in choices regarding the particular entities about which one wishes to communicate. One then selects the particular semantic domains until one finds the specific level of communication, the individual words and their collocates, and then the particular words to use. In some ways this may sound fairly abstract, but fairly sophisticated systemic grammars of languages have been created, including some for the Greek of the New Testament, that show how this meaning potential is realized in linguistic form. One of the major problems in much New Testament study, I think, has been the failure to have linguistic theory inform study of the language of the New Testament. This has been perpetuated by the use of tools that bear witness to models of language that have been superseded, including some that make the word look like the starting and finishing point of linguistic study.

A further development that could well help study of the language of the New Testament, especially its lexicography, involves how individual words are employed in relation to both the usage of the same author elsewhere and other authors of the time. So far, the tools at our disposal certainly are better than previous ones, but still they leave much to be desired. Most modern Bible software (e.g., Accordance, LOGOS, BibleWorks) is good for the New Testament, but it does not go much further than that. The *Thesaurus linguae Graecae* (*TLG*) has a much larger scope, but it relies upon only a fairly basic lexical retrieval system and does not fully address the issues raised above regarding constituents larger than the word. Corpus linguistics is dedicated to the notion of compiling more than simply masses of data; it seeks to assemble genuine corpora of texts that represent the language of a given language community.[40] This is the fundamental difference between simply an archive (such as the *TLG*) and a genuine corpus. A project to assemble a representative corpus is already well underway for English in the Cobuild corpus of written and

---

39. In fact, I have explored this relationship further in Danker's *Festschrift*. See S. E. Porter, "Aspect Theory and Lexicography," in *Biblical Greek Language and Lexicography: Essays in Honor of Frederick W. Danker*, ed. B. A. Taylor et al. (Grand Rapids: Eerdmans, 2004), 207–22.

40. See T. McEnery and A. Hardie, *Corpus Linguistics: Method, Theory and Practice*, CTL (Cambridge: Cambridge University Press, 2012); D. Biber, S. Conrad, and R. Reppen, *Corpus Linguistics: Investigating Language Structure and Use*, CAL (Cambridge: Cambridge University Press, 1998); compare J. Sinclair, *Corpus, Concordance, Collocation* (Oxford: Oxford University Press, 1991); M. Stubbs, *Text and Corpus Analysis* (Oxford: Blackwell, 1996).

spoken English, which totals roughly 650 million words, on many topics and in many genres/registers. These words are drawn upon in machine-readable form for linguistic studies of various types.[41]

For New Testament study, rather than being confined to the language of the New Testament or simply the lexical items of ancient Greek, the ideal would be a fully marked-up electronic corpus of a representative cross-section of the Greek of the Hellenistic world that would allow for sophisticated searches at varying levels, including the morphological, lexical, syntactical, and discourse levels.[42] By performing such sophisticated searches at these varying levels, one could avail oneself of much more useful information regarding patterns of usage in the language. Such information has promise for providing more detailed and sophisticated data for entries in a lexicon, as well as for exegetical studies. For example, rather than simply saying that something is a rare construction, one can know how rare it is compared to other constructions, and the specific environments in which this construction is used. Some preliminary applications have already been attempted, including the use of semantic-domain theory, by which one can quantify various semantic patterns stretching over the whole of Romans, analyze words for "resurrection" in the New Testament and their typical linguistic collocates (especially emphasizing collocation), and analyze "creation" language in Romans 8 based upon a detailed corpus analysis.[43] Further, some studies have

41. See J. Sinclair, ed., *Collins Cobuild English Language Dictionary* (London: HarperCollins, 1987; 2nd ed., 1995); Sinclair, ed., *Collins Cobuild English Grammar* (London: HarperCollins, 1990). An account of the project is given in Sinclair, ed., *Looking Up: An Account of the Cobuild Project in Lexical Computing* (London: Collins, 1987).

42. See M. B. O'Donnell, "Designing and Compiling a Register-Balanced Corpus of Hellenistic Greek for the Purpose of Linguistic Description and Investigation," in *Diglossia and Other Topics in New Testament Linguistics*, ed. S. E. Porter, JSNTSup 193, SNTG 6 (Sheffield: Sheffield Academic Press, 2000), 255–97; compare O'Donnell, "The Use of Annotated Corpora for New Testament Discourse Analysis: A Survey of Current Practice and Future Prospects," in *Discourse Analysis and the New Testament: Results and Applications*, ed. S. E. Porter and J. T. Reed, JSNTSup 170, SNTG 4 (Sheffield: Sheffield Academic Press, 1999), 71–116. Many of his ideas are developed further in M. B. O'Donnell, *Corpus Linguistics and the Greek of the New Testament*, NTM 6 (Sheffield: Sheffield Phoenix Press, 2005).

43. See S. E. Porter and M. B. O'Donnell, "Semantics and Patterns of Argumentation in the Book of Romans: Definitions, Proposals, Data and Experiments," in Porter, *Diglossia*, 154–204; M. B. O'Donnell, "Some New Testament Words for Resurrection and the Company They Keep," in *Resurrection*, ed. S. E. Porter, M. A. Hayes, and D. Tombs, JSNTSup 186, RILP 5 (London: Sheffield Academic Press, 1999), 136–65 (also found in O'Donnell, *Corpus Linguistics*, 315–27); G. P. Fewster, *Creation Language in Romans 8: A Study in Monosemy*, LBS 8 (Leiden: Brill, 2013), 49–72, 94–122. Compare Porter and O'Donnell, "Theoretical Issues for Corpus Linguistics and the Study of Ancient Languages," in *Corpus Linguistics by the Lune: A Festschrift for Geoffrey Leech*, ed. A. Wilson, P. Rayson, and T. McEnery, LSL 8 (Frankfurt am Main: Peter Lang, 2003), 119–37.

investigated how ancient Greek papyri might be incorporated into corpus analyses of this sort.[44]

Of course, here I have moved well beyond what is contained within a traditional printed lexicon such as BDAG. Such tools are now available in electronic form, which facilitates faster searches of the data that they contain. However, even with such tools now widely available in electronic media, we must not think that simply doing this makes any given lexicon into another kind of tool than it is now. It is simply in a different form of retrieval. What I am suggesting is a serious rethinking and expansion of the categories by which we conceptualize the language of the New Testament, one that incorporates lexicography, yet much more besides, including what is traditionally called grammar, and all of that within the larger world of Hellenistic Greek usage.

Conclusion

Lexicons will no doubt continue to have a significant place within New Testament studies. The major questions concern the conceptualization of such lexicons and the types of information that they provide. The traditional lexicon, though no doubt continuing to be used, appears to have reached the extent of its theoretical development and requires major reconceptualization in light of recent developments in semantic theory and corpus studies and retrieval. Some such efforts have already been made; however, more are needed. This situation provides an opportunity for new lexicons to be developed that move beyond the traditional boundaries of the word to incorporate lexical semantic studies that aid exegesis.

44. See especially S. E. Porter and M. B. O'Donnell, "Building and Examining Linguistic Phenomena in a Corpus of Representative Papyri," in *The Language of the Papyri*, ed. T. V. Evans and D. D. Obbink (Oxford: Oxford University Press, 2010), 287–311. Compare S. E. Porter, "The Babatha Archive, the Egyptian Papyri and Their Implications for Study of the Greek New Testament," in *Early Christian Manuscripts: Examples of Applied Method and Approach*, ed. T. J. Kraus and T. Nicklas, TENT 5 (Leiden: Brill, 2010), 213–37.

PART 2

Approaching Analysis

5

Linguistics and Biblical Interpretation

Introduction

Interpretation of the Bible should rightly involve a significant linguistic component, since biblical studies, regardless of whatever else it may be, is a textually based discipline. After all, the Old and New Testaments, whatever else they may be, are written texts. More particularly, they are written texts in two (or three) ancient languages for which there are now no native speakers as informants or interpreters. We have only our reconstructed knowledge of the languages, and our reconstructions are based on these and other related texts. Unfortunately, the biblical texts have been so thoroughly studied for so long that many interpreters do not expect new insights from careful study of the ancient languages. Some scholars seem to think that classical philology has squeezed out whatever useful information there is to be had from Hebrew or Greek studies. Yet classical philology, with its appreciation and assessment of texts from the standpoint of their artistic and literary merit, raises questions that are very different from those that occupy modern linguists.

Modern linguistics cannot be described as a single approach with one set of assumptions. In all of its manifestations, however, it reflects an orientation to language that is very different from that which was characteristic of classical

philology.[1] The following principles concerning linguistic research are generally accepted: (1) linguistics is empirically based and explicit (a feature greatly
enhanced by the development of corpus linguistics, in which entire corpora of
texts are studied); (2) linguistics is systematic in its method and is concerned
with the structure of language; (3) linguistics emphasizes synchronic over
diachronic analysis (though not overlooking the latter in its treatment of the
former); and (4) linguistics is descriptive in nature, rather than prescriptive.
As a result of these principles, modern linguistics neither studies the history
of a language in order to determine its usage nor traces the etymology of a
word in order to determine its meaning (although linguistic transparency can
be important). Unlike classical philology, linguistics is not concerned simply
with the best authors and most beautiful texts. Unlike traditional grammar,
linguistics does not apply Latin-based categories to any and all languages,
and its analyses are not incumbent upon the analyst's ability to understand
or translate.

A conscious effort—it is as much a frame of mind as it is a set of procedures—
is required to successfully apply modern linguistics in the field of biblical studies. There are two main reasons for this, I think. One is the fact that many
of the standard critical tools for studying the biblical languages predate the
development of modern linguistics. (And some of those that are more recent continue to be prelinguistic, methodologically speaking.) The study of
the biblical languages is thus hindered by the lack of availability of modern
resources.[2] A second reason is that much of the work of modern linguistics
has been oriented toward modern languages, especially English. Transference from the modern context of scientific discovery to contexts of ancient
literature has been left to those within the classical disciplines, and this has
clearly retarded the pace of development. Nevertheless, there have been a number of important recent advances that merit attention. These include several
introductory volumes, as well as more intensive work in at least three broad
areas.[3]

1. S. E. Porter, "Studying Ancient Languages from a Modern Linguistic Perspective: Essential
Terms and Terminology," *FN* 2 (1989) 147–72.
2. See S. E. Porter and J. T. Reed, "Greek Grammar since BDF: A Retrospective and Prospective
Analysis," *FN* 4 (1991) 143–64. Notable exceptions are C. H. J. van der Merwe, J. A. Naudé,
and J. H. Kroze, *A Biblical Hebrew Reference Grammar* (Sheffield: Sheffield Academic Press,
1999); S. E. Porter, *Idioms of the Greek New Testament*, 2nd ed., BLG 2 (Sheffield: Sheffield
Academic Press, 1994).
3. See D. A. Black, *Linguistics for Students of New Testament Greek: A Survey of Basic
Concepts and Applications* (Grand Rapids: Baker Books, 1988); P. Cotterell and M. Turner,
Linguistics and Biblical Interpretation (London: SPCK, 1989); S. Groom, *Linguistic Analysis
of Biblical Hebrew* (Carlisle: Paternoster, 2003).

Advances in Linguistic Interpretation of the Bible

The advances that modern linguistics has brought to the study of the Bible fall into three main categories. I will briefly define each category and then select one example for more detailed presentation and discussion.

Morphology, Syntax, and Related Areas

Morphology is concerned with the smallest units of meaningful structure in a language. Syntax is concerned with the arrangement of elements at the level especially of the clause or sentence. Traditional study of language has been concerned with isolating particular units within the language, often confined to units no larger than the word (occasionally the sentence), and tracing the history of their development (e.g., the development of the dative case in Greek, or the history of the prefixed or suffixed form in Hebrew). Insights from modern linguistics into the subjects of morphology and syntax have increased the knowledge of these languages even at this basic level of exploration. Suggestive work has been done in a variety of areas related to morphology and syntax. These include the morphology of the tense systems in Hebrew and Greek, the Greek case system and case-frame analysis, conjunctions and transition markers, and Hebrew and Greek sentence structure and word order, among other elements.[4]

Verb structure is one of the areas that has shown the most significant research and gain in insight. In this area, Hebrew study first advanced more significantly than Greek study, although recently Greek study has made significant strides. The major issue for discussion in verb structure is whether

4. See, e.g., J. P. Louw, "Linguistic Theory and the Greek Case System," *AC* 9 (1966): 73–88; S. Wong, "What Case Is This Case? An Application of Semantic Case in Biblical Exegesis," *JD* 1 (1994): 49–73; P. L. Danove, *Linguistics and Exegesis in the Gospel of Mark: Applications of a Case Frame Analysis and Lexicon*, JSNTSup 218, SNTG 10 (Sheffield: Sheffield Academic Press, 2001); S. L. Black, *Sentence Conjunctions in the Gospel of Matthew: καί, δέ, τότε, γάρ, οὖν and Asyndeton in Narrative Discourse*, JSNTSup 216, SNTG 9 (Sheffield: Sheffield Academic Press, 2002); J. Holmstrand, *Markers and Meaning in Paul: An Analysis of 1 Thessalonians, Philippians and Galatians*, ConBNT 28 (Stockholm: Almqvist & Wiksell, 1997); F. I. Andersen, *The Sentence in Biblical Hebrew*, JLSP 231 (The Hague: Mouton, 1974); C. L. Miller, ed., *The Verbless Clause in Biblical Hebrew: Linguistic Approaches* (Winona Lake, IN: Eisenbrauns, 1999); K. Shimasaki, *Focus Structure in Biblical Hebrew: A Study of Word Order and Information Structure* (Bethesda, MD: CDL Press, 2002); A. W. Pitts, "Greek Word Order and Clause Structure: A Comparative Study of Some New Testament Corpora," in *The Language of the New Testament: Context, History, and Development*, ed. S. E. Porter and A. W. Pitts, ECHC 3, LBS 6 (Leiden: Brill, 2013), 311–46. See also the bibliography for writings by S. E. Porter, M. B. O'Donnell, J. T. Reed, W. V. Cirafesi, and G. P. Fewster.

the verbal forms are concerned more with time or with kinds of action, or even with something else. The traditional emphasis was upon the verbal forms being tense-forms—that is, having strict temporal values. In Hebrew studies, Heinrich Ewald and S. R. Driver caused a revision of this framework, arguing that the two major Hebrew verbal stems refer to the kind of time as either complete or incomplete.[5] A similar progression took place in discussion of the Greek tense-forms, with the strictly temporal view of the eighteenth and nineteenth centuries giving way, at the end of the nineteenth century and the beginning of the twentieth, to the concept of *Aktionsart* ("kind of action"), which attempted to characterize the objective nature of the verbal action. In the middle of the twentieth century, and especially in discussion since the mid 1980s, more and more scholars began to see that *Aktionsart* had not gone far enough,[6] and that Greek tense-forms are concerned to express not primarily the time of an event but rather an author's perspective in characterizing it. In both Hebrew and Greek studies there has been some reaction to these theories, but most recent work has reinforced a form of aspectual theory for tense structure. There continues to be refinement and further definition of what the verbal aspects mean in relation to each other and their contexts of use.[7]

5. H. Ewald, *Syntax of the Hebrew Language of the Old Testament*, trans. J. Kennedy (Edinburgh: T&T Clark, 1881); S. R. Driver, *A Treatise on the Use of the Tenses in Hebrew*, 3rd ed. (Oxford: Clarendon, 1892).

6. There is still much debate regarding *Aktionsart*, or what is sometimes called lexical aspect (as opposed to grammatical aspect). The major shortcomings of virtually all discussions of the procedural character of events (of which *Aktionsart* is a part) are that there are no agreed-upon definitions, no consistent criteria by which such procedures are determinable, and no means of analysis without invoking linguistic units larger than the word, up to the entire sentence, at which point the discussion is of something significantly other than that of *Aktionsart* or lexical aspect. See F. G. H. Pang, "Aktionsart as Epiphenomenon: A Stratal Approach to Process Typologies," in *Greeks, Jews, and Christians: Historical, Religious and Philological Studies in Honor of Jesús Peláez del Rosal*, ed. L. R. Lanzillotta and I. M. Gallarte (Córdoba: Ediciones el Almendro, 2013), 449–74; see also, in the present volume, discussion in chap. 12.

7. For the Greek New Testament, see S. E. Porter, *Verbal Aspect in the Greek of the New Testament, with Reference to Tense and Mood*, SBG 1 (New York: Peter Lang, 1989; 2nd ed., 1993); B. M. Fanning, *Verbal Aspect in New Testament Greek*, OTM (Oxford: Clarendon, 1990); K. L. McKay, *A New Syntax of the Verb in New Testament Greek: An Aspectual Approach*, SBG 5 (New York: Peter Lang, 1994); S. E. Porter, *Studies in the Greek New Testament: Theory and Practice*, SBG 6 (New York: Peter Lang, 1996); C. R. Campbell, *Verbal Aspect, the Indicative Mood, and Narrative: Soundings in the Greek of the New Testament*, SBG 13 (New York: Peter Lang, 2007). See also R. J. Decker, *Temporal Deixis of the Greek Verb in the Gospel of Mark with Reference to Verbal Aspect*, SBG 10 (New York: Peter Lang, 2001); D. L. Mathewson, *Verbal Aspect in the Book of Revelation: The Function of Greek Verb Tenses in John's Apocalypse*, LBS 4 (Leiden: Brill, 2010). For the Septuagint, see T. V. Evans, *Verbal Syntax in the Greek Pentateuch: Natural Greek Usage and Hebrew Interference* (Oxford: Oxford University Press, 2001); A. Voitila, *Présent et imparfait de l'indicatif dans le pentateuque grec: Une étude sur la syntaxe de traduction*, PFES 79 (Helsinki: Sociéte d'Exégèse de Finlande; Göttingen: Vandenhoeck & Ruprecht,

The implications of this shift in perspective can be only briefly summarized. Most important is a shift from seeing the tense-forms as indicating the time of an action to seeing them as indications of how an action is conceived by a writer. Once this fundamental point is established, one is able to analyze relations between the processes being depicted. One is able to recognize that the tense-forms structure large units and hence do not simply indicate the time of a single event (see below on discourse analysis).

Semantics and Lexicography

Ever since James Barr's seminal *The Semantics of Biblical Language*, biblical scholars have been aware of what linguists already knew: words cannot be equated with concepts nor meanings determined by word histories.[8] Nevertheless, it has been very difficult for biblical scholars to rid themselves of some deeply rooted preconceptions, since theological presuppositions are strong motivators. Traditional lexicography often relied upon etymologizing as an aid to establishing the theological significance of a word,[9] and then the entire theological framework was read into a single occasion of the word's use. This led to numerous generalizations not only about language, but also about how the Hebrew or Greek mind worked. Recent developments in lexicography have the potential to free biblical scholars from these unhelpful remnants of the biblical theology movement.[10] These developments in lexicography have gone hand in hand with developments in the field of semantic theory, which studies how words mean and how they mean in relation to each other.[11]

Modern biblical lexicography, especially that of the New Testament, has been greatly helped by the development of semantic-field theory (in biblical studies usually called semantic-domain theory). Semantic-field theory recognizes that the vocabulary of any language is not ordered alphabetically, unlike the

---

2001). For Hebrew, see A. Niccacci, *The Syntax of the Verb in Classical Hebrew Prose*, trans. W. G. E. Watson, JSOTSup 86 (Sheffield: JSOT Press, 1990); J. A. Cook, *Time and the Biblical Hebrew Verb: The Expression of Tense, Aspect, and Modality in Biblical Hebrew* (Winona Lake, IN: Eisenbrauns, 2012).

8. J. Barr, *The Semantics of Biblical Language* (Oxford: Oxford University Press, 1961).

9. According to John Lee, etymologizing appears to be making a strong return in New Testament Greek lexicography—a bad sign for several reasons, not least the poor performance of those doing it. See J. A. L. Lee, "Etymological Follies: Three Recent Lexicons of the New Testament," *NovT* 55 (2013): 383–403, esp. 401.

10. See Porter, *Studies in the Greek New Testament*, 46–74; also, in the present volume, chaps. 3 and 4.

11. For biblical treatments of these issues, see J. P. Louw, *Semantics of New Testament Greek*, SemSt (Philadelphia: Fortress; Chico, CA: Scholars Press, 1982); M. Silva, *Biblical Words and Their Meaning: An Introduction to Lexical Semantics*, rev. ed. (Grand Rapid: Zondervan, 1994).

standard lexicon. Instead, the vocabulary of a language is organized around semantic fields or domains. Semantic-field theory notes that words are used in terms of contextual relations, not in isolation, and that the words are used by speakers and writers to divide the world of experience, feelings, and events into the various realms that words can be used to delimit. Major difficulties with semantic-field theory are those of establishing the fields, determining and differentiating meaning components, and then quantifying the relations of the words within the fields. A major step forward in lexicography of all sorts has been the semantic-domain lexicon by J. P. Louw and Eugene Nida.[12] This lexicon attempts to classify the entire vocabulary of the New Testament—treating this as a dialect of ancient Greek—into semantic domains. Within these domains, the various lexical items are listed and glossed. The lexicon has been criticized for failing to encompass a wider scope than simply the Greek of the New Testament, and for failing to include syntactical information. There is also the difficulty that it tends to include all of the words on the same level, rather than realizing that they have hyponymic relations (hierarchical relations, such as "flower" being higher in a hierarchy with "tulip" and "rose" beneath). The attempt to quantify meanings has been aided by the Spanish New Testament Greek lexicon project, which attempts to provide a schematized semantic framework for each word in the lexicon.[13] A project is currently underway that attempts to construct a similar type of semantic-domain lexicon for the Hebrew Bible.[14]

The implications of modern lexicography for the study of the Bible are several. They include a freeing of the language from the kinds of theological strictures that have tended to envelop it in the past, whereby every word was thought to be a theological cipher. There is also the recognition of how it is that words mean in a language, both in terms of being used to refer to entities in the world and, perhaps more importantly, in terms of how they mean in relation to each other.

Text-Linguistics or Discourse Analysis

The third and last category for discussion here is text-linguistics or discourse analysis.[15] European scholarship has tended to call this discipline "text-

12. J. P. Louw and E. A. Nida, *Greek-English Lexicon of the New Testament Based on Semantic Domains*, 2 vols. (New York: United Bible Societies, 1988). See also E. A. Nida and J. P. Louw, *Lexical Semantics of the Greek New Testament*, SBLRBS 25 (Atlanta: Scholars Press, 1992).

13. J. Mateos and J. Peláez, *Diccionario Griego-Español del Nuevo Testamento*, 5 vols. (Córdoba: Ediciones el Almendro; Fundación Épsilon, 2000–).

14. See http://sdbh.org.

15. For fuller treatment of some of the following issues, see chap. 8.

linguistics" (and in some ways this is the better term, since we are dealing with texts), while English-language scholarship has tended toward the term "discourse analysis." One of the shortcomings of much traditional language study is that it has confined itself to the word or, maximally, to the sentence as the basic unit of analysis. The result has been an emphasis upon word studies, sentence diagramming (based on the principles of English analysis), and the like. Recent developments in modern linguistics (should) have forced scholars to recognize that language is simply not used in this way, and that study of it, no matter how much attention it pays to individual parts of the language (and there is no denying that they are important), must always pay attention to the larger contextual, semantic, and linguistic frameworks in which language is used. "Text-linguistics" (or "discourse analysis") is a broad term, encompassing a number of methods that have been developed in order to study entire discourses.

In New Testament studies today, several models of discourse analysis are being employed.[16] These include methods developed by the Summer Institute of Linguistics (SIL) with its Bible translation work;[17] a model from South Africa that emphasizes the colon (minimally a subject and predicate) as the unit of analysis and the logical relations among them;[18] a European model that attempts to combine semantics, pragmatics, communications theory, and rhetoric into a single linguistic model;[19] and an English-Australian model that draws upon the work of systemic functional linguistics and applies it in a more formally based way to ancient Greek.[20] There is also an eclectic

16. S. E. Porter and D. A. Carson, eds., *Discourse Analysis and Other Topics in Biblical Greek*, JSNTSup 113, SNTG 2 (Sheffield: Sheffield Academic Press, 1995); D. A. Black, with K. Barnwell, and S. Levinsohn, eds., *Linguistics and New Testament Interpretation: Essays on Discourse Analysis* (Nashville: Broadman, 1992); S. E. Porter and J. T. Reed, eds., *Discourse Analysis and the New Testament: Approaches and Results*, JSNTSup 170, SNTG 4 (Sheffield: Sheffield Academic Press, 1999); S. E. Porter and A. W. Pitts, "New Testament Greek Language and Linguistics in Recent Research," *CBR* 6 (2008): 214–55, esp. 235–41.

17. For example, S. H. Levinsohn, *Discourse Features of New Testament Greek: A Coursebook on the Information Structure of New Testament Greek*, 2nd ed. (Dallas: SIL International, 2000).

18. For example, J. P. Louw, *A Semantic Discourse Analysis of Romans*, 2 vols. (Pretoria: University of Pretoria, Department of Greek, 1987).

19. For example, B. Olsson, *Structure and Meaning in the Fourth Gospel: A Text-Linguistic Analysis of John 1:1–11 and 4:1–42*, ConBNT 6 (Lund: Gleerup, 1974); B. C. Johanson, *To All the Brethren: A Text-Linguistic and Rhetorical Approach to 1 Thessalonians*, ConBNT 16 (Stockholm: Almqvist & Wiksell, 1987); L. Hartman, *Text-Centered New Testament Studies: Text-Theoretical Essays on Early Jewish and Early Christian Literature*, ed. D. Hellholm, WUNT 102 (Tübingen: Mohr Siebeck, 1997).

20. For example, J. T. Reed, *A Discourse Analysis of Philippians: Method and Rhetoric in the Debate over Literary Integrity*, JSNTSup 136 (Sheffield: Sheffield Academic Press, 1997); G. Martín-Asensio, *Transitivity-Based Foregrounding in the Acts of the Apostles: A Functional-Grammatical Approach to the Lukan Perspective*, JSNTSup 202, SNTG 8 (Sheffield: Sheffield

method that draws heavily upon literary analysis and related fields.[21] Likewise, in study of the Hebrew Bible, several different models of discourse analysis have been utilized, many of them overlapping with forms of the ones mentioned above.[22]

What distinguishes these models of discourse analysis is the attempt to find a means of discussing an entire discourse. As a result, numerous categories of modern linguistic investigation are brought into play. These include morphology, syntax, semantics, and pragmatics, but also larger categories of thought such as situational context and even the larger context of culture.[23] A full-fledged discourse analysis will not be concerned only with the smallest units within a language but will also be concerned with how these smaller units form ever more complex and larger units. This model may also be turned on its head, so that an analyst will work from the largest units, such as meaning, down to its constituent linguistic units. Those concerned with discourse analysis, therefore, draw upon all of the available linguistic tools in order to analyze texts.

There are at least three major areas with which biblical discourse analysts have been concerned, all of them primarily revolving around the elements that go to make up a text.[24] One is discourse boundaries. Discourse boundaries are the means by which the boundaries of a text, and of the individual units within a text, are established. A number of different features can be used, often in conjunction with each other, to indicate these boundaries, including connecting words, shifts in person or tense-form, or lexicographical shifts. A second area is cohesion and coherence. Cohesion is concerned with the means by which a text holds together; the task of the discourse analysis is to discover what features are used to establish the cohesion of a text. Elements of cohesion can include various lexical items and the use of lexical items within the same domains. It can also include various morphological features that link elements, such as person endings or tense-forms.

Academic Press, 2000); C. L. Westfall, *A Discourse Analysis of the Letter to the Hebrews: The Relationship between Form and Meaning*, LNTS 297 (London: T&T Clark, 2005); J.-H. Lee, *Paul's Gospel in Romans: A Discourse Analysis of Rom. 1:16–8:39*, LBS 3 (Leiden: Brill, 2010).

21. G. H. Guthrie, *The Structure of Hebrews: A Text-Linguistic Analysis*, NovTSup 73 (Leiden: Brill, 1994).

22. For example, R. E. Longacre, *Joseph: A Story of Divine Providence; A Text Theoretical and Textlinguistic Analysis of Genesis 37 and 39–48* (Winona Lake, IN: Eisenbrauns, 1989); D. A. Dawson, *Text-Linguistics and Biblical Hebrew*, JSOTSup 177 (Sheffield: Sheffield Academic Press, 1994); W. R. Bodine, ed., *Discourse Analysis of Biblical Literature: What It Is and What It Offers*, SemSt (Atlanta: Scholars Press, 1995).

23. Porter, *Idioms*, 298–307.

24. See Guthrie, *Structure of Hebrews*; Reed, *Discourse Analysis of Philippians*.

There are also a variety of connecting words, phrases, or larger elements that can be used to establish cohesion. Larger patterns of usage can also be employed to establish cohesion. Many discourse analysts are also concerned with the coherence of a text. Cohesion is concerned with the structural elements by which a text is held together; coherence is concerned with the ideational level, the level at which the ideas communicated make sense. The informational structure of a discourse is often important for establishing coherence. A third area is prominence.[25] Once it has been established that one has a discourse unit to analyze, and when one can establish both its cohesion and its coherence, the discourse analyst will often wish to analyze how it is that certain ideas, persons, or events are made to stand out against others in the text. The ways that prominence is established vary, and often they include a variety of elements, such as the use of more heavily marked tense-forms, shifts in word order and syntax that focus particular elements, and the use of redundant structures to draw attention to themselves. As one may well imagine, in the analysis of even a relatively small text, there is an abundance of data for consideration, and this must result in a process of sifting the information.

The benefits of discourse analysis include the fact that the kinds of information gained from other areas of linguistic investigation, such as syntactical data, are utilized in terms of a broader and more inclusive framework. One of the hallmarks of modern linguistic analysis is that elements of a language are not studied in isolation, but must be seen in their larger linguistic and nonlinguistic contexts. Discourse analysis argues that the appropriate context is the discourse. With this larger context established, the interpretation of the individual elements can then take place. Recently corpus linguistics has argued further that another context for consideration is the largest possible corpus of texts available, and as a result efforts are being made to establish such corpora for comparative linguistic analysis.[26]

25. S. E. Porter, "Prominence: A Theoretical Overview," in *The Linguist as Pedagogue: Trends in the Teaching and Linguistic Analysis of the Greek New Testament*, ed. S. E. Porter and M. B. O'Donnell, NTM 11 (Sheffield: Sheffield Phoenix Press, 2009), 45–74; S. Booth, *Selected Peak Marking Features in the Gospel of John*, AUSTR 78 (New York: Peter Lang, 1996); Martín-Asensio, *Transitivity-Based Foregrounding*; J.-M. Heimerdinger, *Topic, Focus and Foreground in Ancient Hebrew Narratives*, JSOTSup 295 (Sheffield: Sheffield Academic Press, 1999).

26. See M. B. O'Donnell, "The Use of Annotated Corpora for New Testament Discourse Analysis: A Survey of Current Practice and Future Prospects," in *Discourse Analysis and the New Testament: Approaches and Results*, ed. S. E. Porter and J. T. Reed, JSNTSup 170, SNTG 4 (Sheffield: Sheffield Academic Press, 1999), 71–117. For additional bibliography, see chap. 4 in the present volume.

Conclusion

Modern linguistics is not a simple panacea for difficult exegetical questions. Nor is it an optional add-on for interpreters once they have exhausted traditional exegetical approaches. Modern linguistics encompasses developments that have taken place in the analysis of language over the last one hundred years. In the same way that other social sciences have developed and have been brought to bear in biblical studies, in the same way that new historical data and new frameworks have been incorporated in exegesis, and in the same way that various theological positions have been developed—so too modern linguistics must become a part of biblical study. The promise of linguistics is not necessarily that new insights are to be gained (although many new ones have already been realized), nor that it will overthrow all traditional opinions (although a number of unfounded traditional opinions have been called into question). The promise of linguistics is that it can provide a proper interpretive foundation for a text-based discipline—which, after all, is what biblical studies is supposed to be.

6

A Multidisciplinary Approach to Exegesis

Introduction

Exegesis as a concept is closely related to a number of other notions, such as interpretation and hermeneutics. Hermeneutics is concerned with the nature of understanding itself, while interpretation encompasses the many different ways that we go about attempting to arrive at understanding.[1] Exegesis is concerned with the practices and procedures used to understand written texts.

Traditionally, the avowed goal of exegesis has been to determine the original intent of the author in terms of that writer's historical situation (i.e., "what the text meant"). This, at least, is the view of exegesis that undergirds the grammatico-historical method. Originating in the eighteenth century, the grammatico-historical method is an objectivist method of interpretation that follows strict canons of historicity and takes a self-consciously atheological or even antidogmatic bias. It is sometimes called historical exegesis or even "exegesis proper." The grammatico-historical approach to exegesis continues

---

1. On the distinction between hermeneutics and interpretation, see S. E. Porter, "Biblical Hermeneutics and *Theological* Responsibility," in *The Future of Biblical Interpretation: Responsible Plurality in Biblical Hermeneutics*, ed. S. E. Porter and M. R. Malcolm (Downers Grove, IL: IVP Academic, 2013), 29–50, esp. 31–37.

to be promoted in a number of circles, but more recent developments certainly have reduced its dominance.

In general, developments in exegesis have expanded the interests and concerns of the enterprise. For example, it has been suggested that in order to determine what a text meant, one must know where it came from, what it has meant in the history of its interpretation, and even what it means today. This suggestion expands and problematizes the notion of exegesis. Such an expanded notion demands that exegetes pay attention not only to a text's linguistic elements, but also to its prehistory in terms of origins and its posthistory in terms of reception. Interpretation that attempts to encompass these concerns is usually called historical-critical exegesis. Despite claims to the contrary regarding its demise, it continues to be widely used in biblical interpretation.

More recent exegetical developments are not simply refinements of the historical methods; rather, they are quite diverse in their approaches. Even a brief survey must include at least the following methods. *Literary exegesis* has come to embrace a number of often-unarticulated approaches that focus on their relationship to the text, whether in reference to the text itself or to readers responding to the text. Narrative-critical approaches are one form of such exegesis. *Rhetorical exegesis* is concerned with the persuasive character of the text. This persuasive character is often analyzed by using ancient categories of arrangement and argumentative development or certain general principles of persuasiveness. *Linguistic exegesis* involves the use of relatively recent methods of language study, in contrast to the methods of classical philology. Included here are discourse analysis, pragmatics, and various semantic theories. *Social-scientific exegesis*, whether of a descriptive or a prescriptive variety, attempts to exegete the social structures present in a text in the light of either ancient or modern organizational patterns. *Theological exegesis* employs several methods of interpretation. Some of these methods treat the development and eventual shape of the canon as a determinative factor in interpretation; others view the history of Christian interpretation as decisive. *Ideological exegesis* draws together a variety of exegetes who bring various ideological or advocacy positions to bear on the exegetical task, including those related to gender, sexuality, politics, and the like. Certainly more methods could be added to this short list.[2]

---

2. The above is based upon S. E. Porter and K. D. Clarke, "What Is Exegesis? An Analysis of Various Definitions," in *Handbook to Exegesis of the New Testament*, ed. S. E. Porter, NTTS 25 (Leiden: Brill, 1997), 3–21, esp. 3–11. This volume has helpfully guided my understanding of multidisciplinary exegesis. For brief discussions of some of the more important recent approaches, see S. L. McKenzie and J. Kaltner, eds., *New Meanings for Ancient Texts: Recent Approaches to Biblical Criticisms and Their Applications* (Louisville: Westminster John Knox, 2013). Many of these would fall under the category of ideological criticism, discussed below.

No doubt because of how they have been viewed by traditional exegetes, advocates for some of these more recent methods have sometimes distanced themselves from other forms of exegesis. Some have even laid claim to exclusivist perspectives. There have been some historical critics, for example, who have continued to maintain that exegesis is to be equated with historical criticism, and that other methods of exegesis are at best window dressing or at worst clever exercises performed by interpreters who have not learned historical criticism or who are afraid of its outcomes. There have been some reader-response critics who have tried to make everything into reader-response criticism. I could go on.[3] Yet amid all of this posturing, one positive development has emerged. As today's various methods have vied for centrality on the exegetical stage, it has become more clearly apparent that all exegesis is positioned in some way. All exegetical approaches and methods are located in relation to other methods and in relation to the times and places in which they have developed.[4] All approaches and methods enshrine a set of presuppositions, and these presuppositions extend beyond the individual methods themselves in order to encompass the individuals that employ them. It has also become clear that there are many different exegetical methods—whether one accepts them all or not—and that we need to find ways to acknowledge them and possibly even incorporate them into a recognizable multifaceted exegetical approach. I have advocated such a multifaceted approach in previous publications, and I wish to further discuss my approach in this chapter.[5]

In formulating my approach to exegesis, I have come to realize that it is problematic for a single method to make exclusive claims or to pronounce authoritative interpretations. As the history of exegesis over the last thirty or so years has indicated, insights are to be gained from a variety of approaches to the text. A multidisciplinary approach is warranted, and a variety of perspectives must be taken in the exegetical quest for meaning. However, I have also come to see that not all exegetical methods offer the same sorts of insights and that they do not all function on the same level. This, I think, is an essential starting point for the pursuit of a multidisciplinary approach. It is not enough to eliminate exclusivity. Careful judgments must be made about the

3. I will not cite any literature here, but I will say that I have heard such comments from several historical critics.

4. In other words, the final word has not been said regarding exegesis. There was a time before the historical-critical method, and no doubt there will be a time after it. There is definitely a political dimension to interpretation and exegesis, sometimes not widely acknowledged or recognized in biblical studies.

5. The two primary publications where I have identified myself with a multidisciplinary approach are Porter, *Handbook to Exegesis*; S. E. Porter and D. Tombs, eds., *Approaches to New Testament Study*, JSNTSup 120 (Sheffield: JSOT Press, 1995).

interrelatedness of (previously) competing forms of exegesis. The importance of this observation may be seen in the fact that there are competing approaches to exegesis even among those who recognize the importance of multidisciplinarity. Many multidisciplinary analyses employ two or more methods, but often they are employed serially and not in a coordinated fashion. Notice too that integrative approaches tend to be branded as a distinct approach (usually with a hyphen or two) and then reinserted into the competitive methods market.[6]

There are understandable reasons for all of this. Each method is a complex discipline in its own right, and it is not entirely clear how all of the available methods might fit together to create something better than simply the composite of their individual parts. Some methods may even be mutually contradictory. For example, the source-critical approach may be inescapably at odds with certain canonical or literary approaches.[7] Perhaps more significantly, many methods have been developed in reaction to other methods. In an academic climate where methods (and their proponents) are postured in opposition to one another, it is unlikely that they will be brought into constructive conversation with one another. More likely, each will want to remain distinct so that each method is allowed to have its distinctive voice heard. Despite these obstacles, I think that attempts to integrate the various exegetical methods are merited. In what follows, I will offer one such attempt.

Philippians 2:6–11 and a Multidisciplinary Exegetical Method

Taking as a point of departure some of the methods discussed in my *Handbook to Exegesis of the New Testament*, I will attempt to weave a multidisciplinary approach that includes as much as is possible from each individual method. Along the way, I will illustrate the kinds of exegetical discoveries that each discipline has to offer, using Philippians 2:6–11 as the basis for these illustrations. Here is Philippians 2:6–11:

> ὃς ἐν μορφῇ θεοῦ ὑπάρχων οὐχ ἁρπαγμὸν ἡγήσατο τὸ εἶναι ἴσα θεῷ,
> [7]ἀλλὰ ἑαυτὸν ἐκένωσεν μορφὴν δούλου λαβών, ἐν ὁμοιώματι ἀνθρώπων γενόμενος·
> καὶ σχήματι εὑρεθεὶς ὡς ἄνθρωπος [8]ἐταπείνωσεν ἑαυτὸν γενόμενος ὑπήκοος μέχρι θανάτου, θανάτου δὲ σταυροῦ.

6. The volume I edited on exegetical methods presents various approaches but does not bring them together into an integrative method that highlights the strengths of each individual discipline.

7. I say this because the former approach works with pretextual subunits, while the latter works with whole texts or even collections of texts.

⁹διὸ καὶ ὁ θεὸς αὐτὸν ὑπερύψωσεν καὶ ἐχαρίσατο αὐτῷ τὸ ὄνομα τὸ ὑπὲρ πᾶν ὄνομα,

¹⁰ἵνα ἐν τῷ ὀνόματι Ἰησοῦ πᾶν γόνυ κάμψῃ ἐπουρανίων καὶ ἐπιγείων καὶ καταχθονίων,

¹¹καὶ πᾶσα γλῶσσα ἐξομολογήσεται ὅτι κύριος Ἰησοῦς Χριστὸς εἰς δόξαν θεοῦ πατρός.

Although I will not explicitly present the thought process that has resulted in my particular conclusions, I will try to indicate my reasoning at certain key points.[8]

At the outset of this discussion, let me state that I believe there are such things as authorial intentions, though I am skeptical of being able to recover them in any immediate way (and certainly I do not believe that we can recover psychological motivations). From the perspective of the exegete, however, these intentions are recoverable only to the extent that they are embedded within the linguistic expression of a text.[9] Moreover, authorial intentions are rarely embedded explicitly, but more often are discernable only insofar as a text can be positioned with reference to the typical communicative situations that are characteristic of a particular culture. In other words, from the perspective of the exegete, posited authorial intentions are extrapolations made on the basis of contextually interpreted linguistic evidence. I should also add that I believe there is such a thing as the original meaning of a text,[10] though this too must be a complex notion spanning various linguistic levels of analysis and encompassing the notions of culture and situation. For most nonliterary texts, the interpretation of meaning in this broad sense leads fairly directly to conclusions about authorial intentions. For literary texts, the relationship between meaning and intention is much more complex.

Exegetes have long been familiar with the necessity of accounting for the textual "context" of a biblical passage. Here I am using the term "discourse" to describe this traditional concern, and I am using the term "context" with reference to extratextual factors essential for the interpretation of a text. Context in this sense implicates both an immediate context of situation (i.e., the type of situation indicated by the linguistic features of the text) and a wider context of culture (i.e., the cultural system that defines the parameters in which such a discourse can potentially occur). These three environments—discourse,

8. For a similar method for outlining an exegetical method, see R. J. Erickson, *A Beginner's Guide to New Testament Exegesis: Taking the Fear out of Critical Method* (Downers Grove, IL: InterVarsity, 2005).

9. Understood in this way, the notion of authorial intention can encompass intentions such as deception, which involves a deliberate disjunction between a speaker's communicative intentions and those which are embedded in his or her speech.

10. See Porter, "Biblical Hermeneutics," 22–23.

context of situation, and context of culture—provide a useful rubric within which we can encompass the major elements of a multidisciplinary approach to exegesis. Exegesis typically moves out of the relatively explicit environment of specific texts, through reconstructions of their immediate situations, and eventually toward a description of the relatively implicit categories that define a culture. This movement usually is found within elementary books on exegesis. The actual interpretive process is, of course, much more complex. Even if, especially with ancient languages but also with contemporary language usage, we begin with expression, there is a complex reciprocal interstratal movement between specific instances of language (expressed by means of the lexicogrammar) and their meanings in their context of situation and more generalized understandings of their content and context of culture. For the sake of formulating such a model, the categories can therefore be arranged as a stratal hierarchy arranged from broadest to narrowest focus. The context of culture is realized in a context of situation by a discourse:

> *Context of culture*
> *Context of situation*
> *Discourse*

Most of the exegetical methods discussed in the *Handbook to New Testament Interpretation* can be located by means of this hierarchy (if not the kind of interstratal understanding). Organizing them in this way highlights the fact that the various approaches found within a given category generally have a similar orientation and hence share a number of assumptions. I treat them in reverse order, from most concrete to most abstract.

Discourse Level

The discourse level would include what is usually called textual criticism, language analysis, and discourse analysis, among those outlined in the handbook. It is here, I believe, that traditional notions of textual meaning have their basis in actual textual data.

I do not differentiate textual criticism as lower criticism from other, higher forms of criticism. There are several reasons for doing this. One of the most important, I believe, is that much textual criticism has been done apart from larger discourse considerations, and that textual criticism should be placed within the larger consideration of discourse factors. This includes the text of the particular passage being considered, but also the discourse features of the manuscripts involved. Rather than treating manuscripts as simply repositories of individual readings, they should be considered as ancient artifacts bearing witness to the use of texts by early Christian communities. In Philippians 2:6–11 there are few variants worth noting (at least according to the Nestle-Aland text). The text is apparently well established in 𝔓⁴⁶, Sinaiticus (01 ℵ), and Vaticanus (B 03), with few departures. In verse 7 𝔓⁴⁶ has "person" (ἀνθρώπου) rather than "people" (ἀνθρώπων); Bezae (D 06) and the Majority Text delete the article before "name" in verse 9; Alexandrinus (A 02), Ephraemi rescriptus (C 04), Claromontanus (DP 06), and a number of others, including the Majority Text, have the future (ἐξομολογήσεται) rather than the aorist subjunctive (ἐξομολογήσηται) in verse 11 (which may be an instance of vowel exchange for phonetic reasons); and K (017) has Χριστὸς κύριος in verse 11. Though these points of variation might warrant further study in another context, I will not discuss them any further here. They do not greatly affect the text, which is well established on discourse grounds.

Language analysis is also included within the discourse level. This is appropriate in the light of linguistic study of ancient Greek, which has moved language study beyond what was previously gained through traditional language study. These gains go far beyond simply new nomenclature and labeling procedures and now include insights into the structure and meaning of language. One of the most important of these gains is a comprehensive view of language, in which meaningful analysis proceeds from morphology through to discourse, or from discourse to morphology, depending upon one's purpose and perspective. The lexicogrammar of a language includes the lexicon as the most delicate level of grammar, in which the cotextualized meaning of a lexeme is modulated by meaningful grammatical structures (I have become convinced of lexical monosemy, at least at the discourse unit level, as the best explanation of the common semantic features of lexemes across cotexts and contexts).[11] The choice to instantiate a meaning with a particular lexeme and its grammatical form, within this language as used within its interpretive community and analyzed by means of its encoded formal structures, is a part of what it means to constrain the meaning of a given element. This constraint can be seen by means of the various ranks at which this element may function, whether it is at the morphological, word-group, or clausal level. With an ancient language, these constraints provide the basis for reconstructing the meanings of word groups, clauses, and hence the meanings of larger units, such as paragraphs. No doubt some ambiguity will be involved in such interpretive reconstructions, but I note that ambiguity is not unintelligibility since the interpreter must decide how meaning is modulated by cotext and

11. See my comments in earlier chapters to this effect, especially chaps. 3 and 4.

context; a text does not mean anything or everything that an interpreter wishes it to mean. The higher one proceeds beyond clausal syntax, the more potential there is for ambiguity as the immediate grammatical and lexical constraints are reduced.

Concerning Philippians 2:6–11, I notice a few lexicogrammatical features. The first is that the entire unit of verses 6–11 is a single set of secondary clauses and secondary embedded clauses that are connected to the secondary clause of verse 5b (here organized to display primary, secondary, and secondary embedded clauses with brackets):

⁵[τοῦτο φρονεῖτε ἐν ὑμῖν primary]
  [ὃ καὶ ἐν Χριστῷ Ἰησοῦ, secondary]
    ⁶[ὃς [[ἐν μορφῇ θεοῦ ὑπάρχων secondary embedded]] οὐχ
    ἁρπαγμὸν ἡγήσατο [[τὸ εἶναι ἴσα θεῷ, secondary embedded]]
    secondary]
    ⁷[ἀλλὰ ἑαυτὸν ἐκένωσεν [[μορφὴν δούλου λαβών, secondary
    embedded]] [[ἐν ὁμοιώματι ἀνθρώπων γενόμενος· secondary
    embedded]] secondary]
    [καὶ [[σχήματι εὑρεθεὶς ὡς ἄνθρωπος secondary embedded]]
    ⁸ἐταπείνωσεν ἑαυτὸν [[γενόμενος ὑπήκοος μέχρι θανάτου,
    θανάτου δὲ σταυροῦ. secondary embedded]] secondary]
    ⁹[διὸ καὶ ὁ θεὸς αὐτὸν ὑπερύψωσεν secondary]
    [καὶ ἐχαρίσατο αὐτῷ τὸ ὄνομα τὸ ὑπὲρ πᾶν ὄνομα, secondary]
    ¹⁰[ἵνα ἐν τῷ ὀνόματι Ἰησοῦ πᾶν γόνυ κάμψῃ ἐπουρανίων καὶ
    ἐπιγείων καὶ καταχθονίων, secondary]
    ¹¹[καὶ πᾶσα γλῶσσα ἐξομολογήσηται [[ὅτι κύριος Ἰησοῦς
    Χριστὸς secondary]] εἰς δόξαν θεοῦ πατρός. secondary]

Several syntactical observations can be made here.[12] Verse 5a has C–P–A word order, with the cataphoric demonstrative pronoun put in thematic position, and the antecedent for the neuter-singular relative pronoun in verse 5b in the verbless secondary clause (S–A). Reference to Christ Jesus in verse 5b is the antecedent for the relative pronoun in verse 6, which functions as the subject in all the secondary clauses in verses 6–8. The secondary clauses in verses 6–8 all have secondary embedded clauses within them. The clausal ordering of the secondary clauses is S–A–A–C–P (v. 6), C–P–A (2x) (v. 7a), and A–P–C–A (v. 7b). The patterns here—without the A elements—are S–C–P,

12. The letters used here indicate functional designations for particular components used at the clausal level. S = Subject, P = Predicator, C = Complement, A = Adjunct. For more detailed information about this type of clausal annotation, see http://opentext.org/model/introduction.html. For more on Greek word order, see chap. 19 in the present volume.

C–P, and P–C. In verses 9–11 there are shifts in subject, marked in the first clause (v. 9a) by the doubled conjunction and S–C–P order, with the fully grammaticalized subject, God. The ordering in the following clause is P–C–C, with secondary clauses following from this one—also with new subjects fully grammaticalized—with A–S–P–A (v. 10) and S–P–A–A ordering (the first Adjunct is also a secondary verbless clause, C–S) (v. 11). The structural patterns without the A elements are S–C–P, S–P, S–P, and C–S. The initial clause has the present tense-form φρονεῖτε, indicating imperfective aspect (v. 5); all of the other verbs in the passage are in the aorist tense-form, with one exception, the use of ὑπάρχων in verse 6. Although further observations can be made, the syntax of this passage is straightforward, including the way verbs are used to structure this discourse.

Discourse analysis—itself an interdisciplinary if not multidisciplinary arena of study—involves taking linguistic analysis beyond the level of the clause or sentence, so that larger structures are attended to. These include patterns that make a text a cohesive discourse (the so-called textual metafunction): lexical choice and participant choice that indicate the topic of a discourse (the so-called ideational metafunction), and the social factors embedded in the discourse, especially regarding participants (the so-called interpersonal metafunction). This social use and analysis of language forms a natural connection between linguistic usage and the higher strata of the column that I have identified, especially the contexts of situation and culture.

In Philippians 2:6–11 a number of observations could be made regarding each of the aforementioned metafunctions. I will simply list a few for each. Concerning the mode of discourse (i.e., involving the textual metafunction), this passage is surprisingly sparse in terms of conjunctions, instead using what might be termed a type of colon arrangement to structure the clauses into meaningful units. There is a use of the C–P/P–C order in the first half, and emphasis upon the explicit subject with S–C–P, S–P, and C–S ordering in the second. This is further supported by parallel use of embedded or secondary clauses, which often anticipate or repeat the content of the main clause: emptied by taking form of servant, being in likeness of humans; being found in the form of a human, he humbled himself, becoming obedient to death; God exalted him and gave him the name, so that every knee might bow and every tongue might confess. Καί is used connectively in verses 7 and 11, and ἀλλά contrastively in verse 7. The shift in subject from the first half to the second is marked with διὸ καί in verse 9. There is also the use of semantic chains, including words for "likeness" (image, likeness, form), "demotion" (empty, humble, obedience), and possibly "exaltation." The choice of lexis within the grammatical configurations recounts a movement from likeness to demotion to exaltation, and this forms the basis for the major theme of the movement of Christ Jesus in this passage. The interpersonal relations are related to this subject matter. Christ Jesus is first stated to be equal with God but not grasping such equality, and instead he, as agent, demoted himself by taking human form and likeness, but God elevated him to a position where others worship him. Thus there are two status levels indicated, that of God and that of humans, with Christ Jesus moving between the two.

Context of Situation

"Context of situation," a term taken and adapted from systemic functional linguistics to indicate the specific implied context of a given discourse as reconstructed on the basis of its discourse features,[13] also provides a useful term with which to categorize a number of exegetical methods. These include methods such as source, form, and redaction criticism, rhetorical criticism, and literary criticism. In the handbook, rhetorical and narratological criticism were placed together,[14] but I think that narratological criticism is merely a type of formalist literary criticism (following after the New Criticism in literary circles), and so does not merit a separate category (to say nothing of its own brand name).

Source, form, and redaction criticism have long been the stock-in-trade of historical criticism. For many, these criticisms have been equated with the exegetical task itself, as if identifying a form—whether it is a miracle story, pronouncement, parable, or something else—equals identifying its meaning. Such has been the case with much exegesis of the so-called Christ hymn of Philippians 2:6–11. One of the standard treatments of the passage, by Ralph Martin, is an exposition of form and source criticism.[15] The result of form- and source-critical analysis of this passage, such as by Martin, has often been classification of this passage as a preexisting hymn, although theories

13. See S. E. Porter, "Dialect and Register in the Greek of the New Testament: Theory," in *Rethinking Contexts, Rereading Texts: Contributions from the Social Sciences to Biblical Interpretation*, ed. M. D. Carroll R., JSOTSup 299 (Sheffield: Sheffield Academic Press, 2000), 190–208; also M. Ghadessy, ed., *Register Analysis: Theory and Practice* (London: Pinter, 1993); H. Leckie-Tarry, *Language and Context: A Functional Linguistic Theory of Register*, ed. D. Birch (London: Pinter, 1995); D. Biber and S. Conrad, *Register, Genre, and Style*, CTL (Cambridge: Cambridge University Press, 2009).

14. See D. L. Stamps, "Rhetorical and Narratological Criticism," in Porter, *Handbook to Exegesis*, 219–40. Let me be clear that I placed them together, and that Stamps wrote the essay as requested.

15. R. P. Martin, *Carmen Christi: Philippians 2:5–11 in Recent Interpretation and in the Setting of Early Christian Worship*, SNTSMS 4 (Cambridge: Cambridge University Press, 1967; revised and reprinted, Grand Rapids: Eerdmans, 1983).

concerning its original form or source vary. Thus, after performing his form- and source-critical analysis, Martin concludes that Philippians 2:6–11 is possibly derived from an earlier Semitic text, now translated into Greek and used in a eucharistic setting.

It is interesting to observe how scholars have responded to Martin's analysis. Stephen Fowl, for example, states that what is important for exegetical significance is how the passage is read in its larger context, not whether it did or did not originate elsewhere.[16] Gordon Fee argues that the passage is authentically Pauline rather than being an earlier hymn (on form-critical grounds) placed in the Philippians context.[17] Robert Gundry argues that the passage is poetic in nature (and probably Pauline), on the basis of features such as concentric patterning, chiasm, and sound patterns.[18] Although all of these analyses have something to offer, they all miss the very important point that, while Martin may be correct that Philippians 2:6–11 instantiates a particular type of textual structure, this reveals neither its meaning nor its function in Paul's Letter to the Philippians. Rather, form- and source-critical analyses are second-order analyses that have moved up the stack of strata, so to speak. They are dependent upon language-based exegesis for its ability to observe specific linguistic features, but their argumentation and their conclusions operate on a distinct theoretical plane.[19]

To my mind, form, source, and redaction criticisms can be embraced as useful and important parts of the exegetical landscape when they are understood appropriately as second-level exegetical methods. They can possibly offer insights into the prehistory of a text, how it has possibly developed, and how and perhaps even why it has been incorporated into the larger discourse. In these ways, they can help exegetes to understand more fully the creative process by which a text developed, and thereby they can provide contextual information that may be relevant to the interpretation of meaning. It follows from this that to criticize form or source criticism appropriately, one must

16. S. E. Fowl, *The Story of Christ in the Ethics of Paul: An Analysis of the Function of the Hymnic Material in the Pauline Corpus*, JSNTSup 36 (Sheffield: JSOT Press, 1990), 49–101.

17. G. D. Fee, "Philippians 2:5–11: Hymn or Exalted Pauline Prose?," *BBR* 2 (1992): 29–46.

18. R. H. Gundry, "Style and Substance in 'The Myth of God Incarnate' according to Philippians 2:6–11," in *Crossing the Boundaries: Essays in Biblical Interpretation in Honour of Michael D. Goulder*, ed. S. E. Porter, P. Joyce, and D. E. Orton, BIS 8 (Leiden: Brill, 1994), 271–93.

19. This is clearly seen when one examines many of the standard form-critical works, such as R. Bultmann, *History of the Synoptic Tradition*, trans. J. Marsh (Oxford: Blackwell, 1963). Bultmann's observations about New Testament forms in the Gospels follow from a language-based exegesis of the texts, by means of which the characteristic features of the forms are identified. Yet his use of language-based exegesis is carried out not with a view to the Gospels as whole discourses in their own right, but with a view to claims about the typical discourse situations that correlate with individual pericopes.

correctly discern what form and source critics are doing. Exegetical methods at this level do not answer the same questions as those at the discourse level; rather, they act as a control on or as a guide to interpretation at the discourse level. So, although Fowl is no doubt correct that interpretation in context should be preeminent, this does not undermine the important fact that texts sometimes do have prehistories. While Fee may well be accurate in his conclusion, he minimizes the contribution of form criticism by equating form criticism with a type of exegesis that he does not accept. Gundry may well also be correct in what he affirms, but he does not follow the indications of what amounts to his own form-critical analysis. These shortcomings reveal the importance of a multidisciplinary approach to exegesis.

Rhetorical criticism is also best seen as functioning at least at the level of the context of situation, if not the context of culture. The Greco-Roman world was an active rhetorical culture, even if none of the writers of the New Testament, including Paul, was probably a trained rhetorician. Though some have held to this position, rhetoric was not simply "in the air" for everyone to inhale. Rhetoric was a technical discipline for those trained in it. The question is whether any of the New Testament authors availed themselves of the technical instruction in ancient rhetoric. There are two directions in which this rhetorical analysis has been developed. Some believe that the works of the New Testament can be analyzed from a rhetorical-critical exegetical standpoint. Such analyses have been provided by Duane Watson, Gregory Bloomquist, Ben Witherington, and David Alan Black,[20] among others, for the book of Philippians. They try to determine its species of rhetoric, provide an analysis of its arrangement, and explicate its types of proofs. The result has been rhetorical commentaries. Watson and Witherington consider Philippians 2:6–11 to be part of the *probatio* of Paul's letter (2:1–3:21; 2:1–4:3), Black considers it part of a probatio that is part of the *argumentatio* (2:1–30 within 1:27–3:21), and Bloomquist places it as part of the argumentatio (1:18b–4:7). I am not convinced that applying the categories of ancient Greco-Roman rhetoric to the writings of the New Testament is warranted, either as something that the ancients would have recognized as legitimate or as something that is appropriate in the light of the development of rhetoric as a means to create a speech, rather than as a means of composing a literary text such as a letter or gospel. However, the major shortcoming of such analyses, in my opinion, is that they tend to equate rhetorical labeling with first-level exegesis. The identification of rhetorical devices in the New Testament may have implications for the study

20. See S. E. Porter, "Paul of Tarsus and His Letters," in *Handbook of Classical Rhetoric in the Hellenistic Period: 330 B.C.–A.D. 400*, ed. S. E. Porter (Leiden: Brill, 1997), 533–85, esp. 555–57.

of the New Testament texts, but rhetorical labeling in and of itself is not a viable way of interpreting the meaning of those texts as discourses.

However, there is a second and more useful way to conceive of rhetorical criticism in relation to exegesis. General principles of persuasion are found in most, if not all, cultures, and they can serve the exegetical task by bringing to the fore various techniques that authors use for their persuasive power. The biblical authors make use of these general concepts of persuasive discourse. In Philippians 2:6–11 we might well see the use of the humiliation and then exaltation of Christ Jesus as providing an example (exemplum) for the readers to imitate. The structure of the passage itself (from 2:1–11) begins with a series of conditional clauses, which are fulfilled by the example of what it means to think in the same way as Christ Jesus did.

Literary criticism is the third category I will treat. Literary criticism, within which I place narrative criticism as today perhaps the most common expression of it,[21] encompasses a range of reading strategies, including those that rely upon historical factors behind the text, those that focus upon the text as a well-turned artifact, and those that position themselves in front of the text with readerly interests, which also entails those with poststructuralist and deconstructive tendencies. Most of those who have fashioned themselves as literary readers of the New Testament have been of either the second (focus upon the text) or third (in front of the text) type.[22] Those who have concentrated upon the text as text, including narrative critics, usually have emphasized things such as the narrative structure and development of the text, the plotline, its characters, point of view, setting, and the use of such techniques as irony. Such readings have much to offer in appreciating the literary qualities of a text. However, these kinds of readings have often been criticized for trying to distance themselves from authorial intention and hence from socioliterary location, and for imposing categories from fiction upon nonfiction (and secular fiction on the sacred text as well). The dispute over authorial intentionality is legitimate, but it is often marred by misconceptions concerning intentionality itself, the role of intentions in the kind of literary criticism being discussed, and the locus of intentionality and its reconstruction. Such literary criticism was never meant to dismiss intentionality, only the kind of specific intentionality that could not be reconstructed from a

21. See, e.g., P. Merenlahti, *Poetics for the Gospels? Rethinking Narrative Criticism*, SNTW (London: T&T Clark, 2002); J. L. Resseguie, *Narrative Criticism of the New Testament: An Introduction* (Grand Rapids: Baker Academic, 2005).

22. See S. E. Porter, "Literary Approaches to the New Testament: From Formalism to Deconstruction and Back," in Porter and Tombs, *Approaches to New Testament Study*, 77–128. Compare P. Collier and H. Geyer-Ryan, eds., *Literary Theory Today* (Ithaca, NY: Cornell University Press, 1990).

text such as a lyric poem but had to be found in the psychology of the author. The criticism regarding applying categories of fictional analysis to biblical texts fails to recognize that one of the major differences between fictional and nonfictional narrative is extratextual referentialty, not literary features per se. I believe that within the discourse level I have defined earlier, there is a place to locate at least some of the features noted above, although their character of being nontextually based probably means that they are still best discussed in regard to the context of situation and are dependent upon the language-based exegesis of the initial stratum. Those who are concerned with reading in front of the text, and who thus engage in reader-oriented and deconstructive strategies, are—surprising as it may seen—even more clearly dependent upon language-based exegesis. Both methods are predicated upon "playing" with the text, by taking its meanings and manipulating them for various interpretive purposes, whether those purposes are of formulating readerly responses or deconstructing these meanings. Paul de Man, one of the leading figures in deconstruction, disputes objective meanings in texts by playing the rhetorical meaning off against the grammatical meaning—though he admittedly has to find grammatical meaning in order to engage in such play.[23]

Context of Culture

Context of culture involves the culturally based frames of reference in which interpretation occurs.[24] This stratum of interpretation involves genre criticism, ideologically based criticism, social-scientific criticism, canonical criticism, and the study of backgrounds, whether Greco-Roman or Jewish. If I were compiling an introductory handbook again, I would now also include a chapter on the effective history of the text as well as a chapter on theological interpretation of Scripture, and I would locate both of these within context of culture.

It is open to dispute whether genre belongs, or at least is best discussed (stratified), at the stratum of context of culture or of situation, since it both serves as an abstract type and is instantiated within given texts.[25] I believe it is best discussed at the level of context of culture because it has an inherent

23. P. de Man, "Semiology and Rhetoric," in *The Critical Tradition: Classic Texts and Contemporary Trends*, ed. D. H. Richter (Boston: Bedford, 1998), 906–16, esp. 908–9.

24. See M. A. K. Halliday and R. Hasan, *Language, Context, and Text: Aspects of Language in a Social-Semiotic Perspective* (Geelong, Australia: Deakin University Press, 1985). I recognize that in my discussion of context I depart in significant ways from the ways that these concepts are handled in systemic functional linguistics. I am doing that here in the light of my overall exegetical purpose. For other discussion, see chaps. 8, 9, and 13.

25. This involves a much fuller discussion within literary criticism and especially linguistics, in particular systemic functional linguistics. For some of this discussion, see J. R. Martin and

level of abstraction that is culturally dependent, in which generic features are instantiated in and realized by texts within contexts of situation. There is much legitimate discussion of the nature of genres, including how they evolve and develop. Genres appear to be useful categories for classifying types of literature on the basis of the presence or absence of key features. These classifications establish reading expectations within a given cultural context. Some models of exegesis focus upon genre classification as governing exegesis, almost as if genre criticism and exegesis were the same thing. That is, determining the genre of a text governs legitimate interpretation of it. No doubt there is a sense in which the cultural expectations surrounding a literary genre have a role to play in textual expectations. Nevertheless, one knows to impose a generic classification only from the repertoire of culturally available genres and thus on the basis of the textual data first determined by language-based exegesis. Hence, genre criticism should be kept separate from exegesis, and interpretation should begin with an identification of the language-specific characteristics of a text. Genre criticism of Philippians 2:6–11 is problematized by the issue of whether one is simply classifying the particular passage, or whether one is classifying the entire book in which it appears. The entire book certainly is an example of an ancient letter, but one that has benefited from the generic innovation of its author, Paul, who developed the ancient letter form by revising and expanding the thanksgiving and developing the paraenesis. Determining the genre of the particular passage is dependent upon one's form-critical findings. Nevertheless, one might well say that, regardless of generic classification, the text itself follows a pattern of superiority, humiliation, exaltation—a pattern that might be found in other texts as well.

Ideological criticism includes a variety of approaches, including various social and economic theories, such as liberation criticism, womanist and feminist criticism, and various other gender-based criticisms. These have now become what is often called cultural studies.[26] What these various types of criticism have in common is that they are responding to texts at the cultural level, as a a type of rejection of literary theory, or at least of traditional theory.[27] They draw upon language-based interpretation in order to challenge either the text

D. Rose, *Genre Relations: Mapping Culture* (London: Equinox, 2008). For more traditional discussion, see J. Frow, *Genre* (London: Routledge, 2006).

26. See, e.g., S. D. Moore, *The Bible in Theory: Critical and Postcritical Essays*, SBLRBS 57 (Atlanta: Society of Biblical Literature, 2010). For representative essays, see S. During, ed., *The Cultural Studies Reader* (London: Routledge, 1993).

27. See T. Eagleton, *After Theory* (London: Allen Lane, 2003). There has been a significant backlash against the rise of ideological or cultural studies. See, e.g., C. Bremond, J. Landy, and T. Pavel, eds., *Thematics: New Approaches* (Albany: SUNY Press, 1995); W. Sollors, ed., *The Return of Thematic Criticism* (Cambridge, MA: Harvard University Press, 1993).

or its application. Hence, some ideological critics have wanted to dispute with Paul over his view of women, or criticize or endorse other ideological stances of the Bible. The key observation here is that they find such stances in the biblical text and wish to dispute or endorse them on the basis of a set of culturally influenced values. There are no doubt instances of oppression and liberation to be found in Philippians 2:6–11, as well as gendered language (masculine-singular pronouns, for example, although some of these are specifically referential and others are systemic to Greek).[28] The question is how this language relates to larger ideological issues. In any case, the ideological critique must be based upon recognition of language use, for good or bad.

Social-scientific criticism includes a large number of socially based stances, including both descriptive and prescriptive approaches.[29] Descriptive approaches attempt to describe the social relations visible in the text with regard to things such as social status, gender, economics, and the like. For example, one can reconstruct the social configuration of the earliest Pauline churches. Prescriptive approaches draw upon theoretical models from the contemporary social-scientific culture and then try to draw correlates with the ancient world. Hence, one can identify apocalypticism or millenarianism as theoretical constructs relevant to the early church.[30] Both of these social-scientific approaches are useful if properly understood and handled. However, both run the risk of equating their particular method with language-based exegesis, to the point of determining the text's meaning on the basis of the description or prescription sought. Thus some seem to equate social-scientific readings with exegesis, to the point of labeling commentaries as such, whereas in my experience the language-based reading of the text is still clearly the basis for discovery of socially and culturally based configurations. It is possible to see a social ordering in Philippians 2:6–11 with regard to Jesus's relationship to God. This relationship reflects the kind of hierarchies found in the ancient world as well as in the church. One must go into the rest of the letter (e.g., 1:1, but elsewhere also) to explore further social relations within the early church involving Paul, his followers, and members of the Philippian church, and

28. The issue of gender in language is a complex one. For some insights, see G. Corbett, *Gender*, CTL (Cambridge: Cambridge University Press, 1991).

29. The contrast is seen in E. A. Judge, *The First Christians in the Roman World: Augustan and New Testament Essays*, ed. J. R. Harrison, WUNT 229 (Tübingen: Mohr Siebeck, 2008); R. Rohrbaugh, ed., *The Social Sciences and New Testament Interpretation* (Peabody, MA: Hendrickson, 1996). Compare A. Giddens, *Social Theory and Modern Sociology* (Stanford, CA: Stanford University Press, 1987).

30. See, e.g., S. Hunt, ed., *Christian Millenarianism: From the Early Church to Waco* (London: Hurst, 2001).

whether these follow particular social organizational models (e.g., voluntary associations or modern configurations).

Canonical criticism, at least of the New Testament, is not a well-developed interpretive model, despite the best efforts of some well-intentioned interpreters.[31] I believe this is partly caused by failure to recognize that canonical criticism functions as a third-order (or perhaps even fourth-order) interpretive framework. That is to say, canonical criticism operates at least as high as the level of the context of culture. It is not a language-based exegetical method, but rather an exegetical approach or orientation that relies upon language-based data—whether it be for evidence of development within the text itself, seams between texts, or the like—but focuses upon the placement of individual books within the canon. For example, I think that much can be made of the placement of the book of Acts in various early manuscripts and canonical lists. Its placement tells us something about how the book of Acts, together with the books that precede or follow it, is to be interpreted in relationship to the growth and development of the early church and its Scriptures.[32] This is a valuable contribution to biblical interpretation, but it is not to be confused with language-based interpretation.

The study of backgrounds, whether Greco-Roman or Jewish, is of primary importance for exegesis.[33] After all, knowledge of the world in which the New Testament developed is much of what the context of culture consists, including not only genre but also other literary, religious, and historical realities. Despite what some scholars seem to imply, however, this does not mean that we can equate background knowledge with exegesis. The study of background data allows us to theorize the possible textual worlds relevant to a context of culture, but in the end each text instantiates a specific situational configuration, and it is in relation to this configuration that the text must be interpreted. In fact, it is by means of such interpretations that we construct context of culture. Context of culture has a reciprocal relationship with texts, in which the culture provides the encompassing environment for texts and informs their interpretation, and yet each interpreted text speaks back to the culture.

Many proposals regarding Philippians 2:6–11 have been based upon background information. These include James Dunn's notion that this passage

---

31. The model for New Testament study is Brevard Childs, as in B. S. Childs, *The New Testament as Canon: An Introduction* (Valley Forge, PA: Trinity Press International, 1994).

32. See R. W. Wall and E. E. Lemcio, *The New Testament as Canon: A Reader in Canonical Criticism*, JSNTSup 76 (Sheffield: JSOT Press, 1992), 110–28.

33. J. B. Green and L. M. McDonald, eds., *The World of the New Testament: Cultural, Social, and Historical Contexts* (Grand Rapids: Baker Academic, 2013), is an attempt in this direction, though perhaps too brief on just about every topic.

involves a bipartite progression whereby Christ Jesus is equated with Adam, begins as the human made in God's form or image, and then is exalted.[34] Others have tried to identify recognizable Greek hymnic structure in the passage. On this basis they have speculated that certain portions, which violate the perceived Greek poetic style, have been added or deleted. Still others have tried to interpret the text in the light of gnostic or Iranian myths regarding a heavenly man.[35]

As I mentioned above, if I were compiling a handbook to exegesis today, I would specifically add (at the least) chapters on effective history and theological interpretation of Scripture. I mention these here because I believe that they too constitute third-order interpretive positions. Effective history is concerned with the function, use, and interpretation of Scripture—the accumulated meanings of the text as it has been transmitted and continually interpreted and reinterpreted.[36] Such knowledge is helpful for a variety of reasons. It gives insight into the history of interpretation and the developing insights of interpreters, both within and outside the church. It further shows the developments of related doctrines as they respond to the emerging interpretations. On the other hand, although knowledge concerning the history of interpretation is hard to ignore and harder still to overcome (especially in Protestant circles dominated by so many competing theological voices), this knoweldge is still third-level interpretive knowledge. It provides useful and helpful interpretive guidance, but it is not determinative for understanding the text itself.

Theological interpretation of Scripture has been a prolific and growing area of biblical interpretation over the last several years.[37] There are a number of scholars who wish to argue that, in the light of developments in postmodernism, interpretation of the Bible should be seen as an intracommunity activity: it is the believing community that appropriates the legacy of interpreting the Bible. This approach to interpretation is to be commended, as it has made a

---

34. J. D. G. Dunn, *Christology in the Making: A New Testament Inquiry into the Origins of the Doctrine of the Incarnation* (Philadelphia: Westminster, 1980), 98–128.

35. Martin, *Carmen Christi*, surveys such options throughout.

36. See A. C. Thiselton, *The First Epistle to the Corinthians*, NIGTC (Grand Rapids: Eerdmans, 2000). Compare H.-G. Gadamer, *Truth and Method*, trans. J. Weinsheimer and D. G. Marshall, 2nd ed. (New York: Continuum, 2002); H. R. Jauss, *Toward an Aesthetic of Reception*, trans. T. Bahti (Minneapolis: University of Minnesota Press, 1982).

37. Some recent, basic guides include D. J. Treier, *Introducing Theological Interpretation of Scripture: Recovering a Christian Practice* (Grand Rapids: Baker Academic, 2008); J. B. Green, *Practicing Theological Interpretation: Engaging Biblical Texts for Faith and Formation* (Grand Rapids: Baker Academic, 2012). Compare S. E. Porter, "What Exactly Is Theological Interpretation of Scripture, and Is It Hermeneutically Robust Enough for the Task to Which It Has Been Appointed?," in *Horizons in Hermeneutics: A Festschrift in Honor of Anthony C. Thiselton*, ed. S. E. Porter and M. R. Malcolm (Grand Rapids: Eerdmans, 2013), 234–67.

significant effort in reclaiming the Bible from the secular academy and restoring its place as the unique possession of the church. Not all is so optimistic, however, since theological interpretation has major limitations: (1) it draws selectively from a great diversity of opinion, while simultaneously asserting the primacy of its interpretations; (2) it often (at least in some of its manifestations) tries to recognize the results of historical criticism while simultaneously invoking interpretations that are precritical or premodern in their origins; (3) theological interpreters tend to view their method as exegesis rather than as the arbitration between interpretive options that it really is; (4) in at least some forms, it is predicated upon a postmodern stance and hence relies upon the church for its limited authoritative basis.

Finally, I suppose that one could also place practical exegesis within the context of culture. By this, I mean that if one wished to expand exegesis, one could also include practical exegetical abilities, such as preaching, teaching, and other forms of application. This is a reasonable multidisciplinary perspective on exegesis, one used by a number of people who want to link exegesis with homiletics.[38] There are even certain theological institutions that teach "exegesis and homiletics" courses, no doubt for the reason that they do have essential goals in common. I wonder, however, whether this is wise. I have often noticed a tendency to equate particular methods with exegesis itself. There is a danger that homiletics will share in this confusion such that the mechanics of preaching come to be treated as exegesis.

Conclusion

Having described a multidisciplinary exegetical method and briefly (and all too superficially) exemplified that method by using Philippians 2:6–11, I wish to make several concluding observations.

1. The first is the recognition that there are many different approaches to exegesis of the Bible, many of which are identified as exegetical methods. One of the conundrums of talking about exegesis (and certainly teaching it) is determining what exegesis is, and how these different methods do and do not play into a coordinated exegetical method.

2. I have assumed a multidisciplinary approach to exegesis in this essay, but I have attempted to bring some clarity by positing an organizing principle to

38. W. L. Liefeld, *New Testament Exposition: From Text to Sermon* (Grand Rapids: Zondervan, 1984); W. C. Kaiser Jr., *Toward an Exegetical Theology: Biblical Exegesis for Preaching and Teaching* (Grand Rapids: Baker, 1981).

exegetical diversity. I have attempted to show how a framework can be made to encompass many, if not most, of the exegetical methods that are currently being employed.

3. A model of multidisciplinary exegesis must state how the various exegetical approaches are related. The model that I have presented organizes them in terms of three ordered strata, with discourse-based exegetical methods at the bottom as foundational, situational-based methods in the middle, and cultural-based methods on the top. Of course, I do not pretend that this answers all of the important questions concerning how these methods relate to each other, let alone concerning how actual exegesis should take place.

4. In all of this, I have endeavored to underscore the fact that discourse-based approaches have a foundational role to play in exegesis, and that they must be in continual dialogue with higher-order approaches. Methods that are removed from close linguistic study must nevertheless, at some stage in their utilization, establish themselves in relation to the actual language of a text. At the same time, close study of a text's language must occur in relation to higher levels of exegesis.

7

Sociolinguistics
and New Testament Study

The State of the Discussion

In recent years, social-scientific criticism has made especially impressive in-roads in New Testament studies. Whereas in the late 1970s the only social-scientific critic one had perhaps heard of was John Gager,[1] now there are many social-scientific critics engaging with the New Testament.[2] The sign of its integration into the warp and woof of New Testament exegesis is perhaps indicated by the fact that at academic conferences there are social-scientific methods being employed not only in sections specifically called social-science criticism (or something like that), but also throughout the program, in such traditional bastions as Gospels and Pauline studies and other areas. One now even has social-scientific approaches to other forms of criticism, such as

1. J. G. Gager, *Kingdom and Community: The Social World of Early Christianity* (Englewood Cliffs, NJ: Prentice-Hall, 1975); compare Gager, *Reinventing Paul* (Oxford: Oxford University Press, 2000).
2. See, e.g., D. deSilva, "Embodying the Word: Sociological Exegesis of the New Testament," in *The Face of New Testament Studies: A Survey of Recent Research*, ed. S. McKnight and G. Osborne (Grand Rapids: Baker Academic, 2004), 118–29.

rhetorical studies, historical backgrounds, and the like. What literary criticism finally effected in the 1990s (after decades of struggle) has apparently been brought to fruition by social-scientific criticism in much less time, and even more pervasively.

Nevertheless, when one looks at standard grammatical treatments of the language of the Greek New Testament, one finds that little of what has happened in sociolinguistic research has been taken into account.[3] Of course, one also finds that linguistics has not really and truly permeated the exegetical scene either, apart from a few works of significance over the last few years or so.[4] Linguistic works that are sociolinguistically oriented are even fewer in number and have had a correspondingly lesser impact on the discipline.[5] One exception to this is the area of discourse analysis, which has resulted in much research over the last several decades and promises to produce more in the years to come.[6] Even here, however, linguistic work is often being done in virtual isolation from other exegetical work, and few of the discourse analyses are strongly sociolinguistically oriented.[7]

One piece of work that still stands out as leading the way in sociolinguistic

3. The advent of sociolinguistics dates to the 1960s and the work of two major figures, Charles Ferguson and Joshua Fishman. See C. A. Ferguson, *Language Structure and Language Use*, ed. A. S. Dil (Stanford, CA: Stanford University Press, 1971); J. A. Fishman, *Language in Sociocultural Change*, ed. A. S. Dil (Stanford, CA: Stanford University Press, 1972). Two useful introductions to sociolinguistics are R. A. Hudson, *Sociolinguistics*, 2nd ed., CTL (Cambridge: Cambridge University Press, 1996); R. Wardhaugh, *An Introduction to Sociolinguistics*, 5th ed. (Oxford: Blackwell, 2006). A challenging critique of many of the assumptions of sociolinguistics is found in G. Williams, *Sociolinguistics: A Sociological Critique* (London: Routledge, 1992), although his Marxist or poststructuralist corrective may also be questioned.

4. The literature on exegesis is ambivalent about linguistics, with a number of introductions mentioning it but few providing substantive comments on it or full integration of a linguistically sound approach into their exegetical method.

5. This does not mean that there have not been major pieces of work done in recent times that should command attention (see below).

6. I include discourse analysis as a type of sociolinguistics. This is reflected in the fact that discourse analysis was discussed early on among sociolinguists, and it is concerned with language and society. The following show the relationship: F. J. Newmeyer, ed., *Linguistics: The Cambridge Survey*, vol. 4, *Language: The Socio-Cultural Context* (Cambridge: Cambridge University Press, 1988), including ethnography of speaking (210–28), organization of discourse (229–50), and conversation analysis (251–76); D. Schiffrin, *Approaches to Discourse* (Oxford: Blackwell, 1994), including interactional sociolinguistics (97–136) and ethnography of communication (137–89) as approaches to discourse analysis; R. Mesthrie, ed., *The Cambridge Handbook of Sociolinguistics* (Cambridge: Cambridge University Press, 2011), with part 2 focusing on interaction, style, and discourse (103–56).

7. See S. E. Porter, "Discourse Analysis and New Testament Studies: An Introductory Survey," in *Discourse Analysis and Other Topics in Biblical Greek*, ed. S. E. Porter and D. A. Carson, JSNTSup 113, SNTG 2 (Sheffield: JSOT Press, 1995), 14–35; brought up to date in S. E. Porter and A. W. Pitts, "New Testament Greek Language and Linguistics in Recent Research," *CBR* 6 (2008): 214–55, esp. 235–41.

studies of the New Testament is an article by Moisés Silva, first published in 1980 in *Biblica*, titled "Bilingualism and the Character of Palestinian Greek."[8] In this article Silva analyzes the type of Greek found in the New Testament and engages with scholars such as J. Vergote, who emphasizes the Semitic elements found in New Testament Greek to the point of positing a Judeo-Christian dialect different from other forms of Greek. Silva also engages with the work of earlier scholars such as Adolf Deissmann and James Hope Moulton, who emphasize similarities between the Greek of the New Testament and that of the documentary papyri.[9] To move discussion forward, Silva invokes Ferdinand de Saussure's categories of *langue* and *parole*.[10] On the one hand, he argues that the *langue* of the New Testament writers, along with that of the writers of the papyri, was clearly the Greek of the Hellenistic world; on the other hand, he acknowledges certain New Testament peculiarities in the *parole*, or style or expression, of that language. Some of the factors that influenced these peculiarities are accounted for with reference to the subject matter of the New Testament writings, the personal backgrounds of the New Testament writers, and the influence of previous sacred texts, most particularly the Septuagint. Silva's article was distinctive in relation to other work being done by biblical scholars at the time. However, Silva's

8. M. Silva, "Bilingualism and the Character of Palestinian Greek," *Bib* 61 (1980): 198–219; reprinted in *The Language of the New Testament: Classic Essays*, ed. S. E. Porter, JSNTSup 60 (Sheffield: JSOT Press, 1991), 205–26. Other sociolinguistically oriented work to note (not mentioned below) includes E. A. Nida, "Translating Means Communicating: A Sociolinguistic Theory of Translation," *BT* 30 (1979): 101–7, 318–25; B. J. Malina, "The Social Sciences and Biblical Interpretation," *Int* 36 (1982): 229–42; F. P. Cotterell, "The Nicodemus Conversation," *ExpTim* 96 (1985): 237–42; Cotterell, "Sociolinguistics and Biblical Interpretation," *VE* 16 (1986): 61–76; J. P. Louw, ed., *Sociolinguistics and Communication*, UBSMS 1 (London: United Bible Societies, 1986); B. J. Malina, "John's: The Maverick Christian Group, the Evidence of Sociolinguistics," *BTB* 24 (1987): 167–82; S. E. Porter, "The Language of the Apocalypse in Recent Discussion," *NTS* 35 (1989): 582–603; Porter, *Verbal Aspect in the Greek of the New Testament, with Reference to Tense and Mood*, SBG 1 (New York: Peter Lang, 1989), 141–56; B. Zerhusen, "An Overlooked Judean *Diglossia* in Acts 2?," *BTB* 25 (1995): 118–30; S.-I. Lee, *Jesus and Gospel Traditions in Bilingual Context: A Study in the Interdirectionality of Language*, BZNW 186 (Berlin: de Gruyter, 2012); J. M. Watt, "Some Implications of Bilingualism," in *The Language of the New Testament: Context, History, and Development*, ed. S. E. Porter and A. W. Pitts, ECHC 3, LBS 6 (Leiden: Brill, 2013), 9–27; J. A. Snyder, *Language and Identity in Ancient Narratives*, WUNT 2/370 (Tübingen: Mohr Siebeck, 2014). There are also other articles in *The Bible Translator* to note.

9. J. Vergote, "Grecque biblique," in *Dictionnaire de la Bible, Supplément 3*, ed. L. Pirot (Paris: Librarie Letouzey et Ane, 1938), cols. 1321–69; A. Deissmann, *The Philology of the Greek Bible: Its Present and Future* (London: Hodder & Stoughton, 1908); J. H. Moulton, *A Grammar of New Testament Greek*, vol. 1, *Prolegomena*, 3rd ed. (Edinburgh: T&T Clark, 1908).

10. See F. de Saussure, *Course in General Linguistics*, trans. W. Baskin; ed. C. Bally, A. Sechehaye, and A. Reidlinger (London: Fontana, 1959), esp. 17–20.

simple invocation of *langue* and *parole* raises a number of questions. Many linguists, especially functionalists, do not accept Saussure's purported distinction: from the midpoint of the twentieth century, it has been under attack from various quarters.[11] A major criticism has been that these categories are not sociolinguistically based, since they focus upon language either in the abstract or individualistically—although these categories have recently been sociolinguistically reinterpreted.[12] Silva is concerned, as he believes Saussure was, to preserve the *langue*, even if it means that the *parole* is minimized. Sociolinguistics, and perhaps also Saussure, has a different set of interests with regard to the relationship between the abstract and the particular in language knowledge and use than Silva seems to indicate, with more concern for the system and instance. Nevertheless, Silva's article captures, from the standpoint of a biblical scholar, many of the issues involved in a sociolinguistic study of New Testament Greek, and it should be commended for bringing these into the discussion.

In the light of the status that social-scientific criticism has gained since the publication of Silva's article, it is perhaps worthwhile to trace the origins of sociolinguistics and to consider some of the themes it has come to view as important, especially those that have a direct impact on New Testament studies. This survey will indicate that there is indeed a place for further sociolinguistic development in New Testament studies.

Anthropologically Based Linguistics and the Sapir-Whorf Hypothesis

This is not the place to trace the entire history of anthropology (or even linguistic anthropology) or its relation to what has become known as the Sapir-Whorf hypothesis.[13] For my purposes it is sufficient to note that much of North American linguistics, along with a good bit of linguistics elsewhere, has been ideologically driven. It has been concerned with supposed differences between Western and non-Western languages, and (since the two came to be

11. For a history of discussion, see W. T. Gordon, "*Langue* and *parole*," in *The Cambridge Companion to Saussure*, ed. C. Sanders (Cambridge: Cambridge University Press, 2004), 76–87. Gordon offers critiques of the views of such people as J. R. Firth.

12. See P. J. Thibault, *Re-Reading Saussure: The Dynamics of Signs in Social Life* (London: Routledge, 1997), esp. 113–30.

13. Linguistic anthropology precedes the development of sociolinguistics, although many of its concerns overlap. For an introduction to linguistic anthropology, see A. Duranti, *Linguistic Anthropology*, CTL (Cambridge: Cambridge University Press, 1997); and for representative scholarship, Duranti, ed., *Linguistic Anthropology: A Reader* (Oxford: Blackwell, 2001).

linked) Western and non-Western thinking. For example, one of the first and most important American linguists was Franz Boas.[14] After coming from Europe to the United States, Boas was intrigued by Native American languages. Concerned with the possibility of their becoming "dead" languages, Boas undertook serious investigations of these languages. He was not trained as a linguist, at least as we would define that term today, but nevertheless he completed a number of important studies, including chronicling the grammars of Native American languages. An important point of emphasis in his work was the differences in structure between Native American and European languages. Another of the important points that his work brought to the fore was the importance of collecting and analyzing instances of natural language. His research was based upon actual firsthand acquaintance with communities using these languages: corpora of texts were accumulated and analyzed in the course of his descriptions. Hence—and here is a third distinguishing feature of his research—the cultural situations in which his sampled texts were spoken became important to their analysis. To some extent this result grew out of the difficulties of gathering the information, including acquiring the languages, since there was not a long history of knowledge of and acquaintance with them, as there was for Western languages (both ancient and modern). The techniques that Boas pioneered in these areas became very important for some subsequent linguists in the United States (see below).[15] However, those who know the continuing history of linguistics in America will realize that this seminal approach to linguistics was almost entirely abandoned in the middle of the twentieth century. A handful of linguists maintained the tradition of gathering and analyzing instances of natural language—in particular those interested in Bible translation—but mainstream linguistics in North America took a serious turn away from concern for actual usage. Entire books on the English language were published that did not analyze a single naturally occurring English sentence. Some have legitimately labeled these developments with terms such as "mentalism" and "psycholinguistics." Whatever terms one uses, much of this research cannot be properly called sociolinguistics,

14. F. Boas, *Handbook of American Indian Languages*, 3 vols., Smithsonian Institution: Bureau of American Ethnology 40 (Washington, DC: Government Printing Office, 1911–38), esp. the introduction (1:5–83); see also Boas, *Race, Language and Culture* (New York: Free Press, 1940; repr., Chicago: University of Chicago Press, 1982), esp. the four essays under "Language" (199–239).

15. E. Sapir, *Language: An Introduction to the Study of Speech* (New York: Harcourt, Brace, 1921); Sapir, *Selected Writings in Language, Culture, and Personality*, ed. D. G. Mandelbaum (Berkeley: University of California Press, 1984); L. Bloomfield, *Language* (New York: Holt, Rinehart & Winston, 1933).

since there is nothing social about it (and, some might say, little that is linguistic).

The linguist Edward Sapir, and also his student Benjamin Lee Whorf,[16] developed certain dimensions of Boas's earlier work. Continuing to deal with Native American languages, from the 1930s onward, Sapir and Whorf emphasized what has become known as linguistic relativism. Linguistic relativism not only describes and appreciates differences between languages; it also links these with mentality and culture. Its hypothesis is that the language one speaks is closely connected to the way one thinks. That is, all thought takes place in one's language, so that the parameters of one's thinking are set by one's language. Although this hypothesis is frequently referred to as the Sapir-Whorf hypothesis, it was not new to these two linguists; rather, its heritage goes back at least to the eighteenth century, and it was aggressively developed in the nineteenth century.[17] Wilhelm von Humboldt was one of the major advocates.[18] Some of the major thinkers, philosophers, statesmen, and educators who lived during this time, especially as they were part of the rise of nationalism, came to advocate various early forms of linguistic relativism. Unfortunately, it is a fairly short step from linguistic relativism to value judgments that denigrate entire people groups, their abilities to think, and the quality of their culture, simply on the basis of their language. With hindsight, one can see serious trouble developing, much of it unforeseen by those who advocated a close relationship between language and mentality.

The radical or extreme form of the Sapir-Whorf hypothesis—which Whorf seems to have advocated, even though many wish to tone down his statements and present him as advocating a milder theory[19]—directly links language and

16. B. L. Whorf, *Language, Thought, and Reality*, ed. J. B. Carroll (Cambridge, MA: MIT Press, 1956). It should be noted that Whorf's work dates back to the 1930s. For a thorough critical discussion of his work, with previously unpublished documents included, see P. Lee, *The Whorf Theory Complex: A Critical Reconstruction* (Philadelphia: John Benjamins, 1996).

17. I. M. Schlesinger, "The Wax and Wane of Whorfian Views," and V. John-Steiner, "Cognitive Pluralism: A Whorfian Analysis," both in *The Influence of Language on Culture and Thought: Essays in Honor of Joshua A. Fishman's Sixty-Fifth Birthday*, ed. R. L. Cooper and B. Spolsky (Berlin: de Gruyter, 1991), 7–44, 61–74.

18. W. von Humboldt, *On Language: On the Diversity of Human Language Construction and Its Influence on the Mental Development of the Human Species*, ed. M. Losonsky, trans. P. Heath (Cambridge: Cambridge University Press, 1999), originally published in German, *Über die Verschiedenheit des menschlichen Sprachbaues und ihren Einfluss auf die geistige Entwickelung des Menschengeschlechts* (Berlin: Königlichen Akademie der Wissenschaften, 1836).

19. See, e.g., Schlesinger, "Wax and Wane." Schlesinger appears to believe that Whorf simply could not have held to such a theory, despite his statements to the contrary (e.g., Whorf, *Language, Thought, and Reality*, esp. 213–14). See also J. Leavitt, *Linguistic Relativities: Language Diversity and Modern Thought* (Cambridge: Cambridge University Press, 2011). Leavitt argues that many of the more deterministic descriptions come from misreadings of Whorf and Boas. Ambiguity

mentality in a deterministic way. In this strong sense, linguistic relativism (i.e., the idea that language is not a universal but relative to a given culture) becomes deterministic so that language ineluctably sets the parameters for thought and communication. Extensive research followed from Whorf's pronouncements as some tried to quantify his suppositions. It is fair to say that this research did not substantiate the theory as Whorf imagined it, even for the Native American groups in relation to which the theory was developed. Even the theory's famous claims about color terms being language-dependent have been disputed, since people are still able to make distinctions in shades of color, whether or not they have distinct words for them. In any case, it would be naive to establish a general theory about language and cognition on the basis of color terms alone.[20]

With the rise of universal grammar (UG), together with its emphasis upon linguistic universals, attention within linguistics shifted away from the Sapir-Whorf hypothesis.[21] Within biblical studies, however, the hypothesis remained a discussion point, thanks to the biblical theology movement, which accepted a close link between language and mentality.[22] Most biblical scholars are familiar with the problems of linguistic relativism because of the work of James Barr: in *The Semantics of Biblical Language* (1961) and then in *Biblical Words for Time* (1962), he attacked the theory.[23] In *The Semantics of Biblical Language*, Barr took on the work of a number of scholars, most particularly that of Thorlief Boman, who was an advocate of a form of the Sapir-Whorf hypothesis.[24] However, Barr did this less from a sociolinguistic perspective than by indicating the kinds of inconsistencies that such a framework introduced into exegesis of the biblical text. For example, Boman was unable to sustain the kinds of generalizations that he wished to promote regarding differing views of reality on the basis of the differing tense systems of Greek and Hebrew. Barr performed a similar useful task in *Biblical Words*

---

regarding Sapir and Whorf and their implications has attended the discussion throughout. See H. Hoijer, ed., *Language in Culture: Conference on the Interrelations of Languge and Other Aspects of Culture*, CSCC (Chicago: University of Chicago Press, 1954). See also M. Crick, *Explorations in Language and Meaning: Towards a Semantic Anthropology* (London: Malaby, 1986), 62–63. Crick suggests that the entire enterprise may be misformulated.

20. Schlesinger, "Wax and Wane," 30.

21. For discussion, see J. Macnamara, "Linguistic Relativity Revisited," in Cooper and Spolsky, *Influence of Language*, 45–60.

22. For a summary, see B. S. Childs, *Biblical Theology in Crisis* (Philadelphia: Westminster, 1970), esp. 44–47.

23. J. Barr, *The Semantics of Biblical Language* (Oxford: Oxford University Press, 1961); Barr, *Biblical Words for Time* (London: SCM, 1962; 2nd ed., 1969).

24. T. Boman, *Hebrew Thought Compared with Greek*, trans. J. L. Moreau (London: SCM, 1960).

for Time by showing that categorical usages of terms for time were lacking in the biblical documents, contrary to the advocacy of such a position by Oscar Cullmann.[25]

Although Barr popularized a critique of linguistic relativism, few biblical scholars are aware of subsequent research that has been published since he wrote in 1961.[26] The Sapir-Whorf hypothesis is far from dead. Granted, recent research by linguists John Lucy and Daniel Slobin indicates that the radical form of the hypothesis cannot and probably never will be sustained.[27] There is simply too much contrary evidence that cannot be explained—for example, the ability of people to learn other languages (e.g., Whorf learning Hopi!), the ability to paraphrase from one language to another, and the ability to distinguish a concept even where a language does not have a particular word for it. Moreover, recent work in psycholinguistics questions the assumption that all thought takes place in concrete language.[28] Nevertheless, moderate forms of the hypothesis can and probably should be recognized, though I hesitate to call these moderate forms the Sapir-Whorf hypothesis, since I think that Whorf did advocate a radical form of linguistic relativism. Lucy and Slobin have shown that language possibly influences the way one thinks, and possibly has a bearing on how one expresses certain thoughts. For example, in his recent work Lucy has tried to develop more rigorous criteria by which to test the influence of language on thought. In some of his tests, as a result, he thinks he has shown that there are distinct differences in the way various users of languages handle numbers.[29] More noteworthy is the work of Slobin. In a well-titled chapter, "From 'Thought and Language' to 'Thinking for Speaking,'" he simply argues that we learn ways of thinking for speaking in a language, and that language affects the way we think when speaking.[30] Slobin identifies several important points here. The first is that necessary flexibility and accommodation take place in our thinking processes,

25. O. Cullmann, *Christ and Time*, trans. F. V. Filson (London: SCM, 1951).

26. This includes the work of those inspired by Barr, such as A. Gibson, *Biblical Semantic Logic: A Preliminary Analysis* (Oxford: Blackwell, 1981; repr., London: Sheffield Academic Press, 2001).

27. J. A. Lucy, *Grammatical Categories and Cognition: A Case Study of the Linguistic Relativity Hypothesis*, SSCFL 13 (Cambridge: Cambridge University Press, 1992); Lucy, *Language Diversity and Thought: A Reformulation of the Linguistic Relativity Hypothesis*, SSCFL 12 (Cambridge: Cambridge University Press, 1992); D. I. Slobin, "From 'Thought and Language' to 'Thinking for Speaking,'" in *Rethinking Linguistic Relativity*, ed. J. J. Gumperz and S. C. Levinson, SSCFL 17 (Cambridge: Cambridge University Press, 1996), 70–96. *Rethinking Linguistic Relativity* also has other essays of interest.

28. See John-Steiner, "Cognitive Pluralism," 65–69.

29. Lucy, *Grammatical Categories and Cognition*.

30. Slobin, "'Thought and Language,'" 76, 91.

which can be adjusted for the purpose of speaking in a language according to various contexts, and that the limitations of the structures and resources of the language have a bearing on how we think in and use this language, even if they do not determine it.[31]

The Context of Situation and Diglossia

Even more important for the development of sociolinguistics were early theories about the relationship between language and its social contexts.[32] The work of two early scholars, anthropologist Bronislaw Malinowski and linguist J. R. Firth, strongly emphasized this dimension of linguistic study. Drawing upon his knowledge of non-Western languages, Malinowski noted the importance of extralinguistic context in a 1923 essay that appeared as a supplement in C. K. Ogden and I. A. Richards's monumental book, *The Meaning of Meaning*.[33] Today Malinowski's essay seems a bit unscientific, in the sense that his conclusions seem to be based on a fairly informal and casual gathering of a few bits of evidence regarding some "primitive" languages.[34] There is definitely a Western-European perspective evidenced in his approach. Nevertheless, it must be kept in mind that his work was carried out in the early part of the twentieth century, at the advent of such comparative studies. One needs to be very careful not to dismiss Malinowski too quickly.

One person who did not overlook the significance of Malinowski's work was J. R. Firth. Before his appointment as the first professor of general linguistics in the United Kingdom (1944), Firth spent much time abroad in non-Western cultures and became a master of many different languages. This made him sympathetic to the work of Sapir, Whorf, and Malinowski, which helped him to move British linguistics in a direction quite distinct from that being pursued in the United States. In particular, Firth was a keen advocate of Malinowski's context of situation. He developed his ideas on this topic in an early essay in

---

31. Some of these factors are taken into account in ethnography of communication. See D. Hymes, *Foundations in Sociolinguistics: An Ethnographic Approach* (Philadelphia: University of Pennsylvania Press, 1974); J. J. Gumperz and D. Hymes, eds., *Directions in Sociolinguistics: The Ethnography of Communication* (Oxford: Blackwell, 1972).

32. An important collection of essays in the area is P. Giglioli, ed., *Language and Social Context: Selected Readings* (Harmondsworth: Penguin, 1972).

33. B. Malinowski, "The Problem of Meaning in Primitive Languages," in C. K. Ogden and I. A. Richards, *The Meaning of Meaning: A Study of the Influence of Language upon Thought and of the Science of Symbolism* (New York: Harcourt, Brace & World, 1923), 296–336.

34. His conclusions, however, have been reevaluated. See, e.g., A. B. Weiner, *The Trobrianders of Papua New Guinea* (Fort Worth: Harcourt Brace Jovanovich, 1988), esp. 4–9.

1935, and it remained a continuing emphasis throughout his work.[35] According to Firth, the context of situation is determinative in the sense that the social context in which language is used provides the parameters for what is said. (This is where the concept of collocation, which Firth developed, becomes important.) It is unfortunate that Firth left so many of his ideas undeveloped and never systematically elaborated his approach. Nevertheless, his collections of essays are full of interesting insights, often returning to the idea that language usage always occurs within a context. The natural result of such a perspective is to more fully appreciate how different contexts might be at play and what factors contribute to establishing the contexts.

In addition to work on context of situation, various sociolinguistic distinctions are important for biblical studies. Dialectology is concerned to study how people living in different areas speak in different ways.[36] The obvious difference is pronunciation, but syntactical and lexical differences also occur.[37] Although dialectology may not be well known to biblical scholars, there are some intriguing examples in the Bible that may reflect regional dialects, such as the issue of Shibboleth/Sibboleth and the episode in the Gospels where Peter is singled out for his speaking or sounding like a Galilean.[38] There is also much more that can and should be done in the area of pronunciation of the biblical languages, including the Greek of the New Testament, especially since it is fairly well established that the so-called Erasmian pronunciation, based upon Renaissance Latin pronunciation, does not reflect how the ancients sounded.[39] This does not mean that adopting Modern Greek pronunciation, however, is the necessary answer: it has its own problems for language learners with its lack of distinction in pronunciation among a number of different vowels. There is also much more work to be done on dialectal differences within Koine

35. J. R. Firth, "The Technique of Semantics," *TPS* (1935): 36–72; Firth, *Papers in Linguistics, 1934–1951* (Oxford: Oxford University Press, 1957); Firth, *Selected Papers of J. R. Firth, 1952–59*, ed. F. R. Palmer (London: Longmans, 1968).

36. J. C. Catford distinguishes between varieties of language that are permanent, which include dialect and idiolect, and those that are transient, which include register (*A Linguistic Theory of Translation* [Oxford: Oxford University Press, 1965], 84–85). M. A. K. Halliday distinguishes between varieties according to user (dialect) and use (register) (M. A. K. Halliday and R. Hasan, *Language, Context, and Text: Aspects of Language in a Social-Semiotic Perspective* [Geelong, Australia: Deakin University Press, 1985], 41).

37. J. K. Chambers and P. Trudgill, *Dialectology*, CTL (Cambridge: Cambridge University Press, 1980).

38. This episode is handled excellently in J. M. Watt, "Of Gutterals and Galileans: The Two Slurs of Matthew 26.73," in *Diglossia and Other Topics in New Testament Linguistics*, ed. S. E. Porter, JSNTSup 193, SNTG 6 (Sheffield: Sheffield Academic Press, 2000), 107–20.

39. C. Caragounis, "The Error of Erasmus and Un-Greek Pronunciations of Greek," *FN* 8 (1995): 151–85.

Greek, including the Greek of the New Testament. There is a perception that, in some ways at least, Koine Greek was a dialectless language. Nevertheless, I think that it is worth investigating the influence of geography, status, education, and multilingualism, among others, on the varieties of Greek within the New Testament.[40]

A closely related distinction, probably more important for biblical scholars, relates to social dialects. Social dialects are concerned with differences based upon social factors such as age, gender, education, social standing, and the like. Early work in this area was done by William Labov in the 1960s, when he studied various pronunciations in Martha's Vineyard and New York City.[41] These two seminal studies, and many others since then, have confirmed that social factors need to be taken into account in linguistics. At roughly the same time as these types of specific studies were being performed, some linguists were developing theories to describe how various language varieties relate to each other. Charles Ferguson, employing a term that had been in use for some time already, wrote his famous paper on "diglossia," in which he presents what is now the classic form of this hypothesis.[42] He differentiates contexts in which there are "high" and "low" varieties of a language. High varieties usually are written and reflect a more complex syntax learned in school; low varieties usually are spoken by the uneducated and have a simpler syntax. Joshua Fishman took the concept of diglossia and extended it into a theory of multilingualism, so much so that there has had to be a rethinking of this terminology.[43] Interestingly, the result of linguistic discussion on multilingualism in the 1950s and 1960s was a further emphasis upon the context of situation. That is, the various forms of language that may be used, often by the same speaker, depend upon parameters of context, including communicative purpose, subject matter, and also various personal and institutional factors (such as education, gender, etc.). The implications of this research for biblical studies, both Greek and Hebrew, are considered in *Diglossia and Other Topics in*

40. See S. E. Porter, "Dialect and Register in the Greek of the New Testament: Theory," in *Rethinking Contexts, Rereading Texts: Contributions from the Social Sciences to Biblical Interpretation*, ed. M. D. Carroll R., JSOTSup 299 (Sheffield: Sheffield Academic Press, 2000), 190–208, esp. 191–96, drawing upon the work of C. J. Hemer, "Reflections on the Nature of New Testament Greek Vocabulary," *TynBul* 38 (1987): 65–92. See also A. Mullen and P. James, eds., *Multilingualism in the Graeco-Roman Worlds* (Cambridge: Cambridge University Press, 2012).

41. W. Labov, *Sociolinguistic Patterns* (Philadelphia: University of Pennsylvania Press, 1972).

42. C. A. Ferguson, "Diglossia," *Word* 15 (1959): 325–40.

43. See J. M. Watt, "Current Landscape of Diglossia Studies: The Diglossic Continuum in First-Century Palestine," in Porter, *Diglossia*, 18–36. See also Watt, *Code-Switching in Luke and Acts*, BILS 31 (New York: Peter Lang, 1997).

New Testament Studies.[44] That volume includes a discussion of the functional distribution of Koine Greek in first-century Palestine, in which six different assessments are made of dimensions of language usage that can distinguish functional diglossic categories (or registers) among selected Pauline Letters.[45]

Systemic Functional Linguistics and Register

The development of the concept of register fits within the developments noted above regarding context. Despite the newness of the terminology to New Testament scholars, the concept of register has been important for a number of years.[46]

In one sense, many of the sociolinguistic studies that were carried out in the 1950s and 1960s were register studies. This includes not only Ferguson's study of high and low diglossic varieties, but also work by such well-known sociolinguists as John Gumperz, Geoffrey Leech, and David Crystal and Derek Davey, among many others.[47] Dwight Atkinson and Douglas Biber have examined a wide range of register studies and have reported that these studies have been done not only by linguists, but also by scholars working in communication studies, rhetoric, education, anthropology, and other related disciplines.[48] They categorize register studies into four groups: "Synchronic descriptions

44. Porter, *Diglossia*.

45. S. E. Porter, "The Functional Distribution of Koine Greek in First-Century Palestine," in Porter, *Diglossia*, 53–78.

46. For an earlier and lengthier discussion of register, see Porter, "Dialect and Register," 197–207; see also C. D. Land, "Varieties of the Greek Language," in Porter and Pitts, *Language of the New Testament*, 243–60. Important works from systemic functional linguistics on register include M. A. K. Halliday, *Learning How to Mean: Explorations in the Development of Language* (London: Edward Arnold, 1975), 125–33; Halliday, *Language as Social Semiotic: The Social Interpretation of Language and Meaning* (London: Edward Arnold, 1978); M. Gregory and S. Carroll, *Language and Situation: Language Varieties and Their Social Contexts* (London: Routledge & Kegan Paul, 1978), esp. 64–74; Halliday and Hasan, *Language, Context, and Text*, esp. 29–43; M. Ghadessy, ed., *Register Analysis: Theory and Practice* (London: Pinter, 1993), with various essays, esp. R. de Beaugrande, "'Register' in Discourse Studies: A Concept in Search of a Theory," 7–25; H. Leckie-Tarry, *Language and Context: A Functional Linguistic Theory of Register*, ed. D. Birch (London: Pinter, 1995); A. Lukin et al., "Halliday's Model of Register Revisited and Explored," *LHS* 4 (2011): 187–213. For an extended example, see chap. 13 in the present volume.

47. G. N. Leech, *English in Advertising: A Linguistic Study of Advertising in Great Britain*, ELS (London: Longmans, 1966); D. Crystal and D. Davy, *Investigating English Style*, ELS (London: Longman, 1969); J. J. Gumperz, *Discourse Strategies*, SIS 1 (Cambridge: Cambridge University Press, 1982).

48. D. Atkinson and D. Biber, "Register: A Review of Empirical Research," in *Sociolinguistic Perspectives on Register*, ed. D. Biber and E. Finegan, OSS (New York: Oxford University Press, 1994), 351–85. Basil Bernstein is a particularly important figure, especially within the field of education; see Bernstein, ed., *Class, Codes and Control*, vol. 2, *Applied Studies towards a Sociology of Language* (London: Routledge & Kegan Paul, 1973).

of a single register; diachronic descriptions tracing the evolution of a single register; synchronic descriptions of the patterns of variation among multiple registers; and diachronic descriptions tracing changes in the patterns of variation among multiple registers."[49]

Some of the register studies mentioned above can legitimately be called register studies. However, some of them might be better called genre studies, since they focus upon a particular linguistic form, such as poetry or the language of advertising, or stylistics, since they try to define a user's idiolect. Biber himself notes that, in these so-called register studies, terms such as "register," "genre," "style," "sublanguage," and "text-type" have all been used in semantically overlapping ways.[50] There have also been differences regarding the type of linguistic characteristics studied, and also whether and in what way quantitative and/or qualitative methods are utilized. I am not sure that all of these types fit the concept of register that I have in mind, so I will narrow my focus from a general survey of sociolinguistics to a particular type of sociolinguistics.

One of the great breakthroughs in register studies, I believe, came in the work of Michael Halliday and those who followed his example in systemic functional linguistics (SFL). Halliday has never laid out a systematic exposition of his thought on register, and one must go to several different articles and books to piece together his thoughts on the subject.[51] Here I will briefly mention some important concepts that Halliday develops. The first is the context of culture, which consists of those broad cultural features that have a bearing upon language use. Paying attention to the context of culture helps the linguist to remember that language, real and natural language, is used within culturally shaped contexts. Within the broad and flexing boundaries of the context of culture is the context of situation. The context of situation is the linguistic situation that elicits a particular instance of language, or discourse. This means that the context of situation usually involves a speaker or writer and a hearer or reader, though not always. Even though both types of context noted above are potentially broad, one already notices an improvement upon the notion of context as it usually appears in New Testament studies.

In Halliday's work, the concept of register attempts to describe how the components of the context of situation correlate with the variety of language

49. D. Biber, *Dimensions of Register Variation: A Cross-Linguistic Comparison* (Cambridge: Cambridge University Press, 1995), 6–7.

50. Ibid., 7–10. See also D. Biber and S. Conrad, *Register, Genre, and Style*, CTL (Cambridge: Cambridge University Press, 2009), esp. 15–23.

51. See especially Halliday and Hasan, *Language, Context, and Text*; Halliday, *Language as Social Semiotic*; compare Porter, "Dialect and Register," 197–207.

being used. Halliday differentiates three components of the context of situation: field, tenor, and mode. Field is concerned with the subject of a discourse, tenor with its participants, and mode with its medium and other organizing principles. According to Halliday, these three parameters correlate with various meanings and, in conjunction with these, linguistic features (they are realized in the lexicogrammar), which can be described in general terms or observed in actual texts.[52] The descriptive scheme used to document these correlations is far too complex for this simple summary. Field is related to Halliday's ideational metafunction, including the transitivity network, which describes who does what to whom in what way and when, as well as to certain lexical choices. Tenor is related to interpersonal metafunction, including participant structure as well as mood/modality (or Greek attitude). Mode is related to textual metafunction, such as differences in the expression of discourse (i.e., writing versus speech, etc.) and also to textual properties such as cohesion. These basic features have been developed further in many different directions, but they still seem to stand at the heart of what has become register analysis in SFL.[53]

The benefits of SFL register analysis are several. Most important, it bridges the chasm between sociolinguistic studies concerned with language communities and studies concerned with actual discourses. SFL's register analysis can easily become a form of discourse analysis, in which instances of natural language are examined. It also bridges an important gap between semantics and linguistic form. Since ancient languages are restricted to their epigraphic remains, a method that is able to link form and meaning is to be highly desired. Finally, by conceptualizing various features as expressing respective semantic systems, SFL's framework helps to prevent selective analyses that account for only a small handful of linguistic features. The breadth and variable delicacy of register analysis makes it ideal for data processing, which is now beginning to be aided by the use of machine-retrievable data.

It would be invidious for me to single out too many particular works for special mention in a category on New Testament register and discourse studies. Some forms of discourse analysis, such as the South African model, the continental and Scandinavian model, or even the Summer Institute of Linguistics (SIL) model, are more long-standing and more widespread. However,

---

52. See G. Martín-Asensio, "Hallidayan Functional Grammar as Heir to New Testament Rhetorical Criticism," in *The Rhetorical Interpretation of Scripture: Essays from the 1996 Malibu Conference*, ed. S. E. Porter and D. L. Stamps, JSNTSup 180 (Sheffield: Sheffield Academic Press, 1999), 98.

53. For a conspectus on SFL, see M. A. K. Halliday and J. J. Webster, eds., *Continuum Companion to Systemic Functional Linguistics* (London: Continuum, 2009).

that trend has been shifting. It will be clear to those who know this field, especially as I have represented it in my survey of various types of discourse analysis, that SFL analysis has only reached modest levels of popularity.[54] However, recent work shows that SFL research is beginning to mount in both quantity and quality.[55] Hopefully, this trend will continue, and we will see important strides taken as SFL register analysis is applied in New Testament studies. Of course, I must confess to having somewhat of an insider's view of such things, since I have strongly promoted the SFL linguistic theory and framework.

The Future of New Testament Linguistic Studies

In the space that remains in this chapter, I will identify some specific trends that I hope will develop in future linguistic research into the Greek New Testament.

Development of Methods

A shortcoming of New Testament studies in general is that typically it is methodologically derivative. This certainly has proved true in regard to its use of sociolinguistics. Some of the earliest sociolinguistic work in biblical studies simply took over the methods of others and then applied them to the New Testament. As valuable as such research has been, New Testament linguists must eventually come to terms with the data they are dealing with and develop their own methods. This surely is one of the reasons why linguistics has had so little impact in New Testament Greek studies. Many mainstream methods, developed almost entirely with modern English in mind, have not been further developed in order to address the issues involved in dealing with an epigraphic language that has no native informants.

It is easy to get discouraged when one compares a discipline as complex as biblical studies with other disciplines, which are able to pour more resources into methodological experimentation. However, I find comfort in the fact that in many ways those of us who have been studying the Greek of the New Testament are well ahead of those in related areas, such as classical studies, who are undertaking similar investigations. For example, in 1996 it was argued that the tense-forms in Herodotus are not primarily temporal markers,

---

54. See Porter, "Discourse Analysis and New Testament Studies," updated in S. E. Porter and A. W. Pitts, "New Testament Greek Language and Linguistics in Recent Research," *CBR* 6 (2008): 214–55, esp. 235–41.

55. I mentioned several of these in chap. 6 above.

but rather serve a discourse function, and the same book has argued that the perfect tense-form emphasizes the state of the subject—conclusions that were argued within biblical studies already in the 1970s and 1980s.[56] Also, a 1990s collection of essays by classical scholars includes essays calling into question the traditional notion of the historic present and emphasizing the discourse-shaping function of particles.[57] Again, these are conclusions that were reached in study of New Testament Greek much earlier.

In terms specifically related to SFL, it is reassuring to see that in more recent research, serious methodological advances have been made, and I anticipate seeing more such developments in the future.[58] At this stage it is probably appropriate to refer simply to New Testament Greek register studies, since the model as outlined above has been developed in ways beyond those ever anticipated by Halliday and his followers.

Major Interpretive Issues in New Testament Studies

As I have mentioned in various places and at various times before, one of the uphill battles of any method seen to be new and different—that is, anything other than the historical-critical method—is that it must both produce new and exciting results and at the same time confirm what has been discovered in the past. To come up with something new is to risk being dismissed, since tried-and-true methods have not yet come up with such results. On the other hand, to confirm historical-critical results meets with the ho-hum response that, of course, we already knew that and do not need this new method with its impenetrable jargon to tell us what we already have known.

In the light of this "damned if you do and damned if you don't" attitude, it is especially encouraging to see that recent work in sociolinguistics is helpfully addressing questions being asked by more traditional forms of New Testament criticism; it is adding to the discussion in ways that do not necessarily threaten to overturn the entire enterprise. I select several brief examples for illustrative purposes.

56. C. M. J. Sicking and P. Stork, *Two Studies in the Semantics of the Verb in Classical Greek*, Mnemosyne 160 (Leiden: Brill, 1996).

57. E. J. Bakker, ed., *Grammar as Interpretation: Greek Literature in Its Linguistic Contexts*, Mnemosyne 171 (Leiden: Brill, 1997).

58. See, e.g., J. T. Reed, *A Discourse Analysis of Philippians: Method and Rhetoric in the Debate over Literary Integrity*, JSNTSup 136 (Sheffield: Sheffield Academic Press, 1997). Compare T. Klutz, *The Exorcism Stories in Luke-Acts: A Sociostylistic Reading*, SNTSMS 129 (Cambridge: Cambridge University Press, 2004).

The first is Jeffrey Reed's study, unfortunately largely neglected, of the literary integrity of Philippians.[59] Reed ably shows that this is a debate with a long history, but one that has reached a stalemate. Most attempts to address the issue, especially those applying rhetorical analyses, raise more questions than they answer.[60] In the first part of his book, Reed offers a very comprehensive exposition of an SFL model of discourse analysis. He then applies his model to the question of the integrity of Philippians. Of particular importance here is analysis of the texture of Philippians in terms of semantic chains, ideational meanings, process types and their participants, interpersonal meanings, and textual meanings. One can see the SFL categories of register being directly applied to this traditional issue. The result is a study that does not settle for easy answers, but instead shows that some of the theories for and against literary integrity have more linguistic force than others. He also proposes a scale to aid in making claims regarding integrity, rather than simply saying that Philippians is or is not one letter.

A second study is my exploration of the question of criteria for authenticity in historical-Jesus research.[61] This study begins by analyzing the history of discussion of the historical Jesus through its several supposed phases, then concentrates upon the form critics' development of the criteria. It reveals that the criteria themselves have reached something of a standoff in recent research. In the second part of the monograph, two major questions are explored. The first is whether the complex linguistic milieu of first-century Palestine can shed light on questions in historical-Jesus research. The second is whether it is possible to develop new criteria on the basis of the use of Greek by Jews in Palestine. Three potential criteria are proposed, relating to contexts of use (i.e., contexts where Greek might have been used by Jesus and his conversational partners), textual variance (where Synoptic accounts agree or disagree), and register variation, which is most important here. The results of the study indicate that it is worth exploring the use of Greek in Palestine and testing the proposed criteria. The relationship between sociolinguistic-based language criteria and historical-Jesus research has received necessary increased attention.[62]

---

59. Reed, *Discourse Analysis of Philippians*. I am pleased to see that the relatively recent commentary by Walter Hansen (*The Letter to the Philippians*, PilNTC [Grand Rapids: Eerdmans, 2009]) makes some reference to Reed's work.

60. See, e.g., D. F. Watson, "A Rhetorical Analysis of Philippians and Its Implications for the Unity Question," *NovT* 30 (1988): 57–88; D. A. Black, "The Discourse Structure of Philippians: A Study in Textlinguistics," *NovT* 37 (1995): 16–49.

61. S. E. Porter, *The Criteria for Authenticity in Historical-Jesus Research: Previous Discussion and New Proposals*, JSNTSup 191 (Sheffield: Sheffield Academic Press, 2000).

62. See, e.g., H. Ong, "Language Choice in Ancient Palestine: A Sociolinguistic Study of Jesus' Language Use Based on Four 'I Have Come' Sayings," *BAGL* 1 (2012): 63–101; Ong, "An Evaluation

The third publication is Gustavo Martín-Asensio's monograph on transitivity-based foregrounding in the book of Acts.[63] This study utilizes the concept of transitivity as proposed by Halliday and developed by others, such as Paul Hopper and Sandra Thompson.[64] It also draws on other potential markers of foregrounding, such as word order and verbal aspect, to analyze several of the central passages in Acts. These include Stephen's speech in Acts 7 and the shipwreck in Acts 27, among others. Martín-Asensio provides a useful analysis of these episodes by means of register; he offers both confirmatory evidence for traditional interpretations and new readings of these well-known accounts. For example, on the basis of transitivity, he argues that in the account of the shipwreck in Acts 27, Paul is not the central or instigating figure, but that God is. This analysis may depart from several previous interpretations of this passage, but it confirms other critical analysis that sees the importance of God as the instigator of events throughout the book of Acts.

There are, of course, other works worth mentioning. I note these because each one is specifically placed within ongoing debates not only in linguistics but also in the wider field of New Testament studies, where their approaches and conclusions can be brought to bear in new ways.

Use of Other Methods

A third trend in future work will be, I believe, the incorporation of other methods into ever more powerful sociolinguistic models. I have already mentioned that some register-based work has tried to incorporate textual variance in an attempt to gain insights into historical-Jesus research. Others have tried to integrate SFL with other forms of social-scientific criticism, such as forms of critical discourse analysis.[65] One of the most interesting potential areas is corpus linguistics. Corpus linguistics uses defined, categorized, marked, and searchable corpora of texts. Although there are varying schools of thought on corpus linguistics—a major distinction being that some view corpora as

---

of the Aramaic and Greek Language Criteria in Historical Jesus Research: A Sociolinguistic Study of Mark 14:32–65," *FN* 25 (2012): 37–55; Ong, "Can Linguistic Analysis in Historical Jesus Research Stand on Its Own? A Sociolinguistic Analysis of Matthew 26:36–27:26," *BAGL* 2 (2013): 109–38.

63. G. Martín-Asensio, *Transitivity-Based Foregrounding in the Acts of the Apostles: A Functional-Grammatical Approach to the Lukan Perspective*, JSNTSup 202, SNTG 8 (Sheffield: Sheffield Academic Press, 2000).

64. See P. J. Hopper and S. A. Thompson, "Transitivity in Grammar and Discourse," *Language* 56 (1980): 251–99.

65. S. E. Porter, "Is Critical Discourse Analysis Critical? An Evaluation Using Philemon as a Test Case," in *Discourse Analysis and the New Testament: Approaches and Results*, ed. S. E. Porter and J. T. Reed, JSNTSup 170, SNTG 4 (Sheffield: Sheffield Academic Press, 1999), 47–70.

bodies of lexical data, while others view them as repositories of grammatical data—corpus-based research has great potential. When combined with a powerful theoretical model, it has the potential to extend the depth of our generalizations in ways heretofore unimagined.[66] The results of corpus-driven studies are beginning to make significant contributions to issues in New Testament studies, including papyrology and textual criticism, lexical semantics, and research on the Old Testament in the New Testament.[67] In addition, to facilitate such analysis, the OpenText.org project is attempting to compile a workable corpus of texts relatively concurrent with the Greek New Testament.[68]

Conclusion

Within New Testament studies, sociolinguistics is emerging from the shadows of other methods of New Testament study. There are a number of areas in which sociolinguistics might have a productive role to play within New Testament analysis. I have attempted to indicate several where there has been previous discussion and where encouraging advances already are underway. In particular, I have examined register studies as one of the most potentially beneficial for exegetical insights. With continued theoretical and methodological advancement, and with the development of new research tools, we should be able to arrive at a number of important findings by quantifying the registers of various specific New Testament texts, by showing how these registers correlate with features of their own contexts of situation, and by showing how these situations fit within a larger context of culture.

---

66. M. B. O'Donnell, "Designing and Compiling a Register-Balanced Corpus of Hellenistic Greek for the Purpose of Linguistic Description and Investigation," in Porter, *Diglossia*, 255–97. Compare S. E. Porter and M. B. O'Donnell, "Theoretical Issues for Corpus Linguistics and the Study of Ancient Languages," in *Corpus Linguistics by the Lune: A Festschrift for Geoffrey Leech*, ed. A. Wilson, P. Rayson, and T. McEnery, LSL 8 (Frankfurt am Main: Peter Lang, 2003), 119–37.

67. See M. B. O'Donnell, *Corpus Linguistics and the Greek of the New Testament*, NTM 6 (Sheffield: Sheffield Phoenix, 2005); S. E. Porter and M. B. O'Donnell, "Building and Examining Linguistic Phenomena in a Corpus of Representative Papyri," in *The Language of the Papyri*, ed. T. V. Evans and D. D. Obbink (Oxford: Oxford University Press, 2010), 287–311; Gregory P. Fewster, *Creation Language in Romans 8: A Study in Monosemy*, LBS 8 (Leiden: Brill, 2013), esp. 29–72, 123–43; Fewster, "Testing the Intertextuality of ματαιότης," *BAGL* 1 (2012): 39–61.

68. M. B. O'Donnell, S. E. Porter, and J. T. Reed, "OpenText.org: The Problems and Prospects of Working with Ancient Discourse," in *A Rainbow of Corpora: Corpus Linguistics and the Languages of the World*, ed. A. Wilson, P. Rayson, and T. McEnery, LE 40 (Munich: Lincom, 2003), 109–19.

8

Discourse Analysis

Introduction and Core Concepts

hat is discourse analysis?[1] This is a simple question, but it would be wrong to suggest that there is a simple answer. There is no such thing as discourse analysis.[2] After all, discourse analysis is not a thing: it is things.

There are two main reasons why I say that discourse analysis is more than one thing. First, discourse analysis is "things" in the sense that there is no single, agreed-upon definition of what it is.[3] Analyses that appropriate the label

---

1. I should note that discourse analysis is sometimes referred to as "text-linguistics," a term which I myself prefer but which is not as popular today. I like the term "text-linguistics" for a variety of reasons, not least because it includes the term "text," which is what discourse analyses ought to focus upon.

2. This raises the question of what is discourse. This is a subject of lively discussion in light of structuralist and post-structuralist thought. See S. Mills, *Discourse* (London: Routledge, 1997); D. Howarth, *Discourse* (Maidenhead: Open University Press, 2000).

3. There are a huge and growing number of introductions to discourse analysis. Here are a few of them that merit listing (in roughly chronological order) outside of New Testament studies: R.-A. de Beaugrande and W. Dressler, *Introduction to Text Linguistics*, LLL (London: Longman, 1981); J. E. Grimes, *The Thread of Discourse*, JLSM 207 (The Hague: Mouton, 1975); M. Coulthard, *An Introduction to Discourse Analysis*, 2nd ed., ALLS (London: Longman, 1985); T. A. van Dijk, *Text and Context: Explorations in the Semantics and Pragmatics of Discourse*, LLL (London: Longman, 1977); R. de Beaugrande, *Text, Discourse, and Process: Toward a*

"discourse analysis" may bear a closer resemblance to one another than they do
to other forms of criticism, such as source criticism or historical criticism, but
they cannot be equated as though they represent a single unanimous theoretical
or even descriptive perspective. Second, discourse analysis is "things" in the
sense that it is made up of numerous constituent parts that can be combined
in numerous and different ways.[4] Any worthwhile analysis will draw together
various discrete linguistic components in order to create a particular form of
discourse analysis for a particular occasion and purpose.

In this short chapter I want to describe some of the things that generally
distinguish discourse analysis from other interpretive approaches. I do not
develop any original hypotheses, but rather try to clear the ground for chapters
that follow, so if I happen to say anything that is of interest, or anything that
goes beyond a simple recounting of things previously said (both by myself
and by many others), then that is simply by accident.

Forms of Discourse Analysis

Outside of biblical studies, and more particularly outside of New Testament
studies, there are any number of different ways of dividing up the field of

Multidisciplinary Science of Texts, ADP 4 (London: Longman, 1980); M. Coulthard and
M. Montgomery, eds., Studies in Discourse Analysis (London: Routledge & Kegan Paul, 1981);
H. Kalverkämper, Orientierung zur Textlinguistik, LA 100 (Tübingen: Niemeyer, 1981); G. Brown
and G. Yule, Discourse Analysis, CTL (Cambridge: Cambridge University Press, 1983); M. Stubbs,
Discourse Analysis: The Sociolinguistic Analysis of Natural Language (Oxford: Blackwell, 1983);
R. Salkie, Text and Discourse Analysis (London: Routledge, 1995); A. Georgakopoulou and D.
Goutsos, Discourse Analysis: An Introduction, 2nd ed. (Edinburgh: Edinburgh University Press,
2004); T. A. van Dijk, ed., Discourse as Structure and Process, DS 1 (London: Sage, 1997); J. P.
Gee, An Introduction to Discourse Analysis: Theory and Method (London: Routledge, 1999);
M. Hoey, Textual Interaction: An Introduction to Written Discourse Analysis (London: Routledge,
2001); M. A. K. Halliday, Text and Discourse, ed. J. J. Webster (London: Continuum, 2002);
B. Johnstone, Discourse Analysis, 2nd ed. (Oxford: Blackwell, 2008); N. Fairclough, Analysing
Discourse: Textual Analysis for Social Research (London: Routledge, 2003); J. R. Martin and
D. Rose, Working with Discourse: Meaning beyond the Clause, 2nd ed. (London: Continuum,
2007); H. G. Widdowson, Text, Context, Pretext: Critical Issues in Discourse Analysis (Oxford:
Blackwell, 2004); B. Paltridge, Discourse Analysis (London: Continuum, 2006); T. A. van Dijk,
ed., Discourse Studies: A Multidisciplinary Introduction (London: Sage, 2011).
    4. This is evidenced in a number of overviews of discourse analysis. See, e.g., D. Schiffrin,
Approaches to Discourse (Oxford: Blackwell, 1994); D. Schiffrin, D. Tannen, and H. E. Hamilton,
eds., The Handbook of Discourse Analysis (Oxford: Blackwell, 2001); M. Wetherell, S. Taylor,
and S. J. Yates, eds., Discourse Theory and Practice: A Reader (London: Sage, 2001); V. K. Bhatia,
J. Flowerdew, and R. H. Jones, eds., Advances in Discourse Studies (London: Routledge, 2008);
K. Hyland and B. Paltridge, eds., The Bloomsbury Companion to Discourse Analysis (London:
Bloomsbury, 2011).

discourse analysis. One way is to observe whether the discourse analyst is concerned with spoken discourse or written discourse. (Of course, we in New Testament studies are concerned virtually entirely with written discourse, even if we posit oral sources for some of our documents.) Different forms can also be distinguished as anthropological versus linguistic, ethnographic versus dialectic, and so on. The list of possible criteria is quite lengthy.

In terms of New Testament studies, I have on previous occasions provided a taxonomy of four major types of discourse analysis, along with a fifth, eclectic category.[5] The first is continental discourse analysis.[6] Continental discourse analysis typically combines the old syntax, semantics, and pragmatics model of grammar with communications models and rhetorical models. Another is South African discourse analysis.[7] This model is based upon so-called colon analysis. The individual colon, which involves a subject and verb, forms the basis of analysis and is the highest unit of formal analysis. Larger units are said to involve semantic relations, an approach akin to the kind of lumping done in other forms of semantic grouping analysis. A third form of discourse analysis is based around the work of the Summer Institute of Linguistics (SIL). A variety of work is represented here, much of it related to Kenneth Pike's tagmemics and Robert Longacre's top-down discourse model.[8] Pike's work, to my mind, has never been fully appreciated, probably because he wrote a very large book

5. S. E. Porter, "Discourse Analysis and New Testament Studies: An Introductory Survey," in *Discourse Analysis and Other Topics in Biblical Greek*, ed. S. E. Porter and D. A. Carson, JSNTSup 113, SNTG 2 (Sheffield: JSOT Press, 1995), 14–35; developed further in S. E. Porter and A. W. Pitts, "New Testament Greek Language and Linguistics in Recent Research," *CBR* 6 (2008): 214–55, esp. 235–41. Two collections of essays in New Testament studies worth noting are D. A. Black, with K. Barnwell and S. H. Levinsohn, eds., *Linguistics and New Testament Interpretation: Essays on Discourse Analysis* (Nashville: Broadman, 1992), with a range of essays mostly SIL-oriented; S. E. Porter and J. T. Reed, eds., *Discourse Analysis and the New Testament: Approaches and Results*, JSNTSup 170, SNTG 4 (Sheffield: Sheffield Academic Press, 1999), with a wide range of essays.

6. See, e.g., C. Breytenbach, *Nachfolge und Zukunftserwartung nach Markus*, ATANT 71 (Zurich: Theologischer Verlag, 1984).

7. See, e.g., J. P. Louw, *A Semantic Discourse Analysis of Romans*, 2 vols. (Pretoria: University of Pretoria, Department of Greek, 1987).

8. See, e.g., K. L. Pike, *Language in Relation to a Unified Theory of the Structure of Human Behavior*, 2nd rev. ed., JLSMa 24 (The Hague: Mouton, 1967); Pike, *Linguistic Concepts: An Introduction to Tagmemics* (Lincoln: University of Nebraska Press, 1982); R. E. Longacre, *The Grammar of Discourse*, 2nd ed. (New York: Plenum, 1996). Also to be included here is the work of S. H. Levinsohn, *Discourse Features of New Testament Greek: A Coursebook on the Information Structure of New Testament Greek*, 2nd ed. (Dallas: SIL International, 2000); and S. E. Runge, *Discourse Grammar of the Greek New Testament: A Practical Introduction for Teaching and Exegesis* (Peabody, MA: Hendrickson, 2010), with Runge combining Levinsohn's work with cognitive linguistics to examine a select number of topics (three) in the area of textual formation (SFL mode).

that very few people want to read all the way through. If we took the time to understand Pike, however, I am sure that we would understand much more, since his theory is designed as a unified field theory of human action. The fourth form of discourse analysis that I wish to mention is based on systemic functional linguistics (SFL). Several varieties of discourse analysis use systemic functional linguistics, primarily today the Sydney (formerly London) school and the Cardiff school.[9] I believe that this model has the most to offer discourse analysis, although I also recognize that it has not been widely accepted by others. I refuse to believe that this has anything to do with the model (or with me).

We might also include a fifth group of discourse analysts. They are not really a group, if by that one means a coherent group of practitioners; instead, they are people who do not really fit into any one of the other groups. Some of them are highly eclectic in their methods, choosing bits and pieces from several of the models. (Whether it is better to pick and choose than to utilize one of the forms of discourse analysis that has already been developed is a debatable point.) Most of them try to combine discourse considerations with various other types of criticism, such as literary criticism especially.[10] Still others simply draw from the other readily available exegetical methods. These forms of discourse analysis often present themselves as discourse analysis in the language of "the common man," almost as a matter of pride.

9. At one time, there were many more centers of SFL excellence, including Birmingham, Nottingham, Liverpool, Sheffield, and London, to name some of them. The major works of M. A. K. Halliday (too numerous to list all of them) include M. A. K. Halliday, *Explorations in the Functions of Language* (London: Edward Arnold, 1973); Halliday, *Language as Social Semiotic: The Social Interpretation of Language and Meaning* (London: Edward Arnold, 1978); Halliday, *Halliday's Introduction to Functional Grammar*, rev. C. M. I. M. Matthiessen, 4th ed. (London: Routledge, 2014); Halliday, *The Collected Works of M. A. K. Halliday*, ed. J. J. Webster, 10 vols. (London: Continuum, 2002–7); M. A. K Halliday and R. Hasan, *Cohesion in English*, ELS (London: Longman, 1976); Halliday and Hasan, *Language, Context, and Text: Aspects of Language in a Social-Semiotic Perspective* (Geelong, Australia: Deakin University Press, 1985); M. A. K. Halliday and C. M. I. M. Matthiessen, *Construing Experience through Meaning: A Language-Based Approach to Cognition*, OLS (London: Continuum, 1999). Besides Sydney, the Cardiff school is the most active today, represented by the work of R. P. Fawcett, *Cognitive Linguistics and Social Interaction: Towards an Integrated Model of a Systemic Functional Grammar and the Other Components of a Communicating Mind* (Heidelberg: Julius Groos; Exeter: Exeter University, 1980); Fawcett, *Invitation to Systemic Functional Linguistics through the Cardiff Grammar: An Extension and Simplification of Halliday's Systemic Functional Grammar*, 3rd ed. (London: Equinox, 2008); Fawcett, *A Theory of Syntax for Systemic Functional Linguistics* (Philadelphia: John Benjamins, 2000). In New Testament studies, see J. T. Reed, *A Discourse Analysis of Philippians: Method and Rhetoric in the Debate over Literary Integrity*, JSNTSup 136 (Sheffield: Sheffield Academic Press, 1997).

10. See, e.g., G. H. Guthrie, *The Structure of Hebrews: A Text-Linguistic Analysis*, NovTSup 73 (Leiden: Brill, 1994). Compare M. A. Rudolph, "Beyond Guthrie? Text-Linguistics and New Testament Studies," *FN* 26 (2013): 27–47.

Important Terminology and Areas for Development

In this section I want to disambiguate some of the terms used in discourse analysis. Before I begin this exercise, however, I should state that it is very important for one to have a clear idea of the method that one is using. I am a firm believer in method (as well as theory). I do not believe that much good interpretation, and even less good linguistics, goes on without a clear sense of what counts for evidence within a given framework, what that framework is and its limits of application, and the kinds of legitimate expectations one has of any given method. Method needs to be central to the intellectual enterprise. I recommend that any discourse analyst first establish a clear method. If that method is eclectic, one needs to know why and in what ways it is eclectic. The challenge of eclecticism is to see whether disparate elements gleaned from competing conceptual models can actually be made to fit together into a single, coherent framework. In this sense, I am less concerned with whether one selects a continental, South African, SIL, or SFL approach than I am with knowing what approach has been chosen and why, and what one can legitimately expect from that approach. It is necessary to carefully distinguish between methods and results, but one can debate questions of method only if a method is clearly presented. Some, but by no means all, of the important core concepts in discourse analysis are the following.

Bottom-Up and Top-Down Analysis

Now to some crucial distinctions. A major distinction in discourse models is whether they are bottom-up or top-down models. A bottom-up model begins with relatively small units of language and assembles them in increasingly larger units until arriving at the highest level of appropriate analysis. A top-down model begins with relatively large units, often ones that are larger than the grammatical structures of a language (such as a given discourse), and moves down to lower levels of appropriate analysis. One may be tempted to think that "all roads lead to Rome," but my experience is that these two roads in the woods go off into separate parts of the forest. Bottom-up models of analysis are typically more concerned with the forms of the language, such as morphology, words, phrases/groups, and the like, while top-down models are less concerned with forms and more concerned with functions or conceptual categories. A bottom-up analysis, for example, will often appear to be similar to the old structuralist models that dominated linguistics in the first half of the twentieth century. The popular perception of these models is that they were concerned only with things such as constituency relations, but were not concerned with semantics or meaning. This is not exactly true, but it does accurately capture where such models placed their priorities.

Similar priorities are held by bottom-up models of discourse analysis. Individual constituents are seen to join together to form larger units. So one begins with morphology or words but soon builds up to phrases/groups and then clauses or sentences. By way of contrast, top-down models often begin with genre or literary type. These genres or literary types are then broken down into smaller units, such as paragraphs, and these may be categorized according to their types, according to what they do within the specific genres. A major problem with bottom-up analysis is that there always has to be an eye on meaning in order to determine how constituents relate to each other. Even with one eye on meaning, however, it remains difficult to talk about the formal features of a language as one moves to higher levels of abstraction. When one reaches the paragraph (or equivalent), there is a noticeable difference in structure (or perhaps no discernible syntactical structure), compared to smaller units, such as the clause. On the other hand, a major problem with top-down analysis is that it does not deal with formal structures as well as does bottom-up analysis—that is, in correlating meaning with structure. Too often, as one moves from larger to smaller units, attention is given to semantics but not to the formal elements that give rise to the semantics. As a result, there can be a tendency for the discourse analyst to impose a macrostructure on all of the microstructures without showing how the smaller elements sustain the larger ones.

Moving beyond the Clause or Sentence

A further element that is important in discourse analysis, and continues to be a challenge to all linguistic models, is how one moves beyond the clause or sentence. The sentence has proved to be a continual barrier, so much so that major approaches to linguistics collide at the intersection of the sentence and what is beyond it. Most linguists concerned with discourse wish to acknowledge that there are levels or ranks beyond or larger than the sentence, but they struggle to describe them. For example, what are the levels between the sentence and the discourse? We typically speak of paragraphs, but there are also groupings of paragraphs.[11] As a result, some linguists wish to talk about levels above the sentence, even if those levels are not said to have

11. The paragraph is notoriously difficult to define. See Brown and Yule, *Discourse Analysis*, 95–100; S. E. Porter, "Pericope Markers and the Paragraph: Textual and Linguistic Considerations," in *The Impact of Unit Delimitation on Exegesis*, ed. R. de Hoop, M. C. A. Korpel, and S. E. Porter, Pericope 7 (Leiden: Brill, 2008), 175–95.

grammatical or syntactical structure. Other linguists, recognizing units beyond the sentence, wish to see this level or these levels as having structure, almost as if they have the same kind of syntax as a sentence does (supersentences, with reference to supersentential syntax). One can see that these differing perspectives have implications. The former approach recognizes something but categorizes it in such a way that makes description inherently problematic. This inevitably has a stultifying effect upon linguistic exploration, since research naturally focuses on those levels that can be more easily talked about and exemplified. The latter approach optimistically directs its attention to supersentential elements but is perpetually frustrated by the fact that one cannot clearly describe the structural features of those units. They may be there, but we cannot identify them in the same way that we can identify, for example, the subject of a clause.

What Is a Text?

One of the most important questions related to discourse analysis is what it means for a text to be a text.[12] After all, discourse analysis is built on the paired assumptions that there are such things as texts and that they merit analysis as wholes. It is only natural that discourse analysis should explore why these two presuppositions are valid. In this respect, one of the first issues to be confronted is the role of coherence. Coherence entails that a text displays a certain degree of intellectual and ideational intelligibility. When the speech of those with various mental diseases is analyzed, however, there does not appear to be coherence. (Of course, this principle applies more broadly. Undergraduate papers, for example, often lack coherence.) In response to the issue of coherence, some discourse analysts have opted to study cohesion.[13] Cohesion entails that there are various features of texts that hold them together. These linguistic features may not consistently give rise to coherence, but they are quantifiable, and they do play a role in making a text a text. Almost any element of the text can be seen to have cohesive properties. Obvious elements include the use of conjunctions, the presence of participant chains, the repeated use of lexis from certain semantic domains, and the deployment of various

12. This is actually a more philosophical question than it at first appears. See J. J. E. Gracia, *A Theory of Textuality: The Logic and Epistemology* (Albany: SUNY Press, 1995); J. Mowitt, *Text: The Genealogy of an Antidisciplinary Object* (Durham, NC: Duke University Press, 1992).

13. M. Hoey makes clear that the two are different, with coherence being an evaluation of the text and cohesion a property of the text (*Patterns of Lexis in Text*, DEL [Oxford: Oxford University Press, 1991], 12).

morphologically based devices, such as tense-forms, voice-forms, and mood-forms. Every one of these features (and many more besides) plays a role in creating what is called a text. Unfortunately, the area of textuality is woefully underexplored in New Testament studies. We often inherit genres or literary types from previous study—for example, Gospel or epistle—and then we read the characteristics of those genres into a given instance of text. We assume a level of connectedness on the basis of macrostructure, rather than attempting to describe the way in which a particular text is constructed as a text.[14]

Semantics

A further topic for discussion is semantics. How do we describe meaning in texts? By this, I do not mean what has typically been identified as semantics. In fact, most of the time semantics is given a modifying word to help us understand the limit of its application, so that we have "lexical semantics" or "formal semantics" or the like. By "semantics" here, I mean all of the various ways in which we can talk about meaning. A tendency in New Testament studies, as in all forms of ancient language study, is to equate meaning with translation. That is, the way we judge that we understand what something means in one language is to be able to put it into some other expression in another language. I find this highly problematic, and I hope that we can find better ways to talk about meaning without resorting to translation. At the very least, we should use paraphrases, since this permits a greater focus on meaning and forces interpreters to work harder at understanding the original text in its original language. I instead argue that we need to think much more astutely about meaning and meaning making as what authors attempt to do, with semantics as the content stratum concerned with what we are trying to do with language (whether we divide this into discourse semantics and clausal semantics or not, I leave for another discussion).[15]

14. Form criticism has been a popular way of describing individual units, but form criticism typically dissolves discourse coherence and explores instead the underlying cohesion of smaller units. Discourse analysis could play a potentially important role in form criticism, provided it can show better methods by which texuality can be described and discussed.

15. There is a difference of opinion within SFL regarding semantics, whether semantics is the label for an entire content stratum, between context and lexicogrammar, or whether semantics consists of what amounts to discourse semantics and clausal semantics. For the difference between the two approaches, see Halliday, *Introduction to Functional Grammar*, 26; J. R. Martin, *English Text: System and Structure* (Philadelphia: John Benjamins, 1992), 1, 14–20. The major issue has been how to mediate the content strata. See C. S. Butler, "Discourse Systems and Structures and Their Place within an Overall Systemic Model," in *Systemic Perspectives on Discourse*, vol. 1, *Selected Theoretical Papers from the 9th International Systemic Workshop*, ed. J. D. Benson and W. S. Greaves (Norwood, NJ: Ablex, 1985), 213–28.

Levels of Linguistic Description

The concept of levels of language is another useful notion. One of the problems of much discourse analysis is that the discipline has not taken time to differentiate levels of analysis. Each level or rank of language has its own structures, and appropriate methods of describing, analyzing, and interpreting these structures must be identified and utilized. So, a phrase or word group has the kind of structure that must be described in terms of how the individual elements revolve around a central or head term. This kind of analysis is different from the kind of syntactical analysis that is necessary to describe a clause. Further, the relation of groups of clauses will be different than the description of an individual clause. At each rank, there will be various ways that elements are arranged, so that one can determine patterns of greater or lesser frequency. The architecture of a language entails that levels of language are formed by constituents that unite various smaller units together. Thus, at the level of the clause, one can speak ideationally of various agents involved in various processes, sometimes directed toward a person or thing and sometimes not, or interpersonally of the subject in relation to the predicator. How these actions are performed, how agency is expressed, and the relation of these events to reality are all elements that can be described at various levels.

Markedness and Prominence

Levels of language lead to the concept of markedness. "Markedness" is a term that began in phonology to describe the presence or absence of particular phonological features. It has been extended to entail a number of different means by which more or less significant elements may be identified. Sometimes these revolve around frequency of appearance, with significance determined in reverse proportion to frequency; other times they revolve around morphology; and still others revolve around complexity of concept. Related to markedness is the notion of prominence or salience. I think it is worth exploring how, at each level in a language, certain features are emphasized, whether that is by syntagmatic or paradigmatic means (i.e., ordering or substitution). One way of speaking of this is in terms of prominence or salience. Prominence is motivated markedness. That is, it involves marked features that are (by whatever means) shown to be motivated in a particular context, so that a given dimension of a text is brought to the fore.[16]

16. For discussion of the notions of markedness and prominence as well as further development, see S. E. Porter, "Prominence: A Theoretical Overview," in *The Linguist as Pedagogue: Trends in the Teaching and Linguistic Analysis of the Greek New Testament*, ed. S. E. Porter and M. B. O'Donnell, NTM 11 (Sheffield: Sheffield Phoenix Press, 2009), 45–74.

Sociolinguistics

A neglected area in much discourse analysis is the sociolinguistic dimension. Texts, as we know, are written by authors to readers. These authors and readers occupy particular sociological space, and hence in their writing and reading they are sensitive to social groups and social contexts. This is an element of discourse analysis that has not been given the kind of attention that it deserves, especially in New Testament studies.[17] The social status of the participants in a discourse helps to frame the nature of the discourse, and the dynamics of their interaction give insight into the meaning of the discourse. Similarly, when reading a Gospel, one ought to explore the various levels of social interaction within the Gospel narrative itself—for example, between Jesus and the Pharisees, or between Jesus and his disciples. When Jesus calls his disciples "friends" in John's Gospel, there is a shift in social expectations that affects the flow of the narrative. These kinds of relations are understudied because they are undertheorized in discourse analysis.

The Meaning of a Text

Another concept worth exploring is that of the meaning of a text. By this, I mean something different from the semantics of a text. The semantics are concerned with the various ways in which an element is shown to be meaningful (I have touched on only a few of them above). The meaning of a text, however, is something slightly different. The meaning of a text is what the text is about, or better, what is being said about what the text is "about." How exactly does one determine what a text is about? One straightforward way is to examine the words that are used, but this is easier said than done. There is no simple calculus by which one can take the different words and find out with what a text is concerned. A better way might be to explore the various semantic domains into which the words of a text fall. This will reveal broader areas of meaning, but it will also result in statements of meaning that are somewhat broad and that may not adequately capture the meaning of a specific text.[18] A still better approach might be to examine the syntactical patterns in which words or domains appear. For example, this might reveal how a particular discourse participant interacts with other participants or semantic domains.

17. See chap. 7.
18. See my essay, coauthored with M. B. O'Donnell, which attempts an analysis of this sort on the book of Romans: "Semantics and Patterns of Argumentation in the Book of Romans: Definitions, Proposals, Data and Experiments," in *Diglossia and Other Topics in New Testament Linguistics*, ed. S. E. Porter, JSNTSup 193, SNTG 6 (Sheffield: Sheffield Academic Press, 2000), 154–204.

Ultimately, we may need to realize that what a text is about is expressed in highly complex relations between its various linguistic elements and at a high level of abstraction from its linguistic substance.

Corpus Linguistics

A last concept that I wish to note is the importance of extending one's results beyond a single text. This hints at the possibilities of corpus linguistics. Corpus linguistics is less a method than it is a tool to aid in the kind of discourse analysis that I am describing. One way of establishing the meaning of a given linguistic element in a text is to see its importance in relation to similar or different phenomena in other texts. Corpus applications to ancient languages must be done differently than the kind of megacorpus building that is done with modern languages. With ancient languages, the available pool of texts is fixed and finite (and random), and rather than this being a liability, it must be incorporated into the corpus conception and building. As a result, a structured sample corpus provides the best possibilities. This corpus should contain a representative sample of texts and should thereby reproduce the broad cultural environment against which specific phenomena need to be examined.[19]

Conclusion

No doubt various practitioners of discourse analysis will complain that I have omitted or undervalued critical concepts, or at least concepts critical to them and their particular analytical approach. There is truth to this complaint, of course, since the field of discourse analysis is large and highly complex. Even with the confined interests of New Testament studies, there is more data available for analysis than one study can usually handle. Each practitioner of discourse analysis eventually focuses on particular concepts or linguistic elements that he or she finds important and useful. I have drawn from my own exploration of this topic in order to give a glimpse at what I have found helpful or frustrating or worth developing. I leave it to others to sort out the mess that I have created.

19. For a detailed description of how this might be accomplished, see M. B. O'Donnell, "Designing and Compiling a Register-Balanced Corpus of Hellenistic Greek for the Purpose of Linguistic Description and Investigation," in Porter, *Diglossia*, 255–97. See also O'Donnell, *Corpus Linguistics and the Greek of the New Testament*, NTM 6 (Sheffield: Sheffield Phoenix Press, 2005).

9

The Ideational Metafunction
and Register

Introduction

In a previous publication I have described register using J. C. Catford's distinction between language varieties. He distinguishes two types: varieties that are permanent and varieties that are transient. The permanent varieties include idiolect and dialect, varieties related to who a speaker is in terms of geography, time, social status, and individuality. The transient varieties vary according to changing situation; Catford calls them register, style, and mode.[1] I still think that this is a useful distinction to make, because it attempts to parse a complex interplay between features over which the individual language user has more or less control.

---

1. J. C. Catford, *A Linguistic Theory of Translation* (Oxford: Oxford University Press, 1965), 84–85. See S. E. Porter, "Dialect and Register in the Greek of the New Testament: Theory," in *Rethinking Contexts, Rereading Texts: Contributions from the Social Sciences to Biblical Interpretation*, ed. M. D. Carroll R., JSOTSup 299 (Sheffield: Sheffield Academic Press, 2000), 190–208, esp. 190. Compare C. D. Land, "Varieties of the Greek Language," in *The Language of the New Testament: Context, History, and Development*, ed. S. E. Porter and A. W. Pitts, ECHC 3, LBS 6 (Leiden: Brill, 2013), 243–60.

Having said that, over time I have become less and less satisfied with Catford's distinction: I believe that it attempts to bifurcate and parse categories that are not easily distinguished. There are two areas in which I believe that recent work in register studies has advanced understanding and should be taken into account more fully.[2] The first area is that of social context.[3] Register is an attempt to describe the components and realized metafunctions of what M. A. K. Halliday calls "variety according to use," and hence to describe the context of situation that circumscribes the environment in which an utterance is made.[4] The resultant analysis has placed high emphasis upon lexicogrammatical realizations. I argue that these are entirely appropriate within a systemic functional model that is attempting to describe an epigraphic language such as ancient Greek.[5] However, certain elements of social context that have linguistic bearing have not been taken fully into account. These include patterns of language use related to social status. Some recent attempts have been made to incorporate this into analysis, but these are only in their early stages.[6]

The second area is that of the relationship of genre to register. This is not a new dispute, but one that remains unresolved. Current scholarly positions are not quite legion, but nevertheless many.[7] Some equate genre and register,

2. M. A. K. Halliday has done more to develop and foster the notion of register than any other. See especially Halliday, *Learning How to Mean: Explorations in the Development of Language* (London: Edward Arnold, 1975), 125–33; Halliday, *Language as Social Semiotic: The Social Interpretation of Language and Meaning* (London: Edward Arnold, 1978); and Halliday's chapters in M. A. K. Halliday and R. Hasan, *Language, Context, and Text: Aspects of Language in a Social-Semiotic Perspective* (Geelong, Australia: Deakin University Press, 1985). For summary and critique, see R. de Beaugrande, "'Register' in Discourse Studies: A Concept in Search of a Theory," in *Register Analysis: Theory and Practice*, ed. M. Ghadessy (London: Pinter, 1993), 7–25, which notes (p. 14) that Halliday has backed away from the concept of register (see also other essays in Ghadessy's volume); A. Lukin et al., "Halliday's Model of Register Revisited and Explored," *LHS* 4 (2011): 187–213. Register in New Testament studies in recent years has been developed independently of Halliday and others in systemic functional linguistics.

3. See esp. H. Leckie-Tarry, *Language and Context: A Functional Linguistic Theory of Register*, ed. D. Birch (London: Pinter, 1995).

4. Halliday and Hasan, *Language, Context, and Text*, 41.

5. See N. J. C. Gotteri, "Toward a Systemic Approach to Tense and Aspect in Polish," in *Meaning and Form: Systemic Functional Interpretations*, ed. M. Berry et al., ADP 57 (Norwood, NJ: Ablex, 1996), 499–507, esp. 505–6, in what Gotteri rightly calls formal systemic-functional grammar.

6. See, e.g., S. E. Porter and M. B. O'Donnell, "Building and Examining Linguistic Phenomena in a Corpus of Representative Papyri," in *The Language of the Papyri*, ed. T. V. Evans and D. D. Obbink (Oxford: Oxford University Press, 2010), 287–311; S. E. Porter, "Buried Linguistic Treasure in the Babatha Archive," in *Proceedings of the 25th International Congress of Papyrology, Ann Arbor, July 29–August 4, 2007*, ed. T. Gagos, ASP Special Edition (Ann Arbor: Scholarly Publishing Office, The University of Michigan Library, 2010), 623–32.

7. See, e.g., Leckie-Tarry, *Language and Context*, 6–8. Other important discussions of register (and genre) include M. Gregory and S. Carroll, *Language and Situation: Language Varieties and*

treating both as configurations within the context of situation. Others distinguish between genre and register, placing register within the context of situation and genre within the context of culture. Still others identify completely different strata for each of them. Some distinguish register as broad or primary literary types (or genres), while reserving the term "genre" for more narrow or secondary literary types (or genres). Still others reverse this pattern and see register as specific unique manifestations of usage, while genre is reserved for the broader or macropatterns. Finally, some distinguish between the occasional nature of register and the socioinstitutionally fixed patterns of genre. There is also the issue of whether a given text, whether it is characterized by genre or register, constitutes a single instance or whether it can consist of multiple instances. I am inclined to think that the term "genre" should be jettisoned altogether: it carries far too much semantic freight to be useful. The term itself invokes far too many presupposed notions, many of them accumulated from ambiguous discussion in various literary circles. I would want to distinguish between register as local and particular typifications of linguistic usage that function within a context of situation, while reserving the term "textual type" for broader textual usage patterns that are recognized within a given context of culture, and may or may not have correlations with the kinds of socioculturally recognized literary forms (i.e., genres) institutionalized within a culture. This, however, is only a preliminary proposal and requires much more theorizing.

Within this context, my task here is to address the question of the ideational metafunction, which realizes the field component of register within the context of situation.[8] My previous discussion, while it may appear to be tangential, is in fact germane to my comments on the ideational metafunction.

Basic Concepts of the Ideational Metafunction

The ideational metafunction is the semantic realization of the field of a discourse.[9] As I have noted previously, the label "field of discourse" is probably the most easily understandable when compared to tenor and mode.[10] We are all familiar with "fields" of study, and that is generally what is meant by the

Their Social Contexts (London: Routledge & Kegan Paul, 1978), esp. 64–74; Ghadessy, *Register Analysis*; D. Biber and S. Conrad, *Register, Genre, and Style*, CTL (Cambridge: Cambridge University Press, 2009).

8. See Leckie-Tarry, *Language and Context*, 23–25.

9. For a fuller treatment, see M. A. K. Halliday and C. M. I. M. Matthiessen, *Construing Experience through Meaning: A Language-Based Approach to Cognition*, OLS (London: Continuum, 1999).

10. Porter, "Dialect and Register," 199.

field of a discourse. On the other hand, the field of discourse and the ideational metafunction have been the most difficult to define and exemplify in analysis. I think there are two reasons for this. The first is that more attention has been paid to defining the tenor and mode because they are inherently problematic. Tenor, originally called "style" by Halliday,[11] seems like a musical term related to pitch levels. However, it has probably the most narrowly defined semantic and formal features relating to social roles (including language as exchange), relationships, and statuses. Mode is probably the most easily definable and, in some ways, the most useful, because it is concerned with textual features and their organizational patterns, including thematization, cohesion, and information structure.

What exactly is the ideational metafunction concerned with? Whereas the notion of field may be relatively clear, the concept of the ideational semantic component is not, because it seems too inclusive. Virtually everything that is included within tenor and mode has metafunctional realizations that can in some way be seen as contributing something to discourse semantics. So these are ideational also, are they not? They are not, in terms of register analysis. Register analysis is concerned with identifying various components that are realized by specific metafunctions (semantic content), which are then in turn realized by means of variable formal linguistic features (lexicogrammar). The formal elements of the language may be classified formally, but their function identifies their semantics and hence the role they play within any given meta-function. Thus, the social status of a participant—such as Jesus, or a priest, or a Pharisee, or a diseased woman—is part of the interpersonal metafunction, while the participant per se is a component in the ideational metafunction.

Here I treat at least four major dimensions of the ideational metafunction.[12]

Subject Matter

I use the phrase "subject matter" to describe what a discourse is about.[13] This notion has been referred to in various ways. Expressions such as "extralinguistic entities" and "intralinguistic entities" have been used. Helen Leckie-Tarry has recently employed the terms "arena/activities."[14] The two sets of terms

11. M. A. K. Halliday, A. MacIntosh, and P. Strevens, *The Linguistic Sciences and Language Teaching*, LLL (London: Longmans, 1964), 90. Unfortunately, the term "style" has proved to be even more problematic than "tenor."
12. Besides the works of Halliday and others noted above, see Porter, "Dialect and Register," 206–7.
13. Halliday has also used this phrase (see *Language as Social Semiotic*, 142–43).
14. Leckie-Tarry, *Language and Context*, 36.

reveal something of the complexity of the ideational metafunction. The terminology of extralinguistic and intralinguistic entities divides around formal linguistic elements. Extralinguistic entities may or may not have a relationship to language. They would include entities for which language may only play a subordinate or minor role. On the other hand, intralinguistic entities are those that have their existence only through language. In this sense, language is the determining feature to create a fundamental distinction between entities. There is strength in this analysis in that the focus is upon language, and this is, after all, a linguistic model. However, as has been noted, this bifurcation around language can be criticized because it fails to reflect a more fundamental relationship of language and society, or language and culture. Leckie-Tarry adopts the terms "arena/activities" because of the societal dimension. She says that they refer "particularly to the locations of the interaction, both in terms of their inherent features, and in terms of the social institutions which determine them."[15] She goes further and says that arena/activities are what she calls "the most basic element of context," and play "the most critical role in the specification of register."[16] Then she exemplifies this in terms of how invoking a particular arena or activity invokes the appropriate social institution as well.

This differentiation raises important questions for those pursuing register analysis in New Testament studies. There has been a spate of recent work on social institutional issues in New Testament studies. Some of these are confined to social description, and others are social-theory driven.[17] It would seem that Leckie-Tarry's suggestion has potential for this discussion in New Testament studies since the various subject matters that might be invoked in a discourse are all socially located, and since social location carries with it a number of features that will often be important within a discourse (I will return to the issue of schemas below). A classic example, perhaps, is the parable of the Pharisee and tax collector (Luke 18:9–14), where there was the probable presumption in ancient times that the Pharisee was the righteous person, and the tax collector the one unacceptable to God. The impact of the parable is made through Jesus's indicating that it was the tax collector who was forgiven, not the Pharisee, thus playing on the social location and status of these particular social positions. However, one of the shortcomings of social-theory driven biblical analysis has been the tendency to invoke the theory without necessary regard for what can be supported from the available ancient evidence. The language-based criterion should not be too easily

15. Ibid.
16. Ibid.
17. See chap. 6 in the present volume.

abandoned. There is therefore a place for a distinction between entities that are intralinguistically invoked and those that are extralinguistically invoked. Returning to the parable of the Pharisee and the tax collector, I notice that the telling of the parable itself both sets up the expectation and thwarts it in the way the two characters are introduced. The parable does not simply rely upon a presupposed pool of characteristics of each, but iterates them in how the two approach and stand. Thus the reversal at the end is anticipated by the parable itself—that is, by the language of the parable.

I suggest that the notion of subject be retained as a very broad one. It would include subjects that are extralinguistic, but that are linguistically invoked in the text. This would include entities that are grammaticalized within the text. Extralinguistic elements have existence without language, but only have existence in the particular text as they are referenced by the language user. What are invoked by the reference are the element and any other sense connotations that can be supported by that particular text and its cotext. Also to be included are intralinguistic entities. These do not refer to extratextual elements, but are invoked within a denotative world of sense relations. Within the text itself, both extralinguistic and intralinguistic elements will have social location. Some of these will be located within the world outside of the text, with pertinent elements of this world invoked linguistically; others will be located only within the world inside of the discourse, but they too will have relative social location within the terms of the discourse.

Semantic Domains

The field of discourse is explicitly related to semantic domains (realized by lexical items). In earlier writing I referred to the lexicon as the way in which the experiential semantic component of the field of discourse was expressed.[18] The lexicon is the most delicate level of structure, I believe, within the systemic-functional network. Leckie-Tarry refines this description by including semantic domains within the field of discourse.[19] I believe that this is a useful refinement, because not only is the lexicon invoked in that individual lexical items are paradigmatically selected to fill the elements of the grammar, but also these lexical items are selected according to their more abstract domains of meaning. In this sense, the subject of the discourse is a complex (and not

18. Porter, "Dialect and Register," 207.
19. Leckie-Tarry, *Language and Context*, 37. Semantic domains have long been important for R. Hasan (see "The Grammarian's Dream: Lexis as Most Delicate Grammar," in *New Developments in Systemic Linguistics*, vol. 1, *Theory and Description*, ed. M. A. K. Halliday and R. P. Fawcett [London: Pinter, 1987], 184–211). See also, in the present volume, chap. 3.

self-evident) extrapolation from the various semantic domains. The most frequent semantic domain in the book of Romans is domain 33 in the Louw-Nida lexicon, "Communication."[20] However, this being the most frequent domain does not mean that "communication" is the subject of the discourse (letter), apart from saying that Paul clearly uses words concerning communication, and hence communication may be one of the assumed purposes of the discourse.

Leckie-Tarry realizes that the invoked subject has a large effect on setting the parameters of the semantic domain, but that the semantic domains will increase specificity of the subject. Leckie-Tarry does not seem to acknowledge several factors, however. One is that the subject and the semantic domain have a tentative relationship to each other. Another is that more than a single semantic domain may be utilized within a given discourse or episode within a discourse, and that these semantic domains may function on different discourse levels. She does recognize that a semantic domain may have a bearing on tenor and mode, but she seems to think that these are on a local level (e.g., semantic chains, etc.). I think that the distinction is a metafunctional one; that is, the given linguistic element functions (or means) according to its metafunctional use.

Participants/Actors

The notion of participants in a discourse is problematic because of the apparent overlap with the tenor of discourse. I believe that it is worthwhile, however, to specify who these participants are, because of what they bring to the ideational metafunction. The ideational metafunction is not concerned with the discourse-immanent social relations of the participants—that is, with how they are specified in terms of their activity within the discourse. The ideational metafunction is concerned with who the participants are and what characteristics and qualities they bring to a discourse.[21] There are two types of characteristics that they bring, and these are similar to the intralinguistic and extralinguistic features noted above with regard to subject matter. The two types are overt and inferred characteristics. Overt characteristics include things such as gender, position, title, race, class, age, education, and occupation. Inferred characteristics include the kind of social, cultural, and related knowledge that a participant might bring. The parable of the Pharisee and tax collector well illustrates the ideational and interpersonal metafunctions.

---

20. J. P. Louw and E. A. Nida, *Greek-English Lexicon of the New Testament Based on Semantic Domains*, 2 vols. (New York: United Bible Societies, 1988).
21. See Leckie-Tarry, *Language and Context*, 36–37.

We have knowledge of Pharisees and tax collectors from our knowledge of the lexical stock of the language (ideational component), but the position of forgiveness and hence elevation of the tax collector is conveyed by the discourse (interpersonal component).

Transitivity Network

The notion of the transitivity network and the role that it plays in the ideational metafunction is one of the most important that Halliday has contributed, even though it is also one of the most problematic and is far from being fully realized in register analyses (e.g., Leckie-Tarry seems to eliminate it entirely from her analysis).[22] The three components above—subject matter, semantic domains, and participants—constitute the basic semantic material of the ideational metafunction. What the author is saying about these semantic components is expressed through the transitivity network. Through the transitivity network, an author linguistically invokes participants and subject matter through lexical choices and grammatically expresses some perspective on the subject matter. Transitivity as a system functions at the clause level, since it is at the clause level that the various components of transitivity are realized.

Perhaps one of the major difficulties in dealing with transitivity is that it is sometimes unclear how clausal components relate to transitivity as an element of the ideational metafunction. In most treatments of transitivity, transitivity realizes the field of discourse, and essentially it is a treatment of agency and process types,[23] even if it has clear relationships with elements otherwise included in other components of the context of situation and their metafunctions, such as interpersonal (tenor) and textual (mode). This can be particularly problematic for analysis of Greek, in which the verbal tense-form encodes so much information, including aspect, attitude, and causality, realized by the tense-form, mood-form, and voice-form. However, one must remember that the structure in which something is realized (whether this is morphological or syntactical, or both, depending upon the feature and the language) has nothing to do with the systemic location of that feature. Even

22. The best study from a systemic functional linguistic standpoint in New Testament studies is G. Martín-Asensio, *Transitivity-Based Foregrounding in the Acts of the Apostles: A Functional-Grammatical Approach to the Lukan Perspective*, JSNTSup 202, SNTG 8 (Sheffield: Sheffield Academic Press, 2000).

23. For example, S. Eggins, *An Introduction to Systemic Functional Linguistics* (London: Pinter, 1994), 220–70. Compare M. A. K. Halliday, "The Functional Basis of Language," in *Class, Codes and Control*, vol. 2, *Applied Studies towards a Sociology of Language*, ed. B. Bernstein (London: Routledge & Kegan Paul, 1973), 343–66, with a very helpful chart on p. 360. For New Testament Greek, see Martín-Asensio, *Transitivity-Based Foregrounding*, 36.

though these semantic features are encoded in the verbal forms, they realize elements of two different metafunctions: ideational for the first two and interpersonal for the third. Attitude, realized by mood-form of the verb, is not ideational but interpersonal, as it semantically realizes the participants' view not of the process but of the relation of the process to reality.[24] Those elements of transitivity that are included within the ideational metafunction include (besides process types and participant roles) verbal aspect, which indicates the user's perspective on how an action takes place (realized by tense-forms); causality, which indicates the nature and type of cause of the action (realized by the voice system); and, at the clausal syntax level, agency, which indicates those entities involved in causality (agents, patients, etc.).

Strengths and Possibilities of the Ideational Metafunction

There are a number of strengths of a register analysis—that is, the effort to linguistically characterize a text as prototypically representing a particular register of discourse, and more specifically understanding the semantics of the ideational metafunction as realization of the field of discourse within a context of situation. The single most important benefit of a register analysis is seen in its application to an epigraphic language such as ancient Greek. Since the data for analysis cannot be improved upon by the intuitions of native informants, linguistic analysis must be confined to data drawn from the limited range of texts at hand. Therefore, any linguistic model that can mine limited data for maximal results will have an advantage over other models. Such a model is found in systemic functional linguistics (SFL) in general and register analysis in particular. As noted above, register analysis, at least as I conceive of it, prioritizes the close relationship of function and form. In other words, functional distinctions (the metafunctions) are realized in formal distinctions (the lexicogrammar), and formal distinctions are expressions of functional ones. This allows for non-intuition-based semantic distinctions, but it also emphasizes that this is a formally based analytic. Meaningful networks of systemic semantic choices are predicated upon the ability to realize formally based choices. However, the finite number of formal choices may be analyzed in various ways. The elements that function within a transitivity pattern (e.g., agent realized by a noun group) may also function in the textual metafunction as a thematized element. The participants of a discourse will also have various

---

24. See S. E. Porter, *Verbal Aspect in the Greek of the New Testament, with Reference to Tense and Mood*, SBG 1 (New York: Peter Lang, 1989), 163–67, esp. 165.

levels of participant engagement within the discourse and thus contribute to the interpersonal function.

The ideational metafunction also has, I am coming to realize, a relationship to other more psycholinguistically oriented analysis. The early origins of register analysis—long before Halliday was on the scene—included the recognition that what we now call the various metafunctions are related to the ways in which we as human language users process information. This is a further reason for the realization that, with register analysis, finite data can be used for recursive analysis, when it is filtered through various mental filters. Early models of what later came to be characterized as the metafunctions spoke about language as being expressive, as making appeals, and as creating representations, and also noted that all three of these elements function simultaneously but in different ways.[25] The representative is equivalent to the ideational, and the expressive and appeal are equivalent to the interpersonal, leaving a need for Halliday to develop the textual.[26] Nevertheless, this model of expression, appeal, and representation grew out of a psycholinguistic framework of conception, in which the speaker, hearer, and object are interrelated through psycholinguistic processing.

Some recent discussion of register has introduced the notion of schemata, from cognitive linguistics, into the equation.[27] Within an SFL framework, Leckie-Tarry describes schemata as "internal cognitive information derived from specific contexts" that "may be activated and used."[28] She sees schemata as functioning to link the context of situation with the context of culture, in the sense that the schema is the link that joins the specific data of a context of situation and correlates it in a contributory or corrective way with schemata that are part of the context of culture as larger systems of expectations, knowledge, and the like. I do not think that Leckie-Tarry needs to give the schemata such independent existence that verges upon a separate stratum (of context?). I am also not sure where such a level of schemata would exist within a register system. Are schemata another stratum or type of substratum? If they are, then the question of how they connect with context of situation and context of culture has not been answered. If they are not, then they appear to be either a part of context of situation or context of culture.

25. Note Karl Bühler's communication model that I apply in chap. 17, on Pauline opponents.
26. This, at least, is how Halliday describes things in *Language as Social Semiotic*, 48, 50. One might instead conceive of the expressive as textual.
27. On the field of cognitive linguistics, within which schemata (also known as scenarios, scripts, etc.) are found, see W. Croft and D. A. Cruse, *Cognitive Linguistics*, CTL (Cambridge: Cambridge University Press, 2004).
28. Leckie-Tarry, *Language and Context*, 22–23.

They probably cannot be part of context of situation, because, as I noted above, context of situation is a broad descriptor that includes the potential situations of which a register is a particular and specific type, characterized by the accumulation of distinct linguistic features that identify a particular linguistically mediated context for a given discourse. These schemata could be part of the context of culture, but the context of culture is a broad and inclusive construct that, whatever its sociolinguistic reality, is invoked and accessed through language.

I believe that schemata are better identified as a part of the ideational metafunction in the following way, which I believe is consonant with SFL.[29] Ideational knowledge is perhaps retained and organized by means of schemata. The language user has ideational knowledge that is identified, organized, and accessed schematically and then lexicogrammatically instantiated in the discourse. Sometimes the schemata are simply invoked unmodified, but in some instances they are modified because of the particular context of situation, and this modification is then linguistically indicated by means of various lexicogrammatical choices. A schema thus organizes social, cultural, and related information within a given discourse, modified as indicated by the other semantic features of the ideational metafunction.

Challenges and Limitations of the Ideational Metafunction

The challenges and limitations of the ideational metafunction are also to be noted. In the sense that the opportunities above are not realized, they will constitute limitations on the development of the ideational metafunction. Here I specifically include the interplay with psycholinguistics and schemata. Some of the challenges and limitations that others have identified include the social positioning element, the relation of written and spoken language, clarification of such subcategories as experiential and logical subcomponents of the ideational metafunction,[30] and rhetoric. I wish to emphasize several other challenges and limitations of the ideational metafunction that I believe are worth noting but that have not been satisfactorily resolved.

The first is the relationship between the subcomponents of the ideational metafunction, in particular how the various semantic domains are created and then related to and used to establish the subject matter of the discourse. As

29. See ibid., 23.
30. Halliday and others have had a continuing ambiguous relationship to the experiential and logical metafunctions within (or apart from?) the ideational metafunction.

fine a tool as Louw-Nida's semantic-domain lexicon is—and I do not wish
to detract from it—there are problems in assessing how the various domains
are established and distinguished, and how they are populated. There is the
further issue of how words mean. Elsewhere I have explored the question of
how it is that words mean, and whether they are monosemous or polysemous,
and how one differentiates these.[31] In one sense, this is a question that needs
to be answered before one can go about creating a lexicon of words. Nevertheless, assuming that such a question can be answered (and I am inclined
to think that it can, and the answer is not that words only mean in context,
which is to say that they are only and entirely socially constructed ad hoc
in a given instance of use), then one can go about establishing a lexicon.
The semantic-domain lexicon that I envision would have explicit criteria for
identifying modulations of the broad sense of a lexeme (e.g., collocation),
in order to categorize them consistently. It is here that the issue of the link
between semantic domains and subject matter emerges. There is no easy
way to determine how many tokens of a given type are needed to establish a
pattern, and thus less certainty when it comes to tokens of a given semantic
domain. With a large number of semantic domains, increased difficulties
are created.[32]

The second challenge is the role of transitivity in a discourse model. Halliday's efforts with transitivity, though fundamental and important, are confined
to the level of the clause. The clause has so far proved to be an insuperable
barrier in linguistic analysis, even for SFL in many ways (apart from discussion
of the textual metafunction, in particular, cohesion).[33] Many linguistic models
have not even reached the level of the clause yet, so in that sense we should
be pleased that SFL has attained this peak, even if it is only an intermediate
one. However, full-fledged discourse models must go beyond the clause. Some
linguists have attempted to do so by creating supersentential models, but these

31. For further explication of this point in terms of the monosemy-polysemy distinction,
see chap. 3 in the present volume; also S. E. Porter, "Greek Linguistics and Lexicography," in
*Understanding the Times: New Testament Studies in the 21st Century; Essays in Honor of D. A.
Carson on the Occasion of His 65th Birthday*, ed. A. J. Köstenberger and R. W. Yarbrough
(Wheaton, IL: Crossway, 2011), 19–61; Porter, "Matthew and Mark: The Contribution of Recent
Linguistic Thought," in *Mark and Matthew: Comparative Readings*, part 1, *Understanding the
Earliest Gospels in Their First-Century Settings*, ed. E.-M. Becker and A. Runesson, WUNT
271 (Tübingen: Mohr Siebeck, 2011), 97–119; G. P. Fewster, *Creation Language in Romans 8:
A Study in Monosemy*, LBS 8 (Leiden: Brill, 2013), 18–48.

32. See, again, chap. 3 in the present volume.

33. See even M. A. K. Halliday, *An Introduction to Functional Grammar* (London: Edward
Arnold, 1985), and its successive editions up to the fourth (*Halliday's Introduction to Functional
Grammar*, rev. C. M. I. M. Matthiessen [London: Routledge, 2014]), where movement "beyond
the clause" consists almost exclusively of discussion of cohesion.

have yet to prove reliable, especially as many of them seem to be top-down models rather than bottom-up. Nevertheless, one of the areas of challenge, especially for a register model that is discourse oriented, is to develop a framework that exploits transitivity at a larger-than-clause level, including clause complexes and beyond.

A third challenge is how notions such as logical ordering, sometimes apparently referred to as rhetoric, enter into a register model.[34] Halliday sometimes places the logical subcomponent within the ideational metafunction,[35] but other times within the textual metafunction[36] (although he tries to be clear on why he does this, the result is some confusion over the notions). Others have placed what has been called rhetoric in the interpersonal component, no doubt because of its relation to persuasion and the role that participants and their linguistic relations play in that function (the interpersonal metafunction is concerned with clause as exchange).[37] The term "rhetoric" is problematic for a number of reasons, not least because of the somewhat recent revival of classical rhetoric within contemporary studies, including those of the New Testament. Certainly the categories of ancient rhetoric are not what are being discussed here. Rather, what is being discussed is the kind of logical ordering that would be found in, for example, the arrangement of parts of an ancient letter, or the formal structure that can be determined in a narrative work, such as a gospel. This is not to be confused with literary type or literary form (mentioned above), which are either individual literary and linguistically based units, or entire structures—although logic is a part of how they are arranged. The logical component is also not the kind of pure logic that Halliday seems to envision when he identifies various logical relations, although there is some relation here as well.[38] I am identifying a component in which the elements of the text, whether it follows a particular literary type or form or not, are seen to be organically related, without imposing an abstract logical notion on them. I believe that this element needs to be incorporated in register analysis, and that it probably fits best in the ideational component, because it has to do with how a subject is arranged for communicative content purposes, not just to create a text, as it would in the textual component.

34. See J. L. Kinneavy, *A Theory of Discourse: The Aims of Discourse* (New York: Norton, 1971).
35. For example, Halliday, "Functional Basis of Language," 106.
36. Halliday, *Language as Social Semiotic*, 223; and Halliday in Halliday and Hasan, *Language, Context, and Text*, 121.
37. See Porter, "Dialect and Register," 203–4.
38. See Halliday, *Language as Social Semiotic*, 128–33.

Conclusion

The ideational metafunction within the larger notion of register analysis provides an important component to textual analysis. Recent work on register
has helped us to refine the categories further from where they were in earlier
discussions. What is needed now, I believe, is more widespread application of
register analysis to a wide range of texts. Such analyses no doubt will help us
to refine the elements of the various discourse components. However, the major
goal is to be able to say something about the characteristics of the context of
situation that is typified by a particular register.

10

Time and Aspect
in New Testament Greek

A Response to K. L. McKay

Introduction

I consider it a singular honor that Kenneth McKay (1922–2009) saw fit to devote an entire article published in *Novum Testamentum*[1] to responding to my major monograph on verbal aspect.[2] This was at least the third major response to my work,[3] for which I was indeed grateful, since all of these were

1. K. L. McKay, "Time and Aspect in New Testament Greek," *NovT* 34 (1992): 209–28.
2. S. E. Porter, *Verbal Aspect in the Greek of the New Testament, with Reference to Tense and Mood*, SBG 1 (New York: Peter Lang, 1989). This monograph provides detailed study of much more than verbal aspect, including major work on the mood/attitude system of Greek, the issue of Semitisms, multilingualism, sociolinguistics, conditional statements, and periphrastic constructions, among others.
3. The others may be found in an extensive review by J. Mateos in *FN* 4 (1991): 73–76, and a symposium sponsored by the Consultation on Biblical Greek Language and Linguistics at the Society of Biblical Literature annual meeting in Kansas City in November 1991. This extended discussion also involved review of the volume by B. M. Fanning, *Verbal Aspect in New Testament Greek*, OTM (Oxford: Clarendon, 1990). Our work was assessed by D. D.

quite useful in furthering my thinking about the topic of verbal aspect, tense, and time.[4] I was forced to reexamine my assumptions and my application of my theory to the Greek language, in particular that of the New Testament. I was also able to see an adoption of some of my terminology and perspective in the work of others.[5] The publication of my *Idioms of the Greek New Testament*,[6] which, not unexpectedly, makes use of the theory developed in

Schmidt and by M. Silva, whose reviews appeared in *Journal of Biblical Literature* (111 [1992]: 714–18) and *Westminster Theological Journal* (54 [1992]: 179–83), respectively. The papers that Fanning and I presented and the responses by Schmidt and Silva are published as part 1 in S. E. Porter and D. A. Carson, eds., *Biblical Greek Language and Linguistics: Open Questions in Current Research*, JSNTSup 80 (Sheffield: JSOT Press, 1993). Other, later monographs have also given extended treatment to my work.

4. An exception in this regard is the "response" by C. C. Caragounis (*The Development of Greek and the New Testament: Morphology, Syntax, Phonology, and Textual Transmission*, WUNT 167 [Tübingen: Mohr Siebeck, 2004; repr., Grand Rapids: Baker Academic, 2007], esp. 316–36) to the work of McKay and Fanning and especially to my work, which does not merit extended consideration (neither of the others has responded either). The book is a highly questionable exposition of the apparent assumption that Greek can be understood only by Greeks (who understood everything about their language anyway), and it decries alternative explanations of the language and its linguistic development. This seemingly is an example of what fellow Greek Christophoros Charalambakis labels "linguistic chauvinism" ("Modern Greek Archaisms Reconsidered," in *For Particular Reasons: Studies in Honour of Jerker Blomqvist*, ed. A. Piltz et al. [Lund: Nordic Academic Press, 2003], 71–84, esp. 82n12). Caragounis's unlinguistic treatment (in fact, a dismissal of linguistics) includes numerous problems of understanding, and what comes across as a didactic style by one who knows best. One example of misunderstanding must stand for the whole. Caragounis chastises me for stating, "Most credit for making grammarians aware of the issues of verbal kind of action goes to Curtius, who was the first to attempt a reconciliation of comparative linguistics and Greek philology" (Porter, *Verbal Aspect*, 26, referring to G. Curtius, *Elucidations of the Student's Greek Grammar*, trans. E. Abbott, 2nd ed. [London: John Murray, 1875], a translation of Curtius's *Griechische Schulgrammatik* [1852]) (Caragounis cites pp. 26–29, not the exact page number of my quotation). He states that I seem "to believe that before Curtius, Greeks had no idea of aspect!" (*Development of Greek*, 323). Even a casual reading of my statement indicates no such thing. However, that I am not too far off in my estimation of Georg Curtius's role within scholarly discussion, contrary to Caragounis, is indicated by the comments in the concluding essay of a book edited by Caragounis on A. N. Jannaris, who held to some views similar to those of Caragounis and tended to compare ancient with modern Greek synchronically. Fellow Greek scholar Georgios Giannakis states, "From the area of grammar another similar example [regarding historical explanation] concerns the notion of verbal aspect, which was a well established category for the verbal system of Greek since Curtius' treatment of it already in 1852 and subsequently" ("Can a Historical Greek Grammar Be Written?—An Appraisal of A. N. Jannaris' Work," in *Greek, a Language in Evolution: Essays in Honour of Antonios N. Jannaris*, ed. C. C. Caragounis [Hildesheim: Georg Olms, 2010], 304) (on Jannaris's supposed mistake regarding the relation of the perfect and aorist tense-forms on the basis of his synchronic view, see 304–5).

5. See, among many others, D. A. Carson, *The Gospel according to John*, PilNTC (Grand Rapids: Eerdmans, 1991); M. A. Seifrid, *Justification by Faith: The Origin and Development of a Central Pauline Theme*, NovTSup 68 (Leiden: Brill, 1992), 226–44, on Romans 7:7–25. Many later commentaries, as well as other works, have utilized my research.

6. Now in its second edition. See S. E. Porter, *Idioms of the Greek New Testament*, 2nd ed., BLG 2 (Sheffield: Sheffield Academic Press, 1994), 20–49, and passim.

my *Verbal Aspect in the Greek of the New Testament*, has enabled even more widespread adoption. In spite of my reexamination, and even after so much time, there are several points made in McKay's article that are still worth engaging, since I think that at times he has misrepresented my views and made some arguments about verbal aspect that lack consistency with his own previously articulated theories. After briefly outlining my own perspectives on Greek verbal aspect, I will engage some of these issues.

The Greek Verbal System

My hypothesis can be stated simply, although the monograph attempts at great length and in significant detail to defend the positions taken. I believe that, rather than indicating absolute (past, present, future) temporal distinctions, the so-called verbal tense-forms in Greek grammaticalize the author's reasoned subjective choice of how to conceive of a process or event. There are three verbal aspects, morphologically correlated in a direct way with the three major tense-forms: the perfective (aorist), imperfective (present/imperfect), and stative (perfect/pluperfect) aspects.[7] I argue that verbal aspect is the essential semantic component of tense-form usage in Greek, rather than absolute tense, and that this is true in both the indicative and the nonindicative moods. Consequently, I am primarily concerned with describing one element of the linguistic code (system) of the Greek language—the semantics of the verbal system—that enables the aspects to be used in a variety of functional discourse situations.

To establish the validity of my thesis, I turn to two primary streams of evidence. The first is the abundant evidence in the grammarians themselves, in the recognizable and widespread instances of verbal usage that simply do not conform to their expected categories (e.g., present tense-forms used in past contexts, such as the historic [or perhaps better, narrative] present), and also in their formulation of a theory of verbal structure. The second is a linguistic approach to the Greek language that attempts to identify rigorous criteria by which to find, assess, and interpret the evidence. As a result, I rely upon a theory of contrastive substitution to establish that the difference among uses of the tense-forms of Greek is one not of absolute temporal

---

7. For a defense of my understanding of the stative aspect, see S. E. Porter, "Greek Linguistics and Lexicography," in *Understanding the Times: New Testament Studies in the 21st Century; Essays in Honor of D. A. Carson on the Occasion of His 65th Birthday*, ed. A. J. Köstenberger and R. W. Yarbrough (Wheaton, IL: Crossway, 2011), 19–61, esp. 46–54. See also chap. 12 in the present volume.

reference but rather of verbal aspect.[8] To aid in distinguishing these verbal aspects, I introduce four distinct though related formulations, including a series of verbal oppositions (well known from modern linguistic theory), a visualization (first used in discussion of Slavonic languages, also aspectually based, but here applied for the first time to the Greek tense system), planes of discourse (invoking categories from discourse analysis), and a systemic display (using systemic functional linguistics).[9] The systemic network is the heart of my analysis, since it attempts to provide a calculus for determining the relative semantic weight of the verbal aspects, but in coordination with the Greek mood system as well.[10] The relative semantic weight of the aspects is determined by the accumulation of semantic features as one appreciates the various choices that must be made in selecting one verbal form over another, not upon some abstract translational equivalent. I do not know of any other treatment that attempts such a thorough and rigorous analysis for the verbal structure of the Greek of the New Testament, including the work of McKay.

The response to my analysis that Greek does not grammaticalize absolute tense has ranged from endorsement[11] to calling this into question,[12] although

8. Contrastive substitution, whether explicitly called this or not, is widely used in linguistic writing to illustrate the differences between instances, by the alteration of one variable within the expression. In this case, I varied verbal tense-forms to illustrate their contrastive semantics.

9. The only major change that I would make to this presentation is to make clear that these four conceptualizations span from an isolated system up to the discourse function of the aspects, and probably would be better presented in those terms.

10. This network is further developed in S. E. Porter and M. B. O'Donnell, "The Greek Verbal Network Viewed from a Probabilistic Standpoint: An Exercise in Hallidayan Linguistics," *FN* 14 (2001): 3–41, where the virtual independence of the Greek verbal aspect system from the other Greek verbal systems is demonstrated.

11. See, e.g., the review by F. Gignac in *Catholic Biblical Quarterly* (54 [1992]: 366–67); and R. J. Decker, *Temporal Deixis of the Greek Verb in the Gospel of Mark with Reference to Verbal Aspect*, SBG 10 (New York: Peter Lang, 2001).

12. Schmidt, in his review of my book, seems to believe that he has made an argument against my position with reference to my supposed "complete disregard of a morphologically distinct feature, such as the augment" (*JBL* 111 [1992]: 717). Apparently, Schmidt did not read my treatment of the augment (labeled "The Augment") in *Verbal Aspect*, 208–9. After a survey of scholarly opinion, which varies from seeing the augment as a reality indicator, to originally a scansional feature in poetry (some scholars who argue for the temporal use of the verb tense-forms still reject the augment as a temporal indicator), I quote McKay's reasonable conclusion: "It is quite clear that by the classical period it was simply a formal feature of the imperfect, aorist and pluperfect indicative. By the Hellenistic period it was so devoid of special significance that it ceased to be attached to the pluperfect, and in later centuries it disappeared altogether except when accented" (*Greek Grammar for Students: A Concise Grammar of Classical Attic with Special Reference to Aspect in the Verb* [Canberra: Australian National University, 1974], 223). See further chap. 11 in the present volume, where I also deal with the matter of the augment and temporality, as well as other arguments against my position.

none, to my satisfaction, has marshaled a convincing argument against it.[13] The primary reason for this, I believe, is that the ground of my support relies not only on my analysis from a thoroughgoing linguistic perspective, but also on my ability to successfully categorize the range of usage recognized by previous Greek grammarians. It must be clarified, however, that to state that Greek does not grammaticalize absolute temporal reference with its verb tense-forms says nothing about the ability of users of the Greek language to refer to past, present, and future time, or other dimensions of time. In fact, I go further than most traditional grammarians and utilize omnitemporal (gnomic) and timeless reference as appropriate categories to discuss meanings of larger units, such as clauses within discourses. When speakers wish to make such temporal distinctions, they have a variety of means by which these may be specified, including various deictic indicators such as discourse types themselves.[14] The result is that there are a number of predictable patterns of verbal usage—for example, the aorist tense-form in past-time contexts such as narrative and the present tense-form in present time contexts, although these are legitimate implicatures of the verbal aspects determined within cotext on the basis of the narrative or descriptive discourse rather than on the basis of the simple use of a particular verb form.

Points of Contact between Porter and McKay

McKay and I therefore agree on a large number of grammatical formulations, including that of our essential perspective. McKay begins his article in this way: "If it is true, as now appears to be certainly the case, that the inflexions of the ancient Greek verb signal aspect (as well as voice and mood) but not

13. Including S. E. Runge, "Contrastive Substitution and the Greek Verb: Reassessing Porter's Argument," *NovT* 56 (2014): 154–73. Runge seems to be confused about a number of issues that require further discussion elsewhere. Nevertheless, these include the nature of linguistic inquiry, the limitations of linguistic typology, the functions of contrastive substitution, the place and role of linguistic modeling, the problems of assuming one's conclusion, the difference between grammatical aspect and procedural aspect (*Aktionsart*), and possibly other issues. I do not recognize many characteristics of linguistics and its procedures in Runge's depiction, nor do I understand what appears to be his high personal investment in what is simply a matter of academic disagreement. Many of my subsequent comments on McKay apply to Runge as well.

14. My explicit reference to discourse deixis (Porter, *Verbal Aspect*, 101–2) and my use of this category throughout my work, especially in my explication of conditional statements, make it very difficult to understand Schmidt's statement that my treatment of conditional statements diverts focus from the topic of aspect (*JBL* 111 [1992]: 716), especially since he then states that "future discussion of verbal aspect will need to demonstrate greater sensitivity to narrative grammar" (p. 717).

time . . ."[15] It will become clear to readers of my *Verbal Aspect in the Greek of the New Testament* that I am in fact deeply indebted to the seminal work that McKay has done in the area of verbal aspect. Not only do I devote several pages to responding to his work, but also I cite him extensively throughout the monograph. In my discussion I note several things worth repeating about his analysis of verbal aspect, found mainly in his grammar, but reflected also in his several articles. First, he recognizes the difference between *Aktionsart* as a lexical distinction and verbal aspect as a category "by which the author (or speaker) shows how he views each event or activity in relation to its context,"[16] clearly emphasizing the importance of the "subjective attitude of the speaker or writer" in selection of verbal aspect.[17] Not all grammarians have been as careful to make this distinction, which McKay and I believe is so fundamental.[18] Second, he specifies four aspects: the imperfective (present and imperfect forms) for an activity in process, the aorist for expressing a "whole action or simple event," the perfect for "the state consequent upon an action," and the future for "expressing intention."[19] Though he is not consistent in his own work (see below), McKay assumes four verbal aspects, although in actual fact he treats three when he comes to analyzing texts. Third, he uses time distinctions for divisions beneath the classifications of aspect. Fourth, we agree on the significance of verbal aspect in catenative constructions—that is, the aspect of both the finite verb and infinitive.[20] In *Verbal Aspect in the Greek of the New Testament*, I briefly offer several points of criticism of McKay's work, which I want to expand upon briefly here and which will become of even more relevance below.

First, McKay assumes but does not justify or argue for his theory, in particular his renaming of the verbal aspect grammaticalized by the present and imperfect forms as imperfective while maintaining the names of the other tenses. For example, in the article to which I am responding, he states that he continues "to use the terminology" of his previous work, kept mostly "for convenience."[21] This reveals a fundamental flaw in McKay's own analysis, a flaw that has further ramifications for his analysis of the Greek language and of my work. The flaw is the classic one of failing to distinguish between a grammatical

15. McKay, "Time and Aspect," 209.

16. McKay, *Greek Grammar*, 136.

17. Ibid., 137.

18. See, e.g., N. Turner, *A Grammar of New Testament Greek*, vol. 3, *Syntax* (Edinburgh: T&T Clark, 1963), 59; Fanning, *Verbal Aspect*, in his approach to grammatical aspect and lexical aspect or *Aktionsart*.

19. McKay, *Greek Grammar*, 136.

20. McKay, "Time and Aspect," 216n15.

21. Ibid., 211n4.

form and its meaning. (I am quite surprised to find that convenience is used as any kind of criterion for determining essential terminology in this endeavor.) Unfortunately, as even McKay's article to which I am responding seems to do, having stated his theory, McKay abandons his theoretical structure for a treatment of the Greek language that is based upon typical uses. This is a common problem in investigating tense-form distinctions in languages, since the names for tense categories often are based only on typical functions of the tense-forms concerned, and do not capture the full range of functions that a given category may express. Hence there is pressure to defend the traditional category, often for no apparently good reason.

Second, McKay introduces a lexical distinction between action and stative verbs that not only is of dubious value for Greek, but also is based upon English conceptions (to say nothing of requiring differentiation on the basis of various criteria, including use beyond the word).

Third, McKay cannot find a way to abandon the traditional categories of description, which leads to contradiction. On the one hand, he wants the aorist to be a specific aspect describing an event as pure and undefined, but then says that the action may be momentary, prolonged, and so on.

Fourth, his definition of the aspects and his use of them are inconsistent. McKay says that the future expresses intention while also indicating that it refers to futurity. He is even more inconsistent in his article when he states that rather than my definition of the future as grammaticalizing the semantic feature or meaning of [+expectation], he prefers "an explanation which recognizes that the range of future forms approximates most closely to those of the three obvious aspects."[22] McKay seems to lump together the future form and various periphrases, is confusing semantics and pragmatics, or what the form itself means and what it means in context, and has abandoned his own definition of the future as expressing intention (intention is not the definition of any of his other verbal aspects).

The confusion of form and function is seen very clearly in McKay's response to my classification of conditional statements. In response to several previously offered schemes that work more by impressionistic criteria regarding time of occurrence, I attempt to invoke more rigid formal criteria. One example of this is with regard to the unreal conditional (second-class conditional).[23] I classify examples with the aorist or imperfect, even with the negative μή, as instances of the first-class conditional when they do not include all of the formal elements necessary to make a given sentence a clear instance of the second-class

22. Ibid., 215n41.
23. See ibid., 214–15.

conditional, in particular lack of ἄν in the apodosis. McKay objects to this on two different grounds. The first is my use of the translation appropriate for the first-class conditional when translating such an instance, which seems to me to be perfectly reasonable in the light of the criteria I have established. The second is his appeal to knowledge of the circumstances that warrant the translation as an unreal conditional. McKay has again failed to get beyond translation or to deal directly with what I state. My treatment of the second-class conditional emphasizes the necessity of appealing in the first instance not to what the interpreter may or may not know of the truthfulness or falsity of the claim being made, but rather to the form of the conditional itself. In other words, the second-class conditional is to be viewed as a nonfactive put in the form of a contrafactive.

As a result of his analysis of Greek verb structure, despite the problems noted above, McKay is able to give insight into several traditionally troublesome Greek phenomena, such as the distinction between the aorist and the imperfect, the lack of temporal significance of the aorist participle, the aspectual character of the so-called historic present, and the gnomic and present-time uses of the aorist tense. It is not surprising, therefore, that McKay states that I have encouraged him by my more thorough demonstration of truths that he already pointed to,[24] even hinting that he probably agrees in more instances than he disagrees.

In particular, he accepts my account of the narrative or historic present as "an eminently reasonable summary culminating in a conclusion broad enough to acknowledge the problems while offering the most likely line for their solution."[25] In fact, my discussion and explanation of the historic present is based upon and an expansion of McKay's own explanation.[26] This expansion specifying the use of the historic present to mark significant events, however, is not to be minimized, but is an important part of my theory that goes beyond McKay (see below).

Although he disagrees with several of the examples that I cite in defense of the imperfect tense-form as grammaticalizing the semantic feature of remoteness, McKay is in fundamental agreement with the category itself, it being one that he himself has proposed. For example, regarding 2 Corinthians 11:1, he apparently agrees that this is an example indicating the remote use of the imperfective aspect, but he disagrees with the translation I provide, suggesting an alternative.[27]

24. Ibid., 210.
25. Ibid., 212.
26. See ibid., 193–98.
27. Ibid., 213.

McKay also accepts "the possibility of the aorist tense being used with present or future time reference,"[28] although he does not think that it occurs as much in the New Testament as I think it does. We do agree, however, that the use of the aorist indicative ἔγνων in Luke 16:4 indicates present time in context. McKay further states, "In past narrative the tenses predominantly used are obviously the imperfect and the aorist, the latter being the unmarked (less significant) one, used where there is no reason to use something else,"[29] a point with which I not only concur but also find making use of my own language to describe the phenomenon (I arrive at this conclusion since McKay rejects the language of marking in his grammar).[30] Regarding non-past-time contexts, one of the examples that I cite of the timeless use of the aorist, Matthew 13:44, is described by McKay as "undoubtedly" the case.[31]

It is no surprise, therefore, that at several points McKay's summary and conclusion reflect not only my theoretical perspective on Greek verbal structure, but also language very similar to my own. For example, he acknowledges that "time can be implied in NT Greek even though the verb forms do not in themselves signify time."[32] I prefer to reverse the phrases, beginning with the fact that verb forms do not grammaticalize objective temporal reference and then moving to the realization that, as part of larger constructions (clause and above), they can be used in definable temporal contexts, since, as stated above, my purpose is primarily to define the semantic structure of the Greek verbal system rather than the variety of functions that the form can carry out as parts of larger linguistic units. I do in fact recognize that the verb tense-forms can be used in contexts that do indicate temporal reference, if not by means of or for the verb forms but for the propositions in which they are found.[33] McKay further clarifies that "time is not morphologically expressed, but is determined by context."[34] He goes on to specify various deictic indicators, including discourse and temporal indicators,[35] which categories I first introduced into the discussion.[36] In fact, it looks as if McKay and I share a

28. Ibid., 218.

29. Ibid., 221.

30. McKay, *Greek Grammar*, 137. Here, McKay uses Plato, *Phaedrus* 246–256, in almost the same way I do. I point out the perfects, the aorists, and so on. I even make the distinction regarding being outside the narrative flow (but on p. 242, not p. 241 as McKay cites).

31. McKay, "Time and Aspect," 223.

32. Ibid., 225.

33. Porter, *Verbal Aspect*, 82.

34. McKay, "Time and Aspect," 226. Compare C. Breytenbach, "Abgeschlossenes Imperfect? Eine notwendig gewordene Anmerkungen zum Gebrauch des griechischen Imperfekts in neutestamentlichen Briefen," *TLZ* 118 (1993): 85–91.

35. McKay, "Time and Aspect," 226–27.

36. Porter, *Verbal Aspect*, 101–2.

similar essential perspective regarding the structure or, as I prefer, code of the Greek language and its verbal system. We agree that the morphologically based verb tense-forms grammaticalize not objective tense, but rather verbal aspect. His major problem with my work seems to be with my treatment of particular instances rather than with my theoretical model.

Yet there is much more in McKay's article that I find disappointing. My reservations with his critique of my work extend beyond simply disputing a number of Greek examples, many of which have been disputed in various ways and in various guises by biblical scholars and grammarians for generations. If it were only a matter of disputing a number of examples, I would not be writing this rejoinder. But I believe that McKay's article leaves a wrong impression in the minds of some readers who have not taken the time or effort to read my (admittedly big) monograph. First, I believe that McKay has misread me at several points. Second, I believe that he has taken me grossly out of context on more than one occasion. Third, I believe that he has shown a failure to apply his own method rigorously enough. Fourth, I believe that his exposition of several texts is open to serious question. I will deal directly with the first three points, while making the fourth point along the way.

McKay begins his article with a discussion of translation.[37] I agree that those translating from Greek, a language in which the "verb signal[s] aspect but not time,"[38] into a "modern time-based language such as English will find passages in which it is difficult to be sure what time referencing in the modern version will most faithfully represent the intention of the ancient writer."[39] Furthermore, "there are many passages in which the time reference is not overtly indicated,"[40] and new principles for determining temporal reference must be found. These statements would be particularly germane if my work were designed as a guide to translation of Greek into English, or even if I placed any reasonably high emphasis upon this. Much of McKay's criticism of my work can be reduced to a difference of opinion regarding transla-tion. Elsewhere McKay complains that "there are many clumsy translations in the book," in which some of them seem "to be a more or less word for word translation."[41] In fact, here is what I actually say about this matter of translation:

37. Compare G. J. Swart, "Non-past Referring Imperfects in the New Testament: A Test Case for an Anti-anti-anti-Porter Position," *HvTSt* 61 (2005): 1085–99, which essentially compares translations.
38. McKay, "Time and Aspect," 209.
39. Ibid.
40. Ibid.
41. Ibid., 211n3.

Producing translations is not to be seen as the sole purpose of studying a language. Exploiting the translational value of ancient texts has long been an item of high priority for scholars; . . . the ability or lack of ability to translate a given linguistic item into another language, or even into a concise description in a metalanguage, must be viewed with appropriate skepticism. . . . Most examples within this work are translated, but the purposes of the translations vary from being literalistic renderings to interpretative glosses, depending upon the particular point being made, and they are not to be used to evaluate the particular concept being discussed.[42]

Unfortunately, this is the very thing that McKay repeatedly does. He has clearly failed to grasp one of the major points of how my work is structured.

Much of his critique of my work may well be very useful if one were trying to apply it to problems of translation, but with respect to what the work is trying to accomplish, his critique misses the mark widely. As an example, in his discussion of the imperfect, as stated above, McKay agrees that it grammaticalizes the sense of remoteness, but he claims to disagree with the examples that I cite to illustrate the point. It must not be overlooked that McKay and I, regardless of what specific examples we find convincing at this point, agree that the imperfect grammaticalizes remoteness, and that other grammarians should not attempt to use our dispute of examples as an argument against the agreed-upon concept. But to be fair to what I do say, what I state is that there are examples that do not follow the time-based conception of the imperfect; in other words, that it is past in reference.[43] The glosses that I provide attempt to show that. For example, McKay and I simply disagree over John 11:8: νῦν ἐζήτουν σε λιθάσαι οἱ Ἰουδαῖοι. He contends that a better rendering is that the Jews "were just now seeking" to stone Jesus, since in 10:31–41 they were seeking him. I contend that in the discourse context—which, I repeat, underlies my analysis throughout *Verbal Aspect in the Greek of the New Testament*—this verse clearly indicates not only that the Jews had been seeking to kill Jesus (10:31–41), but also that they were presently in that kind of attitude (see 11:45–57); hence arises the disciples' question of Jesus's wisdom in returning to Judea. McKay's translation seems highly unlikely, since the earlier attempts to kill Jesus had ended in 10:40, with several events intervening. "Just now" as a rendering of νῦν to describe this chain of events seems forced, but McKay is forced into it by his understanding of νῦν, not of verbal aspect. I contend that my explanation is better because it includes the past as well as the action in progress mentioned further in 11:45–57. What in the

42. Porter, *Verbal Aspect*, 16.
43. Ibid., 210.

first instance I was attempting to do was give an example that departed from the strictly past-referring use of the imperfect, and I believe I effectively did that. Furthermore, McKay disputes my translations (again, not necessarily my understandings) of Acts 25:22; Philemon 13; Romans 9:3; Galatians 4:20; and 2 Corinthians 10:11. For each of them, he suggests a different translation but one that retains essentially the same temporal reference that I argue for, non-past. Since my point was in the first instance to dispute the past-referring use of the imperfect, McKay has simply made my point again for me, and for this I am grateful.

McKay also criticizes me for using the gloss "might" instead of "may" to render the subjunctive. In keeping with what I state above, my intention was to provide a useful and consistent indicator in the translation, especially for those with little or no Greek, not to produce the most elegant English rendering. It seems to me that substitution of "may" for "might" is not a great help in McKay's view of how translation is to be used. It may be beside the point, but several contemporary English translations use "might" as a rendering of the Greek subjunctive, including the New Internation Version at Ephesians 2:7, for example. Besides, quibbling over these two renderings of the subjunctive, when I go to significant efforts to make clear how I perceive the difference between the subjunctive and the optative in relation to the indicative, seems to me to be an exegesis of the difference between the two English words, having little to do with understanding Greek. To illustrate further that my translations or glosses were designed for a different purpose than for teaching the language, my *Idioms of the Greek New Testament*, which had gone to the printer before McKay's article appeared, does in fact use several translations very similar to those he uses in his article, as well as using other words than simply "might" for the subjunctive.[44]

Not only does McKay fail to understand what my work is about, but also he takes several of my discussions completely out of context. In assessing my citation of Romans 11:7 in my discussion of the narrative or historic present, although McKay acknowledges that the citation is found in parentheses, he interprets it to mean that this instance is simply an example used to show the subjective choice of the author to use the present tense-form with past reference. Then at some length he debates the possible understandings of this verse and comes up with a different translation, but one that is essentially past in reference in English, as is my gloss.[45] If he had read the entire context in

44. See Porter, *Idioms*, 56–59.
45. My translation was not meant to be a question, or it would have had a question mark with it.

which this passage is cited in parentheses, McKay would have seen that in fact the several pages in which this passage is found are concerned neither with how to render the historic present nor with defining it in terms of simply the author's subjective choice (both of which McKay concentrates upon), but rather with how the historic present can be used at various places where the author wishes to draw attention to an event. In fact, McKay's argument for the significance of this passage in Paul's argument provides further proof for the very point I was making in its citation.

Third, McKay reveals himself to be keenly traditional in his analysis, almost as if his theoretical position exists only in the abstract. For example, in commending my work in theoretical linguistics, he states that he is "concerned that theory can sometimes lose sight of fact."[46] This statement is telling in what it reveals. It seems to imply that there are two categories of things: (1) theories that exist independent of data and (2) facts that exist independent of theory. I do not mean to engage in a philosophical discussion at this point, except to say that it seems rather naive—especially since McKay knows the history of discussion of Greek grammar and has presented his own revisionary work in verbal aspect—to claim that there are such things as facts apart from a theory to explain them. It seems to me that what we have is simply raw data that must be organized by some sort of theory before it becomes fact. What we are discussing is whose theory better describes the data so that it can be used as factual material. As we have seen above, McKay agrees with my theory (which is quite similar to his), yet he pulls back at the point where he contends that the facts are not consistent. I maintain that he ought to be consistent with his own theory or reexamine some of his supposed facts. Many examples could be cited at this point, including his appeal to the aorist participle in Luke 6:49 and Matthew 13:18 to indicate a change to past reference (he himself argues elsewhere that the participle does not grammaticalize time).[47] Regarding the use of ἐξέστη in Mark 3:21, McKay's explanation obscures the point. I translate the aorist verb as "is out of his mind" to capture that this exclamation is seen to be contemporary with the narrative thread. McKay recognizes that the "aspectual force is that of complete action or event," but then he draws an unwarranted conclusion, "so that the time reference is logically past."[48] In what sense this is logically past on the basis of the aspectual force of the aorist verb escapes me. This example seems very much to be the same as the example of Luke 16:4, which McKay grants is a "genuine present use" of an aorist verb.

46. McKay, "Time and Aspect," 210.
47. Ibid., 222.
48. Ibid., 219.

An excellent illustration of McKay's confusion between code or system and text is his attempt at a more plausible explanation of Matthew 23:23. McKay concedes that there is a long list of woes against the scribes and Pharisees in Matthew 23:13–31, "in which their faults are described uniformly with timeless (or omnitemporal) present tenses to indicate their habitual activities, with the single exception of the aorist ἀφήκατε . . . in verse 23."[49] He further grants that "this sudden introduction of complete action could be simply a means of emphasis (you completely set aside), with the habitual notion continuing by implication from the preceding context, and one might argue that as it turns to a general summary of many of the criticisms already made, this is natural."[50] I would argue for this kind of explanation. But McKay is not content with this explanation. He speculates further that "the logic of the reference amounts to pointing out that as their regular activities (apart from tithing) are so much at variance with the spirit of the law they must in fact have abandoned it long since."[51] Does this not sound more than a little implausible, or at the least expecting a bit much from the Greek speaker and reader? McKay continues, "It is probably true that an ancient Greek speaker would not be fully conscious of the time element of this logic, but it is quite likely that he would not be so oblivious of it that he could not recognize it if questioned about the precise significance of his statement."[52] It is clear that only one who begins with a model that posits a time-based conception of the Greek tense-forms (and who perhaps has some capacity for channeling denied to other grammarians) could arrive at such an implausible and forced explanation. If one begins with a timeless conception of the tense-forms, this passage is much more plausibly explained, without forcing the evidence beyond recognition. But McKay even here is driven by his, in my estimation, unwarranted concern for translation: "But there can be no doubt that the person translating into English . . . should deduce this effect."[53] I contend that it is better to

49. Ibid., 215.
50. Ibid. Compare McKay's comments on omnitemporal and habitual clauses in "Aspectual Usage in Timeless Contexts in Ancient Greek," in *In the Footsteps of Raphael Kühner: Proceedings of the International Colloquium in Commemoration of the 150th Anniversary of the Publication of Raphael Kühner's Ausführliche Grammatik der griechischen Sprache, II. Theil: Syntaxe, Amsterdam, 1986,* ed. A. Rijksbaron, H. A. Mulder, and G. C. Wakker (Amsterdam: Gieben, 1988), 193–208, which appear to diverge from his 1992 article reviewed here. Interestingly, several of the ancient references he cites are identical. In fact, the concepts of timelessness and habituality themselves are at odds, if verbal aspect is a grammatical category used without temporal significance.
51. McKay, "Time and Aspect," 215.
52. Ibid.
53. Ibid.

ensure that one's estimation of Greek is not dictated by one's translational concerns, as McKay's apparently is.

In the same sentence McKay further claims that his exposition of Greek is "less confusing to the person who learns Greek mainly to understand the text of the NT"[54] than is my exposition. First, I find it debatable whether a system so at odds with itself regarding such fundamental notions as theory and facts can reasonably be called "less confusing," much less to the learner of Greek whom McKay has in mind. Second, the response to my *Idioms of the Greek New Testament* has indicated that my system is proving to be less than confusing to students. Third, one cannot help but ask whether what McKay and I are doing is simply designed to help learners of Greek by providing the most facile method. I would like to think that we are engaged in a project that includes this as one of its goals yet is much larger than this, including gaining a better understanding of various dialects of Greek, the nature of the Greek language, and possibly of language itself. If this material becomes difficult, and if it is left to others to "translate" it for the uninitiated, then that will be one of the conclusions.

Finally, it is clear from how McKay treats certain examples that one must be careful when invoking the concept of context. Context is a necessary concept in interpretation, but one that must be rigorously defined or at least utilized in a consistent way. To illustrate the pitfalls of the concept of context, I notice that for McKay, context appears in many instances to be something that confirms his time-based functional evaluation of the tense-forms. As we have seen above, these are not always the most plausible or self-evident understandings of context. In other instances, McKay invokes the concept of the lexical meaning of the word as a part of the context, in particular the distinction between action and stative verbs, and as relating in some way to aspect. However, he goes on to make the following distinction, which radically undermines what he has just said: he refers to "a lexical distinction in verb types which is analogous to aspect, and which causes some variations in the translatable effects of the grammatical aspects,"[55] but he also suggests that "it is nearer Aktionsart."[56] First, he states that it is analogous to aspect, which seems to me to indicate that it is in some way parallel though not the same thing. Second, he says that it causes some variations in the translatable effects, which says nothing of its effect on verbal aspect itself or how it is understood. Third, he admits that it is nearer to *Aktionsart*, a category that he himself distinguishes from

---

54. Ibid., 210.
55. McKay, *Greek Grammar*, 137
56. McKay, "Time and Aspect," 216n16.

aspect. Context cannot be the sole provider of meaning, however, or nothing means anything (I note, as I have above, that *Aktionsart* as lexical aspect is undermined by necessary analysis at the clausal level and beyond, which seems to be referred to often as context). To have meaning, appeal must be made to something outside context (or within context), which I argue is verbal aspect.

Conclusion

McKay's work in verbal aspect has made important headway in the study of the Greek verbal system. It is not, however, without faults, as his review of my work well illustrates. There are several points at which McKay's theoretical framework is not applied consistently, and many of the critiques raised against my own work reflect these problems. To quote McKay, in the light of the comparisons articulated in this essay, I maintain that my system of verbal structure best satisfies the requirements of a satisfactory analysis: "The test of any hypothesis therefore is not that it resolves all doubts but that it offers the most consistent explanation, leaving few anomalies."[57]

57. McKay, *Greek Grammar*, 214.

11

Three Arguments regarding Aspect and Temporality

A Response to Buist Fanning, with an Excursus on Aspectually Vague Verbs

Introduction

In a paper published in the Festschrift for Stephen Levinsohn,[1] Buist Fanning indicates that he believes "there are still no satisfying answers to objections that have been raised against the non-temporal [i.e., Stanley Porter's] view" of the Greek verbal system.[2] These three objections are "the augment as a past

---

1. B. M. Fanning, "Greek Presents, Imperfects, and Aorists in the Synoptic Gospels," in *Discourse Studies and Biblical Interpretation: A Festschrift in Honor of Stephen H. Levinsohn*, ed. S. E. Runge (Bellingham, WA: Logos Bible Software, 2011), 157–90. His paper was first delivered at a conference in New Orleans in 2009, and I responded to it orally during a question time. I note that Fanning appears to have recrafted his objections in significant ways from his oral presentation in New Orleans.

2. Ibid., 163. He is referring, of course, to the position put forward by, among others and in varying ways and to differing degrees, S. E. Porter, *Verbal Aspect in the Greek of the New Testament, with Reference to Tense and Mood*, SBG 1 (New York: Peter Lang, 1989); K. L. McKay, *A New Syntax of the Verb in New Testament Greek: An Aspectual Approach*, SBG 5

time indicator," "the imperfect in relation to the present" tense-form, and use of "performative or 'instantaneous' presents."[3] In this chapter I will examine these three objections in some detail. Whereas Fanning states that he believes there are no satisfying answers to these objections, I believe that he is clearly wrong, that good answers have already been offered for these objections, but that perhaps he has not been fully aware of them or has not been willing to accept the force of their argument.

The Greek Augment and Time

Fanning cites Trevor Evans's "treatment" of the augment as the basis for his objecting to the nontemporal view that the augment is not a past-time indicator in Greek, the view that I hold, as will be made clear below. Let us examine Evans's treatment to see if there is force to his objection.[4]

There are essentially three parts to Evans's discussion of the "significance of the augment." The first is a section of unfortunate hyperbole, where he characterizes my treatment by using unnecessarily pejorative language.[5] The one important feature of this section is his clear misunderstanding of the form-function correlation. He wishes, as might be expected, to connect the augment to indexing of past time, and he seems to indicate that I, because I do not take it as a past-time indicator, simply disregard it. On this point, he is wrong;

(New York: Peter Lang, 1994); R. J. Decker, *Temporal Deixis of the Greek Verb in the Gospel of Mark with Reference to Verbal Aspect*, SBG 10 (New York: Peter Lang, 2001); and, to a certain degree (although see below), C. R. Campbell, *Verbal Aspect, the Indicative Mood, and Narrative: Soundings in the Greek of the New Testament*, SBG 13 (New York: Peter Lang, 2007). See now also D. L. Mathewson, *Verbal Aspect in the Book of Revelation: The Function of Greek Verb Tenses in John's Apocalypse*, LBS 4 (Leiden: Brill, 2010). Fanning is opposed to such a position.

3. Fanning, "Greek Presents," 163. Fanning has a section (pp. 159–63) that reflects what appears to be an attempt to salvage the vestiges of his temporal view of Greek tense-forms. At the end, he admits to the subjective nature of verbal aspect (as well as mood, etc.), and then wishes for what he calls "tense" (I think he means temporal reference) to be seen as subjective as well. That is no doubt correct, but the attempt to equate tense-form usage with absolute placement along a temporal line (though of course inherently subjective, according to the position of the speaker) is an unconvincing means to find absolute time.

4. T. V. Evans, *Verbal Syntax in the Greek Pentateuch: Natural Greek Usage and Hebrew Interference* (Oxford: Oxford University Press, 2001), 45–50. I must confess that I have found this section very unclear as to what exactly Evans is trying to say and what he is trying to fight against and assert. After reading it several times, I believe that, in fact, he may actually be proving my case for me.

5. Ibid., 45, where he refers to my treatment (Porter, *Verbal Aspect*, 208–9) with terms such as "glaring weakness," "superficial treatment," "surprisingly brief," offering only a "token alternative." On whether these are fair characterizations, see below. See also W. V. Cirafesi, *Verbal Aspect in Synoptic Parallels: On the Method and Meaning of Divergent Tense-Form Usage in the Synoptic Passion Narratives*, LBS 7 (Leiden: Brill, 2013): 33–36.

I take the augment, in agreement with K. L. McKay, as a formal marker of certain types of indicative forms, in particular the aorist, imperfect, and pluperfect.[6] Evans's second section is a comparative philological and diachronic treatment, beginning with the assumption that the augment was originally an "independent particle" that was then prefixed to "'past' tenses of the indicative"[7] (Evans is unclear whether the augment made these tenses past-referring or whether they were already so; his theory only works if they are the former). According to Evans, the augment became fixed in Classical Greek, but then through grammaticalization and morphological reduction was removed in numerous instances in post-Classical Greek. In the third section Evans turns to function, where his explanation becomes muddled and contradictory.[8]

Evans begins with the assumption of the augment as a past-time temporal indicator attached to certain indicative verbal forms that, he also seems to assume, have past-time reference. The circularity of this argument is noteworthy[9] and does not support the case for the augment as temporal, but merely assumes it. In any case, as Evans further states, even when the augment loses its "original function"[10] (or rather, assumed function), the temporal reference of augmented (or formerly augmented) forms is retained, as the verbal endings now indicate this. Perhaps I have missed something important here, but it appears that Evans is unclear regarding what he is asserting about the augment. He seems to want to make an argument for the traditional view that the augment is a past-time indicator. However, he never actually does this in his history of discussion. He instead makes the assumption that the augment indicates past time, but then says that it becomes attached to particular forms and then is lost in post-Classical Greek. I note that, whatever he may be saying regarding its earlier meaning or function, in post-Classical Greek, as the results of grammaticalization (semantic reduction) and morphological

6. See S. E. Porter, *Idioms of the Greek New Testament*, 2nd ed., BLG 2 (Sheffield: Sheffield Academic Press, 1994), 35, where I more specifically refer to the augment's origins as an adverb used in certain narrative contexts. Upon further reflection, I believe that it is quite possibly a discourse marker that Greeks attached to certain forms to indicate a type of discourse, especially event sequential discourse, such as narrative. This merits further exploration. See note 12 of chap. 10.

7. Evans, *Verbal Syntax*, 45.

8. I think that Evans uses the terms "grammaticalized" and "grammaticalization" in potentially confusing ways. Grammaticalization is the process by which various linguistic elements change in their functions. For a helpful introduction to this concept, see P. J. Hopper and E. C. Traugott, *Grammaticalization*, CTL (Cambridge: Cambridge University Press, 1993). "Grammaticalized" indicates the realization of semantic meaning in grammatical form.

9. The circularity of this argument has been pointed out before, especially by Decker, *Temporal Deixis*, 39; Campbell, *Verbal Aspect*, 88.

10. Evans, *Verbal Syntax*, 47.

reduction, the augment does not indicate past-time reference. Apart from his apparent (though poorly supported or argued) assumption regarding the augment, which I believe is unwarranted,[11] I do not think that I disagree with his conclusion regarding it not indicating past-time reference—excluding the fact that I do not believe that the verbal endings convey temporal reference either. In that sense, I am not sure what it is that Evans is disagreeing with me about, since both of us apparently think that the augment was not a temporal indicator in New Testament Greek.

Nevertheless, Evans continues by saying that this, meaning his position, "is obviously unacceptable" to me.[12] Evans states that I do draw attention to dissenting voices regarding the augment,[13] but that I rely for my argument primarily upon a treatment by J. A. J. Drewitt.[14] Drewitt argues that the augment is "purely scansional" and not temporal in Homer, on the basis of distribution

11. Campbell (*Verbal Aspect*, 88) also thinks that Evans simply makes the assumption (along with others) that the augment indicates past time. However, Campbell accepts Evans's other arguments regarding the historical development of the augment and his critique of J. A. J. Drewitt (which, as I point out, do not support the arguments that they are purported to defend). Then, in a very unconvincing instance of unlinguistic thought, after criticizing Evans, Campbell simply states the following: "If, however, the theory that the augment is an indicator of past time is based on an assumption, then another theory based on a different assumption may be equally valid. As McKay suggested long ago, it is here proposed that the augment is an indicator of remoteness rather than past time" (p. 90). McKay's reference is not an argument, but a question he raises ("The Use of the Ancient Greek Perfect Down to the Second Century AD," *BICS* 12 [1965]: 19n22). Campbell does not make an argument, but only an assumption, based upon a question. For an argument, such as it is, see Campbell, *Verbal Aspect*, 48–52.

12. Evans, *Verbal Syntax*, 47. I note that, in defense of the traditional view that the augment is a past-time indicator, Evans cites as examples K. Brugmann and B. Delbrück, *Grundriss der vergleichenden Grammatik der indogermanischen Sprachen*, 2nd ed., 5 parts in 9 vols. (Strasburg: Trübner, 1897–1916; repr., Berlin: de Gruyter, 1967), 2.3/1:10–11; P. Chantraine, *Grammaire homérique*, 2 vols., CPC 1/4 (Paris: Klincksieck, 1958–63), 1:479; B. Comrie, *Tense*, CTL (Cambridge: Cambridge University Press, 1985), 103; Fanning, *Verbal Aspect*, 15–16n26 (a much shorter discussion than mine); Ö. Dahl, *Tense and Aspect Systems* (Oxford: Blackwell, 1985), 83. I note that one source is a comparative grammar, two are general linguistic treatments, one is an incidental treatment within a treatment of New Testament Greek, and only one an actual grammar of Greek. This is hardly overwhelming evidence. Admittedly, Evans cites others in his comparative survey, but these above are the ones he cites as examples in defense of his point.

13. J. Wackernagel, *Vorlesungen über Syntax mit besonderer Berücksichtigung von Griechisch, Lateinisch und Deutsch*, 2 vols. (Basel: Birkhäuser, 1926–28); ET, *Lectures on Syntax with Special Reference to Greek, Latin, and Germanic*, trans. D. Langslow (Oxford: Oxford University Press, 2009), 1:181 (ET, 233); E. Schwyzer, *Griechische Grammatik auf der Grundlage von Karl Brugmanns "Griechischer Grammatik,"* 4 vols., HA 2/1 (Munich: Beck, 1939–71), 2:285 (Evans also includes Schwyzer, *Griechische Grammatik*, 1:652). See Evans, *Verbal Syntax*, 47–48n151. He does not mention P. Friedrich, "On Aspect Theory and Homeric Aspect," *IJAL* Memoir 28, 40 (1974): S1–S44.

14. J. A. J. Drewitt, "The Augment in Homer," *CQ* 6 (1912): 44–59, 104–20. Evans does not note, nor does he cite anywhere else, A. Platt, "The Augment in Homer," *JPhil* 19 (1891): 211–37, which I also cite, and which also argues that the augment is not a time indicator.

of the augment as found in the aorist tense-form, which includes its regular use in similes and gnomic use (non-past use) and its relative lack of appearance in iterative usage and in the narrative proper. This distribution applies also to speeches. Thus, Drewitt concludes, "It is not the augment that creates or emphasizes the past meaning in any tense."[15] What are Evans's arguments against Drewitt? There is only one, and it will strike many as special pleading, besides perhaps being inaccurate. Evans claims that the "twentieth-century revolution in Homeric studies has undermined the value of Drewitt's study, essentially a synchronic analysis. . . . The mixed nature of Homeric language provides no reliable evidence for the diachronic development."[16]

There are three fatal problems here. The first is that, whereas Evans may be concerned with diachronic development of Greek and convinced that so-called earliest or original use is determinative for later use, he is misguided regarding Homeric Greek. The issue is not diachronic development, but rather the use and function of the augment, which Drewitt has shown is not temporal already by the time of Homeric use, regardless of what it was before. Further, Evans himself agrees that, whatever the origins of the augment, by the time of post-Classical Greek it cannot be counted upon to indicate past time (see the discussion above), so in that sense his argument is wasted. The second major problem is that Drewitt's study is about the function of the augment, not the diachronic history of Greek. We are concerned with how the augment, whatever its comparative philological relations, functions in Greek, whether in Homer or later. Within Homer as an author, the augment does not indicate past time (as Evans's tacit admission indicates in his appeal to diachronic over synchronic evidence). The augment, by the time of Homer, was not used to indicate past time, a situation that further erodes (by Evans's own formulation) in the postclassical situation.

The third major problem is that Evans is distorting twentieth-century Homer studies and their influence upon the discussion of the augment. Homer scholars recognize the peculiar nature of Homeric Greek as reflecting a variety of historical and dialectal factors,[17] but they generally do not take the Analytic (i.e., form-critical or diachronic) view that Evans seems to endorse, and more particularly, they recognize the influence of Homer's language being oral poetry, with its fixed formulas and other oral features, and how that has shaped the

15. Drewitt, "Augment," 44. Interestingly, Evans (*Verbal Syntax*, 48n154) seems to try to chastise me for not pursuing Drewitt's idea that the augment originally was a "present" indicator. The fact is that I do mention it (Porter, *Verbal Aspect*, 209), but this would further argue against Evans's own position.

16. Evans, *Verbal Syntax*, 48.

17. This can be seen in virtually every introduction to Homer and his language. See, e.g., J. Griffin, ed., *Homer: Iliad, Book Nine* (Oxford: Clarendon, 1995), 28–45.

development and form of the text.[18] More recent work in Homeric scholarship has gone even further to analyze the epic poems narratologically, a form of synchronic rather than diachronic criticism.[19] Evans may be right that Homer does not give evidence of diachronic development (by which I mean what preceded Homer), but the clear patterns that Drewitt has observed and that go beyond the kind of heterogeneity that Evans notes remain, and in that sense Drewitt does indeed "disprove standard interpretation of the augment,"[20] at least for Homer (Evans himself has, perhaps unwittingly, shown this for post-Classical Greek in his discussion of its supposed semantic and morphological erosion).

More can be said, however, regarding Evans's facile dismissal of Drewitt. In an essay published in 2001 on the augment, Egbert Bakker provides an interesting survey of work on the Greek augment, a study that bears further examination.[21] Bakker first clarifies that Pierre Chantraine, though associated with the view that the augment indicates past time, saw the augment as doing so "more clearly" than forms that do not have the augment.[22] This was meant to deal with the particular situation of the difference between narrative and speech. The augment in Homer is more frequent in speech than in narrative. In this sense, in narrative, the augment is not a past-time indicator, as that is indicated by context, but rather is an emphatic marker, whereas in speeches it may be a time indicator to emphasize or even establish past reference.[23] As Bakker points out, however, the "sense of pastness . . . is by no means self-evident" for the augment.[24] Bakker cites several works on the augment that illustrate this point. These include A. Platt, for whom the augment functions like reduplication and hence is non-past in sense, and Drewitt, who sees the augment as a particle or interjection, and possibly indicating connection with the present. Despite Evans's dismissal of Drewitt's work (and complete lack

18. See, e.g., A. B. Lord, *The Singer of Tales* (New York: Atheneum, 1968), especially part 1; G. S. Kirk, *The Songs of Homer* (Cambridge: Cambridge University Press, 1962).

19. See, e.g., S. Richardson, *The Homeric Narrator* (Nashville: Vanderbilt University Press, 1990).

20. Evans, *Verbal Syntax*, 49.

21. E. J. Bakker, "Similes, Augment, and the Language of Immediacy," in *Speaking Volumes: Orality and Literacy in the Greek and Roman World*, ed. J. Watson, Mnemosyne 218 (Leiden: Brill, 2001), 1–23. I note that Bakker states (contrary to Evans) that it is "my conviction that the common conception of diachronic layering in Homer needs rethinking in light of our changing ideas on language and performance" (p. 1).

22. Bakker cites Chantraine, *Grammaire homérique*, 1:479.

23. Bakker, "Similes," 3. Bakker notes, however, that on speeches Chantraine follows D. B. Monro, *A Grammar of the Homeric Dialect*, 2nd ed. (Oxford: Clarendon, 1891), 62, but that Monro in an appendix (p. 402) follows the findings of Platt, "Augment in Homer," which is contrary to Chantraine's perspective.

24. Bakker, "Similes," 3.

of knowledge of Platt), Bakker states that "the statistical tendencies on which Platt's and Drewitt's account is based require careful interpretation in light of the various factors involved. . . . Yet the tendencies are sufficiently strong to merit more attention than they have received thus far."[25]

Bakker finds a way forward in the research of Louis Basset, in which he invokes work by Émile Benveniste distinguishing between *histoire* as objective narrative (referencing the past) and *discours* as subjective discourse (referencing the present).[26] Basset links the augmentless verbs with *histoire* (and the French *passé simple*) and the augmented verbs with the *passé composé*, especially as found in speeches by characters. Bakker then cites examples, among which are three uses of aorist indicative verbs in a speech by Diomedes to Hector, "all augmented, [that] do not refer to past events" (*Iliad* 11.362–363).[27] Hence, according to this view, the usage of the augment is semantic in that it distinguishes between narration and discourse. The findings of these predecessors encourage Bakker himself to investigate the augment in relation to the aorist and imperfect in the *Iliad*. Bakker examines the augment with the aorist in narrative and characters' speeches, with the aorist in similitudes, with aorists with the -σκ suffix, in speech introductions, with backgrounded verbs,[28] in narrative related by characters, and in character speech proper.

Then Bakker arrives at a number of conclusions, many of them interesting but beyond the scope of this essay. What is important to note is his overall conclusion: "We saw that for Platt and Drewitt there is a connection between the augmented aorist and 'present tense' which is statistically manifest in that augment is more common in character speech and less common in narrative. The distribution of the augment across the various subdivisions presented in the previous section, however, suggests that 'tense' may as such not be the appropriate dimension."[29] He thinks that the augment is instead a specificity indicator, a deictic marker indicating nearness of the speaker's immediate

25. Ibid., 4. Bakker speculates that one of the reasons for Drewitt being neglected or not taken as seriously as he should be is the battle between Analysts (i.e., diachronists) and Unitarians (i.e., synchronists) in Homeric scholarship. Interestingly, Evans seems to dismiss Drewitt in the light of his not being an Analyst (Evans seems to endorse an Analyst agenda), whereas Drewitt himself made comments on the relative age of passages on the basis of the augment, an Analyst characteristic.

26. Ibid., 4–5, citing L. Basset, "L'augment et la distinction discours/récit dans l'*Iliade* et l'*Odyssée*," in *Études homériques: Séminaire de recherche*, ed. M. Casevitz, TMO 17 (Lyon: Maison de l'Orient, 1989), 9–16, citing É. Benveniste, *Problèmes de linguistique generale*, 2 vols. (Paris: Gallimard, 1966), 1:238–45.

27. Bakker, "Similes," 6.

28. For his perspective on backgrounding, see E. J. Bakker, "Foregrounding and Indirect Discourse: Temporal Subclauses in a Herodotean Short Story," *JPrag* 16 (1991): 225–47.

29. Bakker, "Similes," 15.

situation. In other words, the augment in Homer is part of an array of deictic and evidential indicators used to mark immediacy. For Bakker, this formulation explains the use of the augment in speech introductions but its lack of uses with -σκ suffixes or with verbs indicating backgrounded events or in negation or in narrative as a whole.[30]

Bakker's actual conclusion is less important for my purposes (although it certainly is problematic for Evans's assertions) than are the following points. First, Bakker shows that the approach and research of Drewitt (along with Platt) is in fact still relevant for study of the augment, certainly in Homeric Greek, if not in other Greek as well. Second, the conclusions of Drewitt—the augment is not a past-time indicator, whatever alternative is suggested—are not outmoded and superseded but are in fact current and relevant for studies of the augment. Third, Bakker shows that, besides the findings that the augment is not a past-time indicator, a variety of positions are being propounded for the function of the augment, none of them necessarily convincing to everyone—even though many, if not most, of these reject the past-time assumption. Fourth, if we begin from the foundation that the augment was not a past-time indicator, at least by the time of Homer (as the evidence that Bakker marshals indicates), then there is no necessity to see a past-time use in later Greek, from the classical period onward. Fifth, Bakker shows that, if Drewitt and similar conclusions are to be believed (and Bakker has done his best to confirm them), then there are strong negative implications for Evans's attempt to refute my conclusion, along with Drewitt and others, that the augment is not a past-time indicator.

The major implication is that Bakker, following in a long line of other scholars, shows that the augment in Homer is not a past-time indicator (whatever else it may have been), so there is no need to carry forward the sense of its being a past-time indicator to successive periods of Greek usage.[31] As Evans himself also claims, in agreement with other scholars, the augment, through grammaticalization and morphological reduction, was both morphologically and semantically reduced, so that by the time of the postclassical period it was at best a formal feature for some verbal forms in the indicative.[32]

Thus, rather than Evans's claims providing an argument against my theory regarding the nontemporality of the Greek verbal system, Evans actually

30. Ibid., 15–18.
31. I realize that Bakker says, "In classical Greek, augment is the obligatory marker of past tense" ("Similes," 2), but this assertion (regarding time) does not follow from his own analysis and is not argued for in his paper. I suspect that he simply means that it is an obligatory marker of particular tense-forms.
32. See also K. L. McKay, *Greek Grammar for Students: A Concise Grammar of Classical Attic with Special Reference to Aspect in the Verb* (Canberra: Australian National University, 1974), 223.

becomes an ally and supporter of my position, once he is corrected by Bakker regarding work on Homeric augmentation.

The Wallace Argument regarding the Imperfect and Present Tense-Forms

Buist Fanning looks to Daniel Wallace's intermediate grammar regarding the imperfect and present tense-forms for his second argument against the nontemporal view.[33] Under the category of linguistics,[34] Wallace contends that since "the imperfect is derived from the present's principal part, . . . [this] suggests that there must be some similarity and some difference between such corresponding tenses." He contends that the "nontemporal view does not easily handle" an explanation of that difference.[35] Wallace seems to contend that the temporal view, which he advocates (along with Fanning), solves the problem: since temporal reference by means of grammaticalized verbal forms occurs only in the indicative, this explains the primary and secondary tense-forms in the indicative, whereas they would be redundant outside the indicative. For Wallace, this means that the present indicative indicates present time and the imperfect indicative indicates past time, but that without temporal reference there would be "no difference between these two tenses," especially since they "are both often seen in the same contexts."[36] There are two further purported problems that Wallace also wishes to introduce. The first concerns the so-called historic present. Wallace contends, "Most grammars regard the aspectual value of the historical present to be reduced to zero," stating that these verbs are used for actions "in the midst of aorists without the slightest hint that an internal or progressive aspect is intended. Yet if the nontemporal view of tense were true, we would expect the aspect to be in full flower."[37] The second problem concerns the aorist indicative. Wallace contends that if the aorist indicative were not an indicator of time, we would expect it to be used for "an instantaneous present event." Further, Wallace thinks that we should

---

33. D. B. Wallace, *Greek Grammar beyond the Basics: An Exegetical Syntax of the New Testament* (Grand Rapids: Zondervan, 1996), 507–9, although this reference is potentially unclear, as it is in the middle of a larger section. If I had time and space, I would deal with the larger argument, which is full of problems and potentially misleading statements.

34. I find it difficult to know what is particularly linguistic about this part of Wallace's treatment.

35. Wallace, *Greek Grammar*, 507. Wallace also includes the perfect and pluperfect here, but Fanning's argument is addressed to the present and imperfect.

36. Ibid., 508.

37. Ibid.

also expect to find "an instantaneous present (in which the aspect is entirely suppressed and the present time element is all that remains)."[38]

I find it difficult to know where to begin a response to such a perplexing menagerie of concepts and ideas. Wallace makes problematic statements regarding linguistics (the purported category of his discussion), verbal aspect, temporality in the Greek verbal system, and how these elements function individually or systemically. Nevertheless, I will try to sort out some of these issues.

The first, and perhaps the most important, problem is that Wallace apparently does not understand verbal aspect, confusing it instead with what is sometimes called *Aktionsart*, or procedural or lexical aspect, among other terms (as opposed to grammatical aspect, the aspect that is morphologically encoded in the tense-forms).[39] Thus he seems to equate *Aktionsart*, which is concerned with how an action "actually happened," with aspect, when he speaks of aorist indicative verbs not being used "for an instantaneous present event" or of finding "an instantaneous present."[40] He also speaks of "an internal or progressive aspect" as if aspect were indicating how an action actually occurs.[41] The overwhelming majority of recent discussion of the Greek verbal structure has concluded, unlike Wallace, that verbal aspect (morphological aspect) is the semantic feature encoded by the Greek tense-forms (whatever else may or may not be encoded), across the various moods, including infinitives and participles, regardless of its relationship to temporal distinctions and *Aktionsart*.[42] Since Wallace does not seem to understand that aspect is concerned not with how actions actually occur, but rather with their grammaticalized depiction by the author, it is perhaps no wonder that he finds it difficult to understand an aspectual view of Greek tense-form usage. In fact, Wallace's comments seem in some ways to indicate that he takes a nonaspectual view.[43] I suspect that he simply misunderstands the entire concept, especially in his attempt to defend a temporal view of the indicative.

The second problem is that Wallace, whether consciously or intentionally or not, potentially misleads the reader by distinguishing between what he calls the nontemporal and the traditional views of the tense-forms. Wallace makes it seem as if the nontemporal view is a very recent position compared to the traditional view, which must (of course) be better because it is of long standing.

38. Ibid., 509. Wallace is critical of Fanning's view of the instantaneous present (Fanning, *Verbal Aspect*, 202–5), which is discussed below.
39. See Porter, *Verbal Aspect*, 32–35.
40. Wallace, *Greek Grammar*, 509.
41. Ibid., 508.
42. This would include McKay, Porter, Fanning, Decker, Evans, and Campbell, as perhaps the best known among many others.
43. See also Wallace, *Greek Grammar*, 509n37.

Even here, however, Wallace apparently is confused. He introduces the distinction by saying, "Traditionally, NT grammars have viewed time as a part of the Greek tenses, when such tenses combine with the indicative mood."[44] There are two major problems with this assertion. First, it is not historically accurate. It depends upon how one defines "traditional," but many, if not most, New Testament Greek grammars argued for time-based tense-form meaning in all moods (not just the indicative) until sometime in the early twentieth century (although some even much later).[45] The second problem is that, in a footnote, Wallace admits that there is a qualification to his statement, one that I see as virtually vacating his argument: "These same grammars [the traditional grammars] usually point out that time is secondary and that *originally* the Greek tenses did not grammaticalize time (so *BDF*, 166 [§318])."[46] What actually happened is that in the early twentieth century a number of grammarians began to recognize that tense-forms were not temporal in the nonindicative moods (including infinitive and participle), with many later in the century further recognizing that tense-forms were not temporal even in the indicative, or at least that temporality was secondary to aspectuality. This latter position includes not only McKay and Porter, as Wallace states, but also Fanning, Campbell, and others. In other words, the nontemporal view in various forms has been around for some time, and what Wallace calls the traditional view is, in fact, not the prominent view held until the twentieth century but instead a modified view that reflects characteristics of the nontemporal view. This misleading characterization persists in Wallace's treatment, to the point that he ends up making a number of misstatements regarding especially the traditional view.

A third problem is that Wallace creates a false problem with the so-called nontemporal view, one that can work—and even here it does not work, as I will show—only if Wallace assumes his conclusion that the tense-forms are temporal indicators. Wallace believes that the nontemporal view cannot handle the fact that in the indicative mood there is an imperfect tense-form with the same aspect as the present tense-form, and a pluperfect tense-form with the same aspect as the perfect tense-form. In other words, if they have the same aspect, what distinguishes their meaning? For Wallace, it is a temporal distinction between past and present in the indicative, whereas such a distinction (on an aspectual basis) would be unnecessary outside of the indicative (what he, again, characterizes as a traditional view; but since

44. Ibid., 504.
45. For various surveys that illustrate this, see Porter, *Verbal Aspect*, 17–65 and passim.
46. Wallace, *Greek Grammar*, 504n24, with reference to F. Blass and A. Debrunner, *A Greek Grammar of the New Testament and Other Early Christian Literature*, trans. R. W. Funk (Chicago: University of Chicago Press, 1961), 166.

aspectual distinctions were only made beginning in the twentieth century, his nomenclature or historical understanding is inaccurate). Wallace even goes so far as to construct a chart where time distinguishes the forms, so that when the temporal distinction is removed, he says that there is no difference between the two sets of tense-forms.

Besides assuming his conclusion, already recognized above, Wallace fails to notice that there are other possible distinctions between the two sets of tense-forms than temporal ones, so that even in the indicative where they may share common aspect, they may have other distinct semantic features. Several suggestions of such distinctions have been made, but Wallace mentions none of them, and so he misleads his reader into thinking the choice is between a temporal conception of these tense-forms in the indicative and nothing else. Some of these suggested distinctions may be aspectual, spatial, or even temporal while retaining an aspectual distinction (I mention possibilities, without necessarily endorsing any of them). Wallace himself inadvertently suggests that this may be the case when he recognizes that, for example, a present verb and an imperfect verb may be used in the same context. He is unclear what he means by context, but if it means used with the same temporal reference (as his subsequent discussion of the so-called historic present seems to indicate) and close by each other (and his treatment of the historic present, noted below, furthers this difficulty), then he has not solved the problem of his own making, as there are now two forms based upon the same stem with the same temporal reference. Several linguists and grammarians have suggested spatial/temporal features as distinguishing these forms, by utilizing the notion of remoteness (the imperfect grammaticalizes the semantic feature of remoteness, as opposed to the present tense-form, which does not).[47] Since Wallace does not address these proposals (Porter's was available by the time of his publication), his refutation can only be seen as skewed and unconvincing, since he does not consider all of the evidence.

Fourth, Wallace treats the historic (or narrative) present as a supposed problem for the nontemporal view. He first of all contends, "Most grammars regard the aspectual value of the historical present to be reduced to zero."[48] He does not identify "most grammars," and I certainly do not know them, since in my thorough study of the issue I found only a limited number that hold to this view—a view that has been thoroughly dismissed for its failure to explain important examples of things such as concentrations of uses of

47. See, e.g., Porter, *Verbal Aspect*, 95; Campbell, *Verbal Aspect*, 48–52 (although on a dubious conceptual basis); see also McKay, "Ancient Greek Perfect," 19n22, which raises the question.
48. Wallace, *Greek Grammar*, 508.

the historic present or works that begin with the historic present.[49] Passing silently by this obvious problem, Wallace contends that there are places where historic presents appear amid uses of aorist indicatives without indicating what he calls "internal or progressive aspect."[50] However, he says, "If the nontemporal view of tense were true, we would expect the aspect to be in full flower."[51] Again we see that Wallace is assuming his conclusion; he posits that the historic present has what he calls "zero aspect" (a term that few use), then not surprisingly "finds" this lack of aspect because he conceives of the action in categories resembling those of *Aktionsart* rather than aspect, and then uses this to conclude that the nontemporal view must be wrong. Besides failing to understand aspect, Wallace gives no indication of what it would mean for him that aspect was in "full flower." However, by his own previous definition, the question is not whether aspect is present or not in the indicative (it is), but time. There is not a problem of aspect if one has present and aorist indicative tense-forms in the configuration that he proposes. Thus, Wallace has created an artificial problem. There is, however, a genuine problem for his position here. In his own position the only way he can avoid the issue of "redundancy of tenses" (the terminology he gives for his own manufactured conundrum) with the historic present in relation to the imperfect, since they have the same aspectual values and are found in similar contexts, is to posit zero aspect for the historic present—a forced assumption and conclusion at best.

Finally, Wallace suggests that with the nontemporal view, "we should expect to see the aorist indicative regularly used for an instantaneous present event, . . . [and] we would not expect to see an instantaneous present (in which the aspect is entirely suppressed and the present time element is all that remains)."[52] He grants that there are gnomic uses of the aorist indicative but questions the so-called instantaneous aorist. Similarly, he thinks that the nontemporal position cannot explain the use of ἁρπάζω in Matthew 13:19 or John 10:29. Beside the logical difficulty of question framing (Wallace attempts to frame the question in such a way as to arrive at only his answer) and the fact that Fanning himself contends to have found examples of the instantaneous present (see below), the obvious problem is that Wallace does not understand aspect by characterizing uses of the aorist or present in terms of instantaneous action (how actions actually occur—i.e., *Aktionsart*) rather than how they are characterized. According to a theory of aspect, we would expect to be able to find present

49. Porter, *Verbal Aspect*, 190–92. See also K. L. McKay, "Further Remarks on the 'Historical' Present and Other Phenomena," *FL* 11 (1974): 247–51.
50. Wallace, *Greek Grammar*, 508.
51. Ibid.
52. Ibid., 509.

tense-forms used of events that are of any duration (including short), because aspect is concerned with authorial perspective, not objective reality. The same is true of uses of the aorist. Further, Wallace appears—if he has a conception of aspect at all—to give temporality predominance over aspect, at least in the indicative. This raises a number of questions of its own regarding the Greek verbal system and how to account for its aspectuality outside the indicative, and how the indicative and nonindicative relate to each other around the issues of aspect and temporality. This is especially a problem since, by his own characterization, temporal reference is a cancelable feature of the meaning of the Greek tense-forms (as it is not found outside of the indicative). Wallace provides no explanation of such relations. However, despite his assertion, there are numerous instances where the aorist or present indicative form is used with present reference (some are even for events of short duration).[53]

Wallace's attempt to defend what he (mistakenly) calls the traditional view of the temporality of the verb, as opposed to the supposed nontemporal view, must be deemed a failure, not least because of Wallace's own apparent confusion over the very notions of aspect, *Aktionsart*, and perhaps even temporality.

The Performative or Instantaneous Present

Buist Fanning's final line of defense is what he calls the performative or instantaneous present. In some ways, this distinction is related to one of the points that Wallace attempts to make, already mentioned above. Fanning formulates the performative and instantaneous present in two different places in his book on verbal aspect, the former in a section on the effect of time on aspect and the latter in another chapter on aspect in the indicative mood.

Concerning the performative present, Fanning says that the performative present is "another common way in which temporal meaning affects the aspectual function."[54] Citing J. L. Austin, Fanning says that a "performative action is one which is accomplished in the very act of speaking: it is not one which is about to happen or in process of happening or which has just occurred; it is an action *identical* with and thus simultaneous with the act of speaking."[55]

---

53. A good number of these are to be found in Porter, *Verbal Aspect*, 211–30.

54. Fanning, *Verbal Aspect*, 187. Fanning, not I, claims that there are common ways in which temporal meaning "affects" aspect. I believe that he has his categories reversed (at best). In any case, this and the instantaneous present are the only two examples he cites in his later article as being crucial to refuting the nontemporal position.

55. Fanning, *Verbal Aspect*, 187–88, citing J. L. Austin, *How to Do Things with Words* (Oxford: Clarendon, 1962). I am not sure that Fanning has rightly understood Austin's speech-act theory and its implications for the study of Greek. For a critique of speech-act theory, see

At this point, the situation becomes more difficult for Fanning—a problem of his own making. He offers an extensive quotation of Erwin Koschmieder's description of such usage, but he notes that Koschmieder is speaking of the Hebrew perfect form. Fanning (fatally for his position) admits that Koschmieder "related this only to the perfective or aoristic aspect (illustrated with examples of the Hebrew perfect), and did not note a similar meaning for the imperfective aspect in the Greek indicative present."[56] Fanning apparently fails to see that his commendatory citation of Koschmieder undermines his very argument regarding the important linkage between the Greek present tense-form, present temporality, and imperfective aspect, because of his endorsement that a perfective aspect (in this instance in Hebrew) can perform the same function. This indicates that both the perfective and imperfective aspect can have present temporal reference, not that such usage is unique to the present tense-form.

Fanning, however, goes further. He believes, despite the evidence just given (by himself), that he has found the explanation for such usage: "The performative use of the present indicative is due to an emphasis on the present . . . time-value: there is such stress on the action occurring at exactly the moment of speaking that the 'internal viewpoint' of the present is compressed and a possible durative or continuing sense is thus reduced. The present in this case does not denote 'the present moment and a range of time on either side of it' as it usually does; instead, the occurrence is pressed into the time of 'precisely now.'"[57] Fanning says something very similar regarding the instantaneous present, which he contends has the sense of an action that "is 'done' at the moment of speaking." The instantaneous present includes both the performative present already noted (Fanning is somewhat redundant at this point) and the "use of the present to describe acts of speaking narrowly focused on the present moment." Like the performative present, the instantaneous present of speaking "is pressed into the time of 'precisely now.'"[58] He concludes that it "is the combination with present-tense meaning in the indicative which affects the present aspect in this way."[59]

I will pass by Fanning's ill-conceived and problematic definition of imperfective aspect as indicating simply "internal viewpoint," durativity, and temporal

---

G. Leech and J. Thomas, "Language, Meaning and Context: Pragmatics," in *An Encyclopaedia of Language*, ed. N. E. Collinge (London: Routledge, 1990), 173–206.

56. Fanning, *Verbal Aspect*, 188, referring to E. Koschmieder, "Zu den Grundfragen der Aspekttheorie," *IF* 53 (1932): 287–88. Fanning admits that there is "a use of the NT Greek *aorist* with this sense" (n114), but he wrongly (see below) attributes such use to Semitic influence.

57. Fanning, *Verbal Aspect*, 188–89. It seems that Fanning is confusing grammatical aspect and lexical aspect or *Aktionsart* at this point.

58. Ibid., 202.

59. Ibid.

extension.[60] What is more important to note is that he clearly believes, and even goes so far as to state, that the present temporal constraint reduces or focuses the imperfective aspect into something that much more resembles perfective aspect. There are many problems with this formulation. One is the idea that morphological aspect can simply be constrained by certain temporal restrictions, with the result that, contrary to aspectual theory and even Fanning's own perspective (where temporality is a cancelable feature confined to the indicative), aspect is subordinated to tense or temporality. Another problem is that Fanning, as noted above, as much as admits that this is not a function unique to the present tense-form. In fact, it is a function that, in his estimation, can occur only if the present "becomes" perfective or aoristic (his term) in aspect. Finally, he fails altogether to address, apart from a dismissive footnote, what might also be called performative aorists, those instances of use of the aorist tense-form when it "performs" some action, an action seen to be occurring at the time of utterance. Previous grammarians have recognized such a category of aorist usage, often related to verbs of emotion or of action of short duration and widely recognized as occurring in extrabiblical Greek.[61] More than that, some of these examples occur with verbs of thinking and speaking, and thus are also similar to Fanning's so-called instantaneous present of speaking. An excellent example is Luke 16:4, where the unjust steward, who has been caught cheating his master, contemplates what he is to do. Then, all of a sudden, the idea comes to him, at which exact point he says ἔγνων, "I know" (cf. Matt. 25:24; Luke 8:46). This utterance is recorded as occurring at the moment of thought; that is, his moment of recognition occurs at the same moment as speaking, and his knowledge is indicated at that conjunction. Similar examples probably occur in Matthew 23:23; John 11:14; 2 Corinthians 5:13; and James

---

60. Fanning appears here simply to accept one definition of aspect, one presented especially by B. Comrie, *Aspect: An Introduction to the Study of Verbal Aspect and Related Problems*, CTL (Cambridge: Cambridge University Press, 1976). He has become transfixed by a metaphor.

61. See Porter, *Verbal Aspect*, 226–27, for discussion, and the forced explanation of A. Rijksbaron, *The Syntax and Semantics of the Verb in Classical Greek: An Introduction* (Amsterdam: Gieben, 1984), 28–29. Note that this is transformed in the third edition of 2002 into "the aorist indicative of performative verbs ('tragic aorist')" (pp. 29–30). E. Bakker refers to the "dramatic aorist" or "present aorist," saying that in this usage the action is asserted as constituting "the present speech moment" ("Pragmatics: Speech and Text," in *A Companion to the Ancient Greek Language*, ed. E. Bakker, BCAW [Chichester: Blackwell, 2010], 162). Bakker believes that this performative usage reflects the semantic domain of the aorist as performative in the sense that Austin refers to it. Rather than being considered "peculiar use," it is "in fact central to the meaning of this 'tense.'" McKay, contrary to Fanning, goes so far as to say that "the circumstances in which aoristic completeness in a temporally present action is important are rare in literature, but when they do occur the verb is used in the aorist" (*Greek Grammar*, 223). Note, however, that McKay's estimation of numbers of instances may be inaccurate.

2:6, among others.[62] This is not a unique usage in either the Greek of the New Testament or other ancient Greek.

The invocation of the performative or instantaneous present can hardly be said to argue against the nontemporal view. In fact, the supposition of such usage must misconstrue the notion of aspect in several ways and artificially and unnecessarily reduce its aspectual force, as well as subordinating it to a preconceived notion of time, in order to define a usage that is in fact not unique to the present tense-form or even to Greek. The aorist tense-form also is used with similar temporal constraints, and thus shows not that Greek is temporal but in fact that the tense-forms, even in the indicative, are nontemporal—or better, temporally constrained on the basis of cotext (including various types of deictic indicators), when different tense-forms can be used in identical temporal contexts. Fanning's third objection thus also fails.

Conclusion

Despite Fanning's confidence regarding refutation of the so-called nontemporal view of the Greek tense-forms, when the arguments—or, in some instances, lack of arguments—are actually pursued, they reveal that there is little substance to them. An examination of the three proposed responses to the nontemporal view—the issue of the Greek augment, the supposed linguistic arguments of Wallace regarding the imperfect, and the performative or instantaneous present—all fail to be convincing. Moreover, they not only fail to be convincing, but also often fail to have logical or interpretive soundness. They are riddled with misunderstandings, misstatements, and mischaracterizations of their own positions, as well as often of matters of Greek grammar and linguistics, and in the end offer little to nothing of substance to the debate. In fact, with their clear dismissal, there appear to be—at least if Fanning is to be believed in the formulation of the issue—no logical or linguistic impediments to accepting the so-called nontemporal view of the Greek indicative verb.

Excursus: Aspectually Vague Verbs

In my *Verbal Aspect in the Greek of the New Testament*, I included a discussion of Greek periphrastic constructions that went further than most previous studies by treating both elements of the construction: the participle and what

---

62. See Porter, *Verbal Aspect*, 227–28.

qualifies as an auxiliary verb. In that discussion I argued that Greek had a single auxiliary verb suitable for use in periphrastic constructions, the verb εἰμί, because it was aspectually vague; that is, historically it lacked a full verbal paradigm (no meaningful contrastive morphology), and hence no choice of aspect in its tense-forms. Even though there are other aspectually vague verbs, they do not enter into such grammatical relationships with participles, and hence they are not used in periphrastic constructions. This presents a clear theory regarding formation of the periphrastic, in which there is no lack of aspectual congruence between the auxiliary verb and the participle, as is sometimes found in catenative constructions.[63]

Trevor Evans finds my reasoning "unsatisfactory" because it "lacks diachronic scope and yields an artificially narrow definition of periphrasis."[64] I will not pursue the issue of defining periphrasis, but will simply say concerning periphrasis that Evans's response holds no probative weight, as he offers no articulation of what it might mean for a definition to be artificially narrow, especially when he arbitrarily introduces an entirely different—and I would say unhelpful and fundamentally inconsistent—criterion for determining a periphrastic construction, the lexical semantics of the auxiliary verb. However, I will briefly respond to his first objection, that my definition of aspectual vagueness "lacks diachronic scope." By this, he apparently means that in my tracing of the diachronic development of aspectually vague verbs, I have overlooked some helpful information. Evans gives four brief examples that supposedly support his case, and I will address them here.

The first is the verb εἰμί. Evans states that this verb "develops the function of a future in Attic Greek" in suppletion of ἔρχομαι/ἦλθον.[65] This, in fact, proves my point, as the Greek future form is itself aspectually vague.[66] The second example that he cites is one that I discuss, the restricted development and use of an aorist form of φημί (which he does not dispute). However, he contends that this verb supletes εἶπον. This is asserted by some scholars in the English scholarly tradition that Evans seems to follow,[67] but it probably is incorrect at least by the time of the New Testament, which saw restricted

---

63. See Porter, *Verbal Aspect*, 442–47. My study here is based upon a previous study, S. E. Porter and N. J. C. Gotteri, "Ambiguity, Vagueness and the Working Systemic Linguist," *SWPLL* 2 (1985): 105–18, which places the issue of aspectual vagueness within a larger systemic and definitional context.

64. Evans, *Verbal Syntax*, 222.

65. Ibid.

66. Porter, *Verbal Aspect*, 109, 403–40.

67. Evans (*Verbal Syntax*, 223), when asserting that εἶπον is the aorist of φημί, fails to note that λέγω is probably the present tense-form that supletes εἶπον. He provides no documentation at this point, but this view is found in, e.g., LSJ and other English sources.

use of this verb. Instead, λέγω suppletes εἶπον, at least in the first century.[68] Even if I am wrong about φημί, and it is no longer aspectually vague or used suppletively,[69] it does not, however, affect the results regarding εἰμί, as the former is not used in periphrasis. The third example is semantic overlap between εἰμί and γίνομαι, where Evans claims that ἐγενόμην can "arguably function [for εἰμί] as its aorist."[70] He provides no argument, only an assertion that multiplies complexity beyond necessity. Besides, this form of argument as much as concedes lack of aspectual choice for εἰμί. The fourth example concerns εἰμί, ἧμαι, and κεῖμαι, where Evans admits that they "have probably not been fully integrated into the aspectual system because their lexical semantics do not foster marking for more than one aspect (the imperfective)."[71] This final example is perplexing, because it actually admits that certain -μι verbs are not fully aspectual, has a confused notion of aspect that shifts grammatical aspect to lexical aspect, and fails to notice that verbal aspect is not a semantic feature in isolation but rather is founded upon contrast. None of Evans's examples proves compelling or disputes the aspectual vagueness of εἰμί, and certainly none of them calls into question the notion of aspectual vagueness.

Because Evans has apparently completely confused the notion of aspect itself, to say nothing of aspectual vagueness, it is no wonder that, with his emphasis upon lexical semantics of the auxiliary, he must conclude, "[It] is inescapably true that the analysis of Greek verbal periphrasis, especially substitute periphrasis, contains a considerable element of subjectivity."[72] Indeed, if, with Evans, one misconceives the notion of aspect and attempts to solve the problem by means of lexical meaning of the auxiliary (along with other problems that he creates in discussion of periphrasis that are not germane to

---

68. See P. Chantraine, *Morphologie historique du grec*, 3rd ed., NCUC 34 (Paris: Klincksieck, 1991), 153–54, 156.

69. Evans (*Verbal Syntax*, 222–23n10) claims that my explanation of ἔφην along formal and functional lines is "potentially confusing, especially on the complexities of Greek stem formation," citing A. L. Sihler, *New Comparative Grammar of Greek and Latin* (New York: Oxford University Press, 1995), 506, 559, because of the "functional imprecision regarding aspectual force typical of Greek verbs of saying in the post-Classical period." First, Evans appears to be imprecise and confused at this point, because Sihler is concerned not with aspect but with *Aktionsart* or lexical aspect, in particular discussing eventive stems in Proto-Indo-European or punctual eventive (aorist) stems. Second, I do not deny that the augmented form of φημί formally resembles the imperfect formation, and that in a number of instances and types of verbs the aorist and imperfect forms are morphologically similar (so Sihler, *New Comparative Grammar*, 506, 559; and the notions of vagueness explored in Porter and Gotteri, "Ambiguity," 108–12). Nevertheless, the lack of morphological contrast means that the verb is aspectually vague.

70. Evans, *Verbal Syntax*, 223.

71. Ibid.

72. Ibid., 233.

my discussion here), his conclusion seems inevitable. But his conclusion is not necessarily satisfactory or correct, and I think it is not.

For some reason unknown to me, Evans wishes to dispute aspectual vagueness as a useful semantic category for a restricted number of verbs. His attempts at refutation fail to convince, and they leave him with an unsatisfactory explanation of Greek periphrastic constructions, which are better explained with the aid of aspectual vagueness.

12

The Perfect Tense-Form
and Stative Aspect

*The Meaning of the Greek Perfect Tense-Form
in the Greek Verbal System*

Introduction

The study of verbal aspect emblemizes a much larger issue within Greek-language study. That issue concerns the importance, for any who claim to be students of the Greek New Testament, of understanding and positively responding to recent advances in the study of Greek language and linguistics. Verbal aspect is the most advanced of these areas; by far the most important and sustained work has been done since the 1980s, with my own work perhaps serving as the first comprehensive and innovative English-language treatment of the subject with reference to the Greek of the New Testament.[1] However, as much as has been done in study of verbal aspect, there remains a surprising

---

1. For a brief history of aspect study in New Testament Greek, see S. E. Porter and A. W. Pitts, "New Testament Greek Language and Linguistics in Recent Research," *CBR* 6 (2008): 214–55, esp. 215–22, to which is now to be added the work of Constantine Campbell, cited below. For a

lack of sustained linguistic analysis of other important areas of the Greek language. In fact, I fear that, for the vast majority of New Testament scholars, the importance of Greek linguistics for study of the Greek New Testament remains outside of their purview and possibly even comprehension (perhaps apart from a relatively limited understanding of aspect studies). In a recent conversation with a colleague, a New Testament scholar who has written and continues to write commentaries on the Greek New Testament, he said, "Stan, what is that area that you work in again?" To which I replied, somewhat facetiously, "New Testament?" "No, no," he said, "linguistics, that's it, linguistics"—for him apparently a foreign territory dedicated to the arcane and unnecessary. At least linguistics is clearly unnecessary for him as he goes about his exegetical work without recognition that when he engages in exegesis of the Greek text, he is invoking a linguistic conceptual framework that guides the decisions he makes regarding his understanding of the Greek of the New Testament.

Most such exegetes probably believe that their use of what is often called "traditional grammar," which sometimes involves their characterization of themselves as being "grammarians" as opposed to "linguists," either is sufficient for the work they wish to do or marks out a territory of equal yet distinct validity that is free from the distractions of linguistic theory. I strongly disagree with such a characterization, simply because there is no such thing as theory-neutral language examination. The use of the "traditional" tools of Greek language study simply invokes the often prelinguistic (in the sense of prelinguistically informed) language study of an earlier era—that is, without regard for its assumptions and presuppositions or its relationships, whether developmental or incommensurable, with later linguistic thought. I refer to such "traditional grammar" with two different labels. The kind of rationalistic, verbally time-oriented, Latin-based approach, still found in (surprisingly) much language discussion, is what I call "1822 grammar," referring to the date of the first edition of Georg Winer's grammar, translated many times and still used into the twentieth century.[2] The comparative philological approach, with its reliance upon *Aktionsart* theory, I call "1896 grammar," referring to the date of the first edition of Friedrich Blass's grammar, still used in either its latest

---

fuller study up to the time of publication, see S. E. Porter, *Verbal Aspect in the Greek of the New Testament, with Reference to Tense and Mood*, SBG 1 (New York: Peter Lang, 1989), 17–65.

  2. G. B. Winer, *Grammatik des neutestamentlichen Sprachidioms* (Leipzig: Vogel, 1822), revised several times, most especially by P. W. Schmiedel, 8th ed. (Göttingen: Vandenhoeck & Ruprecht, 1894), and translated several times, most especially by W. F. Moulton as *A Treatise on the Grammar of New Testament Greek, Regarded as a Sure Basis for New Testament Exegesis*, 3rd ed. (Edinburgh: T&T Clark, 1882).

English or German edition.[3] A lot of 1822 and 1896 grammar is still being produced in New Testament studies. Some of it can be found, disappointingly, in Greek grammars that continue to be published, and much more of it, unfortunately, in the commentaries that continue to be written.[4] What we need, I think, is far less 1822 and 1896 grammar, and far more "1992 grammar" (and later), which refers to the date of the first edition of my *Idioms of the Greek New Testament*.[5] Far from being a perfect grammar, in it I attempt to consciously integrate a modern linguistic framework into New Testament Greek study. Whereas there are some elements in the diachronic progression of traditional grammar that are compatible with subsequent study, there are many areas that are incommensurable; and a grammar written after 1992 may well be an 1822 or 1896 grammar in disguise.

Discussion of verbal aspect is, or at least should be, part of modern linguistic study of the Greek language of the New Testament. Despite neglect of it within wider New Testament studies, I believe that we have made significant progress in addressing this particular linguistic issue (among others),[6] although I also see much room for further discussion. The semantics of the perfect tense-form is one such area, as there are three major divergent views of the meaning of this form, propounded in three major works on the New Testament Greek verbal system from an aspectual standpoint.[7] These three major works themselves should indicate that we need to engage in similar sustained and intensive research in other areas of Greek linguistics as well. As will become clear in the remainder of this chapter, not every one of these

3. F. Blass, *Grammatik des neutestamentlichen Griechisch* (Göttingen: Vandenhoeck & Ruprecht, 1896), revised numerous times, first by A. Debrunner and then F. Rehkopf, 18th ed. (Göttingen: Vandenhoeck & Ruprecht, 2001), and translated several times, most especially of the 9th/10th edition of Blass and Debrunner by R. W. Funk as *A Greek Grammar of the New Testament and Other Early Christian Literature* (Chicago: University of Chicago Press, 1961).

4. For my recent exploration of some of these issues, see S. E. Porter, "The Linguistic Competence of New Testament Commentaries" and "Commentaries on the Book of Romans," both in *On the Writing of New Testament Commentaries: Festschrift for Grant R. Osborne on the Occasion of His 70th Birthday*, ed. S. E. Porter and E. J. Schnabel, TENT 8 (Leiden: Brill, 2012), 33–56, 365–404.

5. See S. E. Porter, *Idioms of the Greek New Testament*, 2nd ed., BLG 2 (Sheffield: Sheffield Academic Press, 1994).

6. Some of the others, on which I have written, are word and constituent order, paragraphing, and discourse analysis, among others. See the bibliography in the present volume.

7. Porter, *Verbal Aspect*; B. Fanning, *Verbal Aspect in New Testament Greek*, OTM (Oxford: Clarendon, 1990); C. R. Campbell, *Verbal Aspect, the Indicative Mood, and Narrative: Soundings in the Greek of the New Testament*, SBG 13 (New York: Peter Lang, 2007); Campbell, *Verbal Aspect and Non-indicative Verbs: Further Soundings in the Greek of the New Testament*, SBG 15 (New York: Peter Lang, 2008) (it is puzzling that Campbell's material is in two volumes, as their combined length is less than that of either Porter or Fanning).

three major works has fully captured the meaning of the Greek perfect tense-form in the Greek verbal system. The reason is that they have not recognized and realized that the use of language—or more specifically linguistic forms that grammaticalize meanings, in this case, the Greek perfect tense-form—is always for or to perform a specific function, such as for communicative purposes or social interaction. Hence, use of each tense-form within the verbal system of a particular language has its own semantic function, each of which is systemically differentiated from one another. The use of a particular tense-form—the perfect, for instance—by the language user indicates a reasoned (systemically though not necessarily consciously) subjective choice by which the user wishes to conceptualize (or to not conceptualize, based upon a decision to not choose the other tense-forms) the verbal process. Thus the choice of the perfect tense-form by a language user indicates, in opposition to choice of the other tense-forms, that the user conceives of the verbal process as stative—the perception of the action as a condition or state of affairs in existence. This has been and still is my contention (and rightly, I firmly believe) since the publication of my 1989 monograph. In what follows, I first address what I see as some of the areas of agreement among the three major theories of verbal aspect that I examine in this chapter,[8] and then I briefly outline several points of disagreement. Second, I briefly present and offer a critique of the other two views. Then I conclude by reiterating my view of the meaning of the perfect tense-form as encoding stative aspect.

Points of Agreement and Disagreement

There are a number of points of agreement among the three major theories of verbal aspect, but perhaps the single most important point of agreement is that the semantic category of verbal aspect is essential for understanding the meaning of the ancient Greek verb, including the Greek of the New Testament.

---

8. There are other views of the semantics of the perfect tense-form, but these are the major ones propounded in New Testament Greek studies. Many of these other proposals, unfortunately sometimes much like the views of Fanning and Campbell (see below), rely far too heavily upon confusion of aspect (grammatical or morphological aspect) and *Aktionsart* (lexical or procedural aspect); that is, they confuse the meaning of the tense-form with the meaning of the individual verbal lexical item (although see below some statements on *Aktionsart*, in which I indicate that there are problems inherent in *Aktionsart* theory to the point of questioning whether it is mostly a discussion of ontology rather than grammar or linguistics). The need to differentiate between aspect and *Aktionsart* was recognized early on in aspect studies; see, e.g., L. J. Brinton, *The Development of English Aspectual Systems: Aspectualizers and Post-Verbal Particles*, CSL 49 (Cambridge: Cambridge University Press, 1988), 3.

Most who have studied verbal aspect probably would go further and say that understanding the Greek verb is an essential component of understanding the Greek language, in a way that most other elements are not as essential, because of how verbs are used in ancient Greek (as components of noun groups, verbal groups, etc.; through rank shifting, etc.). Implications of this statement include the recognition that those who do not include analysis of verbal aspect (and, I contend, other linguistic elements) within their study of the Greek text are not satisfactorily examining the Greek New Testament.

A second point of agreement concerns the definition of verbal aspect. Despite nuances and some variations regarding particular verbal aspects (such as the meaning of the perfect tense-form), it is also commonly agreed that verbal aspect is perspectival in nature: it is concerned with a grammatical means of enshrining authorial perspectives on processes, whether conscious or otherwise and within the constraints of the resources of the Greek language verbal system. Verbal aspect is not itself a temporal or a spatial/locational category, even if it is related to them, and it is not the same as *Aktionsart*, which purports to be concerned with action types represented by individual lexical items.

A third point of agreement is that verbal aspect is always important, not just occasionally so. In other words, verbal aspect is an essential part of the Greek verbal system and hence of the ancient Greek language: it is not a secondary or tertiary feature that can be invoked when exegetically convenient or played off haphazardly against other conceptions of how verbs function in Greek. This seems to be a point that some commentators miss when invoking verbal aspect in an ad hoc fashion when it suits their exegetical purposes.

A fourth point of agreement is that the aorist tense-form encodes perfective aspect and the present (imperfect) tense-form encodes imperfective aspect, however these aspects are actually defined (and they vary considerably). Most proponents of aspect theory also see some type of binary relationship between the perfective and nonperfective aspects.

A fifth point of agreement is that verbal aspect has textual and hence exegetical significance, possibly even discourse significance. This exegetical significance may vary, with aspect's scope having clausal-to-discourse functionality, but in any case it is seen to be exegetically significant. This means that substantiated exegetical discussions will be grounded in linguistically informed understanding of the Greek verbal system, as well as other features of the Greek language.

These points of agreement (there may be others) are fundamental, because they set the broad parameters within which discussion of verbal aspect occurs and form the parameters in which analysis of the Greek New Testament should occur. I am not convinced that all of those who engage in study of aspect, including the other two major proponents identified here, are always aware of the implications of these fundamental points of agreement or of the constraints that they place on overall analysis (e.g., that if verbal aspect is fundamental, then temporal reference or *Aktionsart* cannot be, or that promoting binary opposition between perfective/imperfective aspect does not exclude other binary choices), but this leads to points of disagreement.

Indeed, there also are several points of disagreement among the major theorists with reference to understanding Greek verbal aspect. This should not worry those who are looking at aspectual studies from the outside, since these are the kinds of disagreements that obtain in any intellectual discourse—although there is always the hope and effort expended toward resolution. I will briefly list such disagreements here.

1. *The role of linguistic theory in aspect studies.* As indicated above, Porter clearly advocates that linguistic theory is fundamental to linguistic understanding and utilizes a particular linguistic theory, while Fanning and Campbell are clearly less explicit about it and possibly do not really have an articulable theory. Porter adopts a defined model of systemic functional linguistics (SFL).[9] Fanning adopts some of the terminology and concepts of recent aspectual studies (e.g., perfective versus imperfective aspect, binarity, among some others), but he nowhere states what his linguistic theory is, and I cannot determine whether there is an explicit one, apart from his adapting some of the orientations of those he draws upon and his fundamental move of bringing aspect and *Aktionsart* together.[10] He draws upon various linguistic thoughts and traditional grammar in an eclectic way, as will be shown below. Campbell briefly identifies the opposition between Chomskyan and functional viewpoints, and claims to endorse a "functional approach," but he does not state exactly what this means apart from the fact that language is "a communicative tool."[11] Without a linguistic theory as the basis of examination

9. Porter, *Verbal Aspect*, 7–16, 75–109, in which see the major theorizers within SFL.

10. Fanning, *Verbal Aspect*, 29–50, which Campbell seems also to endorse (see C. R. Campbell, *Basics of Verbal Aspect in Biblical Greek* [Grand Rapids: Zondervan, 2008]). Fanning (pp. 420–21) outlines how aspect interacts with other components, and Campbell presents this as a formal equation (semantics of aspect + lexeme + context = *Aktionsart*). This formula is highly misleading, apart from acknowledging that the category of *Aktionsart* is different from and cannot be equated with aspect (on which we all apparently agree). However, it makes *Aktionsart* a category that is larger than context (whatever that can possibly mean) and does not recognize the complexity of any of the individual components. Fanning and Campbell were both anticipated by J. Mateos, *El aspecto verbal en el Nuevo Testamento*, ENT 1 (Madrid: Ediciones Cristiandad, 1977), 22 (although Mateos does not attempt to create such a formula).

11. Campbell, *Verbal Aspect* (2007), 19. He fails to note that there are a variety of functional models, including SFL, but others as well, such as tagmemics, stratificational grammar, and continental functionalism.

of the language, it is very difficult to determine what counts as evidence and how any such evidence should be interpreted.

2. *The concept, importance, and place of binarism, or binary opposition.* Porter has a more differentiated understanding, while Fanning and Campbell seem to apply it in a narrow sense, to the point of claiming that there is one fundamental binary opposition in Greek, perfective/imperfective. Porter's more robust theory of binary opposition provides for gradated binary choices that together form systems within a systemic network. Thus, Porter differentiates aspectual from nonaspectual systems, and then within such systems differentiates perfective/nonperfective aspect and then imperfective/stative aspect.[12] As far as I can tell, both Fanning and Campbell simply refer to the perfective/imperfective opposition, without defining it within the larger verbal network and as if this were the only binary opposition permitted within the Greek verbal edifice. This by definition excludes the treatment of anything other than the forms that grammaticalize these aspects, to a large extent creating (unnecessarily, I contend) their problem with the perfect tense-form and its aspect.

3. *The specific definitions of the aspects.* Porter is less concerned to define them independently but wishes to define them systemically, while Fanning and Campbell rely heavily upon Bernard Comrie's definitions, to the point of stereotyping actions on the basis of Comrie's metalanguage.[13] The systemic dimension is crucial, as it examines the aspects as part of a coordinated systemic network, not as individual entities.

4. *The role of semantics and the relationship between semantics and pragmatics.* Porter emphasizes semantics in at least a modified SFL sense, in which semantics includes much that is often placed under the category of pragmatics, and hence wishes to differentiate discussion of aspect from other complicating factors (such as *Aktionsart*).[14] Fanning and Campbell seem to want to hold

---

12. For the Greek verbal network, see Porter, *Verbal Aspect*, 109.

13. See B. Comrie, *Aspect: An Introduction to the Study of Verbal Aspect and Related Problems*, CTL (Cambridge: Cambridge University Press, 1976). Comrie's work has been fundamental in this discussion, even though he himself tends to confuse aspect and *Aktionsart*, a tendency among many linguists who have followed him. The result of use of Comrie's definitions by Fanning and Campbell is a focus upon viewpoint, to the extent of characterizing aspect as simply confined to internal versus external "temporal constituency" (p. 3), and attempting to find such a conception in translation of every example.

14. See Porter, *Verbal Aspect*, 15, where semantics is applied to meanings in context. On semantics in an SFL framework, see M. A. K. Halliday and C. M. I. M. Matthiessen, *Construing Experience through Meaning: A Language-Based Approach to Cognition*, OLS (London: Continuum, 1999), 4. I realize that there are problems with the systemic-functional (Hallidayan) conception of tense and aspect, due to a variety of factors, including the fact that the basic SFL architecture was developed before aspect became a major category in general linguistic theory (i.e., pre-Comrie). For a critique of SFL's handling of tense and aspect, see C. Bache, *English*

to a firm line between semantics and pragmatics, even if they often end up conflating the categories and muddying the discussion of aspect. This becomes clear in discussion of the meaning of the perfect tense-form (see below).[15]

5. *Temporal reference in the Greek verbal system*. Porter and Campbell reject temporality as a grammaticalized feature,[16] while Fanning argues for it in the indicative, with bleeding of it over into the nonindicative, and especially for the perfect tense-form, which, for him, enshrines past and present reference (see below).

6. *Spatial location in the Greek verbal system*. Porter has a limited role for it, especially in relation to the meaning of the imperfect tense-form and the pluperfect tense-form,[17] while Campbell replaces temporality with spatiality simply on the basis of an assumption,[18] and Fanning does not utilize it at all.

7. *The place of* Aktionsart *in discussion of verbal aspect*. Porter minimizes the role of *Aktionsart* and considers it to involve a (problematic) debate about lexis, not aspect, and hence to be unimportant for defining aspectual semantics.[19] Fanning embraces it fully as an "inherent" feature of the meaning of the Greek verb, and, though distinguishing aspect and *Aktionsart*, believes that they must be considered together.[20] Campbell includes it among other features,[21] with both Fanning and Campbell confusing discussion of aspect

---

Tense and Aspect in Halliday's Systemic Functional Grammar: A Critical Appraisal and an Alternative (London: Equinox, 2008), esp. 18.

15. The more rigid divide between semantics and pragmatics that has continued in much discussion of verbal aspect apparently was introduced by D. A. Carson in "An Introduction to the Porter/Fanning Debate," in *Biblical Greek Language and Linguistics: Open Questions in Current Research*, ed. S. E. Porter and D. A. Carson, JSNTSup 80 (Sheffield: JSOT Press, 1993), 18–25, esp. 24–25, where he endorses a more radical distinction between the two, apparently followed by Fanning (even if not explicitly), Decker, and Campbell, among others. I owe this insight (among others) to my colleague Francis Pang. For some of the difficulties with contemporary thought in pragmatics, see M. Ariel, *Defining Pragmatics*, RSL (Cambridge: Cambridge University Press, 2010), 23–89.

16. I argue that temporal reference is indicated at the clausal level and above through deictic indicators, syntax, and other clausal and beyond features, but that the semantics encoded by the perfect tense-form are stative, as noted below. For discussion of temporality and nontemporality in the Greek verbal system, see chap. 11 above, where I discuss Fanning's and Campbell's theories.

17. Porter, *Verbal Aspect*, 95.

18. Campbell, *Verbal Aspect* (2007), 14–16.

19. Porter, *Verbal Aspect*, 87. By this, I do not mean that grammatical and lexical aspect (if this is even the right terminology) are to be examined on the same plane, as if in order to understand a clause, one simply (simplistically!) adds aspect plus *Aktionsart* (and perhaps other components) to arrive at interpretation. This seems to be the way aspect and *Aktionsart* are sometimes handled by Fanning and Campbell. This is particularly difficult when *Aktionsart* studies cannot decide whether *Aktionsart* functions at the rank of word, word group, clause, or even larger unit.

20. Fanning, *Verbal Aspect*, 50.

21. Campbell, *Verbal Aspect* (2007), 33–34.

and its central role by their attention to *Aktionsart* and, to a large extent, making their discussion focus upon *Aktionsart*.

There may be other points of disagreement among the major proponents, but these illustrate some of the fundamental differences. They are sufficient, however, to illustrate some major issues that separate the three major proponents and that account for three distinctly different definitions of the meaning of the perfect tense-form.

Fanning and Campbell on the Meaning of the Perfect Tense-Form

When we turn to discussion of the perfect tense-form among the three major advocates,[22] there are also a number of specific areas of disagreement to identify, in addition to the broader linguistic differences already noted above. At this point I will not discuss in detail my understanding of the perfect tense-form and stative aspect (which I do below), but will respond to some more specific disagreements with Fanning and Campbell on the meaning of this important element within the larger Greek verbal structure. These disagreements revolve around major differences in theory and method, and also major differences in formulation and interpretation.

I treat Fanning first, as his work appeared soon after and independently of mine. Fanning does not define or utilize a linguistically robust theory of aspect, or even display a particularly clear linguistic theory at all. I would characterize his view of aspect as extensional; that is, he divides the linguistic terrain into a number of different subfields, and for some reason (not clear to me) selects one.[23] To determine the aspectual meaning of both the aorist and the present tense-forms, he surveys the three or four major views as found in the traditional grammars and a few other works, and then decides which one seems right to him. Then he redefines the particular aspect by using Comrie's terminology for perfective or imperfective aspect.[24] Fanning also appears to have a very limited notion of binary opposition: he confines it to the aorist/present or perfective/imperfective opposition. This means that the

---

22. I realize that there is a certain fragility to debating an individual node in a systemic network, as it can neglect the larger questions of system. We must remember that discussion of stative aspect must be seen in relation to perfective and imperfective aspect, as well as other features of the Greek verbal network. See also Halliday and Matthiessen, *Construing Experience*, 466. For other views of the meaning of the perfect tense-form, besides those of Fanning and Campbell, see A. Sauge, *Les degrés du verbe: Sens et formation du parfait en grec ancien* (Bern: Peter Lang, 2000).

23. See Ö. Dahl, *Tense and Aspect Systems* (Oxford: Blackwell, 1985), 9.

24. Fanning, *Verbal Aspect*, 97–98, 103.

perfect does not neatly fit and is technically excluded from this binary system. And indeed, for him, it does not fit and is unnecessarily excluded. Fanning contends that the perfect grammaticalizes a combination of tense, aspect, and *Aktionsart*. However, each area is suspect in this formulation. Regarding tense, Fanning recognizes an "inherent" temporal ordering between occurrence and consequence. He then says that this "works its way out in actual expression as a temporal one, producing a dual time-reference of 'past and present' together."[25] In other words, this is not part of the semantics of the perfect tense-form at all. Regarding *Aktionsart*, Fanning relies upon the philosopher Zeno Vendler's well-known characterization of actions as of four types, one of which is "state."[26] I have argued, and others more recently have confirmed (especially Francis Pang) this,[27] that *Aktionsart* characterizations are inherently problematic and not features of the Greek verbal system, but at best are phenomena that may be analyzed at word, group/phrase, clause, or even higher levels.[28] Even though Fanning appears to rely upon them as part of what an aspect means, when it comes to the perfect he refers to "the Aktionsart-feature of stative situation."[29] This is clearly not at all what Vendler's typology of action means, but appears to indicate that one feature of use of the perfect tense-form—that is, its semantics—is a "stative situation" regardless of the individual lexeme used. Regarding aspect, Fanning sees the perfect as perfective, probably reflecting his failure to move beyond simple binary opposition or indicating his adoption of the supposed resultive action as determinative. In other words, when all is said and done, despite some rough edges where he attempts to salvage the traditional definition of the perfect tense-form, once we move beyond trying to fit the perfect into the perfective/imperfective opposition, Fanning's definition (which is unsubstantiated by his theoretical framework, if he indeed has one) is in many ways simply an affirmation of

25. Ibid., 112.

26. Z. Vendler, "Verbs and Times," *PR* 66 (1957): 43–60; reprinted in Vendler, *Linguistics in Philosophy* (Ithaca, NY: Cornell University Press, 1967), 97–121. The other three are activities, achievements, and accomplishments. The problems with all typologies are discussed in W. Croft, *Verbs: Aspect and Clausal Structure* (Oxford: Oxford University Press, 2012), 128–29.

27. F. G. H. Pang, "Aktionsart as Epiphenomenon: A Stratal Approach to Process Typologies," in *Greeks, Jews, and Christians: Historical, Religious and Philological Studies in Honor of Jesús Peláez del Rosal*, ed. L. R. Lanzillotta and I. M. Gallarte (Córdoba: Ediciones el Almendro, 2013), 449–74.

28. See also Halliday and Matthiessen, *Construing Experience*, 466–506, where they take *Aktionsart* (or the equivalent) as "epiphenomenal" (p. 475)—that is, beyond the systems of language. I wonder whether it is not simply a matter of debate over philosophical categories. The result is that much discussion of *Aktionsart* (or lexical aspect as it is often called) is a debate over ontology (the nature of being) rather than over linguistics.

29. Fanning, *Verbal Aspect*, 119.

the perfect as encoding stative aspect. This is seen in his own characterization of the perfect as indicating a stative situation.

Campbell's definition of the perfect takes a different approach but ends up with a similar extensional definition.[30] On the one hand, he seems to want to use what he calls a "functional approach,"[31] but on the other hand, this appears to mean simply a comparison of translations. In other words, Campbell clearly does not have an explicit linguistic method, but relies heavily upon translation (i.e., English).[32] He unfortunately makes all-too-frequent appeal to what he calls the "natural" meaning of a passage; the problem is that the "natural" meaning is what we are trying to figure out, and so we cannot appeal to it as a judge (in fact, there are no such things as natural or plain meanings, only interpreted meanings). Translation is a very poor indicator of meaning (even if we must inevitably use it), since translation should not determine meaning but should come only after the meaning has been decided. Campbell rejects the notion of stative aspect as the meaning of the perfect tense-form for a number of highly questionable reasons. One of these is his contention that "stativity is regarded by most linguists as an *Aktionsart* value rather than an aspect," what he calls a "consensus among both Greek linguists and general linguists alike."[33] This is an odd reason for someone to use who then proceeds to define the perfect tense-form in a way never before used by any Greek or general linguist (or probably since—there are good reasons for this, as I will show below). Furthermore, he is clearly wrong (even if in his formulation he contends that it is only "most"), as a number of general linguists use this very category in their discussions of aspect (whether they end up accepting it or not, and whether they are always entirely clear on the difference between aspect and *Aktionsart*),[34] and some

30. For another critique of Campbell, within a larger linguistic context, see S. E. Porter, "Greek Linguistics and Lexicography," in *Understanding the Times: New Testament Studies in the 21st Century; Essays in Honor of D. A. Carson on the Occasion of His 65th Birthday*, ed. A. J. Köstenberger and R. W. Yarbrough (Wheaton, IL: Crossway, 2011), 19–61, esp. 46–54.

31. Campbell, *Verbal Aspect* (2007), 19.

32. Translation is his focus in C. R. Campbell, "Breaking Perfect Rules: The Traditional Understanding of the Greek Perfect," in *Discourse Studies and Biblical Interpretation: A Festschrift in Honor of Stephen H. Levinsohn*, ed. S. E. Runge (Bellingham, WA: Logos Bible Software, 2011), 139–55.

33. Campbell, *Verbal Aspect* (2007), 172.

34. See Porter, "Greek Linguistics," 48. These "general linguists" include the following (by no means an attempt at a comprehensive list): N. E. Collinge, "Some Reflexions on Comparative Historical Syntax," *AL* 12 (1960): 79–101, esp. 95–96, where he says that the "perfect (set apart by stem metaphony and internal apophony and special endings) denoted simple state"; D. Cohen, *L'aspect verbal*, LN (Paris: Presses universitaires de France, 1989), 67, 110–11, where he speaks of Greek as having three aspects (present, aorist, and perfect) and defines the perfect as indicating "statif" as opposed to process by the present and aorist (p. 111); H. J. Verkuyl, *A Theory of*

(in New Testament Greek studies) are open to its being used of the Greek perfect.[35]

Aspectuality: The Interaction between Temporal and Atemporal Structure, CSL 64 (Cambridge: Cambridge University Press, 1993), 11, where, though questioning the ability to differentiate between aspect and *Aktionsart*, he states that "one may describe one and the same situation as a state, a process or an event," reflecting language of subjective authorial choice very much in keeping with standard aspectual terminology; T. F. Mitchell and S. A. al-Hassan, *Modality, Mood and Aspect in Spoken Arabic: With Special Reference to Egypt and the Levant*, LAL 11 (London: Kegan Paul International, 1994), 65, 78–90, where, in a chapter specifically on aspect, they speak of Arabic as grammaticalizing stativity in especially the participle (though there is some confusion between aspect and what I would call *Aktionsart*, this is not a distinction that they make; they speak of grammaticalizing the stative in a particular form, the participle); L. A. Michaelis, *Aspectual Grammar and Past-Time Reference*, RLGS 4 (London: Routledge, 1998), 172–88, where she evaluates "an aspectual property attributed to the general perfect construction: stativity" (p. 172), where stativity is clearly an aspectual category even if she attributes it to the English perfect ("have x" construction); J. Clackson, *Indo-European Linguistics: An Introduction*, CTL (Cambridge: Cambridge University Press, 2007), 119–21, where, after noting the distinction between imperfective and perfective aspect, he states, "The perfect principally denotes a state: for example, the perfect *tēthnēke* [sic] means 'he is dead,' distinct from present *thnēiskei* 'he is dying,' imperfect *éthnēiske* 'he was dying' and aorist *éthane* 'he died'" (p. 121). This does not mean that even these scholars fully support the use of this terminology, only that they endorse the notion and use it in their discussions of aspect, such as they are. John Lyons, in *Semantics*, 2 vols. (Cambridge: Cambridge University Press, 1977), 2:706–7, which admittedly tends to confuse aspect and *Aktionsart*, distinguishes between lexicalized features (lexical aspect or *Aktionsart*) and grammaticalized aspect (morphological aspect as being discussed here), with stativity as a category that he attributes to each, but including grammatical aspect ("Whether a language grammaticalizes either stativity or progressivity [or both, or neither] is something that cannot be predicted"); cf. Lyons, *Introduction to Theoretical Linguistics* (Cambridge: Cambridge University Press, 1968), who says, "The Greek perfective [by which he means the perfect tense-form] refers to the *state* which results from the completion of the action or process" (p. 314). See now also K. Bentein, "Perfect," in *Encyclopedia of Ancient Greek Language and Linguistics*, ed. G. K. Giannakis (Leiden: Brill, 2014), 3:46–49, esp. 46–47, where he recognizes "stativity" as a major view of the meaning of the perfect (including McKay [see note 35 below], Porter, and C. M. J. Sicking and P. Stork, "The Synthetic Perfect in Classical Greek," in *Two Studies in the Semantics of the Verb in Classical Greek*, Mnemosyne 160 [Leiden: Brill, 1996], 119–298). Even Andrew Sihler, *New Comparative Grammar of Greek and Latin* (New York: Oxford University Press, 1995), 564–79, in his treatment of stative verbs (as opposed to eventive and punctual stems, the latter associated with the aorist form), links it directly with the Greek perfect tense-form (pp. 572–79).

35. See Porter, "Greek Linguistics," 48. These include (among others) P. Chantraine, *Histoire du parfait grec*, CL 21 (Paris: Champion, 1927), 4, and passim (with some reservations); P. Friedrich, "On Aspect Theory and Homeric Aspect," *IJAL* Memoir 28, 40 (1974): S1–S44; K. L. McKay, *Greek Grammar for Students: A Concise Grammar of Classical Attic with Special Reference to Aspect in the Verb* (Canberra: Australian National University, 1974), 146–47; McKay, *A New Syntax of the Verb in New Testament Greek: An Aspectual Approach*, SBG 5 (New York: Peter Lang, 1994), 31–34 (as well as a number of articles [see below]); J. P. Louw, "Verbale Aspek in Grieks," *Taalfasette* 15 (1971): 13–26, esp. 26; Louw, "Die Semantiese Waarde van die Perfektum in Hellenistiese Grieks," *AC* 10 (1967): 23–32, esp. 23–24; R. J. Decker, *Temporal Deixis of the Greek Verb in the Gospel of Mark with Reference to Verbal Aspect*, SBG 10 (New York: Peter Lang, 2001), 103, and passim; P. L. Fernandez, *L'aspect verbal en grec ancien: Le choix des thèmes verbaux chez Isocrate*, BCILL 111 (Louvain-la-Neuve: Peeters, 2003), 53–54; D. L.

There is, however, a more important issue at stake in this discussion that makes such a (false) claim moot. The fact that Vendler used the term "state" to describe a type of action (or *Aktionsart*) does not mean that the terms "state" or "stative" are the exclusive purview of *Aktionsart* or lexical aspect. Such a claim is preposterous, and it limits the scope of our linguistic terminology simply either to the terms that we already know or to those who claim them first. This is not the case. Aspects must be defined on their own terms and within their own systems, and as an aspect, "stative" means something different than it does within *Aktionsart*.

Campbell then defines the aspect of the perfect tense-form on the basis that it is used at the discourse level in a way similar to that of the present tense-form—that is, within what he calls discourse as opposed to narrative[36]— and therefore it functions similarly to the present tense-form and hence reflects imperfective aspect. But this clearly cannot be right since, even at the discourse level, the appearance or presence of both the present tense-form and the perfect tense-form requires an explanation with reference to their specific function(s) in the discourse. Otherwise, why would speakers/writers use two different forms that are merely functioning in the same manner? Here I will interact with Campbell's analysis, which I find completely unpersuasive.

He arrives at his conclusion by, among other things, completely ignoring the use of κέκραγεν in the narrative of John 1:15 so as to concentrate upon γέγονεν as opposed to uses of the present tense-form in John's statement (discourse); hence his extensive definition. (He also seems to ignore, but perhaps is in fact relying upon, the supposition that the perfect was originally an intensive present, according to some linguists.)[37] Yet surprisingly, after defining the meaning of the perfect on the basis of its parallel use with the present tense-form in discourse, Campbell then acknowledges that there is a difference between the two tense-forms and gives the perfect tense-form the designation of heightened proximity but still imperfective aspect (unfortunately, he simply assumes

---

Mathewson, *Verbal Aspect in the Book of Revelation: The Function of Greek Verb Tenses in John's Apocalypse*, LBS 4 (Leiden: Brill, 2010), 29–39. See also T. S. Foley, *Biblical Translation in Chinese and Greek: Verbal Aspect in Theory and Practice*, LBS 1 (Leiden: Brill, 2009), 140; J.-H. Lee, *Paul's Gospel in Romans: A Discourse Analysis of Rom. 1:16–8:39*, LBS 3 (Leiden: Brill, 2010), 68–69; W. V. Cirafesi, *Verbal Aspect in Synoptic Parallels: On the Method and Meaning of Divergent Tense-Form Usage in the Synoptic Passion Narratives*, LBS 7 (Leiden: Brill, 2013), 40–45; along with Porter, *Verbal Aspect*, 245–90; Porter, *Idioms*, 21–24, 39–42. This is not to say that any of these argue for the same verbal structure as any other, only that they employ the term "stative" as a means of characterizing the meaning (aspect) of the perfect tense-form.

36. There are better terms for this, such as "nonnarrative" or "exposition." The term "discourse" is ambiguous.

37. According to E. Schwyzer, *Griechische Grammatik auf der Grundlage von Karl Brugmanns "Griechischer Grammatik,"* 4 vols., HA 2/1 (Munich: Beck, 1939–71), 2:263.

without argument or external support that spatial relations best describe the entire Greek verbal edifice instead of time or anything else). Besides the circularity, his definition is fundamentally flawed because it fails to acknowledge the morphology of the three-tense-form Greek verbal system (the future excluded, due to its irregular paradigm) and is instead based upon a tenuous discourse theory and procedure. Moreover, what exactly is the meaning of "heightened proximity"? Two things are either proximate to each other, or they are not; the "heightened" qualifier is both senseless and superfluous. Campbell, like Fanning, seems constrained by the failure to move beyond binarity.

However, even more problematic is that his definition of aspect, on the basis of his own conception of it in discourse, is not transferable to nonindicative usage. Campbell contends that indicative usage applies to discourse, but that nonindicative usage applies to the clause (a dubious distinction at best). Having defined the semantics of the perfect tense-form on the basis of discourse usage, Campbell has no means of defining it for nonindicative (or nondiscourse) usage, so he simply assumes and asserts it.[38] However, if Campbell had recognized the triaspectual nature of Greek, and had had a more robust definition of binarity (rather than only accepting one binary opposition in the Greek verbal system between perfective and imperfective, as does Fanning), he could have arrived at three aspects, with the imperfective and the more than imperfective (we can probably call this stative) fitting well within the Greek verbal network. Campbell as much as admits that the stative aspect is a satisfactory explanation of the use of the Greek perfect when, in his analysis of translations of instances of the Greek perfect (and finding the stative explanation much to be preferred to Fanning's explanation), he admits that stativity explains 90.5 percent of the uses of the Greek perfect in the New Testament. The 9.5 percent that he questions, however, he questions simply on the basis that they should be translated with the English past tense, something he believes that stative aspect does not provide.[39] He is wrong in this regard. Instances of the Greek perfect tense-form can have past reference when various contextual indicators place the process within such a past-time context, as demonstrated by the example in John 1:15 above.[40] With recognition of the capability of the perfect tense-form and stative aspect being used

38. Campbell, *Verbal Aspect* (2008), 24–29. I find it odd that Campbell defines the perfect participle as encoding imperfective aspect and discusses it in these terms, only invoking the idea of the "enhanced" imperfective with heightened proximity after discussing examples (pp. 28–29). As for the examples, he admits that stative aspect can account for most of the same examples. It appears that Campbell is determined to assert his theory, regardless of anything else.

39. Campbell, "Breaking Perfect Rules," 148.

40. See Porter, *Verbal Aspect*, 260–65, where numerous such examples of past usage of the perfect tense-form are presented.

in past contexts, 100 percent of Campbell's examples, according to his own analysis, can be explained by stative aspect. This both eliminates the need for his peculiar imperfective analysis and supports stative aspect as in fact being the best explanation according to his own formulation of the issues.[41]

This concludes my summary of the two other views of the meaning of the perfect tense-form among the three major views within New Testament Greek study, with extended critique of the theories of Fanning and Campbell. The principal shortfall of their theories is that they fail to recognize the triaspectual structure of the Greek verbal system, which necessitates that they contrive unconvincing explanations of what is in fact more easily explainable in other ways, especially in terms of stative aspect. In fact, their own arguments reveal that they come close to formulating such a view, despite their best efforts to avoid it.

Defining the Semantics of the Perfect Tense-Form

From what I have said above, one probably can gain a clear idea of where I am proceeding in defining the semantics of the perfect tense-form. However, I also must note that, even though I am defining the aspectual value encoded by the perfect tense-form, one should also consider one such aspect always in (opposite) relationship to the other aspects. This fundamental systemic orientation underlies the following discussion.[42]

First, one needs a clear linguistic model that provides for clear and principled thinking about language in general and Greek in particular. I am a firm advocate of what Nigel Gotteri calls "formal Systemic Functional Grammar,"[43]

41. In a review of Campbell's *Basics of Verbal Aspect*, R. Crellin ("Basics of Verbal Aspect in Biblical Greek," *JSNT* 35 [2012]: 196–202) criticizes Campbell's use of spatiality and definition of the meaning of the perfect tense-form as imperfective. Crellin's own solution on the basis of lexical aspect confuses the notion of aspect (see R. Crellin, "The Greek Perfect Active System: 200 BC–AD 150," *TynBul* 64 [2013]: 157–60). This also calls into question the conclusions of M. Palu, *Jesus and Time: An Interpretation of Mark 1.15*, LNTS 468 (London: T&T Clark, 2012), 129–35.

42. See Porter, *Verbal Aspect*, 7–16, 75–109, esp. 109. The independence of the aspect system from other systems of the Greek verbal network is shown in S. E. Porter and M. B. O'Donnell, "The Greek Verbal Network Viewed from a Probabilistic Standpoint: An Exercise in Hallidayan Linguistics," *FN* 14 (2001): 3–41; and the independence of the aspect system from lexical choice (i.e., from *Aktionsart*) in S. E. Porter, "Aspect Theory and Lexicography," in *Biblical Greek Language and Lexicography: Essays in Honor of Frederick W. Danker*, ed. B. A. Taylor et al. (Grand Rapids: Eerdmans, 2004), 207–22.

43. N. J. C. Gotteri, "Toward a Systemic Approach to Tense and Aspect in Polish," in *Meaning and Form: Systemic Functional Interpretations*, ed. M. Berry et al., ADP 57 (Norwood, NJ: Ablex, 1996), 505.

holding that within a systemic and functional (SFL) framework, there is a relation between form and meaning. This framework can be expressed by means of
semantic system networks that capture the meaning potential of the language
and graphically display the meaning choices. Such system networks recognize
that meaning implies choice, and that choice indicates meaning, especially as
captured within series of binary oppositions.[44] Complex choices can be understood, and are profitably defined, as series of broader to more delicate binary
choices. The Greek verbal edifice comprises a series of such binary choices,
displayed in systems and networks. Hence, choice of perfective aspect (realized
in the aorist tense-form) implies not choosing the other alternatives (the nonperfective aspects). If nonperfective aspect is chosen, this then requires a choice
between imperfective (realized in the present tense-form, including the imperfect)
or stative aspect (realized in the perfect tense-form, including the pluperfect).

Second, a paradigm-function morphological framework best describes
Greek morphology,[45] in which the Greek language has three clearly defined
morphologically determined tense-form systems[46] (the future form is excluded
from this because it is not as clearly defined morphologically, and hence not
fully aspectual and thus aspectually vague). A sophisticated set of binary
choices can graphically explain the relationships among these morphologically
based paradigms. I believe that the perfective/nonperfective binary choice is
the primary aspectual choice, and that the nonperfective choice results in the
more delicate choice between imperfective/stative, realized by the present and
perfect tense-forms.[47] In this sense, Campbell is right (yet not because he only
recognizes the imperfective aspect), but for the wrong reasons, regarding the
meaning of the perfect tense-form: it is systemically and hence semantically
related to the present tense-form, but not simply indicating "heightened proximity" or being hyperimperfective (regardless of its possible diachronic origins).

Third, in defining the semantics of the perfect tense-form, we need to
be careful not to confuse a number of issues. These include translational

44. See W. B. McGregor, "Attribution and Identification in Gooniyandi," in Berry et al.,
Meaning and Form, 395–430, esp. 425, where he also notes that functional categories "are also
established *whenever* there is a contrast at the level of form."

45. See G. T. Stump, *Inflectional Morphology: A Theory of Paradigm Structure*, CSL 93
(Cambridge: Cambridge University Press, 2001), esp. 32–34. This morphological approach essentially states that morphology is meaningful within its respective paradigms.

46. Besides Collinge, noted above, for a recent exposition, note Clackson (*Indo-European
Linguistics*, 119, 121), who says that the "three-way split between a present, aorist and perfect
stem seems to be an original distinction [in Greek and Sanskrit] which has been lost in other
languages" (p. 119). Compare Comrie, *Aspect*, who states that "In ancient Greek, the morphology of the perfect precludes combination with the Aorist/Imperfect aspectual distinction since
different stems are used for the three verb forms" (p. 62).

47. See the systemic network in Porter, *Verbal Aspect*, 109.

descriptions, various discourse functions, *Aktionsart* categories (a particular area of conflation and hence misunderstanding), and the like, all of which have confused other efforts. In one sense, as I have previously suggested, I would be content with the tense-forms simply being numbered, since their names often confuse their meanings and function.[48] However, there is sufficient precedent, even in Fanning and Campbell, to warrant the designation "state" or "stativity" as the best means of labeling the semantic category of the perfect tense-form. By this, I do not mean the category found in *Aktionsart*, even if there is some possible similarity. What I mean is that, as with all aspectual choices, the use by an author of the perfect tense-form encodes the action as reflecting a complex state of affairs of the subject. This may involve a previous action (although this may be true for the action encoded by any of the aspects), but the emphasis is upon this subject-related state of affairs.[49] In this sense, there may be some overlap with *Aktionsart* theory in that both are using the notion of state or stativity. However, what the use of grammatical aspect (as opposed to lexical aspect, or *Aktionsart*) says is that, by using this particular tense-form, the author chooses to describe the particular process as a state or as stative, regardless of the lexeme selected and its supposed *Aktionsart*.

Fourth, we can do a better job of defining the meaning of the perfect tense-form if we examine it systemically and through the categories of markedness. As I noted above, the perfect tense-form is the realization of (at least) two meaningful semantic choices. The nonperfective choice is marked in relation to the perfective, and the stative (realized by the perfect) in opposition to the imperfective (realized by the present). The perfect tense-form is distributionally marked in relation to the present and aorist, occurring the least frequently. The perfect tense-form also has material markedness, with its unthematic root, endings, and reduplication integral to the stem as part of its paradigm. The perfect, regarding implicational markedness, has the greatest morphological

---

48. S. E. Porter, "Tense Terminology and Greek Language Study: A Linguistic Re-Evaluation," *SWPLL* 3 (1986): 77–86. I do not actually suggest numbering the tense-forms, but indicate their complexity.

49. This is stated clearly by Louw, "Semantiese Waarde," esp. 31; argued at length in various ways by McKay, *Greek Grammar*, 146; McKay, *New Syntax*, 31; McKay, "The Use of the Ancient Greek Perfect Down to the Second Century AD," *BICS* 12 (1965): 1–21; McKay, "On the Perfect and Other Aspects in the Greek Non-Literary Papyri," *BICS* 27 (1980): 23–49; McKay, "On the Perfect and Other Aspects in New Testament Greek," *NovT* 23 (1981): 289–329; and recently restated in D. Pastorelli, "La formule johannique (Jean 14:25; 15:11; 16:1, 4, 6, 25, 33): Un exemple de parfait transitif," *FN* 19 (2006): 73–88. Campbell (*Verbal Aspect* [2007], 169–70) makes far too much of trying to play McKay and Louw off of each other regarding stativity and its relation to the subject and the process, when they both essentially argue for the stative aspect with regard to the subject as opposed to the object or result.

regularity (as opposed to the thematic and nonthematic roots and various types of augmentation and suffixes of the aorist and present tense-forms) but also the greatest defectivation. This defectivation results in few instances of the perfect subjunctive and loss of the optative, in which these tense-forms are formed periphrastically.[50] Semantic markedness forms a cline, from the semantics of the aorist to the present to the perfect. This is the movement from the undifferentiated whole or complete action, grammaticalized by the aorist; to the contoured (whether internally or not) or progressive action of the present; to the most highly defined, complex, and contoured of the perfect, what I have labeled as the stative. Campbell is correct in noting (even though he does not formulate it this way) that the most heavily marked tense-form occurs more frequently in the most heavily marked contexts, including exposition (his discourse), even if he does so by neglecting its use in narrative. We can see this distribution not as sole means to a definition but probably as an instance of markedness assimilation, in which marked forms tend (though not invariably) to appear in marked contexts.[51]

Sixth, the definition of stative aspect that I have offered is similar to the definitions that have been proposed by a number of previous scholars. These include, to some extent, Martín Ruipérez, who speaks of a "resultant state," that is, a state (C) that results from action AB, different from the action itself and not the event itself.[52] In this sense, the stative aspect in some ways subsumes either aspect or both the perfective and imperfective aspects, hence its markedness and semantic complexity (note that this is not the so-called resultive perfect, where the result rests on the object of the action, a category that does not in fact exist).[53] Perhaps most important is the work of J. P. Louw, which is not used by Fanning on the perfect, and is cited though apparently not clearly understood by Campbell. Louw defines the aspect of the perfect as stative ("statief" or "statiewe aspek" in Afrikaans).[54] Louw points out that some examples simply cannot be explained by the traditional explanation of the perfect, and, I would contend, cannot be explained by either perfective or imperfective aspect on their own. Examples that Louw cites include the

50. See Porter, *Verbal Aspect*, 246–48.
51. See E. L. Battistella, *The Logic of Markedness* (Oxford: Oxford University Press, 1996), 61–65.
52. M. S. Ruipérez, *Estructura del sistema de aspectos y tiempos del verbo griego antigua: Análisis funcional sincrónico* (Salamanca: Colegio Trilingue de la Universidad, 1954), 45.
53. See Porter, *Verbal Aspect*, 257–59.
54. Louw, "Verbale Aspek," 26; compare Louw, "Semantiese Waarde," 27. Contrary to those who wish to minimize its aspect (perhaps because it falls outside of their preconceived framework of what aspect entails, or because they simply cannot understand it), Louw ("Verbale Aspek," 26) says that aspect is particularly strong in the perfect tense-form.

following verbs.[55] For example, ἐλπίζω, in the perfect ἤλπικα, means "I have set my hope on," or "I hope," or "I am in a hopeful state" (whether based upon another event or not, and it cannot be resultive because it is intransitive). The verb οἶδα means "I know," indicating the knowing state of the subject (Louw notes that one never translates the verb as "I discovered [εἶδον] and now it is discovered," but always in terms of knowing: "I know"). A further example is John 16:30: νῦν οἴδαμεν ὅτι οἶδας πάντα ("now we know that you know all things"), where the knowing states of the subjects are contrasted, not the result of knowing. There are similar examples with γινώσκω or, in the perfect, ἔγνωκα, such as John 8:52: νῦν ἐγνώκαμεν ("now we know") that Jesus (supposedly) has a demon. The verb κράζω, in the perfect κέκραγα (and κέκραγεν in John 1:15), indicates "I shout" (or in John 1:15, "he shouts"),[56] which in no way can be explained as indicating a state of the subject or object as the result of a completed action. The verb δέχομαι, in the perfect δέδεγμαι, means "I receive," as in Acts 8:14, where the Jerusalem apostles heard that the Samaritans δέδεκται ("received," or "were in a state of reception of") the word of God (note the past context).[57] Finally, the verb κρίνω, in the perfect κέκρικα, indicates a state of judgment, as in John 16:11: the ruler of this world κέκριται ("is judged," or "stands judged"). Other examples can be cited, but they indicate the same thing: any previous action or any idea of an object-oriented result is not part of what the perfect means in its stative aspect.

This stative aspect (grammatical aspect) is found whether the perfect tense-form is used in the indicative or in the nonindicative, and whether it is found in narrative or nonnarrative. Examples of narrative use include the following:[58] John 1:15, noted above; John 12:40: τετύφλωκεν αὐτῶν τοὺς ὀφθαλμοὺς ("he blinded their eyes"), used in parallel with a subsequent aorist with perfective aspect (καὶ ἐπώρωσεν αὐτῶν τὴν καρδίαν, "and hardened their heart"), quite possibly an instance of tense-form reduction (and a quotation of Isa. 6:10); 2 Corinthians 2:13: οὐκ ἔσχηκα ἄνεσιν τῷ πνεύματί μου ("I did not have rest in my spirit"; i.e., "I was not in a restful state"), used in parallel with a subsequent aorist with perfective aspect (ἀλλὰ ἀποταξάμενος αὐτοῖς ἐξῆλθον εἰς

55. Louw, "Semantiese Waarde," 23–24. The following examples are taken from Louw's article and from Porter, *Verbal Aspect*, 253–56.

56. Louw ("Semantiese Waarde," 27) prefers the translation "scream" in order to capture the intense meaning of the perfect in this instance.

57. Instances with an object are probably best understood as the subject (regardless of person), "*x*-ed the *y* and now (logically, not temporally) is in a state of having done so." This formulation is based upon A. Willi, *The Languages of Aristophanes: Aspects of Linguistic Variation in Classical Attic Greek* (Oxford: Oxford University Press, 2003), 130–31, but differs from his.

58. See Porter, *Idioms*, 40–41. Campbell's (*Verbal Aspect* [2007], 187, 208–10) explanation of this as a "historical present" similar to a "historic perfect" is unnecessary and misleading.

Μακεδονίαν, "but taking leave of them, I went into Macedonia"), again possibly an instance of tense-form reduction; Revelation 5:7: ἦλθεν καὶ εἴληφεν ("he came and took"), in parallel with an aorist tense-form and followed by an aorist in the narrative (καὶ ὅτε ἔλαβεν τὸ βιβλίον, "and when he took the book" [5:8]). I note that in narrative there are instances where the perfect and the aorist are used in parallel. Perhaps there is a further correlation in narrative to the one that Campbell claims to have found in nonnarrative, in which the perfect tense-form encoding stative aspect is used in contrastive parallel with the mainline tense-form in each of these basic text types. This claim, however, rightly moves from the semantics of the perfect tense-form to its discourse function, and one that, I believe, establishes the priorities correctly for discussion. The semantics of the form within the Greek verbal system are established first (at the level of code), before extended application to various discourse contexts (in text). Otherwise, one will not be looking at the meaning of the perfect tense-form itself, but will instead be looking at the meaning of its usage in context—two different things.

Some other examples worth considering include the following.[59] The verb ἐγγίζω, in the perfect ἤγγικα, is used to speak of a near state: the kingdom stands near or is at hand (Matt. 3:2 // Mark 1:15; Matt. 4:17; 10:7; Luke 10:9, 11); Jesus tells his disciples that his hour or his betrayer stands near (Matt. 26:45–46 // Mark 14:42); Paul says that the night is cut short and the day is near (Rom. 13:12); and James 5:8 says that the coming of the Lord is at hand. The verb θνήσκω, in the perfect τέθνηκα, indicates a dead state. In John 11:44, Lazarus, ὁ τεθνηκώς ("the dead one"), came out of the tomb (so much for any abiding state of death indicated by the perfect tense-form according to traditional views). The verb πιστεύω, in the perfect πεπίστευκα, is used in John 6:69 (along with γινώσκω): καὶ ἡμεῖς πεπιστεύκαμεν καὶ ἐγνώκαμεν ὅτι σὺ εἶ ὁ ἅγιος τοῦ θεοῦ ("and we believe and know that you are the holy one of God"). C. K. Barrett renders the verbs this way: "We are in a state of faith and knowledge; we have recognized the truth and hold it."[60] The verb διανοίγω, in the perfect διήνοιγα, is used in the participle form in Acts 7:56: τοὺς οὐρανοὺς διηνοιγμένους ("the open heavens"; i.e., "the heavens standing open"). Other examples include Galatians 5:11, where, after dismissing charges that he is preaching circumcision, Paul affirms that in this way the scandal of the cross κατήργηται ("stands abolished"). In Hebrews 7:6, the author states that Melchizedek δεδεκάτωκεν ("tithed") Abraham, though the two men were not related, and εὐλόγηκεν ("blessed") the one possessing the promise.

59. See Porter, *Verbal Aspect*, 255–56.
60. C. K. Barrett, *The Gospel according to St. John*, 2nd ed. (London: SPCK, 1978), 306.

This admittedly brief exposition of the semantics of the perfect tense-form shows how it relates to the larger issue of the Greek verbal system, defines stative aspect of the perfect tense-form as a clear aspectual category, and provides a range of examples of how to understand its semantics in context. From these examples, it should now be clear which theory among the three major views stands out as the most plausible one in defining the meaning of the perfect tense-form.

Conclusion

There is much in common among leading advocates of the Greek of the New Testament regarding its verbal structure. However, there are also crucial points of difference. Included within these is the meaning of the perfect tense-form. In fact, the meaning of the perfect tense-form has been a point of continuing disagreement among the scholars discussed above. However, much of the disagreement is simply the result of misunderstanding by those who fail to differentiate and define the appropriate semantic categories (and even a carelessness in their own definitions that shows they are not too far from the stative truth). These categories especially include the difference between aspect and other semantic or pragmatic categories (such as *Aktionsart*), the importance of thinking beyond simple binarism, the need to formulate understanding not simply on the basis of translation, and, most important, the need to have a robust linguistic theoretical framework upon which analyses and arguments are based—failures of which are major shortcomings of other theories. There is, however, a more plausible and defensible semantic characterization of the meaning of the perfect tense-form. I argue on a number of fronts—not least the failure of these other theories, but also on the basis of formal and functional aspectual semantic categories—that stative aspect is a useful functional category to describe the meaning of the perfect tense-form.

PART 3

Doing
Analysis

13

A Register Analysis of Mark 13

Toward a Context of Situation

Introduction

This chapter extends and refines my earlier work on register analysis as the study of a variety of language and on the register of Mark 13 in particular. My earlier work developed a definition of the concept of register and then applied register analysis to Mark's Gospel.[1] The systemic functional linguistic (SFL) notion of register has proved to be one of the most productive in New Testament discourse analysis, even if Halliday or others probably would not recognize the form that it has taken or how it has been used by those examining ancient Greek. The concept of register has proved very important in the discourse model that Matthew Brook O'Donnell and I, along with others, have been developing by fits and starts since the 1990s. One of the distinct advantages of the notion of register in discourse studies is that it provides a means by which the data of a

1. S. E. Porter, "Dialect and Register in the Greek of the New Testament: Theory" and "Register in the Greek of the New Testament: Application with Reference to Mark's Gospel," both in *Rethinking Contexts, Rereading Texts: Contributions from the Social Sciences to Biblical Interpretation*, ed. M. D. Carroll R., JSOTSup 299 (Sheffield: Sheffield Academic Press, 2000), 190–208, 209–29. See also chap. 7 in the present volume.

language can be described, categorized, and then usefully analyzed in service of broader discourse notions. In my earlier application of register analysis, I analyzed the mode, tenor, and field of Mark's Gospel. Regarding mode, I concluded that this oral/written narrative, with Jesus as major character, coheres by means of by a variety of elements, such as connectives, syntax, and person reference.[2] Regarding tenor, I observed that this monolingual text utilizes third person, with some instances of first and second person, especially in discourse by the main character, Jesus. Instances of the third person are particularly noteworthy because of their distancing of the participant from the action. Last, regarding field, I discussed the subject of the Gospel as the good news of Jesus Christ, "Son of God."[3] Transitivity choices reveal that the text's focus is upon the actions done by or to Jesus.

My first examination of Mark 13 sought to develop a new criterion for determining authenticity in historical-Jesus research (i.e., the criterion of discourse features).[4] Here I wish to examine Mark 13 from a different standpoint, this time asking how the register factors indicate its context of situation.[5]

Register Analysis of Mark 13

Mark 13:5–37 is the largest unit of discourse in Mark's Gospel. Although originally it may not have been (yet also it may have been) delivered as a single discourse, there are good reasons for seeing it as at least a unified (if not single) discourse and for analyzing it as such.[6] Its unity and cohesion suggest a definable context of situation, albeit perhaps one that is in some ways different from that of the Gospel of Mark itself.[7] This stands to reason, since the

2. See Porter, "Register in the Greek," 216–27. See now also G. Martin, "Procedural Register in the Olivet Discourse: A Functional Linguistic Approach to Mark 13," *Bib* 90 (2009): 457–83.

3. The variant in Mark 1:1 is well supported by the textual evidence.

4. S. E. Porter, *The Criteria for Authenticity in Historical-Jesus Research: Previous Discussion and New Proposals*, JSNTSup 191 (Sheffield: Sheffield Academic Press, 2000), 210–37, which I freely draw upon. See also J. A. L. Lee, "Some Features of the Speech of Jesus in Mark's Gospel," *NovT* 27 (1985): 1–26.

5. Many of the additional data come from information generated by the OpenText.org project, whose principals are S. E. Porter, J. T. Reed, and M. B. O'Donnell.

6. Discourse analysis is not a tool that can be used to determine textual integrity, although it can provide a means of examining evidence for those wishing to argue for or against it. This is shown by J. T. Reed, *A Discourse Analysis of Philippians: Method and Rhetoric in the Debate over Literary Integrity*, JSNTSup 136 (Sheffield: Sheffield Academic Press, 1997), 412–18. The range of critical opinion on Mark 13 is usefully surveyed in G. R. Beasley-Murray, *Jesus and the Last Days: The Interpretation of the Olivet Discourse* (Peabody, MA: Hendrickson, 1993), 1–349.

7. The issue of whether a given discourse can have multiple contexts of situation or only a single context of situation, and whether there are such things as registers or subregisters is not

context of situation of the Gospel is different from the context of situation that generated any given discourse unit, including this so-called Little Apocalypse. Recent Gospel studies have only recently begun to catch up with register studies in the sense that these studies have noted that there are features of the Gospels that point away from them being exclusively or even primarily written for a particular early Christian community but rather for a broader, even if not universal, audience.[8] Yet there are features of each Gospel that implicate distinct contexts of situation, and these should not be neglected or denied. I will treat the three components of context together with their corresponding linguistic metafunctions in order to determine the register of this discourse—that is, its prototypical character. One of the strengths of SFL is its reciprocal interstratal analysis that moves from context to content, including semantics to lexicogrammar. Language is a system of meanings that are realized in lexicogrammar. My analysis is concerned with examining the lexicogrammar in order to assess the semantics expressed by it. This provides a logical means that allows for the proper categorization of the data and the drawing of pertinent conclusions regarding the register of the passage and its context of situation—that is, the type of context in which such a discourse would typically be expressed.

Mode of Discourse and Textual Metafunction

With regard to textual features of discourse, I will concentrate on cohesion, or the means by which the text displays its unity as a whole,[9] and information flow, or the means by which the subject matter of the passage (discussed under field of discourse) is presented.

COHESION

There are a number of features that indicate the cohesion of the discourse. (1) The first is the conjunctions.[10] One of the noteworthy (and often commented

---

discussed here. The question of registers within registers, or subregisters, remains a debated point. If a register is a variety of language, even though it is linguistically circumscribed, then there seems to be no reason why there cannot be subvarieties that evidence similar, if not identical, lexicogrammatical patterns.

8. See R. Bauckham, ed., *The Gospels for All Christians: Rethinking the Gospel Audiences* (Grand Rapids: Eerdmans, 1998).

9. See M. A. K. Halliday and R. Hasan, *Cohesion in English*, ELS (London: Longman, 1976), 1–2. A now neglected work contemporary with Halliday and Hasan is W. Gutwinski, *Cohesion in Literary Texts: A Study of Some Grammatical and Lexical Features of English Discourse*, JLSMi 204 (The Hague: Mouton, 1976). For studies of classical Greek, see S. Bakker and G. Wakker, eds., *Discourse Cohesion in Ancient Greek*, ASCP 16 (Leiden: Brill, 2009).

10. Conjunctions are a common feature for analysis in studies of cohesion. See Halliday and Hasan, *Cohesion in English*, 226–73; D. Schiffrin, *Discourse Markers*, SIS 5 (Cambridge:

upon) features of Mark's Gospel is the use of the conjunction καί ("and") to introduce sections and subsections of the Gospel. For example, of the 88 sections in the Westcott-Hort edition of the Greek New Testament, according to John Hawkins, 80 sections begin with καί, while δέ begins (postpositively) six, showing Mark's much more frequent usage of καί against δέ than in Matthew and Luke.[11] Apparently Mark uses this conjunction as a means of uniting together his episodes/pericopes and signaling when a new one begins[12]—whether one accepts this feature of Markan syntax as simply a feature of Koine Greek (perhaps enhanced in Markan usage), whether one treats it as a distinctive characteristic of Markan style, or (least likely) whether one considers it a clear Semitism.[13]

A noteworthy feature of Mark 13, however, is significantly reduced use of conjunctions, to the point of raising questions about unity and cohesion. This pattern includes reduction in the use of the introductory conjunctive καί. According to the subsections in the Nestle-Aland Greek New Testament (27th ed.), καί is used to open 114 of 143 subsections of Mark's Gospel, including

Cambridge University Press, 1987), esp. 128–90. See also S. H. Levinsohn, *Textual Connections in Acts*, SBLMS 31 (Atlanta: Scholars Press, 1987), esp. 83–156; Levinsohn, *Discourse Features of New Testament Greek: A Coursebook on the Information Structure of New Testament Greek*, 2nd ed. (Dallas: SIL International, 2000), esp. 13–30; D. A. Black, with K. Barnwell, and S. Levinsohn, eds., *Linguistics and New Testament Interpretation: Essays on Discourse Analysis* (Nashville: Broadman, 1992); S. L. Black, *Sentence Conjunctions in the Gospel of Matthew: καί, δέ, τότε, γάρ, οὖν and Asyndeton in Narrative Discourse*, JSNTSup 216 (Sheffield: Sheffield Academic Press, 2002); S. E. Porter and M. B. O'Donnell, "Conjunctions, Clines and Levels of Discourse," *FN* 20 (2007): 3–14. However, it has been argued that lexis organizes text, shifting the emphasis to lexis for discussion of cohesion. See M. Hoey, *Patterns of Lexis in Text*, DEL (Oxford: Oxford University Press, 1991).

11. J. Hawkins, *Horae synopticae* (Oxford: Clarendon, 1909), 151. There are numerous internal uses of conjunctive καί as well, as is discussed below. E. Maloney notes the frequency of use of καί over δέ throughout Mark's Gospel (without differentiating levels of usage) (*Semitic Interference in Marcan Syntax*, SBLDS 5 [Chico, CA: Scholars Press, 1981], 66).

12. To use the functional language of Levinsohn (*Discourse Features*, 13–31), Mark's use of καί usually seems to indicate continuity or points of departure.

13. On the use of conjunctive καί as a feature of Greek, see S. Trenkner, *Le style kai dans le récital attique oral* (Brussels: Éditions de l'Institut d'Études Polonaises en Belgique, 1948), esp. 5–7 on the New Testament; E. Mayser, *Grammatik der griechischen Papyri aus der Ptolemäerzeit*, 3 vols. (Berlin: de Gruyter, 1906–34), 2:3, 184–86; M. Reiser, *Syntax und Stil des Markusevangeliums im Licht der hellenistischen Volksliteratur*, WUNT 2/11 (Tübingen: Mohr Siebeck, 1984), 99–137. On the use of καί as a characteristic of Markan style, see Hawkins, *Horae synopticae*, 150–52; V. Taylor, *The Gospel according to St. Mark* (London: Macmillan, 1959), 48–49; and many other commentators. On the use of καί as a Semitism, see M. Black, *An Aramaic Approach to the Gospels and Acts* (Oxford: Clarendon, 1946; repr., Peabody, MA: Hendrickson, 1998 [with "Introduction: An Aramaic Approach Thirty Years Later," by C. A. Evans, v–xxv]), 61–69; Maloney, *Semitic Interference*, 66–74; see also S. P. Brock, review of *An Aramaic Approach to the Gospels and Acts*, by Matthew Black, *JTS* 20 (1969): 274–78.

13:1 and 13:3, both narrative portions outside of the words of Jesus, but is used in only one of nine subsections within 13:5–37, at verse 21.[14] In other words, roughly 80 percent of all of the subsections of the Gospel begin with καί (i.e., 4 out of 5), while within 13:5–37 only about 11 percent of the sections begin with καί (the percentage of the subsections of the Gospel as a whole beginning with καί would increase if 13:5–37 were not entered into the calculation). By contrast, within the discourse of Mark 4:3–32 every one of the subsections except the opening of the speaking in verse 3 begins with καί (5 of 6, not including the one at 4:1, which begins with καί). Within 13:5–37, rather than καί, two other linguistic elements apparently are used to create textual cohesion. One of these is conjunctive δέ, used in verses 9, 14, 18, 28, and 32—that is, in 5 out of 9 instances (56%).[15] The other elements are asyndeton (vv. 30, 33) and ἀλλά (v. 24). Although the sample is too small for us to speak definitively, the ratios for usage of καί and δέ in Mark's Gospel are here apparently reversed (though clearly maintained in Mark 4). Within the discourse itself there is a proportionate reduction in the use of conjunctions, especially when compared to 4:3–32. Of the 91 nonembedded clauses in 13:5–37 are 51 that have a conjunction (56% of the clauses), of which 23 are instances of καί (45%) and 7 are δέ (14%).[16] Thus, 40 percent of the conjunctions used are conjunctions other than those two. By comparison, of the 105 nonembedded clauses in 4:3–32 are 70 that have a conjunction (67%), of which 51 are instances of καί (73%) and 2 are δέ (3%), thus accounting for 76 percent of all of the conjunctions. Another linguistic feature in the Mark 13 discourse is asyndeton. Elliott Maloney has analyzed the types of asyndeton in Mark's Gospel. Mark 13:5–37 has ten instances where sentences are placed together without a conjunction or other kind of linking word (vv. 6, 7, 8 [3x], 9, 23, 30, 31, 34), and one instance of two imperatives placed together (v. 33).[17]

14. Some later manuscripts do attempt to add καί, however; see Codex Bezae (D) at Mark 13:15.

15. This corrects the figures found in Porter, *Criteria for Authenticity*, 225, with the point being made even more firmly.

16. Mark 13 has the lowest frequency per verse of use of καί (1.1 per verse compared to a range of 1.2 in Mark 15 to 2.0 in Mark 5 and Mark 6), whether verses 1–5a are included or not (without these verses the frequency is 1.0 per verse). Mark 13 also has the lowest frequency of verse-initial καί of any chapter in Mark's Gospel (.35 per verse compared to .40 in Mark 10 to .83 in Mark 3), whether verses 1–5a are included or not (without these verses the frequency is .31 per verse); this is roughly half that of the frequency of verse-initial καί for the entire Gospel (.65 per verse). The frequency of καί per 1,000 words in the whole of Mark's Gospel is 84.45, with Mark 13 having a frequency of only 59.42 per 1,000 words.

17. See Maloney, *Semitic Interference*, 77. In the first version of this paper I should have stated that I was looking at 6 of 22 "chief instances" of asyndeton on the basis of Hawkins, *Horae synopticae*, 137–38.

Although asyndeton is typically thought to be poor Greek, Maloney goes on to note that both forms of asyndeton are common features of Hellenistic Greek, and thus one of the means of creating cohesive discourse in the Hellenistic/Roman period literature.

At first glance, the use of conjunctions in Mark 13 might argue against cohesion and for the discourse being a random collection of individual statements linked by a later redactor. On more than one occasion, of course, this has been argued for. However, another way of examining this evidence is to accept that the discourse is cohesive, but along different lines, and that this fact helps to distinguish this discourse from the Gospel's narration. Whereas the narrator of the Gospel relies upon the use of καί, here the author, while still using καί, uses it less frequently and in fact utilizes other cohesive means, including the conjunction δέ and asyndeton, as the means for creating cohesion.

INFORMATION FLOW AND LEXICAL ANALYSIS

Another textual feature is information flow.[18] I realize that information flow can be defined to include a number of elements (especially those related to the ordering of elements), but here I will include lexical analysis.[19] The vocabulary of a discourse often is analyzed in an undifferentiated way, examining only individual lexical items. One of the advantages of register analysis is that the choice of lexical items is seen to contribute to different dimensions of the discourse. For the most part, vocabulary usually is treated as indicating the subject matter of the discourse (which will be briefly discussed below regarding the field of discourse). Yet the choice of lexical items is also a means by which an author structures and shapes the discourse and directs the flow of information. This often occurs in terms of how words from the same semantic domain are selected, and how these items are distributed throughout the discourse.

With regard to Markan vocabulary, one can find some interesting patterns in Mark 13. The first dimension that I wish to discuss concerns the author's characteristic vocabulary, and how that relates to the vocabulary of Mark 13. The characteristic vocabulary of an author is that set of lexical items that is regularly drawn upon to shape the discourse and convey the flow of information. Of the 41 words that Hawkins determines are characteristic of Mark's Gospel, only 4 instances of these words occur in the words of Jesus in 13:5–37

18. On information flow, see Reed, *Discourse Analysis of Philippians*, 101–19.
19. See R. Hasan, "The Grammarian's Dream: Lexis as Most Delicate Grammar," in *New Developments in Systemic Linguistics*, vol. 1, *Theory and Description*, ed. M. A. K. Halliday and R. P. Fawcett (London: Pinter, 1987), 184–211.

(out of 357 uses of this characteristic vocabulary throughout the Gospel).[20] Whereas the characteristic vocabulary appears at a rate of roughly 1 in every 31 words over the entire Gospel (11,099 words in 1:1–16:8), these words only appear at the rate of roughly 1 in every 132 words in 13:5–37 (530 words). The characteristic vocabulary is more than four times as frequent in the Gospel as it is in 13:5–37. In other words, there appears to be a shift in the information flow, since this Markan section must rely upon highly noncharacteristic vocabulary.

The second dimension that I wish to consider is, in some ways, the reverse of the first. It involves the use of unusual vocabulary or phrasing in 13:5–37, some of which has been changed in the other Gospels.[21] These odd or unusual features are, by definition, ones that the author does not use elsewhere in the Gospel. For example, the word προμεριμνᾶτε ("worry") in 13:11 is not found elsewhere in the New Testament, but is found in the unprefixed form in Matthew 10:19 and Luke 12:11; the articular prepositional phrase (ὁ εἰς τὸν ἀγρόν) in 13:16 is changed so as to use ἐν in Matthew 24:18 and Luke 17:31; the phrase ἔσονται γὰρ αἱ ἡμέραι ἐκεῖναι θλῖψις in 13:19 is avoided in Matthew 24:21 and Luke 21:23; and the pronouns οἵα . . . τοιαύτη in 13:19 are not found elsewhere in Mark, in the Matthean parallel, or in Daniel, to which an allusion is being made.[22] These odd features, which are part of the pattern of information flow of 13:5–37, are avoided in the other Gospels as well as elsewhere in Mark.

A third dimension involves the distribution of lexical items within semantic domains. As will be discussed below, semantic domains are useful in establishing the field of a discourse. However, the repeated use of words from a semantic domain also serves to create cohesion (sometimes called semantic chains). Three categories of domains have significant usage within Mark 13.

20. These include εὐαγγέλιον in 13:10, οὔπω in 13:7, πρωΐ in 13:35 and τοιοῦτος in 13:19. See Hawkins, Horae synopticae, 12–13. E. J. Pryke (Redactional Style in the Marcan Gospel: A Study of Syntax and Vocabulary as Guides to Redaction in Mark, SNTSMS 33 (Cambridge: Cambridge University Press, 1978], 136–38) presents a list of 140 Markan redactional vocabulary (1,423 occurrences), but the list cannot be used because, reflective of its problems, it includes words that have a single occurrence, includes syntactical units, and seems to be determined on the basis of sometimes questionable and subjective syntactical analysis. For a reconsideration of some issues related to Markan vocabulary, see R. Mackowski, "Some Colloquialisms in the Gospel according to Mark," in Daidalikon: Studies in Memory of Raymond V. Schoder, SJ, ed. R. F. Sutton Jr. (Wauconda, IL: Bolchazy-Carducci, 1989), 229–38.

21. This point as formulated assumes Markan priority. One could, however, simply note that in 13:5–37 certain less usual lexical and syntactical choices are made. On issues in lexicography with regard to the Greek of the New Testament, see S. E. Porter, Studies in the Greek New Testament: Theory and Practice, SBG 6 (New York: Peter Lang, 1996), 49–74; also chaps. 3–4 in the present volume.

22. See Hawkins, Horae synopticae, 133–34.

The first category includes words for "Time" (37 instances; domain 67),[23] "Affirmation, Negation" (24 instances; domain 69), "Communication" (23 instances; domain 33), and "Be, Become, Exist, Happen" (22 instances; domain 13). Words from at least three of these domains appear in every subunit of 13:5–37 (vv. 5–8, 9–13, 14–17, 18–20, 21–23, 24–27, 28–29, 30–31, 33–37) except for one (v. 32), in which only two are used ("Time" [domain 67] and "Be, Become, Exist, Happen" [domain 13]). Words for time are by far the most common in this discourse (see below), and they occur in every subunit of the discourse apart from one (vv. 30–31). The same can be said for words of "Affirmation, Negation" (domain 69) (the one unit in which these words do not occur is vv. 28–29). The other domains appear in all but two of the subunits ("Communication" [domain 33] words do not appear in vv. 24–27 and v. 32; "Be, Become, Exist, Happen" [domain 13] words do not appear in vv. 14–17 and v. 32). Thus words for time are used at a density of 1 instance every 4 clauses (not counting embedded clauses) and 8.5 every subunit. The other three domains appear at roughly 1 for every 5 clauses and 3 every subunit.

The second set of domains includes "Geographical Objects and Features" (15 instances; domain 1), "Linear Movement" (13 instances; domain 15), "Relations" (13 instances; domain 89), and "Quantity" (12 instances; domain 59). What is noticeable about this second set of words is that they feature far less significantly in creating cohesion, since their usage is much less systematic. In fact, there are only two subunits in which these words appear in proportions that are near or in excess of those of the first group. In verses 14–17 there is an equal number of instances of the first and second major domain groups, and in verses 24–27 there is a significantly larger number of examples from the second group than the first. The average for the second group is 1 instance per 8 to 10 clauses and approximately 1.5 to 2 instances per unit.

The third group of domains includes "Learn" (9 instances; domain 27), "Possess, Transfer, Exchange" (8 instances; domain 57), "Control, Rule" (7 instances; domain 37), "Kinship Terms" (8 instances; domain 10), "Constructions" (5 instances; domain 7), and "Physiological Processes and States" (6 instances; domain 23). These words are only used haphazardly in the discourse, apart from usage in verses 14–17 and verses 32–35, but in neither as much as the words from the first group.

Thus the first domain group, apart from its contribution to the subject matter of the discourse, serves an important function in creating cohesion in the

23. I use the semantic domains in J. P. Louw and E. A. Nida, *A Greek-English Lexicon of the New Testament Based on Semantic Domains*, 2 vols. (New York: United Bible Societies, 1988).

discourse. The second domain group performs a somewhat similar process, though in a less systematic way, while the third domain group is used only for specific informational purposes and contributes little to the cohesive flow of information itself.

Placing vocabulary statistics, as well as other factors, within this contextual category helps to isolate their function within Mark's Gospel. On the basis of the data gathered and analyzed above, there are several clear indications that Mark 13:5–37 is made cohesive in a manner that distinguishes it from the rest of Mark's Gospel.[24]

Tenor of Discourse and Interpersonal Metafunction

The tenor of a discourse is concerned with participant relations and how they are represented by linguistic features such as grammaticalized, reduced (e.g., pronouns), and implied forms (e.g., verb-form endings), and how the actions of the participants are related to reality (mood and attitude).[25] The tenor of Mark 13 can be analyzed with reference to interaction that is narrated, and also with reference to the interaction represented by Jesus's discourse itself.

Before Jesus's speech itself begins (13:1–4), the directive focus of the discourse is from the disciples toward Jesus. The disciples are grammaticalized in the first clause of the discourse (v. 1), while Jesus is referred to with three reduced (pronoun) forms. One of Jesus's disciples addresses him with commands, demanding information from him about the temple and when its destruction will occur (v. 1). Jesus, referred to with a grammaticalized form, then answers this disciple with a question and a statement about the devastation (v. 2). In verse 3 Jesus is again referred to with a reduced form (pronoun), but now four disciples are referred to with grammaticalized forms—"Peter," "James," "John," and "Andrew"—who command Jesus to tell them when the destruction will occur and what signs to expect (v. 4). "Jesus," again referred to with a grammaticalized form, then gives his discourse.

The participants in the discourse and the attitudinal semantics are worth noting. Regarding the participants, there are clearly two categories of

---

24. Clearly, a more thorough study of the semantic domains throughout Mark's Gospel needs to be done.

25. On participant reference, see Levinsohn, *Discourse Features*, 113–26; G. Martín-Asensio, *Transitivity-Based Foregrounding in the Acts of the Apostles: A Functional-Grammatical Approach to the Lukan Perspective*, JSNTSup 202, SNTG 8 (Sheffield: Sheffield Academic Press, 2000), esp. 87–111; on mood and modality, see S. E. Porter, *Verbal Aspect in the Greek of the New Testament, with Reference to Tense and Mood*, SBG 1 (New York: Peter Lang, 1989), 163–78; Porter, *Idioms of the Greek New Testament*, 2nd ed., BLG 2 (Sheffield: Sheffield Academic Press, 1994), 50–61.

participants in the discourse. The first is Jesus and his four disciples, Peter, James, John, and Andrew (the primary participants). All are referred to by using grammaticalized forms before the discourse begins, but only by reduced and implied forms within the discourse itself (the possible exception is reference to the "Son" in v. 32).[26] Nevertheless, these forms are used relatively frequently. Jesus has 8 instances of reduced or implied reference within the discourse itself, along with the two grammaticalized references and 7 reduced or implied references in verses 1–5a, before the discourse proper. The four disciples have 15 reduced and 27 implied references to them within the discourse. Clearly these four disciples are the major participants with Jesus in this dialogue. However, there are other secondary participants as well (those invoked but not interactive with the primary participants). In fact, there are thirty other indirect participants in the discourse, though none of them is referred to more than 13 times, and four of them only 1 time. Even those that appear the most within this group, such as human beings, God, and false Christs, tend (apart from human beings) to appear in concentrated instances. For example, over half of the references to God appear in verses 19 and 20; similarly, over half of the references to false Christs appear in verses 5–6 and 22.

Within the discourse itself, Jesus clearly is instigating and directing comments to his listeners by means of use of the imperative mood-form.[27] As Willem Vorster states, "It is remarkable that almost everything which is said to, and thus about the four [disciples] to whom the speech is directed, is done by way of imperatives."[28] Indeed, Mark 13 has a larger number of imperatives than any other single chapter in Mark (23 in total, and 21 in vv. 5–37 [1 per 1.5 verses], with the two in verses 1 and 4 used by the disciples).[29] This is the case even though it is much smaller than several other chapters that have large numbers of imperatives (e.g., Mark 9 has 11 imperatives in 50 verses [1 per

26. There is reference to "the Christ" in verse 21, but this is not to Jesus but rather to one claiming to have found the Christ.

27. On the directive function of the imperative form, see Porter, *Verbal Aspect*, 335–61; Porter, *Idioms*, 53–56.

28. W. S. Vorster, "Literary Reflections on Mark 13:5–37: A Narrated Speech of Jesus," in *Speaking of Jesus: Essays on Biblical Language, Gospel Narrative and the Historical Jesus*, ed. J. E. Botha, NovTSup 92 (Leiden: Brill, 1999), 410. The use of the imperative βλέπετε (found in Mark 4:24 [= Luke 8:18]; 12:36; 13:5 [= Matt. 24:4; Luke 21:8], 9, 33) is used by P. Vassiliadis to argue for a Markan sayings-of-Jesus source (ΛΟΓΟΙ ΙΗΣΟΥ: *Studies in Q*, USFISFCJ 8 [Atlanta: Scholars Press, 1999], 153–59).

29. The imperative in 13:1 is ἴδε. On this form, see J. C. Doudna, *The Greek of the Gospel of Mark*, JBLMS 12 (Philadelphia: Society of Biblical Literature and Exegesis, 1961), 63–65. I count it as an imperative in my calculations, based on morphology, even though it may function in "unimperative" (explicative or fixed form) ways.

4.5 verses], Mark 10 has 15 in 52 verses [1 per 3.5 verses], and Mark 14 has 18 in 65 verses [1 per 3.6 verses]). The ratios indicate that the frequency of imperatives in 13:5–37 is more than twice that of any other chapter in the Gospel. Mark 13:5–37, according to Keith Dyer, also has 5.1 percent of the total verses of Mark's Gospel, but 13.6 percent of the imperatives.[30] In other words, in this discourse the frequency of imperatives is out of keeping with Markan usage elsewhere in the Gospel. This is further evidenced by Jesus's mode of speaking with the disciples before the discourse proper begins, and by his communication elsewhere in the Gospel. In 4:3–32 Jesus uses only five imperative forms throughout.

Part of the result of this usage in 13:5–37 is a sense of urgency created by the commanding posture of the discourse, in which Jesus is seen to be the one who instigates directive pronouncement. This is not a conversation or a dialogue, but a direct address.[31] Mark 4, by contrast, contains a number of statements by Jesus and his telling of several parables, so the indicative mood-form grammaticalizing assertive attitude is used 64 times in 105 clauses, or 1 per 1.6 clauses (by contrast, in 13:5–37 the indicative mood-form is used in 21 of 91 clauses, or 1 per 4 clauses, less than half as frequently as in Mark 4). Furthermore, in 13:5–37 Jesus frequently uses the future form (grammaticalizing expectation), 21 times in 91 clauses (by contrast, in 4:3–32 the future form is only used 5 times in 105 clauses). The use of expectative semantics also is directive in nature. The mode of discourse in Mark 13 is not characteristic of how Jesus is elsewhere depicted as speaking in Mark's Gospel,[32] and therefore it throws its depiction of Jesus into relief.

Attitude is only one feature relevant to the tenor of Mark 13. In itself, however, it is instructive for helping to isolate and quantify a particular orientation to communication between Jesus and his conversational partners, the disciples, that is distinctive from what is found elsewhere in Mark's Gospel.

30. K. D. Dyer, *The Prophecy on the Mount: Mark 13 and the Gathering of the New Community*, ITS 2 (Bern: Peter Lang, 1998), 81n49. Dyer also notes that 13:5–37 contains 22.6 percent of the future form verbs in Mark's Gospel (26 out of 115 instances), even though it contains only 5.1 percent of the total words. Our statistics vary, but the point is the same.

31. See R. H. Gundry, *Mark: A Commentary on His Apology for the Cross* (Grand Rapids: Eerdmans, 1993), 752; contra D. E. Aune, *Prophecy in Early Christianity and the Ancient Mediterranean World* (Grand Rapids: Eerdmans, 1983), 186–87, 399–400.

32. Note how typical it is for Jesus to begin his speaking in Mark's Gospel (in passages longer than one verse that are not simple instructions) with questions that lead directly to his statements (e.g., 2:8–9, 19, 25; 3:24; 4:13, 21, 30; 7:18; 8:17; 10:18, 36; 12:24, 35). He virtually never is seen to follow a question with a command (using an imperative) (except 14:6). See 4:3; 6:8; 8:15, 33; 9:39; 12:38, where he begins with an imperative.

Field of Discourse and Ideational Metafunction

The field of discourse is concerned with what a discourse is about—that is, its subject matter. The recognition that syntax conveys meaning has been fully adopted by SFL,[33] so much so that syntactical structures within the lexicogrammar can be components of the instantiation of the ideational metafunction. There are a number of factors to consider, including transitivity (realized in clausal structure) and subject matter. Transitivity involves who does what action to whom, and how, and thus includes (at least) the types of processes, aspect, and causality.[34] Subject matter is related to the choice of vocabulary but goes beyond simply identifying semantic domains and their distributions.

TRANSITIVITY

Traditional analysis of a passage such as Mark 13 includes discussion of syntax and style. Some useful observations can still be made from this perspective by means of transitivity. Mark 13 does not conform to typical Markan stylistic syntactical features. Of fourteen syntactical features that are considered by E. J. Pryke to be guides to Mark the editor and redactor's style,[35] 13:5–37 has only five instances of three of these features.[36] In other words, 13:5–37 does not have a very large number of the redactional features that are said to characterize Markan style, but it has more of the style of non-Markan material, which must have originated from earlier sources. This non-Markan material may, of course, have come from a number of different sources, with the words spoken by Jesus being construed as authentic source material by this reasoning. These Markan linguistic features include the following. (1) The first is

33. Although from a different framework, note the perspective in C. Ferris, *The Meaning of Syntax: A Study in the Adjectives of English*, LLL (London: Longman, 1993), esp. 1–18.

34. See M. A. K. Halliday, *Halliday's Introduction to Functional Grammar*, rev. C. M. I. M. Matthiessen 4th ed., (London: Routledge, 2014), 332–55; Martín-Asensio, *Transitivity-Based Foregrounding*, esp. 87–110. On aspect, see Porter, *Verbal Aspect*; Porter, *Idioms*, 20–28. There is no systematic study of causality realized by the voice system. For some preliminary comments, see M. B. O'Donnell, "Some New Testament Words for Resurrection and the Company They Keep," in *Resurrection*, ed. S. E. Porter, M. A. Hayes and D. Tombs, JSNTSup 186; RILP 5 (Sheffield: Sheffield Academic Press, 1999), 136–64, esp. 155–61.

35. See Pryke, *Redactional Style*, 32–135. His study is much more satisfactory than that of F. Neirynck (*Duality in Mark: Contributions to the Study of the Markan Redaction*, BETL 31 [Leuven: Leuven University Press, 1988]), since Pryke attempts to analyze the relative frequencies of the syntactical tendencies and to account for redactional influence, whereas Neirynck is content simply with lists, without further interpretation.

36. Features listed by Pryke not to be found in 13:5–37 include genitive absolute, participle as a main verb, πολλά accusative, ἄρχομαι + infinitive, εὐθύς and καὶ εὐθύς, πάλιν, "redundant" participles, periphrastic tenses, "impersonals," ὥστε + infinitive, and two or more participles before or after the main verb.

two uses of parenthetical clauses, in verses 10 and 14b, both instances of what Pryke calls catechetical, liturgical, and biblical usage.[37] In 13:10 the parenthetical statement, καὶ εἰς πάντα τὰ ἔθνη πρῶτον δεῖ κηρυχθῆναι τὸ εὐαγγέλιον, is called by Pryke "a Marcan redactional passage which the evangelist believes expresses the mind of Christ, although it may not be His exact words. The main reasons for regarding this verse as parenthetical and redactional are the vocabulary and the fact that the poetry of the passage and its main theme are interrupted by the parenthetical phrase."[38] In 13:14b the parenthetical statement is ὁ ἀναγινώσκων νοείτω, and there is a diversity of scholarly opinion on its origins.[39] (2) The second feature is two uses of λέγω ὅτι in verses 6 and 30. According to Pryke, relying on the work of others before him, the author of the Gospel avoids indirect speech and prefers direct speech, of which these are two instances.[40] (3) The last feature is the use of explanatory γάρ in verse 11b.[41] If the first and third features are clearly redactional, as Pryke contends, these two portions of verses perhaps can be seen to have been edited when the discourse was placed within its surrounding narrative, without necessarily affecting one's view of the authenticity of the remaining material. This leaves one supposed Markan syntactical redactional feature within 13:5–37, one at least arguably necessary to its discursive nature. By this analysis, there is very little evidence of Markan syntactical redaction of 13:5–37.

Dyer has approached the issue of syntax from a different angle. In a response to the challenges of stylometry, he has chronicled the instances of unique clusters of three-word syntax sequences in Mark 13 and the rest of the Gospel. In response to the work of David Peabody, as well as noting the features cited by Frans Neirynck,[42] Dyer has also plotted recurrent six-word syntactical sequences in Mark's Gospel. According to him, unique syntax ostensibly indicates "distinctive traditions," whereas recurrent syntax indicates

37. Pryke, *Redactional Style*, 53; compare C. H. Turner, "Marcan Usage: Notes, Critical and Exegetical, on the Second Gospel [3]," *JTS* 26 (1924–25): 145–46.

38. Pryke, *Redactional Style*, 53, citing the vocabulary of ἔθνη, πρῶτον, δεῖ, κηρύσσω, εὐαγγέλιον.

39. Ibid., 56. See A. Y. Collins, *The Beginning of the Gospel: Probings of Mark in Context* (Minneapolis: Fortress, 1992), 78.

40. Pryke, *Redactional Style*, 73, citing C. H. Turner, "Marcan Usage: Notes, Critical and Exegetical, on the Second Gospel [7]," *JTS* 28 (1926–27): 9–15; J. Sundwall, "Die Zusammensetzung des Markusevangeliums," *AAAH* 9 (1934): 8; M. Zerwick, *Untersuchungen zum Markus-Stil: Ein Beitrag zur Durcharbeitung des Neuen Testamentes*, SPIB (Rome: Pontifical Biblical Institute, 1937), 4ff., 45.

41. Pryke, *Redactional Style*, 126.

42. D. B. Peabody, *Mark as Composer*, NGS 1 (Macon, GA: Mercer University Press, 1987); Neirynck, *Duality in Mark*. Dyer (*Prophecy on the Mount*) rightly draws attention to the shortcomings of the work of Neirynck and Peabody.

"inter-connected traditions or Markan redaction."[43] It is not entirely clear, however, what linguistic status these three- and six-word syntactical sequences have; much more research is necessary to quantify what they might indicate. Dyer uses them in an attempt to isolate redactional and nonredactional syntax within Mark 13, differentiating the influence of the author on particular groups of verses. Thus his analysis of recurrent syntax shows a particularly high concentration in 13:24–27 (71.8% recurrent syntax). What is worth noting here, however, is that regarding his three-word syntactical sequences, there is a larger percentage of unique syntax in 13:3–37 (21.7%), especially verses 14–23 (35.3%), than there is in any other section of the Gospel (other sections that are close are 1:1–16 with 20.3% and 10:32–34 with 20.5%, but the latter may be too small for meaningful calculation).[44] As interesting as these indicators are, one must be cautious in attributing more status to them than is warranted at this stage in research, since there is no cross-correlation with other Greek writers, or even detailed exploration of their meaning within Mark's Gospel.

Transitivity includes the kind of verbal process, the aspect and causality of that process, and those involved in the process. One can see the importance of transitivity by comparison of the discourses in 4:13–32 and 13:5–37. In the first subunit of Mark 4, verses 3–9, even though the discourse begins with a command regarding a mental process, "hear" (v. 3), followed by a second command using a fixed verbal form, "see," the bulk of the unit consists of a series of 19 assertive verbs: 15 of these are aspectually perfective, while 4 are imperfective; and 16 of these are causally active, while 1 is ergative and 2 are passive. All but 2 of these verbs describe material processes as well. There is a confluence of imperfective verbs at the climax of the parable. The interpretation of the parable in 4:14–20, after the intervening words on interpretation of parables marked by the stative aspect (v. 11), has a similarly consistent pattern of verbal usage. This time, however, the backbone of the interpretation, rather than using perfective aspect, uses the imperfective in 11 of 13 verbal instances; similarly 10 of 13 verbs are causally active, with 3 ergative. The verbal processes are more mixed than in the parable itself, with virtually equal numbers of relational (8 instances) and material (7 instances) processes (the rest are mental processes, such as hearing). The next set of three parables, verses 21–33, follows a similar pattern to the telling of the first parable. In other words, there is a consistent transitivity pattern in which the narrative utilizes the perfective causally active verb, while interpretation uses the imperfective causally active verb as the standard pattern.

43. Dyer, *Prophecy on the Mount*, 147.
44. Ibid., 88.

The discourse in Mark 13 has different transitivity patterns than those in Mark 4. It presents features that are like neither the narrative of the parables nor the expository material of the parable explanation. Like 4:3, here 13:5 begins with a command. However, there is a mix of mood-forms (as noted above), and an alternation in tense-forms (18 aorists, 23 presents, 5 perfects). The first two uses of the perfective aspect are with the projective attitude (vv. 5, 6), and the first instance of an aorist indicative does not occur until verse 20. There are only two clusters of perfective aspect grammaticalized by aorist indicative forms, those in verses 14–16 and 20–21. Apart from two instances of impersonal verbs, present indicatives occur only in verses 28, 30, and 37 (two with verbs of speaking, hence as verbal processes). These are indicators that the discourse is not a narrative or an exposition. As the process types confirm, the discourse is concerned with material (or behavioral) processes. There are 38 instances of material processes, compared to 13 instances of relational, 9 of verbal, and 16 of mental processes. The mental processes are clearly linked in the vast majority of instances to nonassertive attitude, whether these are in terms of projection (vv. 5, 11, 30, 34) or, more importantly, directives (vv. 5, 14–16, 21, 33, 35, 37), and especially expectation of not-yet-existent events (vv. 6, 8, 9, 12, 13, 22, 24, 25, 27, 31). This tendency toward direction and expectation is supported by the use of active causality (49 instances of active, 9 of passive, and 11 of ergative causality). The semantic features of material process, active causality, and direction or expectation are found in 19 clauses of the 91 nonembedded.

The only other treatment of this passage in this way that I have found is by Rodney Decker, who similarly concludes that there is a mix of time-setting (often using the genitive absolute) and speculation about future events in the discourse.[45] As he says, "The most striking temporal feature of Mark 13 is, of course, the high frequency of the future form [and he includes future-referring forms as well] as Jesus tells the disciples what can be expected in the future."[46]

SUBJECT MATTER

The second feature of the field of discourse is the subject matter. The subject matter usually is indicated by the choice of lexical items within their respective semantic domains.[47] In terms of the subject matter of this discourse, there has been much debate over the origins of the apocalyptic imagery and thought,

45. See R. Decker, *Temporal Deixis of the Greek Verb in the Gospel of Mark with Reference to Verbal Aspect*, SBG 10 (New York: Peter Lang, 2001), 131–36.
46. Ibid., 136.
47. On the importance of semantic-domain theory, see E. A. Nida and J. P. Louw, *Lexical Semantics of the Greek New Testament*, SBLRBS 25 (Atlanta: Scholars Press, 1992). See also chaps. 3–4 in the present volume.

and whether it is possible or likely that Jesus could have stated what he does about the impending troubles, which seem to many so much like the destruction of Jerusalem that occurred in AD 70.[48] In a brief study of the vocabulary of Mark 13, Norman Perrin reported that "of the 165 words in the Nestle text of Mark 13:5–27, [a count of] 35 (= 21.2 per cent) do not occur elsewhere in the Gospel, and of these 35 words 15 are to be found in the Book of Revelation." Similarly, "investigation of the vocabulary of Mark 13:28–37 reveals a total vocabulary of 79 words, of which 13 (= 16.4 per cent) do not occur elsewhere in the Gospel. Of these 13 words only 2 are to be found again in Revelation."[49] Perrin's findings tend to show (the size of the chapter is too small to argue for far-reaching conclusions) that Mark 13 has a higher proportion of unique, and possibly apocalyptic, vocabulary than elsewhere in the Gospel.[50] This is confirmed by the nature of the vocabulary used within the discourse. As noted above, there is a heavy use of words for time. These statistics, however, have been called into question by Dyer.[51] He notes that Perrin, using Robert Morgenthaler, counts a lexical item only once, regardless of its number of occurrences. When the total number of words is used in the calculations, the proportion of unique words falls. Dyer's recalculated figures are that 13:5–27 has 41 unique words out of 381 total words (= 10.8%), and 13:28–37 has 14 of 152 (= 11.7%). To show that these figures are not as distinctive as Perrin claims, Dyer draws parallels with Mark 4 (with 493 words in vv. 3–32). According to Dyer, there are 60 unique words out of 493 words (= 12.2%) in 4:3–32. Dyer's conclusion is that "the vocabulary of Mark 13 is no more distinctive than the other major discourse in the Gospel, Mark 4."[52] Although he uses this to argue against the uniqueness of Mark 13, the evidence that he has gathered can also be interpreted to show, at least in a limited way, that Mark 13 and Mark 4, both with subject matter distinctive from that of the rest of the Gospel and discourses of Jesus, are independent from the general subject matter of the Gospel. The

48. See T. R. Hatina, "The Focus of Mark 13:24–27: The Parousia, or the Destruction of the Temple?," *BBR* 6 (1996): 43–66; N. H. Taylor, "Palestinian Christianity and the Caligula Crisis, Part II: The Markan Eschatological Discourse," *JSNT* 62 (1996): 13–41; E. Adams, "Historical Crisis and Cosmic Crisis in Mark 13 and Lucan's *Civil War*," *TynBul* 48 (1997): 329–44.

49. N. Perrin, *The Kingdom of God in the Teaching of Jesus* (London: SCM, 1963), 131, using R. Morgenthaler, *Statistik des neutestamentlichen Wortschatzes* (Zurich: Gotthelf-Verlag, 1958), 186–87. Compare M. E. Boring, *Sayings of the Risen Jesus: Christian Prophecy in the Synoptic Tradition*, SNTSMS 46 (Cambridge: Cambridge University Press, 1982), 186–95, esp. 193–95, citing and expanding on Perrin's statistics, citing more parallels with Revelation.

50. There is question whether the apocalyptic vocabulary shared by Mark 13 and Revelation comes from Mark, Revelation, common apocalyptic tradition, or elsewhere. See Dyer, *Prophecy on the Mount*, 77.

51. Ibid., 75–77.

52. Dyer, *Prophecy on the Mount*, 77.

nature of the subject matter of Mark 13 is no doubt responsible in large part for various theories on the origins of this discourse prior to the Gospel's author receiving it.[53] These words include those that refer to the "beginning" and the "end," "morning" and "middle of the night," seasons ("harvest," "winter"), and especially words for "near," "when/whenever," "hour," "days," and "then." In other words, there are several words that point to contemporary time, but even more words that are used to speak of future time. This correlates with the fact that roughly two-thirds of the uses of time words in Mark 13 occur with the nonindicative mood-forms, with only one-third with the indicative.

The data regarding syntax, transitivity, and subject matter indicate that the field of discourse of Mark 13 also has a number of distinctive features when compared to the rest of the Gospel.[54] The vocabulary may well indicate, in conjunction with the transitivity framework, a type of "apocalyptic discourse."

Conclusion regarding the Context of Situation of Mark 13

Scholarship is far from a consensus on the origin of the so-called apocalyptic discourse of Mark 13.[55] Nevertheless, the features analyzed above, gathered from a number of standard treatments of Markan linguistic features, and supplemented by several of my own, when placed within a different conceptual model—register analysis—provide support for a number of conclusions regarding this discourse. One is that this discourse appears to have a number of unique features when compared with the rest of the Gospel. On the basis of a limited amount of available evidence, I believe that it can be shown in relation to mode, tenor, and field as components of context that there are distinctive features for this discourse in each area. Some of these are seen in relation to the entire Gospel, while others are seen in comparison with other parts of the Gospel, especially Mark 4. This preliminary analysis begs for more detailed discussion of the rest of the Gospel, and comparison with the other Gospels, especially Matthew 24 and Luke 21. In any case, it appears that the results confirm that the context of situation of this text seems to be decidedly different from that of the Gospel as a whole, and even Mark 4.

53. The major theories have revolved around the apocalyptic dimension of the discourse, and in particular whether a written source, often labeled the Little Apocalypse, lies behind what is found in 13:5–37.

54. See D. Wenham, *The Rediscovery of Jesus' Eschatological Discourse*, GP 4 (Sheffield: JSOT Press, 1984), esp. 359–64, 373–74.

55. For a survey of opinion, see G. R. Beasley-Murray, *Jesus and the Kingdom of God* (Grand Rapids: Eerdmans, 1986), 322–23.

Another conclusion concerns the nature of these unique features. Some of them may simply be attributable to differences in subject matter, although the indicators seem to reach beyond this. Others may well point to a distinct context of situation that differs from that of the Gospel as a whole. So little is known of the origins of Mark's Gospel, or more particularly, of the individual discourses within it,[56] that it is difficult to ascertain a "material situational setting" for either.[57] That does not mean that we cannot discuss possible contexts of situation for Mark 13 and for the Gospel as a whole. I have previously argued, on the basis of some of the evidence cited above, that Mark took an earlier unitary tradition attributed to Jesus as a teaching discourse about the future and addressed to his disciples, then placed it within his Gospel, making only a few adaptations according to his style, but leaving many if not most of the features of the earlier tradition untouched. The cohesion of the discourse, especially in its lexical patterns, also argues for this conclusion. If we accept Markan priority in Synoptic source criticism, further support for this hypothesis can be found in how Matthew and Luke have made further changes to this discourse. The Gospel itself fits within a context of situation as a narrative about the life of Jesus, written for widespread distribution and perhaps with oral delivery intended.

A third conclusion is that this material seems to have originated in and to maintain a concern for speculative issues. The traditional way to describe this is as the Little Apocalypse. The potential validity of such a conclusion, without our accepting many of the authorial and form-critical conclusions that might attend to such a position, is reinforced in a number of ways by the features of the text. These include the use of the mood-forms to describe attitude, with those features being grammaticalized that point to the world of projection, direction, and expectation. The vocabulary itself is concerned with issues of time, whether here or elsewhere, such as in the future. There is far less of a sense of asserting the case rather than projecting a world not realized. This includes a possible ethical dimension conveyed by verbs of mental processes. In other words, the features of mode, tenor, and field indicate that Jesus offered to four of his disciples—Peter, James, John, and Andrew—an answer to their initial questions regarding when and how, and a glimpse of what to expect in future days.

56. See M. Hengel, "Entstehungszeit und Situation des Markusevangeliums," in Hengel, *Markus-Philologie: Historische, literargeschichtliche und stilistische Untersuchungen zum zweiten Evangelium*, ed. H. Cancik, WUNT 33 (Tübingen: Mohr Siebeck, 1984), 1–45; ET, in M. Hengel, *Studies in the Gospel of Mark*, trans. J. Bowden (London: SCM, 1985), 1–30.

57. R. Hasan, "Ways of Meaning, Ways of Learning: Code as an Explanatory Concept," in *Language, Society and Consciousness*, ed. J. J. Webster (London: Equinox, 2005), 215–27.

14

The Grammar of Obedience

Matthew 28:19–20

Introduction

A number of questions are raised by the Great Commission passage in Matthew's Gospel. I will focus upon two of them. One concerns the relation of the individual clausal units within 28:19–20, especially how the last statement on teaching, with its two secondary embedded clauses, relates to the other parts of the primary clause, including any other secondary or embedded structures as well as primary structures.[1] A second question is how this subject of obedience, assuming that it is well founded within this passage of Matthew 28, is treated in the New Testament theological and exegetical literature. The topic of "teaching them obedience" is, after all, a kind of general statement that one might find within theological and ethical discourse on the New Testament. I would like to think that such syntactical, exegetical, and theological analyses are linked together so that one proceeds to the other in a coherent and understandable way.

1. I use the terminology of the OpenText.org project. See below for further use of this terminology.

In the light of this, I wish first to treat this passage within New Testament theology, then within the exegetical literature, and then in terms of the syntax itself.

Matthew 28:19–20 in New Testament Theology

Within the English-language tradition to which I confine myself with regard to this passage (i.e., New Testament theologies written in English or translated into English), there are several ways in which this passage is treated.[2]

1. *Complete absence.* It may come as something of a surprise to notice that this passage, Matthew 28:19–20, does not appear to be mentioned, to say nothing of being cited or utilized, in at least one New Testament theology.[3] There is only one apparent reason for this: a number of authors appear to consider this passage inauthentic alongside the original Jesus material and hence not worth treating in any detail. The passage apparently is not given any type of authentic standing in relation to Jesus or the church, and therefore not as commanding obedience, or even very much attention.

2. *Appearance story.* Rather than simply neglecting the passage altogether (as noted above), some New Testament theologies treat Matthew 28:19–20 as part of an appearance story in which Jesus reveals himself to his followers.[4] Therefore, it is considered similar to passages in Luke (chap. 24) and John's Gospel (chap. 21) when Jesus appears to his disciples after his resurrection. Whereas this view at least takes the idea of Jesus's appearances seriously, there are still difficulties. One is that the classification of "appearance stories" all too easily becomes another way of talking about later church authors creating stories where Jesus after his death "appears" to people to speak to them, and thus the genuineness of these postresurrection appearances is called into question.[5] Another problem is that these passages are generally conflated so that their individuality is lost; all of the so-called appearance stories are deemed to

2. I am not trying to be inclusive and exhaustive in citing the secondary literature. I cite representative examples to make the point, and do not cite incidental references. For a good overall summary of many of the major issues, see E. J. Schnabel, *Early Christian Mission*, 2 vols. (Downers Grove, IL: InterVarsity, 2004), 1:348–67.

3. For example, W. G. Kümmel, *The Theology of the New Testament*, trans. J. E. Steely (Nashville: Abingdon, 1973).

4. G. Strecker, *Theology of the New Testament*, trans. M. E. Boring (Berlin: de Gruyter, 2000), 267; I. H. Marshall, *New Testament Theology* (Downers Grove, IL: InterVarsity, 2004), 111. Marshall identifies it as a numinous experience.

5. L. Goppelt, *Theology of the New Testament*, trans. J. Alsup, 2 vols. (Grand Rapids: Eerdmans, 1981), 1:212, 244; B. S. Childs, *Biblical Theology of the Old and New Testaments: Theological Reflection on the Christian Bible* (Minneapolis: Fortress, 1992), 277.

be similar in kind and distributed throughout the Gospels. There is, however, no other episode like the Great Commission in the Gospels—the passage in the longer ending of Mark notwithstanding (16:15)—and its unique features warrant separate consideration.

3. *Simple quotation.* There is at least one New Testament theologian who, rather than offering any particular classification or interpretation, simply quotes the passage.[6] The advantage of such an approach is that there is a recognition of the importance and integrity of the entire passage, but the citation in English enshrines a particular interpretation of the passage, almost as if it were self-evident, and moves very quickly over a number of pressing exegetical issues that pertain to this particular passage (as I hope to show below).

4. *Other uses.* Several New Testament theologians use this passage in relation to one or more other issues that are important to them. For example, the following topics that are mentioned or introduced in the passage are focused upon by a number of New Testament theologians (this is not an inclusive list): the tripartite name of Father, Son, and Holy Spirit, as a baptismal formula or an element of Christology;[7] the place of Jesus's commandments in relation to Moses's commandments;[8] ordinances, especially baptism;[9] and the people of God.[10] In other words, even though particular issues are selected for treatment, as if they were being treated in isolation or on their own, there is no consideration or recognition of the fact that each of these particular issues is part of a larger grammatical structure that helps to dictate the relation of the individual elements, to each other and to the rest of the Gospel.

In my research—and I do not pretend to have surveyed every New Testament theology ever written, or even all of those written within the last twenty-five

6. P. F. Esler, *New Testament Theology: Communion and Community* (Minneapolis: Fortress, 2005), 113, as part of a discussion of Paul Ricoeur. On Ricoeur, see S. E. Porter and J. C. Robinson, *Hermeneutics: An Introduction to Interpretive Theory* (Grand Rapids: Eerdmans, 2011), 105–30.

7. R. Bultmann, *New Testament Theology*, trans. K. Grobel, 2 vols. (London: SCM, 1952–55), 1:134, thinking that it might be a later interpolation; E. Stauffer, *New Testament Theology*, trans. J. Marsh (London: SCM, 1955), 160, 237, 250, 252; J. Jeremias, *New Testament Theology*, trans. J. Bowden (London: SCM, 1971), 57, 258; G. E. Ladd, *A Theology of the New Testament* (Grand Rapids: Eerdmans, 1974), 272; Goppelt, *Theology*, 1:202, 204. Compare U. Schnelle, *Theology of the New Testament*, trans. M. E. Boring (Grand Rapids: Baker Academic, 2009), 432–39.

8. F. Thielman, *Theology of the New Testament: A Canonical and Synthetic Approach* (Grand Rapids: Zondervan, 2005), 92, 184.

9. G. Vos, *Biblical Theology: Old and New Testaments* (Grand Rapids: Eerdmans, 1948), 340; L. Morris, *New Testament Theology* (Grand Rapids: Zondervan, 1986), 143.

10. T. R. Schreiner, *New Testament Theology: Magnifying God in Christ* (Grand Rapids: Baker Academic, 2008), 679–80.

years—one has to go back to George Stevens, as far as I can tell, to find a detailed, sustained, and extended treatment (actually a defense of the authenticity) of the Great Commission in a New Testament theology.[11] Stevens treats both the language of the commission and the categories of thought suggested by this usage, including some of those mentioned in number 4 (above). Since Stevens, the only two volumes of those I have surveyed that give more than passing mention to the passage are Donald Guthrie's New Testament theology, which offers a sustained interpretation, and the new treatment of the Synoptic Gospels by R. T. France in the revision of George Ladd's New Testament theology.[12] I suspect that this neglect is caused by the fact that so many of the treatments of this passage are either entirely or partially dismissive of it because of the authors' underlying critical theories. The passage, according to these advocates, was either inauthentic, created by the later church, or in some way a transposed form of another type of story—all to the detriment of the Great Commission in recent theological discussion. I believe, however, that there is much more to this episode than has often been recognized, especially of a theological nature, once attention is paid to the entire text, including its grammar. On the basis of the language of this passage, clearer relations can be indicated among teaching, obedience, and other notions, such as making disciples and baptism.

Matthew 28:19–20 and the Commentaries

Whereas the major New Testament theologies tend to be, at best, selective in their reference to this Matthean passage, at least since the time of George Stevens, the same is not the case for recent commentary discussion. Earlier English-language commentaries, however, also tend to be choosy in their treatment of the passage. One of the reasons for this is that Matthew was a neglected book in English-language commentary literature for much of the twentieth century.[13] Only in the waning years of the last century were significant commentaries written that paid attention to important exegetical detail. Nevertheless, some of these commentaries still have a tendency to be highly selective in the issues that they treat and often neglect grammatical

11. G. B. Stevens, *The Theology of the New Testament* (Edinburgh: T&T Clark, 1911), 146–48.

12. D. Guthrie, *New Testament Theology* (Leicester: Inter-Varsity, 1981), 715–16; R. T. France, "Matthew, Mark, Luke," in *A Theology of the New Testament*, by G. E. Ladd, ed. D. A. Hagner, rev. ed. (Grand Rapids: Eerdmans, 1993), 226.

13. Particularly disappointing is W. C. Allen, *A Critical and Exegetical Commentary on the Gospel according to S. Matthew*, ICC (Edinburgh: T&T Clark, 1907), 305–8, with half the space devoted to the triune formula, and six lines to verse 20.

issues.[14] Such issues as are treated include what "all the nations" mean, or the origins of the tripartite baptismal formula.[15] However, in recent years, a number of full-length exegetical commentaries have treated more of the significant exegetical issues, although some have simply reasserted standard opinions without significant support. Although I have surveyed more commentaries than I cite here, I can mention three exegetical commentaries that provide some of the better traditional grammatical treatments of this passage.[16] D. A. Carson's commentary, though not purportedly on the Greek text, offers a full and rigorous examination of most of the major issues.[17] The fairly recent commentary by R. T. France provides a surprisingly full account of the passage.[18] His comments are shaped by theological and other issues at many places, with the result that a number of the grammatical issues are subsumed in footnotes; nevertheless, with sufficient checking of these notes and several different places in the extended discussion, one is able to piece together a set of useful observations. Finally, Grant Osborne gives useful comments on the Greek of the passage in his recent exegetical commentary, which proceeds in a traditional verse-by-verse format.[19]

Despite the greater attention to exegetical detail in some recent commentaries, which helps to overcome a number of the limitations of earlier treatments, there are still some shortcomings in the exegetical discussions. These shortcomings mostly revolve around syntactical issues. The tendency within commentaries is still either (1) to treat most of the grammatical issues as if they were a series of discrete and separate issues to be asked and answered, rather than viewing them as a complex set of linguistic inquiries, in which larger units than the word or even phrase have bearing on interpretation of an entire clause or clause complex, or (2) to accept the received exegetical/

---

14. Very disappointing in this regard is J. Nolland, *The Gospel of Matthew*, NIGTC (Grand Rapids: Eerdmans, 2005), 1265–72.

15. The new ICC is much like the old. See W. D. Davies and D. C. Allison Jr., *A Critical and Exegetical Commentary on the Gospel according to Saint Matthew*, 3 vols., ICC (Edinburgh: T&T Clark, 1997), 3:684 (on "nations"), 685–86 (on the baptismal formula).

16. For linguistic evaluation of recent research on Matthew, see S. E. Porter, "Matthew and Mark: The Contribution of Recent Linguistic Thought," in *Mark and Matthew: Comparative Readings*, part 1, *Understanding the Earliest Gospels in Their First-Century Settings*, ed. E.-M. Becker and A. Runesson, WUNT 271 (Tübingen: Mohr Siebeck, 2011), 97–119. Compare S. E. Porter, "The Linguistic Competence of New Testament Commentaries," in *On the Writing of New Testament Commentaries: Festschrift for Grant R. Osborne on the Occasion of His 70th Birthday*, ed. S. E. Porter and E. J. Schnabel, TENT 8 (Leiden: Brill, 2012), 33–56, which examines some commentaries on Matthew.

17. D. A. Carson, "Matthew," in vol. 8 of *The Expositor's Bible Commentary*, ed. F. E. Gaebelein (Grand Rapids: Zondervan, 1984), 595–99.

18. R. T. France, *The Gospel of Matthew*, NICNT (Grand Rapids: Eerdmans, 2007), 1114–19.

19. G. R. Osborne, *Matthew*, ZECNT (Grand Rapids: Zondervan, 2010), 1079–83.

grammatical conclusion, even if it does not make good sense in the context. Even the commentaries above are sometimes guilty of these tendencies.

Matthew 28:19–20 and Its Grammar

In this section, I wish to examine the lexicogrammar of Matthew 28:19–20a. In particular, I want to examine it syntactically, utilizing recent advances in linguistic theory, to provide a linguistically informed reading of this passage. To do so, I will need to utilize the resources of the OpenText.org textual annotation project (www.opentext.org).

The OpenText.org project differentiates primary, secondary, and (secondary) embedded clauses, and offset (projected) material to indicate dialogue.[20] Matthew 28:19–20a consists of a single primary clause with the structure A–P–C–A–A (Adjunct–Predicator–Complement–Adjunct–Adjunct). The Predicator consists of the word group composed of the single finite verb μαθητεύσατε. This verb is an imperative, and it is the only imperative and the only finite verb in a primary clause in the two verses. The Predicator has a Complement. The Complement for this verb (which can be transitive or intransitive) is πάντα τὰ ἔθνη. The Predicator is preceded by a secondary embedded clause with πορευθέντες as its Predicator. The Predicator is followed by two further Adjuncts, each of them consisting of a secondary embedded clause. The first of these secondary embedded clauses is formed around the Predicator βαπτίζοντες and the second around the Predicator διδάσκοντες. The second Adjunct also contains two further embedded clauses, one using the infinitive as Predicator (τηρεῖν) and the other a relative clause (ὅσα ἐνετειλάμην).

The major syntactical discussion involved in this relatively straightforward clause complex revolves around three issues: the semantics of finite and nonfinite forms of verbs, the temporal relations of participles to finite verbs that can be indicated through syntactical ordering, and the nontemporal relations that can be indicated at the clause level or above, in part through syntactical ordering.

Semantics of Finite and Nonfinite Verbs

The typical translation of Matthew 28:19 and its first two verbal forms is this: "go and make disciples. . . ." This rendering is found in a range of translations,

---

20. OpenText.org avoids language of subordination, and prefers to describe primary clauses as those that carry the discourse line (horizontal plane), while secondary clauses provide offline material (vertical plane). Secondary embedded clauses have their own Predicator but occur within a primary or secondary clause to provide further off-line development.

such as the Authorized of 1881 (this AV renders "make disciples" as "teach"), Barclay (with the slight modification "you must therefore go and make . . ."), Beck, BBE, Cassirer, CEV, ESV, GNB, HCSB, Moffatt, NASB (original and revised), NET (with a footnote to Daniel Wallace's grammar justifying the imperatival translation [see below]), NEB, NLT, Lattimore, LB, NJB, NKJV (and its recent revision), NIV, Phillips (with "you are then to go and make . . ."), Rieu, REB, RSV, NRSV, TNIV, Schonfield, Tyndale, and Weymouth. In other words, just about every translation from Tyndale to the present has chosen to render the aorist participle and then aorist imperative forms with two English imperatives.

This translational tendency clearly precedes the justification for such a practice given by Daniel Wallace in his grammar. The note in the NET recognizes that there are three participles, but claims that the one rendered "go" "fits the typical structural pattern for the attendant circumstance participle (aorist participle preceding aorist main verb, with the mood of the main verb, usually imperative or indicative) and thus picks up the mood (imperative in this case) from the main verb." The NET commentators take as a further implication that "semantically the action of 'going' is commanded, just as 'making disciples' is."[21] Several commentaries also seem to accept a similar explanation.[22]

There are a number of unclear statements in this explanation, including reference to the "structural pattern" of the "attendant circumstance participle" and what it means that the participle "picks up" the mood of the main verb. Wallace attempts an explanation. Matthew 28:19–20 is treated as a disputed example in his grammar. His defense of the traditional rendering includes four "observations." The first is the issue of the "structural pattern for the attendant circumstance participle: aorist participle preceding an aorist main verb."[23] Earlier Wallace defines the attendant circumstance participle as being "used to communicate an action that, in some sense, is coordinate with the finite verb. In this respect it is not dependent, for it is translated like a verb. Yet it is still dependent *semantically*, because it cannot exist without the main verb."[24] There are at least three points at which this attempt at an explanation is confusing. First, one must decide in advance what constitutes a coordinate notion (not structure, because the participle is always a participle by form); second, the explanation confuses the issue of syntax and semantics, since

---

21. Note to Matt. 28:19 in the NET, citing D. B. Wallace, *Greek Grammar beyond the Basics: An Exegetical Syntax of the New Testament* (Grand Rapids: Zondervan, 1996), 645.

22. For example, Carson, "Matthew," 595; L. Morris, *The Gospel according to Matthew*, PilNTC (Grand Rapids: Eerdmans, 1992), 746n30; D. A. Hagner, *Matthew*, 2 vols., WBC 33A–B (Dallas: Word, 1993–95), 2:886; Schnabel, *Early Christian Mission*, 1:356; C. A. Evans, *Matthew*, NCBC (Cambridge: Cambridge University Press, 2012), 243, though with some ambivalence.

23. Wallace, *Greek Grammar*, 645.

24. Ibid., 640.

the participle in relation to a finite verb is always syntactically dependent, regardless of one's translation; and third, the description elevates translation to the level of syntactical explanation and analysis. Wallace goes on to attempt to clarify this matter by claiming that the participle is always dependent, because it is used in relation to a finite verb—but so are many if not most uses of dependent verbal participles (apart from absolute or independent uses). Further, Wallace argues that sense takes precedence over translation, but then he uses the criterion of making "good sense" to determine this (he mixes "sense" as a technical term with common sense). His explanation of his supposed validation passage for the attendant circumstance participle further confuses the issue. He recognizes that, in Matthew 2:13, the typical understanding for an adverbial participle could explain the use, but rejects it on the basis of the urgency of the aorist imperative, which explanation is dependent on a view of the meaning of the aorist imperative rather than the syntactical construction at hand.[25]

In his explanation of 28:19–20, Wallace appeals to the notion that classifying the initial aorist participle as an adverbial participle (rather than an attendant circumstance participle) turns the Great Commission into "the Great Suggestion."[26] There are several problems with this explanation. One is that it makes a particular theological explanation determinative for grammar, but it also further reinforces a particular view of the aorist imperative. However, this is an unnecessary explanation. The command is to make disciples of all nations. It is difficult to know what is lost or tempered by not having the participle understood as imperatival as well, especially since the word for "going" is still there (surely Wallace cannot mean that the use of only a single imperative means that the command is less pertinent).[27] His third supporting point is even less germane, when he states that this passage must be interpreted in its historical context. He observes that the disciples did not leave Jerusalem and fulfill the Great Commission until after Stephen's martyrdom.[28] In other words, even with the two commands, as Wallace sees it, the disciples took it as a suggestion until further motivation was provided. In other words, syntax alone does not determine motivational or human results.

25. Ibid., 643. On the aorist imperative, see S. E. Porter, *Verbal Aspect in the Greek of the New Testament, with Reference to Tense and Mood*, SBG 1 (New York: Peter Lang, 1989), 335–61, esp. 351–52, where it is shown that urgency is not the meaning of the aorist imperative.

26. Wallace, *Greek Grammar*, 645.

27. Compare France, *Matthew*, 1114n27. France recognizes that one cannot press the verb "going" too far in indicating that "Jesus speaks here of moving to a new area or field of mission. . . . In due course a mission to 'all the nations' will no doubt involve disciples moving outside their home territory."

28. Wallace, *Greek Grammar*, 645.

Wallace treats the participle in relation to the main verb in an inconsistent way that attempts to deal only with tense and mood. He fails to explain the use of the participle in relation to the main verb and in respect to how a syntactically embedded structure (participle) functions in relation to a primary clause structure (based around a finite verb)—in other words, in terms of the discourse-shaping use of syntax. Carson also confuses the issue when he says that he finds it "difficult to believe that 'go' has lost all imperatival force,"[29] when the participle as a participle never had any imperatival force to lose. Wallace is right to observe the syntax, in which the participle precedes the finite verb. He also notes that there is an inevitable sense in which the actions are coordinated, and the action of the participle is antecedent to that of the main verb. He is also correct to note that, in this instance, the two verbs are aorist tense-forms. What Wallace fails to draw is a conclusion from this regarding the linear ordering of Greek,[30] the proper understanding of the relation of translation to syntax, and how tense-forms function in discourse. The aorist tense-form as the perfective aspect of πορευθέντες is used to establish the circumstance for the action of the finite verb of the primary clause, μαθητεύσατε. This circumstance is one of "going." Within the secondary embedded structure forming an Adjunct, placed before the Predicator of the primary clause, it logically indicates background information to the command: going is background to the making of disciples.[31] There is nothing here that minimizes the Great Commission to a suggestion. To the contrary, the syntactical structure retains the focus upon the making of disciples, which is at the syntactical heart of this command because it identifies the lexis of the finite verb of the Predicator.[32]

How one renders Matthew 28:19–20 is another issue entirely. The Greek structure of a secondary embedded clause as Adjunct and Predicator of the primary clause does not "share" mood, but an English rendering might find it convenient to put the two on a parallel semantic plane in given contextual circumstances. However, this is probably not the best explanation for this passage, despite the history of translation. One reason to alter the rendering is that too much has probably been made of "going" (as Wallace does) rather than on "making disciples." A rendering with "going" indicated as in some way subordinate in focus to "make disciples" helps to avoid any misperceptions

29. Carson, "Matthew," 595.
30. Porter, *Verbal Aspect*, 381.
31. This statement is based upon the semantics of aspect and the participle. See Porter, *Verbal Aspect*, as well as comments below.
32. See the comments of E. Schweizer, *The Good News according to Matthew*, trans. D. E. Green (Atlanta: John Knox, 1975), 532.

that might result from simply taking the English as if it represented Greek with two imperative forms. This is the way Robert Gundry renders the construction, the only commentator that I have found who does so: "Going, therefore, make disciples of all the nations."[33]

Temporal Relations Indicated through Syntactical Ordering

There are two sets of participles to consider in the construction in Matthew 28:19–20. The first set is the participle πορευθέντες as the Predicator of the secondary embedded clause as Adjunct that precedes the Predicator of the primary clause, μαθητεύσατε, and the second set is the two participles, βαπτίζοντες and διδάσκοντες, that follow the Predicator of the primary clause, each a Predicator of its own secondary embedded clause used as Adjuncts in this clausal complex.[34]

I have already discussed the semantics of the first participle above, but the issue of temporal relations in clausal syntax must be examined more closely. In his definition of the attendant circumstance use of the participle, Wallace acknowledges that, besides both verbs being in the aorist tense-form and the main verb being an imperative, the participle not only precedes the main verb but also precedes it in terms of "time of event" (he also states that "usually there is a very close proximity").[35] Above I noted that the preceding participle was used in a discourse function to indicate the backdrop for the action of the Predicator of the primary clause's finite verb. The semantic relation of the "dependent participle to its main verb" is a complex one that may involve temporal and/or nontemporal relations. What Wallace captures in his time-based description of the participle is that the participle may be used to indicate sequential ordering of events, not because of the tense-form of the participle (Wallace admits this), but because of the syntax of the clause itself. As indicated by the cotext, the focus on making disciples is logically and temporally indicated through syntax as preceded by the act of going. The going is not the focus, but it is the assumption and prior action required before the process of making disciples can be undertaken. The use of the aorist participle in the secondary embedded clause as Adjunct before the Predicator of the primary

33. R. H. Gundry, *Matthew: A Commentary on His Literary and Theological Art* (Grand Rapids: Eerdmans, 1982), 595.

34. These two secondary embedded clauses as Adjuncts following the Predicator (and Complement) of the primary clause are connected by asyndeton. It functions here as a low-level means of linking material with "the closest of connections." See S. L. Black, *Sentence Conjunctions in the Gospel of Matthew: καί, δέ, τότε, γάρ, οὖν and Asyndeton in Narrative Discourse,* JSNTSup 216, SNTG 9 (Sheffield: Sheffield Academic Press, 2002), 182.

35. Wallace, *Greek Grammar,* 642.

clause is a frequently occurring pattern in ancient Greek, including the Greek of the New Testament.[36]

In their comments, both the NET and Wallace also recognize that there is a distinction to be made between the preceding aorist participle and the two present tense-form participles, each as Predicator of its own secondary embedded clause as Adjunct, that follow the Predicator of the primary clause. At this point, the NET and Wallace partially diverge. The NET recognizes that the two present participles following the finite verb as Predicator of the primary clause do not fit Wallace's criteria for the attendant circumstance use of the participle—that is, his so-called structure criteria. The NET continues, however, by noting that there are interpreters who do see these participles as having imperatival force or other types of semantic relations, such as means, manner, or result.[37] Wallace does not go so far. He notes also that these two present tense-form participles do not fit his criteria, but he takes them as adverbial participles indicating that the "means by which the disciples were to make disciples was to baptize and then to teach."[38] Wallace's conclusion is somewhat surprising: he seems to be saying that what constitutes the making of a disciple in Matthew's Gospel is baptism and teaching. This raises the kind of theological issue that Wallace is often quick to try to avoid. It is also unclear what grammatical and theological criteria he is applying to arrive at this conclusion. Carson refutes this understanding in stating that "baptizing and teaching are not the means of making disciples, but they characterize it."[39] In other words, they may be characteristic of discipleship, though not necessarily all that is involved in it.

Wallace is correct, however, in recognizing that these two present tense-form participles follow the finite verb of the primary clause. The pattern of present tense-form participles as Predicators in secondary embedded clauses as Adjuncts following the Predicator of the primary clause is frequent. Wallace goes on, however, by asserting that the participles indicate the means by which the action of the finite verb is performed. I will return to this in the section below. However, there is more to consider at this stage. I have noted (above) a syntactical ordering pattern in Greek, in which logically antecedent action is often indicated by syntactically placing a participle (as the Predicator of a

---

36. For discussion of the ordering principle regarding participles, see Porter, *Verbal Aspect*, 377–88; Porter, *Idioms of the Greek New Testament*, 2nd ed., BLG 2 (Sheffield: Sheffield Academic Press, 1994), 187–90; Porter, "Time and Order in Participles in Mark and Luke: A Response to Robert Picirilli," *BBR* 17 (2007): 261–67. The present chapter develops some of these ideas further.

37. For example, Carson, "Matthew," 597; Hagner, *Matthew*, 2:886, 887, 888.

38. Wallace, *Greek Grammar*, 645.

39. Carson, "Matthew," 597.

secondary embedded clause as Adjunct) before the verb of the Predicator of the primary clause (the so-called main or finite verb). In Greek there is also a syntactical ordering pattern in which logically concurrent or subsequent action is often indicated by placing such a participle after its main verb. The latter structure is the syntactical pattern that is indicated in this situation. The question becomes one of determining whether the action is—whatever type of other relationship is indicated—concurrent or subsequent. In a sense, Wallace has already inadvertently answered this question by stating that the relationship is one of "means." He defines means in terms of the participle answering the question of how an action takes place, and defines or in some way makes specific the action indicated by the main verb (he also uses the terms "epexegetical," "defines," and "explains").[40] Thus, according to Wallace, "means" indicates logically concurrent action, in that the verbal action indicated by the participle is an action that in some way elucidates the action of the main verb. The problem with Wallace's analysis is that his use of "means" indicates a level of pragmatic relation that is not indicated by the syntax, but one that restricts the temporal relations. The syntactical ordering principle only indicates that the action of baptizing and teaching are concurrent or subsequent to the action of making disciples.

Cotextual Relations and Semantics: Nontemporal Relations Syntactically Indicated

I have stated (above) that the syntactical ordering principle indicated the logical temporal possibilities of the participles as Predicators in secondary embedded clauses, in relation to the Predicator of the primary clause. The syntactical ordering principle establishes the logical temporal ordering, but it does not address issues of how the events referred to are otherwise related. I also noted that Wallace treats the adverbial functions simply as semantic features, rather than as cotextual semantic relations. In other words, if we treat semantics as the meaning of the form or forms involved, regardless of the level of exposition (at the clause and beyond), and treat discourse semantics as what a user means when the semantics are considered cotextually,[41] then

---

40. Wallace, *Greek Grammar*, 628–29.

41. See J. R. Martin, *English Text: System and Structure* (Philadelphia: John Benjamins, 1992), 1, and passim; J. R. Martin and D. Rose, *Working with Discourse: Meaning beyond the Clause*, 2nd ed. (London: Continuum, 2007), 5, and passim, referring to discourse semantics—that is, the cotextual meaning of the instantiations of the lexicogrammar. See Porter, *Verbal Aspect*, 15, and the distinctions made in N. J. C. Gotteri, "A Note on Bulgarian Verb Systems," *JMALS* 8 (1983): 49–70, esp. 49. See also N. J. C. Gotteri, "Toward a Systemic Approach to Tense and

we can see that the nontemporal relations are cotextually indicated—that is, at the discourse level. Matthew 28:19–20a has three potential cotextual relations in which the verbal semantics interact: the initial aorist participle and the main verb, the following two present participles and the main verb, and the relation between the two present participles.

I will deal with the cotextual semantic relations of the initial aorist participle and the main verb first. Wallace has usefully noted a number of examples even in Matthew's Gospel where the same verb for "going" is syntactically placed before the Predicator of the primary clause (Matt. 2:8; 9:13; 11:4; 17:27; 21:6; 22:15; 25:16; 26:14; 27:66; 28:7).[42] The cotextual force of these constructions appears to be to indicate directionality toward an action, perhaps even indicating a prerequisite intention before the main action can be executed. This is shown by the usually initial (or close to it) positioning of the participle (prime position), no matter where the Predicator of the primary clause structurally occurs, often separated by other elements, such as an expressed subject.

The second cotextual semantic relation involves the following two present participles and the main verb. As noted above, Wallace asserts that what I am calling cotextual relations are semantic ones, by placing categories of means, manner, and so on under the rubric of the adverbial participle. Wallace hence states that the "means by which the disciples were to make disciples was to baptize and then to teach."[43] However, Carson can state, "The syntax of the Greek participles for 'baptizing' and 'teaching' forbids the conclusion that baptizing and teaching are to be construed solely as the *means* of making disciples. . . . Similarly baptizing and teaching are not the *means* of making disciples, but they characterize it."[44] Neither actually provides clear criteria by which his particular judgment is made. The logically concurrent semantics of the construction indicate that the two embedded participles indicate functions that constitute the primary clausal function of making disciples.

The third cotextual semantic relation is potentially the most interesting for analysis here, because not only is there a relationship between the two participles and the Predicator of the primary clause, but also there is a cotextually determined semantic relationship between the two subsequent secondary embedded clauses. These two embedded structures offer several insights. One is that these two participles provide a pertinent illustration of the function of verbal aspect, as against both *Aktionsart* and temporal conceptions. On

---

Aspect in Polish," in *Meaning and Form: Systemic Functional Interpretations*, ed. M. Berry et al., ADP 57 (Norwood, NJ: Ablex, 1996), 499–507.

42. Wallace, *Greek Grammar*, 645n77.
43. Ibid., 645.
44. Carson, "Matthew," 597.

the basis of usage of the verbs for "baptize" and "teach" elsewhere in the New Testament, one probably would want to argue, according to *Aktionsart* theory, for "baptize" as punctiliar and "teach" as continuous (or other such terminology). However, both appear here in the present tense-form, grammaticalizing imperfective aspect. Some less likely explanations come to mind. One could—just hypothetically, by stretching—posit that "baptize" refers to the baptisms of all of the people, and hence it is a recurring or iterative event, in a similar way that "teach" in the present tense-form indicates continuous or possibly iterative action. One certainly is not interested in arguing for continuous baptism. Another less likely option is that "baptize" is used in the present tense-form because it is part of a construction that speaks of baptizing in terms of three names: "the name of the Father, and the Son, and the Holy Spirit." That is unlikely. With regard to time of action, if the present participles are seen to be present-time referring (simply on the basis of verbal morphology), then we have the conundrum of baptism and teaching being concurrent events. This is possible, but again unlikely. A plausible explanation, as opposed to those above, is the cotextual one that the linear and orderly syntax of the Greek establishes that baptism and teaching occur as closely related (note similar syntax) but sequential events; that is, baptism occurs first and is then followed by teaching, just as the two secondary embedded clauses are syntactically ordered. In relation to aspectual theory, or rather in conjunction with aspectual theory, the process that "baptizing" is conceptualizing could be the single initiatory event found elsewhere in the New Testament (even using the present participle), while "teaching" indicates a continuous pattern of teaching and instruction of those who have been baptized. The aspectual semantics do not specify the type of baptism or teaching (nor does any other theory of verbal meaning).

Understanding the Great Commission in Context

With this grammatical analysis firmly in place, I can examine the Great Commission statement in an attempt to understand fully the linguistic indications of the Greek syntax. There are at least two conclusions to draw.

The first is that the making of disciples involves "all nations." The syntax indicates this with the P–C syntax of the primary clause.[45] Some have taken "all nations" as a collective noun, and hence interpreted the clause as indicating that it involves making disciples of particular people groups rather than

45. See Davies and Allison, *Matthew*, 3:684.

individuals. Others have taken "all nations" to mean all nations except the Jews, and thus have interpreted the clause as marking a significant shift in the ministry of Jesus.[46] I am not here specifically concerned with the lexical semantics of this passage. However, there is no indication that "all nations" means all nations except the Jewish people. Jesus's mission began with the Jewish people and, if the rest of the New Testament is to be believed, will involve them again at the end of the church era, when he returns. In the light of how disciples are understood in the Gospels, including Matthew's Gospel, disciple making is an individual process, whether entire people groups become followers of Jesus or not.

The second conclusion is that the participle constructions are cotextually indicated for various roles within this clause complex, in syntactically embedded relations (as Adjuncts at clause level) to the Predicator of the primary clause.[47] The initial aorist participle sets the assumptive background for the act of disciple making, logically and temporally precedes the action of the main verb, and is cotextually indicative of an intention toward disciple making. Thus, rather than confining the understanding of the relation of the participle to the main verb as one of sharing imperatival force, the initial participle performs a discourse function. This discourse function involves setting the stage for the making of disciples by Jesus instructing his followers to move in a certain direction. The movement is a necessary concomitant circumstance to the process of the primary clause.

The two following present participles, as indicated by the syntax, enjoy a different semantic relationship (though they are Predicators of secondary embedded clauses serving as Adjuncts in the same clause complex) and are used for a different cotextual function. There is a long history of interpretation, going back to Johann Albrecht Bengel, recognizing that the imperative "make disciples" is "a general imperative which is filled out (although not exhausted) by what follows: baptism and instruction in obedience belong to discipleship."[48] Thus, rather than trying to confine the understanding of the two participles simply by adverbial labeling, the syntax indicates that logically they are temporally concurrent or subsequent, in relation to both the Predicator of the primary clause and to each other.[49] In order words, the syntax probably indicates that the action of the two participles is logically concurrent in that the two actions of baptizing and teaching indicate, at least in part, what

46. For opinions, see Carson, "Matthew," 596; compare Schnabel, *Early Christian Mission*, 1:361.
47. See Schweizer, *Matthew*, 532.
48. Davies and Allison, *Matthew*, 3:686.
49. As noted above, see Porter, *Verbal Aspect*, 377–88.

it means to make disciples. W. C. Allen believes that baptism here "implies belief in Christ," because New Testament baptism involves expressing belief, and then after baptism being a disciple.[50] The syntax itself further indicates that there is a sequencing order to these two events, that baptism precedes teaching. Although many interpreters take this passage as focusing upon the centrality of the baptism function, or reversing the ordering so that teaching precedes baptism, none of these explanations is plausible in the light of the syntactical and other arguments presented above.[51] Leon Morris states that baptism "is no more than the beginning," as the person must then be taught.[52]

The second of the secondary embedded participle clauses after the main Predicator also has two further embedded structures, an embedded clause with infinitive as Predicator and an embedded secondary relative clause. W. D. Davies and D. C. Allison see the imperative "make disciples," the two participles "baptizing" and "teaching," and the infinitive "to keep" as what they call "ecclesiastical verbs" that appear in a particular order.[53] They rightly do not overly exegete these verbs, but it is worth noting that this is the clause that has given rise to the notion of this passage being about obedience. In some ways, this subject of obedience sums up everything that Jesus has taught throughout Matthew's Gospel.[54]

Thus, I can conclude with an interpretive translation that attempts to capture the sense of the passage as I have examined it above: "Going, therefore, make disciples of all the nations, including baptizing them into the name of the Father and the Son and the Holy Spirit, teaching them to keep all that I have commanded you."

Conclusion

The Great Commission is developed around a relatively straightforward grammatical construction in Matthew 28:19–20, or at first sight it at least appears to be so. This construction focuses upon four significant verbal constructions: one Predicator of a primary clause and three secondary embedded participle Predicators. In this chapter I argue that although the grammar by which Jesus's followers are commanded to be taught to obey what he commands is relatively easy to describe, the syntax and semantics of the passage establish

50. Allen, *Matthew*, 305.
51. See France, *Matthew*, 1115n32.
52. Morris, *Matthew*, 749.
53. Davies and Allison, *Matthew*, 3:686.
54. See Hagner, *Matthew*, 2:888; Guthrie, *New Testament Theology*, 715–16.

priorities that move in unexpected ways. The notion of going (to make disciples), rather than being grammatically prominent, is the background to the command to make disciples, realized by the finite verb in the Predicator of the primary clause. The command to make disciples is defined by two further prominent concepts, grammaticalized by two more participles: baptism and teaching. This passage seems to indicate a disciple-making ministry for Jesus's followers that involves first baptism and then teaching those baptized to obey his commands. The making of a disciple involves the public witness of baptism followed by and mirrored in a life of Christian obedience. According to Matthew in his quoting of Jesus, this is what it means to evidence being a disciple of Jesus Christ.

15

Verbal Aspect and Synoptic Relations

Introduction

It has been twenty-five years since my study of verbal aspect, *Verbal Aspect in the Greek of the New Testament, with Reference to Tense and Mood*, was published.[1] This was the first full-scale monograph devoted to verbal aspect in the Greek of the New Testament published in English. Buist Fanning and I had been in something of a slow-motion race to see who could finish his doctorate first and then get his monograph into print. Whatever readers may think of my monograph and the theories that I argue for, at the least it can be said that I was the first. One's first book, probably like one's first child (I imagine, since although I have authored and published more than twenty books, I have no children), always has a special place in one's memory. I still remember the first Society of Biblical Literature annual conference at which this volume was publicized. As I approached the booth of my publisher, Peter

---

I wish to thank an anonymous student at Westminster Graduate School of Theology in Seoul, South Korea, when I presented this paper on October 31, 2010, for his helpful comments that led to the correction of several errors. The errors that remain are of my own doing.

1. S. E. Porter, *Verbal Aspect in the Greek of the New Testament, with Reference to Tense and Mood*, SBG 1 (New York: Peter Lang, 1989).

Lang, the publisher's representative saw me and called out in a loud voice for many around to hear, "Stan, you've outsold the pope." The pope of the time also had a book published by Peter Lang that year, and it was featured at the same conference alongside mine, which was the inaugural volume in the Studies in Biblical Greek series. Apparently my monograph had sold more copies during the course of the conference than the pope's book. Pity the pope. I am not sure how many copies of my book were sold during that conference, but I am quite certain the pope expected to do much better than he did.

Despite these beginnings—whether they are modest or sensational, I leave for you to decide—the study of verbal aspect has become significant in at least some quarters of New Testament studies over the last twenty-five years. As a result, in the past twenty-plus years, several other monographs have been published specifically on the topic of verbal aspect, some articles have analyzed and/or utilized verbal aspect in some ways and to varying degrees, and some monographs have incorporated various insights from aspectual analysis into their findings (see the bibliography of this volume). All of this is fine and good. I applaud it and welcome more of it. I especially welcome work that pushes beyond what has been done before and that explores new areas. There are even some commentaries that make use of insights from study of verbal aspect and related concepts.

There is one major area, however, where verbal aspect is clearly missing from the scene compared to other areas of biblical study: critical analysis of textual relations.[2] Textual relations encompasses a number of different types of relations, mostly concerning matters such as origins or dependency, such as those found perhaps in some Pauline Letters and by most accounts in the Synoptic Gospels. In this chapter I wish to determine if there is a means by which we can gain some insight into Synoptic relations on the basis of a study of verbal aspect.[3] I will do this in three steps. The first step is to define the phrase "verbal aspect" as I intend to use it in this essay. The second is to take a look at the types of linguistic criteria utilized in current Synoptic source theories. The third is to examine how verbal aspect might serve as an indicator of Synoptic relations, by first examining a number of texts with relatively clear dependency relations to formulate some opinion on the

---

2. For a recent effort, see B. M. Fanning, "Greek Presents, Imperfects, and Aorists in the Synoptic Gospels," in *Discourse Studies and Biblical Interpretation: A Festschrift in Honor of Stephen H. Levinsohn*, ed. S. E. Runge (Bellingham, WA: Logos Bible Software, 2011), 157–90. For my response to the challenge that Fanning poses, see chap. 11 in the present volume.

3. Since this chapter was written, W. V. Cirafesi has published his *Verbal Aspect in Synoptic Parallels: On the Method and Meaning of Divergent Tense-Form Usage in the Synoptic Passion Narratives*, LBS 7 (Leiden: Brill, 2013). He is more concerned to explain individual variations than determine overall patterns.

general patterns of use and then to apply this to some specific passages in the Synoptic Gospels.

What Is Verbal Aspect?

"Verbal aspect" is a phrase used in linguistics to describe synthetic or analytic semantic categories that describe systems of meaningful choice regarding processes within languages. Although I realize that not all agree with this, I distinguish verbal aspect from so-called lexical aspect or *Aktionsart*, as well as tense or temporality. In my *Verbal Aspect in the Greek of the New Testament*, I define verbal aspect in systemic functional linguistic (SFL) terms as follows: "Greek verbal aspect is a synthetic semantic category (realized in the forms of verbs) used of meaningful oppositions in a network of tense systems to grammaticalize the author's reasoned subjective choice of conception of a process."[4] Here is not the place to enter into a thorough discussion of all of the dimensions of verbal aspect.[5] Building from this definition, I wish to focus upon what I consider to be important in discussing how verbal aspect may figure into analysis of Synoptic relations.

There are two axioms of structural linguistics that I have found particularly insightful, especially as they relate to the issue of verbal aspect. The first is the structuralist maxim *Tout se tient*, or "Everything hangs together," and the other is "Meaning implies choice." Some scholars do contend in their discussions of verbal aspect, or at least act as if it were true, either that the Greek verbal aspect system is unorganized and without principle, or that there are not significant choices to be made. Nevertheless, I think that these two linguistic principles are deeply enshrined in the way language works, including the Greek verbal system. Six sets of observations grow out of this definition and these axioms. (1) The first is that verbal aspect is a semantic category, reflecting some type of meaning that is defined by and has a role to play in the language. (2) The second is that verbal aspect is realized in the forms of verbal tense-forms. There is a correlation between form and function within the Greek verbal system, whereby the selection of meanings within the verbal network is realized in the individual forms of the verbs themselves.[6] (3) The

---

4. Porter, *Verbal Aspect*, 88. What follows draws upon this work.

5. Several other chapters in this volume have already discussed various dimensions of verbal aspect. See especially chaps. 10, 11, and 12.

6. See N. J. C. Gotteri, "Toward a Systemic Approach to Tense and Aspect in Polish," in *Meaning and Form: Systemic Functional Interpretations*, ed. M. Berry et al., ADP 57 (Norwood, NJ: Ablex, 1996), 499–507.

third is that there is a network of aspect systems within the Greek language. There has been some confusion over this and other notions, especially related to the systemic nature of the Greek verbal network. Whether or not one believes that individual users are able to articulate the structure of their language has little or no bearing on whether descriptive linguistics benefits from being able to articulate such structural relations. Virtually all discussions of the Greek verbal system recognize some system of systemic relations, and SFL provides probably the best means of graphically representing the semantic potential of the language in this regard.[7] (4) The fourth is that this system has meaningful oppositions. By definition and articulation, such systems within networks differentiate semantic choices on the basis of (usually) binary choices—that is, semantic oppositions. This notion of opposition has proved difficult to grasp by some discussants of verbal aspect, because unfortunately they have been unable to appreciate or articulate the value of binary oppositions for describing complex sets of semantic choices as semantic paths through a network, and have arbitrarily either tried to limit Greek to two aspects, or tried to posit a triadic set of equal semantic choices. Binary oppositions enable fine-tuning of semantic choice relations—that is, increasingly delicate choices within the Greek verbal edifice.[8] (5) The fifth is that the choice of verbal aspect is grammaticalized by means of tense-forms; that is, the author's reasoned, subjective choice is instantiated in grammatical substance. The first subpart of this point is that the author's choice is reasoned. This has been wrongly equated by some to mean that this is always a conscious choice. This is not necessarily a conscious choice, but rather a choice demanded and constrained by the verbal system itself, and therefore not arbitrary but reasoned. The second is the element of subjectivity. Subjectivity in this context does not mean to be without basis but rather to be reflective of the choices offered within the language of the author's perspective on the process. (6) The sixth and final point is that verbal aspect grammaticalizes how an author wishes for a process to be conveyed. One of the primary tasks of verbal aspect is to serve as a discourse indicator, by which an author is able to shape and convey the processes of a given discourse.

As I have mentioned above, there are many other important concepts that could be discussed with reference to verbal aspect, but I will pass over those here because I believe that what I have laid out is sufficient in order to push forward discussion of the issue of how verbal aspect plays a role in Synoptic

7. The independence of the aspectual system within the Greek verbal edifice has been confirmed by S. E. Porter and M. B. O'Donnell, "The Greek Verbal Network Viewed from a Probabilistic Standpoint: An Exercise in Hallidayan Linguistics," *FN* 14 (2001): 3–41.

8. This is represented in Porter, *Verbal Aspect*, 109.

relations, even if I am not able fully to explore all of the semantic implications of such choices in the examples that I treat below.

Greek Grammar and the Synoptic Problem

One of the serious shortcomings of much critical New Testament literature is appreciation, recognition, and, most important, utilization of the latest research in linguistics. Even though I am not greatly knowledgeable regarding the inner workings of automobiles, when I last bought a new one, I chose to buy a 2009 Honda Accord, not Henry Ford's Quadricycle, his first car manufactured in 1896. This 1896 "car" (if the term applies) had four bicycle tires, a steel frame, but no body, and at the time was dubbed "experimental." Now modern automobiles, even economy cars such as mine, have electronic everything, automatic transmissions, and highly efficient engines. Yet most New Testament scholars are content to drive their way to understanding the text of the New Testament with nothing more innovative or faster or efficient than Blass, Debrunner, and Funk's *Greek Grammar*, originally published in 1896—the Quadricycle of Greek grammars.[9] The same is true, and even more so, in critical analysis of textual relations. Most recently developed linguistic tools of New Testament study are sidelined as experimental methods and outside the purview of traditional historical and critical methods. As a result, many such available tools have not been utilized in mainstream scholarly criticism. A case in point is analysis of issues of language surrounding the Synoptic problem. I will briefly treat two types of resources: commentaries written after 1989 and introductions to the Synoptic problem written after 1989. I have chosen 1989 because that was the year my *Verbal Aspect in the Greek of the New Testament* was published.

There are a number of commentaries that have been written since 1989 that have had the opportunity to use work on verbal aspect in their analysis of the Synoptic problem. Included in this group of commentaries are those that are particularly focused on matters of language. I would expect to find suitable comments in such commentaries. In my examination of these commentaries, it is surprising how many of them have virtually no comments at all, not just on grammatical matters but even on any substantive issues regarding the Synoptic problem. It is not uncommon to discover, even in commentaries that

9. F. Blass, *Grammatik des neutestamentlichen Griechisch* (Göttingen: Vandenhoeck & Ruprecht, 1896). The many revisions of this grammar, including by Albert Debrunner and Friedrich Rehkopf, as well as by Robert Funk the translator, have not significantly altered the basic orientation of the grammar, despite repeated "new" editions (see the bibliography for this volume).

purport to be close readings or examinations of the text of the New Testament, especially the Greek text, that linguistic comments are virtually nowhere to be found in statements about the text, with nothing in the discussion of the Synoptic problem, if such treatments themselves are included at all (which they sometimes are not). There may be a bigger problem revealed here than simply whether the latest linguistic tools are being employed in Greek textual analysis. The larger issue may be whether there is any substantive examination of the language at all.

In the commentaries that do have some discussion of language matters, there unfortunately is a lack of substantial or important use of linguistic tools or even very many detailed comments on the Greek text itself. I offer several examples, without trying to be comprehensive.[10] In one commentary on Matthew, the author states regarding "single pericopes drawn from Mark" that "Matthew's version is almost consistently more terse." By this, he means that "Matthew has edited out unnecessary words, improving the syntax considerably." In other words, "It is unlikely that Mark would have produced his Greek while looking at Matthew's Greek." Yet strangely, one of the features of Mark's Greek is "directness and vividness."[11] Besides general comments regarding the "quality" of Mark's and Matthew's Greek, there are a number of vague grammatical comments that are not substantiated in any way with reference to any theory, old or new, regarding Greek. The comments regarding Mark's vividness may well be statements regarding his use of the narrative present, although this is uncertain. Another commentary has a subsection on the Greek style of the Synoptic Gospels. The author's assessment of the style of Matthew and Luke is that it is "generally better Greek style" than that in Mark, which is described as "characteristic, inferior Greek style."[12] Besides these general observations on the quality of Greek, stated without further ado, there is no statement regarding anything that can be seen as concerning the verbs. Finally, a commentary reports, "It has often been observed that Mark's literary style lacks the polish and sophistication that one regularly encounters in Matthew and Luke," though no reference is offered. The author continues,

10. I have examined commentaries on other books with some of the same issues in mind, and found similar results, in S. E. Porter, "Matthew and Mark: The Contribution of Recent Linguistic Thought," in *Mark and Matthew: Comparative Readings,* part 1, *Understanding the Earliest Gospels in their First-Century Settings,* ed. E.-M. Becker and A. Runesson, WUNT 271 (Tübingen: Mohr Siebeck, 2011), 97–119; Porter, "The Linguistic Competence of New Testament Commentaries" and "Commentaries on the Book of Romans," both in *On the Writing of New Testament Commentaries: Festschrift for Grant R. Osborne on the Occasion of His 70th Birthday,* ed. S. E. Porter and E. J. Schnabel, TENT 8 (Leiden: Brill, 2012), 33–56, 365–404.

11. D. A. Hagner, *Matthew,* 2 vols., WBC 33A–B (Dallas: Word, 1993–95), 1:xlvii.

12. J. Marcus, *Mark 1–8,* AB 27 (New York: Doubleday, 2000), 44.

"Markan style is Semitic, nonliterary, and sometimes may even be described as primitive." In discussing Synoptic relations, the author posits that if Mark used Matthew and/or Luke, he would have needed to rewrite them in "a cruder and less polished form."[13]

When we turn to recent works on the Synoptic problem, we do not find much better or more informative results. One such introduction to the Synoptic Gospels justifies Markan priority on the basis of Matthew or Luke altering Mark: "Included in this argument would be grammatical, stylistic, and content changes." Further, this means that, by comparison, "the writing style of Mark is rough and its grammar is awkward and poor." Matthew and Luke are said to "smooth these out." None of the examples suggested to illustrate this perspective refers specifically to any changes regarding verbal tense-forms; comments are confined to conjunctions, lexical choice, Latinisms or Aramaicisms, and theological issues.[14] A second work in the same vein refers to Mark's supposed lack of use of oral traditions, and says that this "troubling situation is intensified by a striking feature of Mark's style." This is characterized as Mark being "the most blatantly colloquial, the most 'oral' in nature." Four features are singled out as illustrating this orality: Mark's "lively pace" (e.g., "and immediately . . ."), "its present tenses" (e.g., "and Jesus says . . ."), "its love of visual detail" (e.g., Mark's reference to "green grass" in 6:39), and "its abrupt ending" (at Mark 16:8).[15] There is no explanation of how these relate to the other Gospels, or even how they function within Mark's Gospel. There is no reference to any other scholar who makes the point that these are features of ancient Greek orality.

The final example occurs in a book devoted to the Synoptic problem. Within one chapter on Markan priority is a subsection titled "Mark's Poorer Writing Style: The Argument from Grammar."[16] Here the author notes that an argument "frequently brought forward in favor of the priority of Mark involves the inferior quality of the Markan grammar." The author defines grammar broadly "to include matters of vocabulary, style, idiom, and sentence construction." The conclusion that the author draws is that "Mark appears to have possessed lesser literary skills," because Matthew and Luke display "a more polished and improved literary form."[17] The evidence for this is found

13. C. A. Evans, *Mark 8:27–16:20*, WBC 34B (Nashville: Nelson, 2001), xlix.

14. M. G. Reddish, *An Introduction to the Gospels* (Nashville: Abingdon, 1997), 29.

15. M. Goodacre, *The Synoptic Problem: A Way through the Maze*, BibSem 80 (London: Sheffield Academic Press, 2001), 62.

16. R. H. Stein, *Studying the Synoptic Gospels: Origin and Interpretation*, 2nd ed. (Grand Rapids: Baker Academic, 2001), 56–67.

17. Ibid., 56.

in three categories: "Colloquialisms and Inferior Writing Style," "Aramaic Expressions," and "Redundancy." I will pass over the question of whether these are suitable categories to illustrate the point that the author is contending and will mention several of his specific examples.[18] The author notes Mark's "rather clumsy redundancy" and cites 213 examples of redundancy or duplicate expressions that he calls "clearly a Markan stylistic feature."[19] Included in his statistics is the fact that 49 of these instances involve either Matthew or Luke retaining the supposedly redundant expression. What the author does not notice is how many of these involve verbal expressions, and whether such verbal expressions involve a change of tense-form. In his discussion of colloquialisms and other indicators of supposed inferior writing style, the author singles out five examples. Two involve lexical choice (passed over in the author's comments is the fact that one change of lexeme also involves a change in tense-form), one a purportedly awkward change in number from plural to singular, one the use of a singular verb with a plural (nonneuter) subject, and one a change of verbal voice-form. Since there is no instance of treating a change of tense-form, perhaps the example of change of voice-form can serve as an illustration of some of the difficulties involved in such analysis. The author observes that Mark 10:20 uses an aorist middle verb that is purportedly changed in Matthew 19:20 and Luke 18:21 to the active form. As the author states, "Mark has used a less common form of the verb," the aorist middle, "which Matthew and Luke have changed to the more common aorist active."[20] He draws the conclusion that this change makes more sense than Mark changing the more common form to the less common. In a footnote the author admits that in the first edition of the book he labeled this usage by Mark as "incorrect grammar," which was argued against by another

---

18. I have trouble accepting that they are suitable categories. Under Aramaic expressions, the author (Stein, *Studying the Synoptic Gospels*) simply notes that Mark is a "more Semitic or 'Hebraizing' gospel" (p. 59), and he looks at seven Aramaic expressions. He explains the deletion of these expressions by Matthew and Luke in at least five of the parallels as making "good sense" on their part, because of the difference in audience. The only point that addresses the quality of Mark's Greek style is the note that Henry Cadbury "has further pointed out that careful writers of Greek avoided foreign words" (p. 63, citing H. J. Cadbury, *The Making of Luke-Acts* [London: SPCK, 1958], 123–26). He also acknowledges that some have disagreed with Cadbury on this point (E. P. Sanders, *The Tendencies of the Synoptic Tradition*, SNTSMS 9 [Cambridge: Cambridge University Press, 1969], 187–88), which he quickly dismisses as "not convincing" (p. 63n19). However, he does not actually address the literary situation that he has created for Mark: a Gospel addressed to a Semitic audience. Cadbury's disclaimer is addressed to authors writing to Greek audiences.

19. Stein, *Synoptic Gospels*, 63, 66. The references are given in C. M. Tuckett, *The Revival of the Griesbach Hypothesis: An Analysis and Appraisal*, SNTSMS 44 (Cambridge: Cambridge University Press, 1983), 20, 194.

20. Stein, *Synoptic Gospels*, 57.

scholar.[21] Our author concedes this point, although wants to make sure it is noted that even if the form is not incorrect, it is less normal. As he asks, "Is it more likely that Matthew and Luke would change Mark's aorist middle, which is contrary to the general trend, or that Mark would have changed the normal aorist active in Matthew and Luke to the less normal aorist middle?"[22] How should one answer such a speculative question? The most that the author has shown is that Mark uses the less usual form. How this has anything to do with Mark's inferior writing style is beyond me; one could argue that it reflects a more sophisticated style, which then is demoted by Matthew and Luke. In other words, why give up a good example, even if it can no longer really support the case one is making?

This quick survey, which is only representative of several prominent works on the topic, clearly has not answered the question of the relationship of verbal aspect to the Synoptic problem. In fact, I think it illustrates that much discussion of linguistic issues regarding the Synoptic problem is quite underdeveloped and ripe for a thorough rethinking and reexamination. More to the point of this chapter, however, is the relative paucity of examples that draw upon any sustainable theories about tense-form usage, and certainly any hard evidence regarding patterns of usage apart from assuming one particular theory of Synoptic origins (Markan priority). In other words, the prescient question remains: which change is more likely? This question remains unanswered.

Assessing Verbal Aspect and Synoptic Relations

In order to see whether verbal aspect can provide a way forward in assessing Synoptic relations, I decided to examine changes in verbal tense-forms between texts where it can be established which text is dependent upon the other. I would be interested in any further examples that can be studied similarly. To provide some control on the study, I identified one set of data: uses of the Old Testament quoted in the New Testament. I realize that there are problems with such a set of data, such as knowing the text of the source citation, other changes introduced into the text that may have had a direct impact on the use of tense-forms, and the like; however, for the sake of discussion in this preliminary exercise, I decided to compare straight across in Greek sources.

---

21. Ibid., 57n11. He cites D. A. Black, "Some Dissenting Notes on R. Stein's *The Synoptic Problem* and Markan 'Errors,'" *FN* 1 (1988): 95–96. Black has his own problems in this article, when he identifies the middle voice as reflexive. See S. E. Porter, *Idioms of the Greek New Testament*, 2nd ed., BLG 2 (Sheffield: Sheffield Academic Press, 1994), 67–70.

22. Stein, *Synoptic Gospels*, 57n11.

This set of data provides information directly from the New Testament writers. As a second set of data, I decided to use an extrabiblical author roughly contemporary with the New Testament. I have also analyzed how Josephus in his *Jewish Antiquities* uses the Maccabean literature at places where there is enough sustained text to provide for synoptic comparison. In this section I summarize the patterns that I see within these bodies of literature, and then I examine whether these offer insight into select Synoptic Gospel passages, with the intention of seeing if the results can illustrate in any way, in particular with regard to possible changes in tense-form, the relations of the Synoptic Gospels. I have no vested interest in defending any particular view of Synoptic origins, especially in relation to the standard theories of Markan priority or Matthean priority. I suspect that the relations among the Gospels probably were much more complex than we typically imagine, and that the process was less like that of a German scholar in his study copying from a source book than the standard theories imagine, and certainly less like that of a modern scholar compiling a text by using a cut-and-paste function.[23]

Patterns of Verbal Change in Old Testament Passages Cited in the New Testament

I have analyzed the changes that are made in selection of verbal aspect in all of the citations of Old Testament passages in the New Testament, from the Gospels, Acts, and the Pauline Letters.[24] In this corpus of material, as far as I have identified, there are roughly 508 instances of a verbal tense-form being used in the source text and then a corresponding form being used in the receptor text. I have not counted instances where a passage is cited but a verb within the source text is not carried over into the receptor text. This could prove to be an interesting area of exploration, because deletion might be a pertinent factor in determining source relations. However, I am concentrating on verbal form change indicating change of aspect. In some instances it is clear that there has been a lexical change, and that the new lexeme used in the receptor text is used for the source lexeme. I note these changes as pertinent, and also include the few instances of analytical constructions (e.g., catenative constructions or periphrastics). The tense-forms represented include all of

23. See S. E. Porter, "The Legacy of B. F. Westcott and Oral Gospel Tradition," in festschrift, ed. J. Neusner et al. (Leiden: Brill, forthcoming). I have sympathies with Westcott's theory of oral and mnemonic development, which adds a further dimension to the analysis that cannot be taken into account here

24. I acknowledge the fact that we do not know the source text used in many instances, but I base this comparison on Rahlf's edition of the Septuagint.

the major categories of tense-forms, including the aorist, present/imperfect, perfect/pluperfect, future forms, and aspectually vague verbs.[25]

There are forty-five instances where the receptor author has used a different verbal tense-form than that found in the source text. In some instances there are interesting examples of lexical changes and mood-form changes that I will also note. The following tense-form changes are to be found.

Aorist Tense-form

Aorist to Present/Imperfect: Matthew 7:23 citing Psalm 6:8 (6:9 LXX) (ἀπόστητε > ἀποχωρεῖτε); Mark 4:12 citing Isaiah 6:9–10 (ἀκούσωσιν > ἀκούοντες ἀκούωσιν, with the quotation creating a different type of parallelism than in the source text; συνῶσιν > συνιῶσιν); Luke 8:10 citing Isaiah 6:9–10 (twice: ἀκούσωσιν > ἀκούοντες; συνῶσιν > συνιῶσιν) = four instances, with two forms replacing the original one in one instance.

Aorist to Future: Matthew 26:31 citing Zechariah 13:7 (twice imperative to future: πατάξατε > πατάξω;[26] ἐκσπάσατε > διασκορπισθήσονται); Mark 14:27 citing Zechariah 13:7 (twice imperative to future: πατάξατε > πατάξω; ἐκσπάσατε > διασκορπισθήσονται); John 2:17 citing Psalm 69:9 (68:10 LXX) (κατέφαγεν > καταφάγεται); Acts 7:6–7 citing Genesis 15:13–14 (subjunctive to future: δουλεύσωσιν > δουλεύσουσιν);[27] Romans 3:4 citing Psalm 51:4 (50:6 LXX) (subjunctive to future: νικήσῃς > νικήσεις;[28] Romans 9:33 citing Isaiah 28:16 (subjunctive to future: καταισχυνθῇ > καταισχυνθήσεται); Romans 10:11 citing Isaiah 28:16 (subjunctive to future: καταισχυνθῇ > καταισχυνθήσεται) = nine instances, with eight of these being changes of nonindicative mood-forms to the future form.

There is no instance of a change from the aorist tense-form to the perfect/pluperfect form or from the aorist to an aspectually vague verb form other than future.

Present Tense-form

Present/Imperfect to Aorist: Matthew 8:17 citing Isaiah 53:4 (twice: φέρει > ἔλαβεν; ὀδυνᾶται > ἐβάστασεν); Matthew 10:35–36 citing Micah 7:6 (ἀτιμάζει >

25. For clarification of some of these terms, see Porter, *Verbal Aspect*, esp. 75–109, and several of the chapters in the present volume, including chaps. 10, 11, and 12.

26. This form may be parsed as an aorist active subjunctive, but the parallelism in both the Septuagint and the New Testament probably indicates that the author meant to use a future form. The same applies to Mark 14:27.

27. I recognize that these two forms may simply reflect phonetic interchange. See F. T. Gignac, *A Grammar of the Greek Papyri of the Roman and Byzantine Periods*, 2 vols. (Milan: Cisalpino-Goliardica, 1976–81), 1:208–11. Note the following κρίνω, which may either be a present subjunctive, κρίνω, or a future form, κρινῶ. But the same form is found in both the LXX and Acts 7:7.

28. This may also involve phonetic interchange. See ibid., 1:239–42.

ἦλθον διχάσαι, with an aorist catenative);[29] John 15:25 citing Psalm 35:19 (34:19 LXX) and 69:4 (68:5 LXX) (μισοῦντες > ἐμίσησαν) = four instances.

Present/Imperfect to Future: Luke 12:53 citing Micah 7:6 (ἀτιμάζει > διαμερισθήσονται; note that the next verb in Micah 7:6, ἐπαναστήσεται, is not rendered in Luke 12:53); Romans 2:6 citing Proverbs 24:12 (ἀποδίδωσιν > ἀποδώσει);[30] 1 Corinthians 2:16 citing Isaiah 40:13 (συμβιβᾷ > συμβιβάσει) = three instances.

Present/Imperfect to Aspectually Vague (other than Future):[31] Matthew 4:15–16 citing Isaiah 9:1–2 (twice: πορευόμενος > καθήμενος; κατοικοῦντες > καθημένοις) = two instances.

There is no instance of the present/imperfect tense-form being changed to the perfect/pluperfect tense-form.

PERFECT TENSE-FORM

Perfect/Pluperfect to Aorist: Acts 7:33–34 citing Exodus 3:5, 7–8, 10 (ἀκήκοα > ἤκουσα); Acts 7:40 citing Exodus 32:1, 23 (γέγονεν > ἐγένετο);[32] Romans 3:15–17 citing Isaiah 59:7–8 and possibly Proverbs 1:16 (οἴδασιν > ἔγνωσαν) = three instances.

Perfect/Pluperfect to Aspectually Vague (other than Future): John 12:15 citing Zechariah 9:9 (ἐπιβεβηκώς > καθήμενος) = one instance.

There is no instance of the perfect/pluperfect tense-form being changed to the present/imperfect tense-form or to the future form.

FUTURE FORM

Future to Aorist: Matthew 18:16 citing Deuteronomy 19:15 (σταθήσεται > σταθῇ in the subjunctive); Mark 4:12 citing Isaiah 6:9–10 (ἰάσομαι > ἀφεθῇ in the subjunctive); Mark 10:19 citing Exodus 20:12–16 or Deuteronomy 5:16–20 (four times, using the negated aorist subjunctive: φονεύσεις > φονεύσῃς; μοιχεύσεις > μοιχεύσῃς; κλέψεις > κλέψῃς; ψευδομαρτυρήσεις > ψευδομαρτυρήσῃς, with the final command retained with the present imperative);[33] Luke 18:20 (four times, using the negated aorist subjunctive: μοιχεύσεις > μοιχεύσῃς; φονεύσεις > φονεύσῃς; κλέψεις > κλέψῃς; ψευδομαρτυρήσεις > ψευδομαρτυρήσῃς, with the final command retained with the present imperative); Luke 20:28 citing

---

29. I recognize that the words in Matt. 10:35 are not usually considered part of the quotation, but they appear to serve the same function within the discourse as the word cited in Mic. 7:6.

30. Psalm 62:12 (61:13 LXX) reads σὺ ἀποδώσεις.

31. On aspectually vague verbs, those -μι verbs that never developed a full aspectual paradigm, see Porter, *Verbal Aspect*, 442–47. See also chap. 12.

32. Note that in the LXX text of Exod. 32:1 there is a sequence of perfect tense-forms: οἴδαμεν and γέγονεν. There may well be discourse implications for the use of the second perfect.

33. This may involve phonetic interchange, along with the following example. See Gignac, *Grammar*, 1:239–42.

Deuteronomy 25:5 and Genesis 38:8 (λήμψεται > λάβῃ, using the subjunctive); Acts 2:31 citing Psalm 16:10 (15:10 LXX) (ἐγκαταλείψεις > ἐγκατελείφθη); Romans 11:4 citing 1 Kings 19:18 (καταλείψεις > κατέλιπον); 1 Corinthians 5:13 citing Deuteronomy 17:7, 19:19, 22:21, 24, 24:7 (ἐξαρεῖς > ἐξάρατε, using the imperative) = fourteen instances, including eleven changes to the aorist subjunctive and one to the aorist imperative.

Future to Present/Imperfect: Matthew 15:4b citing Exodus 21:16 (τελευτήσει > τελευτάτω); Mark 4:12 citing Isaiah 6:9–10 (βλέψετε > βλέπωσιν, with subjunctive); Luke 8:10 citing Isaiah 6:9–10 (βλέψετε > βλέπωσιν, with subjunctive); Luke 23:46 citing Psalm 31:5 (30:6 LXX) (παραθήσομαι > παρατίθεμαι); Romans 9:33 quoting Isaiah 28:16 (ἐμβαλῶ > τίθημι) = five instances, including two changes to the present subjunctive.

There is no instance of the future form being changed to the perfect/pluperfect tense-form or to an aspectually vague verb.

Aspectually Vague Verbs (Other Than Future Forms)

There is no instance of an otherwise aspectually vague verb (other than future forms) being changed to an aspectual form, or even to the future form (however, there are a number of instances of the future form of εἰμί being used).

Several preliminary and no doubt statistically untested conclusions can be drawn from this information. (1) There is no instance of a major aspectual elevation occurring, in which a less marked form is elevated to the most marked form. In other words, there is no instance in which an aorist, present/imperfect, or a future form is elevated to a perfect/pluperfect form. There are four instances of minor aspectual elevation in which the aorist is elevated to the present/imperfect (two of these involve the same cited passage), but no instance of the present/imperfect to the perfect/pluperfect.

(2) There are, however, a number of instances of tense-form and aspectual reduction, where a more marked form is reduced to a less marked form. Examples of this include present/imperfect reduced to aorist, future, or aspectually vague; and perfect/pluperfect reduced to aorist or aspectually vague (there is no instance of the perfect/pluperfect reduced to present/imperfect). These instances of tense-form and aspectual reduction account for 13 of the 45 instances of tense-form changes.

(3) There are a number of instances in which there is what I would call an aspectualization of the process, by which an aspectually vague verb, in particular a future form, is changed to an aspectual verb. These instances would include those in which a future form is changed from the source to the receptor text into an aorist or present/imperfect form (there are no changes from aspectually

vague to perfect/pluperfect). These aspectualizations account for 19 of the 45 changes. I note further that in 13 of these 19 the change is from the future form to the aorist or present subjunctive, thereby maintaining similar attitudinal semantics of the nonindicative mood-forms in the aspectualization process.[34]

(4) There are also 12 instances in which aorist, present/imperfect, or perfect/pluperfect forms are changed to the not fully aspectual or vague future form, a process of de-aspectualization. This is related to aspectual reduction, but goes further and uses an aspectually vague verb, especially the future form.

(5) There are also instances of tense-form alternation between the aorist (perfective) and present (imperfective). This lower-level aspectual movement (minor aspectual elevation or reduction) seems to occur in relatively similar proportions. Let me simply note one other feature, not directly related to aspectual alteration, that I could not help but observe as I was examining this material. There is a tendency for the New Testament writers to delete prefixed prepositions of verbs in the source text and use the simpler form in the receptor text. Examples of this occur in Matthew 2:15 (μετεκάλεσα > ἐκάλεσα), Matthew 2:18 (ἀποκλαιομένη > κλαίουσα), Matthew 11:10 (ἐξαποστέλλω > ἀποστέλλω, where the two prefixed prepositions are reduced to one),[35] Matthew 19:5 (προσκολληθήσεται > κολληθήσεται), Mark 1:2 (ἐξαποστέλλω > ἀποστέλλω), Luke 7:27 (ἐξαποστέλλω > ἀποστέλλω), possibly Acts 3:25 (ἐνευλογηθήσονται > εὐλογηθήσονται), where there is a textual dispute[36]—all in examples where there is no aspectual change. There are 6 instances here, possibly 7, with 1 occurring 3 times. An example where a preposition is added is Luke 20:28 (ἀνάστησον > ἐξαναστήσῃ).

Josephus and His Use of the Maccabees in Jewish Antiquities

A number of passages in Josephus's *Jewish Antiquities* draw especially on 1 Maccabees, but also some draw on 2 Maccabees.[37] They occur in *Antiquities*

34. For discussion of the semantics of the future form in relation to the attitudinal semantics grammaticalized by the subjunctive mood-form, see Porter, *Verbal Aspect*, esp. 409–16.

35. It appears that Matt. 2:10 is citing Mal. 3:1, rather than Exod. 23:20, on the basis of the second clause.

36. Both the United Bible Societies and the Nestle-Aland texts fail us at this point by not making a decision. The textual evidence is split between P74, ℵ (01), A^c, D, and the Majority text for the prefixed form, and A*, B, a few other manuscripts and Irenaeus for the unprefixed form. The prefixed form probably is to be preferred, but the issue of retention or deletion of the prefixed preposition perhaps should factor into the discussion.

37. I use the text of J. Sievers, *Synopsis of the Greek Sources for the Hasmonean Period: 1–2 Maccabees and Josephus, War 1 and Antiquities 12–14*, SubBi 20 (Rome: Pontifical Biblical Institute, 2001), and I thank my colleague Andrew W. Pitts for his help in analyzing the data.

12–13 concerning the Hasmoneans. These parallels are ideally suited for my present purpose due to our knowledge of their chronological relationship and the contemporaneity of Josephus to the writing of the New Testament. The major problem is that despite a number of places where Josephus does appear to follow his source fairly literalistically, there are numerous places where he does not do so, but instead either paraphrases or transforms the Greek in such a way as to eliminate verbal tense-form correspondence, such as by grammaticalization with nominal constructions. Despite this unfortunate complication, similar general patterns can still be observed. In the vast majority of instances where there is verbal tense-form correspondence, the source text is taken over into the receptor text unchanged, at least as far as aspectual choice is concerned. This includes retention especially of aorist and present/imperfect forms, even if the mood-form is changed (e.g., 1 Macc. 5:14 and *Ant.* 12.331, with changes from imperfect to present participle [ἀνεγιγνώσκοντο > ἀναγινωσκομένων], or 1 Macc. 6:2 with aorist indicative to aorist infinitive in *Ant.* 12.354 [κατέλιπεν > καταλιπεῖν], or aorist indicative in 1 Macc. 6:62 to aorist participle in *Ant.* 12.383 [εἰσῆλθεν > εἰσελθών]).

There are, however, also a number of changes that Josephus makes from his source into the receptor text. Most of these are very similar to those noted above for the use of the Old Testament. For example, there is an example of tense-form or aspectual reduction, with a change of aspect from the stative (perfect participle) to the imperfective (imperfect form). What makes this example particularly interesting is that the perfect participle (stative aspect) is found in both of Josephus's sources at this point, 2 Maccabees 6:10 (περιτετμηκυῖαι) and 1 Maccabees 1:60 (περιτετμηκυίας), but changed to the imperfect form (imperfective aspect) in *Antiquities* 12.256 (περιέτεμνον). There are some examples of change from the perfective to the imperfective aspect (minor aspectual elevation), which we have already noted above in the New Testament, even though I have not yet found any examples of change from the imperfective to the perfective aspect (minor aspectual reduction). These instances of shifts include a change from the aorist indicative form (perfective aspect) in 1 Maccabees 6:63 to the imperfect form (imperfective aspect) of *Antiquities* 12.386 (ἐπολέμησεν > ἐπολέμει), or change of the aorist infinitive (perfective aspect) to the present infinitive (imperfective aspect), which occurs three times in 1 Maccabees 10:44–45 (οἰκοδομηθῆναι, ἐπικαινισθῆναι, οἰκοδομηθῆναι) and *Antiquities* 13.57 (οἰκοδομεῖν, ἀνακαινίζειν, οἰκοδομεῖσθαι). Perhaps the most noteworthy change, since it was not observed in the foregoing discussion of the Old and New Testaments, is a change from the perfective to the imperfective aspect that reflects a change from a narrative aorist to a narrative (or sometimes so-called historic) present. There are a number of instances of this change.

In fact, this is the single most obvious change that I have so far discovered in Maccabees and Josephus. These occur in, for example, 1 Maccabees 7:2 and *Antiquities* 12.390 (συνέλαβον ἀγαγεῖν > ἀνάγουσιν), 1 Maccabees 10:21 and *Antiquities* 13.46 (συνήγαγεν > συνάγει), 1 Maccabees 11:22 and *Antiquities* 13.123 (ἔγραψεν > γράφει), and 1 Maccabees 11:56 and *Antiquities* 13.144 (κατεκράτησεν > κρατεῖ, which also involves reduction of the prefixed preposition). This may be a stylistic feature of Josephus, except that Josephus's use of the narrative present, though relatively high (though not apparently the highest) among postclassical writers, seems generally to conform to usage of this discourse-structuring device, and therefore is susceptible to explanation in these instances where he departs from his source.[38]

The evidence from Josephus is considerably smaller than that found in the use of the Old Testament by the New Testament authors, but there are a number of similar patterns. These include the retention of aspect in the vast majority of instances, at least one example of tense-form/aspectual reduction from the perfect to the present/imperfect form (stative to imperfective aspect), and some alteration within perfective and imperfective aspect. The one noticeable feature of Josephus's use of his sources is changing of the perfective to the imperfective aspect when the change results in creating a so-called narrative present, but with no examples of the reverse found.

Examples of Aspectual Change in the Synoptic Gospels

In this section I select several Gospel passages for brief examination. I examine passages where there is significant material in each of the Synoptic Gospels. These examples are not meant to be definitive, but rather to illustrate factors often not taken into consideration in discussing Synoptic relations.

THE TEMPTATION OF JESUS

The standard critical theory, if I am not mistaken, is that the Matthean (4:1–11) and Lukan (4:1–13) accounts of the temptation are in some way derived from the Markan (1:12–13) account and radically expanded by using Q material.[39] However, there are two considerations to weigh in the light of my discussion above. The first is that Mark 1:12 uses a narrative present,

---

38. See Porter, *Verbal Aspect*, esp. 134–35; compare K. Eriksson, *Das Präsens historicum in der nachklassischen griechischen Historiographie* (Lund: Håkan Ohlsson, 1943), esp. 15–17.

39. For example, W. D. Davies and D. C. Allison Jr., *A Critical and Exegetical Commentary on the Gospel according to Saint Matthew*, 3 vols., ICC (Edinburgh: T&T Clark, 1988–97), 1:350–51; F. Bovon, *Luke 1: A Commentary on the Gospel of Luke 1:1–9:50*, trans. C. M. Thomas, ed. H. Koester, Hermeneia (Minneapolis: Fortress, 2002), 139.

ἐκβάλλει, to introduce the unit, whereas Matthew 4:1 uses an aorist indicative (ἀνήχθη) and Luke 4:1 uses an aorist indicative (ὑπέστρεψεν) and imperfect (ἤγετο) to introduce the scene. The second is that Mark continues in verse 13 with two instances of the verb form ἦν, the first possibly used as a component of a periphrastic construction (ἦν . . . πειραζόμενος) and the other as the finite verb of the group/clause construction. In contrast to the initial narrative present in Mark, both Matthew and Luke use participles, Matthew with an aorist participle dependent upon a following aorist verb (νηστεύσας . . . ἐπείνασεν), and Luke with a present participle dependent upon the preceding imperfect verb (ἤγετο . . . πειραζόμενος). Admittedly, this is not a lot of evidence, but these two factors point to Mark's account as the one that is derived from either the Matthean or Lukan account, as the pattern seems to represent a shift—at least in the Matthean account—from perfective to imperfective aspect for the use of a narrative present tense-form (found in Josephus), and there is no instance of an aspectually vague verb being aspectualized in either the New Testament or the Josephus evidence examined. In this case, Matthew and Luke would have had different sequences of the temptation, the specifics of which are deleted by Mark in his account, along with making other verbal changes.

THE PARABLE OF THE SOWER AND ITS INTERPRETATION

The introduction of the parable of the sower (Matt. 13:1–9; Mark 4:1–9; Luke 8:4–8) is similar in Matthew 13:1–2 and Mark 4:1, but different in Luke 8:4. Matthew 13:1 uses what is probably an aspectually vague verb, ἐκάθητο, while Mark uses a catenative construction, ἤρξατο διδάσκειν; however, Mark then uses the narrative present συνάγεται, whereas Matthew has συνήχθησαν. It is difficult to establish the dependency relation between these two openings, although it may reflect Matthew as the source based upon some of the patterns in Josephus. As the parable continues, the Lukan account (8:5–6) uses prefixed verbs twice, κατεπατήθη and κατέπεσεν, with the equivalents in Matthew and Mark being the unprefixed forms. However, there are other prefixed forms used by these Gospels (e.g., ἐξῆλθεν in Luke 8:5; Matt. 13:3; Mark 4:3; ἐξανέτειλεν in Matt. 13:5; Mark 4:5). There is some further verbal tense-form interchange between perfective and imperfective forms in both directions, such as συμφυεῖσαι in Luke 8:7 and ἀνέβησαν in Matthew 13:7 and Mark 4:7; and ἐποίησεν in Luke 8:8 and ἐδίδου in Matthew 13:8 and Mark 4:8—which could indicate movement in either direction. This slender evidence may indicate that the Lukan account of the parable of the sower is the source text for Matthew and Mark, on the basis of the use of prefixed forms. This slight tendency may be strengthened by the interpretation of the parable (Matt. 13:18–23; Mark 4:13–20; Luke 8:11–15). In Luke's account of the interpretation, his opening in Luke 8:11–12 in the primary clause Predicator components relies upon three uses of forms of the verb εἰμί. In two of these instances the equivalents in Matthew 13:18 (the first instance) and Mark 4:13–14 (the first two instances) are aspectualized verbs (in Matthew ἀκούσατε, in Mark οἴδατε and σπείρει) (I take the future form, γνώσεσθε, as a component of a secondary clause, serving as Complement). However, I also note that in Mark 4:13, the beginning of Mark's interpretation of the parable, Jesus is quoted as using the stative aspect with οἴδατε. The corresponding verb in Matthew 13:18 is the aorist imperative ἀκούσατε, and in Luke 8:11 a form of εἰμί, both instances of major tense-form and aspectual reduction.

In this particular set of parallels, there is evidence that pushes in various directions. The use of the prefixed forms and the use of forms of the verb εἰμί indicate that Luke is the source text, while this evidence is not unequivocal alongside the evidence of the perfective-imperfective alteration and apparent tense-reduction of the perfect form in Mark.

PETER'S CONFESSION

Peter's confession, found in Matthew 16:13–20; Mark 8:27–30; Luke 9:18–21; and somewhat in John 6:67–71, is usually said to originate with Mark's account, although some have argued that Matthew is closer to the original and may have been the source of the others.[40] In terms of the criteria that I am using here, there are reasons for these mixed conclusions. As might be expected, many verbal features of the text are identical throughout the accounts. However, several instances of variation are worth noting. The first concerns prefixed and unprefixed tense-forms. Mark 8:27 and Luke 9:18 have the prefixed form ἐπερωτάω, although Mark uses the imperfective aspect (ἐπηρώτα, imperfect tense-form) and Luke the perfective (ἐπηρώτησεν, aorist tense-form). In Mark 8:29, however, the author uses the same prefixed form, ἐπηρώτα, while Luke 9:20 has εἶπεν and Matthew 16:15 has the narrative present λέγει. The unusual feature of this instance is that there is an aspectual change from the imperfective in Mark to the perfective in Luke (but no change between Matthew and Mark). Later in the same verse, Matthew and Luke use the aorist εἶπεν, while Mark uses the narrative present (imperfective) λέγει. Deletion of the prefixed preposition (in 16:13) tends to indicate that Matthew is the source text, but this is not maintained. Both Matthew and Mark use the narrative present, which tends to reflect the receptor text, although Matthew's does not follow

40. See S. E. Porter, "Vague Verbs, Periphrastics, and Matthew 16:19," *FN* 1 (1988): 155–73; revised and reprinted in S. E. Porter, *Studies in the Greek New Testament: Theory and Practice*, SBG 6 (New York: Peter Lang, 1996), 103–24.

the traditional pattern by shifting lexemes. Thus, there are various verbal factors that push toward either Matthew or Mark as the source text.

A similar opposition of verbal factors is found in the pericope regarding Jesus and his coming death (Matt. 16:21–23; Mark 8:31–33; Luke 9:22). The similarities between the Matthean and Markan accounts are numerous. However, Mark 8:33 has the prefixed verb form ἐπιστραφείς, while Matthew 16:23 has the unprefixed form of the same verb, στραφείς; and Mark 8:33 uses the narrative present, λέγει, while Matthew 16:23 uses the aorist εἶπεν. Compare also Matthew 19:23 and Luke 18:24 with εἶπεν, and Mark 10:23 with λέγει.

THE RICH YOUNG MAN

The story of the rich young man (Matt. 19:16–22; Mark 10:17–22; Luke 18:18–23, treated here as parallels) is interesting because it contains some of the passages that have gone into formulating the observations above on tense-form change in the use of the Old Testament in the New Testament. There are several verbal factors to observe, including the quoted material. The first is the use of the prefixed forms ἐπηρώτα in Mark 10:17 and ἐπηρώτησεν in Luke 18:18, while Matthew 19:16 uses εἶπεν—which points to Mark and Luke as the source account, and Matthew as the receptor. This pattern does not follow the one identified in the sample texts, whereby there is not a shift in aspect, but it does resemble the pattern noted above in Peter's confession. The second factor is the use of the stative aspect, with the verb οἶδας, in both Mark 10:19 and Luke 18:20. The parallel construction in Matthew (19:17) appears to have been completely rewritten, but reflects major tense-form and aspectual reduction to the aorist imperative, τήρησον. This second feature also points to Matthew as the receptor account. The third consideration is the quotation of the Old Testament commandments. Matthew's account (19:18–19) uses future forms (including his lone statement regarding loving one's neighbor as oneself), while Mark (10:19) and Luke (18:20) use aorist subjunctives—except for the last command regarding honoring one's parents, which uses the present imperative in all three Gospels. Both the Exodus 20 and Deuteronomy 5 accounts in the Septuagint use the future form, except for the command to honor one's parents (present imperative). The analysis of the use of the Old Testament in the New Testament above indicated that it was more likely that a source was changed from a future form to an aorist, especially subjunctive, than it was from an aorist subjunctive to a future. If we assume that the movement in these Synoptic verses was within the three Gospel texts, it appears more likely that Mark and Luke were receptors of Matthew as the source, rather than the other way around. A fourth consideration occurs with verbs of speaking in Matthew 19:20; Mark 10:20; and Luke 18:21. Matthew has the narrative present λέγει,

Mark the aspectually vague verb ἔφη, and Luke the aorist εἶπεν. This feature points to Luke as the source and to Matthew and Mark as the receptors. However, in the next verse, Matthew uses the aspectually vague ἔφη, while Mark and Luke use εἶπεν. This fourth factor perhaps helps to confirm Matthew as a receptor text, and possibly indicate Luke as the source.

The evidence in this passage is difficult to assess due to a number of competing factors, although one can see some slight tendencies. Whether one thinks that Mark or Luke was the source (on the basis of the verbal criteria, Luke may be the source), Matthew appears to be the one who used their tradition.

The Triumphal Entry

The triumphal entry (Matt. 21:1–9; Mark 11:1–10; Luke 19:28–40) has a number of features to examine. The first concerns the introduction of the episode. The same two verbal lexemes are used in the introduction to the episode in all three Gospels. Matthew 21:1 uses two major indicative verbs, ἤγγισαν and ἀπέστειλεν. Luke 19:28–29 uses ἤγγισεν embedded within the account but still in relation to the two villages Bethphage and Bethany, as well as using ἀπέστειλεν. Mark 11:1, however, uses the two verbs with imperfective aspect as narrative presents, ἐγγίζουσιν and ἀποστέλλει (as well as λέγει in Mark 11:2, and φέρουσιν and ἐπιβάλλουσιν in Mark 11:7). This presumably indicates Mark as the receptor account. The second feature revolves around the use of forms of λύω and ἄγω/φέρω in Matthew 21:2; Mark 11:2; and Luke 19:30. Matthew and Luke use the aorist participle and aorist indicative, but Mark the aorist imperative and present imperative. Although we did not note such a tense-form reduction pattern above, it is possible that this is what has happened here, indicating Mark as the source (however, there is interchange between perfective and imperfective aspect, which is indecisive). A third factor to consider is that Matthew 21:3 and Mark 11:3 use the aorist subjunctive εἴπῃ, while Luke 19:31 uses the present subjunctive ἐρωτᾷ. This may also indicate tense-form and aspectual reduction, although possibly simply tense-form interchange. A fourth factor is the use of the future form ἐρεῖτε in Matthew 21:3 and Luke 19:31, while Mark 11:3 uses the aorist imperative εἴπατε. This may well indicate Mark as the source text on the basis of the tendency to reduce to the aspectually vague future form. A fifth factor is the use of the prefixed imperfective form ὑπεστρώννυον in Luke 19:36, while Matthew 21:8 and Mark 11:8 use the unprefixed aorist ἔστρωσαν. The overall evidence is mixed, but probably points away from Luke as the source.

A similar passage is the question about authority in Matthew 21:23–27; Mark 11:27–33; and Luke 20:1–8. Mark uses a number of imperfective verbs as narrative presents (e.g., ἔρχονται, λέγουσιν, λέγει) but also has several prefixed verbs (e.g., ἐπερωτήσω, ἀποκρίθητε).

PRECEDENCE AMONG THE DISCIPLES

This passage (Matt. 20:24–28; Mark 10:41–45; Luke 22:24–30) has a number of the features already noted above, such as the use of the narrative present λέγει in Mark 10:42, as opposed to an aorist in Matthew 20:25 and Luke 22:25 (εἶπεν in both); or a prefixed verb, κατακυριεύουσιν, in Matthew 20:25 and Mark 10:42, but unprefixed in Luke 22:25, κυριεύουσιν. Here I wish to deal with several considerations that have not been noted as widely as some others. The first is the use of the stative aspect, with the form οἴδατε in Matthew 20:25 and Mark 10:42, while Luke has no corresponding form, but does have similar wording. It is unclear how one would analyze such evidence, but the surrounding syntax seems to indicate that Luke has used a source similar to that of Matthew and Mark. The second is what has taken place in regard to the use of the future form ἔσται in Matthew 20:26 and Mark 10:43. Again, there is nothing equivalent in the Lukan text, even though the parallel seems clear. The question is whether this has been a reduction of the aspectually vague verb to nothing (in Luke) or whether there is addition of a verb to a passage with none (in Matthew and Mark). The evidence regarding a source of this passage is equivocal, with Matthew probably having the marginal claim, and Luke clearly as the receptor text.

THE WOMEN VISITING THE TOMB

The final episode that I will consider is found in Matthew 28:1–8; Mark 16:1–8; and Luke 24:1–12, when the women visit the tomb of Jesus. There are a number of competing features to be found in this episode. The first is Mark's use of the imperfective aspect as a narrative present, ἔρχονται, whereas Matthew 28:1 uses the aorist ἦλθεν and Luke 24:1 the aorist ἦλθον. The second feature concerns use of stative aspect. Both Mark in 16:4 and Luke in 24:2 use perfect tense-forms: ἀποκεκύλισται and ἀποκεκυλισμένον. There is no parallel in Matthew. Later in the account, Mark in 16:5 uses a perfect, περιβεβλημένον, while Matthew has no verb and Luke 24:4 simply describes the man's appearance (ἐν ἐσθῆτι ἀστραπτούσῃ). The features are too few to speak definitively, but it appears that Mark probably is the source of the other two accounts.

Conclusion

I wish to draw several preliminary conclusions from this study.

1. These are recognizably preliminary and very minimalist findings. They are based on a very limited study of Synoptic and extra-Synoptic material, and they need to be expanded greatly to ensure that the kinds of patterns

identified are indeed found across a wide range of evidence. I think that there are two ways in which this evidence needs to be expanded. The first is to identify a larger number of useful texts in which clear chronological dependency relations can be established so as to study the use of tense-form change. The second is to expand the categories of analysis so that tense-form change can be correlated with other types of verbal changes, such as mood, voice, and the like, to discover if alteration patterns can be established.

2. Even though the observations made here are quite limited, and perhaps not in and of themselves useful for solving the Synoptic problem, they have a more explicit basis than is evidenced in much other work that pronounces on the nature of the Synoptic problem, as noted at the outset of this chapter. For that reason alone, the type of study performed here should be greatly expanded.

3. Many of the observations and tentative conclusions that I have drawn are probably not what one might have expected or hoped for, and in fact do not clearly lead to definitive conclusions. This is to be expected, since the goal of this chapter was not to solve enduring problems, but rather to bring new insights and avenues of exploration to those problems. One area requiring further study is the semantic implications of tense-form changes. In other words, if we are able to establish patterns of tense-form change, then we should be able to examine the semantic and discourse implications of those changes as they are found within various discourses, such as the Synoptic Gospels.

4. Almost assuredly, the relations among the Synoptic Gospels are far more complex than most theories recognize, and certainly more complex than most discussions are willing to admit. The evidence from examining only the verbs in the Gospels in the light of trends and patterns of movement in other texts indicates that dependency relations for any given passage are neither consistent nor definitive. Standard Gospel source theories (including variations on the two- and four-source hypotheses, Matthean priority, etc.) are woefully inadequate for satisfactorily addressing and explaining the complexity of these relationships. This observation is worthwhile in and of itself because it indicates a class of variables that ought to be considered in future investigations of this abiding and significant problem. Similar avenues of constructive investigation, such as analysis of other linguistic categories, should also be utilized in future explorations.

16

Study of John's Gospel
New Directions or the Same Old Paths?

Introduction

This chapter grows out of several projects on the Gospel of John. One of these is a monograph on various topics in Johannine studies that includes a chapter on literary study of John's Gospel.[1] This is a topic that I have been involved in for some time—one of my earliest published chapters was on John's Gospel[2]—and in which I continue to have interest. The second project, and perhaps the more important of the two, is an annotated bibliography on the Johannine corpus.[3] There is nothing like wading through several thousand pieces of secondary literature to make one either completely abandon the topic of the bibliography and despair of one's sanity or (and perhaps both) learn incredible

---

1. See S. E. Porter, *John, His Gospel, and Jesus* (Grand Rapids: Eerdmans, forthcoming).
2. S. E. Porter, "Can Traditional Exegesis Enlighten Literary Analysis of the Fourth Gospel? An Examination of the Old Testament Fulfilment Motif and the Passover Theme," in *The Gospels and the Scriptures of Israel*, ed. C. A. Evans and W. R. Stegner, JSNTSup 104, SSEJC 3 (Sheffield: Sheffield Academic Press, 1994), 396–428.
3. S. E. Porter and A. K. Gabriel, *Johannine Writings and Apocalyptic: An Annotated Bibliography*, JOST 1 (Leiden: Brill, 2013).

amounts about the topic (much of it things that one did not even really want or need to know). In my case, I thoroughly enjoyed the opportunity to revisit old friends and make many new friends along the way. This bibliography, though it concentrated almost exclusively upon English-language sources (whether originally written in English or not), took seriously the range and history of Johannine scholarship, but included, as one might legitimately expect, a major section on literary study of John's Gospel. In this volume we traced the history and development of Johannine understanding over the last one hundred or so years, including not only the major works recognized by virtually all scholars, but also many lesser works that marked significant points along the way.

In the course of such a project, a number of trends begin to emerge. These trends, I believe, tell us something about the areas of interest in Johannine studies; who is writing on what; and how an idea comes to the fore, is explored, and then finally either dropped or resolved, before scholars move on to other topics and ideas. One of these topics is literary interpretation of John's Gospel. In this chapter, I briefly trace what I see as the major trends in contemporary Johannine literary-critical scholarship from a literary and linguistic perspective, with the idea of asking whether we are heading in new directions—and what these new directions are—or whether we are heading down the same old paths as before. As might be expected, the answer to such questions is not easy. Nevertheless, along the way, I put forth what I consider to be some new directions that might be pursued, as well as tracing some of the same old paths encountered in Johannine scholarship. My goal is to advance scholarship on literary analysis of John's Gospel, especially in the area of linguistic analysis, by noticing where there have been areas of serious advancement, while at the same time perhaps exposing areas that have stagnated or not progressed beyond where they were some time ago.

Literary Analysis of John's Gospel

Alan Culpepper was not the first to analyze a New Testament book, or even a Gospel, from a literary standpoint. However, he was among the first, and certainly he remains one of the most important. Culpepper published his *Anatomy of the Fourth Gospel* in 1983,[4] and his was the first volume I know of that was wholly dedicated to presenting a literary reading of John's Gospel. By doing so, Culpepper in many ways set the agenda for subsequent readings,

---

4. R. A. Culpepper, *Anatomy of the Fourth Gospel: A Study in Literary Design* (Philadelphia: Fortress, 1983).

of which there have been many. Culpepper was not the first to engage in a literary reading of a Gospel, however. That distinction perhaps belongs to David Rhoads, who not only first used the term "narrative criticism" in relation to reading the Gospels in his 1982 article,[5] but also published a literary analysis of Mark's Gospel in conjunction with the literary scholar Donald Michie.[6] I will take a temporary diversion in my account to say something about Rhoads and Michie's volume, because it is in itself an intriguing work in the history of interpretation. The foundation of Rhoads and Michie's first edition is Seymour Chatman's *Story and Discourse*, a well-known synthetic treatment of American narratology.[7] For the second edition, Rhoads and Michie, who also bring into the authorial mix Joanna Dewey,[8] rely instead upon Wesley Kort's *Story, Text, and Scripture*.[9] There are clearly some organizational and content differences that such a shift makes, although one perhaps is forgiven for thinking that they are not as many as one might have imagined. But something happened from 1982, when *Mark as Story* was first published, until the second edition was published in 1999, with its perspective retained in the third edition of 2012, along with the addition of an epilogue by Mark Powell.[10]

Before examining what happened, I must place Culpepper's and Rhoads and Miche's works within their appropriate interpretive context. Both Culpepper and Rhoads and Michie are heavily reliant upon Chatman, who is dependent upon Roman Jakobson and his communications model.[11] I need not go into the specifics, but this means that both Culpepper and Rhoads and Michie trace their literary-critical heritage back to structuralism, and especially to the kind of analysis that grew out of the Prague Linguistic Circle in some fundamental ways.[12] Jakobson stands at the center of much Prague school linguistics, with

5. D. Rhoads, "Narrative Criticism and the Gospel of Mark," *JAAR* 50 (1982): 411–34; reprinted in Rhoads, *Reading Mark: Engaging the Gospel* (Minneapolis: Fortress, 2004), 1–22.

6. D. Rhoads and D. Michie, *Mark as Story: An Introduction to the Narrative of a Gospel* (Philadelphia: Fortress, 1982).

7. S. Chatman, *Story and Discourse: Narrative Structure in Fiction and Film* (Ithaca, NY: Cornell University Press, 1978).

8. D. Rhoads, J. Dewey, and D. Michie, *Mark as Story: An Introduction to the Narrative of a Gospel*, 2nd ed. (Minneapolis: Fortress, 1999).

9. W. Kort, *Story, Text, and Scripture: Literary Interests in Biblical Narratives* (University Park: Pennsylvania State University Press, 1988).

10. Rhoads, Dewey, and Michie, *Mark as Story*, 3rd ed. (Minneapolis: Fortress, 2012), 157–62.

11. R. Jakobson, "Concluding Statement: Linguistics and Poetics," in *Style in Language*, ed. T. A. Sebeok (Cambridge, MA: MIT Press, 1963), 350–77, which is an expansion of the work of fellow Prague school linguist Karl Bühler. For an analysis based upon Bühler, see chap. 17 in the present volume, on Pauline opponents.

12. For a summary of some of the history and issues related to the rise of structuralism, and the Prague school in particular, see S. E. Porter and J. C. Robinson, *Hermeneutics: An Introduction to Interpretive Theory* (Grand Rapids: Eerdmans, 2011), 155–67.

its functional-structural approach. One of the most productive continental developments for structuralism was narratology, which was deeply rooted in French structuralism, but also spread to North America by a variety of people, both French and otherwise. Chatman probably is the best-known popularizer of narratology within the North American context.

Others related to this intellectual development, directly and significantly relied upon in Culpepper's treatment, are the narratologist Gérard Genette (who himself uses the work of the American New Critics Cleanth Brooks and Robert Penn Warren, themselves highly influenced by continental structuralism);[13] Boris Uspensky, the Russian formalist related to the Moscow school from which Jakobson hailed;[14] Wayne Booth, the American Aristotelian critic also influenced by narratology;[15] and Robert Scholes and Robert Kellogg, whose book *The Nature of Narrative*, reflecting structuralist principles, was in North America long a standard on narrative.[16] I should also mention the influence of Wolfgang Iser, the reader-response and reception theorist;[17] Frank Kermode, the literary critic;[18] Northrop Frye, the Aristotelian-influenced mythical typologist;[19] and Meir Sternberg, the narratologist.[20] Of course, there are also a number of influential biblical scholars noted along the way by Culpepper, although they do not influence the theoretical foundations very much, it seems to me.

An examination of Rhoads and Michie reveals something similar, even if not to the same broad theoretical extent. In other words, in 1982–83 two major works on literary interpretation of the Gospels were published. In

13. G. Genette, *Narrative Discourse: An Essay in Method*, trans. J. E. Lewin (Ithaca, NY: Cornell University Press, 1980). See also C. Brooks and R. P. Warren, *Understanding Fiction* (New York: Crofts, 1943).

14. B. Uspensky, *A Poetics of Composition: The Structure of the Artistic Text and Typology of a Compositional Form*, trans. V. Zavarin and S. Wittig (Berkeley: University of California Press, 1973).

15. W. Booth, *The Rhetoric of Fiction* (Chicago: University of Chicago Press, 1961). See also Booth, *A Rhetoric of Irony* (Chicago: University of Chicago Press, 1974).

16. R. Scholes and R. Kellogg, *The Nature of Narrative* (New York: Oxford University Press, 1966).

17. W. Iser, *The Implied Reader: Patterns of Communication in Prose Fiction from Bunyan to Beckett* (Baltimore: Johns Hopkins University Press, 1974); Iser, *The Act of Reading: A Theory of Aesthetic Response* (Baltimore: Johns Hopkins University Press, 1978).

18. F. Kermode, *The Sense of an Ending: Studies in the Theory of Fiction* (New York: Oxford University Press, 1967); Kermode, *The Genesis of Secrecy: On the Interpretation of Narrative* (Cambridge, MA: Harvard University Press, 1979).

19. N. Frye, *Anatomy of Criticism: Four Essays* (Princeton: Princeton University Press, 1957).

20. M. Sternberg, *Expositional Modes and Temporal Ordering in Fiction* (Baltimore: Johns Hopkins University Press, 1978). Sternberg now is perhaps better known in biblical circles for his densely written book *The Poetics of Biblical Narrative: Ideological Literature and the Drama of Reading*, ISBL (Bloomington: Indiana University Press, 1985).

their theoretical roots they demonstrated close ties to continental literary and linguistic structuralism as found in various manifestations, especially dealing with narrative. These included especially Prague school linguistics, Russian formalism, French narratology, and North American New Criticism, all closely related in complex ways, as well as a number of (then) cutting-edge literary-critical approaches, some of them developments of New Criticism, such as reader-response, reception theory, and Aristotelian criticism. These were heady days for New Testament criticism as it drank deeply from the well of linguistic and literary criticism.

Something happened on the way to the forum, however. I realize that I run the risk of oversimplification when I summarize the trajectory in the subsequent thirty or so years, but I see two major trends emerging. The first trend is that few readers of the Gospels, at least those writing monographs, were willing to shoulder the same critical burden as were Culpepper and, to a slightly less degree, Rhoads and Michie. They instead offered narrative readings.

The result is emergence of a tame form of New Criticism, with its emphasis upon the relatively fixed categories of plot, setting, character, and sometimes point of view (although not nearly as much on the last as one might think or hope) as the major form of literary criticism of John's Gospel. This form of criticism soon came to be called narrative criticism. I readily acknowledge that some critics have taken examination of John's Gospel in other directions—deconstruction, feminist criticism, and more—but I am not concerned with that here. Instead I am considering those still functioning within the literary-critical mode as I have defined it above. The change in the Rhoads, Michie, and Dewey volume from Chatman to Kort well illustrates this transition. The result is a much more constrained form of literary criticism, one that focuses upon the traditional categories of criticism as deeply enshrined by the New Criticism. Gone is attention to rhetoric as defined in Chatman, and left is simply narrator, settings, plot, and character. I cannot pretend to have surveyed every literary work on John's Gospel, but several of them illustrate this transformation.

One of the first was Jeffrey Staley's *The Print's First Kiss*, which follows up on one of the major ideas of Culpepper's volume, the implied reader.[21] The implied reader has been an important part of literary study since the influence of Iser, and picked up by a number of others. The notion is implicated, however, by the communications model of Jakobson and hence Chatman, and further utilized by Booth. Irony was also one of the standard tropes examined

---

21. J. L. Staley, *The Print's First Kiss: A Rhetorical Investigation of the Implied Reader in the Fourth Gospel*, SBLDS 82 (Atlanta: Scholars Press, 1988) (completed in 1985).

in New Critical circles, especially seen in the work of Booth. At the same time as Staley's work was being done, Paul Duke was writing *Irony in the Fourth Gospel*, with heavy reliance on Booth; and Gail O'Day was discussing irony and its relationship to revelation in John's Gospel, though she draws primarily on other biblical scholars, such as Duke.[22] The 1980s already revealed a focus upon a set of standard and narrower topics in literary criticism.

In what I still consider to be one of the finest literary readings of John's Gospel—or any Gospel, for that matter—Mark Stibbe examines *John as Storyteller* from four perspectives on narrative criticism.[23] Stibbe's narrative criticism encompasses what I. A. Richards called practical criticism[24] to appreciate John's narrative artistry, genre criticism of John's Gospel, a social or situated analysis of John's Gospel (Stibbe notes that this dimension is missing in most narrative criticism, including Culpepper's [something to which I will return]), and narrative-historical analysis. He then reads John 18–19 from these four perspectives. In the same year, Margaret Davies published an intriguing book that attempts to bring together literary and historical dimensions of study of John's Gospel.[25] She takes a narrative approach that strives to be comprehensive, with the literary element concentrating upon various metaphors. By contrast, Dorothy Lee simply offers a literary critical reading of John's Gospel, without significant reference to extrabiblical literary scholars, while Staley returns for a second significant probe of John's Gospel from a reader-oriented perspective.[26] These four studies, all within the field of literary study, could not be more different in orientation to the major literary questions. The early to mid-1990s showed some signs of both revival and repose within the Johannine literary camp.

By the time of the mid to late 1990s onward, literary criticism had definitely taken on a relatively set and formalist character. Craig Koester wrote a book

22. P. D. Duke, *Irony in the Fourth Gospel* (Atlanta: John Knox, 1985); G. R. O'Day, *Revelation in the Fourth Gospel: Narrative Mode and Theological Claim* (Philadelphia: Fortress, 1986).

23. M. W. G. Stibbe, *John as Storyteller: Narrative Criticism and the Fourth Gospel*, SNTSMS 73 (Cambridge: Cambridge University Press, 1992).

24. I. A. Richards, *Practical Criticism: A Study of Literary Judgment* (New York: Harcourt, Brace, 1929). Stibbe does not, however, mention Richards in his work, as far as I can tell, instead relying upon a number of previous biblical scholars for examples of what he is calling practical criticism.

25. M. Davies, *Rhetoric and Reference in the Fourth Gospel*, JSNTSup 69 (Sheffield: Sheffield Academic Press, 1992).

26. D. A. Lee, *The Symbolic Narratives of the Fourth Gospel: The Interplay of Form and Meaning*, JSNTSup 95 (Sheffield: Sheffield Academic Press, 1994); J. L. Staley, *Reading with a Passion: Rhetoric, Autobiography, and the American West in the Gospel of John* (New York: Continuum, 1995). See also Lee's more recent *Flesh and Glory: Symbol, Gender, and Theology in the Gospel of John* (New York: Crossroad, 2002).

on symbolism in John's Gospel, again one of the topics central to the New Critics, with their appreciation of well-crafted poetic writing; by 2003 his book was revised but not substantially changed.[27] Larry Jones offers a more focused study of the symbol of water.[28] D. F. Tolmie similarly, in his *Jesus' Farewell to the Disciples*, studies the Farewell Discourse in John's Gospel by using narrative criticism especially dependent upon Shlomith Rimmon-Kenan,[29] as well as others such as Iser, A.-J. Greimas (see below), and Chatman, concluding that the reader is guided to a viewpoint on discipleship.[30] David Beck's *The Discipleship Paradigm* focuses on readers and characterization (in his case, anonymous characters) in John's Gospel.[31] Derek Tovey can simply refer to "the literary approach to the Gospels," which for him primarily includes discussion of point of view and narrative, as well as speech-act theory.[32] In a study of female characters, Adeline Fehribach is slightly better, making reference to some of the standards, such as Culpepper, Iser, and Booth.[33]

At the turn of the millennium, the same general pattern as represented in the 1990s continues into the new era. Andrew Lincoln, in his book *Truth on Trial*, essentially adopts the narrative perspective of Culpepper, complete with reference to Chatman, Scholes and Kellogg, and Duke.[34] Larry Darnell George does likewise, although without nearly as much explicit reference to scholars so much as to New Criticism in general.[35] In a work that directly reflects the kinds of concerns and orientation of Rhoads and Michie, James Resseguie (to whom we will return again) presents a narrative-critical study of John's Gospel's use of rhetoric, setting, character, and plot in order to discern the Gospel's point of view.[36] Beck was concerned with anonymous

---

27. C. R. Koester, *Symbolism in the Fourth Gospel: Meaning, Mystery, Community*, 2nd ed. (Minneapolis: Fortress, 2003).

28. L. P. Jones, *The Symbol of Water in the Gospel of John*, JSNTSup 145 (Sheffield: Sheffield Academic Press, 1997).

29. S. Rimmon-Kenan, *Narrative Fiction: Contemporary Poetics* (London: Methuen, 1983).

30. D. F. Tolmie, *Jesus' Farewell to the Disciples: John 13:1–17:6 in Narratological Perspective*, BIS 12 (Leiden: Brill, 1995).

31. D. R. Beck, *The Discipleship Paradigm: Readers and Anonymous Characters in the Fourth Gospel*, BIS 27 (Leiden: Brill, 1997).

32. D. Tovey, *Narrative Art and Act in the Fourth Gospel*, JSNTSup 151 (Sheffield: Sheffield Academic Press, 1997).

33. A. Fehribach, *The Women in the Life of the Bridegroom: A Feminist Historical-Literary Analysis of the Female Characters in the Fourth Gospel* (Collegeville, MN: Liturgical Press, 1998).

34. A. T. Lincoln, *Truth on Trial: The Lawsuit Motif in the Fourth Gospel* (Peabody, MA: Hendrickson, 2000).

35. L. D. George, *Reading the Tapestry: A Literary-Rhetorical Analysis of the Johannine Resurrection Narrative (John 20–21)*, StBL 14 (New York: Peter Lang, 2000).

36. J. L. Resseguie, *Strange Gospel: Narrative Design and Point of View in John*, BIS 56 (Leiden: Brill, 2001).

characters; Stan Harstine studies one character, Moses; and Margaret Beirne focuses on gender pairs, calling her approach literary but without providing any substantive discussion of what that means.[37] Although Jo-Ann Brant examines John's Gospel as a Greek tragedy, she is heavily indebted to those who have come before her, including some structuralists, Culpepper, and a few other recognizable literary critics.[38] Warren Carter's treatment of the storytelling (along with the interpretive and evangelistic) element of John's Gospel reads much the same as his predecessors.[39] He discusses genre, plot, characters, and style (including irony and other tropes). Kasper Larson's *Recognizing the Stranger*, though it definitely attempts to locate itself within treatment of the classical recognition scene, makes use of categories prized in literary criticism, in particular recognition and response by characters.[40] Even Douglas Estes, in his provocative *The Temporal Mechanics of the Fourth Gospel*, which attempts to introduce notions of time from modern physics into his discussion of John's Gospel, creates a platform for such exposition on narrative criticism that finds its support in poststructuralism, structuralism, New Criticism, and Russian formalism, all of the same sources that have been mentioned above.[41]

The first decade of the twenty-first century drew to a close much as did the opening, although without as much adventure as before. Cornelis Bennema offers a series of character studies in the Gospel of John, Susan Hylen does similarly with ambiguous characters, Nicolas Farelly examines the disciples (again), and Andreas Köstenberger, as part of his biblical theology of John, offers a literary-theological reading that employs a "close narrative reading" of the Gospel.[42] Even though reading as a literary scholar, not a biblical scholar, Thomas Gardner purports to be reading John in the same way he would read

37. S. Harstine, *Moses as a Character in the Fourth Gospel: A Study of Ancient Reading Techniques*, JSNTSup 229 (Sheffield: Sheffield Academic Press, 2002); M. M. Beirne, *Women and Men in the Fourth Gospel: A Genuine Discipleship of Equals*, JSNTSup 242 (Sheffield: Sheffield Academic Press, 2003).

38. J. A. Brant, *Dialogue and Drama: Elements of Greek Tragedy in the Fourth Gospel* (Peabody, MA: Hendrickson, 2004).

39. W. Carter, *John: Storyteller, Interpreter, Evangelist* (Peabody, MA: Hendrickson, 2006).

40. K. B. Larson, *Recognizing the Stranger: Recognition Scenes in the Gospel of John*, BIS 93 (Leiden: Brill, 2008).

41. D. Estes, *The Temporal Mechanics of the Fourth Gospel: A Theory of Hermeneutical Relativity in the Gospel of John*, BIS 92 (Leiden: Brill, 2008).

42. C. Bennema, *Encountering Jesus: Character Studies in the Gospel of John* (Milton Keynes: Paternoster, 2009); S. E. Hylen, *Imperfect Believers: Ambiguous Characters in the Gospel of John* (Louisville: Westminster John Knox, 2009); N. Farelly, *The Disciples in the Fourth Gospel: A Narrative Analysis of Their Faith and Understanding*, WUNT 2/290 (Tübingen: Mohr Siebeck, 2010); A. J. Köstenberger, *A Theology of John's Gospel and Letters* (Grand Rapids: Zondervan, 2009), 176.

poetry; he especially invokes the work of Kenneth Burke,[43] Culpepper and his followers, and Kermode.[44] His sequential reading of the Gospel has a definite New Critical feel to it, not surprising in light of the sources—mostly biblical literary readers—that he turns to.

This summative treatment of some of those who have published in the area shows the major influence upon literary criticism of John's Gospel by means of a pattern set by Culpepper and Rhoads and Michie. Their perspective, formulated in the light of the structuralist agenda and its emphasis upon literary criticism, became fixed in more narrowly defined and constrained forms of literary criticism that became more internally rather than externally oriented.

The second major trend that resulted in fixing the state of literary-critical study, along with the numerous works that seem to narrow and constrain the conspectus of the field, are two books on narrative criticism. The first is Mark Alan Powell's *What Is Narrative Criticism?*[45] The second is James Resseguie's *Narrative Criticism of the New Testament.*[46] Powell's work, published in 1990, after the first wave of literary studies, calls narrative criticism a "new approach" to studying the Bible. He defines narrative criticism side-by-side with and in relationship to structuralism, rhetorical criticism, and reader-response, although he admits that "narrative criticism" is not a label of a type of criticism used within English or literature departments, but that it is unique to biblical studies.[47] Then he singles out the key characteristics of narrative criticism. These include story and discourse, including point of view, narration, symbolism and irony, and narrative patterns; events, which I take to be what is usually called plot; characters; and settings. Among the secular literary critics that he cites are Booth, Chatman, E. M. Forster,[48] Roger Fowler,[49] Genette, Iser, Kermode, Kort, Scholes, Kellogg, Uspensky, René Wellek,[50] and Warren, along with a number of other narratologists, such as Mieke Bal,

---

43. K. Burke, *A Grammar of Motives* (Berkeley: University of California Press, 1969).

44. T. Gardner, *John in the Company of Poets: The Gospel in Literary Imagination*, SCL 6 (Waco: Baylor University Press, 2011).

45. M. A. Powell, *What Is Narrative Criticism? A New Approach to the Bible* (London: SPCK, 1990).

46. J. L. Resseguie, *Narrative Criticism of the New Testament: An Introduction* (Grand Rapids: Baker Academic, 2005).

47. Powell, *Narrative Criticism*, 19. This uniqueness in itself should make one suspicious of it.

48. E. M. Forster, *Aspects of the Novel* (New York: Harcourt, Brace & World, 1927).

49. R. Fowler, ed., *Style and Structure in Literature: Essays in the New Stylistics* (Oxford: Blackwell, 1975).

50. Wellek's best-known work is R. Wellek and A. Warren, *Theory of Literature*, 3rd ed. (New York: Harcourt, Brace & World, 1956).

Wallace Martin, and Gerald Prince.[51] As for studies of biblical narrative, he cites, among others, Culpepper, Frye, Kermode, Kort, Rhoads, Michie, and Sternberg, along with some others whom I have not cited because they have not done work especially on John's Gospel, such as Robert Alter, William Beardslee, Hans Frei, Jack Kingsbury, Tremper Longman, Edgar McKnight, Norman Petersen, Lynn Poland, Mary Ann Tolbert, and Robert Tannehill.[52] Powell's book attempts to be an introduction to the subject, and therefore it treats narrative criticism as a "thing" in distinction to other things—that is, as a type of unique biblical criticism in distinction to other types of literary criticism. At times he oversimplifies or is even possibly wrong (such as his statement that literary criticism is based on communications models based in speech-act theory, and his statement that structuralism is not a method but a philosophy, overlooking narratology). Most of the time, however, he describes the results of others' thinking and summarizes these results in only a few pages. The result is a fixed form of description of most topics, including such important areas as point of view, plot, and the like.

The work by Resseguie, published fifteen years later, in 2005, is surprisingly similar, despite the amount of time intervening. Resseguie introduces narrative criticism by defining it in relation to New Criticism and reader-response criticism. He then discusses some particular elements of it: rhetoric, which includes narrative framing and rhetorical figures and tropes (such as irony), but not rhetoric in the sense used by Chatman; setting; character; point of view; and plot. Apart from his chapter on rhetoric, which is less about rhetoric and more

51. M. Bal, *Narratology: Introduction to the Theory of Narrative*, trans. C. van Boheemen (Toronto: University of Toronto Press, 1985); W. Martin, *Recent Theories of Narrative* (Ithaca, NY: Cornell University Press, 1986); G. Prince, *A Grammar of Stories: An Introduction*, DPLSMi 13 (The Hague: Mouton, 1973); Prince, *Narratology: The Form and Functioning of Narrative*, JLSMa 108 (Berlin: Mouton, 1982).

52. R. Alter, *The Art of Biblical Narrative* (New York: Basic Books, 1981); W. Beardslee, *Literary Criticism of the New Testament*, GBSNT (Philadelphia: Fortress, 1969); H. W. Frei, *The Eclipse of Biblical Narrative: Study in Eighteenth and Nineteenth Century Hermeneutics* (New Haven: Yale University Press, 1974); J. D. Kingsbury, *The Christology of Mark's Gospel* (Philadelphia: Fortress, 1983); Kingsbury, *Matthew as Story*, 2nd ed. (Philadelphia: Fortress, 1988); Kingsbury, *Conflict in Mark: Jesus, Authorities, Disciples* (Minneapolis: Fortress, 1989); Kingsbury, *Conflict in Luke: Jesus, Authorities, Disciples* (Minneapolis: Fortress, 1991); T. Longman, *Literary Approaches to Biblical Interpretation* (Grand Rapids: Zondervan, 1987); E. V. McKnight, *The Bible and the Reader: An Introduction to Literary Criticism* (Philadelphia: Fortress, 1985); N. R. Petersen, *Literary Criticism for New Testament Critics*, GBSNT (Philadelphia: Fortress, 1978) (though he treats John's Gospel elsewhere; see below); L. M. Poland, *Literary Criticism and Biblical Hermeneutics: A Critique of Formalist Approaches*, AARAS 48 (Chico, CA: Scholars Press, 1985); M. A. Tolbert, *Sowing the Gospel: Mark's World in Literary-Historical Perspective* (Minneapolis: Fortress, 1989); R. Tannehill, *The Narrative Unity of Luke-Acts: A Literary Interpretation*, 2 vols. (Minneapolis: Fortress, 1986–90).

about style, this outline is very similar to that of Powell, along with many of the previously mentioned works. One feature to notice—besides the fact that Resseguie occasionally applies these categories to secular literature, by such noteworthy authors as Ernest Hemingway and Kate Chopin—is the brevity of his actual definitions. He defines rhetoric, character, point of view, and plot in no more than two to three pages each, and setting in just one page. It appears that Resseguie either is defining crucial terms in narrative criticism by means of example, whether biblical or otherwise, or assumes that these terms are commonplaces within biblical literary analysis. In any case, they are not simple concepts that can be adequately mastered by just a few pages of definition.

Certainly at this juncture I could cite other works concerned with establishing the narrative criticism of the New Testament. However, I think that those summarized above have offered a significant and confirmatory understanding of what such criticism entails. The utilization of a tame form of narrative criticism and the two books that codified narrative criticism represent the two major influences and trends in development of Johannine literary criticism.

An Assessment of Directions in Johannine Literary Criticism

There are many problems with literary criticism of the Gospels and of John's Gospel in particular, and especially narrative criticism. These are more than adequately displayed in the several works that I have all too briefly cited above. The major problem is not that narrative criticism has come to represent literary criticism within the field of New Testament studies—although that is, I believe, a serious enough criticism—especially when it is a term not used within secular literary criticism. The problem is not the terminology, but rather what is represented by the use of the term "narrative criticism" itself. It is difficult to say what term would be preferred in secular literary criticism, because the terminological terrain is quite different than in biblical studies. Few literary scholars that I know of are as explicit about their methodological approaches as are biblical scholars, and I remember few if any of them referring to what they are doing and saying using something like "Now I am going to offer a literary reading," because all that they ever offer is literary readings.

The backdrop of contemporary literary criticism is highly complex, involving at least the following influences: historically based criticism with emphasis upon the author (there is still a lot of this kind of criticism done, especially but not only by textual critics); various criticisms based on the text, such as residuals of the New Criticism found in things such as close readings and narratology; a number of reader-oriented types of criticism, although perhaps less reader-response and deconstruction than was once on offer—all overlaid with acute awareness of the role of ideology, whether in the form of New Historicism (Marxist-influenced criticism), feminism, postcolonialism, gender studies, and so on—plus a backlash against much of this in what is sometimes called thematic criticism, where the notion of "meaning" has had a resurgence.[53] All of this is to say that the situation for literary criticism is much more dynamic and fluid than that in the vast bulk of New Testament literary criticism.[54] In fact, that is my major complaint about contemporary New Testament literary criticism: it has become static, losing a sense of the dynamic interplay of textual features that was originally envisioned and forecast by its early interpreters, and hence not resulting in conveying the dynamism of the text in vibrant readings.

This can be seen in any number of ways. One is in the adoption of the name "narrative criticism" itself. As I have attempted to show, narrative criticism is a refinement and progressive narrowing of a number of different types of criticism, including the influence of structuralism, New Criticism, and narratology, among others. As I have already noted, there are close ties among these three. Structuralism, with its roots in Saussurean linguistics and more particularly Prague school linguistics, is the common origin of the others. New Criticism had strong influence from structuralism by way of such people as Wellek, besides its being grounded in a North American and British phenomenological criticism with its philosophical origins in logical positivism. Narratology was an application of structuralism to literary texts broadly conceived. Narrative criticism is a haphazard amalgamation of these, with probably its strongest basis in the English-language New Criticism. If we are to examine the three major foci of hermeneutics—author, text, and reader—all of these criticisms focus upon the text. In fact, I believe it is arguable that one of the reasons for the emergence of reader-centered criticism was the perceived stasis of textually oriented interpretation, whether European or North American. New Criticism placed a high emphasis upon such stasis when it spoke of the literary work as an autonomous artifact, the image of the well-wrought urn,[55] independent of author and receptor,

53. I cannot hope to cite examples of each of the above. However, I do wish to note the advent of thematic criticism, as in some ways a point of stability for those despairing of the directions of literary criticism. See, e.g., C. Bremond, J. Landy, and T. Pavel, eds., *Thematics: New Approaches* (Albany: SUNY Press, 1995); W. Sollors, ed., *The Return of Thematic Criticism* (Cambridge, MA: Harvard University Press, 1993).

54. One of the few exceptions is Stephen Moore, but even he has moved on from literary criticism to various types of cultural and gender studies, which he perhaps sees as a contemporary form of narratology (see comments below). See Porter and Robinson, *Hermeneutics*, 285–92.

55. This is the title of a book of essays by Cleanth Brooks, and it came to represent one of the major texts of the New Criticism. See C. Brooks, *The Well Wrought Urn: Studies in the Structure of Poetry* (New York: Harcourt, Brace & World, 1947).

subject to critical scrutiny through close readings of texts, especially poetry. The same criticism has been made of structuralism and narratology. Typical narratological analysis is not so much concerned with the dynamic interplay of different characters within a text, but rather with the static underlying structures and actants that the characters represent. Whether it is Vladimir Propp and his taxonomy of the Russian folktale, or A.-J. Greimas and his six major actants, the result of narratology is a static analysis of character, as part of the larger stasis of a work in which story time is the surface manifestation of an underlying narrative, and hence sequential, time.[56]

In a work that attempts to move beyond such stasis, Ross Chambers says:

> It seems strange that literary criticism and theory have paid so little attention to the performative function of storytelling, preferring to limit themselves arbitrarily to the study of narrative structure and the discourse of narration conceived in each case as a set of relationships internal to a context-free text. As a consequence, we possess a fine "grammar" of stories, deriving from the work of Propp, Greimas, Bremond, Todorov, Prince, and others. We possess, too, a useful "rhetoric" of narration, elaborated by Booth and especially by Genette, as a grammar of possible relationships between text as narration ("discourse") and text as narrated ("story"). All this work has been summated, added to, and worked into a synthesis by Seymour Chatman in a handbook entitled, precisely, *Story and Discourse*. But what is lacking is recognition of the significance of situational phenomena—of the social fact that narrative mediates human relationships and derives its "meaning" from them; that, consequently, it depends on social agreements, implicit pacts or contracts, in order to produce exchanges that themselves are a function of desire, purposes, and constraints.[57]

Narrative criticism is, then, simply the reification of this stasis to its most codified and sterile form—but without recognizing the context of situation.[58]

I do not think that it always had to be this way in biblical studies. However, some early decisions were made that pushed in this direction. I will be the first to admit, even though Jason Robinson and I selected Culpepper to be the

56. V. Propp, *The Mythology of the Folk Tale*, trans. L. Scott (Austin: University of Texas Press, 1968 [1928]); A.-J. Greimas, *Structural Semantics: An Attempt at a Method*, trans. D. McDowell, R. Schleifer, and A. Velie (Lincoln: University of Nebraska Press, 1983 [1966]).

57. R. Chambers, *Story and Situation: Narrative Seduction and the Power of Fiction* (Minneapolis: University of Minnesota Press, 1984), 4. Some of the other key figures that Chambers refers to not already noted above are: C. Bremond, *Logique du récit* (Paris: Seuil, 1973); T. Todorov, *The Poetics of Prose*, trans. R. Howard (Oxford: Blackwell, 1977).

58. I intentionally use "context of situation" with reference to systemic functional linguistics (SFL). Other essays in this volume treat matters related to context, and in particular an SFL-defined context of situation.

representative of literary hermeneutics, that Culpepper was not a theoretical innovator.[59] Clearly, his contribution was in bringing a previous and important discussion within literary and linguistic circles to bear on New Testament study in a thorough and inviting way. In several ways, he had much in common with the work of Rhoads and Michie, which preceded his by a year or so. On the one hand, Culpepper did bring the literary and linguistic together in his own synthesis, though highly influenced by the kinds of common concerns that were then, and are still now, important in literary interpretation. Rhoads and Michie were more inclined to take the model of Chatman (already identified above as the summation of such an approach) and apply it to interpretation. Culpepper, who was trained as a historical critic but undertook a literary initiation under the tutelage of Kermode during a sabbatical in England, also had a dynamic element to his work that brought him into dialogue with reader-response and reception history, something that Chambers notes as moving in the right direction to reinvigorate interpretation with a situational component. As Chambers says, "We owe it to the *Rezeptionsästhetik* movement in Germany that there is now some perception of the act of reading as based on a relational 'contract' with a text (cf. the work of W. Iser) and as a historical, that is, historically determined *and* determining, process (cf. the work of H. Jauss)"; however, Chambers states that for literary criticism "the implications of the contextual nature of meaning for the analysis of *narrative texts themselves* remain to be explored."[60]

What is true of literary criticism is true of biblical criticism as well. We note that in the work that followed in the wake of Culpepper, there was a focus upon the individual elements of the narrative structure, mostly upon character, to the point of static character comparisons within the narrative being the focus of much work. Rhoads and Michie themselves even replaced the foundation of their work in a second edition, not with something more reception-oriented, but with a work that is more self-consciously biblical in perspective, closing the noose more tightly around the work of biblical literary criticism. Even standard resources on the topic tend toward the highly static and formulaic in their definitions of the major categories.

There are, however, a few exceptions to this pattern that are worth noting. Perhaps there are others, but a couple merit mention. Helen Orchard, in her *Courting Betrayal*, observes that there are those who noted such a static tendency in Culpepper's work from the start, observed even by those who are

---

59. See Porter, and Robinson, *Hermeneutics*, 274–85.

60. Chambers, *Story and Situation*, 4. Besides Iser, see H. R. Jauss, *Toward an Aesthetic of Reception*, trans. T. Bahti (Minneapolis: University of Minnesota Press, 1982).

literary readers.[61] There were some who thought that cutting off the Gospel's relationship to its origins—the historical or authorial-oriented focus—was detrimental. Even such a literary reader as Stibbe makes this point when he states that "the value of the gospel as narrative history and as community narrative" was obscured.[62] Lynn Poland, in her assessment of formalism, such as the New Criticism, notes that its "stress on the literary work's discontinuity with the full range of human experience and value make it difficult to describe how literature actually does, in fact, extend and transform our perceptions."[63] Orchard's solution is to recognize the "hermeneutical value of the social function of the Gospel,"[64] within a broadly literary pattern. This feature of social function added to a literary approach seems to have either fallen on deaf ears or been obscured from blind readers, probably because it looks at first glance like simply an added feature to give this approach something distinctive.

Another approach is found in the so-called sequential reading of John's prologue by Peter Phillips.[65] Phillips addresses some of the same concerns by creating an intriguing mix of methods. The authors that he brings into the mix include Genette, Elizabeth Struthers Malbon, Culpepper, Staley, Iser, Catherine Emmott, Stephen Moore, and Sternberg.[66] Also noteworthy is his combination of literary theory noted in the people mentioned above, with rhetoric mostly dependent upon ancient conceptions, and sociolinguistics seen through the eyes of Norman Petersen and antilanguage, Anna Wierzbicka and conceptual synonymy, and Bruce Malina and speech-accommodation theory.[67]

61. H. C. Orchard, *Courting Betrayal: Jesus as Victim in the Gospel of John*, JSNTSup 161 (Sheffield: Sheffield Academic Press, 1998), 32–37. I do not include the nonliterary readers, who objected to this orientation from the start. These would include, among others, M. C. de Boer, "Narrative Criticism, Historical Criticism and the Gospel of John," *JSNT* 47 (1992): 35–48; S. McKnight, *Interpreting the Synoptic Gospels* (Grand Rapids: Baker Books, 1988), 128; J. D. G. Dunn, *The Partings of the Ways: Between Christianity and Judaism and their Significance for the Character of Christianity* (London: SCM, 1991), 16, all cited by Orchard. It is unclear to me what literary interpretation would have to do—besides become historical criticism—to convince them.

62. Stibbe, *John as Storyteller*, 11.

63. Poland, *Literary Criticism*, 132.

64. Orchard, *Courting Betrayal*, 36.

65. P. M. Phillips, *The Prologue of the Fourth Gospel: A Sequential Reading*, LNTS 294 (London: T&T Clark, 2006).

66. See E. S. Malbon, "Ending at the Beginning: A Response," *Semeia* 52 (1991): 175–84; C. Emmott, *Narrative Comprehension: A Discourse Perspective* (Oxford: Oxford University Press, 1999); S. D. Moore, *Literary Criticism and the Gospels: The Theoretical Challenge* (New Haven: Yale University Press, 1989).

67. N. R. Petersen, *The Gospel of John and the Sociology of Light: Language and Characterization in the Fourth Gospel* (Valley Forge, PA: Trinity Press, 1993), based upon M. A. K. Halliday, *Language as Social Semiotic: A Social Interpretation of Language as Meaning* (London: Edward Arnold, 1978); A. Wierzbicka, *Understanding Cultures through Their Key Words: English, Russian, Polish, German, and Japanese* (New York: Oxford University Press, 1997);

This is quite an intriguing concoction that Phillips has assembled—much too complex to analyze here, except to say that I am not entirely clear how such methodologically diverse, even fundamentally opposed, approaches to language can be made to play nicely together in one book. When it comes to his sequential reading, Phillips attempts such an amalgamation. However, I wonder if what he is really getting at is a way to offer guidelines for limiting the scope of reading while appreciating its situatedness; the importance of the sequential element is examining how the text presents itself to us or we experience it—that is, sequentially, without imposing all of the extraneous knowledge that might be within the work or that we know from outside, something very important for the divulging of the *logos*. The issue of situatedness certainly is commendable, but I am not sure that all of what he is bringing to the equation helps, when many of the theories that he introduces bring a number of apparently conflicting conceptual perspectives to bear. For example, Emmott's narrative analysis is a combination of narrative study with cognitive linguistics, which tends toward a maximalist semantics; then Wierzbicka's emphasis upon cultural influence tends toward a minimalist semantics. Phillips seems to want a minimalist semantics, but his grounding in a broad view of culture is bound to expand the parameters of semantics. I cannot believe that many will be bold enough to attempt other such readings. I am not sure that Phillips has succeeded, although he certainly is to be commended for trying.

Many of these same contributors have participated in a recent volume that celebrates Culpepper's work twenty-five years later.[68] Moore offers an intriguing analysis of how such New Testament narrative criticism fits within the larger field of narratological study. Although there are some interesting insights into their relationship, including the fact that narrative criticism has always been more concerned with interpretation than theory, I think that he misses the point that the resultant stasis and the traditional worldview mean that narrative criticism is a far cry from being in any way commensurable with poststructuralist narratology.[69] In other words, narrative criticism is still located where it has long been; it is narratology that has changed.

B. Malina, "John's: The Maverick Christian Group, the Evidence of Sociolinguistics," *BTB* 24 (1994): 167–82.

68. T. Thatcher and S. D. Moore, eds., *Anatomies of Narrative Criticism: The Past, Present, and Futures of the Fourth Gospel as Literature*, SBLRBS 55 (Atlanta: Society of Biblical Literature, 2008).

69. S. D. Moore, "Afterword: Things Not Written in This Book," in Thatcher and Moore, *Anatomies of Narrative Criticism*, 253–58. Few New Testament readers are likely to wish to pursue the antirealist perspective of P. O'Neill, *Fictions of Discourse: Reading Narrative Theory* (Toronto: University of Toronto Press, 1994).

Some Possible New Directions in Johannine Literary-Critical Scholarship

There are many good reasons to explore the issue of situatedness in literary readings of John's Gospel. The obvious one is the stasis that has come over much recent literary interpretation, as I have chronicled above. I am not saying that every reading of John's Gospel from a literary standpoint is static, but I am saying that the standard method of literary reading, as so-called narrative criticism, and the major categories of interpretation brought to bear in such readings—these are static in definition, orientation, and general application. From a simple pragmatic standpoint, another approach is warranted, since there are only so many readings such as this that have interest or can find a place in Johannine scholarship, even if there is an emphasis upon the pragmatics of interpretation over the ideology of method.

There are many other reasons to explore other types of readings, in particular the kind of situated readings that I am calling for. One of these is developments in other areas of linguistic and literary scholarship that provide new avenues for exploration—but with the attendant risk, of course, of moving beyond the contemporary stasis into a more dynamic reading and interpreting environment. There may be some vested interests that wish to preserve these static readings, thinking that in some way their stasis indicates a kind of textual and interpretive stability that stands behind and endorses such readings. Here is not the place to explore this notion in more detail, except to note that from what I have said above, such readings are deeply embedded in interpretive and hermeneutical presuppositions that indicate anything but necessarily stable and authoritative meanings.

A more important reason to explore such situated meanings, however, might be a theological one. That is, the narratives depicted and the characters represented, as well as the situation into which we all enter as humans before God, are depictions of relationships, grounded in theological and personal situatedness (I clearly am not confining situatedness to a historical situation). In John's Gospel, Jesus sees and describes himself in a situated relationship with God. One of John's significant themes is the relationship of Jesus and God, with Jesus indicating that they have a common existence, but that he is also the Son of the Father. This is a dynamic relationship that is situated in both theological and worldly (even if only in a narrative world) realization. Similarly, those who follow Jesus enter into dynamic relationship with him. There are those who enter into relationship for a time but then fall away. There are those who enter into relationship and endure but who nevertheless have ups and downs in that relationship, such as Peter. There are those whose relationship is more ambiguous, such as Nicodemus. By their entrance into relationship with Jesus, however, these people also enter into relationship with God; and once Jesus leaves, he says that he will send the Paraclete to continue yet create a new relationship with him. More than simply theologically, understanding of the Johannine narrative requires attention to situatedness and dynamism.

What interpretive approaches do we have at our disposal in order to be able to effect such readings?[70] I will offer three approaches that might bring a dynamic element to interpretation, without attempting to be inclusive or complete. These readings are situated in the sense that they are firmly located in the dynamism of the text. If I had more space, I would extend that situatedness beyond these individual pericopes and the entire biblical works to consider this layer of context (context being variably described according to the approach employed).

Literary Stylistics

The first approach to examine is literary stylistics.[71] Many will not be familiar with literary stylistics, which was an earlier attempt to bring literary and linguistic insights together. As the direct result of the concern for literature that grew out of Russian formalism and Prague school linguistics, literary stylistics was short lived before being replaced by various types of discourse analysis. However, I think that there are features of literary stylistics that merit renewed investigation.

Literary stylistics encompasses a number of features. These include the belief that analysis of literature demands methods of linguistic analysis that move beyond the sentence; appreciation of the literary dimensions of texts by accounting for both "habitualization" and "defamiliarization," both stasis and dynamism within a text; the description and quantification of literary observations; attention to frequency and expectation, which individuate various literary works; features thought to be primarily literary being seen to be linguistic as well, such as genre; attempts to go beyond description to criticism and evaluation; offering an account of the style of individual texts

70. Other approaches have been suggested. For example, besides those suggested by Moore, "Afterword," see P. Merenlahti, *Poetics for the Gospels? Rethinking Narrative Criticism* (London: T&T Cark, 2002), esp. 115–30, suggesting alternatives that are more literary or rhetorical. See also the recent work of B. M. Stovell, *Mapping Metaphorical Discourse in the Fourth Gospel: John's Eternal King*, LBS 5 (Leiden: Brill, 2012).

71. The description below comes from S. E. Porter, "Why Hasn't Literary Stylistics Caught On in New Testament Studies?," in *Discourse Studies and Biblical Interpretation: A Festschrift in Honor of Stephen H. Levinsohn*, ed. S. E. Runge (Bellingham, WA: Logos Bible Software, 2011), 35–57.

and the style of an author; the perceived hiddenness of literary texts that can
be demystified by linguistic description; and the transferability of features of
literary stylistics from a single literary text to other texts. From this brief entirely summative description, I hope that, even though literary stylistics as an
embodied theory and approach remains vague, it is clear that literary stylistics
has the potential for bringing both concreteness to literary observations and
a dynamic interpretation that moves beyond mere description, to the point of
providing potential comparative literary-linguistic study.

I only know of two works of literary stylistics in New Testament studies,
the one by Aída Spencer, *Paul's Literary Style*,[72] and the second an article
that I wrote on a Synoptic comparison (Matt. 9:18–26; Mark 5:21–43; Luke
8:40–56).[73] This does not mean that literary stylistics has no potential for New
Testament studies, and in particular Johannine studies, but only that few have
attempted it to date.

Let me suggest just one example as a means of exploration of literary stylistics: a contrast between the Johannine temple incident (John 2:14–17) and
that incident as recorded in the Synoptics (Matt. 21:12–13; Mark 11:15–17;
Luke 19:45–46). Here I do not treat John 2:18–22, for which there is no clear
parallel (those suggested in Matt. 21:23–27; Mark 11:27–33; and Luke 20:1–8
are not true parallels to John, but clearly a separate incident). This treatment
can only be brief, but it is suggestive. John's account is the longest with 75
words (in the Nestle-Aland edition), with Mark's being 65, Matthew's 46,
and Luke's 25. In fact, there are only six words that John's account has in
common with the Synoptic accounts, and some of these are of dubious worth.
These are the initial καί, the reference to the temple though in another case,
τοὺς πωλοῦντας, and another καί. In other words, if similarity of wording
is the basis for establishing a common account, then this passage fails. The
Johannine account is sufficiently different so that stylistically it has very little
in common with the Synoptic accounts, apart from essential features to establish that this event occurred in the temple and involved those selling (which
accounts for the narrative flow of the accounts). As for the Synoptics, there
is clearly a verbal relation among the accounts that cuts across many usual
(form-critical) observations. Mark's account is the longest and most detailed,

---

72. A. B. Spencer, *Paul's Literary Style: A Stylistic and Historical Comparison of II Corinthians
11:16–12:13, Romans 8:9–39, and Philippians 3:2–4:13* (Jackson, MS: Evangelical Theological
Society, 1984; repr., Lanham, MD: University Press of America, 1998).
73. S. E. Porter, "Verbal Aspect and Discourse Function in Mark 16:1–8: Three Significant
Instances," in *Studies in the Greek Bible: Essays in Honor of Francis T. Gignac, S.J.*, ed. J. Corley
and V. Skemp, CBQMS 44 (Washington, DC: Catholic Biblical Association of America, 2008),
123–37.

with a reference both to Jesus entering Jerusalem and then not permitting anyone to carry anything through the temple and to his teaching there, and with a fuller quotation from Isaiah 56:7 regarding this being for all the nations.

Other features of the Johannine account are also worth noting from a literary stylistic standpoint. Jesus is the protagonist in each account, but whereas in the Synoptics he enters and then drives out those who are selling, within John's Gospel Jesus finds those selling the animals and the money changers. The Synoptics make Jesus the direct agent, whereas in John he is at first the experiencer of what he observes, and only after that does he drive them out. John then includes the details of Jesus making a whip from the individual cords, driving the animals out along with their sellers, and pouring out the coins of the money changers when he overturns their tables. Jesus is the agent of all of these actions—making, driving, pouring, and overturning. There is more to the Johannine account than that, however. Each primary clause is connected to the subsequent one using καί; however, each of the Predicators of the primary clauses is preceded by some other linguistic element within the clause structure. Thus Jesus, having made the whip from cords (an introductory adjunctive participle clause), as John states (with each clausal Predicator having a preceding linguistic element): "all things, he drove out . . . , and of the money changers, he poured out . . . , and the tables, he overturned . . . , and to the pigeon-sellers, he said . . ."

The Synoptics relate their events in a far more compact and less overtly artful way, although certainly there are individual stylistic differences among the Synoptic accounts, especially in their use of verbal tense-forms.[74] In this instance, however, Luke simply uses a secondary participle clause, a primary clause, and then another participle clause. Matthew is also relatively straightforward, with the episode based around four primary clauses, the third of which has the Complement before the Predicator, as in John. Mark is also a relatively straightforward narrative, with a number of clauses connected by καί, and the same clause as in Matthew having the Complement before the Predicator.

The Synoptics have Jesus directly address those involved through the Old Testament quotations. In John's account, after actually driving the animals and the moneychangers out, Jesus in his own words commands them (using the aorist imperative) to take these things away, and then more emphatically instructs them (using the negated present imperative) not to make his Father's house a house of business. Whereas the Synoptics use the indicative for

74. See chap. 15 in the present volume; see also W. V. Cirafesi, *Verbal Aspect in Synoptic Parallels: On the Method and Meaning of Divergent Tense-Form Usage in the Synoptic Passion Narratives*, LBS 7 (Leiden: Brill, 2013).

introducing the Old Testament quotations, Jesus in John's Gospel makes a statement that attributes the temple to being God's dwelling place and indicates a close family relationship between God and himself—perhaps by implication claiming that the temple is also thereby his own house. The narrator—only in John's Gospel, in a function that he also performs elsewhere and that is not always evident in the Synoptics—notes that Jesus's disciples were mindful of or remembered (an aorist passive verb) a quotation from Psalm 69:9 regarding zeal for his house. In the light of this, it is no wonder that the Jews in John's account ask for a sign that authorizes his actions. Jesus then continues the ambiguous reference to himself in relation to the temple by speaking of destroying "this temple" and raising it.

In this Johannine episode there is a developmental pattern that is worth noting. The pattern is one of incremental progression from lesser to greater significance. Jesus enters and experientially observes before he takes action. He instructs regarding the physical accoutrements before he pronounces regarding God's house. The Synoptics treat their accounts entirely differently, with a more regulated account, apart from the one instance in Mark and Matthew, somewhat similarly with John, where information on the tables being overturned is fronted.

More could be said about this episode within John's Gospel and in relation to the Synoptics, but I have shown enough to illustrate how literary stylistics might interpret such passages. The result is a much more dynamic evaluation of the text, even of one where there is only one active and fronted participant. Even here, the way the participant acts is depicted differently than in other types of criticism. It goes well beyond the task that I have set for myself in this chapter, but the Johannine and Synoptic accounts are sufficiently different—apart from the material related to overturning tables—that I think it is worth considering, from a literary stylistic standpoint, whether we have two separate incidents recorded in these accounts.

Discourse Analysis

The next approach to consider is discourse analysis, which, like any other field of scholarly methodology, is constantly undergoing examination and development; but it is a field where there are rules of engagement and, what is more important, scholarly gains to be secured from its practice.[75] Discourse

75. For example, see D. Schiffrin, D. Tannen, and H. E. Hamilton, eds., *The Handbook of Discourse Analysis* (Oxford: Blackwell, 2001). For additional comments, see chap. 8 in the present volume.

analysis addresses the major shortcoming of most, I dare say all, forms of linguistics: viewing the sentence as the maximal unit of structure and hence, usually, of meaning. There are any number of different types of discourse analysis used in New Testament studies, but all of them share the principle that discourse is a dynamic phenomenon. Continental discourse analysis, with its incorporation of rhetoric, as well as communication theories such as that of Jakobson, recognizes that a text is not a static representation of character or actions, but rather is part of a larger communication dynamic that depicts in order to motivate and persuade. The colon analysis from South Africa, though it identifies subject-predicate structures, must create a larger conceptual framework of interdependence for these colons. The tagmemic dimension of Summer Institute of Linguistics discourse analysis is performed within a unified theory of human behavior, in which the use of language is one important and dynamic part. Various memes fill ever increasingly larger slots, until the entirety of human experience is represented. Even the eclectic method of discourse analysis, as haphazard and unsystematic as it is, has some dynamic elements—less because of its use of literary analysis than because of linguistic analysis—in which the understanding of individual units of discourse within the larger discourse are understood in varying ways.[76]

As an example I will take the episode with Jesus and Peter at the close of the Gospel of John (21:15–19). These are controversial verses, not necessarily because of their theological content, but because of their linguistic content, and so they are appropriate to address by discourse analysis. In this instance, attention to matters of discourse helps to explain a persistent problem in Johannine exegesis. In John's account, when Jesus and some disciples finish eating, Jesus speaks to Simon Peter, recorded using the narrative present in Complement-Predicate-Subject clausal element order. We assume that Jesus asks Peter a question, but that is not entirely certain from the Greek text. Jesus may ask him, "Simon son of John, do you love me more than these?" Or he may simply say to him, "Simon son of John, you love me more than these." The Greek text, of course, had no punctuation, and the question is an editor's decision. The response by Peter does not necessarily decide this issue, as the affirmation, ναί, can be used in contexts other than in answer to a question, such as an affirmation or asseveration—just as Peter seems to do when he says, "Indeed, Lord, you know that I love you." I note that Jesus asks the question with the use of ἀγαπάω, and Peter answers with φιλέω. The typical debate, found in virtually every commentary, is whether ἀγαπάω and

76. The above taxonomy is found in S. E. Porter and A. W. Pitts, "New Testament Greek Language and Linguistics in Recent Research," *CBR* 6 (2008): 214–55, esp. 235–41.

φιλέω are true synonyms or contextual synonyms, or, if not either, what lexical semantic relationship they have. Actually, the debate is rarely that clear, with many commentators confusing the concepts. Many say, on the basis of the usage in John 21, that the two verbs are synonymous, thus apparently taking what may be contextual synonymy for true (or complete) synonymy.[77] These two verbs, φιλέω and ἀγαπάω, are not true or complete synonyms. One of the differing components in the meanings of these words appears to be related to levels of esteem (a vertical scale) for ἀγαπάω and interpersonal associations (a horizontal scale) for φιλέω. The definition of a true synonym is that the two lexemes are interchangeable in all contexts. That simply is not true for these Greek lexemes: there is a major identifiable pattern of usage that is different. Therefore, the question is not whether they are true synonyms (they are not), but whether they are contextually synonymous. A case can be made that they are. However, I think that a nuanced discourse analysis indicates that they are not.[78]

As indicated, Jesus either asks Peter whether he loves (ἀγαπάω) him or states that Peter loves (ἀγαπάω) him. Peter responds that, indeed, Jesus knows that Peter loves (φιλέω) him. Why is it that Jesus then asks Peter a second time and even a third time regarding his love? One possible answer is the very fact that Peter does not answer with the same verb. We can only speculate regarding what Jesus would have said if Peter had answered that he loved (ἀγαπάω) Jesus. However, he does not say this. The shift in lexemes, I think, is sufficient to raise questions whether these lexical items are contextually synonymous. An illustration in English perhaps makes this clear (I recognize that this is an English example, but I use it for the sake of comparison, not to establish the semantics of these Greek lexemes). If someone were to ask (or say), "With what esteem do you hold the president of the United States?," and someone were to answer, "I think that he is a very accessible person relationally," most of us would argue that holding someone in esteem is different from whether we like someone or not.

Something similar is probably going on in John 21. Jesus asks (or says to) Peter whether he holds him in higher esteem than he does any other person (the fullest form of his question), and Peter answers that he thinks Jesus is a relational and accessible person. In fact, he states it strongly: "You know

77. An example of this is A. J. Köstenberger, *John*, BECNT (Grand Rapids: Baker Academic, 2004), 596.
78. See D. Shepherd, "'Do You Love Me?': A Narrative-Critical Reappraisal of ἀγαπάω and φιλέω in John 21:15–17," *JBL* 129 (2010): 777–92. Shepherd wrongly contends that the two verbs are semantically synonymous, but that narrative-critically they are to be distinguished. This is an odd position for which to argue, as cotext (context of usage) determines synonymy.

[οἶδας] that I think you are a great person." Jesus tells him to feed (βόσκε) his sheep (ἀρνία). As a result, with his first question unanswered, Jesus asks (or tells) Peter again, "Simon son of John, do you love [ἀγαπᾷς] me?" using a shorter form of the question. Peter answers a second time, "You know [οἶδας] that I love [φιλῶ] you," repeating his first answer. Jesus then changes his response and says, "Shepherd [ποίμαινε] my sheep [πρόβατα]." I think that, even though βόσκω and ποιμαίνω are possibly contextual synonyms, the logic of the discourse indicates otherwise for these lexemes as well. Jesus has reduced and toned down his first question to a simpler second question, and he has received a similarly unsatisfactory answer. Jesus has asked (or stated to) Peter whether he holds Jesus in high esteem beyond any other, then simply whether he holds Jesus in high esteem without comparison of him to anyone else, and Peter again has strongly asserted that he simply likes Jesus. In his second response, Jesus changes from the specific task of feeding his figurative flock (ἀρνίον is only used figuratively in the New Testament) to the more general word for shepherding (ποιμαίνω probably is a superordinate of βόσκω) and the broader term for sheep (again, a hyponymous relationship exists between the superordinate πρόβατον and the hyponym ἀρνίον).[79] As with Jesus's formulation of the question/statement a second time, this statement reflects a general shifting down in expectations for Peter, which he fails a second time.

As a result, Jesus asks/states a third time whether Simon son of John loves him, this time using the verb φιλέω: "Do you love [φιλεῖς] me?" Peter, perhaps indicating some exasperation—although not necessarily because Jesus has failed to grasp contextual synonymy, but more because he simply cannot affirm what Jesus asks of him—answers a third time in an emphatic double assertion (using the marked pronouns as well as doubling the "knowing" clause): "Lord, all things you [σύ] know [οἶδας], you [σύ] know [γινώσκεις] that I love [φιλῶ] you." Jesus answers, "Feed [βόσκε] my sheep [πρόβατα]." The use of βόσκω with πρόβατα probably indicates Jesus's resignation to Peter having a less responsible task by use of the broader, more generic term for sheep. I would not say that there is a lot of difference here, but the context seems to indicate that there is some. The words for knowing reinforce this. The verb οἶδα is a hyponym of γινώσκω, but it always conveys the stative aspect and hence is frontgrounded in discourse against the imperfective γινώσκω. Even Peter recognizes that something has gone on within the dialogue. He acknowledges that Jesus knows (οἶδα) all things, but can only force himself to admit

79. On hyponymy, see J. Lyons, *Introduction to Theoretical Linguistics* (Cambridge: Cambridge University Press, 1968), 453–55; Lyons, *Semantics*, 2 vols. (Cambridge: Cambridge University Press, 1977), 1:293–95. For further exploration of this linguistic category in the interests of theology, see chap. 21 in the present volume.

that Jesus knows (γινώσκω) that he loves (φιλέω) him. Jesus then concludes by telling Peter the way that his life will proceed, from the independence of youthfulness to the dependence of old age, where he will need to be led by others, sometimes to places where he will not want to go. The narrator concludes the paragraph by indicating that this indicates by which type of death Peter would honor God.

In any discourse analysis there are always more data than can be accommodated in a single analysis. In this one, I have concentrated upon the textual flow and shown how attention to patterns larger than the sentence, including an entire dialogue, can help us to gain insight into the discourse itself, and in particular the development of thought as expressed in a number of lexemes that have proved to be interpretively problematic. In this instance, the discourse flow indicates that the Johannine use of any number of different potentially synonymous pairs—including ἀγαπάω and φιλέω, βόσκω and ποιμαίνω, ἀρνίον and πρόβατον, and οἶδα and γινώσκω—are contextually given different senses. We know that none of the pairs is truly synonymous, and I believe that the discourse itself shows that they are not contextually synonymous either. The tripartite question and answer of Jesus and Peter, which progressively focuses Jesus's question regarding Peter's love, moves from a question of esteem to one simply of relation, when Jesus sees that Peter is unable to make the affirmation of love in terms of esteem.

Systemic Functional Linguistics and Register Analysis

I could have placed SFL (systemic functional linguistics) register analysis under the preceding section as a type of discourse analysis, but I wish to say something more about this. SFL register analysis is not specifically a form of discourse analysis, but the SFL conception of register has proved useful in the analysis of discourse, for the reasons that I have been discussing in this chapter.[80] Register analysis is a powerful concept for examination of texts because it explains the relationships among the context of situation—with its potential field, tenor, and mode—its construal by means of the metafunctions of language, and their realizations in the lexicogrammar. The metafunctions realize the field, tenor, and mode of a given context of situation. By analyzing the metafunctions within a discourse, and their realizations in the lexicogrammar, in relationship to the components of register (field, tenor, and mode), one is

---

80. For a survey of literary analysis by SFL proponents, see A. Lukin and J. J. Webster, "SFL and the Study of Literature," in vol. 1 of *Continuing Discourse on Language: A Functional Perspective*, ed. R. Hasan, C. Matthiessen, and J. Webster, 2 vols. (London: Equinox, 2005), 413–56. No work in New Testament studies is cited.

able to create a linguistic profile of the given discourse, which constitutes its register, whether the potential registers are more broadly conceived types of discourse or specific instantiations of language usage. SFL register analysis follows in a long, though now often neglected, history of functional language research and analysis.[81] First developed by the Prague school linguists, especially in the work of Bühler, whose work was fundamental to other Prague school linguists as well as J. R. Firth and Michael Halliday, this functionalist perspective has permeated a number of other linguistic models, but especially SFL. The contribution of SFL register analysis and its attention to the meaning potential of language and how register constrains the metafunctions of language is that it covers the various functions that languages perform. Admittedly, there are differences of opinion on those metafunctions and their number, but for the sake of discussion, I will work with three. The experiential metafunction is concerned with realizing the content of the discourse, the interpersonal deals with the social relations or exchange potential of the text, and the textual works with what it means to be a text. Each of these allows for the discourse to be seen as a dynamic linguistic expression, in which these metafunctions are realized by various linguistic means. The register itself is a level of abstraction that attempts, in a generalized way, to capture at one particular point the alignment of these various independent dynamic elements.[82]

An example from John's Gospel is the episode in John 4 with the Samaritan woman (esp. vv. 1–42). This is a lengthy passage, so I can again only give a glimpse of what a register analysis might indicate, in the order of textual, ideational, and interpersonal metafunctions.

The textual metafunction structures the dialogue along two axes, as is to be expected in Greek discourse. There is the online or mainline narrative frametale, what I often refer to as the narrative backbone that also represents the background against which the highlighted action occurs.[83] There is only

81. This does not mean that all issues of register are resolved. Indeed, one of the most important is the relationship of register to various subunits within a larger discourse, and whether there are various subregisters of the whole, or parts that constitute a larger linguistic stratum, such as a genre.

82. See S. E. Porter, "Dialect and Register in the Greek of the New Testament: Theory," in *Rethinking Contexts, Rereading Texts: Contributions from the Social Sciences to Biblical Interpretation*, ed. M. D. Carroll R., JSOTSup 299 (Sheffield: Sheffield Academic Press, 2000), 190–208, and the literature cited there. See now also D. A. Lamb, *Text, Context and the Johannine Community: A Sociolinguistic Analysis of the Johannine Writings*, LNTS 477 (London: Bloomsbury, 2014).

83. There has been some unnecessary confusion in some circles regarding my use of "background," as if it is behind the major discourse focal plane of the text. In narrative, the background can be, as in a painted picture (to use an analogy), the surface of the canvas against which the highlighted (foregrounded or frontgrounded) material is represented, and constitutes

one clause within the narrative frametale with an explicit Subject as the prime (first element) of the clause. This occurs in verse 6, at the transition from the introduction of the scene and before Jesus's encounter with the Samaritan woman (ὁ Ἰησοῦς). Verses 27 (οὐδείς) and 32 (ὁ) have reduced forms used as the prime. Once the encounter begins, there is no other participant in a prominent position at the clause level. There are uses of explicit Subjects at the level of the clause complex that indicate thematization, but these themes follow the rheme (nonthematic or remaining material), so that the pattern is rheme-theme throughout (see, e.g., vv. 10, 11, 13, 15, 17 [2x], 19, 21, 25, 26, 27, 28, 31, 33, 34), with two exceptions in verses 27 and 32.[84] The result is to demote the participants of the discourse. In contrast to this is the off-line material—that is, the material that is expressed in secondary clauses, whether expansions or projections; both are found in this discourse unit. These secondary clauses include numerous explicit Subjects used at the clause level in prime position to promote participant structure; that is, the Subject is introduced as prominent, and as thematic material, so that the information structure cohesively unites the unit (e.g., in secondary clauses: e.g., vv. 8, 12 [3x]; in projected [including secondary] clauses: e.g., vv. 9, 10 [2x], 11, 12, 13, 14 [2x], 18, 20 [2x], 22 [2x], 23 [2x], 25, 26, 29, 33, 34, 35 [3x], 36 [2x], 38 [3x]). The frametale relies upon aorist indicative verbs for conveying material processes, and the narrative utilizes present indicatives for verbs of saying.

---

a focal plane. This discourse focal plane provides the mainline for narrative, although that of nonnarrative (exposition) is provided by the foregrounded material (a second discourse focal plane). See S. E. Porter, *Verbal Aspect in the Greek of the New Testament, with Reference to Tense and Mood*, SBG 1 (New York: Peter Lang, 1989), 102–7. Some have also questioned my use of the term "frontground," as if it is wrong to differentiate a third discourse focal plane when some work in cognitive thinking (perhaps simplistically?) identifies only two. A third issue is that some works seem to have more fore/frontgrounding than others, such as is indicated by John's Gospel's use of the perfect tense-form. I would note that the concept of foregrounding (including what I would call frontgrounding) is not unique to cognitive linguistics (which tends to confine itself to figure and ground), and that there is reference in Prague school functionalism to forms of all of the above issues. See, e.g., B. Havránek, "The Functional Differentiation of the Standard Language," in *A Prague School Reader on Esthetics, Literary Structure, and Style*, ed. P. L. Garvin (Washington, DC: Georgetown University Press, 1964), 3–16, esp. 10–12, especially with reference to the maximum foregrounding of poetry. See also S. E. Porter, "Verbal Aspect as a Prominence Indicator: A Response to Jody Barnard," in *Greeks, Jews, and Christians: Historical, Religious, and Philological Studies in Honor of Jesús Peláez del Rosal*, ed. L. R. Lanzillotta and I. M. Gallarte (Córdoba: Ediciones el Almendro, 2013), 421–48, esp. 430–31. To note, Miroslaw Marczak wrote a doctoral dissertation titled "The Significance of Peak and Frontground in Discourse Analysis and Translation: A Case Study in Acts 19–26" (University of Wrocławski, 2005). Though I have not read it, I note the linguistic categories invoked in the title (whether we define them identically or not).

84. I rely here upon the graphic displays found at the OpenText.org cite for clausal analysis of John's Gospel.

The ideational metafunction is focused upon the secondary clauses, as expansions or projections. At least five major semantic domains are invoked in the dialogue between Jesus and the Samaritan woman: domain 93, "Names of Persons and Places" (Samaritans, Jews, Jacob, Jerusalem, Christ); domain 23, "Physiological Processes and States" (e.g., drinking, eating, living, thirsting, food); domain 2, "Natural Substances" (e.g., water); domain 10, "Kinship Terms" (husband, wife, man); and domain 53, "Religious Activities" (prophet, worship, Messiah).[85] The dialogue ends up being a complex interplay between two people from different places and backgrounds discussing more fundamental issues regarding these differences through a discussion of physiological processes related to eating and drinking. The discussion of physiological processes entails two levels: a congruent level (between the entities and what is said of them) and a metaphorical discussion that ends up being about the woman's spiritual needs and the kinds of personal relationships that she has. This leads to further bilevel discussion between Jesus and his disciples once they return from their shopping excursion, because they have not been part of the metaphorical discussion of water. This use of lexical metaphor—in which two or more semantic domains are juxtaposed to each other so that the meanings of one domain are placed upon another—links the discussion of physical substances to spiritual realities, which are made explicit elsewhere in the dialogue.

Finally, the interpersonal metafunction is concerned with the relations among Jesus, the Samaritan woman, and the disciples, and how they are expressed in the lexicogrammar. All three characters are introduced with an explicit subject, although Jesus, named twice, occurs within the secondary clauses that introduce the episode. Even though the dialogue essentially is between two people, until the disciples return, there are numerous textual elements that mark their relationship. In verse 7 the woman is labeled as a woman from Samaria, and Jesus is called by name. In verse 9 she is again called a Samaritan woman, and in verse 10 Jesus is specifically said to give his reply. Apart from verse 16, Jesus is always referred to with the full noun expression when he speaks to the woman (without the article in vv. 10, 13), even though the Samaritan woman from verse 9 onward is progressively downgraded from the full reference to her as a Samaritan woman—until the closing reference in verse 42. From the full reference to her as the woman from Samaria or the Samaritan woman, she then becomes always simply the woman (ἡ γυνή). The disciples, when they return, are referred to both times as "the disciples" (vv.

85. See J. P. Louw and E. A. Nida, *A Greek-English Lexicon of the New Testament Based on Semantic Domains*, 2 vols. (New York: United Bible Societies, 1988).

27, 33). The crowd from Samaria is never identified with a full expression in a primary clause, only in a secondary clause or by an implied reference (vv. 30, 39–40). There is a clear hierarchy in the conversation, reflected here by the grammatical choices. Jesus is the commanding figure due to the full references used of him, followed by the Samaritan woman, the disciples, and then the Samaritans. This is reinforced by the words of address that are used, especially between Jesus and the woman. The first time, she refers to Jesus using the personal pronoun, σύ, a form of direct, personal address, but after that, when she begins to note that he is not like other people she has met, in three of five times she uses the vocative κύριε, in one she uses the marked perfect οἶδα ("I know"),[86] while in one, when she speaks about a sensitive subject, she simply speaks to him without direct address when she admits that she has no husband (v. 17). In this passage the interpersonal semantic perspective is directly expressed in the lexicogrammar, especially in how the conversants speak to each other.

A register analysis of this episode shows that the field of the discourse is a complex interplay regarding Jews and Samaritans over their identities, played out as a conversation about water as a metaphor for eternal life. The field includes several levels of ideational content, and in that sense a number of metaphorical expressions are used, so much so as to form a level of metaphorical content. The tenor of the discourse is one between fluctuating values of equality and inequality. Whereas Jesus, the Samaritan woman, and even the disciples appear to start on a level field of textual importance, it is clear early on that the dialogue is between Jesus and the woman. Both are given status in the dialogue, though the woman's address of Jesus with "lord" and other elements indicate her ready recognition of his status, whereas he does not seem to give her the equivalent regard or elevation. The narrative itself is not advanced by the on-line narrative progression, because the frametale merely serves to introduce and distinguish the participants. The development takes place in the off-line material, which is structured to display the substance of the discussion. The result of such an analysis of the components of register provides for the interpreter to formulate the register of the discourse and to describe its context of situation. A context of situation—not to be confused with the term "situatedness" used above—is not a historical but an extratextual and in that sense extralinguistic analysis of the type of situation that would have elicited the linguistic responses found within the discourse. In this case,

---

86. See S. E. Porter and M. B. O'Donnell, "The Vocative Case in Greek: Addressing the Case at Hand," in *Grammatica intellectio Scripturae: Saggi filologici di Greco biblico in onore di Lino Cignelli OFM*, ed. R. Pierri, SBFA 68 (Jerusalem: Franciscan Printing Press, 2006), 35–48; Porter, *Verbal Aspect*, 245–90.

the context of situation is a discovery dialogue between a man and a woman over mundane topics, conveyed originally orally but now through written medium, in which the man asserts and the woman recognizes his superior status on the basis of his knowledge, to the point of challenging the woman to act upon her newly found knowledge regarding her life.

Conclusion

This chapter has attempted to offer two major contributions. The first is a conspectus of the directions in which literary criticism of John's Gospel has gone. What began as a promising interaction among various literary and linguistic critics has become an ossified literary criticism, called narrative criticism. Rather than being dynamic and interactive among text and situation, the focus has been upon the text simply as literary artifact, to the point of rarifying analysis so that it often focuses upon isolated and static elements of literary criticism of the Gospel text. John's Gospel indicates that such a static reading was never intended, and the Gospel merits better literarily and linguistically situated analysis. The second result is to introduce, even if only briefly and in insufficient detail, three possible ways forward in such dynamic and situated analysis. I have suggested, without wanting to be definitive or prescriptive, that literary stylistics, discourse analysis (no matter how it might be defined), and SFL register analysis provide three such interpretive ways forward. In examining each of these, I have not tried to select the passage on the basis of anticipated results, but have chosen three different passages as a means of illustrating what I think is the next stage in literary analysis of John's Gospel. We need to move away from the kinds of narrative criticism that are being almost routinely suggested and toward those that capture the dynamic capacities of the text and move interpretation to a new level of interactive analysis.

17

Method and Means of Analysis of the Opponents in the Pauline Letters

Introduction

Who were Paul's opponents? How do we define them? How do we identify and describe them? And how do we talk about them in terms of the Pauline

I thank Dr. Mark Seifrid and Dr. Udo Schnelle for the initial invitation to deliver this essay to the New Testament Theology Seminar of the Society for New Testament Studies annual meeting in Vienna, August 4–8, 2009, and to the participants for their helpful questions and comments. J. Ramsey Michaels notes in the introduction to his commentary on 1 Peter that his qualification for writing an entire commentary on the book was his having written one article on 1 Peter earlier in his career (J. R. Michaels, *1 Peter*, WBC 49 [Waco: Word, 1988], x). I can tell a similar story. In 2005 I wrote a single article on Paul's opponents, in particular in the Letter to the Romans, and edited the volume in which this article appeared, also on Paul's opponents (S. E. Porter, "Did Paul Have Opponents in Rome and What Were They Opposing?," in *Paul and His Opponents*, ed. S. E. Porter, PAST 2 [Leiden: Brill, 2005], 149–68). The result was an invitation to the Society for New Testament Studies meeting to think in a more sustained way about the methods and means of analysis of the opponents in the Pauline Letters. The truism that no good deed goes unpunished seems to have been repeated in this exercise. What I thought at the time was my lone concentrated venture into discussing Paul's opponents has now come back to revisit me, not as an entire commentary, but as a further effort to think about this very difficult topic of what we mean by "Paul's opponents."

Letters? For a number of reasons, the enterprise of determining and discussing Paul's opponents is not an easy task. One obstacle is the definition of what it means to be an opponent. After all, the term "opponent" involves a complex of historical, sociological, theological, and perhaps even psychological factors that are clearly perspectival in nature, depending upon which side of any particular issue or question one may stand. Paul may have seen certain people as opponents, but they may or may not have seen themselves as opposed to Paul, and they may or may not have seen Paul as opposed to them. The word "opponent" may not be applicable in all instances, since in some cases the people in question may have been viewed not so much as opponents but as antagonists or simply as people holding opinions different from Paul's.

A second difficulty is the articulation of a method that is sufficient for both definition and identification of opponents. The definition and identification process would seem, even in the way it is framed, to privilege one perspective: Paul's. Would it not be preferable to move beyond a single personal perspective in order to attempt a description of what must have been a complex state of conflictual affairs? Of course, even if this question is answered affirmatively, is there a method sufficiently rigorous to move beyond epiphenomena to define such a complex phenomenon?

A third consideration is the realistic limitation of trying to create the historical, social, and theological context on the basis of limited data in order to pursue such an enquiry. The Pauline Letters reflect one side of a conversation that makes no attempt to be representative, egalitarian, or even balanced according to the modern interpreter's agenda. The perceptive observation that reading Paul's Letters is like listening to one end of a telephone conversation provides perspective on the capacity for interpretive reconstruction.[1]

A fourth problem is the recurring issue of the place of so-called mirror readings in historical reconstruction. A common complaint is that mirror readings reflect more of the interpreter than they do of the interpreted, or rather that the interpreter and the interpreted become one in the same and find it difficult to move beyond this potentially vicious recursion.[2]

In this chapter, I wish to tackle, at least in an initial and superficial way, some of these issues. I will begin with a brief overview of several attempts to analyze Paul's opponents. I will then put forward a new approach to describing

---

1. See M. D. Hooker, "Were There False Teachers in Colossae?," in *Christ and Spirit in the New Testament: Essays in Honour of C. F. D. Moule*, ed. B. Lindars and S. S. Smalley (Cambridge: Cambridge University Press, 1973), 315.

2. This limitation is not unique to biblical studies, but is found in many disciplines, including history and literary study. See, e.g., M. Krieger, *A Window to Criticism: Shakespeare's Sonnets and Modern Poetics* (Princeton: Princeton University Press, 1964), 3–4.

the opponents in Paul's Letters. I will conclude with some tentative samples to see if this new approach offers anything of merit in the discussion of the Pauline opponents.

Three Recent Approaches to the Opponents in Paul's Letters

Critical study of Paul's opponents can be coordinated with the advent of critical study of Paul's Letters—in other words, with F. C. Baur's study of the Christ party in the Corinthian community and the opposition of Petrine and Pauline Christianity within the early church.[3] Baur's opposition between competing parties has formed a template for subsequent discussion, even if scholars have modified the major viewpoints represented in such antagonism. Besides Judaizers—frequent opponents in the light of Baur's hypothesis—a number of other parties have been suggested since Baur as well, such as gnostics, pneumatics, and syncretists. Efforts have regularly been made to find a common opponent or set of opponents for the widest number of the Pauline Letters. Those who have found a form of Judaizers include, besides Baur, Gerd Lüdemann and Michael Goulder,[4] while those arguing for gnosticism include Walther Schmithals and Kurt Rudolph.[5] Most tend to distinguish the opponents letter by letter. However, there are even a few who find no opponents at all—a rare position.[6]

A survey of all of the various views of the opponents in Paul's Letters goes beyond what is necessary at this point. To set the groundwork for this study, I want to examine briefly three fairly recent studies of Paul's opponents. I recognize that discussion of Paul's opponents is found in a manifold variety of studies, including most commentaries on the Pauline Letters, introductions to the New Testament where these letters (and others) are examined, and a wide variety of individual studies, especially articles and book chapters, that

3. F. C. Baur, "Die Christuspartei in der korinthischen Gemeinde, der Gegensatz des Petrischen und Paulinischen Christentum in der ältesten Kirche, der Apostel Petrus in Rom," *TZT* 4 (1831): 61–206; Baur, *Paul, the Apostle of Jesus Christ: His Life and Work, His Epistles and Teachings; A Contribution to a Critical History of Primitive Christianity*, trans. A. Menzies, 2 vols. (London: Williams & Norgate, 1873–75; reprinted in 1 vol., Peabody, MA: Hendrickson, 2003).

4. G. Lüdemann, *Opposition to Paul in Jewish Christianity*, trans. M. E. Boring (Minneapolis: Fortress, 1989); M. Goulder, *A Tale of Two Missions* (London: SCM, 1994); Goulder, *Paul and the Competing Mission in Corinth*, LPS (Peabody, MA: Hendrickson, 2001).

5. W. Schmithals, *Gnosticism in Corinth: An Investigation of the Letters to the Corinthians*, trans. J. E. Steely (Nashville: Abingdon, 1971); Schmithals, *Paul and the Gnostics*, trans. J. E. Steely (Nashville: Abingdon, 1972); K. Rudolph, *Gnosis: The Nature and History of Gnosticism*, trans. R. McL. Wilson (New York: HarperCollins, 1984), 300–301.

6. J. Munck, *Paul and the Salvation of Mankind* (London: SCM, 1959), 135–67.

treat Paul's opponents in a given letter or context. In another situation, a survey of all of these treatments might be interesting, if for no other reason than to see the scope of the continuing discussion among a range of scholars, but it would progress this study no further. Instead, what I wish to treat here are three significant studies that have methodological issues at heart. In other words, they are concerned not just with who Paul's opponents may be in a given book or as a whole, but with how we define and identify such opponents.[7]

John J. Gunther and a Conspectus of Paul's Opponents

In 1973 John Gunther published a major study of Paul's opponents.[8] There are five characteristics of his study that I wish to note. (1) The first is that he does not define the notion of opponents, but simply invokes it at the outset. As he states on the first page of the foreword, "There has been no systematic study of Paul's various opponents in light of what is known of Jewish sectarianism and heterodoxy";[9] and on the first page of text, regarding sources, he notes, "Scholarly opinion in the 19th and 20th centuries has been very diverse concerning the identification of the opponents whose teachings were warned against in letters of the Pauline corpus."[10] And so it goes. (2) Gunther does not hesitate to draw directly upon a range of previous scholarship concerned with the purported opponents. As a result, he chronicles 7 or 8 opponents in Galatians; 13 for 2 Corinthians; 18 in Philippians 3; 8 in Romans 16; 43 in Colossians (which he acknowledges has the widest range of divergent opinions regarding Paul's opponents!); and 19 in the Pastoral Epistles, a large number that he attributes to the obscurity of

---

7. I could have included here several other studies (see Sumney's summary of most of them, in Sumney's works cited below): N. A. Dahl, "Paul and the Church at Corinth according to 1 Corinthians 1:10–4:21," in *Christian History and Interpretation: Studies Presented to John Knox*, ed. W. R. Farmer, C. F. D. Moule, and R. Niebuhr (Cambridge: Cambridge University Press, 1967), 313–35, who provides four principles for identifying opponents (pp. 317–18); J. M. G. Barclay, "Mirror-Reading a Polemical Letter: Galatians as a Test Case," *JSNT* 31 (1987): 73–93, who differentiates types of statements and their certainty (pp. 88–90); C. H. Cosgrove, *The Cross and the Spirit: A Study in the Argument and Theology of Galatians* (Macon, GA: Mercer University Press, 1988), 31–38, who, on the basis of epistolary form, uses the salutations, thanksgivings, and central argumentative section (body) but dismisses autobiographical and hortatory material; M. D. Nanos, *The Irony of Galatians: Paul's Letter in First-Century Context* (Minneapolis: Fortress, 2002), 62–72, who looks to "situational discourse units." Note that many if not most of these factors are taken into account in the model I posit below.

8. J. J. Gunther, *St. Paul's Opponents and Their Background: A Study of Apocalyptic and Jewish Sectarian Teachings*, NovTSup 35 (Leiden: Brill, 1973).

9. Ibid., vii.

10. Ibid., 1.

the letters.[11] This is quite a wide-ranging set of options. (3) The third is a concern for the difficulty of identifying the opponents. As Gunther states, "The detection of opposing viewpoints is admittedly a hazardous undertaking, as Paul did not intend to present them clearly or plausibly, much less perpetuate memory of them."[12] (4) Gunther is concerned with method. He takes several steps in this regard. One is to identify signs that reveal the opponents, such as direct and indirect statements that are negative in nature; another is statements that are positive but that oppose statements elsewhere; a third is attempts to preempt the opponents' position. However, he works from the position of testing the assumption that the Pauline works identified above can be analyzed as being opposed by Jewish sectarian and apocalyptic thinkers. (5) Gunther develops a rough means of numerical assessment of the topics that constitute Jewish sectarian and apocalyptic thought, and their mutual appearance in letters. He believes that the higher a determined number, the stronger is the appearance of the particular feature.

Gunther's study assumes that there are such things as opponents, that opponents are of a particular type and background, and that their identification is a quantifiable proposition. Although each of these suppositions can and has been challenged, Gunther's work remains a valuable source for the range of previous scholarly opinion that he has marshaled, even if discussion has moved forward in some regards.

Jerry L. Sumney and Identifying Paul's Opponents

Jerry Sumney is probably responsible more than any other recent scholar for attempting to bring order, coherence, and consistency to discussion of Paul's opponents. He has done so in three major works.

The first, a revision of his doctoral dissertation, addresses the larger question of Paul's opponents while focusing in particular on 2 Corinthians.[13] As Sumney reports early in his study, though many scholars mention and treat the opponents, "few have given much attention to method," with the result often being that method is confined to "scattered statements" that must be gathered.[14] After surveying what he identifies as the four major proposals regarding the opponents found in 2 Corinthians, Sumney elaborates a method for examination of opponents. He first identifies the issues of historical reconstructions

---

11. Gunther also treats Hebrews and Ignatius.

12. Gunther, *St. Paul's Opponents*, 14.

13. J. L. Sumney, *Identifying Paul's Opponents: The Question of Method in 2 Corinthians*, JSNTSup 40 (Sheffield: JSOT Press, 1990).

14. Ibid., 13.

and concludes that they cannot be used to identify opponents but only to test a hypothesis arrived at through other means. Similar to Nils Dahl, he next considers sources other than the primary biblical text and concludes that they must be used with caution, since in most instances sufficient exegesis has not been done on both passages. He finally deals with the assessment of passages within the biblical text, where he concludes that there are three types of contexts—polemical, apologetic, and didactic—to be found among the major sections of the epistolary form. He differentiates five levels of certainty of reference and four levels of reliability. The levels of certainty are from (1) explicit statements in any context, to (2) allusions in polemical and apologetic contexts, (3) allusions in polemical contexts that require mirror reading and in didactic contexts and thanksgivings, (4) themes in thanksgivings and greetings, and (5) the remaining uncertain evidence. The levels of reliability range from (1) explicit statements and allusions found in didactic contexts and explicit statements, allusions, and major themes found in letter thanksgivings; to (2) affirmations given in apologetic and polemical contexts and major themes found in letter greetings; (3) explicit statements and allusions in apologetic and polemical contexts and greetings and closings; and (4) the remaining explicit statements in hortatory contexts.

In his subsequent major treatment of the opponents in all of Paul's Letters, Sumney essentially repeats the method that he has defined above.[15] He makes several further observations in defense of his approach. The first is that, rather than accepting the criticism that this method reflects a limited historical perspective because it is confined to individual letters, again reflecting Dahl, Sumney believes that this recognizes the complexity of the historical context of ancient letter writing, where one must confine oneself to the given letter as the primary evidence considered.[16] One may wish to draw further conclusions regarding more than one letter, but one must begin with the primary evidence. The second observation is that this method is designed not to provide a full analysis of a given letter's occasion, but only to identify its opponents.[17] Therefore, Sumney does not treat Philemon, Ephesians, or Romans in his work, because he does not believe that they demonstrate any direct statements concerning opponents.[18] However, he does examine the Pastoral Epistles, treating them individually to appreciate the varied contexts in which they were written, rather than attempting to define a common opponent or opponents for all of the letters.

15. J. L. Sumney, *"Servants of Satan," "False Brothers" and Other Opponents of Paul*, JSNT-Sup 188 (Sheffield: Sheffield Academic Press, 1999).
16. Ibid., 23.
17. Ibid., 30.
18. Ibid., 31.

In his third significant treatment (found in the volume that I edited, mentioned above, and noted as the third major contribution below), Sumney provides a conspectus of his previous work, while also extending it in important ways.[19] After he summarizes the history of discussion of Paul's opponents, he then offers letter-by-letter summaries of recent research on Paul's opponents, comments on method, observations on anti-Pauline movements, and finally evaluations of recent Pauline reconstructions. His letter-by-letter summaries are distinguished by the fact that he makes comments on all of the letters attributed to Paul except Philemon. Thus he devotes most of his time to Romans and Galatians, as well as Philippians, Colossians, and 2 Thessalonians, while noting that Romans has elicited little comment, Ephesians has no evidence of gnosticism, and 1 Thessalonians has no clear indication of opponents. Sumney's treatment of the Pastoral Epistles is again noteworthy for both his treatment of the letters at all and his treatment of the letters separately, rather than finding a common opponent or situation. Sumney also notes that there has been some recent attention to questions of method in the study of Paul's opponents. However, he then reinforces the idea that there are two major anti-Pauline movements, one that opposes his apostleship and the other that opposes his theology.[20] He concludes by criticizing two recent attempts at historical reconstruction of the Colossian situation for still failing to impose the kinds of limits that are necessary to determine the nature of Paul's opponents.[21]

Sumney has made a significant and helpful contribution to New Testament scholarship by attempting to define a usable means of distinguishing the opponents in Paul's Letters. Even if his conclusions in many cases agree with previous proposals—the task is not necessarily to find new and previously undiscovered opponents, but rather to assess and, if possible, verify or correct previous proposals—his helpful categorization of types of statements and contexts, and their resultant reliability, provides a significant way forward for this topic.

Paul's Opponents in Recent Discussion

The third treatment to be discussed here is the volume that I recently edited. I have already noted that this volume includes what I consider to be an

---

19. J. L. Sumney, "Studying Paul's Opponents: Advances and Challenges," in Porter, *Paul and His Opponents*, 7–58. I use this article for many of the examples below.

20. Ibid., 48–50.

21. These are T. Martin, *By Philosophy and Empty Deceit: Colossians as a Response to a Cynic Critique*, JSNTSup 118 (Sheffield: Sheffield Academic Press, 1996); C. E. Arnold, *The Colossian Syncretism: The Interface between Christianity and Folk Belief at Colossae*, WUNT 2/77 (Tübingen: Mohr Siebeck, 1995; repr., Grand Rapids: Baker, 1996).

excellent conspectus of the major issues by Sumney, one that recapitulates and extends his previous work in useful ways. This is, however, the only programmatic and methodologically oriented essay in the collection. The other essays are concerned with individual studies of various Pauline Letters in terms of the opponents. Five of the essays are in one way or another (one partially, and one indirectly) addressed to the situation at Galatia, with one (partially) addressed to that of Corinth, another to Rome (the essay I wrote; see note 1 above), and one to Colossae, along with one focusing upon the imperial cult as Paul's major single opponent. Two pertinent observations can be made about the essays in this volume apart from Sumney's. One is that it is surprising how few of them actually invoke either Gunther's or Sumney's work. I realize that it is perhaps my own bias that skews this, but nevertheless their methodological pertinence would seem to require some acknowledgment. Excluding Sumney's essay, Gunther is cited in three of the seven essays, and Sumney in the same three. Of the other three major recent discussions of method that Sumney cites,[22] two are not cited elsewhere at all, one is cited by no one but him, and the last is cited once by the author himself. So by any account, methodological issues do not loom large in this recent discussion. The second observation is that the collection, perhaps not surprisingly, falls back on the same New Testament books that continue to generate excitement regarding Paul's opponents, especially Galatians and the Corinthian letters.

Several generalizations emerge from such a survey. One is that it is difficult to establish firmly what constitutes an opponent. Implicit definitions are what we mostly find.[23] It appears from what Sumney says that a tacit definition is that an opponent is someone who explicitly and even consciously opposes Paul on theological matters, such as questions of Jew versus Gentile, from outside the Christian community (he states that they are "intruding teachers").[24] There is the further difficulty of establishing what is pertinent background for the discussion. Even with a method that attempts to identify types of statements and their reliability, it is not always clear that use of these statements leads to clear results. Nevertheless, they all show that the focus of investigation rests upon the text itself as the starting point for all analysis and the primary source of data.

22. These are the studies by Dahl, Cosgrove, and Nanos.
23. P. W. Barnett defines opponents as "outsiders who have penetrated the Pauline assemblies" ("Opponents of Paul," in *Dictionary of Paul and His Letters*, ed. G. F. Hawthorne, R. P. Martin, and D. G. Reid [Downers Grove, IL: InterVarsity, 1993], 644). This definition probably would serve to restrict the letters in which opponents are found.
24. Sumney, "Studying Paul's Opponents," 14. This is consistent with his treatment of 1 Thessalonians in *"Servants of Satan,"* where he concludes that there are no opponents that are being countered in the letter (p. 227).

A New Approach to Paul's Opponents

In the light of the foregoing discussion of fairly recent secondary literature on Paul and his opponents, several pertinent observations can be made. One is that methodological issues, despite some recent attempts to treat them, remain in the background of discussion. In other words, despite several treatments that delve into such issues, especially the research by Sumney, much of this work remains outside of the continuing discussion of Paul's opponents. The second observation, perhaps not too surprisingly, follows from the first: despite such attempts to determine methodological issues, with their neglect the discussion rather much continues along the same lines. I do not want to say that there has been no progress, because there has been in some ways (I would note Nanos's study of Galatians and would like to think that my study of Romans that prompted this chapter has made a contribution); nevertheless, despite the same evidence and without methodological controls, I find it difficult to know whether one is actually talking about the same concept of what it means to be an opponent of Paul and how one would recognize such a conclusion and test its validity.

There are, as a result, at least two major residual issues in talking about Paul's opponents. The first is defining what such opponency actually means. The second is how the opponents are described. In the course of discussion, I think I have uncovered at least six different major ways in which opponents of Paul are discussed in the secondary literature.

The first question that must be asked in discussing the opponents is, "What constitutes an opponent?" This question often goes unanswered, or an answer is simply assumed, as if we would all recognize an opponent when we saw one, even if we are not explicit on how we would define one. Would Paul have to see them as opponents? Would they need to see themselves as opponents? Are they from outside the church? Or can they be, or should they be, from within? Must they oppose Paul on theological grounds, or can they oppose him on other grounds? These are just some of the complicating factors involved. As a result, more highly polemical contexts attract more proposals of opponents, while less polemical contexts have fewer proposals. In the various attempts to delimit the opponents, it is clear that there are a variety of answers given, often on the basis of the letter that is being treated.

The following are some of the major ways the opponents are described for particular letters. (1) One of the major means of distinguishing Pauline opponents revolves around the question of whether the opponents are those who come from outside the Christian community (e.g., as in Galatians [see 3:1], according to most interpreters); (2) or whether the opponents must, or at least may, come from within (e.g., 1 Corinthians, according to Gordon Fee, who sees local opposition;[25] 1 Thessalonians, with divisive views on eschatology that have led to relaxed ethical and moral standards).[26] (3) Others discuss the opponents in terms of the level and type of contrary theological beliefs that they have (e.g., Galatians, whether the dispute is over the law and legalism, or over what it means to be a member of the people of God;[27] 2 Thessalonians, over the imminence of the day of the Lord;[28] Colossians, with regard to angel worship, mystery cults, or other forms of syncretism;[29] 1 Timothy, over food laws and scriptural interpretation;[30] Titus, with Jewish Christians promoting observance of the law).[31] (4) Sometimes the opponents are defined not with reference to theological beliefs, but rather regarding other types of contrary ideas (e.g., Romans, over the relationship of Jews and Gentiles in church leadership,[32] or over Paul and various personal issues;[33] 2 Timothy, over various speculative ideas).[34] (5) In some discussions of the opponents, they are characterized according to the level of their support for or opposition to Paul (e.g., 2 Corinthians, with opposition to Paul's apostleship).[35] (6) For a final group, the question is raised whether those who are labeled as Paul's opponents must see themselves as his opponents, or whether this is only in

25. G. D. Fee, *The First Epistle to the Corinthians*, NICNT (Grand Rapids: Eerdmans, 1987), 6–15.

26. For example, R. Jewett, *The Thessalonian Correspondence: Pauline Rhetoric and Millenarian Piety* (Philadelphia: Fortress, 1986), 94–106.

27. The first is the traditional estimation, and the second is an encapsulation of more recent discussion. There are other views as well.

28. This is the traditional view, as held by, e.g., G. Milligan, *St. Paul's Epistles to the Thessalonians* (London: Macmillan, 1908), xxxviii.

29. See, e.g., E. Lohse, *Colossians and Philemon: A Commentary on the Epistles to the Colossians and to Philemon*, trans. W. R. Poehlmann and R. J. Karris, ed. H. Koester, Hermeneia (Philadelphia: Fortress, 1971), 2–3; M. Dibelius, "The Isis Initiation in Apuleius and Related Initiatory Rites," in *Conflict at Colossae: A Problem in the Interpretation of Early Christianity Illustrated by Selected Modern Studies*, ed. and trans. F. O. Francis and W. A. Meeks, SBLSBS 4 (Missoula, MT: Society of Biblical Literature, 1973), 61–112; Arnold, *Colossian Syncretism*; F. O. Francis, "Humility and Angelic Worship in Col. 2:18," in Francis and Meeks, *Conflict at Colossae*, 163–96.

30. J. Murphy-O'Connor, "2 Timothy Contrasted with 1 Timothy and Titus," *RB* 98 (1991): 403–18, esp. 415–16.

31. Sumney, "Studying Paul's Opponents," 44.

32. These types of issues are discussed in K. P. Donfried, ed., *The Romans Debate*, rev. ed. (Peabody, MA: Hendrickson, 1991).

33. Porter, "Did Paul Have Opponents in Rome?," 153–67, including such issues as the Romans' frustrations with Paul's travel, questions regarding charismatic experience, his purported avoidance of them, his purported abandonment of Judaism, and questions regarding his apostolic appointment.

34. C. Spicq, *Saint Paul: Les Épîtres pastorales*, ÉBib (Paris: Lecoffre, 1947), 354–55, 360.

35. E. Käsemann, "Die Legitimität des Apostels," *ZNW* 41 (1942): 33–71.

the eyes of Paul (e.g., Philippians, where there are those who preach the same gospel but are opposed to Paul;[36] Colossians, with its syncretism that attempts to add to the gospel;[37] 2 Thessalonians, with those who have misunderstood but not consciously attempted to oppose Paul).[38]

On the surface, it is difficult to know how these can be drawn together to form a common methodological framework for discussion of Paul's opponents, because they seem to be discussing various factors from differing perspectives. Some of the proposals seem to focus upon Paul as person, others upon the individual churches, some upon those outside of the church, and still others on both theological and other kinds of teaching. For Sumney, such a broad expanse of factors is clearly too broad to constitute discussion of opponents. As a result, he wishes to limit his discussion to those who are specifically opposed to Paul as teachers from outside of the church. However, the history of discussion as summarized by Gunther makes clear that others have ranged far more broadly in including the kinds of opponents of Paul who fit many if not most of these broad parameters. One factor that all of the depictions of Paul's opponents have in common is that they are conveyed by language within the letters, as reflective of a situation involving others. If we take these parameters seriously, we can perhaps expand upon them and develop a means by which to clarify and expand discussion of Paul's opponents.

I would like to introduce a particular methodological approach to the question of Paul's opponents in an attempt to find a possible way forward in such discussion. I wish to introduce a new framework so that we do not simply repeat the kinds of studies that we have seen before, which speak at cross-purposes and without a common language of opponency, and result in studies that do not end up addressing the same issues. I am not naive enough to believe that this method will solve all of the interpretive problems (I would be thrilled if it did, of course). In fact, it may well solve none of them, but it is an attempt to find a way of moving discussion forward by providing a comprehensive framework that includes as many of the variables noted above in one approach as is possible.

Here I wish to introduce a model for functional language analysis first proposed by the Viennese psychiatrist, educationalist, and linguist Karl Bühler (1879–1963), and since then used by many others. In 1934 Bühler published his organon model of language and communication, by which language

---

36. Sumney, *"Servants of Satan,"* 166–70.

37. R. E. DeMaris, *The Colossian Controversy: Wisdom in Dispute at Colossae*, JSNTSup 96 (Sheffield: Sheffield Academic Press, 1994).

38. G. Holland, *The Tradition That You Received from Us: 2 Thessalonians in the Pauline Tradition*, HUT 24 (Tübingen: Mohr Siebeck, 1988).

functions as the tool, or organon, that is used for communicative purposes by means of representation.[39] Bühler puts forward what he explicitly states is a reductionistic model:[40] he believes that a comparatively simple set of relative values captures the entire communicative situation. Bühler is now relatively unknown in linguistic and related circles,[41] even though his communications model had a major influence upon structural linguistics, including providing the basis for developments in Prague school linguistics such as Nikolai Trubetzskoy's phonetics and Roman Jakobson's communications model, and a number of functional linguistic models, such as that of Michael Halliday and what is known today as systemic functional linguistics.[42] Even though some key elements of Bühler's organon model have been adopted by others, the model itself bears further exploration, which it has not received in the last eighty or so years: it provides a linguistic and even cognitive framework for

39. K. Bühler, *Theory of Language: The Representational Function of Language*, trans. D. F. Goodwin (Philadelphia: John Benjamins, 1990), 2 (translation of *Sprachtheorie* [Jena: Gustav Fischer, 1934]). For more on the life and work of Bühler, whose constructive career was prematurely curtailed by the German invasion of Austria and his expulsion from the country, see the editor's introduction by A. Eschbach, "Karl Bühler: Sematologist," xiii–xliii. For other essays on language and related topics, see also K. Bühler, *Schriften zur Sprachtheorie*, ed. A. Eschbach (Tübingen: Mohr Siebeck, 2012).

40. Bühler, *Theory*, 30.

41. References to Bühler in linguistics books are exceedingly rare. I have found only one that devotes significant treatment to him (though I do not claim to have examined every one). See G. Pätsch, *Grundfragen der Sprachtheorie* (Halle: Max Niemeyer, 1955), 34–35. Note that this book was written in communist East Germany and so reflects that perspective, though Bühler no doubt would have been antithetical to such a perspective.

42. See P. L. Garvin, "The Prague School of Linguistics," in *Linguistics Today*, ed. A. A. Hill (New York: Basic Books, 1969), 229–38, esp. 231–32; P. Steiner, "The Conceptual Basis of Prague Structuralism," in *Sound, Sign, and Meaning: Quinquagenary of the Prague Linguistic Circle*, ed. L. Matejka (Ann Arbor: University of Michigan, 1976), 381–82n48; M. A. K. Halliday, *Language as Social Semiotic: The Social Interpretation of Language and Meaning* (London: Edward Arnold, 1978), 47–48 (among others of Halliday's references to Bühler). For other important works on the Prague school, see J. Vachek, *The Linguistic School of Prague: An Introduction to Its Theory and Practice* (Bloomington: Indiana University Press, 1966); F. W. Galan, *Historic Structures: The Prague School Project, 1928–1946* (Austin: University of Texas Press, 1985). For anthologies of some important work by Prague linguists, see J. Vachek, ed., *A Prague School Reader in Linguistics* (Bloomington: Indiana University Press, 1964); P. L. Garvin, ed. and trans., *A Prague School Reader on Esthetics, Literary Structure, and Style* (Washington, DC: Georgetown University Press, 1964). For a summary regarding New Testament studies, see J. H. Nylund, "The Prague School of Linguistics and Its Influence on New Testament Language Studies," in *The Language of the New Testament: Context, History, and Development*, ed. S. E. Porter and A. W. Pitts, ECHC 3, LBS 6 (Leiden: Brill, 2013), 155–221. For a placement of the Prague linguistic contribution within structuralism, see S. E. Porter and J. C. Robinson, *Hermeneutics: An Introduction to Interpretive Theory* (Grand Rapids: Eerdmans, 2011), 155–67. I have also explored another dimension of Prague school linguistics in S. E. Porter, "A Functional Letter Perspective: Towards a Grammar of Epistolary Form," in *Paul and the Ancient Letter Form*, ed. S. E. Porter and S. A. Adams, PAST 6 (Leiden: Brill, 2010), 9–31.

addressing a number of the issues raised (above) regarding determining the Pauline opponents.

Bühler's organon model identifies four significant entities that must be taken into account in thinking about language, and hence about the contexts in which language is used. These four entities are the objects and states of affairs themselves, the sender of the message, the receiver of the message, and the concrete language phenomenon itself—that is, the sign or set of signs that would constitute the discourse. Apart from the language phenomenon itself, the other three entities enter into relationship by means of their position in relation to language. This can be reduced to three fundamental functions: the one—to the other—about the things (to use Bühler's language).[43] Thus, an instance of language use involves three functions. It is a symbol in terms of its relationship to the objects or states of affairs depicted; a symptom (or index) because it is dependent upon the sender who produced it; and a signal because it appeals to the hearer or reader. Each of these merits further description.

The sender, whether by means of speech or writing, produces what is called an expression, which is the symptom of the inner condition or state of its user. The receiver, whether by means of hearing or reading, receives the signal of the sender by means of the language signs, in which there is an appeal to the hearer, or by means of which the hearer is triggered in a response, which directs either outward or inward behavior. The objects or states of affairs are represented by the discourse as a coordinated representation.[44] Bühler represents his organon model as shown in figure 17.1.[45]

This model overcomes a number of the limitations of other linguistic models, including some of the proposed means of discussing Paul's opponents. It recognizes that language is not referential, but that it is users who are referential through language. Further, what is conveyed by language is meaning or semantics, not substance. This semantics exists within the context of a communicative contract; that is, there are conventions of communication that must be in place for meaning to be conveyed. Therefore, Bühler's model is a suitable point of at least initial exploration for several reasons: (1) It provides a linguistic model recognizing that meaning is communicated through language, and it focuses upon the discourse. (2) It recognizes that language is a tool for accomplishing various purposes. (3) It takes a representational approach to language, rather than expressive. (4) It focuses on the linguistic

43. Bühler, *Theory*, 30–31. This language is reminiscent of Halliday's description of transitivity in terms of who does what to whom. See M. A. K. Halliday, *Halliday's Introduction to Functional Grammar*, rev. C. M. I. M. Matthiessen, 4th ed. (London: Routledge, 2014), 332–55.
44. Bühler, *Theory*, 35.
45. Ibid.

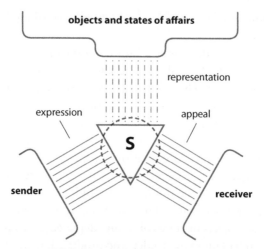

Figure 17.1 Bühler Organon Model

communication, but within its communicative context. (5) It is multivariate so as to capture the mediated view of reality in relation to the speaker and hearer. And (6) it is helpfully reductionistic in its attempt to capture complex communicative functions in definable and communicable relations.

Examples of the Opponents in Paul's Letters

I wish to test the viability of this model by treating three examples. I am selecting three different examples in order to probe the viability of the linguistic model that I have introduced above: (1) Philemon, where there is virtually no discussion of Pauline opponents; (2) Romans, where there is some debate over opponents, but not a huge number of options; and (3) Colossians, where there has been and continues to be much debate, as recently as the major treatment by Sumney (noted above).

Philemon

The first example is Philemon.[46] Philemon usually is not included in discussions of Paul's opponents, and one does not find discussion of Philemon by

46. For the structure of the letter relied upon here, see S. E. Porter, *The Apostle Paul: His Life, Thought, and Letters* (Grand Rapids: Eerdmans, forthcoming), chap. 11. For a different approach to Philemon, see S. E. Porter, "Is Critical Discourse Analysis Critical? An Evaluation Using Philemon as a Test Case," in *Discourse Analysis and the New Testament: Approaches and*

either Gunther or Sumney. The reasons for this are made clear by Sumney: "The occasion of Philemon is the return of Onesimus and the assumed acceptance of the authority of Paul clearly indicates that no opponents are involved."[47] Several objections can be legitimately made to this summary. It presupposes, first, that Paul assumes there is going to be acceptance of his authority; second, that Paul has clear authority over his audience; and third, that as such is the case, no one would oppose him. Only if the Pauline opponents are seen as of necessity being from outside the Christian community, as Sumney and others seem to indicate, is exclusion of Philemon warranted, since we have already noted examples above where scholars have seen internal opposition to Paul and his authority as a major ground for positing opponents. However, there are also numerous indicators within the letter that the author, Paul, does not anticipate ready acceptance of his authority or acceptance of the return of Onesimus.

To facilitate discussion in the light of Bühler's organon model, I will examine Philemon from the three different perspectives of the model. The first concerns the author and his expressive or professive function. Seven items are worth noting. (1) The author addresses a plurality of recipients (vv. 1–3), but then, in the thanksgiving portion of the letter (vv. 4–7), he switches to the second-person singular. This is unprecedented in the Pauline Letters. The only somewhat similar pattern of use of the singular is found in the other personal letters, but there the address is in the singular as well. The movement from plural to singular has the effect of focusing the comments by moving from potentially an inclusive to a decidedly exclusive emphasis. (2) The author attributes a number of complimentary features to the singular recipient in the thanksgiving, including love, faith, fellowship, and resulting joy, comfort, and refreshment. Paul uses the singular possessive pronoun a number of times with these complimentary features: "*your* love and faith,"[48] "fellowship of *your* faith," "*your* love," and "refreshment through *you*" (unfortunately, this cannot easily be made clear in English). (3) There is a concentration of directive language[49] in the body of the letter (vv. 8–22). Paul says that he does not want to "command," so instead he wants to "appeal" (vv. 9–10); he does not want to compel but instead wants Philemon to utilize free will (v. 14); and he instructs Philemon to prepare a room (v. 22). (4) Paul uses a number of lexical

---

Results, ed. S. E. Porter and J. T. Reed, JSNTSup 170, SNTG 4 (Sheffield: Sheffield Academic Press, 1999), 47–70.

47. Sumney, *"Servants of Satan,"* 31.

48. Possibly *"your* love and the faith" as in the revised version of the NASB, but I think that the pronoun probably modifies both in a complex word group.

49. On directive language, see S. E. Porter, *Verbal Aspect in the Greek of the New Testament, with Reference to Tense and Mood*, SBG 1 (New York: Peter Lang, 1989), 335–36.

items related to socially based categories, oriented to the world and especially to the family, reflective of the fictive kinship found in early Christianity.[50] These include "prisoner" (vv. 1, 9), "brother" (vv. 1, 16, 20), "fellow worker" (v. 1), "sister" (v. 2), "fellow soldier" (v. 2), "Father" (v. 3), "Lord" (vv. 5, 20), "fellowship" (v. 6), "old man" (v. 9), "child" (v. 10), "slave" (v. 16), and "partner" (v. 17). In other words, there is much language that characterizes and seeks to create a sense of motivated bonding, on the basis of family-like ties. (5) Paul also uses language of contradiction and contraries to characterize his perception and desired outcome. He speaks not only of ordering versus appealing (vv. 8–9) and compulsion versus free will (v. 14), but also of Onesimus as "once useless" and now "useful" (v. 9), as having been returned even though Paul wished to keep him there (vv. 12–13), as separated for a time so that he might be returned forever (v. 15), not as a slave but as a brother (v. 16), and of obedience and of exceeding what is required (v. 21). (6) Paul uses language of moral suasion, including language of obligation (vv. 14, 18, 19, 21). Paul links the language of obligation to himself in every instance, such as tying his request for Philemon's consent (v. 14) to the debt that Philemon owes to Paul (vv. 18–19), and expressing certainty that Philemon will exceed Paul's stated desires (v. 21). (7) Paul, perhaps recognizing the inherent limitations of the letter as a surrogate for personal presence, and hence without the force of personal confrontation, links the request of the letter to the possibility of personal confrontation in the form of a possible visit (v. 22). He does this along with, both at the outset and closing, soliciting the witness of others both at the letter's origin (vv. 23–24) and its reception (v. 2).

There have been many discussions about the nature of Paul's communication with Philemon, especially the tone and nature of his persuasive tactics.[51] Leaving the tangential issues aside here, I believe that the foregoing list of seven features makes clear that we do not have a straightforward letter of petition or recommendation. The author, Paul, is representing himself as a major and, because elderly, respected member of a social hierarchy, where there is an expectation of compliance. However, he clearly does not necessarily count on such subservience. Hence, while constantly reinforcing the social linkage among the participants, including Paul and those with him and those around Philemon, he makes clear a specific set of expectations that he wishes to have

50. See N. R. Petersen, *Rediscovering Paul: Philemon and the Sociology of Paul's Narrative World* (Philadelphia: Fortress, 1985), 89–199. Compare P. A. Harland, *Associations, Synagogues, and Congregations: Claiming a Place in Ancient Mediterranean Society* (Minneapolis: Fortress, 2003).

51. Some of these and related issues are discussed in B. W. R. Pearson, *Corresponding Sense: Paul, Dialectic, and Gadamer*, BIS 48 (Leiden: Brill, 2001), 46–92.

accomplished by his major designated recipient, acknowledges the potential for thwarting them, and then appeals to several types of compulsive force, including rank, obligation, and witness, as a means of compelling compliance. These are not the words of a person who does not sense potential opposition. More to the point, I believe that Paul's words as the author reflect his belief in a high likelihood of opposition from within the very group that he addresses, in particular from the major recipient of his letter.

In Bühler's model, especially if applied to interpreting letters, the characterization of the speaker or sender is much easier than dealing with the other two dimensions, those of receiver or reader and of the objects and states of affairs represented. Nevertheless, in regard to the reader, I think we can gain some insight into the appeal or triggering of behavior that would have occurred by means of the text, though mediated through the text.[52] There are eight features that are worth noting here. (1) The first is the sense of focused intent that results from being singled out by the shift from plural to singular pronouns. Not only does Philemon have the singular pronouns used of him in the thanksgiving (vv. 4–8), but also the use of the singular second-person pronoun and verb continues throughout most of the body of the letter (vv. 8, 10, 11 [2x], 12, 13, 14 [2x], 15, 16, 17 [2x], 18 [2x], 19 [3x], 20 [2x], 21 [3x]). Only in verse 22b is there a shift to the second-person plural again. (2) The thanksgiving of the letter signals a sense of positive atmosphere in the tone of the letter. Paul's specifically cited elements, reinforced by the use of the second-person singular pronoun, are designed to trigger a positive response in the hearer, as many of the distinguishing features are virtues that characterize faith in Jesus Christ (e.g., love). (3) The use of command-and-appeal language has several effects on the hearer. One is the desire, in the light of the positive thanksgiving, to fulfill Paul's request. Another is to create difficulty in being able to deny the appeal in the light of the authority structure represented. The hearer at this stage, Philemon, probably was wanting to fulfill what the apostle was asking, but not entirely certain of the nature of the request or why Paul mentioned that he could command but had chosen not to do so. (4) Language of social inclusion has the effect of creating recognizable hierarchy that both compels obedience and sets up Philemon as a potential example for others to watch due to his apparent social position. Because of his being one of the addressees of the letter, his ownership of a slave, and the possibility of having a house large enough for gathering, Philemon is one of the leaders; yet by the use of the socially based language, he is included tightly within the fictive

---

52. Of course, we have no way of testing the effect of the appeal of the language, except in terms of the normative communicative responses to such linguistic features.

family network. The language of the thanksgiving is designed to reinforce this positive familial situation, in which there is mutual interdependence. (5) The specific details about Onesimus would trigger a sense of resistance to certainly the appeal and probably the command, due to the importance of slavery as a social institution. Even if Onesimus was a trusted household slave, he was nevertheless a slave, with all of the social (and economic) obligations that this implied.[53] (6) Paul's use of slavery and prisoner language for himself would have triggered more than simply emotive effects, in the light of what Philemon was being called upon to do. This would also have possibly perplexed one, such as Philemon, used to the social norms. (7) The mention of Philemon's obligation or debt to Paul probably would have been the most significant reversal of expectations. If Philemon saw himself as an important social figure, and to this point in the dialogue perhaps capable of resisting the appeal and possibly even the command of the apostle, now he has been characterized as a debtor on the same level as the slave Onesimus, both of whom owe their existence to the slave and prisoner Paul. In other words, Philemon has been linguistically transfigured from being at the top of the social order to the bottom of the order, right alongside Onesimus—in fact, possibly lower than Onesimus, if he is disobedient—in subordination to the prisoner Paul. (8) Philemon must have sensed the linguistic pressure being exerted by the fact that the letter is addressed to Apphia, who is characterized as a "sister" in the faith, and hence one intimately connected with the Christian community, and to Archippus, who is characterized as a fellow combatant for the faith with Paul, along with the church that is ambiguously characterized as "in your [singular] house," quite possibly referring to Philemon's house. There are several potential responses on Philemon's part that would end up characterizing him, while not necessarily as an opponent, as at least a potential opponent of Paul. His opposition would be based not upon theological doctrine in the narrow sense—that is, upon issues such as the law—but rather, in a broader sense, regarding the nature and composition of the Christian community, its hierarchy, its mutual interdependence, the effect of conversion upon internal church composition, and the nature of what Christian community means. At all points, Philemon is a potential opponent of what Paul is suggesting.

The third area for investigation is the relationship of the objects and states of affairs as they are represented in the text. Bühler was very careful in characterizing the world outside of the text in terms of the notions of objects and states

---

53. See M. J. Harris, *Slave of Christ: A New Testament Metaphor for Total Devotion to Christ* (Downers Grove, IL: InterVarsity, 1999); J. A. Harrill, *Slaves in the New Testament: Literary, Social, and Moral Dimensions* (Minneapolis: Fortress, 2006).

of affairs. He notes that the relationship between the thing and the word used of it is conventional and arbitrary (a typical structuralist perspective). Thus, the relationship between a word and its object is not a strictly referential and historical one, but rather a coordinated one, for which the language users do not know its origin or development. The relationship that exists is by virtue of an unstated linguistic contract between the parties involved. Hence, Bühler does not want to use the term "objects" only, but "states of affairs" to show that the language as it is used involves much more than simply individual words, but also syntactical conventions that expand the range and domain of the coordinated relationships.[54] We see, then, that the use of language as a functional "tool" (hence the organon model) invokes much more than simply things, such as the participants, Paul, Philemon, and the others. A complex of entities, including objects and more, such as various states of affairs, is represented by the linguistic expression—much more than I can talk about here, but that is part of what might best be called the cultural context, in which a particular contextual situation (e.g., one in which there was slavery, prisons, and language used in a particular way, etc.) results in a text as an instantiation.[55]

This can be said of the Letter to Philemon as well. The context is one in which there is a physical and symbolically organized institution, a church. This physical organism meets in a particular house and has particular participants. The major issue of the letter is whether one of the major participants in this physical church will allow another, over whom in the physical world he has control due to the slave-master relationship, to be fully included in this physical assembly. The symbolically organized institution, represented by means of social dynamics, consists of people characterized on the basis of a number of functional relations—brother, sister, fellow worker, fellow soldier, prisoner (it is unclear whether Epaphras is a literal prisoner confined for being a Christian, or is characterized by Paul as a fellow prisoner held captive by Christ Jesus [v. 23]). Paul represents this symbolically organized institution as having precedence over the physical one, and he has already inaugurated the transition of Onesimus's status from outsider to insider. Onesimus is now characterized as more than a slave: he is a "beloved brother" (v. 16), both to Paul and to Philemon. Paul is, in effect, attempting to effect a change in Onesimus's status that has implications for both Paul and Philemon: changing the state of affairs from one of subservience to one of full participation. Paul is clearly an advocate for such a change. Philemon, while not depicted

54. Bühler, *Theory*, 36–37.
55. The terms context of culture and context of situation are from Halliday, *Language as Social Semiotic*, 27–31, 67–69.

as an outright opponent, is seen as accustomed to the status quo. The use of the second-person pronoun throughout the thanksgiving and body of the work grammaticalizes several purposes for the representational function of language. One is that it serves as a cohesive device and thereby links all of the material within the thanksgiving and the body of the work, up until the ending of the body of the letter, into a single cohesive unit. The effect is to represent the state of affairs as one in which Philemon is both praised for particular Christian traits and appealed to regarding Onesimus.

As shown above, using this linguistic method to explore the potential of Pauline opposition in Philemon uncovers a number of potentially enlightening results. One is that the discussion of Pauline opponents is fully integrated with a number of other discussions regarding the Pauline Letters, such as the nature of the early Christian community, the social hierarchy of the ancient world and the early Christian church, and the roles and relations of various people within this world. A second is that I believe the question of a Pauline opponent in this letter should at least be entertained on the basis of the findings here, unless one chooses to narrowly confine the notion of opponent to an already-established external group focused upon distinctly Christian theological concepts. Here in his Letter to Philemon, the primary opposition, which Paul has not yet encountered but which he warily anticipates he might need to confront, is addressed from the outset, instead of Paul waiting to hear that a problem has arisen, presumably after his return of Onesimus. Paul's response focuses upon the social composition of the early Christian community, but this notion itself is theological in nature, with implications regarding the nature of Christian salvation and the debts that it reflects and incurs.

Romans

I have chosen Romans as a second example for several reasons. One is that Romans is not an overworked letter in treatments of Paul's opponents. As several scholars have noted, the discussion of Paul's opponents in Romans has been curtailed for various reasons. Though Sumney treats the book in his latest article, in his earlier book he considers but rejects the possibility of discovering Pauline opponents there: "We exclude Romans, even though its purpose is still a matter of much debate, because the church at Rome was not a Pauline church in the sense that those in Corinth, Thessalonica and elsewhere were. Furthermore, since Paul had not been to Rome, anti-Pauline activity is not as probable. In addition, Romans was clearly not written as a response to anti-Pauline activity. We may take it, then, that the primary purposes of Romans do not involve opponents."[56] This disclaimer introduces a number of additional factors to consider when discussing Paul's opponents. One such factor is Sumney's clear prior decision that opponents play no role in the letter's formulation. I would have thought that this conclusion could be reached only after one has studied the letter in detail. However, one of the factors that exclude such study is the prior determination that Romans was "clearly" not composed in response to Pauline opponents. Again, the prior exclusion seems to have dictated the conclusion. There are further factors that limit the possibility of such exploration. One of these is that a Pauline opponent could be located only in a church that Paul founded. Sumney introduces the notion that the church in Rome was not a Pauline church in the way that those in Corinth and Thessalonica were. However, excluding the issue of pseudepigraphy, in which cases the actual author would not have a similar relationship to the churches as Paul did, the church at Colossae was, according to most scholars, one that Paul had not visited, but that he had sent emissaries to establish (although this hypothesis has, perhaps rightly, been questioned).[57] We simply do not know about the origins of the church in Rome. What we do know is that Paul knows enough about that church's members to write a major letter to them. This letter includes significant and developed theological content and reference to a number of apparently personal and related matters, such as his travel itinerary and motivation, that indicate at least familiarity on Paul's part sufficient to warrant such a letter. A final factor is the unlikelihood of anti-Pauline activity in a place that Paul had never visited. The grounds for this assumption are unclear, as it would seem to indicate that one's reputation and teaching could not spread where one had not actually traveled. Yet, I think, we do know that Paul excited interest in places outside his immediate sphere of contact, to the point of arousing opposition (e.g., one of the frameworks for early composition of the Letter of James).[58] Such a case is also to be found within Sumney's treatment of other Pauline Letters, including Colossians and those to Timothy and Titus.

A second reason why I treat Romans is to revisit the treatment of Paul's opponents that I previously published. I see no significant reason to recant my conclusions from that time. However, I wish to treat the issue again with a new methodological approach. The one that I used previously focused upon five major sections where Paul seemed to be directly addressing the Romans.[59]

---

56. Sumney, *"Servants of Satan,"* 31.

57. For the standard views, see Porter, *Apostle Paul*, chap. 12.

58. See Pearson, *Corresponding Sense*, 251–58.

59. In that regard, my method is similar to that of A. J. M. Wedderburn, *The Reasons for Romans*, SNTW (Edinburgh: T&T Clark, 1988), 102–42. Wedderburn draws upon Paul's statements to arrive at conclusions regarding Paul's defense of himself and his message.

However, there is much more in the letter that might be germane to discussion of those who may be opposed to Paul, even though I will need to limit myself in the light of the length of the letter.

Concerning the author and his expressive or professive function, the following seven features may be observed in what Paul says to the Romans.[60]

1. In the salutation of the letter, Paul includes the longest and most developed of all of his salutations, this one expanding upon and elaborating the description of the author.[61] Paul frames his characterization of himself in terms of three major features: a slave, a called apostle, and as set apart for the gospel of God. The use of the term "gospel" (1:1, 3; cf. 1:9, 15, 16) seems to prompt his expansion and extension of a theological treatment of this gospel of which he is the set-apart apostle. He characterizes it as promised beforehand through the prophets, and being concerned with God's Son, who was born of flesh and is also Son of God as declared by the resurrection. If Paul is drawing upon a formulaic piece of tradition in 1:3–4,[62] this may serve to add some weight to what he is saying. In any case, he uses the declaration on the Son, God, and the Spirit to return to his apostleship, designed to bring about faith among the Gentiles, of whom the Romans are part. Not only the unusualness of the length, but also the nature and argument of the extension, point to Paul reinforcing and professing his apostleship to the Gentiles, grounding it in the very nature of Jesus Christ our Lord, who is God's Son, and the Spirit's resurrected result.

2. Paul commends the Romans in his thanksgiving because their faith is being proclaimed in the entire world. The purpose of the thanksgiving is not only to give thanks to God, but also to provide a general orientation to the relationship between Paul and the particular church that he is addressing. In the thanksgiving he mentions the faith of the Romans known to the world (1:8, 12), the gospel that he preaches (1:9, 15), his mentioning of them in his prayers (1:9–10), his desire to see them (1:11), his desire to share a spiritual experience with them (1:11), the desire for mutual encouragement (1:12), his frustrated plans to visit them (1:13), and his desire for fruit among them as among the other Gentiles to whom he is obligated (1:13–14). I do not want to minimize the importance of the two sets of statements that I singled out in my previous treatment (1:9–10, concerning frustration over Paul's arrival; 1:11–12, concerning charismatic experience), but I do wish to place these

60. For the outline of the letter followed here, see Porter, *Apostle Paul*, chap. 10.

61. Apart from Ephesians, Romans is the only church letter ascribed only to Paul as author. The only other church letter that comes anywhere close to the length of the salutation in development of the author is Galatians; compare 1 Timothy and Titus.

62. So most scholars, although this is widely disputed.

observations in the larger context of what Paul is saying in the thanksgiving. The statements regarding Paul not arriving and charismatic experience are made within the context of Paul explaining himself as a preacher of the gospel and imparter of other gifts to the wider Gentile church. This unifies and broadens the emphases of the thanksgiving.

3. As has been observed many times previously, the so-called theme statement of Romans, 1:16–17, encapsulates a number of key ideas that are expanded upon further in Paul's letter. These include the emphasis upon the gospel as reflective of God's power to effect salvation to those who believe, including both Jews and Greeks, because it reflects God's righteousness and establishes a pattern of Spirit-led life. Rather than go through the rest of Romans, I will simply say that I believe these major themes are further explicated in the major portions of the letter, including the human predicament, righteousness as the solution to the human legal problem, reconciliation as encompassing the relationship of God to humanity, salvation as encompassing the life of the believer, and the means by which one lives such a life (as well as the relationship of Jews and Gentiles [see below]).[63]

4. Throughout the body of the letter Paul ties several strands together as he unfolds his theological progression from human sinfulness to life in the Spirit. One is the impartiality of God with regard to both Jews and Gentiles, in his actions and their consequences (1:18; 2:1, 11–12; 3:9; 4:16; 5:12; 6:3, 8); another is the continued place and accountability of the Jews (1:16; 2:9–10, 17; 3:1, 9, 29; 4:1–25); and a third is the inclusion of the Gentiles in this plan (1:14, 16; 2:9–10; 3:9, 29).

5. Romans 9–11 has been a focal point of discussion. Some have taken it as central to understanding Paul, while others have treated it as parenthetical material. Without it being central to the letter, there are a number of topics that Paul introduces in this section that, though not directly pointed at the Roman audience, are important for his discussion. (a) Paul frames these three chapters in relation to his truth telling (9:1; cf. 10:2), using strong diatribal language that creates a sense of moral urgency. He uses a number of repetitive or interrogative constructions to emphasize the seriousness with which he regards the topics he introduces. They may be additional ideas, but they are expressed with a sense of personal urgency. (b) Paul expresses his sorrow and grief over the separation of his "kindred according to the flesh" (9:3)—that is, Israelites, to whom much was given regarding the law, service, and promises,

---

63. Despite all of the discussion of the purpose and occasion of Romans, the content of these chapters in many ways gives support to the traditional supposition of Romans as a compendium of Pauline thought.

but who are now separated from God. He affirms, in no uncertain language, his belief that God has not rejected his people, the Israelites; that God has a future and continuing purpose for them; and that all Israel will be saved (11:25–26).[64] (c) Paul's deep concern is shown in his citation of numerous Old Testament passages in support of his various claims regarding God's purposes toward Israel. This section of Romans has the highest concentration of Old Testament passages, not just in the letter, but also within the entire Pauline corpus. Paul defends his belief in the salvation of Israel by citing Israel's Scriptures.

6. The use of paraenetic material in establishing Paul's opponents has been recognized by earlier interpreters. The problem of this material is dissociating advice from response, and general from particular statements. The paraenetic section of Romans itself has provided plenty of controversy because it seems to combine general exhortation with specific recommendations based upon specific situations, even though Paul had never visited the city. The paraenesis, however, does include some statements that are consistent with the tenor elsewhere. Paul states that people are not to think of themselves more highly than they should, followed by the use of the body metaphor (12:3–6). On Christian behavior, while there are many general directives, though contextually sensitive, they occur within the context of people distinguishing themselves from others. Paul seems to make these comments more specific in 14:1 to 15:13, concerning the weak and strong. However one characterizes the weak,[65] Paul is clearly on the side of the strong, and he addresses those who seem to be the strong as well, even if the weak are close at hand. He states that the strong should accept the weak even though one is strong (14:1; 15:1).

7. In the closing of the letter, Paul communicates regarding his travel plans (15:25–27), asserts his apostolic calling via his approval of gathering support from the Gentiles (15:28–29), and then greets numerous people in Rome (16:1–23). Paul may simply have been offering an explanation of his travel plans to the Romans, but it is more likely that he is making clear that he has a particular purpose to fulfill with the Jerusalem church on behalf of the churches of Macedonia and Achaia, which have generously given on behalf of

---

64. See K. Haacker, *The Theology of Paul's Letter to the Romans*, NTT (Cambridge: Cambridge University Press, 2003), 77–96.

65. It seems that the best explanation is that they are Jews, probably Jewish Christians, who, returning at the expiration of the edict of Claudius, still wished to practice various Jewish rituals, and the majority of the Roman church, consisting of Gentiles, did not believe that such practices were theologically necessary. For a recent discussion of the issues, including the proposal that the weak are non-Christ-believing Jews, and both groups are still part of the synagogue (with which I disagree), see A. A. Das, *Solving the Romans Debate* (Minneapolis: Fortress, 2007), 115–43.

the needs of the Jerusalem Christians. Paul's noting the seal that he will put on the work of the Gentile churches both validates their work and endorses his ability to offer such a seal of approval (15:28). It is only after he has fulfilled this purpose that, Paul says, he intends to visit Rome on his way to Spain. Finally, Paul creates a closing commendation of himself by offering greetings to a number of people who have had association with the church at Rome, virtually all of whom have non-Jewish names.[66]

The language that Paul uses would have served as a signal to trigger a number of responses in his Roman audience. I will concentrate on the opening of the letter, since it would instigate the initial response of the readers. The salutation of Romans is designed to trigger a response by the readers on several accounts. One is the exceptional length, which draws attention to the description of the author. There is bulk to Paul's expanded self-presentation. Another is the content contained within the salutation, including the significance of the possible citation of traditional material (1:3–4). A third is the structure of the argument, which moves from the appositives regarding the author (elaboration), his calling, and his gospel to providing a theological foundation for this description in terms of God, the Son, and the Spirit. The effect is to place the salutation into a theological framework, in the light of which the subsequent material must be understood. In this sense, the entire rest of the letter makes appeal to a strongly theological foundation. Thus, when the letter turns to the particular issues that Paul mentions, the recipients hear these within the wider theological framework. Whereas traditional analysis probably would see the specific comments by Paul triggering the response, and perhaps motivating a larger theological appeal, I think that the way Paul presents his argument in the larger theological sections provides the framework in which the specific comments are to be heard.

There are five significant signals that make an appeal to the hearer in the light of this introductory framing. (1) The first is Paul's effusive praise of the Romans' faith, which is proclaimed throughout the entire world (1:8). Paul appeals to the Romans as faithful followers of Jesus Christ whose reputation and standing, he says, go beyond the bounds of their immediate location. (2) The second is Paul's first direct address of the reason for his not having visited them yet. The listeners hear him frame this in terms of both his work for the gospel of Jesus Christ, God being his witness to his concern for them, and his genuine desire to visit. (3) The third signal is Paul's second direct response to them regarding his desire to impart a spiritual gift and engage in

66. See P. Lampe, "The Roman Christians of Romans 16," in Donfried, *Romans Debate*, 216–30, esp. 218, on 16:3–16 being Paul's recommendation of himself.

mutual encouragement. This response moves beyond the Romans simply receiving benefit from Paul and appeals to them as engaging in reciprocal benefit. (4) The use of the disclosure formula ("I do not want you to be unaware") in the fourth response (1:13) is designed to trigger a direct acknowledgment by the Romans regarding the sincerity and intentionality of Paul's planning, even though thwarted to this point. However, the readers probably would have also noted that with his planned visit, Paul includes obtaining fruit among the Romans, as he had among the rest of the Gentiles, since he is under obligation to both Greeks and barbarians. Paul shows that his thwarted plans to visit the Romans are related to the very kind of spiritual activities of which he has been speaking, and are a part of a larger plan of his dealing with other Gentiles and of preaching the gospel also to those in Rome. (5) The final appeal is made in the theme statement of 1:16–17, which rounds out reference to the gospel by emphasizing Paul's fervency for it as the power of God for salvation to any believer, both Jew and Gentile.

By this time, the hearers of the letter must have realized that although Paul had addressed particular concerns, he views these within his larger theological agenda. In fact, his use of litotes in 1:16, coming at the end of this progression of thought, may signal to the Romans that he senses they may in fact be ashamed of the gospel, as they have equated it with their self-importance regarding a visit from Paul, rather than with the power of salvation for everyone who believes, both Jews and Gentiles. On the basis of what I have said above regarding the speaker and his expression, I think that this language of the opening of Romans would trigger responses throughout the letter that are geared to these major conceptual notions, especially the inclusion of Jews and Gentiles within the plan of God. This includes those in Rome but goes beyond them, all of this drawn together with the list of those greeted in Romans 16 as a form of proof to his hearers that Paul understands his audience and has close connections with a number of those in Rome.

Concerning the objects and states of affairs represented in the text, one of the major issues in recent study of Romans is the composition of the church. Cases have been argued for a predominantly Gentile church, a predominantly Jewish church, and various degrees of mixed congregation. Recently it has been argued that the church was essentially Gentile.[67] While there is much to commend such a viewpoint, on the basis of the evidence that I have noted above in the way that Paul expresses his position and the Romans would have

---

67. See Das, *Solving the Romans Debate*, esp. 53–114. I note that his treatment of the salutation and thanksgiving of Romans to determine the composition of the audience has a number of similarities with my treatment here in establishing the opponents of Paul.

received it, I do not think that the all-Gentile hypothesis answers all of the questions. I think that the language used in the letter points to a complex social composition along at least three axes: ethnic composition, number, and social hierarchy. The ethnic mix of the congregation seems to be one that includes both Gentiles and Jews, although numerically it appears that the Gentiles are in the vast majority, but the numbers of Jews may be growing. To this point, at least with reference to social hierarchy, the Gentiles appear to be predominant in the Roman church context. However, with the growing numbers of Jews—precipitated by the return after the expiration of Claudius's edict probably around the time of his death in AD 54, and indicated by the numerous references to the Jews alongside the Gentiles, the role that Paul envisions for them, and probably the nature of the issue in 14:1–15:13—there may well be some concern that in the future this organizational structure may change, perhaps radically. This is the state of affairs of the Roman church that Paul addresses.

I believe that my initial analysis of the opponents in Romans was correct, but that this subsequent analysis embeds more securely and expands upon that previous study in significant ways. Paul was indeed meeting opposition around specific points that he addresses directly: frustration over his not coming to Rome sooner, the question of what he would have contributed to the Romans if he were to come, rumors that he was avoiding them, and questions regarding his relationship to Judaism and hence the nature of his apostolic appointment. However, I think that Paul's particular responses to these issues are not themselves alone sufficient to explain the possible opposition in Rome. My foregoing analysis, I believe, shows that these particular issues are embedded in larger theological topics of which these are just the ostensive or apparent or identified points of opposition. The larger matter is the nature of Paul's apostleship, which includes a place for both Jews and Gentiles in the promotion of the gospel—Jews and other Gentiles beyond those Gentiles in Rome. It appears that there were those in Rome who pointed out the specifics noted above as a way of calling into question Paul's entire apostolic calling and mission, taking what was perhaps seen as a personal slight of the church at Rome by Paul as an excuse to do so. This probably indicates not an external set of opponents, but rather a group from within the Roman church that opposes Paul and perhaps is agitating the Gentile believers against Paul and against the returning Jews. Paul chooses to address both the particulars and the larger issues by embedding his personal response within the larger issue of how his calling and gospel are grounded in the work of God, his Son, and the Spirit. This gospel is for the Gentiles at Rome, but more than that, for the Gentiles beyond the scope of Rome, as well as the Jews, who continue to have a future function in God's economy.

Colossians

There have been more proposals regarding the opponents at Colossae than for any of the other Pauline Letters, as Gunther has noted and as continues to be the case in succeeding scholarship. The reason for this is the amount of evidence to be considered. As recently as Christian Stettler's article in the book that I edited, he lists the following examples as pertinent: "a syncretistic, Gnostic group which combines an ascetic veneration of the elements; Jewish ritualism and Jewish speculation about angels; Pythagorean philosophy; the propagation of double membership in church and mystery associations; a group close to the Essenes; Jewish mystics; or even John, the author of Revelation, and his apocalyptic circle; . . . syncretism of Lydia and Phrygia; . . . Middle Platonism (with Jewish elements); . . . Cynic philosophy; . . . different social profiles; . . . [and] the Jewish synagogue(s) at Colossae."[68]

Regarding the author expressing his position by means of language, there are four types of expressions that merit particular attention. The first type is the structural or frame comments, the second is Christian content expressions, the third is directive or behavioral comments, and the fourth type is statements of criticized and endorsed behaviors.

1. The frame or structural comments—besides the usual epistolary format—are used as a means of shaping the argument of the letter. The elements include, first, Paul's mention of Epaphras as the one from whom they learned (1:7), as the one who affirms what they have received (1:6), and as the one who provides the knowledge and impetus for Paul's continued interaction (1:8–9). The second major frame device is Paul's mentioning of his suffering and struggles on their behalf and for those at Laodicea (1:24; 2:1) and his absence (2:5). The third is the shift from indicative to imperative at 2:16, which semantically moves from description to direction. The final one is the closing, in which Paul includes greetings from Aristarchus and Epaphras (4:10, 12).

2. In Colossians, Paul includes a number of important theological statements, some of which may already have been traditional by the time the letter was written. The Christian-content expressions are for the most part confined to the body of the letter (1:13–2:15). The major tenets of Christian content include Paul's description of Christ as the means of deliverance and redemption, as the image of God, the instrument of creation, the one with precedence, the head of the church, the firstborn from the dead, the one in whom the fullness of God dwells, the means of reconciliation, the one in whom they are made complete, circumcised, and buried and raised; and Paul's description

---

68. C. Stettler, "The Opponents at Colossae," in Porter, *Paul and His Opponents*, 170–72. For the outline of Colossians, see Porter, *Apostle Paul*, chap. 11. I take Colossians as written by Paul. See Porter, *Paul*, chap. 11.

of the church as the body, of which Paul is a servant in making known the hidden mystery of God, which is Christ. Paul offers the Christian content as if it is in competition with another philosophy (2:8), which is characterized as empty deception and human tradition that follows other principles (labeled the "principles" [στοιχεῖα] of the world; 2:8, 20) and could take them captive (cf. 3:2, which speaks of setting the mind on the things above).

3. Paul begins his directive or behavioral comments at 2:16, the start of the paraenetic section of the letter. As noted above, paraenesis has traditionally proved difficult for determination of its relation to establishment of opponents. However, Paul's frequent use of a number of directive statements seems far more directional than general exhortation. His directive statements include 2:16, 18, 20 (by means of a question); 3:1, 2, 5, 8, 9, 12, 15, 16, 18, 19, 20, 21, 22, 23; 4:1, 2, 5. Paul is clearly engaging in directive expression aimed at his readers.

4. These directive statements are focused upon such issues as food and drink and festivals (2:16), self-abasement and worship of angels (2:18), decrees regarding abstention (2:20–21), focusing on the things above (3:1–2), abnegating bodily desires (3:5), ridding oneself of untoward and destructive emotions and responses (3:8–9), adopting Christian responses and behaviors (3:12–17), following orderly social behavior (3:18–4:1), and practicing prudent behavior (4:2–6). Virtually all of the condemned behaviors are called into question or corrected by Paul through extension, some labeled as being shadows of what is coming (2:17), fraudulent (2:18), inflated (2:18), unattached to Christ (2:19), having the appearance of wisdom (2:23), and being of no value (2:23), while the other behaviors are endorsed.

Paul's language signals certain anticipated responses by his hearers. Paul uses the frame to link the behavior of the Colossians to his ministry, whether direct or mediated by means of Epaphras. By appealing to Epaphras, Paul signals to the audience that he is monitoring their belief and behavior. More to the point is the nature of what is being monitored. I think that the doctrinal instruction is geared to expand the knowledge of Christ and the church among the Colossians, although the way in which Paul presents it clearly signals that this is being given in response to some other teaching or teachings. The material in the paraenetic portion of the letter is presented as directives. Although there is some indication of overlap with the material in the body of the letter, these directives seem much more focused on specific behavior than on general exhortation or doctrine. They cover a range of topics, some of them unique to Colossians and others shared with other Pauline Letters. Paul's strong division between description and direction conveys a strong separation between the two types of material, with the directive material much more particularized and specific, as opposed to the broader notions of the cosmic function of Christ and the nature of his church.

In assessing the relationship of the text to the events and states of affairs, the interpreter must ask whether the situation represented is gnostic, some other type of philosophy (Platonic, Stoic, Pythagorean), Jewish in origin, Hellenistic and pagan, or perhaps something syncretistic. All these and more have been proposed. Recent trends try to make all of the pieces fit together into a syncretistic conflation of strands from a variety of sources.[69] There are clearly some reasons for such a perspective, including the serial way that all of the evidence is presented, the sense of overlap and integration among the various competing factors, the use of positive and negative statements intertwined together, and some common language. No doubt the general tenor of Paul's content is to differentiate the earthly from the heavenly, and to endorse Christ as the one who bridges the gap. He is the fulfillment and only source of the upper level, while earthly things and behaviors are at the human level and threaten to encumber the believer. Does this match any particular oppositional group? There are some clear potential overlaps with gnosticism, but one finds similar differentiations in other philosophies of the time.[70] There are also potential overlaps with any number of different types of thinking. However, the question is whether this was genuinely syncretistic, or simply a reflection of the complex situation in which the church at Colossae found itself.[71] Paul apparently structures the letter to indicate that he had less of a concern for doctrinal issues and more of a concern for behavioral ones, hence his numerous references to behaving in an appropriate manner, regardless of the particular issue (e.g., 1:10; 2:6; 4:5). It may seem less systematic and predictable to take such a view, but it at least seems consistent with the evidence.

Conclusion

I wish to conclude by addressing two issues. First, there is the method that I have used to discuss the Pauline opponents. The use of this method grew out of my perception of the relatively stagnant situation in which discussion of the

69. Arnold, *Colossian Syncretism*, is only one of those to make this proposal.

70. It is fair to say that the gnostic explanation probably has been the most common and widespread. Some proponents include (see Stettler's article) W. G. Kümmel, *Introduction to the New Testament*, trans. H. C. Kee (Nashville: Abingdon, 1975), 338–40; M. Goulder, "Colossians and Barbelo," *NTS* 41 (1995): 601–19. Those who have found parallels in some philosophies of the time include DeMaris, *Colossian Controversy* (Middle Platonism with Jewish elements); and Martin, *Philosophy and Empty Deceit* (Cynic philosophy).

71. The social, religious, and philosophical issues present in Asia Minor are noteworthy and diverse. See S. Mitchell, *Anatolia: Land, Men, and Gods in Asia Minor*, 2 vols. (Oxford: Clarendon, 1993).

Pauline opponents found itself. I wondered whether another method, one that was more consciously attuned to the various acknowledged and unacknowledged factors in discussing Paul's opponents, would provide a way forward in such discussion. One of the primary tasks of such a method was to recognize the importance of the individual discourse (a Pauline letter) in such a discussion, and to find a means to differentiate some of the factors that were often conflated, including the perspective of the author and the recipients, and the external reality—all this by means of use of language. I think that Bühler's organon method has some important merit because it forces the interpreter to differentiate between the use of language by the author, how this language would be perceived by the reader or hearer, and how the language apart from either author or recipient coordinates with these events and states of affairs. The task is complicated by the need to interpret the use of language from the several different perspectives, switching from speaker to hearer, though the language remains the same, with expressions instantiating their meanings. I believe that this method, though it does not eliminate the problem of mirror reading, helps to nuance and distinguish the relationship of the discourse and the events and states of affairs, in distinction from the author and the reader. I think that the method has been moderately successful in these respects.

However, I think that there are some limitations of the method that also need to be addressed.[72] One of the limitations of Bühler's method includes calibration of suitable linguistic criteria to give access to the particular characteristics of the expressive language of the author, in order to distinguish it from the appellative force that such language has on the receiver. I have only been able to hint at such a system here, for example, by differentiating between the force of directive language when used by the speaker in expressing a desire to direct the action of the hearer, and the effect of the use of the directive on the hearer's response—whether that response is welcomed or compelled or resisted. I believe that such an exercise would aid greatly in attempting to differentiate the functional force and effect of the use of language.[73]

Second, whether the method has produced any useful conclusions is another matter altogether. This is one of the dangers of biblical interpretation—the "damned if you do and damned if you don't" syndrome. If you arrive at new

---

72. To be fair to Bühler, he wished to write two further volumes on appeal and representation, besides the one on expression, but was prevented from doing so by the tragic circumstances of his life.

73. One of Halliday's objections to Bühler's method is that "Bühler is not attempting to explain the linguistic system in functional terms," but that he is attempting to perform a psycholinguistic analysis. Halliday notes that, though the representational function is similar to his own ideational, Halliday has to add the textual component to deal with texts (Halliday, *Language as Social Semiotic*, 48). This element is clearly missing in Bühler's analysis.

interpretations, they are easily dismissed, because the history of critical scholarship has not arrived at them already and so they are inherently suspect. If you arrive at interpretations similar to those discovered by previous or more conventional means, these are also easily dismissed, because they do not add to knowledge and have already been discovered by other means. I believe that some of both types of conclusions have been reached by this exploratory approach. On the one hand, I am encouraged to think that Philemon should perhaps be included within the discussion of the Pauline opponents, because the language of the letter indicates that Paul is anticipating and attempting to forestall such opposition by means of his various types of appeal and persuasion. In some ways this is a new conclusion, but it requires that we shift the tacit definition of Pauline opposition to that of an individual within the church, in anticipation of the actual act of opposition. Further, the Letter to the Romans is not always included in such studies of Paul's opponents. Building on work that I have previously done, I believe that including it is legitimate on the basis of Paul's language, the triggers that would have been pulled by this language within the Roman church, and the probable states of affairs; hence my previous conclusions can be expanded and developed further. The result is that what at first appeared to be primarily a question of personal and nontheological opposition over Paul's visit and his role as apostle can be seen as indicating, to Paul at least, a more theologically significant problem grounded in the nature of the gospel that he is proclaiming and its grounding in God, Son, and Spirit.

On the other hand, I note also that with Colossians it is hard to say anything more than has already been said regarding Paul's opponents. The surfeit of previous proposals makes it difficult to form a new synthesis that goes beyond the previous ones. In that sense, the method serves to reinforce previously ascertained conclusions. If there is a contribution that this method makes in this regard, it is that perhaps rather than pushing for the synthesis of the evidence, which usually (in recent times) ends up with the syncretistic hypothesis, the method indicates that in the absence of other firm indicators that compel such amalgamation, one should confine oneself to the evidence; this means leaving the Pauline opposition as one that is, at the least, multifaceted and perhaps, at the most, several different opponents.

18

1 Timothy 2:8

Holy Hands or Holy Raising?

First Timothy 2:8 reads, τοὺς ἄνδρας ἐν παντὶ τόπῳ ἐπαίροντας ὁσίους χεῖρας. In most English versions it is translated as "men . . . raising holy hands" (see, e.g., RSV, ESV, AV, NIV, NASB, JB, CEB, Weymouth, Phillips, Moffatt, Williams, Berkeley), with the adjective "holy" modifying the noun "hands."[1] Only a few translations take it otherwise, such as the NEB: "men of the congregation, who shall lift up their hands with a pure intention"; or the GNB: "men who are dedicated to God and can lift up their hands." Of course, these translations provide no rationale for these singular renderings.

Likewise, virtually no commentator[2] draws attention to the fact that the usual interpretation of this construction understands the adjective ὁσίους as

1. See also Twentieth Century New Testament and Conybeare.

2. For example, H. Alford, *Alford's Greek Testament: An Exegetical and Critical Commentary*, 4 vols. (London: Rivingtons, 1844–57; rev. ed., 1874–75; repr., Grand Rapids: Guardian Press, 1976), 3:317, who disputes G. B. Winer (see below); J. E. Huther, *Critical and Exegetical Hand-Book to the Epistles to Timothy and Titus*, trans. D. Hunter (New York: Funk & Wagnalls, 1885); H. P. Liddon, *Explanatory Analysis of St. Paul's First Epistle to Timothy* (London: Longmans, Green, 1907; repr., Minneapolis: Klock & Klock, 1978); N. J. D. White, "The First and Second Epistles to Timothy and the Epistle to Titus," in vol. 4 of *The Expositor's Greek Testament*, ed. W. R. Nicoll (London: Hodder & Stoughton, 1912; repr., Grand Rapids: Eerdmans, 1980),

modifying the noun χεῖρας, even though grammatically the adjective could well modify the participle, ἐπαίροντας, which in (traditional) predicate structure modifies the articular noun τοὺς ἄνδρας. According to the terminology of OpenText.org, the first analysis takes the adjective (ὁσίους) as a definer

---

55–202; B. Weiss, *Die Briefe Pauli an Timotheus und Titus*, 7th ed., KEK 11 (Göttingen: Vandenhoeck & Ruprecht, 1902), 17, who, against G. B. Winer (see below), says that the words ὁσίους and χεῖρας "gehört sicher zusammen"; R. St. J. Parry, *The Pastoral Epistles: With Introduction, Text and Commentary* (Cambridge: Cambridge University Press, 1920); D. G. Wohlenberg, *Die Pastoralbriefe*, 3rd ed., KNT 13 (Leipzig: Deichertsche, 1923); W. Lock, *A Critical and Exegetical Commentary on the Pastoral Epistles*, ICC (Edinburgh: T&T Clark, 1924); E. F. Scott, *The Pastoral Epistles*, MNTC (London: Hodder & Stoughton, 1936); R. Falconer, *The Pastoral Epistles* (Oxford: Clarendon, 1937); C. Spicq, *Saint Paul: Les Épîtres pastorales*, ÉBib (Paris: Gabalda, 1947), 65, who gives examples; B. S. Easton, *The Pastoral Epistles: Introduction, Translation, Commentary and Word Studies* (London: SCM, 1948); M. Dibelius and H. Conzelmann, *The Pastoral Epistles: A Commentary on the Pastoral Epistles*, trans. P. Buttolph and A. Yarbro, ed. H. Koester, Hermeneia (Philadelphia: Fortress, 1972); D. Guthrie, *The Pastoral Epistles*, 2nd ed., TNTC (London: Tyndale, 1990); J. N. D. Kelly, *A Commentary on the Pastoral Epistles*, BNTC (London: A&C Black, 1963); C. K. Barrett, *The Pastoral Epistles in the New English Bible* (Oxford: Clarendon, 1963), 53, who gives the NEB translation and then says, "literally, to 'lift up holy hands'"; G. Holtz, *Die Pastoralbriefe*, THNT 13 (Berlin: Evangelische Verlagsanstalt, 1966); A. T. Hanson, *The Pastoral Letters: Commentary on the First and Second Letters to Timothy and the Letter to Titus*, CBC (Cambridge: Cambridge University Press, 1966); N. Brox, *Die Pastoralbriefe: Übersetzt und Erklärt*, 4th ed., RNT 7/2 (Regensburg: Pustet, 1969); J. L. Houlden, *The Pastoral Epistles: I and II Timothy, Titus*, PelNTC (Harmondsworth: Penguin, 1976), 64–70, who notes that ὅσιος means "pious" and "devout" rather than "sacred" (ἅγιος); V. Hasler, *Die Briefe an Timotheus und Titus (Pastoralbriefe)*, ZB 12 (Zurich: Theologischer Verlag, 1978); R. Earle, "1 Timothy," in vol. 11 of *The Expositor's Bible Commentary*, ed. F. E. Gaebelein (Grand Rapids: Zondervan, 1978), 339–90; J. Jeremias and A. Strobel, *Die Briefe an Timotheus und Titus; Der Brief an die Hebräer*, 12th ed., NTD 9 (Göttingen: Vandenhoeck & Ruprecht, 1981); G. D. Fee, *1 and 2 Timothy, Titus*, GNC (San Francisco: Harper & Row, 1984); J. Roloff, *Der erste Brief an Timotheus*, EKK 15 (Zurich: Benziger, 1988); T. C. Oden, *First and Second Timothy and Titus*, IBC (Louisville: John Knox, 1989); G. W. Knight III, *The Pastoral Epistles*, NIGTC (Grand Rapids: Eerdmans, 1992); I. H. Marshall with P. H. Towner, *A Critical and Exegetical Commentary on the Pastoral Epistles*, ICC (Edinburgh: T&T Clark, 1999); W. D. Mounce, *Pastoral Epistles*, WBC 46 (Nashville: Nelson, 2000); J. D. Quinn and W. C. Wacker, *The First and Second Letters to Timothy: A New Translation with Notes and Commentary*, ECC (Grand Rapids: Eerdmans, 2000); J. D. G. Dunn, "The First and Second Letters to Timothy and the Letter to Titus," in vol. 11 of *The New Interpreter's Bible*, ed. L. E. Keck (Nashville: Abingdon, 2000), 773–879; L. T. Johnson, *The First and Second Letters to Timothy*, AB 35A (New York: Doubleday, 2001), 198, though he renders the verse "hands lifted up with piety"; B. Witherington III, *Letters and Homilies for Hellenized Christians*, vol. 1, *A Socio-Rhetorical Commentary on Titus, 1–2 Timothy, and 1–3 John* (Downers Grove, IL: InterVarsity; Nottingham: Apollos, 2001); R. F. Collins, *1 and 2 Timothy and Titus: A Commentary*, NTL (Louisville: Westminster John Knox, 2002); A. J. Köstenberger, "1 Timothy," in vol. 12 of *The Expositor's Bible Commentary*, ed. T. Longman III and D. E. Garland, rev. ed. (Grand Rapids: Zondervan, 2006), 487–561; P. H. Towner, *The Letters to Timothy and Titus*, NICNT (Grand Rapids: Eerdmans, 2006); B. Fiore, *The Pastoral Epistles: First Timothy, Second Timothy, Titus*, SP 12 (Collegeville, MN: Liturgical Press, 2007). There are other commentaries, but the point is well enough made regarding scholarship on this issue.

of its head term (χεῖρας), with the entire word group (ὁσίους χεῖρας) as the Complement of a Predicator (ἐπαίροντας), functioning as a rank-shifted Adjunct within a rank-shifted structure that is the Complement of the Predicator βούλομαι. The second analysis takes the adjective (ὁσίους) as a definer of its preceding head term (ἐπαίροντας), with the noun χεῖρας now its own one-word word group. This can be displayed as either [[ἐπαίροντας] [ὁσίους χεῖρας]] or [[ἐπαίροντας ὁσίους] [χεῖρας]]. The word order, while favoring ὁσίους modifying χεῖρας, is not decisive. Martin Dibelius and Hans Conzelmann, in one of a few modern commentaries with detailed discussion of the passage, devote an extended footnote to ὅσιος, claiming that "purity of the hands" is found in a variety of literature, and that the expression "to raise pure hands to heaven" "seems to have been widely used" in the sense of moral purity.[3] But of the examples cited by them, only four are in Greek, and of these only two have an expression using the significant words found in 1 Timothy 2:8 (Galen, *De Antidotis* 2.7; Athenagoras, *Suppl.* [= *Legatio*] 13.3 [not 13.2]). Of these only Athenagoras, *Legatio* 13.3 collocates ὅσιος and χείρ. Thus, one cannot rely upon the commentaries for signaling the difficulties with this construction. If it is not virtually neglected, a tendential interpretation is often assumed.

Perhaps one of the major reasons for this lack of grammatical commentary rests with the grammarians of the Greek New Testament. Most neglect to take the issue seriously, either by ignoring it or by providing potentially misleading discussion of the grammatical structure. For example, Alexander Buttmann states, "ὁσίους, too, in 1 Tim. ii.8, as its very position indicates, is to be joined to χεῖρας, as is done by most of the commentators and the ancients. The Fem. does not occur elsewhere."[4] But in fact, the word order is indecisive, since in Greek a modifier such as an adjective can precede or follow the word that it modifies, and the ancient evidence warrants reconsideration (see below).

A. T. Robertson similarly places ὅσιος under the category of "adjectives with two terminations," while admitting that "ὁσίους may be construed with ἐπαίροντας instead of χεῖρας."[5] He does not satisfactorily resolve the issue. In ancient Greek (see below) this adjective has two and three terminations, not just the two that Robertson's facile categories suggest. Georg Winer is the only grammarian consulted by me who fully appreciates the potential ambiguity of the construction: "But in 1 Tim. ii.8, ἐπαίροντας ὁσίους χεῖρας (where some

3. Dibelius and Conzelmann, *Pastoral Epistles*, 44n2.
4. A. Buttmann, *A Grammar of the New Testament Greek*, trans. J. H. Thayer (Andover, MA: Draper, 1880), 26. According to Buttmann, like ἐπαίροντας, ὁσίους must be considered of common gender, with two terminations in the New Testament, not three.
5. A. T. Robertson, *A Grammar of the Greek New Testament in the Light of Historical Research*, 4th ed. (Nashville: Broadman, 1934), 273.

MSS. have ὁσίας), ὁσίους may be joined with ἐπαίροντας; though Fritzsche is wrong in maintaining that this *must* be the construction (*Rom*. III.161)."[6] But in a telling footnote the translator and editor, W. F. Moulton, says in brackets, "as to 1 Tim. ii.8 see Ellicott in 10c."[7] This prompted James Hope Moulton and Wibert Francis Howard to state, "Ὅσιος apparently has acc. fem. pl. -ους; in 1 Tim 2[8], except in some cursives (incl. 33 and 1). Here Winer admitted the possibility of Fritzsche's construction (ὁσίους with ἐπαίροντας): against this W. F. Moulton referred to Ellicott *in loc*. The fem. has no parallel here, not even in LXX, but an isolated slip, affected by the analogy of other adj. in -ιος fem., is not strange."[8] Moulton's comment that the feminine has no parallel in the New Testament is correct (see below). With such little encouragement in the grammars, however, it is no wonder that there has not been significant discussion of this construction in the commentaries.

In the light of the grammatical ambiguity, the ancient Greek evidence is worth examining to see if such confident neglect is warranted. I do not here dispute that ὁσίους may well modify χεῖρας, since ὁσίους may serve as the feminine as well as the masculine form of the adjective (they are syncretized by some writers). However, on the basis of how these words collocate in Greek literature outside of the New Testament, the varied collocations in the early church writers, and the ambiguity of the syntax, the usual translational understanding is open to serious question. There is good reason to believe that the adjective ὁσίους should be analyzed as masculine in gender, thus describing the act of raising (and by implication those who raise their hands), rather than as feminine and thus describing the hands themselves.[9]

In ancient Greek literature, as far as the *Thesaurus linguae Graecae* (*TLG*) database bears witness (up to the early fifth century AD), the limited use of the root ὁσι- with χείρ in syntactically bound configurations not separated by more than ten characters attests to use of both the masculine and the feminine

---

6. G. B. Winer, *A Treatise on the Grammar of New Testament Greek, Regarded as a Sure Basis for New Testament Exegesis*, trans. W. F. Moulton, 3rd ed. (Edinburgh: T&T Clark, 1882), 80. This is rendered faithfully from the German: G. B. Winer, *Grammatik des neutestamentlichen Sprachidioms*, 6th ed. (Leipzig: Vogel, 1855), 64.

7. Winer, *Treatise*, 80n3. Compare C. J. Ellicott, *Critical and Grammatical Commentary on the Pastoral Epistles* (Boston: Draper & Halliday, 1867), 32: "It is singular that Winer . . . should suggest the possibility of so awkward a connection as ὁσίους ('religione perfusos,' Fritz.) with ἐπαιρ., and still more so that Fritz., *Rom*. Vol. III. p. 1, should actually adopt it, when the common Attic use of adjectives in -ιος, &c. (Elmsl. Eur[ipides] *Heracl[idae]* 245), with only two terminations is so distinctly found in the NT (ver. 9; see Winer *l.c.*), and gives so good a sense."

8. J. H. Moulton and W. F. Howard, *A Grammar of New Testament Greek*, vol. 2, *Accidence and Word-Formation* (Edinburgh: T&T Clark, 1929), 157.

9. Of course, if the adverb ὁσίως had been used, the syntax would be clearer. That is not the point. The question is whether the adjective modifies the following noun or the preceding participle.

forms of the adjective. In secular writers, in the three recorded instances, ὅσια (the feminine form) is always found when the ὁσι-root is linked with χείρ. It is only in Christian writers, many of whom apparently assumed a particular grammatical relation, that the so-called masculine form of the adjective is understood to be feminine in gender, although the feminine form also appears in significant numbers. There are also a number of quotations of 1 Timothy 2:8 that evidence the same ambiguity as the original passage. In the New Testament, as Moulton implied, the ὁσι-root is never found in its feminine form (see Acts 2:27; 13:34, 35; Titus 1:8; Heb. 7:26; Rev. 15:4; 16:5). But there is no instance with the potential ambiguity of 1 Timothy 2:8.

The evidence from ancient Greek writers outside of the New Testament is as follows:

A. Secular writers (all with the feminine form of the adjective)
  1. *Iusiurandum medicum* (fifth–fourth century BC?) 8: ὁσίας . . . χείρας (part of a quotation from a Hippocratic medical oath).
  2. Heliodorus Trag. (pre–first century BC), *Fragmenta* 4171.6: ὁσίας . . . χείρας (the same in all essential points as 1 above).
  3. Galen (second century AD), *De Antidotis* 2.7 (14.145.16): ὁσίας . . . χείρας (the same in all essential points as 1 and 2 above).

B. Christian writers
  1. Ambiguous instances as in 1 Timothy 2:8 (ἐπαίροντας ὁσίους χείρας).
    a. Origen (second–third century AD), *De oratione* 9.1.9; 31.1.10; *In Jeremiam* 5.9.12; *Fragmenta in Jeremiam* 68.24.
    b. Eusebius (fourth century AD), *Commentario in Psalmos* 23.608.17–18; 23.889.23.
    c. Athanasius (fourth century AD), *Homilia de semente* 28.168.46–47.
    d. Basilius (Basil the Great, fourth century AD), *Enarratio in prophetam Isaiam* 1.35.12; *Asceticon magnum sive Quaestiones* 31.1216.38; *Regulae morales* 31.785.45.
    e. John Chrysostom (fourth–fifth century AD), *In Genesim* 53.296.42; 53.318.27–28; *Expositiones in Psalmos* 55.429.50–51; *In Matthaeum* 57.284.19; 58.516.56–57; *In epistulam i ad Timotheum* 62.539.21; 62.539.38, 57.
  2. Masculine and feminine forms syncretized (ὁσίους χείρας)
    a. Athenagoras (second century AD), *Legatio* 13.3.3, an apparent allusion to 1 Timothy 2:8–9,[10] although there is little in the context to make the connection a strong one.

---

10. So W. R. Schoedel, *Athenagoras: Legatio; and, De resurrectione* (Oxford: Clarendon, 1972), ad loc. and index.

b. Origen (second–third century AD), *Contra Celsum* 3.60.4; *Fragmenta in Psalmos 1–150* 23.4.6; *Selecta in Psalmos* 12.1232.39–40; 12.1258.25; 12.1652.41; *Commentarii in evangelium Joannis* 28.5.36.3—all apparent citations or paraphrases of 1 Timothy 2:8.

c. Hippolytus (third century AD), *Commentarium in Danielem* 3.24.7.4—citing 1 Timothy 2:8.

d. Pseudo-Justin Martyr (third–fifth century AD), *Quaestiones et responsiones ad orthodoxos* 470.D.6, citation of 1 Timothy 2:8.

e. Eusebius (fourth century AD), *Commentario in Psalmos* 23.889.21; 23.1272.12–13; 24.44.22—all apparently based upon 1 Timothy 2:8.

f. (Pseudo-)Macarius (fourth century AD), *Sermo* 28 167.25, citation of 1 Timothy 2:8.

g. Didymus Caecus (fourth century AD), *Commentarii in Job* 303.27; *Fragmenta in Psalmos* 571.5; *In Genesim* 85.21—citing or paraphrasing 1 Timothy 2:8.

h. Evagrius (fourth century AD), *De malignis cogitationibus* 32.7—paraphrasing 1 Timothy 2:8.

i. John Chrysostom (fourth–fifth century AD), *De cruce et latrone (homilia 1)* 49.409.24, 26; *In principium Actorum* 51.83.59–60; *In Genesim* 53.282.46; 54.447.52; *In Matthaeum* 57.313.19; *In epistulam i ad Timotheum* 62.540.29, 55; *In Psalmos 101–107* 55.645.65; *Interpretatio in Danielem prophetam* 56.227.13; *De circo* 59.570.61—all but the last paraphrases of 1 Timothy 2:8.

3. Feminine form

a. Origen (second–third century AD), *De oratione* 2.2.11 (ἐπαίροντας ὁσίας χεῖρας); 9.1.2 (ὁσίας χεῖρας)—both citations of 1 Timothy 2:8.

b. Athanasius (fourth century AD), *Epistulae ad Castorem* 28.892.29 (ὁσίας χεῖρας), a citation of 1 Timothy 2:8.

c. Gregory of Nazianzus (fourth century AD), *Epigrammata* (both instances cited in the *Greek Anthology*) 8.215.4 (χεῖρα . . . ὁσίην); 8.218.4 (χείρεσιν . . . ὁσίαις); *Carmina dogmatica* 510.15 (ὁσίας χεῖρας ἐπαίρων).

d. John Chrysostom (fourth–fifth century AD), *De cruce et latrone (homilia 2)* 49.401.3 (ἐπαίροντας ὁσίας χεῖρας); 49.401.5 (ἐπαίρειν χεῖρας ὁσίας), both citations of 1 Timothy 2:8.

Whereas the formal linguistic evidence for reading ὁσίους as feminine or masculine in 1 Timothy 2:8 could point in either direction, and although traditionally many interpreters even from earliest times have taken the form in 1 Timothy 2:8 as feminine, the reading may plausibly be understood as masculine. The evidence for this is found, first, in the fact that virtually all examples from Christian writers are quotations or paraphrases of 1 Timothy 2:8, including those that use the feminine form. This use of the feminine form in citation of a New Testament passage by early church fathers suggests not only that the feminine form remained viable, but also that the tradition of the syncretized form linked with the noun rather than the participle was established early, perhaps misguiding some subsequent interpreters.

Second, the use by several early Christian writers of the feminine form ὁσίας raises the question of why an author would use the feminine as opposed to the masculine or syncretized form. Use of the masculine or syncretized form could simply reflect citation of the ambiguous New Testament passage. Use of the feminine form, however, raises further possibilities. Later interpreters may have used the feminine form to ensure that the reader knew that the adjective modified the noun, especially if it was a distinct grammatical possibility that it modified the participle; they may have used it to disambiguate the New Testament quotation by showing their understanding of it; they may have used it in distinction to the clear possibility—in the light of contemporary use by secular authors—that ὁσίους was masculine and normally would be taken as modifying the participle.[11] Three of the early Christian authors—Origen, Athanasius, and John Chrysostom—use both the masculine and the feminine forms of the adjective, suggesting that there may have been a distinction in the use of the two forms.

Third, the clear (though admittedly small) evidence from secular writers, both before and after the New Testament era, is that whenever a form of ὁσι- collocates with χείρ, the feminine form is used. The secular usage is formulaic, but it should be given serious consideration as illustrating contemporary understanding of the phrasing.

Fourth, the context of 1 Timothy 2, with its concern for proper Christian behavior, further suggests that the adjective is masculine. The author's emphasis is upon instructing his reader(s) to perform acts of Christian piety (prayers, petitions, thanksgivings) for all persons (vv. 1–2). His reader(s) are doing the good and acceptable thing by their behavior (v. 3)—that is, by following the author's example (v. 7) and, for women, by adorning themselves properly (v. 9). The emphasis is clearly upon the people and the quality of their actions.

---

11. Hypercorrection to Attic standards is unlikely, since in Attic Greek the adjective had two and three endings, as it apparently did in later usage as well.

Conclusion

The foregoing evidence, when taken as a whole, confirms the judgment that in 1 Timothy 2:8 the adjective ὁσίους may well modify the participle ἐπαίροντας rather than the noun χεῖρας. A survey of the extrabiblical Greek evidence serves as a corrective to some apparently inaccurate grammatical comments and helps to establish the basis of this reinterpretation. Therefore, the translational understanding of the passage should not be "men lifting holy hands" but something wooden and expressive like "holy lifters of [their] hands" or "holy men lifting [their] hands" or, capturing the adverbial sense of the adjectival modifier, "men lifting [their] hands in holiness."

19

Greek Word Order

Still an Unexplored Area in New Testament Studies?

Introduction

Is Greek word order still an unexplored area in New Testament studies? The brief answer is yes. I could perhaps leave the issue at this point if it were not for the fact that the question alludes to an article that I published in 1993, titled "Word Order and Clause Structure in New Testament Greek: An Unexplored Area of Greek Linguistics Using Philippians as a Test Case."[1] Since this article was written such a long time ago (so it seems to me, at least), my affirmative response raises a more specific question: *Why* is Greek word order still an unexplored area? This is not nearly as easy to answer as the first question. It demands not merely a simple yes or no, but an explicit discussion of causality. In what follows, I will indicate some of the conditions under which any exploration must be pursued in order to qualify as an adequate exploration. This will, I hope, clarify why I think Greek word order remains unexplored.[2]

---

1. S. E. Porter, "Word Order and Clause Structure in New Testament Greek: An Unexplored Area of Greek Linguistics Using Philippians as a Test Case," *FN* 6 (1993): 177–206.

2. For a recent and comprehensive overview of the subject, see J. J. Song, *Word Order*, RSL (Cambridge: Cambridge University Press, 2012). I am pleased to note that some of the types

347

A Brief History of the Study of Greek Word Order

The study of Greek word order is not a recent phenomenon. The ancients themselves made observations regarding word order. Many of these observations were couched in terms of what has come to be labeled "stylistics," a category to which I will return below. However, the ancients also identified some specific possibilities for word order. For example, Aristotle and Longinus made comments on parataxis (Aristotle, *Rhet.* 1409AB; Longinus, *Subl.* 21), and Dionysius of Halicarnassus (*Or.* 14.5) noted hyperbaton (as in Homer).

In the last two hundred years a great many studies have focused on ancient Greek word order.[3] There have been, for example, studies concerned with the placement of individual words. These include, for example, Thomas Middleton's classic study of the use of the article and its placement in relation to a variety of substantives and modifiers,[4] and now two more recent studies by Daniel Wallace and Ronald Peters;[5] and a number of studies of the placement and use of particles (including conjunctions) by such scholars as D. B. Monro, J. D. Denniston, A. C. Moorhouse, Margaret Thrall, Jerker Blomqvist, Susumu Kuno, K. J. Dover, J. Wills, Stephanie Black, Stanley Porter and Matthew Brook O'Donnell;[6] the placement of the interrogative by

---

of distinctions that I made in my 1993 article are also noted in Song's treatment, such as the necessity of having alternative typology patterns.

3. Here I draw heavily upon the compilation of bibliographical data found in I. S. C. Kwong, *The Word Order of the Gospel of Luke: Its Foregrounded Messages*, LNTS 298 (London: T&T Clark, 2005), esp. 10–29. I rely heavily upon his descriptions of the content of many of these works, although the categories of arrangement are my own. I am excluding the grammars of classical and New Testament Greek, even though they often comment on word order, as well as unpublished theses and dissertations. Such a treatment, of course, cannot be complete, nor does it try to be.

4. T. F. Middleton, *The Doctrine of the Greek Article Applied to the Criticism and Illustration of the New Testament*, ed. H. J. Rose (London: Deighton, Bell, 1833), esp. 71–88.

5. D. B. Wallace, *Granville Sharp's Canon and Its Kin: Semantics and Significance*, SBG 14 (New York: Peter Lang, 2009); R. D. Peters, *The Greek Article: A Functional Grammar of ὁ-Items in the Greek New Testament with Special Emphasis on the Greek Article*, LBS 9 (Leiden: Brill, 2014).

6. D. B. Monro, *A Grammar of the Homeric Dialect*, 2nd ed. (Oxford: Clarendon, 1891), 335–38; J. D. Denniston, *The Greek Particles*, 2nd ed. (Oxford: Oxford University Press, 1954), esp. lviii–lxi; A. C. Moorhouse, *Studies in the Greek Negatives* (Cardiff: University of Wales Press, 1959), 69–156; M. E. Thrall, *Greek Particles in the New Testament: Linguistic and Exegetical Studies*, NTTS 3 (Leiden: Brill, 1962), 34–40; J. Blomqvist, *Greek Particles in Hellenistic Prose* (Lund: Berlingska Boktryckeriet, 1969), 108–27; S. Kuno, "The Position of Relative Clauses and Conjunctions," *LI* 5 (1974): 117–36; K. J. Dover, "Abnormal Word Order in Attic Comedy," *CQ* 35 (1985): 324–43; J. Wills, "Homeric Particle Order," *HS* 106 (1993): 61–81; S. L. Black, *Sentence Conjunctions in the Gospel of Matthew: καί, δέ, τότε, γάρ, οὖν and Asyndeton in Narrative Discourse*, JSNTSup 216, SNTG 9 (Sheffield: Sheffield Academic Press, 2002); S. E. Porter and M. B. O'Donnell, "Conjunctions, Clines and Levels of Discourse," *FN* 20 (2007): 3–14.

G. Thompson;[7] the placement of the vocative by J. Banker;[8] the syntax of the vocative by Porter and O'Donnell;[9] and the use of clitics by Graham Dunn,[10] Mark Janse,[11] and A. Taylor.[12] There have also been a number of studies that have concentrated upon what we might call the phrase or word group. These include studies of the ordering of adjective and noun by G. D. Kilpatrick, and studies by L. Bergson, Stanley Porter, Daniel Wallace, W. G. Pierpont, and H. H. Hess.[13]

Most of the studies of word order, however, have concentrated on clausal constituents in some form. These include studies of infinitive clauses with two elements in the accusative by H. R. Moeller and A. Kramer, Jeffrey Reed, and P. W. Cheung;[14] studies of the double accusative as object of a finite verb by Daniel Wallace;[15] study of hyperbaton by A. M. Devine and

---

7. G. Thompson, "The Postponement of Interrogatives in Attic Drama," *CQ* 33 (1939): 147–52.

8. J. Banker, "The Position of the Vocative *adelphoi* in the Clause," *START* 11 (1984): 29–36.

9. S. E. Porter and M. B. O'Donnell, "The Vocative Case in Greek: Addressing the Case at Hand," in *Grammatica intellectio Scripturae: Saggi filologici di Greco biblico in onore di Lino Cignelli OFM*, ed. R. Pierri, SBFA 68 (Jerusalem: Franciscan Printing Press, 2006), 35–48.

10. G. Dunn, "Enclitic Pronoun Movement and the Ancient Greek Sentence Accent," *Glotta* 67 (1989): 1–19.

11. M. Janse, "La phrase segmentée en grec ancien: Le témoignage des enclitiques," *BSLP* 86, no. 1 (1991): xiv–xvi; Janse, "La position des pronoms personnels enclitiques en grec neo-testamentaire a la lumiere des dialectes neo-helleniques," in *La koine grecque antique I: Une langue introuvable?*, ed. C. Brixhe, TMEA 10 (Nancy: Presses universitaires de Nancy, 1993), 83–121; Janse, "Convergence and Divergence in the Development of the Greek and Latin Clitic Pronouns," in *Stability, Variation and Change of Word-Order Patterns over Time*, ed. R. Sornicola et al. (Philadelphia: John Benjamins, 2000), 232–44.

12. A. Taylor, "A Prosodic Account of Clitic Position in Ancient Greek," in *Approaching Second: Second Position Clitics and Related Phenomena*, ed. A. Halpern and A. Zwicky (Stanford, CA: CSLI Publications, 1996), 477–503; Taylor, "The Distribution of Object Clitics in Koine Greek," in *Indo-European Perspectives*, ed. M. R. V. Southern (Washington, DC: Institute for the Study of Man, 2002), 285–315. See also A. Spencer and A. R. Luís, *Clitics: An Introduction*, CTL (Cambridge: Cambridge University Press, 2012).

13. G. D. Kilpatrick, "The Order of Some Noun and Adjective Phrases in the New Testament," *NovT* 5 (1962): 111–14; L. Bergson, *Zur Stellung des Adjektivs in der älteren griechischen Prosa: Die Motive der Voran- bzw. Nachstellung in ihren Hauptzügen*, AUSSGS 1 (Stockholm: Almqvist & Wiksell, 1960); S. E. Porter, "The Adjectival Attributive Genitive in the New Testament: A Grammatical Study," *TJ* 4 (1983): 3–17; D. B. Wallace, "The Relation of Adjective to Noun in Anarthrous Constructions in the New Testament," *NovT* 26 (1984): 128–67; W. G. Pierpont, "Studies in Word Order: Personal Pronoun Possessives in Nominal Phrases in the New Testament," *START* 15 (1986): 3–25; H. H. Hess, "Dynamics of the Greek Noun Phrase in Mark," *OPTT* 4 (1990): 353–69.

14. H. R. Moeller and A. Kramer, "An Overlooked Structural Pattern in New Testament Greek," *NovT* 5 (1962): 25–35; J. T. Reed, "The Infinitive with Two Substantival Accusatives: An Ambiguous Construction?," *NovT* 33 (1991): 1–27; P. W. Cheung, "Revisiting the Case of an Infinitive with Two Substantival Accusatives," *JD* 13 (1999): 69–101.

15. D. B. Wallace, "The Semantics and Exegetical Significance of the Object-Complement Construction in the New Testament," *GTJ* 6 (1985): 91–112.

L. D. Stephens;[16] and study of the placement of the participle in relation
to the finite verb by Stanley Porter.[17] A number of studies are concerned
with word order and types of clauses: B. Giseke examines word order in
subordinate clauses in Homer.[18] H. Ammann sees the verbs in Homer as
usually placed at the ends of clauses, a conclusion found also by J. Aitchison and J. L. Houben.[19] From examination of Herodotus, Thucydides, and
Xenophon, E. Kieckers believes that the usual placement of the Greek verb
is medial.[20] P. Fischer believes that the verb appears after the subject and
object.[21] A. Taylor believes that Greek changes from verb-final in Homer to
verb-final and verb-medial in the Greek of Herodotus (i.e., SOV to SVO).[22]
H. L. Ebeling examines Xenophon and Plato and concludes that Greek is
SOV (as opposed to SVO, OSV, OVS, VSO, and VOS).[23] H. Frisk claims that
in Greek ranging from Herodotus to the papyri, including Matthew, the
subject precedes the predicate in 70–80 of cases; and the object precedes
the predicate in 50–70 percent of instances, apart from Matthew and the
papyri.[24] P. Friedrich believes that the most marked word order in Homer is
VOS, followed by OSV, with SVO, SOV, and OVS being unmarked.[25] G. C.
Wakker notes that nearly 90 percent of purpose clauses are last in a sentence, while conditional clauses are usually initial.[26] J. K. Elliott believes

16. A. M. Devine and L. D. Stephens, *Discontinuous Syntax: Hyperbaton in Greek* (New York: Oxford University Press, 2002).

17. S. E. Porter, *Verbal Aspect in the Greek of the New Testament, with Reference to Tense and Mood*, SBG 1 (New York: Peter Lang, 1989), 377–90; Porter, *Idioms of the Greek New Testament*, 2nd ed., BLG 2 (Sheffield: Sheffield Academic Press, 1994), 187–90; Porter, "Time and Order in Participles in Mark and Luke: A Response to Robert Picirilli," *BBR* 17 (2007): 261–67.

18. B. Giseke, "Über die Wortstellung in abhängigen Sätzen bei Homer," *JCP* 31 (1861): 225–32.

19. H. Ammann, "Untersuchungen zur homerischen Wortfolge und Satzstruktur," *IF* 42 (1924): 149–78, 300–322; Ammann, "Wortstellung und Stilentwickelung," *Glotta* 12 (1922): 107–11; J. Aitchison, "The Order of Word Order Change," *TPS* (1979): 43–65; J. L. Houben, "Word-Order Change and Subordination in Homeric Greek," *JIS* 5 (1977): 1–8.

20. E. Kieckers, *Die Stellung des Verbs im griechischen und in den verwandten Sprachen*, UISK 2 (Strassburg: K. J. Trübner, 1911); Kieckers, "Die Stellung der Verba des Sagens in Schaltesätzen im griechischen und in den indogermanischen Sprachen," *IF* 30 (1912): 145–90.

21. P. Fischer, "Zur Stellung des Verbums im Griechischen," *Glotta* 13 (1924): 1–11, 189–205.

22. A. Taylor, "The Change from SOV to SVO in Ancient Greek," *LVC* 6 (1994): 1–37.

23. H. L. Ebeling, "Some Statistics on the Order of Words in Greek," in *Studies in Honor of Basil L. Gildersleeve* (Baltimore: Johns Hopkins Press, 1902), 229–40.

24. H. Frisk, *Studien zur griechischen Wortstellung* (Göteborg: Wettergren & Kerbers, 1933), 16.

25. P. Friedrich, *Proto-Indo-European Syntax: The Order of Meaningful Elements*, JISM 1 (Butte, MT: Journal of Indo-European Studies 1975), 21–23.

26. G. C. Wakker, "Purpose Clauses in Ancient Greek," in *Getting One's Words into Line: On Word Order and Functional Grammar*, ed. J. Nuyts and G. de Schutter, FGS 5 (Dordrecht: Foris, 1987), 91–92.

that causal clauses are final.[27] J. R. Radney and R. E. Smith think the word order of Koine Greek is VSO.[28] And B. D. Frischer and others have shown how accusative objects appear with equal frequency before or after their main verb.[29]

A few studies have been more comprehensive in nature. These include a number of important studies. C. Short examines various ordering patterns, such as adjective and noun, adverb and verb, noun and its preposition.[30] K. J. Dover studies word order in terms of three determinants: lexical and semantic, syntactical, and logical.[31] Graham Dunn applies a dependency (head and modifier) model to noun and adjective, verb and object, and preposition and noun, in which Greek moves from modifier-head to head-modifier, as reflected in Matthew.[32] M. E. Davison examines various phrasal and clausal patterns, then concludes that Romans and Luke are noun before demonstrative, noun before adjective, noun before modifying genitive, preposition before noun phrase, and VSO/SVO; and Epictetus 1 is demonstrative before noun, adjective before noun, noun before genitive, noun before relative, preposition before noun phrase, and SVO.[33] In independent clauses Stanley Porter finds the frequency of clausal ordering PC, CP, and then P; in dependent clauses, P, CP, PC, and SP; in participial clauses, almost equally P, PC, and CP; and in infinitival clauses P and CP almost equally.[34] And Andrew Pitts, extending and expanding Porter's work by utilizing the resources of the OpenText.org annotated database, largely confirms his conclusions for the entire New Testament, according to various subcorpora such as narrative, Paul's letters, the general literature, and apocalyptic, and differentiating ranks of analysis such as word groups from clauses.[35]

27. J. K. Elliott, "The Position of Causal ὅτι Clauses in the New Testament," *FN* 6 (1993): 177–205.

28. J. R. Radney, "Some Factors That Influence Fronting in Koine Clauses," *OPTT* 2 (1988): 1–79, esp. 1, 8–10; R. E. Smith, "The Unmarked Order of Pronominal Objects and Indirect Objects," *START* 12 (1984): 24–26.

29. B. D. Frischer et al., "Word-Order Transference between Latin and Greek: The Relative Position of the Accusative Direct Object and the Governing Verb in Cassius Dio and Other Greek and Roman Prose Authors," *HSCP* 99 (1999): 357–90. See also B. D. Frischer and F. J. Tweedie, "Analysis of Classical Greek and Latin Compositional Word-Order Data," *JQL* 6 (1999): 85–97.

30. C. Short, "The Order of Words in Attic Greek Prose: An Essay," in *An English Greek Lexicon: With Many New Articles, an Appendix of Proper Names, and Pillon's "Greek Synonyms,"* by C. D. Yonge, ed. H. Drisler (New York: Harper, 1870), i–cxv.

31. K. J. Dover, *Greek Word Order* (Cambridge: Cambridge University Press, 1960). See also Dover, *The Evolution of Greek Prose Style* (Oxford: Clarendon, 1997).

32. G. Dunn, "Ancient Greek Order and the Lehmann Hypothesis," *Te Reo* 28 (1985): 81–94; Dunn, "Syntactic Word Order in Herodotean Greek," *Glotta* 66 (1988): 63–79; Dunn, "Greek Word Order: Three Descriptive Models," *Te Reo* 33 (1990): 57–63.

33. M. E. Davison, "New Testament Greek Word Order," *LLC* 4 (1989): 19–28.

34. Porter, "Word Order and Clause Structure," 192–93.

35. A. W. Pitts, "Greek Word Order and Clause Structure: A Comparative Study of Some New Testament Corpora," in *The Language of the New Testament: Context, History, and Development*, ed. S. E. Porter and A. W. Pitts, ECHC 3, LBS 6 (Leiden: Brill, 2013), 311–46.

Most of these studies are geared toward formally based, syntactically identified, or functionally determined constituents. Some studies are geared toward so-called pragmatic categories, or explanation of the resulting syntax on the basis of function or context. In his extensive study, Short notes that the major factor to affect word order is emphasis.[36] T. D. Goodell treats a variety of factors that affect word order, including syntax, rhetoric, and euphony.[37] G. Thompson believes that the emphatic element of a sentence is placed first in Attic Greek, while this is not necessarily true in Hellenistic Greek (e.g., Matthew's Gospel).[38] H. Frisk posits that initial elements are emphatic.[39] A. Loepfe attempts to identify theme and rheme and use them as the determiners of word order at the clause level.[40] John Callow believes that contrast, emphasis, focus, interrogation, and thematic significance dictate word order in copula clauses.[41] Stanley Porter concludes that use of an explicit subject before a predicate and other elements acts as a topic marker or shifter.[42] Stephen Levinsohn considers a variety of factors that affect word order, including topicality, focality, emphasis, and forefronting.[43] Helma Dik attempts to account for topic and focus by studying selective features of Greek, such as particles and select verbs.[44] Ivan Kwong treats word order as a means of foregrounding.[45] And Stanley Porter and Matthew Brook O'Donnell compare the typological word-order patterns in a representative corpora of documentary papyri, the Babatha archive, and the New Testament, finding them to represent similar Koine Greek patterns.[46]

36. Short, "Order of Words," xli, xliv, xlvi, xlviii.

37. T. D. Goodell, "The Order of Words in Greek," *TAPA* 21 (1890): 13–15, 44.

38. G. Thompson, "On the Order of Words in Plato and Saint Matthew," *Link* 2 (1939): 16.

39. Frisk, *Studien.*

40. A. Loepfe, *Die Wortstellung im griechischen Sprechsatz: Erklärt an Stücken aus Platon und Menander* (Freiburg [Switzerland]: Paulusdruckerei, 1940).

41. J. Callow, "Constituent Order in Copula Clauses: A Partial Study," in *Linguistics and New Testament Interpretation*, ed. D. A. Black and D. S. Dockery (Grand Rapids: Zondervan, 1991), 68–89.

42. Porter, "Word Order and Clause Structure," 194, 200–201.

43. S. H. Levinsohn, *Discourse Features of New Testament Greek: A Coursebook on the Information Structure of New Testament Greek*, 2nd ed. (Dallas: SIL International, 2000); Levinsohn, "A Discourse Study of Constituent Order and the Article in Philippians," in *Discourse Analysis and Other Topics in Biblical Greek*, ed. S. E. Porter and D. A. Carson, JSNTSup 113 (Sheffield: Sheffield Academic Press, 1995), 60–74. Compare S. H. Levinsohn, *Textual Connections in Acts*, SBLMS 31 (Atlanta: Scholars Press, 1987).

44. H. Dik, *Word Order in Ancient Greek: A Pragmatic Account of Word Order Variation in Herodotus*, ASCP 5 (Amsterdam: Gieben, 1995). See also Dik, *Word Order in Greek Tragic Dialogue* (Oxford: Oxford University Press, 2007); Dik, "Interpreting Adjective Position in Herodotus," in *Grammar as Interpretation: Greek Literature in Its Linguistic Contexts*, ed. E. J. Bakker, Mnemosyne 171 (Leiden: Brill, 1997), 55–76.

45. Kwong, *Word Order.*

46. S. E. Porter and M. B. O'Donnell, "Building and Examining Linguistic Phenomena in a Corpus of Representative Papyri," in *The Language of the Papyri*, ed. T. V. Evans and D. D. Obbink

As one can see from this survey, which though broad in scope is clearly not complete, a variety of issues are discussed when the issue of word order is broached.

Major Issues in Exploring Word Order

Despite all of the work listed above, there is still widespread misunderstanding and confusion about the word-order patterns found within the New Testament. Some of these are fundamental issues associated with linguistic typology, in which there is a tendency to prescribe typological patterns rather than describe the language,[47] and others are related to the failure to properly define the endeavor for Greek itself. Most of these issues go beyond the simple dichotomy of whether and to what degree Greek does or does not have flexible word order.[48] The issue is far more complicated than that, because it involves the difference between configurational languages—those typically used for analysis of Greek, such as English and German—and nonconfigurational languages such as Greek.[49] There are three issues that I believe merit consideration in the study of word order in the Greek New Testament. I will treat each of these briefly, drawing occasionally on previous studies.

Defining the Domain of Study

The first issue in considering word order is the domain of study. The rubric "word order" is thrown about fairly often and fairly casually in studies of this sort (entire books are even called "word order"), but the term ends up referring to a number of different things. For example, it can include the study of an individual word or type of word in relation to almost any other domain of study. So we have a study of the use of a particular word in the vocative, and its placement in relation to the clauses in which this word occurs.

(Oxford: Oxford University Press, 2010), 287–311; Porter, "The Babatha Archive, the Egyptian Papyri and Their Implications for Study of the Greek New Testament," in *Early Christian Manuscripts: Examples of Applied Method and Approach*, ed. T. J. Kraus and T. Nicklas, TENT 5 (Leiden: Brill, 2010), 213–37.

47. On issues regarding linguistic typology and its shortcomings, see W. Croft, *Verbs: Aspect and Clausal Structure* (Oxford: Oxford University Press, 2012), 128–29, criticisms formulated by a leading typologist. See also Song, *Word Order*, esp. 10–71; W. Croft, *Typology and Universals*, CTL (Cambridge: Cambridge University Press, 1995), 4–11.

48. See E. v. E. Boas and L. Huitink, "Syntax," in *A Companion to the Ancient Greek Language*, ed. E. J. Bakker, BCAW (Chichester: Blackwell, 2010), 134–50, esp. 148–49.

49. See K. Hale, "Walpiri and the Grammar of Non-Configurational Languages," *NLLT* 1 (1983): 5–47.

There are many studies of the use of particles or conjunctions in relation to phrases, clauses, and even beyond clauses, paragraphs. There are also studies of the elements that make up phrases or word groups. These take a variety of forms. They might include the syntactical (and even semantic) relations of adjectives and nouns, nouns and defining genitives, prepositions and nouns. When we reach the clause level, the situation does not become much clearer. At this level we may have different types of clause constituents and different types of clauses considered. For example, sometimes such studies focus upon a single clause constituent in regard to the other elements of a clause, such as a (variously described) direct or indirect object or double accusative. Sometimes the clause is an infinitival clause (still rightly labeled a clause, even if there is no finite verb), other times a participial clause (when these are not defined as single words or types of words in relation to a larger domain), sometimes a main clause, and other times a subordinate clause. The discussion sometimes extends to the elements of these clauses and even to relations between clauses. Thus we have some typological studies of clause constituents, and some studies of the relationship between conditional, causal, or purpose clauses in relation to their main clauses. Even though these vary considerably as to the scope of what they entail, and are often at different places on the rank scale, all of them are usually and unfortunately referred to as matters of "word order."

The first order of business in study of word order is to define the domain of study. A study of word order must determine what level of study (place on the rank scale) it is interested in analyzing.[50] I believe that differentiating levels of language analysis (the scale of rank) provides a major step forward in isolating and identifying, and then studying, the major components of what is traditionally called "word order." There have been, for example, many studies of particles and conjunctions in ancient Greek. However, many of these fail to provide insight into the larger question of how particles and conjunctions are used, because they fail to clearly define the levels or ranks at which they function. Take conjunctions as an example. A conjunction might be used to join words or word groups together. It may be used to join two clauses together. It may be used to join two or more paragraphs together. The conjunctions used in these differing environments are not all the same conjunctions, and even the same conjunctions function differently according to rank of usage. As a result, a study of conjunctions needs to differentiate which conjunctions

50. The rank scale is a contribution of systemic functional linguistics. See, e.g., M. A. K. Halliday, *Halliday's Introduction to Functional Grammar*, rev. C. M. I. M. Matthiessen, 4th ed. (London: Routledge, 2014), 9–10.

function at which levels, and then to analyze their use in relation to the other conjunctions that could be used at each specific level.[51]

One of the benefits of such differentiated investigation is in terms of language typology. Many typological studies have lumped together findings that apply at different levels or ranks. There may be certain patterns that apply at different levels of investigation. For example, in Davison's study of Romans, Luke, and Epictetus, he finds different patterns of usage at the phrase or group level than he does at the clause level.[52] He finds that Romans and Luke are noun before demonstrative, noun before adjective, noun before modifying genitive, preposition before noun phrase, noun before relative, and VSO/SVO, whereas Epictetus 1 is demonstrative before noun, adjective before noun, noun before modifying genitive, preposition before noun phrase, noun before relative, and SVO. I note that noun before demonstrative, noun before adjective, noun before modifying genitive, and preposition before noun phrase are descriptions at the word-group level or rank. At this level, there are some noteworthy differences between Romans and Luke versus Epictetus. However, noun before relative relates to embedded (rank-shifted) modification, and here the two bodies of evidence are similar. At the level of the clause, however, the New Testament has either, according to Davison, VSO or SVO order, whereas Epictetus has SVO, indicating a significant degree of overlap (but see below on this clausal typology). It would seem that texts differ or are similar with regard to different levels or ranks of analysis. This needs to be taken into account in formulating and conducting word-order investigations.

Consistent Terminology

The studies noted above use a variety of terminologies in their analysis of ancient Greek word order. Some of the categories used are morphological, so that there are studies of particles, vocatives, and the like. There are also categories of terminology related to parts of speech, so that we have nouns, adjectives, verbs, and the like. We also have categories that are syntactically identified, such as subject, verb, and object (although this set of terms is not entirely consistent). There are also categories that are functionally identified, such as subject, predicate, complement, and the like. And some categories are a mixture, such as the defining genitive, which is a morphological and functional category. We find other categories as well.

---

51. An initial step in this direction has been made in Porter and O'Donnell, "Conjunctions," where two different clines of conjunction use are differentiated and the rank scale is utilized.

52. Davison, "New Testament Greek Word Order," 19–28. Note that these are differentiated more clearly in Porter, *Idioms*, 289–95, esp. 290–92.

This terminology adds to the confusion of the discussion in several ways. In some instances, the terminology employed makes it unclear whether studies are talking about the same thing or about different things. In all instances, the theoretical categories used will determine what counts as evidence, and consequently how data are selected, analyzed, quantified, and then typologically compared.

I suggest that word-order studies must, first, define a domain of study, and then find a consistent terminology for that specific domain of study. For instance, we ought to question whether terms like "noun" and "adjective" are appropriate for studying ordering within word groups or phrases. Nouns and adjectives are parts of speech. They are word categories, not word functions. Yet surely ordering within phrases or word groups involves the functional relationships that words enter into at the word-group level. Moreover, it is not only single words that can enter into functional relationships at this level. Larger units perform various functions, some of them very similar to those performed by individual words, in which case it is the ordering of these larger units that must be examined.

A positive example may be seen in the work of Dunn, who uses the terms "head" and "modifier."[53] This is fairly common terminology for a dependency model, in which there is a relationship of dependency between two elements. One is the dominant element, the head, and the other is a modifier. The slots of head and of modifier may be filled with a variety of elements, not simply nouns and adjectives. Thus a head in a phrase may be a noun, or it may be a noun substitute of some sort, such as a participle or any other element that functions as a substantive does when it is the head term in a construction. The modifier slot may be filled with a variety of elements as well, in some analyses including a word in the genitive case, indicating a different type of modifying relationship than is indicated by an adjective in the same case, number, and gender. A related example is the OpenText.org project, which identifies a number of different modifying relationships, including conjunction (as noted above, a conjunction that is used within a group to conjoin elements), specification (typically involving an article, but also prepositions), qualification (often but not always an element in the genitive), definition (often but not always an adjective or appositional word), and relation (often a preposition as the specifier of its own group). One need not necessarily accept the OpenText.org model of word-group analysis in order to see the benefit of developing a distinct terminology for each level of study. Rather than simply confining oneself to terms such as "adjective" and "noun," one can easily encompass

---

53. Dunn, "Ancient Greek Order"; Dunn, "Syntactic Word Order"; Dunn, "Greek Word Order." On dependency grammar, see I. A. Mel'čuk, *Dependency Syntax: Theory and Practice* (Albany: SUNY Press, 1988), 12–42.

a variety of items that may occur in relation to the head term, including not only adjectives but also articles, other nouns, participles, and even infinitives and clauses. This extends the data for analysis by finding a means of analyzing all of the different types of words that may be used for a specific function within the syntax of the Greek word group.

Along similar lines in these studies is a lack of differentiation of form from function, even if there is a necessary correlation and linkage between them. Thus one finds studies that discuss nouns and adjectives, or verbs and adverbs, or particles, or even participles and infinitives. All of these are formal categories. However, these same studies do not explicitly discuss the functions of these forms in the specific domain under consideration. Formal terms are appropriate in certain contexts, to be sure. Yet when studies of word order use explicit formal terms, the functions of these forms are usually implied. It would be better to explicitly state the functional categories and then explain how various formal items function in relation to them.

For advancement to be made in word-order studies, we need both an identification of the forms involved and a set of categories to identify functions. This can be clearly seen at the clausal level. The traditional terminology used in language typology has been long established but is itself inherently inconsistent. The categories typically used are Subject, Verb, and Object (although there are others who simply use Subject and Verb, thus alleviating some of the problems for intransitive verbs).[54] Verb is an indicator of a part of speech and is morphologically grounded. Subject and Object are functionally identified and may consist of similar forms. Thus a noun (as opposed to a verb) may be used as the subject or as the object in such a clause. However, we realize that a verb may also be used as a subject or object (e.g., a participle or infinitive). What is meant even in the use of the terms above is usually a finite verb performing a particular function, rather than a nonfinite verb performing a different function, as it might if it is a participle being used as a substantive and serving as subject of a clause. In the OpenText.org Project, four primary clausal components are adopted: Subject, Predicator, Complement, and Adjunct. Many different elements are capable of performing these functions, even if a Predicator usually consists of at least one verb form.

Explanation

In the study of word order, the most pressing need is persuasive explanations of the patterns observed. The exemplary studies cited above attempt to

54. For discussion of some of these issues, see Song, *Word Order*, 29.

do precisely this. There are two major types of explanatory studies that I will note, before drawing attention to several features that I believe merit further discussion. First, there are explanations that attempt to analyze simply by classifying. Davison, for example, indicates that the Greek of Romans and Luke has a number of patterns: noun before demonstrative, noun before adjective, noun before modifying genitive, preposition before noun phrase, noun before relative. These classifications may be useful for comparing authors or languages, but they have very little explanatory power. Even the much-disputed clausal orderings, such as SVO, OVS, and so on, are classifications without explanation. I observe also that the effort to force Greek into traditional typological categories based on supposed language universals has a distorting effect. Many Greek clauses do not have explicit Subjects, and so these clauses must, by definition, be excluded (calling it a pro-drop language adds to the confusion). Others do not have Objects, and so they too are excluded. Thus some studies have stated that their proposals concerning word order are for clauses in which an explicit Subject appears. However, this merely raises the question of the clauses in which a Subject does not appear (in fact, Greek does not always need an explicit object either). How frequently and in what environments are such clauses used? In order to use some of the traditional categories, one must sacrifice a great deal of descriptive power. The resultant number of clauses analyzed may well not be representative of the typological patterns of the Greek language.

A second type of explanation establishes a pattern of usage and then attempts to find plausible explanations for deviations from that pattern. Functional syntax often attempts to perform such analysis. A variety of terminologies is used in such explanations. "Topic," "focus," "emphasis," "theme," "prominence," "salience," and "markedness" are just some of the terms employed. Despite the inconsistency and lack of clarity that sometimes surrounds such terms, these efforts are at least pursuing viable explanations for variation in word order. It is, of course, unreasonable to expect all such analyses to agree on a common language, since they reflect different orientations to language. What is more, the presence of different theoretical orientations makes it hard to relate technical studies to one another. Are different studies arriving at common understandings by using different frameworks? Are important distinctions being glossed over because similar terms are being used that mask underlying differences? Despite the hazards of entering into terminological debates, I will make at least a few comments on the language being used in current typological-linguistic explanations of word-order variation in New Testament Greek.

The first observation is that virtually all of those who attempt an explanation are convinced that deviation requires comment, and that deviation introduces something important that is not present when the expected pattern is used. This no doubt accounts for the use of the language of markedness. The language of markedness, as is commonly realized, originated in Prague school phonetics to indicate the presence or absence of key features in the production of sounds. It has been extended in other areas to indicate the presence or absence of structural features on the basis of analogy with the presence or absence of articulatory features.[55] Hence, whether it is a single feature or a larger set of features that are not present in the "unmarked" form, such a configuration is often called "marked." There is some sense to such an explanation. I wonder, however, whether the terminology of markedness is the best language to use in such an explanatory environment, because markedness does not necessarily indicate meaning, only difference, especially in terms of other or added features. Labeling something "marked" does not necessarily indicate the function or meaning of the marked element. A further explanatory analysis is required. Thus we may still be able to use the language of markedness to indicate a pattern that is different from another, and as a result probably less frequent across a distributional pattern, and probably more semantically freighted in some way; yet the notion of markedness by itself does not suffice as an explanation of such patterns.

The language of emphasis is also suspect, even though widely used. There is little doubt, even on the basis of what has been said above regarding markedness, that those who use the language of emphasis are trying to capture an explanatory feature that goes beyond simply the idea of markedness. Whereas markedness is probably confined to some type of notation of features (whether they be frequency or structure), the notion of emphasis attempts to bring a descriptive category of meaning into play. Unfortunately, it is probably not a particularly helpful category. With the simple notion of markedness, one can extrapolate from a quantifiable difference and move toward a specific semantic description. The language of emphasis, however, seems to exclude the possibility of semantic distinctions. Emphatic and unemphatic structures are (so it would seem) semantically identical, even if the discourse function of an emphatic structure is in some way contextually enhanced.

Many studies employ terms related to topic—whether "topic" and "comment," "topicality," "focality," or the like, along with the related terminology

---

55. For discussion of some of the history of this discussion, see E. L. Battistella, *The Logic of Markedness* (New York: Oxford University Press, 1996), 7–72; Croft, *Typology*, 64–94; compare S. E. Porter, "Prominence: A Theoretical Overview," in *The Linguist as Pedagogue: Trends in the Teaching and Linguistic Analysis of the Greek New Testament*, ed. S. E. Porter and M. B. O'Donnell, NTM 11 (Sheffield: Sheffield Phoenix Press, 2009), 45–74.

of "theme" and "rheme."[56] There are many different interpretations of such language in linguistic thought. Some are related to simple word order, so that elements in particular positions are defined as being topical or the topic element. Others are related to cognitive categories and indicate informational flow; they are related to concepts such as "given" and "new" information. In any case, such language may provide a useful set of categories for word-order analysis. Above, it was noted that the explicit subject in Greek is an optional element of the clause. This means that clauses are not necessarily required to have an explicit subject. The subject may be inferential, and thus conveyed by means of verbal morphology (which inferential subject, despite the thoughts of some, does not enter into clausal typology). However, there are clear instances when the Greek user needs to indicate an overt subject, whether one can be inferred from the discourse or not. This is done most easily by using the explicit grammaticalized subject, often reduced by use of a pronoun.

Description of Greek clausal ordering of constituent elements thus needs to be able to account for several features. One is the expression of the grammaticalized Subject, whether in full grammatical or reduced form; a second is the ordering of this element in relation to the other elements of the clause and their exponence; and a third is the role of this grammaticalized form within the clause and other larger units. Thus the question is *if* there is a Subject expressed, and *where* that Subject is placed in the clausal ordering, especially in relation to other elements and larger structures. The analysis must be able to explain all of these features in syntactical and/or semantic categories that are transparent and differentiated. For example, an explicit Subject that is the first element in a clause may well have a different clausal and/or discourse function than one that is ordered differently in the clause (i.e., medial or final).

One possible approach to this involves an explicit differentiation between clausal function, clausal ordering, and discourse function, with appropriate terminology of given and new, prime and subsequent, theme and rheme, and topic and comment to differentiate the information structure according to rank, from the clause to the paragraph. At the rank of clause, an important potential feature of the clause—although an optional element—is an explicit grammaticalized Subject. Many Greek clauses do not have a grammaticalized Subject. However, an explicit grammaticalized Subject may be used within

56. These terms are derived from the Prague school of linguistics. For recent discussion, see Halliday, *Introduction to Functional Grammar*, 88–92, 114–21, where he differentiates between theme and rheme and given and new. See also J. Firbas, *Functional Sentence Perspective in Written and Spoken Communication*, SEL (Cambridge: Cambridge University Press, 1992), esp. 79–83.

a clause to perform a variety of discourse functions—such as to introduce a new participant, indicate the function of a participant within a discourse (e.g., within dialogue), or signal a specific function of the participant (e.g., direct speech or statement)—and, in Greek, this Subject can be introduced within the clausal construction at any number of syntactical positions. The grammaticalized Subject indicates new information within the informational structure of "given" and "new" information (the rest of the clause indicates given information; without an explicit Subject the clause simply indicates given information). Within clausal structure, the focus of a clause, its "aboutness," is expressed in the prime or first clausal component position, followed by the other or subsequent material. New information (an explicit grammaticalized Subject) does not necessarily need to be placed first or in prime position, so that the new clausal information may also not be the focus of the clause. However, there are occasions when the explicit grammaticalized Subject is placed in prime position, indicating information of particular significance at the clause level or beyond. An explicit grammaticalized Subject in prime position designates a thematized element, indicating a topic or information for consideration that goes beyond simply the clausal level to the clause complex, and controls the information at this higher level.[57] At the pericope or paragraph level, a thematized element may well indicate the topic for an entire larger unit to elucidate, and hence it may be referred to in terms of topic and comment. The thematized Subject functions as the topic for the paragraph, and the rest of the material of the paragraph comments upon it. One need not accept the labels that I have used here to appreciate that we need a more robust terminology in order to explain the phenomena involved in "word order."

Conclusion

In conclusion, although there has been much discussion of Greek word order, I am not sure that much of it is helpful or insightful in its explanatory value. My proposals are not designed to dictate the way that studies should be conducted in the future. My intention, rather, is to show that there are many loose ends in word-order studies that need tying up. We need to critically evaluate how much real progress has been made, and we need to consolidate the genuine insights that have been made. In order to make this progress, I believe, we

---

57. That is, the first element before Predicator or Complement, regardless of Adjunct components.

need to clearly differentiate between different domains of discussion; we need to determine an appropriate and consistent terminology for each domain of discussion, utilizing terms that do not confuse form and function; and what is most important, we need to pursue theoretical categories that provide us with genuine explanatory power.

20

Proper Nouns in the New Testament

Introduction

"Proper nouns," as linguists prefer to call them (or "proper names," as philosophers prefer), are a particularly understudied area in linguistics, as well as in New Testament research. John Lyons, for example, in his otherwise in many ways exemplary introduction to theoretical linguistics, has but a paragraph on proper nouns, where he discusses one criterion that determines whether a noun is a proper noun.[1] Friedrich Waismann fares slightly better by identifying "three main motifs which guide us in the use of the word."[2] These amount to rather loose criteria, which result in more questions than

This essay was first drafted during my stay as visiting scholar in the Protestant Theological Faculty of Charles University in Prague, Czech Republic, October 24 to November 9, 1997. I thank the faculty for extending their gracious hospitality. I also thank my former colleague Professor Arthur Gibson for helping me to think through several of these philosophical issues. I am sure that he would disagree with many of the results.

1. J. Lyons, *Introduction to Theoretical Linguistics* (Cambridge: Cambridge University Press, 1968), 337.

2. F. Waismann, *The Principles of Linguistic Philosophy*, ed. R. Harré (London: Macmillan, 1965), 196. The looseness of his "motifs" does, however, allow him to engage more specific concerns, such as naming physical objects, "objects in the process of becoming," and identifying whether the demonstrative "this" ought to be considered a proper name.

actual answers. Many do not have as much to offer.[3] Distinctions between "descriptivist theory" and "causal theory" of naming are significant in the philosophical discussion of naming. Descriptivist theories suggest that names become referential by virtue of their intended and repeated attribution,[4] while causal theories emphasize the external/social causal chain that links the use of a name to its referent.[5] But I am concerned here not simply with the concept of proper nouns in general linguistic or philosophical usage. Here I am concerned with proper nouns in the Greek New Testament. Unfortunately, the standard Greek reference tools say little more than the general linguists. A volume as comprehensive as Rafael Kühner and Bernhard Gerth's *Ausführliche Grammatik der griechischen Sprache* gives no attention to proper nouns, according to the index,[6] and neither does William Goodwin's *Greek Grammar*, apart from some comments on syntax (see below). Better is Friedrich Blass and Albert Debrunner's grammar in its English translation by Robert Funk, which at least addresses some of the problems concerning personal nouns. Their discussion is confined, however, to a discussion of foreign names brought into Greek (§§53–55) and to odd declensions of some names (§125).[7] The same is true of Blass and Debrunner's grammar as subsequently revised by Friedrich Rehkopf.[8]

3. More sustained treatments tend to deal with the various philosophical and linguistic complexities associated with naming rather than with identifying strict criteria for identifying proper nouns/names as such. In a brief discussion of the linguistic characteristics of proper names, John Searle argues that proper names are used to refer but do not have sense insofar as they do not describe or specify ("Proper Names," in *Philosophical Logic*, ed. P. F. Strawson, ORP [Oxford: Oxford University Press, 1967], 89–96). R. M. Martin's premise that proper names refer to individual persons, places, and things and are capitalized is entirely unhelpful (e.g., in German all nouns are capitalized). His rejection of descriptivist analysis of proper names is apt, yet defining proper names as "rigid designators" seems to run counter to the fuzziness that many other theorists attribute to the notion of proper names (*The Meaning of Language* [Cambridge, MA: MIT Press, 1987]).
4. The impulse for this perspective derives from Bertrand Russell's work on description in general. See B. Russell, "Descriptions," in *The Philosophy of Language*, ed. A. P. Martinisch, 2nd ed. (Oxford: Oxford University Press, 1990), 212–18; compare J. M. Anderson, *The Grammar of Names* (Oxford: Oxford University Press, 2007), 138–48; M. Morris, *An Introduction to the Philosophy of Language*, CIP (Cambridge: Cambridge University Press, 2007), 49–73.
5. See especially S. A. Kripke, *Naming and Necessity* (Cambridge, MA: Harvard University Press, 1980); compare G. Evans, "The Causal Theory of Naming," in Martinisch, *Philosophy of Language*, 295–307 (who coins the term "causal theory" with reference to Kripke's work [p. 295]); J. R. Searle, "Proper Names and Intentionality," in Martinisch, *Philosophy of Language*, 330–46; Morris, *Philosophy of Language*, 74–93; Anderson, *Grammar of Names*, 155–59.
6. See R. Kühner and B. Gerth, *Ausführliche Grammatik der griechischen Sprache: Satzlehre*, 2 vols., 4th ed. (Leverkusen: Gottschalksche, 1955).
7. F. Blass and A. Debrunner, *A Greek Grammar of the New Testament and Other Early Christian Literature*, trans. R. W. Funk (Chicago: University of Chicago Press, 1961).
8. F. Blass and A. Debrunner, *Grammatik des neutestamentlichen Griechisch*, ed. F. Rehkopf, 17th ed. (Göttingen: Vandenhoeck & Ruprecht, 1990), where the same paragraphs apply.

On the basis of this dearth of discussion, one might be led to believe that there is nothing much to say about proper nouns in either general linguistics or New Testament (or other Greek language) studies. Yet even some preliminary investigation shows that this is not the case. There are at least three difficulties that require attention. First, in order to establish what constitutes a proper noun, should one employ philosophical or linguistic criteria? (And if one opts for the latter, should these be formal or functional criteria?) Second, how does one develop suitable criteria when working with an epigraphic (or dead) language? Third, where should the category of proper nouns be located within a linguistic description?

In order to explore these difficulties, I examine the two standard tests that are used to distinguish proper nouns: (1) they cannot be preceded by an article; (2) they cannot be pluralized.[9] Let me be clear from the outset, however, that these are philosophical tests, and that part of what I intend to discuss is whether these philosophical tests have any linguistic validity, especially in relation to Hellenistic or New Testament Greek.

Criterion 1: The Article

The first test is that a proper noun cannot be preceded by the article. Thus, in English one can go to "the john," but this is something quite different from visiting "the John," where "John" is the name of a person. Thus one does not normally speak of "the Mary," "the Sam," or "the Stephen." Of course, there are even problems with this rule in English, as with phrases such as "the Fred standing in the corner," as opposed to "the Fred who just made that unintelligible remark." One may wish to argue that the article here does not collocate with the proper noun itself but rather with the entire noun phrase. I will leave it to others to decide whether this is more or less convincing than the idea that the article can sometimes be used with a proper noun (since one might well expect the article to collocate with the head term of a phrase just as it collocates with the head term together with its dependents or modifiers).

Whatever one may decide about English, however, this first test does not seem to apply to Hellenistic Greek. In Hellenistic Greek the article regularly appears before proper nouns. Or does it? Perhaps, before conceding this point prematurely, we should at least consider whether there is an alternative explanation for this apparent "oddity." Might it be that the article before proper

9. See A. Gibson, *Biblical Semantic Logic: A Preliminary Analysis* (Oxford: Blackwell, 1981; repr., London: Sheffield Academic Press, 2001), 56–57. Gibson suggests a third philosophical test.

nouns is not really an article but is some other indicator, perhaps something akin to a demonstrative pronoun? After all, according to most grammarians, the Greek article has its origins in the demonstrative pronoun.[10] To my mind, this alternative explanation is implausible. To begin with, it fails to distinguish formal, and even historical, and functional criteria. Ronald Peters has provided a convincing case against the origins of the article in the demonstrative, finding them instead in the relative pronoun. Even if we do not accept all of Peters's conclusions regarding functional extensions,[11] he shows that these common origins provide a useful functional conceptual framework. In other words, the Greek article may perform a number of different functions while it remains a single form. It is not necessary to distinguish different forms in order to encompass diverse functions.[12] In addition, this traditional explanation mistakenly relies on an etymological argument. Whether or not it is true that the article originated as some demonstrative form (and it probably did not), it ceased to be a simple demonstrative much earlier than the Greek that we are concerned with here. Clear evidence of this may be seen in the fact that a separate set of near and remote demonstratives has already developed in Hellenistic Greek and is used to indicate demonstrative relations, including spatial, temporal, and conceptual nearness and remoteness. These forms perform their demonstrative functions even when the article precedes a proper noun. In that sense, Peters's explanation is much to be preferred, since he is able to show formal and functional similarities between the Greek article and relative pronoun in New Testament usage. In the end, I think we must conclude with Goodwin that, in Greek, "Proper names may take the article."[13]

Having observed this basic fact, we are still a long way from a satisfactory explanation. The use of the article with the proper noun has instigated serious and lengthy discussions among Greek grammarians.[14] Thomas Middleton appears to have been the first to formulate rules regarding use of the article before the proper noun. He states that names appear with the article if they have been mentioned previously or if the person who is being referred to is

10. See the survey of opinion in R. D. Peters, *The Greek Article: A Functional Grammar of ó-Items in the Greek New Testament with Special Emphasis on the Greek Article*, LBS 9 (Leiden: Brill, 2014), 5–68.

11. Ibid., 184–87. Peters essentially contends that the article functions as a modifier to concretize the element that it modifies.

12. Many New Testament scholars refer to the Greek "definite article," and the indication of definiteness (of some sort) may be one contextual function of this form. It is, however, not the only one that has been identified, and in fact may not be the best way to characterize the function of the article at all.

13. W. W. Goodwin, *Greek Grammar* (London: Macmillan, 1894), 206 (§943).

14. It is perhaps worth noting that all of the Greek grammarians I have surveyed presume that the article is used before proper nouns.

well known.[15] There appear to be four different courses that discussion has followed since Middleton. First, there are those who have in some ways followed Middleton's path, maintaining these rules in some form or other. These include scholars such as Edwin Abbott, Blass and Debrunner (in both Funk's and Rehkopf's versions), Nigel Turner, and most recently, Jenny Heimerdinger and Stephen Levinsohn.[16] Second, some believe that no set rules can be established, but that unquantifiable factors such as style or even geographical dialect must be considered. These include scholars such as Georg Winer, Basil Gildersleeve, James Hope Moulton, Bernhard Weiss, and Richard Nevius.[17] Third, others believe that general rules can be determined, but that they must be formulated according to the style of a given author. These include scholars such as Gordon Fee and Howard Teeple.[18] Fourth, and most recently, Peters has argued that the article functions with proper nouns to characterize an already-definite instance (the proper noun used of a person) and give it salience, hence the frequent use of the article with proper names when a character is first introduced within a discourse.[19]

For the sake of illustration, let me compare a somewhat recent article by Heimerdinger and Levinsohn with an article by Fee. Heimerdinger and Levinsohn contend, "The only rule [regarding the article with proper nouns] which emerges, and about which there is some consensus of opinion, is a very general one: that names of persons are not usually preceded by the definite [sic] article, in other words reference to them is anarthrous; but the article may be used (reference is arthrous) if the person has already been introduced by name

15. T. F. Middleton, *The Doctrine of the Greek Article Applied to the Criticism and Illustration of the New Testament*, ed. H. J. Rose (London: Deighton, Bell, 1833), 71–88.

16. E. A. Abbott, *Johannine Grammar* (London: A&C Black, 1906), 57–58; Blass, Debrunner, and Funk, *Greek Grammar*, 135–36 (§260); Blass, Debrunner, and Rehkopf, *Griechische Grammatik*, 210–12 (§260); N. Turner, *A Grammar of New Testament Greek*, vol. 3, *Syntax* (Edinburgh: T&T Clark, 1963), 166–67; J. Heimerdinger and S. H. Levinsohn, "The Use of the Definite Article before Names of People in the Greek Text of Acts with Particular Reference to Codex Bezae," *FN* 5 (1992): 15–44.

17. G. B. Winer, *A Treatise on the Grammar of New Testament Greek, Regarded as a Sure Basis for New Testament Exegesis*, trans. W. F. Moulton, 3rd ed. (Edinburgh: T&T Clark, 1882), 140–41; B. L. Gildersleeve, "On the Article with Proper Names," *AJP* 11 (1890): 483–87; J. H. Moulton, *A Grammar of New Testament Greek*, vol. 1, *Prolegomena*, 3rd ed. (Edinburgh: T&T Clark, 1908), 83; B. Weiss, "Der Gebrauch des Artikels bei den Eigennamen," *TSK* 86 (1913): 352–55; R. C. Nevius, "The Use of the Definite Article with 'Jesus' in the Fourth Gospel," *NTS* 12 (1965–66): 81–85.

18. G. D. Fee, "The Use of the Definite Article with Personal Names in the Gospel of John," *NTS* 17 (1970–71): 168–83; H. M. Teeple, "The Greek Article with Personal Names in the Synoptic Gospels," *NTS* 19 (1972–73): 302–17.

19. Peters, *Greek Article*, 247–51, esp. 248–49. Compare S. E. Porter, *Idioms of the Greek New Testament*, 2nd ed., BLG 2 (Sheffield: Sheffield Academic Press, 1994), 107.

before."[20] By contrast, Fee criticizes the claim that "John generally introduces a proper name without the article and then uses it," arguing unambiguously that "if there is one rule not true of Johannine usage, this is it."[21] Each article goes on to offer a full treatment and defense of its respective position.

Together these articles raise a number of important questions that must be answered before any resolution can be reached. One concerns the nature of grammatical rules. Fee rejects rules, which he sees as being quite determinative, and opts instead to describe a number of tendencies. Heimerdinger and Levinsohn, on the other hand, establish a general rule but then go on to discuss various exceptions. A second question concerns how much of the data can be accounted for by appealing to style and personal choice. On the basis of personal style, one might explain different patterns of usage between Matthew and John, but what about the wide divergence between Luke and Acts? Moreover, many uses of the article are relatively fixed as general features and do not seem as susceptible to idiosyncratic variation (e.g., Granville Sharp's rule and Apollonius's canon, to name only two).[22] Perhaps what we explain as stylistic is simply a general pattern of usage that has not yet been clearly identified. A third question concerns what counts as evidence for or against a particular thesis. In several of the scholarly articles that discuss the use of the article, the issue of textual criticism is raised. In a number of places a given manuscript will have the article before a proper noun, whereas another manuscript will not. This clouds the picture somewhat, since both sides are able to skew their results by finding support for their thesis in textual variants.

20. Heimerdinger and Levinsohn, "Use of the Definite Article," 15.

21. Fee, "Use of the Definite Article," 170.

22. By Granville Sharp's rule, I mean the rule as more expansively defined and not narrowly construed (and hence more of a generality than a rigid test), and as found exemplified in Porter, *Idioms*, 110–11 (see also D. B. Wallace, "The Semantic Range of the Article-Noun-Kai-Noun Plural Construction in the New Testament," *GTJ* 4 [1983]: 59–84). For recent debate over Sharp's "rule," see D. B. Wallace, *Granville Sharp's Canon and Its Kin: Semantics and Significance*, SBG 14 (New York: Peter Lang, 2009); S. E. Porter, review of *Granville Sharp's Canon and Its Kin: Semantics and Significance*, by Daniel B. Wallace, *JETS* 53 (2010): 828–32; Porter "Granville Sharp's Rule: A Response to Dan Wallace, or Why a Critical Book Review Should Be Left Alone," *JETS* 56 (2013): 93–100. For Wallace's responses, see "Sharp's Rule Revisited: A Response to Stanley Porter," *JETS* 56 (2013): 79–92; Wallace, "Granville Sharp's Rule: A Rejoinder to Stan Porter," *JETS* 56 (2013): 101–6. Wallace narrows the applicability of Sharp's rule to the point of its only including two examples in the New Testament (even these may be questioned), and too easily dismisses the counterevidence or other counterarguments. I argue for a more expansive interpretation of the rule that allows for conceptual unity rather than strict referential identity. This has far higher explanatory power, utility, and inclusiveness. On Apollonius's canon, see S. D. Hull, "Exceptions to Apollonius' Canon in the New Testament: A Grammatical Study," *TJ* 7 (1986): 3–16.

A final question concerns what counts for a plausible explanation of an exception. As part of their general rule of usage of the article, Heimerdinger and Levinsohn state, "The unmarked way of mentioning a person by name is with the article," and "The omission of the article indicates that attention is being drawn to the person being named."[23] Yet there is ongoing debate regarding criteria for markedness, and even more regarding how to handle loosely defined phenomena such as "attention being drawn" to someone or something in a text. What might seem to be attention to Heimerdinger and Levinsohn may well appear to be nothing more than special pleading to someone else. In this case, Peters's explanation of the use of the article with proper nouns—a recognizable feature of Hellenistic, including New Testament, Greek—is much to be preferred. His explanation of the function of the article to mark salience accounts best for the evidence of the article's use with the proper noun.

Criterion 2: Pluralization

The second test is that of pluralization, and it is the one that I wish to spend the most amount of time upon. There is one instance where pluralization of a proper noun has what appears to some people to be several noteworthy implications, and that is with regard to the possible name of God in the New Testament. Is God's name "God"? Daniel Wallace states, "A good rule of thumb to follow is that a proper name is one that cannot be pluralized. Thus, Χριστός, θεός, and κύριος are not proper names; Παῦλος, Πέτρος, and Ἰησοῦς are."[24] Later, he states more strongly, "A *proper* noun is defined as a noun which *cannot* be 'pluralized'—thus it does *not* include titles. A person's name, therefore, is proper and consequently does not fit the rule [?]. But θεός is not proper because it can be pluralized. . . . Since θεοί is possible (cf. John 10:34), θεός is not a proper name."[25]

This rule may seem to be self-evident, but it is in need of qualification. A very general qualification is that whatever one might think of how it applies to so-called first names or Christian names, it cannot apply to last names or surnames. "Bill" might refer only to this Bill, but one can and does hear reference being made to the Smiths and the Joneses, in which all of the members of the group have the proper name "Smith" or "Jones." I suppose it might

23. Heimerdinger and Levinsohn, "Use of the Definite Article," 17, 18.
24. D. B. Wallace, *Greek Grammar beyond the Basics: An Exegetical Syntax of the New Testament* (Grand Rapids: Zondervan, 1996), 246n77. See also Wallace, *Granville Sharp's Canon*, 251–55.
25. Wallace, *Greek Grammar*, 272n42.

be argued that the referential feature of a proper noun, such that it refers a particular individual, is not present in such plural uses. Thus plural surnames are generic rather than proper because they describe a genre or class of people. This begs the question, however, by deciding that it is the property of specific reference that defines a proper noun.[26] Here, let us simply agree that the rule concerning pluralization does not apply to surnames.

The question is even more complex than that, however. Does the rule of pluralization really apply to first names? I am not sure that it does. Let us consider some evidence in English and ancient Greek. In English, we find people with the name "Sky" or "Sun." Yet we also find plural forms of these words, such as "skies" or "suns," even if we do not apply the plural form to a single individual (though I am willing to bet that someone has named a child "Roses" or the like). One might contend that these are modern names and hence in some way they fail to qualify as "real" names. But what then of such names as "Daisy," "Violet," "Ruby," or "Rose"? These names have been in English usage for over a hundred years, and all of them have plural forms, again even if not always used as names for a person. One might argue that we are witnessing here a process by which common nouns become proper nouns. However, all of these continue to be used as common nouns regardless of whether they are also used as proper nouns. Furthermore, one might well wonder whether this is not true of any proper noun—that it may well, if we go back far enough, have its origins in a common noun, no matter what the fate of that common noun. In fact, this may well indicate that the origin and development of nouns may not be the act of naming; rather, naming may be a derivative use of nouns (but that is another issue for discussion elsewhere).

When we turn to Hellenistic Greek, the situation is very similar. For example, as Herbert Smyth states in his grammar, "The plural of proper names . . . is used to denote a class."[27] He gives as the example Plato's *Theaetetus* 169b with Θησέες, translated "men like Theseus," although a better way of rendering it might be "Theseans." Setting aside once again the fact that the plural is used as a form of generic reference, it remains true that there can be plural forms of some proper nouns, here identifying a class or group by means of the plural proper name. A related example is found in the Greek of the New Testament. In Matthew 16:18 Jesus is reported as saying to Simon Barjonah, "You are Πέτρος." Even if one does not accept that this scene is historically accurate,

26. The issue of generic nouns is treated in Anderson, *Grammar of Names*, 228–37. Anderson notes that in Greek argumental and generic names take the article (p. 233).

27. H. W. Smyth, *Greek Grammar*, rev. G. Messing, rev. ed. (Cambridge, MA: Harvard University Press, 1956), 270.

at some point Peter was given the name "Peter."[28] Certainly the Gospels are all agreed that Jesus himself renamed Simon as Peter (Matt. 4:18; Mark 3:16; Luke 6:14; John 1:42). As is well known, however (despite Wallace's comment to the contrary), Πέτρος is the singular form of a common noun with the plural form πέτροι. It seems to me fruitless to argue that it represents anything less than a proper name, given that this was the name by which Peter came to be known in the Gospels and throughout subsequent history, and given that we have many people today known by the name "Peter" (though we generally neither know nor care that the name comes from a Greek common noun). Πέτρος, it seems to me, is here undergoing a significant functional extension.[29] When Jesus applies the noun to Peter as a name, it is probably being used in a way that consciously expands or shifts its semantic scope.

There are also a number of other nouns that may or may not be proper nouns. For example, what of the noun phrase or word group πνεῦμα ἅγιον ("Holy Spirit")? There are a number of places where the phrase is used in parallel with a proper name. For example, in 2 Corinthians 13:13 Paul closes his letter by referring to the grace of the Lord Jesus Christ and the fellowship of the "Holy Spirit." Moreover, it is the "Holy Spirit" that Jesus tells the disciples that they can expect to come upon them (Acts 1:8), and it is the "Holy Spirit" with which all are later filled (Acts 2:4). Two considerations must be taken into account. The first is that the noun πνεῦμα can be pluralized. As we have already seen above, however, this may not be as difficult a problem as some have suggested. A second consideration is that there are instances where the phrase apparently is not used as a proper name, such as John 1:33, where "holy spirit" (πνεῦμα ἅγιον, but in the dative singular) may refer to the spirit of Jesus, not to a unique figure. Less ambiguous is John 20:22, where Jesus instructs his followers to receive "Holy Spirit" (anarthrous, πνεῦμα ἅγιον). And arguably not ambiguous at all is John 14:26, where ὁ παράκλητος is defined appositionally by "the Holy Spirit" (τὸ πνεῦμα τὸ ἅγιον).[30] An even clearer example has already been mentioned. Is θεός the name of God in the New Testament? It can certainly appear with the article, but we have seen that

28. See S. E. Porter, *Studies in the Greek New Testament: Theory and Practice*, SBG 6 (New York: Peter Lang, 1996), 122.
29. My terminology here reflects a monosemic bias, wherein I assume that words have a single abstract sense that can be extended and restricted by contextual constraints rather than having multiple, discrete meanings entirely dependent upon cotext. An alternative explanation in this instance could be homonymy, but, with respect to proper nouns, this is unlikely as the extensions of meaning are often clearly relatable to a common abstract semantic component. For more detailed comments on monosemy, see chaps. 3 and 4 in the present volume and their attendant bibliography.
30. See Fee, "Use of the Definite Article," 171.

this in no way determines whether it does or does not function as a proper name. To my mind, the criterion of pluralization is not decisive either. Even though the plural θεοί occurs, this does not preclude the possibility that θεός has a relatively circumscribed functional extension—a proper name for the Judeo-Christian God.

Perhaps if we approach this issue from a different angle, we can gain further insight. Let us assume that the proper noun for God in the Old Testament is "YHWH."[31] There may or may not be other proper nouns for God as well (such as "Elohim," an interesting plural form), but the status of "YHWH" as a proper noun seems an indisputable supposition. In the Septuagint the word that is used to translate "YHWH" in the vast majority of instances (over 90%) is the Greek word κύριος. Recent Septuagint scholarship, on the basis of some of the Dead Sea Scrolls of the early Greek versions, has called into question whether the initial Greek translation of the Old Testament used κύριος for "YHWH." However, such scholarship also recognizes that by the first two centuries BC, κύριος was used in this way, and the New Testament confirms this.[32] Κύριος is widely used in the New Testament when Hebrew texts that use "YHWH" are cited in Greek. It seems logical to conclude that the name of God—or at least one of the names—in the New Testament is thus κύριος. Two factors should be noticed here. First, this is a word that clearly has a plural form, κύριοι. Second, κύριος displays a wide range of usage in the New Testament. This wide range of usage indicates that the word κύριος is functionally diverse, being used as a name of God and appearing in other contexts to refer to things such as earthly masters. When the Gospels refer to Jesus as κύριος, this may sometimes mean nothing more than "master." However, one must at least wonder whether Paul applies κύριος to Jesus Christ as the name of God. There are several instances where Paul cites an Old Testament passage that has "YHWH" in the Hebrew but κύριος in the Greek, and then subsequently refers to Jesus by using the word κύριος (e.g., Rom. 10:13; 1 Cor. 1:31; 10:26; 2 Cor. 10:17; 2 Tim. 2:19, and possibly others).[33]

All of this, it seems to me, is germane to consideration of θεός. It is worth considering whether θεός is a name of God in the New Testament. An example that suggests this is John 6:45, which cites Isaiah 54:13. The Isaiah passage refers to those who are "taught of the LORD," using the word κύριος in the

31. See Gibson, *Biblical Semantic Logic*, 151–54.

32. J. A. Fitzmyer, "κύριος, ου, ὁ," in vol. 2 of *Exegetical Dictionary of the New Testament*, ed. H. Balz and G. Schneider (Grand Rapids: Eerdmans, 1991), 328–31, esp. 330.

33. See S. E. Porter, "Images of Christ in Paul's Letters," in *Images of Christ: Ancient and Modern*, ed. S. E. Porter, M. A. Hayes, and D. Tombs, RILP 2 (Sheffield: Sheffield Academic Press, 1997), 101–2.

LXX for a rendering of "YHWH" in the MT. In John's Gospel, however, the word used for the translation of "YHWH" is θεός. This one instance is slender evidence indeed if one is trying to prove that θεός is used as a proper noun for the Judeo-Christian God in the New Testament. Without further instances, we cannot be sure whether or not θεός is a proper noun for God in the New Testament. We can be certain, however, that the philosophical tests regarding proper names do not work very well when applied to the Greek of the New Testament. They do not tell us what is and what is not a proper noun or name in Hellenistic Greek.

Additional Criteria

Having set aside the traditional philosophical criteria, we should consider three other tests. Rather than providing additional clarity, however, these additional criteria simply confuse matters further. The first possible test concerns the so-called nomina sacra found in Greek New Testament manuscripts.[34] In numerous manuscripts, from virtually the earliest New Testament papyri until much later, certain words were often written without their full complement of letters but instead with a line over a shortened form. Short forms like this seem to be similar to abbreviations, but they are peculiar in some ways to Christian copyists and scribes. One might think that nomina sacra provide us with some insight into what was considered to be a sacred name in the New Testament. According to Larry Hurtado, the four words most frequently written as nomina sacra in the earliest manuscripts are θεός ("God"), κύριος ("Lord"), χριστός ("Christ"), and Ἰησοῦς ("Jesus").[35] Schuyler Brown even says that these

34. I thank my colleague Matthew Brook O'Donnell for his suggestions regarding the nomina sacra and their possible relevance to this discussion. Bibliography on the nomina sacra includes L. Traube, *Nomina Sacra: Versuch einer Geschichte der christlichen Kürzung*, QULPM 2 (Darmstadt: Wissenschaftliche Buchgesellschaft, 1967); F. G. Kenyon, "Nomina Sacra in the Chester Beatty Papyri," *Aegyptus* 13 (1933): 5–10; A. H. R. E. Paap, *Nomina Sacra in the Greek Papyri of the First Five Centuries AD: The Sources and Some Deductions*, PLB 8 (Leiden: Brill, 1959); J. O'Callaghan, "*Nomina Sacra*" in Papyris Graecis Saeculi III Neotestamentariis, AnBib 46 (Rome: Biblical Institute Press, 1970); S. Brown, "Concerning the Origin of the Nomina Sacra," *SPap* 9 (1970): 7–19; J. O'Callaghan, "'Nominum sacrorum' elenchus in Graecis Novi Testamenti papyris a saeculo IV usque ad VIII," *SPap* 10 (1971): 99–122; C. H. Roberts, *Manuscript, Society and Belief in Early Christian Egypt* (London: British Academy; Oxford University Press, 1979), 26–48; L. W. Hurtado, "The Origin of the *Nomina Sacra*: A Proposal," *JBL* 117 (1998): 655–73 (repr. in Hurtado, *The Earliest Christian Artifacts: Manuscripts and Christian Origins* [Grand Rapids: Eerdmans, 2006], 95–134); C. M. Tuckett, "'Nomina Sacra': Yes and No," in *The Biblical Canons*, ed. J.-M. Auwers and H. J. de Jonge, BETL 163 (Leuven: Peeters, 2003), 431–58.
35. Hurtado, *Earliest Christian Artifacts*, 97.

are *nomina divina*, or divine names.[36] This may indicate that at least early on
these were considered proper nouns, along with other names such as "Mary"
and "Martha" that are also used in their shortened form. Unfortunately, so
also are "human" (ἄνθρωπος), "heaven" (οὐρανός), "mother" (μήτηρ), and
"cross" (σταυρός), even at a fairly early stage. Ultimately, the nomina sacra
point to significant concepts recognized by early copyists, but not necessarily
to proper nouns per se.

Another test might be to examine the use of the word ὄνομα ("name") and
its collocations in the New Testament. In the Gospels, the standard syntactical
pattern is for the noun ὄνομα to be used appositionally with a proper noun in
the same case. Thus, "You shall call his name Jesus" (Matt. 1:21).[37] In Acts,
the standard syntactical pattern is for the noun ὄνομα to be used in the dative
case, when the proper noun is used in another. Thus a certain man is "Ananias
by name [ὀνόματι]" (Acts 5:1).[38] There also appears to be a third syntactical
pattern, which utilizes a form of the noun ὄνομα with a dependent genitive.
Thus Acts 13:6 speaks of the false prophet having the name "of Bar-Jesus"
(Βαριησοῦ), and 1 Corinthians 1:13 mentions "the name of Paul" (τὸ ὄνομα
Παύλου). Numerous places, especially in Acts, speak of the name "of Jesus
Christ,"[39] or the name "of Jesus."[40] For example, Acts 4:10 speaks of "the
name of Jesus Christ the Nazarene," with verse 12 stating that there is no
other name under heaven by which people are saved, making it clear (at least
to me) that the author sees "Jesus Christ the Nazarene" as a name. This use
of a dependent genitive phrase has suggestive implications for a number of
other instances in the New Testament. For example, Matthew 28:19 speaks
of baptism into "the name of the Father, Son, and Holy Spirit." Which of
these are names, if any, and which are epithets, or descriptive appellatives? Or
what are we to make of the phrase "name of the Lord"?[41] Two factors suggest
that κύριος here may be functioning as a proper noun. First, there are several
instances where the phrase "name of the Lord Jesus (Christ)" is used. "Name
of the Lord" may simply be shorthand, in which case "Lord Jesus Christ"

36. Brown, "Concerning the Origin," 19.
37. See, e.g., Matt. 1:23, 25; 10:2 (in the plural with the names of the disciples); 24:5; 27:57;
Mark 3:16, 17; 5:9; 14:32; Luke 1:5, 13, 26, 27, 31, 63; 2:21, 25; 8:30, 41; 24:13; John 1:6; 3:1;
18:10; Acts 27:1; 28:7; Rev. 9:11.
38. See, e.g., Matt. 27:32; Mark 5:22; Luke 1:5; 5:27; 10:38; 23:50; 24:18; Acts 5:34; 8:9; 9:10,
11, 12, 33, 36; 10:1; 11:28; 12:13; 16:1, 14; 17:34; 18:2, 7, 24; 19:24; 20:9; 21:10.
39. Acts 2:38; 3:6; 8:12, 16; 10:48; 15:26 (with "Lord Jesus Christ"); 16:18; 1 Cor. 1:2, 10;
6:11; Eph. 5:20; 2 Thess. 3:6; 1 John 3:23.
40. Acts 4:18; 5:40; 9:27; 19:5, 13, 17; 21:13; 26:9; 1 Cor. 5:4; Phil. 2:10; Col. 3:17; 2 Thess.
1:12. Compare 1 Pet. 4:14 with "name of Christ."
41. Besides those mentioned below, see Acts 2:21; 9:28; Rom. 10:13; 2 Tim. 2:19; James 5:14.

is a full name. Second, when the phrase is used in the so-called triumphal entry,[42] it is in a quotation of Psalm 118:26, which uses κύριος as a translation of "YHWH" in the MT. Related instances worth mentioning include the phrase "name of God" (Rom. 2:24; 1 Tim. 6:1; Rev. 3:12; 16:9),[43] "name of the only begotten Son of God" (John 3:18; cf. 1 John 5:13), and "name of the Father" (John 10:25; Rev. 14:1). I think that it is debatable whether any of this last set can be seen as proper nouns. They are more likely descriptive epithets. The same probably is true of Revelation 13:17, which mentions the "name of the beast," although many seem to have taken "beast" as a proper name.

A third test is to examine the use of the word καλέω ("call") and its collocations in the New Testament. This test proves less productive than one might at first hope in trying to determine how users of the language thought of the process of "calling" or "naming." The vast majority of instances are simply with the sense of calling, appointing, or choosing rather than a more modulated sense of naming. Other instances, in which καλέω is used with ὄνομα, have already been discussed above.[44] Of the remaining uses, most are simple naming constructions, where someone or something is given a name. For example, the son of Elizabeth and Zechariah is "called John" (Luke 1:60), and the city where Jesus is born is "called Bethlehem" (Luke 2:4).[45] These examples seem to me to be straightforward. There are a number of other phrases, however, that are also worth considering. For example, Matthew 2:23 says that "he will be called a Nazarene," which seems to be an instance of naming. There are also a number of names apparently being given to places, such as "field of blood" (Matt. 27:8) or the mountain called "olives" (Luke 19:29; 21:37; Acts 1:12 [note the plural]). Also to be considered are instances where something is called "house of prayer" (Matt. 21:13; Mark 11:17), "skull" (Luke 23:33), "straight" (Acts 9:11), and "Euraquilo" (Acts 27:14). That these probably are proper nouns is given weight by the phrasing in Acts 1:19, where the author states that the land is called "Hakeldama," or "field of blood," with similar syntax to the examples just cited above. Also similar in syntax, however, are instances where a person is called "son/sons of God" (Luke 1:35; Matt. 5:9), "lord" (Matt. 22:43, 45; 1 Pet. 3:6), "son of the highest" (Luke 1:32), "prophet of the highest" (Luke 1:76), "holy to the Lord" (Luke 2:23), or "sons of the

42. Matt. 21:9 (see also 23:39); Mark 11:9; Luke 19:38; John 12:13.
43. The instance in Rev. 3:12 has two parallel phrases, "name of God" and "name of the city of God." Is "City of God" the name of the city? Augustine perhaps thought so.
44. For example, Matt. 1:21, 23, 25; Luke 1:13, 31.
45. See also Luke 1:59; 2:21; 6:15; 7:11; 8:2; 10:39; 19:2; John 1:42; Acts 1:19, 23; 3:11; 7:58; 10:1; 13:1; 14:12; 15:22, 37; 27:8, 16; 28:1; Rev. 1:9; 11:8; 16:16.

living God" (Rom. 9:26).[46] All of these are better described as epithets. Perhaps least easy to see as a proper noun, and thus perhaps in this instance used as a form of singular address, is "son" in Luke 15:19, 21 in the parable of the prodigal son, "servant" in 1 Corinthians 7:21–22, "apostle" in 1 Corinthians 15:9, "friend of God" in James 2:23, and "children of God" in 1 John 3:1. These instances of καλέω indicate nothing more than that there is a significant gray area with regard to determining what constitutes a proper noun.[47]

Conclusion

I think that several tentative conclusions have been reached. First, the standard philosophical tests related to proper names cannot be applied to proper nouns in the Greek of the New Testament. Whatever merit they may have for discussion of contemporary English problems, or whatever merit they might have when redefined for Greek, they cannot be used as they are. Second, this study points to the fact that, when discussing things such as proper nouns, one must be careful to try to define one's categories in terms of the language being studied rather than by imposing some external or predetermined conceptual framework. A functional rather than a formalist linguistic perspective is to be preferred. Third, what we find in New Testament Greek (and this probably is a general conclusion that applies to many languages) is that proper nouns do not form a category that is separate and distinct from common nouns. Rather, proper nouns are merely a subset of nouns—a fuzzy set whose boundaries must be determined by studying how nouns are actually used. A number of what we might wish to call proper nouns may be merely instances of common nouns as epithets. A number of what we might wish to call common nouns may simply be nouns that are used to refer to a specific, unique individual. Context must be decisive in determining when these nouns are being used as proper nouns (i.e., to name a single and specific individual) and when they are being used as common nouns (i.e., to refer to a token of a type).

46. At Rev. 19:11 there is a textual variant with the word for "calling," and the attributions "faithful" and "true."

47. A similar observation is made by Waismann with respect to the English word "call" (*Principles*, 195–96).

21

Hyponymy and the Trinity

Introduction

After being relegated to the minor leagues by Friedrich Schleiermacher early in the nineteenth century,[1] the topic of the Trinity has been called up to the major leagues again in recent theological discussion and debate.[2] But this trinitarian work is being done on different terms than before. Theologians are realizing more and more the importance of models and analogies for interpretation of a

---

I am grateful to several friends over the years who have commented on various forms of this chapter and have made suggestions from which I—and the chapter, I trust—have benefited. I especially thank my colleague Steven Studebaker for his comments on this chapter.

1. Friedrich Schleiermacher marks the beginning of theological liberalism, with its redefinition of the basis of theology and the nature of Jesus Christ's and the Holy Spirit's divinity, especially in the light of his human-centered and experience-oriented system of belief. See T. Tice, *Schleiermacher* (Nashville: Abingdon, 2006), 42–43.

2. See, e.g., K. Rahner, *The Trinity*, trans. J. Donceel (New York: Seabury, 1974); G. Wainwright, "The Doctrine of the Trinity: Where the Church Stands or Falls," *Int* 45 (1991): 117–32; L. Gilkey, "God," in *Christian Theology: An Introduction to Its Traditions and Tasks*, ed. P. C. Hodgson and R. H. King, rev. ed. (Minneapolis: Fortress, 1994), 88–113, esp. 93–96; A. Stirling, ed., *The Trinity: An Essential for Faith in Our Time* (Nappanee, IN: Evangel, 2000); R. Letham, *The Holy Trinity: In Scripture, History, Theology, and Worship* (Phillipsburg, NJ: P&R, 2004); G. Emery, *The Trinity: An Introduction to Catholic Doctrine on the Triune God*, trans. M. Levering (Washington, DC: Catholic University of America Press, 2011).

concept as complex as the Trinity. Several of these models—the interpersonal, social, process, narrative, and eschatological models—participate in some of the most recent trends and share some of the most avant-garde language in theology.[3] I could profitably enter into the current discussion and offer my own critique, but instead I would like to shift the focus slightly by employing a linguistic model to attempt to bring further insight to the concept of the Trinity. I suggest that the linguistic notion of hyponymy provides a working model that can appreciate the complex and developing relationships of divine epithets employed in New Testament writings.

Hyponymy as a Useful Model

James Barr opened the door for serious account to be taken of modern structural linguistics in theological studies.[4] And in the last nearly fifty years structural semantics has made great strides forward in discussion of the relations that obtain among the vocabulary items of a language, such as synonymy, antonymy, and meronymy.[5] One of these relations is called hyponymy, or inclusion. For example, the meaning of "tulip" is included in the meaning of "flower," just as the meanings of "violet," "rose," and "daisy" are (see fig. 21.1). "Flower" is the superordinate term with respect to its various hyponyms.[6] This relationship is one of genus and species, but hyponymous relations need not be constrained by this. Other hyponymous relations include the superordinate term "military" and the hyponyms "army," "navy," "air force," and "marines," in this instance not an example of genus and species.[7]

3. For discussion of the Trinity and some of the issues, see L. Hodgson, *The Doctrine of the Trinity* (Digswell Place: Nisbet, 1943); J. Macquarrie, *Principles of Christian Theology* (New York: Scribner, 1966), 174–93; Letham, *Holy Trinity*, 271–373.

4. See J. Barr, *The Semantics of Biblical Language* (Oxford: Oxford University Press, 1961). However, I also believe that, as indicated by the widespread neglect of Barr's pronouncements in continuing biblical and theological studies, his volume remains one of the most widely mentioned yet infrequently actually read or understood. If he were read and understood, there would not be such egregious semantic mistakes made by biblical scholars.

5. See, e.g., D. A. Cruse, *Lexical Semantics*, CTL (Cambridge: Cambridge University Press, 1986); D. Geeraerts, *Theories of Lexical Semantics* (Oxford: Oxford University Press, 2010), esp. 47–100.

6. See J. Lyons, *Introduction to Theoretical Linguistics* (Cambridge: Cambridge University Press, 1968), 453–55, using color terms and flowers as primary examples; Lyons, *Semantics*, 2 vols. (Cambridge: Cambridge University Press, 1977), 1:293–95, noting the difficulty of knowing whether the hyponym is included in the superordinate or vice versa. This is an important question, as will be seen below.

7. A question that I do not pursue here is whether the members of the Trinity enjoy a genus and species relationship. Common or intrinsic features of the species of a genus must be identified, as not all features—e.g., color, height, weight, and texture—might be relevant.

In recent theological discussion the concept of the Trinity is well defended, but much current discussion seems to neglect the biblical-theological level. In other words, discussion of the Trinity is often an attempt to grasp the creedal implications of a doctrine that most scholars are agreed grew up in the postapostolic church amid fundamental doctrinal and related conflicts. On the basis of hyponymy, however, I would like to offer a new look at the biblical evidence to see if we can gain insight, if not necessarily into the Trinity per se, at least into the biblical usage of terms such as "God" and "Lord," and their possible relationships.

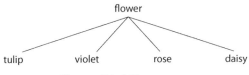

Figure 21.1 Hyponomy

Hyponymy, Trinity, and Early Christian Writings

In the Pauline writings, some of the earliest writings of Christianity, there are numerous tripartite formulas or passages that depict three apparently divine or spiritual beings in some type of relationship. For example, in 2 Thessalonians 2:13–14 Paul says, "God chose you, as a guarantee, unto salvation in holiness of the Spirit and belief of truth, unto which he also called you through our gospel to the obtaining of the glory of our Lord Jesus Christ." I cite also 1 Corinthians 12:4–6, where Paul refers to "the same Spirit . . . same Lord . . . and same God," and 2 Corinthians 13:13, where he prays that "the grace of the Lord Jesus Christ, the love of God, and the communion of the Holy Spirit" would be with his readers. Similar formulas are found in Romans (1:1–4; 8:1–3, 9–11), Galatians (4:6), Ephesians (1:13–14, 17; 2:18, 22; 3:15–17; 4:4–7), Philippians (3:3), Colossians (1:6–9), 1 Thessalonians (1:4–6), and Titus (3:4–6).[8] Many scholars argue that this evidence, however, shows no awareness of what came to be labeled as the Trinity or of any of its theoretical problems, but clearly

---

8. I have elsewhere called these prototrinitarian passages. See S. E. Porter, "Hermeneutics, Biblical Interpretation and Theology: Hunch, Holy Spirit or Hard Work?," in *Beyond the Bible: Moving from Scripture to Theology*, by I. H. Marshall, with essays by K. Vanhoozer and S. E. Porter (Grand Rapids: Baker Academic; Milton Keynes: Paternoster, 2004), 97–127, esp. 122. G. D. Fee (*Pauline Christology* [Peabody, MA: Hendrickson, 2007], 63) has adopted this term in his own work. See his list of such passages in G. D. Fee, *God's Empowering Presence: The Holy Spirit in the Letters of Paul* (Peabody, MA: Hendrickson, 1994), 48n39. Letham (*Holy Trinity*, 52–72) calls them "triadic patterns."

maintains distinct identities, in some instances even indicating hierarchy.[9] This conclusion shows that the interpretive lens by which scholars examine the biblical data has clear exegetical implications, in the same way that I am arguing that examining similar passages by means of hyponymy opens up new interpretive possibilities.

This raises a number of issues, not all of which I can explore in this chapter. However, I begin with an interesting linguistic question that is raised here: are speakers aware of something for which they do not have a simple term in their vocabulary? One of several kinds of hyponymous relationship is where a number of hyponymous terms have no specific superordinate term. For example, ancient Greek has terms for "helmsman," "carpenter," "doctor," "flautist," and "cobbler," all placed under the superordinate term of *dēmiourgos*, yet in English there is no term that includes all of these (see 21.2).[10] Does this mean English speakers are unaware of any relation among these terms and cannot speak of them meaningfully? This is doubtful, even if they do not place them all together in one simple category. Similarly, in English "carrot," "pea," and "potato" are hyponyms of "vegetable," yet in German the nearest equivalent, "Gemüse," does not include "potato." My German friends assure me that, although they do not have an inclusive or superordinate term used in the same way as in English, they know quite a bit about what we call "vegetables." In the Pauline Letters, Paul uses terms such as "God," "Son," and "Spirit," as indicated above, but of course he does not use the term "Trinity." Can it, therefore, be asserted unquestionably that Paul was not aware of the concept of the Trinity? Or better still, can it be asserted that he was not aware of relations among the three, what we might now call the Trinity, because he does not appear to have a simple term to label it? Certainly he did not know the terminology that Tertullian or Basil used.[11] Yet on the basis of the widespread use of the tripartite formulas, it is worth considering that Paul was aware of some type of close relations (what we might even call ontological) among what are now called the three persons, though he did not have a superordinate term at his immediate disposal.

Some might object that Paul did not view the individual members of the hyponymic Trinity to be related to each other as hypostases. Surely this is

---

9. See J. D. G. Dunn, *Christology in the Making: A New Testament Inquiry into the Origins of the Doctrine of the Incarnation* (Philadelphia: Westminster, 1980).

10. See J. Lyons, *Structural Semantics: An Analysis of Part of the Vocabulary of Plato* (Oxford: Blackwell, 1963), 68–71 and 140–43. This situation is further complicated by Paul's apparent use of "Lord" both for God the Father and for the Son. See, e.g., 2 Tim. 2:7, 19.

11. See G. Scott, "The Foundation of the Doctrine of the Trinity: The Early Church," in Stirling, *The Trinity*, 109–38, esp. 120.

wide of the mark on two accounts. The first is that the first formulation of the Trinity per se did not necessarily come fully formed from its womb, but was the result of historical-theological debate. The second is that, if we accept the Christian view of the Trinity—as I do—then we must retrospectively understand that the basis of this conception is in the biblical documents, not simply a later doctrinal imposition, and Paul's Letters (though see below) are as good a place as any to find the basis of this.[12] The argument that he would not understand the relation in the same terms we would is specious, as the term itself was not formulated until later. That Paul *saw* a relationship, perhaps even an ontological one, sufficient enough to bring terms such as "God," "Lord," "Jesus Christ," and "Spirit" together in a meaningful way, is the important point.

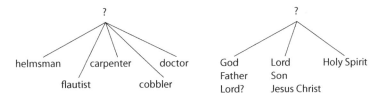

Figure 21.2 Hyponomous Terms without Superordinate Term

If this is the case, hyponymy perhaps helps to clarify Matthew 28:19, the baptismal formula of the so-called Great Commission. On critical grounds, scholars often call this formulation into question, since it is unparalleled in the rest of the Synoptics and is not duplicated in Acts, where baptism is performed in the name of Jesus Christ only, as if an understanding of a relation among the three could not be conceived of this early.[13] On these critical grounds it is easy to doubt that these words were spoken by Jesus and hence must be attributed to much later church development, but several other points must be considered. *Didache* 7.1–3 (possibly dating to the late first century) show that the tripartite baptismal formula did exist in the early church, when readers are instructed to baptize in the name of "the Father and the Son and the Holy Spirit." If Acts 2:38–39 is examined closely, it can be seen that whereas

12. I believe that Paul accepted the God of the Old Testament, the divinity of Jesus Christ (see, e.g., Phil. 2:6–11), and the divinity of the Holy Spirit (see, e.g., Rom. 8:9). In one sense, all I am arguing here is that, on this basis, Paul saw a common divine character among them, even if he lacked the term that we would use to describe this—at least that is what his language usage can be interpreted to indicate.

13. See G. R. Osborne, *Matthew*, ZECNT (Grand Rapids: Zondervan, 2010), 1081. See also further discussion of Matt. 28:19–20 in chap. 14 of the present volume.

the baptism itself is performed in the name of Jesus Christ, reference to the Holy Spirit and Lord God follow on closely. Not only is evidence for tripartite use early, but the concept of hyponymy makes their relationship conceivable—with Jesus himself possibly understanding the terminology and even himself in this light.

The tripartite formulation is included in a looser way elsewhere in the Gospels.[14] For example, in Mark 1:10–17, at Jesus's baptism, the Spirit descends, and a voice from heaven commends Jesus as "my Son." More problematic are the following passages: Luke 24:49, where Jesus gives his followers the promise of his Father, that they are to wait in the city until power comes from on high; Matthew 12:28, where Jesus says, "If I cast out demons by the Spirit of God, then the kingdom of God has come upon you"; and Luke 1:35, where the angel tells Mary that the Holy Spirit will come upon her, the power of the Most High will overshadow her, and the holy offspring will be called "Son of God." These last several examples show ambiguity with regard to what is traditionally called the first member of the Trinity, God the Father, and the Trinity itself, the Triune God. The Gospels seem, however, to show a further development in prototrinitarian thought that attempts to provide a superordinate term for the hyponymous relationship. The Gospel writers seem to go to lengths to refer to a God "above," and finally they settle upon the term "God," Greek θεός. Old Testament usage probably influenced this selection. That name of God then is used both as one of the hyponymous terms and as the superordinate term. (Parenthetically, this may in fact be true of Paul as well, though I am essentially limiting my discussion to places where multiple members of the Trinity are referred to.)

The use of a hyponym as a superordinate term is not particularly surprising. This kind of semantic scheme can be found in English avian terminology, where "drake" refers to the male of the species, and "duck" to the female. But "duck" is also used as the superordinate term. In most instances, the potential ambiguity is not a problem because of context. Perhaps this helps to clarify biblical passages often seen as problematic. For example, in John 1:1 the author says, "In the beginning was the Word, and the Word was with God, and the Word was God." The relationships among the beings represented by the terms are complex, but hyponymy may suggest that they are understood in both relations of equality and hierarchy. John 1:1 makes sense if "the Word was with God" is a formulation about two hyponyms as individual members

14. See A. D. Churchill, "The New Testament and the Trinity," in Stirling, *The Trinity*, 31–105. Churchill treats many of the same passages as I do here, but does not appeal to the use of hyponymy to resolve some of the ambiguities. Compare Letham, *Holy Trinity*, 34–85.

of the Trinity, while "the Word was God" is a formulation that includes both a hyponym, "Word," and its superordinate term, "God," or what would later be called the Triune God, whose status (as well as label) encompasses all of its hyponyms or individual members. The scheme in figure 21.3 must be adapted to take into account the terminology of each subcorpus of New Testament writings, but I think that it indicates a way forward in discussing the issue.

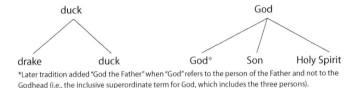

*Later tradition added "God the Father" when "God" refers to the person of the Father and not to the Godhead (i.e., the inclusive superordinate term for God, which includes the three persons).

Figure 21.3 Hyponomy with Hyponym as a Superordinate Term

Incidentally, I wonder, therefore, if some of the terminology devised to describe the Trinity—terms such as "immanent," "economic," and especially "hypostasis"—are not sometimes more confusing than helpful, or at least are not the only terms that can and should be used. They too are terms used in particular models. Let me draw an analogy. I might say, for example, that "orange" and "grapefruit" are "citrus fruits." In other words, they are hyponyms of the superordinate term "citrus fruit." I need not ponder overly long on describing what traits they share, which traits distinguish them, any order or hierarchy, and especially orders of emanation and individuation, since these terms establish functional relationships by use in the context of the hyponymous model. And if English did not have the term "citrus fruit," it is not hard to believe that the terms "orange" and "grapefruit" would still be classed together. I am not trying to be dismissive of longstanding theological debates. However, the use of hyponymy to discuss the biblical evidence might provide a way forward that does not introduce such historical technical discussion too early in the formulation.

Conclusion

There are several benefits of using hyponymy as a model of the Trinity. First, it can serve as an instructive interpretive device, providing a hermeneutical framework for understanding a body of data—the biblical data—often seen as unwieldy and intractable, as an explainable whole. Not only could this provide a helpful teaching model, but also the kinds of assumptions inherent in the model could help to provide useful categories for understanding relations among the various divine epithets used by New Testament writers. It becomes clear that most instances of New Testament usage employ the hyponymous terms, often without a superordinate term in view or mind. Second, hyponymy can help us to understand the evolution of thought regarding the Trinity. It is entirely plausible that Paul himself may well have deeply understood what is now called the Trinity, as evidenced through his conscious use of tripartite formulas that conform to the superordinate and hyponymous lexical pattern. This, then, places the concept of the Trinity early in Christian understanding, much earlier than often posited, even if there was not a specific or single term for it. To put it another way, there is no critical objection to the early formulation of the concept of the Trinity, since prototrinitarian formulas undoubtedly appear in the Pauline Letters, and there is linguistic precedent for such an understanding.[15] Third, this hermeneutical correlation also lends credence to the early church fleshing out the initial Pauline formulation of the Trinity through use of one of the hyponymous terms as the superordinate term, even though a potentially ambiguous term was selected (witness contemporary parlance that speaks of "the trinitarian God" to distinguish from "God the Father").[16] But ambiguity in vocabulary does not necessarily indicate confusion, sloppiness, or lack of understanding. It instead points here to an early doctrinal tension. Fourth, this model may also provide some evidence for Jesus's own consciousness of his own trinitarian relation with the Father and the Spirit. I will not be so bold as to argue stringently for such an understanding, since other critical issues must be taken into account, but I will say only that there is no linguistic argument that stands in its way. In fact, hyponymy as a model for the Trinity suggests an early acceptance of just such a structure of understanding.

15. See A. W. Wainwright, *The Trinity in the New Testament* (London: SPCK, 1962), esp. 248–67.

16. As noted above, later tradition added "God the Father" when "God" refers to the person of the Father and not to the Godhead.

Bibliography

Abbott, E. A. *Johannine Grammar*. London: A&C Black, 1906.

Adams, E. "Historical Crisis and Cosmic Crisis in Mark 13 and Lucan's *Civil War*." *TynBul* 48 (1997): 329–44.

Aitchison, J. "The Order of Word Order Change." *TPS* (1979): 43–65.

Aland, K. "Der neue 'Standard-Text' in seinem Verhältnis zu den frühen Papyri und Majuskeln." In *New Testament Textual Criticism: Its Significance for Exegesis; Essays in Honour of Bruce M. Metzger*, edited by E. J. Epp and G. D. Fee, 157–75. Oxford: Clarendon, 1981.

———. "The Significance of the Papyri for Progress in New Testament Research." In *The Bible in Modern Scholarship: Papers Read at the 100th Meeting of the Society of Biblical Literature, December 28–30, 1964*, edited by J. P. Hyatt, 325–46. Nashville: Abingdon, 1965.

Aland, K., and B. Aland. *The Text of the New Testament: An Introduction to the Critical Editions and to the Theory and Practice of Modern Textual Criticism*. Translated by E. F. Rhodes. 2nd ed. Grand Rapids: Eerdmans, 1989.

Alford, H. *Alford's Greek Testament: An Exegetical and Critical Commentary*. 4 vols. London: Rivingtons, 1844–57. Rev. ed., 1874–75. Reprint, Grand Rapids: Guardian Press, 1976.

Allen, W. C. *A Critical and Exegetical Commentary on the Gospel according to S. Matthew*. ICC. Edinburgh: T&T Clark, 1907.

Alter, R. *The Art of Biblical Narrative*. New York: Basic Books, 1981.

Ammann, H. "Untersuchungen zur homerischen Wortfolge und Satzstruktur." *IF* 42 (1924): 149–78, 300–322.

———. "Wortstellung und Stilentwickelung." *Glotta* 12 (1922): 107–11.

Andersen, F. I. *The Sentence in Biblical Hebrew*. JLSP 231. The Hague: Mouton, 1974.

Anderson, J. M. *The Grammar of Names*. Oxford: Oxford University Press, 2007.

Apel, W. "Aulos." In *Harvard Dictionary of Music*, edited by W. Apel, 63–64. 2nd ed. Cambridge, MA: Belknap Press of Harvard University Press, 1969.

Ariel, M. *Defining Pragmatics*. RSL. Cambridge: Cambridge University Press, 2010.

Arnold, C. E. *The Colossian Syncretism: The Interface between Christianity and Folk Belief at Colossae*. WUNT 2/77. Tübingen: Mohr Siebeck, 1995. Reprint, Grand Rapids: Baker, 1996.

Atkinson, D., and D. Biber. "Register: A Review of Empirical Research." In *Sociolinguistic Perspectives on Register*, edited by D. Biber and E. Finegan, 351–85. OSS. New York: Oxford University Press, 1994.

Aune, D. E. *Prophecy in Early Christianity and the Ancient Mediterranean World*. Grand Rapids: Eerdmans, 1983.

Austin, J. L. *How to Do Things with Words*. Oxford: Clarendon, 1962.

Bache, C. *English Tense and Aspect in Halliday's Systemic Functional Grammar: A Critical Appraisal and an Alternative*. London: Equinox, 2008.

Bakker, E. J. "Foregrounding and Indirect Discourse: Temporal Subclauses in a Herodotean Short Story." *JPrag* 16 (1991): 225–47.

———, ed. *Grammar as Interpretation: Greek Literature in Its Linguistic Contexts*. Mnemosyne 171. Leiden: Brill, 1997.

———. "Pragmatics: Speech and Text." In *A Companion to the Ancient Greek Language*, edited by E. J. Bakker, 151–68. BCAW. Chichester: Blackwell, 2010.

———. "Similes, Augment, and the Language of Immediacy." In *Speaking Volumes: Orality and Literacy in the Greek and Roman World*, edited by J. Watson, 1–23. Mnemosyne 218. Leiden: Brill, 2001.

Bakker, S., and G. Wakker, eds. *Discourse Cohesion in Ancient Greek*. ASCP 16. Leiden: Brill, 2009.

Bal, M. *Narratology: Introduction to the Theory of Narrative*. Translated by C. van Boheemen. Toronto: University of Toronto Press, 1985.

Baldwin, H. S. "Appendix 2: αὐθεντέω in Ancient Greek Literature." In *Women in the Church: A Fresh Analysis of Timothy 2:9–15*, edited by A. J. Köstenberger, T. R. Schreiner, and H. S. Baldwin, 269–305. Grand Rapids: Baker Books, 1995.

———. "A Difficult Word—αὐθεντέω in 1 Timothy 2:12." In *Women in the Church: A Fresh Analysis of Timothy 2:9–15*, edited by A. J. Köstenberger, T. R. Schreiner, and H. S. Baldwin, 65–80. Grand Rapids: Baker Books, 1995.

———. "An Important Word: Αὐθεντέω in 1 Timothy 2:12." In *Women in the Church: An Analysis and Application of 1 Timothy 2:9–15*, edited by A. J. Köstenberger and T. R. Schreiner, 39–51. 2nd ed. Grand Rapids: Baker Academic, 2005.

Banker, J. "The Position of the Vocative *adelphoi* in the Clause." *START* 11 (1984): 29–36.

Barclay, J. M. G. "Mirror-Reading a Polemical Letter: Galatians as a Test Case." *JSNT* 31 (1987): 73–93.

Barnbrook, G., O. Mason, and R. Krishnamurthy. *Collocation: Applications and Implications*. Basingstoke: Palgrave Macmillan, 2013.

Barnett, P. W. "Opponents of Paul." In *Dictionary of Paul and His Letters*, edited by G. F. Hawthorne, R. P. Martin, and D. G. Reid, 644–53. Downers Grove, IL: InterVarsity, 1993.

Barr, J. "Abba Isn't Daddy." *JTS* 39 (1988): 28–47.

———. *Biblical Words for Time*. London: SCM, 1962. 2nd ed., 1969.

———. *The Semantics of Biblical Language*. Oxford: Oxford University Press, 1961.

Barrett, C. K. *The Gospel according to St. John*. 2nd ed. London: SPCK, 1978.

———. *The Pastoral Epistles in the New English Bible*. Oxford: Clarendon, 1963.

Basset, L. "L'augment et la distinction discours/récit dans l'*Iliade* et l'*Odyssée*." In *Études homériques: Séminaire de recherche*, ed. M. Casevitz, 9–16. TMO 17. Lyon: Maison de l'Orient, 1989.

Battistella, E. L. *The Logic of Markedness*. Oxford: Oxford University Press, 1996.

Bauckham, R., ed. *The Gospels for All Christians: Rethinking the Gospel Audiences*. Grand Rapids: Eerdmans, 1998.

Bauer, W. *A Greek-English Lexicon of the New Testament and Other Early Christian Literature*. Translated by W. F. Arndt and F. W. Gingrich. Chicago: University of Chicago Press, 1957. 2nd ed., revised by F. W. Gingrich and F. W. Danker, 1979.

———. *A Greek-English Lexicon of the New Testament and Other Early Christian Literature*. Edited by F. W. Danker. 3rd ed. Chicago: University of Chicago Press, 2000.

———. *Griechisch-Deutsches Wörterbuch zu den Schriften des Neuen Testaments und der übrigen urchristlichen Literatur*. 2nd ed. Gießen: Töpelmann, 1928. 3rd ed.,

Berlin: de Gruyter, 1937. 4th ed., 1952. 5th ed., 1958. 6th ed., revised by K. Aland and B. Aland with V. Reichmann, 1988.

Baur, F. C. "Die Christuspartei in der korinthischen Gemeinde, der Gegensatz des Petrischen und Paulinischen Christentum in der ältesten Kirche, der Apostel Petrus in Rom." *TZT* 4 (1831): 61–206.

———. *Paul, the Apostle of Jesus Christ: His Life and Work, His Epistles and Teachings; A Contribution to a Critical History of Primitive Christianity*. Translated by A. Menzies. 2 vols. London: Williams & Norgate, 1873–75. Reprinted in 1 vol., Peabody, MA: Hendrickson, 2003.

Beardslee, W. *Literary Criticism of the New Testament*. GBSNT. Philadelphia: Fortress, 1969.

Beasley-Murray, G. R. *Jesus and the Kingdom of God*. Grand Rapids: Eerdmans, 1986.

———. *Jesus and the Last Days: The Interpretation of the Olivet Discourse*. Peabody, MA: Hendrickson, 1993.

Beaugrande, R. de. *Linguistic Theory: The Discourse of Fundamental Works*. LLL. London: Longman, 1991.

———. "'Register' in Discourse Studies: A Concept in Search of a Theory." In *Register Analysis: Theory and Practice*, edited by M. Ghadessy, 7–25. London: Pinter, 1993.

———. *Text, Discourse, and Process: Toward a Multidisciplinary Science of Texts*. ADP 4. London: Longman, 1980.

Beaugrande, R.-A. de, and W. Dressler. *Introduction to Text Linguistics*. LLL. London: Longman, 1981.

Beck, D. R. *The Discipleship Paradigm: Readers and Anonymous Characters in the Fourth Gospel*. BIS 27. Leiden: Brill, 1997.

Beirne, M. M. *Women and Men in the Fourth Gospel: A Genuine Discipleship of Equals*. JSNTSup 242. Sheffield: Sheffield Academic Press, 2003.

Bennema, C. *Encountering Jesus: Character Studies in the Gospel of John*. Milton Keynes: Paternoster, 2009.

Bentein, K. "Perfect." In vol. 3 of *Encyclopedia of Ancient Greek Language and Linguistics*, edited by G. K. Giannakis, 46–49. Leiden: Brill, 2014.

Benveniste, É. *Problèmes de linguistique generale*. 2 vols. Paris: Gallimard, 1966.

Bergson, L. *Zur Stellung des Adjektivs in der älteren griechischen Prosa: Die Motive der Voran- bzw. Nachstellung in ihren Hauptzügen*. AUSSGS 1. Stockholm: Almqvist & Wiksell, 1960.

Berkowitz, L., and K. A. Squitier. *Thesaurus Linguae Graecae: Canon of Greek Authors and Works*. New York: Oxford University Press, 1990.

Bernstein, B., ed. *Class, Codes and Control*. Vol. 2, *Applied Studies towards a Sociology of Language*. London: Routledge & Kegan Paul, 1973.

Bhatia, V. K., J. Flowerdew, and R. H. Jones, eds. *Advances in Discourse Studies*. London: Routledge, 2008.

Biber, D. *Dimensions of Register Variation: A Cross-Linguistic Comparison*. Cambridge: Cambridge University Press, 1995.

Biber, D., and S. Conrad. *Register, Genre, and Style*. CTL. Cambridge: Cambridge University Press, 2009.

Biber, D., S. Conrad, and R. Reppen. *Corpus Linguistics: Investigating Language Structure and Use*. CAL. Cambridge: Cambridge University Press, 1998.

Bierwisch, M. "Semantics." In *New Horizons in Linguistics*, edited by J. Lyons, 166–84. Harmondsworth: Penguin, 1970.

Black, D. A. "The Discourse Structure of Philippians: A Study in Textlinguistics." *NovT* 37 (1995): 16–49.

———. *Linguistics for Students of New Testament Greek: A Survey of Basic Concepts and Applications*. Grand Rapids: Baker Books, 1988.

———. "Some Dissenting Notes on R. Stein's *The Synoptic Problem* and Markan 'Errors.'" *FN* 1 (1988): 95–101.

Black, D. A., with K. Barnwell, and S. H. Levinsohn, eds. *Linguistics and New Testament Interpretation: Essays on Discourse Analysis*. Nashville: Broadman, 1992.

Black, M. *An Aramaic Approach to the Gospels and Acts*. Oxford: Clarendon, 1946.

Reprint, Peabody, MA: Hendrickson, 1998 (with "Introduction: An Aramaic Approach Thirty Years Later," by C. A. Evans, v–xxv).

Black, S. L. *Sentence Conjunctions in the Gospel of Matthew: καί, δέ, τότε, γάρ, οὖν and Asyndeton in Narrative Discourse*. JSNTSup 216; SNTG 9. Sheffield: Sheffield Academic Press, 2002.

Blass, F. *Grammar of New Testament Greek*. Translated by H. St. J. Thackeray. London: Macmillan, 1898. 2nd ed., 1905.

———. *Grammatik des neutestamentlichen Griechisch*. Göttingen: Vandenhoeck & Ruprecht, 1896.

Blass, F., and A. Debrunner. *Grammatik des neutestamentlichen Griechisch*. Edited by F. Rehkopf. 17th ed. Göttingen: Vandenhoeck & Ruprecht, 1990. 18th ed., 2001.

———. *A Greek Grammar of the New Testament and Other Early Christian Literature*. Translated by R. W. Funk. Chicago: University of Chicago Press, 1961.

Blomqvist, J. *Greek Particles in Hellenistic Prose*. Lund: Berlingska Boktryckeriet, 1969.

Bloomfield, L. *Language*. New York: Holt, Rinehart & Winston, 1933.

Boas, E. v. E., and L. Huitink. "Syntax." In *A Companion to the Ancient Greek Language*, edited by E. J. Bakker, 134–50. BCAW. Chichester: Blackwell, 2010.

Boas, F. *Handbook of American Indian Languages*. 3 vols. Smithsonian Institution: Bureau of American Ethnology 40. Washington, DC: Government Printing Office, 1911–38.

———. *Race, Language and Culture*. New York: Free Press, 1940. Reprint, Chicago: University of Chicago Press, 1982.

Bodine, W. R., ed. *Discourse Analysis of Biblical Literature: What It Is and What It Offers*. SemSt. Atlanta: Scholars Press, 1995.

Boman, T. *Hebrew Thought Compared with Greek*. Translated by J. L. Moreau. London: SCM, 1960.

Booth, S. *Selected Peak Marking Features in the Gospel of John*. AUSTR 78. New York: Peter Lang, 1996.

Booth, W. *The Rhetoric of Fiction*. Chicago: University of Chicago Press, 1961.

———. *A Rhetoric of Irony*. Chicago: University of Chicago Press, 1974.

Boring, M. E. *Sayings of the Risen Jesus: Christian Prophecy in the Synoptic Tradition*. SNTSMS 46. Cambridge: Cambridge University Press, 1982.

Bovon, F. *Luke 1: A Commentary on the Gospel of Luke 1:1–9:50*. Translated by C. M. Thomas. Edited by H. Koester. Hermeneia. Minneapolis: Fortress, 2002.

Brant, J. A. *Dialogue and Drama: Elements of Greek Tragedy in the Fourth Gospel*. Peabody, MA: Hendrickson, 2004.

Bremond, C. *Logique du récit*. Paris: Seuil, 1973.

Bremond, C., J. Landy, and T. Pavel, eds. *Thematics: New Approaches*. Albany: SUNY Press, 1995.

Breytenbach, C. "Abgeschlossenes Imperfect? Eine notwendig gewordene Anmerkungen zum Gebrauch des griechischen Imperfekts in neutestamentlichen Briefen." *TLZ* 118 (1993): 85–91.

———. *Nachfolge und Zukunftserwartung nach Markus: Eine methodenkritische Studie*. ATANT 71. Zurich: Theologischer Verlag, 1984.

Brinton, L. J. *The Development of English Aspectual Systems: Aspectualizers and Post-Verbal Particles*. CSL 49. Cambridge: Cambridge University Press, 1988.

Brock, S. P. "Review of *An Aramaic Approach to the Gospels and Acts*, by Matthew Black." *JTS* 20 (1969): 274–78.

Brooks, C. *The Well Wrought Urn: Studies in the Structure of Poetry*. New York: Harcourt, Brace & World, 1947.

Brooks, C., and R. P. Warren. *Understanding Fiction*. New York: Crofts, 1943.

Brown, G., and G. Yule. *Discourse Analysis*. CTL. Cambridge: Cambridge University Press, 1983.

Brown, S. "Concerning the Origin of the Nomina Sacra." *SP* 9 (1970): 7–19.

Brox, N. *Die Pastoralbriefe: Übersetzt und Erklärt*. 4th ed. RNT 7/2. Regensburg: Pustet, 1969.

Brugmann, K., and B. Delbrück. *Grundriss der vergleichenden Grammatik der indogermanischen Sprachen*. 2nd ed. 5 parts in 9 vols. Strasburg: Trübner, 1897–1916. Reprint, Berlin: de Gruyter, 1967.

Bühler, K. *Schriften zur Sprachtheorie*. Edited by A. Eschbach. Tübingen: Mohr Siebeck, 2012.

———. *Sprachtheorie*. Jena: Gustav Fischer, 1934.

———. *Theory of Language: The Representational Function of Language*. Translated by D. F. Goodwin. Philadelphia: John Benjamins, 1990.

Bultmann, R. *History of the Synoptic Tradition*. Translated by J. Marsh. Oxford: Blackwell, 1963.

———. *New Testament Theology*. Translated by K. Grobel. 2 vols. London: SCM, 1952–55.

Burke, K. *A Grammar of Motives*. Berkeley: University of California Press, 1969.

Butler, C. S. "Discourse Systems and Structures and Their Place within an Overall Systemic Model." In *Systemic Perspectives on Discourse*. Vol. 1, *Selected Theoretical Papers from the 9th International Systemic Workshop*, edited by J. D. Benson and W. S. Greaves, 213–28. Norwood, NJ: Ablex, 1985.

Buttmann, A. *A Grammar of the New Testament Greek*. Translated by J. H. Thayer. Andover, MA: Draper, 1880.

———. *Grammatik des neutestamentlichen Sprachgebrauchs*. Berlin: Ferd. Dümmler, 1859.

Cadbury, H. J. *The Making of Luke-Acts*. London: SPCK, 1958.

Callow, J. "Constituent Order in Copula Clauses: A Partial Study." In *Linguistics and New Testament Interpretation*, edited by D. A. Black and D. S. Dockery, 68–89. Grand Rapids: Zondervan, 1991.

Campbell, C. R. *Basics of Verbal Aspect in Biblical Greek*. Grand Rapids: Zondervan, 2008.

———. "Breaking Perfect Rules: The Traditional Understanding of the Greek Perfect." In *Discourse Studies and Biblical Interpretation: A Festschrift in Honor of Stephen H. Levinsohn*, edited by S. E. Runge, 139–55. Bellingham, WA: Logos Bible Software, 2011.

———. *Verbal Aspect, the Indicative Mood, and Narrative: Soundings in the Greek of the New Testament*. SBG 13. New York: Peter Lang, 2007.

———. *Verbal Aspect and Non-indicative Verbs: Further Soundings in the Greek of the New Testament*. SBG 15. New York: Peter Lang, 2008.

Caragounis, C. *The Development of Greek and the New Testament: Morphology, Syntax, Phonology, and Textual Transmission*. WUNT 167. Tübingen: Mohr Siebeck, 2004. Reprint, Grand Rapids: Baker Academic, 2007.

———. "The Error of Erasmus and Un-Greek Pronunciations of Greek." *FN* 8 (1995): 151–85.

Carson, C. A. "The Application of American Copyright Law to the Dead Sea Scrolls Controversy." In *On Scrolls, Artefacts and Intellectual Property*, edited by T. H. Lim, H. L. MacQueen, and C. M. Carmichael, 74–98. JSPSup 38. Sheffield: Sheffield Academic Press, 2001.

Carson, D. A. *The Epistles of John*. NIGTC. Grand Rapids: Eerdmans, forthcoming.

———. *The Gospel according to John*. PilNTC. Grand Rapids: Eerdmans, 1991.

———. "An Introduction to the Porter/Fanning Debate." In *Biblical Greek Language and Linguistics: Open Questions in Current Research*, edited by S. E. Porter and D. A. Carson, 18–25. JSNTSup 80. Sheffield: JSOT Press, 1993.

———. "Matthew." In vol. 8 of *The Expositor's Bible Commentary*, edited by F. E. Gaebelein, 3–599. Grand Rapids: Zondervan, 1984.

Carter, W. *John: Storyteller, Interpreter, Evangelist*. Peabody, MA: Hendrickson, 2006.

Catford, J. C. *A Linguistic Theory of Translation*. Oxford: Oxford University Press, 1965.

Chambers, J. K., and P. Trudgill. *Dialectology.* CTL. Cambridge: Cambridge University Press, 1980.

Chambers, R. *Story and Situation: Narrative Seduction and the Power of Fiction.* Minneapolis: University of Minnesota Press, 1984.

Chantraine, P. *Grammaire homérique.* 2 vols. CPC 1/4. Paris: Klincksieck, 1958–63.

———. *Histoire du parfait grec.* CL 21. Paris: Champion, 1927.

———. *Morphologie historique du grec.* 3rd ed. NCUC 34. Paris: Klincksieck, 1991.

Charalambakis, C. "Modern Greek Archaisms Reconsidered." In *For Particular Reasons: Studies in Honour of Jerker Blomqvist,* edited by A. Piltz et al., 71–84. Lund: Nordic Academic Press, 2003.

Chatman, S. *Story and Discourse: Narrative Structure in Fiction and Film.* Ithaca, NY: Cornell University Press, 1978.

Cheung, P. W. "Revisiting the Case of an Infinitive with Two Substantival Accusatives." *JD* 13 (1999): 69–101.

Childs, B. S. *Biblical Theology in Crisis.* Philadelphia: Westminster, 1970.

———. *Biblical Theology of the Old and New Testaments: Theological Reflection on the Christian Bible.* Minneapolis: Fortress, 1992.

———. *The New Testament as Canon: An Introduction.* Valley Forge, PA: Trinity Press International, 1994.

Churchill, A. D. "The New Testament and the Trinity." In *The Trinity: An Essential for Faith in Our Time,* edited by A. Stirling, 31–105. Nappanee, IN: Evangel, 2000.

Cirafesi, W. V. *Verbal Aspect in Synoptic Parallels: On the Method and Meaning of Divergent Tense-Form Usage in the Synoptic Passion Narratives.* LBS 7. Leiden: Brill, 2013.

Clackson, J. *Indo-European Linguistics: An Introduction.* CTL. Cambridge: Cambridge University Press, 2007.

Cohen, D. *L'aspect verbal.* LN. Paris: Presses universitaires de France, 1989.

Collier, P., and H. Geyer-Ryan, eds. *Literary Theory Today.* Ithaca, NY: Cornell University Press, 1990.

Collinge, N. E. "Some Reflexions on Comparative Historical Syntax." *AL* 12 (1960): 79–101.

Collins, A. Y. *The Beginning of the Gospel: Probings of Mark in Context.* Minneapolis: Fortress, 1992.

Collins, R. F. *1 and 2 Timothy and Titus: A Commentary.* NTL. Louisville: Westminster John Knox, 2002.

Comfort, P. W. *The Quest for the Original Text of the New Testament.* Grand Rapids: Baker, 1992.

Comrie, B. *Aspect: An Introduction to the Study of Verbal Aspect and Related Problems.* CTL. Cambridge: Cambridge University Press, 1976.

———. *Tense.* CTL. Cambridge: Cambridge University Press, 1985.

Cook, J. A. *Time and the Biblical Hebrew Verb: The Expression of Tense, Aspect, and Modality in Biblical Hebrew.* Winona Lake, IN: Eisenbrauns, 2012.

Corbett, G. *Gender.* CTL. Cambridge: Cambridge University Press, 1991.

Cosgrove, C. H. *The Cross and the Spirit: A Study in the Argument and Theology of Galatians.* Macon, GA: Mercer University Press, 1988.

Cotterell, F. P. "The Nicodemus Conversation." *ExpTim* 96 (1985): 237–42.

———. "Sociolinguistics and Biblical Interpretation." *VE* 16 (1986): 61–76.

Cotterell, P., and M. Turner. *Linguistics and Biblical Interpretation.* London: SPCK, 1989.

Coulthard, M. *An Introduction to Discourse Analysis.* 2nd ed. ALLS. London: Longman, 1985.

Coulthard, M., and M. Montgomery, eds. *Studies in Discourse Analysis.* London: Routledge & Kegan Paul, 1981.

Crellin, R. "Basics of Verbal Aspect in Biblical Greek." *JSNT* 35 (2012): 196–202.

———. "The Greek Perfect Active System: 200 BC–AD 150." *TynBul* 64 (2013): 157–60.

Cremer, H. *Biblisch-theologisches Wörterbuch der neutestamentliche Gräcität.* Gotha: F. A. Berthes, 1866. 11th ed., rev. by J. Kögel, 1923.

Crick, M. *Explorations in Language and Meaning: Towards a Semantic Anthropology.* London: Malaby, 1986.

Croft, W. *Typology and Universals.* CTL. Cambridge: Cambridge University Press, 1995.

———. *Verbs: Aspect and Clausal Structure.* Oxford: Oxford University Press, 2012.

Croft, W., and D. A. Cruse. *Cognitive Linguistics.* CTL. Cambridge: Cambridge University Press, 2004.

Cruse, D. A. *Lexical Semantics.* CTL. Cambridge: Cambridge University Press, 1986.

———. *Meaning in Language: An Introduction to Semantics and Pragmatics.* 2nd ed. Oxford: Oxford University Press, 2004.

Crystal, D., and D. Davy. *Investigating English Style.* ELS. London: Longmans, 1969.

Cullmann, O. *Christ and Time.* Translated by F. V. Filson. London: SCM, 1951.

Culpepper, R. A. *Anatomy of the Fourth Gospel: A Study in Literary Design.* Philadelphia: Fortress, 1983.

Curtius, G. *Elucidations of the Student's Greek Grammar.* Translated by E. Abbott. 2nd ed. London: John Murray, 1875.

Dahl, N. A. "Paul and the Church at Corinth according to 1 Corinthians 1:10–4:21." In *Christian History and Interpretation: Studies Presented to John Knox,* edited by W. R. Farmer, C. F. D. Moule, and R. Niebuhr, 313–35. Cambridge: Cambridge University Press, 1967.

Dahl, Ö. *Tense and Aspect Systems.* Oxford: Blackwell, 1985.

Danker, F. W. *A Century of Greco-Roman Philology: Featuring the American Philological Association and the Society of Biblical Literature.* SBLCP. Atlanta: Scholars Press, 1988.

———. "Lexical Evolution and Linguistic Hazard." Paper presented at the annual meeting of the Society of Biblical Literature, Boston, Massachusetts, November 21, 1999.

Danove, P. L. *Linguistics and Exegesis in the Gospel of Mark: Applications of a Case Frame Analysis and Lexicon.* JSNTSup 218; SNTG 10. Sheffield: Sheffield Academic Press, 2001.

———. "The Theory of Construction Grammar and Its Application to New Testament Greek." In *Biblical Greek Language and Linguistics: Open Questions in Current Research,* edited by S. E. Porter and D. A. Carson, 119–51. JSNTSup 80; SNTG 1. Sheffield: JSOT Press, 1993.

Das, A. A. *Solving the Romans Debate.* Minneapolis: Fortress, 2007.

Davies, M. *Rhetoric and Reference in the Fourth Gospel.* JSNTSup 69. Sheffield: Sheffield Academic Press, 1992.

Davies, W. D., and D. C. Allison Jr. *A Critical and Exegetical Commentary on the Gospel according to Saint Matthew.* 3 vols. ICC. Edinburgh: T&T Clark, 1988–97.

Davison, M. E. "New Testament Greek Word Order." *LLC* 4 (1989): 19–28.

Dawson, D. A. *Text-Linguistics and Biblical Hebrew.* JSOTSup 177. Sheffield: Sheffield Academic Press, 1994.

de Boer, M. C. "Narrative Criticism, Historical Criticism and the Gospel of John." *JSNT* 47 (1992): 35–48.

Decker, R. J. *Temporal Deixis of the Greek Verb in the Gospel of Mark with Reference to Verbal Aspect.* SBG 10. New York: Peter Lang, 2001.

Deissmann, A. *The Philology of the Greek Bible: Its Present and Future.* London: Hodder & Stoughton, 1908.

de Man, P. "Semiology and Rhetoric." In *The Critical Tradition: Classic Texts and Contemporary Trends,* edited by D. H. Richter, 906–16. Boston: Bedford, 1998.

DeMaris, R. E. *The Colossian Controversy: Wisdom in Dispute at Colossae.* JSNTSup 96. Sheffield: Sheffield Academic Press, 1994.

Denniston, J. D. *The Greek Particles.* 2nd ed. Oxford: Oxford University Press, 1954.

deSilva, D. "Embodying the Word: Sociological Exegesis of the New Testament." In *The Face of New Testament Studies: A Survey of Recent Research,* edited by S. McKnight and G. Osborne, 118–29. Grand Rapids: Baker Academic, 2004.

Devine, A. M., and L. D. Stephens. *Discontinuous Syntax: Hyperbaton in Greek.* New York: Oxford University Press, 2002.

Dibelius, M. "The Isis Initiation in Apuleius and Related Initiatory Rites." In *Conflict at Colossae: A Problem in the Interpretation of Early Christianity, Illustrated by Selected Modern Studies*, edited and translated by F. O. Francis and W. A. Meeks, 63–82. SBLSBS 4. Missoula, MT: Scholars Press, 1973.

Dibelius, M., and H. Conzelmann. *The Pastoral Epistles: A Commentary on the Pastoral Epistles*. Translated by P. Buttolph and A. Yarbro. Edited by H. Koester. Hermeneia. Philadelphia: Fortress, 1972.

Dik, H. "Interpreting Adjective Position in Herodotus." In *Grammar as Interpretation: Greek Literature in Its Linguistic Contexts*, edited by E. J. Bakker, 55–76. Mnemosyne 171. Leiden: Brill, 1997.

———. *Word Order in Ancient Greek: A Pragmatic Account of Word Order Variation in Herodotus*. ASCP 5. Amsterdam: Gieben, 1995.

———. *Word Order in Greek Tragic Dialogue*. Oxford: Oxford University Press, 2007.

Donfried, K. P., ed. *The Romans Debate*. Rev. ed. Peabody, MA: Hendrickson, 1991.

Doudna, J. C. *The Greek of the Gospel of Mark*. JBLMS 12. Philadelphia: Society of Biblical Literature and Exegesis, 1961.

Dover, K. J. "Abnormal Word Order in Attic Comedy." *CQ* 35 (1985): 324–43.

———. *The Evolution of Greek Prose Style*. Oxford: Clarendon, 1997.

———. *Greek Word Order*. Cambridge: Cambridge University Press, 1960.

Drewitt, J. A. J. "The Augment in Homer." *CQ* 6 (1912): 44–59, 104–20.

Driver, S. R. *A Treatise on the Use of the Tenses in Hebrew*. 3rd ed. Oxford: Clarendon, 1892.

Duke, P. D. *Irony in the Fourth Gospel*. Atlanta: John Knox, 1985.

Dunn, G. "Ancient Greek Order and the Lehmann Hypothesis." *Te Reo* 28 (1985): 81–94.

———. "Enclitic Pronoun Movement and the Ancient Greek Sentence Accent." *Glotta* 67 (1989): 1–19.

———. "Greek Word Order: Three Descriptive Models." *Te Reo* 33 (1990): 57–63.

———. "Syntactic Word Order in Herodotean Greek." *Glotta* 66 (1988): 63–79.

Dunn, J. D. G. *Christology in the Making: A New Testament Inquiry into the Origins of the Doctrine of the Incarnation*. Philadelphia: Westminster, 1980.

———. "The First and Second Letters to Timothy and the Letter to Titus." In vol. 11 of *The New Interpreter's Bible*, edited by L. E. Keck, 773–879. Nashville: Abingdon, 2000.

———. *The Partings of the Ways: Between Christianity and Judaism and Their Significance for the Character of Christianity*. London: SCM, 1991.

Duranti, A. *Linguistic Anthropology*. CTL. Cambridge: Cambridge University Press, 1997.

———, ed. *Linguistic Anthropology: A Reader*. Oxford: Blackwell, 2001.

During, S., ed. *The Cultural Studies Reader*. London: Routledge, 1993.

Dyer, K. D. *The Prophecy on the Mount: Mark 13 and the Gathering of the New Community*. ITS 2. Bern: Peter Lang, 1998.

Eagleton, T. *After Theory*. London: Allen Lane, 2003.

Earle, R. "1 Timothy." In vol. 11 of *The Expositor's Bible Commentary*, edited by F. E. Gaebelein, 339–90. Grand Rapids: Zondervan, 1978.

Easton, B. S. *The Pastoral Epistles: Introduction, Translation, Commentary and Word Studies*. London: SCM, 1948.

Ebeling, H. L. "Some Statistics on the Order of Words in Greek." In *Studies in Honor of Basil L. Gildersleeve*, 229–40. Baltimore: Johns Hopkins Press, 1902.

Eggins, S. *An Introduction to Systemic Functional Linguistics*. London: Pinter, 1994.

Ellicott, C. J. *Critical and Grammatical Commentary on the Pastoral Epistles*. Boston: Draper & Halliday, 1867.

Elliott, J. K. "The Position of Causal ὅτι Clauses in the New Testament." *FN* 6 (1993): 177–205.

Emery, G. *The Trinity: An Introduction to Catholic Doctrine on the Triune God.* Translated by M. Levering. Washington, DC: Catholic University of America Press, 2011.

Emmott, C. *Narrative Comprehension: A Discourse Perspective.* Oxford: Oxford University Press, 1999.

Epp, E. J. "Textual Criticism in the Exegesis of the New Testament, with an Excursus on Canon." In *Handbook to Exegesis of the New Testament,* edited by S. E. Porter, 45–97. NTTS 25. Leiden: Brill, 1997.

Erickson, R. J. *A Beginner's Guide to New Testament Exegesis: Taking the Fear out of Critical Method.* Downers Grove, IL: InterVarsity, 2005.

Eriksson, K. *Das Präsens historicum in der nachklassischen griechischen Historiographie.* Lund: Håkan Ohlsson, 1943.

Esler, P. F. *New Testament Theology: Communion and Community.* Minneapolis: Fortress, 2005.

Estes, D. *The Temporal Mechanics of the Fourth Gospel: A Theory of Hermeneutical Relativity in the Gospel of John.* BIS 92. Leiden: Brill, 2008.

Evans, C. A. *Mark 8:27–16:20.* WBC 34B. Nashville: Nelson, 2001.

———. *Matthew.* NCBC. Cambridge: Cambridge University Press, 2012.

Evans, G. "The Causal Theory of Naming." In *The Philosophy of Language,* edited by A. P. Martinisch, 295–307. 2nd ed. Oxford: Oxford University Press, 1990.

Evans, T. V. *Verbal Syntax in the Greek Pentateuch: Natural Greek Usage and Hebrew Interference.* Oxford: Oxford University Press, 2001.

Ewald, H. *Syntax of the Hebrew Language of the Old Testament.* Translated by J. Kennedy. Edinburgh: T&T Clark, 1881.

Fairclough, N. *Analysing Discourse: Textual Analysis for Social Research.* London: Routledge, 2003.

Falconer, R. *The Pastoral Epistles.* Oxford: Clarendon, 1937.

Fanning, B. M. "Greek Presents, Imperfects, and Aorists in the Synoptic Gospels." In *Discourse Studies and Biblical Interpretation:* *A Festschrift in Honor of Stephen H. Levinsohn,* edited by S. E. Runge, 157–90. Bellingham, WA: Logos Bible Software, 2011.

———. *Verbal Aspect in New Testament Greek.* OTM. Oxford: Clarendon, 1990.

Farelly, N. *The Disciples in the Fourth Gospel: A Narrative Analysis of Their Faith and Understanding.* WUNT 2/290. Tübingen: Mohr Siebeck, 2010.

Fawcett, R. P. *Cognitive Linguistics and Social Interaction: Towards an Integrated Model of a Systemic Functional Grammar and the Other Components of a Communicating Mind.* Heidelberg: Julius Groos and Exeter: Exeter University, 1980.

———. *Invitation to Systemic Functional Linguistics through the Cardiff Grammar: An Extension and Simplification of Halliday's Systemic Functional Grammar.* 3rd ed. London: Equinox, 2008.

———. *A Theory of Syntax for Systemic Functional Linguistics.* Philadelphia: John Benjamins, 2000.

Fee, G. D. *1 and 2 Timothy, Titus.* GNC. San Francisco: Harper & Row, 1984.

———. *The First Epistle to the Corinthians.* NICNT. Grand Rapids: Eerdmans, 1987.

———. *God's Empowering Presence: The Holy Spirit in the Letters of Paul.* Peabody, MA: Hendrickson, 1994.

———. *Pauline Christology.* Peabody, MA: Hendrickson, 2007.

———. "Philippians 2:5–11: Hymn or Exalted Pauline Prose?" *BBR* 2 (1992): 29–46.

———. "The Use of the Definite Article with Personal Names in the Gospel of John." *NTS* 17 (1970–71): 168–83.

Fehribach, A. *The Women in the Life of the Bridegroom: A Feminist Historical-Literary Analysis of the Female Characters in the Fourth Gospel.* Collegeville, MN: Liturgical Press, 1998.

Ferguson, C. A. "Diglossia." *Word* 15 (1959): 325–40.

———. *Language Structure and Language Use.* Edited by A. S. Dil. Stanford, CA: Stanford University Press, 1971.

Fernandez, P. L. *L'aspect verbal en Grec ancien: Le choix des thèmes verbaux chez Isocrate*. BCILL 111. Louvain-la-Neuve: Peeters, 2003.

Ferris, C. *The Meaning of Syntax: A Study in the Adjectives of English*. LLL. London: Longman, 1993.

Fewster, G. P. *Creation Language in Romans 8: A Study in Monosemy*. LBS 8. Leiden: Brill, 2013.

———. "Testing the Intertextuality of ματαιότης in the New Testament." *BAGL* 1 (2012): 39–61.

Fiore, B. *The Pastoral Epistles: First Timothy, Second Timothy, Titus*. SP 12. Collegeville, MN: Liturgical Press, 2007.

Firbas, J. *Functional Sentence Perspective in Written and Spoken Communication*. SEL. Cambridge: Cambridge University Press, 1992.

Firth, J. R. *Papers in Linguistics, 1934–1951*. Oxford: Oxford University Press, 1957.

———. *Selected Papers of J. R. Firth, 1952–59*. Edited by F. R. Palmer. London: Longmans, 1968.

———. "The Technique of Semantics." *TPS* (1935): 36–72.

Fischer, P. "Zur Stellung des Verbums im Griechischen." *Glotta* 13 (1924): 1–11, 189–205.

Fishman, J. A. *Language in Sociocultural Change*. Edited by A. S. Dil. Stanford, CA: Stanford University Press, 1972.

Fitzmyer, J. A. "κύριος, ου, ὁ." In vol. 2 of *Exegetical Dictionary of the New Testament*, edited by H. Balz and G. Schneider, 328–31. Grand Rapids: Eerdmans, 1991.

Foley, T. S. *Biblical Translation in Chinese and Greek: Verbal Aspect in Theory and Practice*. LBS 1. Leiden: Brill, 2009.

Forster, E. M. *Aspects of the Novel*. New York: Harcourt, Brace & World, 1927.

Fowl, S. E. *The Story of Christ in the Ethics of Paul: An Analysis of the Function of the Hymnic Material in the Pauline Corpus*. JSNTSup 36. Sheffield: JSOT Press, 1990.

Fowler, R., ed. *Style and Structure in Literature: Essays in the New Stylistics*. Oxford: Blackwell, 1975.

France, R. T. *The Gospel of Matthew*. NICNT. Grand Rapids: Eerdmans, 2007.

———. "Matthew, Mark, Luke." In *A Theology of the New Testament*, by G. E. Ladd, edited by D. A. Hagner, 212–45. Rev. ed. Grand Rapids: Eerdmans, 1993.

Francis, F. O. "Humility and Angelic Worship in Col. 2:18." In *Conflict at Colossae: A Problem in the Interpretation of Early Christianity Illustrated by Selected Modern Studies*, edited by F. O. Francis and W. A. Meeks, 163–96. SBLSBS 4. Missoula, MT: Scholars Press, 1973.

Frei, H. W. *The Eclipse of Biblical Narrative: Study in Eighteenth and Nineteenth Century Hermeneutics*. New Haven: Yale University Press, 1974.

Friedrich, G. "Pre-History of the Theological Dictionary of the New Testament." In vol. 10 of *Theological Dictionary of the New Testament*, edited by G. Kittel and G. Friedrich, translated by G. W. Bromiley, 613–61. Grand Rapids: Eerdmans, 1976.

Friedrich, P. "On Aspect Theory and Homeric Aspect." *IJAL* Memoir 28, 40 (1974): S1–S44.

———. *Proto-Indo-European Syntax: The Order of Meaningful Elements*. JISM 1. Butte, MT: Journal of Indo-European Studies, 1975.

Frischer, B. D., and F. J. Tweedie. "Analysis of Classical Greek and Latin Compositional Word-Order Data." *JQL* 6 (1999): 85–97.

Frischer, B. D., et al. "Word-Order Transference between Latin and Greek: The Relative Position of the Accusative Direct Object and the Governing Verb in Cassius Dio and Other Greek and Roman Prose Authors." *HSCP* 99 (1999): 357–90.

Frisk, H. *Studien zur griechischen Wortstellung*. Göteborg: Wettergren & Kerbers, 1933.

Fritzsche, C. F. A. *Pauli ad Romanos Epistola: Recensuit et cum commentariis perpetuis edidit*. 3 vols. Halis Saxonum: Sumtibus Gebaueriis, 1836–43.

Frow, J. *Genre*. London: Routledge, 2006.

Frye, N. *Anatomy of Criticism: Four Essays.* Princeton: Princeton University Press, 1957.

Gadamer, H.-G. *Truth and Method.* Translated by J. Weinsheimer and D. G. Marshall. 2nd ed. New York: Continuum, 2002.

Gager, J. G. *Kingdom and Community: The Social World of Early Christianity.* Englewood Cliffs, NJ: Prentice-Hall, 1975.

———. *Reinventing Paul.* Oxford: Oxford University Press, 2000.

Galan, F. W. *Historic Structures: The Prague School Project, 1928–1946.* Austin: University of Texas Press, 1985.

Gardner, T. *John in the Company of Poets: The Gospel in Literary Imagination.* SCL 6. Waco: Baylor University Press, 2011.

Garvin, P. L. "The Prague School of Linguistics." In *Linguistics Today,* edited by A. A. Hill, 229–38. New York: Basic Books, 1969.

———, ed. and trans. *A Prague School Reader on Esthetics, Literary Structure, and Style.* Washington, DC: Georgetown University Press, 1964.

Gee, J. P. *An Introduction to Discourse Analysis: Theory and Method.* London: Routledge, 1999.

Geeraerts, D. *Theories of Lexical Semantics.* Oxford: Oxford University Press, 2010.

Genette, G. *Narrative Discourse: An Essay in Method.* Translated by J. E. Lewin. Ithaca, NY: Cornell University Press, 1980.

Georgakopoulou, A., and D. Goutsos. *Discourse Analysis: An Introduction.* 2nd ed. Edinburgh: Edinburgh University Press, 2004.

George, L. D. *Reading the Tapestry: A Literary-Rhetorical Analysis of the Johannine Resurrection Narrative (John 20–21).* StBL 14. New York: Peter Lang, 2000.

Ghadessy, M., ed. *Register Analysis: Theory and Practice.* London: Pinter, 1993.

Giannakis, G. K. "Can a Historical Greek Grammar Be Written?—An Appraisal of A. N. Jannaris' Work." In *Greek, a Language in Evolution: Essays in Honour of Antonios N. Jannaris,* edited by C. C. Caragounis, 295–313. Hildesheim: Georg Olms, 2010.

Gibson, A. *Biblical Semantic Logic: A Preliminary Analysis.* Oxford: Blackwell, 1981. Reprint, London: Sheffield Academic Press, 2001.

Giddens, A. *Social Theory and Modern Sociology.* Stanford, CA: Stanford University Press, 1987.

Giglioli, P., ed. *Language and Social Context: Selected Readings.* Harmondsworth: Penguin, 1972.

Gignac, F. T. *A Grammar of the Greek Papyri of the Roman and Byzantine Periods.* 2 vols. Milan: Cisalpino-Goliardica, 1976–81.

Gildersleeve, B. L. "On the Article with Proper Names." *AJP* 11 (1890): 483–87.

Gilkey, L. "God." In *Christian Theology: An Introduction to Its Traditions and Tasks,* edited by P. C. Hodgson and R. H. King, 88–113. Rev. ed. Minneapolis: Fortress, 1994.

Giseke, B. "Über die Wortstellung in abhängigen Sätzen bei Homer." *JCP* 31 (1861): 225–32.

Goodacre, M. *The Synoptic Problem: A Way through the Maze.* BibSem 80. London: Sheffield Academic Press, 2001.

Goodell, T. D. "The Order of Words in Greek." *TAPA* 21 (1890): 5–47.

Goodwin, W. W. *Greek Grammar.* London: Macmillan, 1894.

Goppelt, L. *Theology of the New Testament.* Translated by J. Alsup. 2 vols. Grand Rapids: Eerdmans, 1981–82.

Gordon, W. T. "*Langue* and *parole.*" In *The Cambridge Companion to Saussure,* edited by C. Sanders, 76–87. Cambridge: Cambridge University Press, 2004.

Gotteri, N. J. C. "A Note on Bulgarian Verb Systems." *JMALS* 8 (1983): 49–70.

———. "Toward a Systemic Approach to Tense and Aspect in Polish." In *Meaning and Form: Systemic Functional Interpretations,* edited by M. Berry et al., 499–507. ADP 57. Norwood, NJ: Ablex, 1996.

Goulder, M. "Colossians and Barbelo." *NTS* 41 (1995): 601–19.

———. *Paul and the Competing Mission in Corinth.* LPS. Peabody, MA: Hendrickson, 2001.

———. *A Tale of Two Missions*. London: SCM, 1994.

Gracia, J. J. E. *A Theory of Textuality: The Logic and Epistemology*. Albany: SUNY Press, 1995.

Green, J. B. *Practicing Theological Interpretation: Engaging Biblical Texts for Faith and Formation*. Grand Rapids: Baker Academic, 2012.

Green, J. B., and L. M. McDonald, eds. *The World of the New Testament: Cultural, Social, and Historical Contexts*. Grand Rapids: Baker Academic, 2013.

Gregory, M., and S. Carroll. *Language and Situation: Language Varieties and Their Social Contexts*. London: Routledge & Kegan Paul, 1978.

Greimas, A.-J. *Structural Semantics: An Attempt at a Method*. Translated by D. McDowell, R. Schleifer, and A. Velie. Lincoln: University of Nebraska Press, 1983.

Griffin, J., ed. *Homer: Iliad, Book Nine*. Oxford: Clarendon, 1995.

Grimes, J. E. *The Thread of Discourse*. JLSM 207. The Hague: Mouton, 1975.

Groom, S. *Linguistic Analysis of Biblical Hebrew*. Carlisle: Paternoster, 2003.

Gumperz, J. J. *Discourse Strategies*. SIS 1. Cambridge: Cambridge University Press, 1982.

Gumperz, J. J., and D. Hymes, eds. *Directions in Sociolinguistics: The Ethnography of Communication*. Oxford: Blackwell, 1972.

Gumperz, J. J., and S. C. Levinson, eds. *Rethinking Linguistic Relativity*. SSCFL 17. Cambridge: Cambridge University Press, 1996.

Gundry, R. H. *Mark: A Commentary on His Apology for the Cross*. Grand Rapids: Eerdmans, 1993.

———. *Matthew: A Commentary on His Literary and Theological Art*. Grand Rapids: Eerdmans, 1982.

———. "Style and Substance in 'The Myth of God Incarnate' according to Philippians 2:6–11." In *Crossing the Boundaries: Essays in Biblical Interpretation in Honour of Michael D. Goulder*, edited by S. E. Porter, P. Joyce, and D. E. Orton, 271–93. BIS 8. Leiden: Brill, 1994.

Gunther, J. J. *St. Paul's Opponents and Their Background: A Study of Apocalyptic and Jewish Sectarian Teachings*. NovTSup 35. Leiden: Brill, 1973.

Guthrie, D. *New Testament Theology*. Leicester: Inter-Varsity, 1981.

———. *The Pastoral Epistles*. 2nd ed. TNTC. London: Tyndale, 1990.

Guthrie, G. H. *The Structure of Hebrews: A Text-Linguistic Analysis*. NovTSup 73. Leiden: Brill, 1994.

Gutwinski, W. *Cohesion in Literary Texts: A Study of Some Grammatical and Lexical Features of English Discourse*. JLSMi 204. The Hague: Mouton, 1976.

Haacker, K. *The Theology of Paul's Letter to the Romans*. NTT. Cambridge: Cambridge University Press, 2003.

Hagner, D. A. *Matthew*. 2 vols. WBC 33A–B. Dallas: Word, 1993–95.

Hale, K. "Walpiri and the Grammar of Non-Configurational Languages." *NLLT* 1 (1983): 5–47.

Halliday, M. A. K. "Categories of the Theory of Grammar." *Word* 17 (1961): 241–92.

———. *The Collected Works of M. A. K. Halliday*. Edited by J. J. Webster. 10 vols. London: Continuum, 2002–7.

———. *Explorations in the Functions of Language*. London: Edward Arnold, 1973.

———. "The Functional Basis of Language." In *Class, Codes and Control*. Vol. 2, *Applied Studies towards a Sociology of Language*, edited by B. Bernstein, 343–66. London: Routledge & Kegan Paul, 1973.

———. *Halliday's Introduction to Functional Grammar*. Revised by C. M. I. M. Matthiessen. 4th ed. London: Routledge, 2014.

———. *An Introduction to Functional Grammar*. London: Edward Arnold, 1985. 3rd ed., revised by C. M. I. M. Matthiessen, London: Continuum, 2004.

———. *Language as Social Semiotic: The Social Interpretation of Language and Meaning*. London: Edward Arnold, 1978.

———. *Learning How to Mean: Explorations in the Development of Language*. London: Edward Arnold, 1975.

———. "Lexicology." In *Lexicology: A Short Introduction*, edited by M. A. K. Halliday and C. Yallop, 1–22. London: Continuum, 2004.

———. "Lexis as a Linguistic Level." In *In Memory of J. R. Firth*, edited by C. E. Bazell et al., 148–62. London: Longmans, 1966.

———. *Text and Discourse*. Edited by J. J. Webster. London: Continuum, 2002.

———. "Text as Semantic Choice in Social Contexts." In *Grammars and Descriptions: Studies in Text Theory and Text Analysis*, edited by T. A. van Dijk and J. S. Petöfi, 176–225. RTT 1. Berlin: de Gruyter, 1977.

Halliday, M. A. K., and R. Hasan. *Cohesion in English*. ELS. London: Longman, 1976.

———. *Language, Context, and Text: Aspects of Language in a Social-Semiotic Perspective*. Geelong, Australia: Deakin University Press, 1985.

Halliday, M. A. K., A. MacIntosh, and P. Strevens. *The Linguistic Sciences and Language Teaching*. LLL. London: Longmans, 1964.

Halliday, M. A. K., and C. M. I. M. Matthiessen. *Construing Experience through Meaning: A Language-Based Approach to Cognition*. OLS. London: Continuum, 1999.

Halliday, M. A. K., and J. J. Webster, eds. *Continuum Companion to Systemic Functional Linguistics*. London: Continuum, 2009.

Hansen, G. W. *The Letter to the Philippians*. PilNTC. Grand Rapids: Eerdmans, 2009.

Hanson, A. T. *The Pastoral Letters: Commentary on the First and Second Letters to Timothy and the Letter to Titus*. CBC. Cambridge: Cambridge University Press, 1966.

Harland, P. A. *Associations, Synagogues, and Congregations: Claiming a Place in Ancient Mediterranean Society*. Minneapolis: Fortress, 2003.

Harrill, J. A. *Slaves in the New Testament: Literary, Social, and Moral Dimensions*. Minneapolis: Fortress, 2006.

Harris, M. J. *Slave of Christ: A New Testament Metaphor for Total Devotion to Christ*. Downers Grove, IL: InterVarsity, 1999.

Harstine, S. *Moses as a Character in the Fourth Gospel: A Study of Ancient Reading Techniques*. JSNTSup 229. Sheffield: Sheffield Academic Press, 2002.

Hartman, L. *Text-Centered New Testament Studies: Text-Theoretical Essays on Early Jewish and Early Christian Literature*. Edited by D. Hellholm. WUNT 102. Tübingen: Mohr Siebeck, 1997.

Hasan, R. "The Grammarian's Dream: Lexis as Most Delicate Grammar." In *New Developments in Systemic Linguistics*. Vol. 1, *Theory and Description*, edited by M. A. K. Halliday and R. P. Fawcett, 184–211. London: Pinter, 1987.

———. "The Nursery Tale as a Genre." In *Ways of Saying, Ways of Meaning: Selected Papers of Ruqaiya Hasan*, edited by C. Cloran et al., 51–72. London: Cassell, 1996.

———. "Ways of Meaning, Ways of Learning: Code as an Explanatory Concept." In *Language, Society and Consciousness*, edited by J. J. Webster, 215–27. London: Equinox, 2005.

Hasler, V. *Die Briefe an Timotheus und Titus (Pastoralbriefe)*. ZB 12. Zurich: Theologischer Verlag, 1978.

Hatina, T. R. "The Focus of Mark 13:24–27: The Parousia, or the Destruction of the Temple?" *BBR* 6 (1996): 43–66.

Havránek, B. "The Functional Differentiation of the Standard Language." In *A Prague School Reader on Esthetics, Literary Structure, and Style*, edited by P. L. Garvin, 3–16. Washington, DC: Georgetown University Press, 1964.

Hawkins, J. *Horae synopticae*. Oxford: Clarendon, 1909.

Heimerdinger, J.-M. *Topic, Focus and Foreground in Ancient Hebrew Narratives*. JSOTSup 295. Sheffield: Sheffield Academic Press, 1999.

Heimerdinger, J., and S. H. Levinsohn. "The Use of the Definite Article before Names of People in the Greek Text of Acts with Particular Reference to Codex Bezae." *FN* 5 (1992): 15–44.

Hemer, C. J. "Reflections on the Nature of New Testament Greek Vocabulary." *TynBul* 38 (1987): 65–92.

Hengel, M. "Entstehungszeit und Situation des Markusevangeliums." In *Markus-Philologie: Historische, literargeschichtliche und stilistische Untersuchungen zum zweiten Evangelium*, edited by H. Cancik, 1–45. WUNT 33. Tübingen: Mohr Siebeck, 1984.

———. *Studies in the Gospel of Mark.* Translated by J. Bowden. London: SCM, 1985.

Hess, H. H. "Dynamics of the Greek Noun Phrase in Mark." *OPTT* 4 (1990): 353–69.

Hodgson, L. *The Doctrine of the Trinity.* Digswell Place: Nisbet, 1943.

Hoey, M. *Lexical Priming: A New Theory of Words and Language.* London: Routledge, 2005.

———. *Patterns of Lexis in Text.* DEL. Oxford: Oxford University Press, 1991.

———. *Textual Interaction: An Introduction to Written Discourse Analysis.* London: Routledge, 2001.

Hoijer, H., ed. *Language in Culture: Conference on the Interrelations of Language and Other Aspects of Culture.* CSCC. Chicago: University of Chicago Press, 1954.

Holland, G. *The Tradition That You Received from Us: 2 Thessalonians in the Pauline Tradition.* HUT 24. Tübingen: Mohr Siebeck, 1988.

Holmstrand, J. *Markers and Meaning in Paul: An Analysis of 1 Thessalonians, Philippians and Galatians.* ConBNT 28. Stockholm: Almqvist & Wiksell, 1997.

Holtz, G. *Die Pastoralbriefe.* THNT 13. Berlin: Evangelische Verlagsanstalt, 1966.

Hooker, M. D. "Were There False Teachers in Colossae?" In *Christ and Spirit in the New Testament: Essays in Honour of C. F. D. Moule*, edited by B. Lindars and S. S. Smalley, 315–31. Cambridge: Cambridge University Press, 1973.

Hopper, P. J., and S. A. Thompson. "Transitivity in Grammar and Discourse." *Language* 56 (1980): 251–99.

Hopper, P. J., and E. C. Traugott. *Grammaticalization.* CTL. Cambridge: Cambridge University Press, 1993.

Houben, J. L. "Word-Order Change and Subordination in Homeric Greek." *JIS* 5 (1977): 1–8.

Houlden, J. L. *The Pastoral Epistles: I and II Timothy, Titus.* PelNTC. Harmondsworth: Penguin, 1976.

Howarth, D. *Discourse.* Maidenhead: Open University Press, 2000.

Hudson, R. A. *Sociolinguistics.* 2nd ed. CTL. Cambridge: Cambridge University Press, 1996.

———. *Word Grammar.* Oxford: Blackwell, 1984.

Hull, S. D. "Exceptions to Apollonius' Canon in the New Testament: A Grammatical Study." *TJ* 7 (1986): 3–16.

Humboldt, W. von. *On Language: On the Diversity of Human Language Construction and Its Influence on the Mental Development of the Human Species.* Edited by M. Losonsky. Translated by P. Heath. Cambridge: Cambridge University Press, 1999.

———. *Über die Verschiedenheit des menschlichen Sprachbaues und ihren Einfluss auf die geistige Entwickelung des Menschengeschlechts.* Berlin: Königlichen Akademie der Wissenschaften, 1836.

Hunt, S., ed. *Christian Millenarianism: From the Early Church to Waco.* London: Hurst, 2001.

Hurford, J. R., B. Heasley, and M. B. Smith. *Semantics: A Coursebook.* 2nd ed. Cambridge: Cambridge University Press, 2007.

Hurtado, L. W. *The Earliest Christian Artifacts: Manuscripts and Christian Origins.* Grand Rapids: Eerdmans, 2006.

———. "The Origin of the *Nomina Sacra*: A Proposal." *JBL* 117 (1998): 655–73.

Huther, J. E. *Critical and Exegetical Handbook to the Epistles to Timothy and Titus.* Translated by D. Hunter. New York: Funk & Wagnalls, 1885.

Hyland, K., and B. Paltridge, eds. *The Bloomsbury Companion to Discourse Analysis.* London: Bloomsbury, 2011.

Hylen, S. E. *Imperfect Believers: Ambiguous Characters in the Gospel of John.* Louisville: Westminster John Knox, 2009.

Hymes, D. *Foundations in Sociolinguistics: An Ethnographic Approach.* Philadelphia: University of Pennsylvania Press, 1974.

Iser, W. *The Act of Reading: A Theory of Aesthetic Response.* Baltimore: Johns Hopkins University Press, 1978.

———. *The Implied Reader: Patterns of Communication in Prose Fiction from Bunyan to Beckett.* Baltimore: Johns Hopkins University Press, 1974.

Jakobson, R. "Concluding Statement: Linguistics and Poetics." In *Style in Language,* edited by T. A. Sebeok, 350–77. Cambridge, MA: MIT Press, 1963.

Jankowsky, K. R. *The Neogrammarians.* JLSMi 116. The Hague: Mouton, 1972.

Janse, M. "Convergence and Divergence in the Development of the Greek and Latin Clitic Pronouns." In *Stability, Variation and Change of Word-Order Patterns over Time,* edited by R. Sornicola et al., 232–44. Philadelphia: John Benjamins, 2000.

———. "La phrase segmentée en grec ancien: Le témoignage des enclitiques." *BSLP* 86, no. 1 (1991): xiv–xvi.

———. "La position des pronoms personnels enclitiques en grec neo-testamentaire a la lumiere des dialectes neo-helleniques." In *La koine grecque antique I: Une langue introuvable?,* edited by C. Brixhe, 83–121. TMEA 10. Nancy: Presses universitaires de Nancy, 1993.

Jauss, H. R. *Toward an Aesthetic of Reception.* Translated by T. Bahti. Minneapolis: University of Minnesota Press, 1982.

Jeremias, J. *Abba: Studien zur neutestamentlichen Theologie und Zeitgeschichte.* Göttingen: Vandenhoeck & Ruprecht, 1966.

———. *The Central Message of the New Testament.* London: SCM, 1965.

———. *New Testament Theology.* Translated by J. Bowden. London: SCM, 1971.

Jeremias, J., and A. Strobel. *Die Briefe an Timotheus und Titus; Der Brief an die Hebräer.* 12th ed. NTD 9. Göttingen: Vandenhoeck & Ruprecht, 1981.

Jewett, R. *The Thessalonian Correspondence: Pauline Rhetoric and Millenarian Piety.* Philadelphia: Fortress, 1986.

Johannson, S. "Grammatical Tagging and Total Accountability." In *Papers on Language and Literature: Presented to Alvar Ellegård and Erik Frykman,* edited by S. Bäckman and G. Kjellmer, 208–20. GSE 60. Göteborg: Acta Universitatis Gothoburgensis, 1998.

Johanson, B. C. *To All the Brethren: A Text-Linguistic and Rhetorical Approach to 1 Thessalonians.* ConBNT 16. Stockholm: Almqvist & Wiksell, 1987.

Johnson, L. T. *The First and Second Letters to Timothy.* AB 35A. New York: Doubleday, 2001.

John-Steiner, V. "Cognitive Pluralism: A Whorfian Analysis." In *The Influence of Language on Culture and Thought: Essays in Honor of Joshua A. Fishman's Sixty-Fifth Birthday,* edited by R. L. Cooper and B. Spolsky, 61–74. Berlin: de Gruyter, 1991.

Johnstone, B. *Discourse Analysis.* 2nd ed. Oxford: Blackwell, 2008.

Jones, L. P. *The Symbol of Water in the Gospel of John.* JSNTSup 145. Sheffield: Sheffield Academic Press, 1997.

Judge, E. A. *The First Christians in the Roman World: Augustan and New Testament Essays.* Edited by J. R. Harrison. WUNT 229. Tübingen: Mohr Siebeck, 2008.

Kaiser, W. C., Jr. *Toward an Exegetical Theology: Biblical Exegesis for Preaching and Teaching.* Grand Rapids: Baker, 1981.

Kalverkämper, H. *Orientierung zur Textlinguistik.* LA 100. Tübingen: Niemeyer, 1981.

Käsemann, E. "Die Legitimität des Apostels." *ZNW* 41 (1942): 33–71.

Kelly, J. N. D. *A Commentary on the Pastoral Epistles.* BNTC. London: A&C Black, 1963.

Kenyon, F. G. "Nomina Sacra in the Chester Beatty Papyri." *Aegyptus* 13 (1933): 5–10.

Kermode, F. *The Genesis of Secrecy: On the Interpretation of Narrative.* Cambridge, MA: Harvard University Press, 1979.

———. *The Sense of an Ending: Studies in the Theory of Fiction.* New York: Oxford University Press, 1967.

Kieckers, E. "Die Stellung der Verba des Sagens in Schaltesätzen im griechischen und in den indogermanischen Sprachen." *IF* 30 (1912): 145–90.

———. *Die Stellung des Verbs im griechischen und in den verwandten Sprachen.* UISK 2. Strassburg: K. J. Trübner, 1911.

Kilpatrick, G. D. "The Order of Some Noun and Adjective Phrases in the New Testament." *NovT* 5 (1962): 111–14.

Kingsbury, J. D. *The Christology of Mark's Gospel.* Philadelphia: Fortress, 1983.

———. *Conflict in Luke: Jesus, Authorities, Disciples.* Minneapolis: Fortress, 1991.

———. *Conflict in Mark: Jesus, Authorities, Disciples.* Minneapolis: Fortress, 1989.

———. *Matthew as Story.* 2nd ed. Philadelphia: Fortress, 1988.

Kinneavy, J. L. *A Theory of Discourse: The Aims of Discourse.* New York: Norton, 1971.

Kirk, G. S. *The Songs of Homer.* Cambridge: Cambridge University Press, 1962.

Kittel, G. *Lexicographia sacra: Two Lectures on the Making of the "Theologisches Wörterbuch zum Neuen Testament."* London: SPCK, 1938.

Klutz, T. *The Exorcism Stories in Luke-Acts: A Sociostylistic Reading.* SNTSMS 129. Cambridge: Cambridge University Press, 2004.

Knight, G. W., III. *The Pastoral Epistles.* NIGTC. Grand Rapids: Eerdmans, 1992.

Koester, C. R. *Symbolism in the Fourth Gospel: Meaning, Mystery, Community.* 2nd ed. Minneapolis: Fortress, 2003.

Kort, W. *Story, Text, and Scripture: Literary Interests in Biblical Narratives.* University Park: Pennsylvania State University Press, 1988.

Koschmieder, E. "Zu den Grundfragen der Aspekttheorie." *IF* 53 (1932): 287–88.

Köstenberger, A. J. "1 Timothy." In vol. 12 of *The Expositor's Bible Commentary*, edited by T. Longman III and D. E. Garland, 487–561. Rev. ed. Grand Rapids: Zondervan, 2006.

———. *John.* BECNT. Grand Rapids: Baker Academic, 2004.

———. *A Theology of John's Gospel and Letters.* Grand Rapids: Zondervan, 2009.

Krieger, M. *A Window to Criticism: Shakespeare's Sonnets and Modern Poetics.*

Princeton: Princeton University Press, 1964.

Kripke, S. A. *Naming and Necessity.* Cambridge, MA: Harvard University Press, 1980.

Kroeger, C. C. "Ancient Heresies and a Strange Greek Verb." *RJ* 29, no. 3 (1979): 12–15.

Kroeger, R. C., and C. C. Kroeger. *I Suffer Not a Woman: Rethinking 1 Timothy 2:11–15 in Light of Ancient Evidence.* Grand Rapids: Baker, 1992.

Kühner, R., and B. Gerth, *Ausführliche Grammatik der griechischen Sprache: Satzlehre.* 2 vols. 4th ed. Leverkusen: Gottschalksche, 1955.

Kümmel, W. G. *Introduction to the New Testament.* Translated by H. C. Kee. Nashville: Abingdon, 1975.

———. *The Theology of the New Testament.* Translated by J. E. Steely. Nashville: Abingdon, 1973.

Kuno, S. "The Position of Relative Clauses and Conjunctions." *LI* 5 (1974): 117–36.

Kwong, I. S. C. *The Word Order of the Gospel of Luke: Its Foregrounded Messages.* LNTS 298. London: T&T Clark, 2005.

Labov, W. *Sociolinguistic Patterns.* Philadelphia: University of Pennsylvania Press, 1972.

Ladd, G. E. *A Theology of the New Testament.* Grand Rapids: Eerdmans, 1974.

Lamb, D. A. *Text, Context and the Johannine Community: A Sociolinguistic Analysis of the Johannine Writings.* LNTS 447. London: Bloomsbury, 2014.

Lampe, G. "The Roman Christians of Romans 16." In *The Romans Debate*, edited by K. P. Donfried, 216–30. Rev. ed. Peabody, MA: Hendrickson, 1991.

Land, C. D. "Varieties of the Greek Language." In *The Language of the New Testament: Context, History, and Development*, edited by S. E. Porter and A. W. Pitts, 243–60. ECHC 3; LBS 6. Leiden: Brill, 2013.

Larson, K. B. *Recognizing the Stranger: Recognition Scenes in the Gospel of John.* BIS 93. Leiden: Brill, 2008.

Leavitt, J. *Linguistic Relativities: Language Diversity and Modern Thought.* Cambridge: Cambridge University Press, 2011.

Leckie-Tarry, H. *Language and Context: A Functional Linguistic Theory of Register.* Edited by D. Birch. London: Pinter, 1995.

Lee, D. A. *Flesh and Glory: Symbol, Gender, and Theology in the Gospel of John.* New York: Crossroad, 2002.

———. *The Symbolic Narratives of the Fourth Gospel: The Interplay of Form and Meaning.* JSNTSup 95. Sheffield: Sheffield Academic Press, 1994.

Lee, J. A. L. "Etymological Follies: Three Recent Lexicons of the New Testament." *NovT* 55 (2013): 383–403.

———. *A History of New Testament Lexicography.* SBG 8. New York: Peter Lang, 2003.

———. "Some Features of the Speech of Jesus in Mark's Gospel." *NovT* 27 (1985): 1–26.

———. "The United Bible Societies' Lexicon and Its Analysis of Meanings." *FN* 5 (1992): 167–89.

Lee, J.-H. *Paul's Gospel in Romans: A Discourse Analysis of Rom. 1:16–8:39.* LBS 3. Leiden: Brill, 2010.

Lee, P. *The Whorf Theory Complex: A Critical Reconstruction.* Philadelphia: John Benjamins, 1996.

Lee, S.-I. *Jesus and Gospel Traditions in Bilingual Context: A Study in the Interdirectionality of Language.* BZNW 186. Berlin: de Gruyter, 2012.

Leech, G. N. *English in Advertising: A Linguistic Study of Advertising in Great Britain.* ELS. London: Longmans, 1966.

Leech, G. N., and J. Thomas. "Language, Meaning and Context: Pragmatics." In *An Encyclopaedia of Language,* edited by N. E. Collinge, 173–206. London: Routledge, 1990.

Lehrer, A. *Semantic Fields and Lexical Structure.* Amsterdam: North Holland, 1974.

Letham, R. *The Holy Trinity: In Scripture, History, Theology, and Worship.* Phillipsburg, NJ: P&R, 2004.

Levinsohn, S. H. *Discourse Features of New Testament Greek: A Coursebook on the Information Structure of New Testament Greek.* 2nd ed. Dallas: SIL International, 2000.

———. "A Discourse Study of Constituent Order and the Article in Philippians." In *Discourse Analysis and Other Topics in Biblical Greek,* edited by S. E. Porter and D. A. Carson, 60–74. JSNTSup 113. Sheffield: Sheffield Academic Press, 1995.

———. *Textual Connections in Acts.* SBLMS 31. Atlanta: Scholars Press, 1987.

Liddon, H. P. *Explanatory Analysis of St. Paul's First Epistle to Timothy.* London: Longmans, Green, 1907. Reprint, Minneapolis: Klock & Klock, 1978.

Liefeld, W. L. *New Testament Exposition: From Text to Sermon.* Grand Rapids: Zondervan, 1984.

Lim, T. H., H. L. MacQueen, and C. M. Carmichael, eds. *On Scrolls, Artefacts and Intellectual Property.* JSPSup 38. Sheffield: Sheffield Academic Press, 2001.

Lincoln, A. T. *Truth on Trial: The Lawsuit Motif in the Fourth Gospel.* Peabody, MA: Hendrickson, 2000.

Lock, W. *A Critical and Exegetical Commentary on the Pastoral Epistles.* ICC. Edinburgh: T&T Clark, 1924.

Loepfe, A. *Die Wortstellung im griechischen Sprechsatz: Erklärt an Stücken aus Platon und Menander.* Freiburg (Switzerland): Paulusdruckerei, 1940.

Lohse, E. *Colossians and Philemon: A Commentary on the Epistles to the Colossians and to Philemon.* Translated by W. R. Poehlmann and R. J. Karris. Edited by H. Koester. Hermeneia. Philadelphia: Fortress, 1971.

Longacre, R. E. *The Grammar of Discourse.* 2nd ed. New York: Plenum, 1996.

———. *Joseph: A Story of Divine Providence; A Text Theoretical and Textlinguistic Analysis of Genesis 37 and 39–48.* 2nd ed. Winona Lake, IN: Eisenbrauns, 2003.

Longman, T. *Literary Approaches to Biblical Interpretation.* Grand Rapids: Zondervan, 1987.

Lord, A. B. *The Singer of Tales.* New York: Atheneum, 1968.

Louw, J. P. "Linguistic Theory and the Greek Case System." *AC* 9 (1966): 73–88.

———. "The Present State of New Testament Lexicography." In *Lexicography and*

Translation, edited by J. P. Louw, 97–117. Roggebaai: Bible Society of South Africa, 1985.

———. *A Semantic Discourse Analysis of Romans*. 2 vols. Pretoria: University of Pretoria, Department of Greek, 1987.

———. *Semantics of New Testament Greek*. SemSt. Philadelphia: Fortress; Chico, CA: Scholars Press, 1982.

———. "Die Semantiese Waarde van die Perfektum in Hellenistiese Grieks." *AC* 10 (1967): 23–32.

———, ed. *Sociolinguistics and Communication*. UBSMS 1. London: United Bible Societies, 1986.

———. "Verbale Aspek in Grieks." *Taalfasette* 15 (1971): 13–26.

Louw, J. P., and E. A. Nida. *Greek-English Lexicon of the New Testament Based on Semantic Domains*. 2 vols. New York: United Bible Societies, 1988.

Lucy, J. A. *Grammatical Categories and Cognition: A Case Study of the Linguistic Relativity Hypothesis*. SSCFL 13. Cambridge: Cambridge University Press, 1992.

———. *Language Diversity and Thought: A Reformulation of the Linguistic Relativity Hypothesis*. SSCFL 12. Cambridge: Cambridge University Press, 1992.

Lüdemann, G. *Opposition to Paul in Jewish Christianity*. Translated by M. E. Boring. Minneapolis: Fortress, 1989.

Lukin, A., and J. J. Webster. "SFL and the Study of Literature." In vol. 1 of *Continuing Discourse on Language: A Functional Perspective*, edited by R. Hasan, C. Matthiessen, and J. Webster, 413–56. 2 vols. London: Equinox, 2005.

Lukin, A., et al. "Halliday's Model of Register Revisited and Explored." *LHS* 4 (2011): 187–213.

Lyons, J. *Introduction to Theoretical Linguistics*. Cambridge: Cambridge University Press, 1968.

———. *Semantics*. 2 vols. Cambridge: Cambridge University Press, 1977.

———. *Structural Semantics: An Analysis of Part of the Vocabulary of Plato*. Oxford: Blackwell, 1963.

Mackowski, R. "Some Colloquialisms in the Gospel according to Mark." In *Daidalikon: Studies in Memory of Raymond V. Schoder, SJ.*, edited by R. F. Sutton Jr., 229–38. Wauconda, IL: Bolchazy-Carducci, 1989.

Macnamara, J. "Linguistic Relativity Revisited." In *The Influence of Language on Culture and Thought: Essays in Honor of Joshua A. Fishman's Sixty-Fifth Birthday*, edited by R. L. Cooper and B. Spolsky, 45–60. Berlin: de Gruyter, 1991.

Macquarrie, J. *Principles of Christian Theology*. New York: Scribner, 1966.

MacQueen, H. L. "Copyright Law and the Dead Sea Scrolls: A British Perspective." In *On Scrolls, Artefacts and Intellectual Property*, edited by T. H. Lim, H. L. MacQueen, and C. M. Carmichael, 99–115. JSPSup 38. Sheffield: Sheffield Academic Press, 2001.

Malbon, E. S. "Ending at the Beginning: A Response." *Semeia* 52 (1991): 175–84.

Malina, B. "John's: The Maverick Christian Group, the Evidence of Sociolinguistics." *BTB* 24 (1994): 167–82.

———. "The Social Sciences and Biblical Interpretation." *Int* 36 (1982): 229–42.

Malinowski, B. "The Problem of Meaning in Primitive Languages." In *The Meaning of Meaning: A Study of the Influence of Language upon Thought and of the Science of Symbolism*, by C. K. Ogden and I. A. Richards, 296–336. New York: Harcourt, Brace & World, 1923.

Maloney, E. *Semitic Interference in Marcan Syntax*. SBLDS 51. Chico, CA: Scholars Press, 1981.

Marcus, J. *Mark 1–8*. AB 27. New York: Doubleday, 2000.

Marczak, M. "The Significance of Peak and Frontground in Discourse Analysis and Translation: A Case Study in Acts 19–26." Doctoral diss., University of Wrocławski, 2005.

Marshall, I. H. *New Testament Theology*. Downers Grove, IL: InterVarsity, 2004.

Marshall, I. H., with P. H. Towner. *A Critical and Exegetical Commentary on the Pastoral Epistles*. ICC. Edinburgh: T&T Clark, 1999.

Martin, G. "Procedural Register in the Olivet Discourse: A Functional Linguistic Approach to Mark 13." *Bib* 90 (2009): 457–83.

Martin, J. R. *English Text: System and Structure.* Philadelphia: John Benjamins, 1992.

Martin, J. R., and D. Rose. *Genre Relations: Mapping Culture.* London: Equinox, 2008.

———. *Working with Discourse: Meaning beyond the Clause.* 2nd ed. London: Continuum, 2007.

Martin, R. M. *The Meaning of Language.* Cambridge, MA: MIT Press, 1987.

Martin, R. P. *Carmen Christi: Philippians 2:5–11 in Recent Interpretation and in the Setting of Early Christian Worship.* SNTSMS 4. Cambridge: Cambridge University Press, 1967. Revised and reprinted, Grand Rapids: Eerdmans, 1983.

Martin, T. *By Philosophy and Empty Deceit: Colossians as a Response to a Cynic Critique.* JSNTSup 118. Sheffield: Sheffield Academic Press, 1996.

Martin, W. *Recent Theories of Narrative.* Ithaca, NY: Cornell University Press, 1986.

Martín-Asensio, G. "Hallidayan Functional Grammar as Heir to New Testament Rhetorical Criticism." In *The Rhetorical Interpretation of Scripture: Essays from the 1996 Malibu Conference,* edited by S. E. Porter and D. L. Stamps, 84–107. JSNTSup 180. Sheffield: Sheffield Academic Press, 1999.

———. *Transitivity-Based Foregrounding in the Acts of the Apostles: A Functional-Grammatical Approach to the Lukan Perspective.* JSNTSup 202; SNTG 8. Sheffield: Sheffield Academic Press, 2000.

Mateos, J. *El aspecto verbal en el Nuevo Testamento.* ENT 1. Madrid: Ediciones Cristiandad, 1977.

———. *Método de análisis semántico: Aplicado al Griego del Nuevo Testamento.* EFN 1. Córdoba: Ediciones el Almendro, 1989.

Mateos, J., and J. Peláez. *Diccionario Griego-Español del Nuevo Testamento.* 5 vols. Córdoba: Ediciones el Almendro, 2000–.

Mathewson, D. L. *Verbal Aspect in the Book of Revelation: The Function of Greek Verb Tenses in John's Apocalypse.* LBS 4. Leiden: Brill, 2010.

Mayser, E. *Grammatik der griechischen Papyri aus der Ptolemäerzeit.* 3 vols. Berlin: de Gruyter, 1906–34.

McEnery, T., and A. Hardie. *Corpus Linguistics: Method, Theory and Practice.* CTL. Cambridge: Cambridge University Press, 2012.

McGregor, W. B. "Attribution and Identification in Gooniyandi." In *Meaning and Form: Systemic Functional Interpretations,* edited by M. Berry et al., 395–430. ADP 57. Norwood, NJ: Ablex, 1996.

McKay, K. L. "Aspectual Usage in Timeless Contexts in Ancient Greek." In *In the Footsteps of Raphael Kühner: Proceedings of the International Colloquium in Commemoration of the 150th Anniversary of the Publication of Raphael Kühner's Ausführliche Grammatik der griechischen Sprache. II. Theil:* Syntaxe, *Amsterdam, 1986,* edited by A. Rijksbaron, H. A. Mulder, and G. C. Wakker, 193–208. Amsterdam: Gieben, 1988.

———. "Further Remarks on the 'Historical' Present and Other Phenomena." *FL* 11 (1974): 247–51.

———. *Greek Grammar for Students: A Concise Grammar of Classical Attic with Special Reference to Aspect in the Verb.* Canberra: Australian National University, 1974.

———. *A New Syntax of the Verb in New Testament Greek: An Aspectual Approach.* SBG 5. New York: Peter Lang, 1994.

———. "On the Perfect and Other Aspects in New Testament Greek." *NovT* 23 (1981): 289–329.

———. "On the Perfect and Other Aspects in the Greek Non-Literary Papyri." *BICS* 27 (1980): 23–49.

———. "Time and Aspect in New Testament Greek." *NovT* 34 (1992): 209–28.

———. "The Use of the Ancient Greek Perfect Down to the Second Century AD." *BICS* 12 (1965): 1–21.

McKenzie, S. L., and J. Kaltner, eds. *New Meanings for Ancient Texts: Recent Approaches to Biblical Criticisms and Their Applications.* Louisville: Westminster John Knox, 2013.

McKnight, E. V. *The Bible and the Reader: An Introduction to Literary Criticism*. Philadelphia: Fortress, 1985.

McKnight, S. *Interpreting the Synoptic Gospels*. Grand Rapids: Baker Books, 1988.

Mel'čuk, I. A. *Dependency Syntax: Theory and Practice*. Albany: SUNY Press, 1988.

Merenlahti, P. *Poetics for the Gospels? Rethinking Narrative Criticism*. SNTW. London: T&T Clark, 2002.

Mesthrie, R., ed. *The Cambridge Handbook of Sociolinguistics*. Cambridge: Cambridge University Press, 2011.

Michaelis, L. A. *Aspectual Grammar and Past-Time Reference*. RSGL 4. London: Routledge, 1998.

Michaels, J. R. *1 Peter*. WBC 49. Waco: Word, 1988.

Middleton, T. F. *The Doctrine of the Greek Article Applied to the Criticism and Illustration of the New Testament*. Edited by H. J. Rose. London: Deighton, Bell, 1833.

Miller, C. L., ed. *The Verbless Clause in Biblical Hebrew: Linguistic Approaches*. Winona Lake, IN: Eisenbrauns, 1999.

Milligan, G. *St. Paul's Epistles to the Thessalonians*. London: Macmillan, 1908.

Mills, S. *Discourse*. London: Routledge, 1997.

Mitchell, S. *Anatolia: Land, Men, and Gods in Asia Minor*. 2 vols. Oxford: Clarendon, 1993.

Mitchell, T. F., and S. A. al-Hassan. *Modality, Mood and Aspect in Spoken Arabic: With Special Reference to Egypt and the Levant*. LAL 11. London: Kegan Paul International, 1994.

Moeller, H. R., and A. Kramer. "An Overlooked Structural Pattern in New Testament Greek." *NovT* 5 (1962): 25–35.

Monro, D. B. *A Grammar of the Homeric Dialect*. 2nd ed. Oxford: Clarendon, 1891.

Moore, S. D. "Afterword: Things Not Written in This Book." In *Anatomies of Narrative Criticism: The Past, Present, and Futures of the Fourth Gospel as Literature*, edited by T. Thatcher and S. D. Moore, 253–58. SBLRBS 55. Atlanta: Society of Biblical Literature, 2008.

———. *The Bible in Theory: Critical and Postcritical Essays*. SBLRBS 57. Atlanta: Society of Biblical Literature, 2010.

———. *Literary Criticism and the Gospels: The Theoretical Challenge*. New Haven: Yale University Press, 1989.

Moorhouse, A. C. *Studies in the Greek Negatives*. Cardiff: University of Wales Press, 1959.

Morgenthaler, R. *Statistik des neutestamentlichen Wortschatzes*. Zurich: Gotthelf-Verlag, 1958.

Morris, L. *The Gospel according to Matthew*. PilNTC. Grand Rapids: Eerdmans, 1992.

———. *New Testament Theology*. Grand Rapids: Zondervan, 1986.

Morris, M. *An Introduction to the Philosophy of Language*. CIP. Cambridge: Cambridge University Press, 2007.

Moulton, J. H. *A Grammar of New Testament Greek*. Vol. 1, *Prolegomena*. 3rd ed. Edinburgh: T&T Clark, 1908.

———. *An Introduction to the Study of New Testament Greek*. 2nd ed. London: Kelly, 1903.

Moulton, J. H., and W. F. Howard. *A Grammar of New Testament Greek*. Vol. 2, *Accidence and Word-Formation*. Edinburgh: T&T Clark, 1929.

Mounce, W. D. *Pastoral Epistles*. WBC 46. Nashville: Nelson, 2000.

Mowitt, J. *Text: The Genealogy of an Antidisciplinary Object*. Durham, NC: Duke University Press, 1992.

Mullen, A., and P. James, eds. *Multilingualism in the Graeco-Roman Worlds*. Cambridge: Cambridge University Press, 2012.

Munck, J. *Paul and the Salvation of Mankind*. Translated by F. Clarke. London: SCM, 1959.

Muraoka, T. *A Greek-English Lexicon of the Septuagint: Twelve Prophets*. Louvain: Peeters, 1993.

Murphy-O'Connor, J. "2 Timothy Contrasted with 1 Timothy and Titus." *RB* 98 (1991): 403–18.

Nanos, M. D. *The Irony of Galatians: Paul's Letter in First-Century Context*. Minneapolis: Fortress, 2002.

Neirynck, F. *Duality in Mark: Contributions to the Study of the Markan Redaction.* BETL 31. Leuven: Leuven University Press, 1988.

Nevius, R. C. "The Use of the Definite Article with 'Jesus' in the Fourth Gospel." *NTS* 12 (1965–66): 81–85.

Newmeyer, F. J., ed. *Linguistics: The Cambridge Survey.* Vol. 4, *Language: The Socio-Cultural Context.* Cambridge: Cambridge University Press, 1988.

Niccacci, A. The *Syntax of the Verb in Classical Hebrew Prose.* Translated by W. G. E. Watson. JSOTSup 86. Sheffield: JSOT Press, 1990.

Nida, E. A. *Componential Analysis of Meaning: An Introduction to Semantic Structures.* The Hague: Mouton, 1975.

———. *Toward a Science of Translating: With Special Reference to the Principles and Procedures Involved in Bible Translating.* Leiden: Brill, 1964.

———. "Translating Means Communicating: A Sociolinguistic Theory of Translation." *BT* 30 (1979): 101–7, 318–25.

Nida, E. A., and J. P. Louw. *Lexical Semantics of the Greek New Testament.* SBLRBS 25. Atlanta: Scholars Press, 1992.

Nida, E. A., J. P. Louw, and R. B. Smith. "Semantic Domains and Componential Analysis of Meaning." In *Current Issues in Linguistic Theory,* edited by R. W. Cole, 139–67. Bloomington: Indiana University Press, 1977.

Nimmer, D. "Assaying Qimron's Originality." In *On Scrolls, Artefacts and Intellectual Property,* edited by T. H. Lim, H. L. MacQueen, and C. M. Carmichael, 159–76. JSPSup 38. Sheffield: Sheffield Academic Press, 2001.

Nolland, J. *The Gospel of Matthew: A Commentary on the Greek Text.* NIGTC. Grand Rapids: Eerdmans, 2005.

Novenson, M. V. "Can the Messiahship of Jesus Be Read off Paul's Grammar? Nils Dahl's Criteria 50 Years Later." *NTS* 56 (2010): 396–412.

Nylund, J. H. "The Prague School of Linguistics and Its Influence on New Testament Language Studies." In *The Language of the New Testament: Context, History, and Development,* edited by S. E. Porter and A. W. Pitts, 155–221. ECHC 3; LBS 6. Leiden: Brill, 2013.

O'Callaghan, J. *"Nomina Sacra" in Papyris Graecis Saeculi III Neotestamentariis.* AnBib 46. Rome: Biblical Institute Press, 1970.

———. "'Nominum sacrorum' elenchus in Graecis Novi Testamenti papyris a saeculo IV usque ad VIII." *SPap* 10 (1971): 99–122.

O'Day, G. R. *Revelation in the Fourth Gospel: Narrative Mode and Theological Claim.* Philadelphia: Fortress, 1986.

Oden, T. C. *First and Second Timothy and Titus.* IBC. Louisville: John Knox, 1989.

O'Donnell, M. B. *Corpus Linguistics and the Greek of the New Testament.* NTM 6. Sheffield: Sheffield Phoenix Press, 2005.

———. "Designing and Compiling a Register-Balanced Corpus of Hellenistic Greek for the Purpose of Linguistic Description and Investigation." In *Diglossia and Other Topics in New Testament Linguistics,* edited by Stanley E. Porter, 255–97. JSNTSup 193; SNTG 6. Sheffield: Sheffield Academic Press, 2000.

———. "Some New Testament Words for Resurrection and the Company They Keep." In *Resurrection,* edited by S. E. Porter, M. A. Hayes, and D. Tombs, 136–65. JSNTSup 186; RILP 5. London: Sheffield Academic Press, 1999.

———. "The Use of Annotated Corpora for New Testament Discourse Analysis: A Survey of Current Practice and Future Prospects." In *Discourse Analysis and the New Testament: Approaches and Results,* edited by S. E. Porter and J. T. Reed, 71–117. JSNTSup 170; SNTG 4. Sheffield: Sheffield Academic Press, 1999.

O'Donnell, M. B., S. E. Porter, and J. T. Reed. "OpenText.org: The Problems and Prospects of Working with Ancient Discourse." In *Proceedings of the Corpus Linguistics 2001 Conference,* edited by P. Rayson et al., 413–22. Lancaster: Lancaster University, 2001.

———. "OpenText.org: The Problems and Prospects of Working with Ancient Discourse." In *A Rainbow of Corpora: Corpus Linguistics and the Languages of the World*, edited by A. Wilson, P. Rayson, and T. McEnery, 109–19. LE 40. Munich: Lincom, 2003.

Öhman, S. "Theories of the Linguistic Field." *Word* 9 (1953): 123–34.

Olsson, B. *Structure and Meaning in the Fourth Gospel: A Text-Linguistic Analysis of John 1:1–11 and 4:1–42*. ConBNT 6. Lund: Gleerup, 1974.

O'Neill, P. *Fictions of Discourse: Reading Narrative Theory*. Toronto: University of Toronto Press, 1994.

Ong, H. T. "Can Linguistic Analysis in Historical Jesus Research Stand on Its Own? A Sociolinguistic Analysis of Matt 26:36–27:26." *BAGL* 2 (2013): 109–38.

———. "An Evaluation of the Aramaic and Greek Language Criteria in Historical Jesus Research: A Sociolinguistic Study of Mark 14:32–65." *FN* 25 (2012): 37–55.

———. "Language Choice in Ancient Palestine: A Sociolinguistic Study of Jesus' Language Use Based on Four 'I Have Come' Sayings." *BAGL* 1 (2012): 63–101.

Orchard, H. C. *Courting Betrayal: Jesus as Victim in the Gospel of John*. JSNTSup 161. Sheffield: Sheffield Academic Press, 1998.

Osborne, G. R. *Matthew*. ZECNT. Grand Rapids: Zondervan, 2010.

Paap, A. H. R. E. *Nomina Sacra in the Greek Papyri of the First Five Centuries AD: The Sources and Some Deductions*. PLB 8. Leiden: Brill, 1959.

Paltridge, B. *Discourse Analysis*. London: Continuum, 2006.

Palu, M. *Jesus and Time: An Interpretation of Mark 1.15*. LNTS 468. London: T&T Clark, 2012.

Pang, F. G. H. "Aktionsart as Epiphenomenon: A Stratal Approach to Process Typologies." In *Greeks, Jews, and Christians: Historical, Religious and Philological Studies in Honor of Jesús Peláez del Rosal*, edited by L. R. Lanzillotta and I. M. Gallarte, 449–74. Córdoba: Ediciones el Almendro, 2013.

Panning, A. J. "αὐθέντης—A Word Study." *WLQ* 78 (1981): 185–91.

Parry, R. St. J. *The Pastoral Epistles: With Introduction, Text and Commentary*. Cambridge: Cambridge University Press, 1920.

Pastorelli, D. "La formule johannique (Jean 14:25; 15:11; 16:1, 4, 6, 25, 33): Un exemple de parfait transitif." *FN* 19 (2006): 73–88.

Pätsch, G. *Grundfragen der Sprachtheorie*. Halle: Max Niemeyer, 1955.

Peabody, D. B. *Mark as Composer*. NGS 1. Macon, GA: Mercer University Press, 1987.

Pearson, B. W. R. *Corresponding Sense: Paul, Dialectic, and Gadamer*. BIS 48. Leiden: Brill, 2001.

Peláez, J. *Metodología del Diccionario Griego-Español del Nuevo Testamento*. EFN 6. Córdoba: Ediciones el Almendro; Fundación Épsilon, 1996.

Pennington, J. T. "Setting Aside 'Deponency': Rediscovering the Greek Middle Voice in New Testament Studies." In *The Linguist as Pedagogue: Trends in the Teaching and Linguistic Analysis of the Greek New Testament*, edited by S. E. Porter and M. B. O'Donnell, 181–203. NTM 11. Sheffield: Sheffield Phoenix Press, 2009.

Perriman, A. C. "What Eve Did, What Women Shouldn't Do: The Meaning of αὐθεντέω in 1 Timothy 2:12." *TynBul* 44 (1993): 129–42.

Perrin, N. *The Kingdom of God in the Teaching of Jesus*. London: SCM, 1963.

Peters, R. D. *The Greek Article: A Functional Grammar of ὁ-Items in the Greek New Testament with Special Emphasis on the Greek Article*. LBS 9. Leiden: Brill, 2014.

Petersen, N. R. *The Gospel of John and the Sociology of Light: Language and Characterization in the Fourth Gospel*. Valley Forge, PA: Trinity Press, 1993.

———. *Literary Criticism for New Testament Critics*. GBSNT. Philadelphia: Fortress, 1978.

———. *Rediscovering Paul: Philemon and the Sociology of Paul's Narrative World*. Philadelphia: Fortress, 1985.

Phillips, P. M. *The Prologue of the Fourth Gospel: A Sequential Reading*. LNTS 294. London: T&T Clark, 2006.

Pierpont, W. G. "Studies in Word Order: Personal Pronoun Possessives in Nominal Phrases in the New Testament." *START* 15 (1986): 3–25.

Pike, K. L. *Language in Relation to a Unified Theory of the Structure of Human Behavior.* 2nd rev. ed. JLSMa 24. The Hague: Mouton, 1967.

———. *Linguistic Concepts: An Introduction to Tagmemics.* Lincoln: University of Nebraska Press, 1982.

Pitts, A. W. "Greek Word Order and Clause Structure: A Comparative Study of Some New Testament Corpora." In *The Language of the New Testament: Context, History, and Development*, edited by S. E. Porter and A. W. Pitts, 311–46. ECHC 3; LBS 6. Leiden: Brill, 2013.

Platt, A. "The Augment in Homer." *JPhil* 19 (1891): 211–37.

Poland, L. M. *Literary Criticism and Biblical Hermeneutics: A Critique of Formalist Approaches.* AARAS 48. Chico, CA: Scholars Press, 1985.

Porter, S. E. "The Adjectival Attributive Genitive in the New Testament: A Grammatical Study." *TJ* 4 (1983): 3–17.

———. "Allusions and Echoes." In *As It Is Written: Studying Paul's Use of Scripture*, edited by S. E. Porter and C. D. Stanley, 29–40. SBLSymS 50. Atlanta: Scholars Press, 2008.

———. "Apocryphal Gospels and the Text of the New Testament before AD 200." In *The New Testament Text in Early Christianity: Proceedings of the Lille Colloquium, July 2000 = Le texte du Nouveau Testament au début du christianisme: Actes du colloque de Lille, juillet 2000*, edited by C.-B. Amphoux and J. K. Elliott, 235–58. HTB 6. Lausanne: Éditions du Zèbre, 2003.

———. *The Apostle Paul: His Life, Thought, and Letters.* Grand Rapids: Eerdmans, forthcoming.

———. "The Argument of Romans 5: Can a Rhetorical Question Make a Difference?" *JBL* 110 (1991): 655–77. Revised and reprinted in Porter, *Studies in the Greek New Testament: Theory and Practice*, 213–38. SBG 6. New York: Peter Lang, 1996.

———. "Aspect Theory and Lexicography." In *Biblical Greek Language and Lexicography: Essays in Honor of Frederick W. Danker*, edited by B. A. Taylor et al., 207–22. Grand Rapids: Eerdmans, 2004.

———. "Assessing Translation Theory: Beyond Literal and Dynamic Equivalence." In *Translating the New Testament: Text, Translation, Theology*, edited by S. E. Porter and M. J. Boda, 117–45. MNTS. Grand Rapids: Eerdmans, 2009.

———. "An Assessment of Some New Testament-Related Assumptions for Open Theism in the Writings of Clark Pinnock." In *Semper Reformandum: Studies in Honour of Clark H. Pinnock*, edited by S. E. Porter and A. R. Cross, 160–82. Carlisle: Paternoster, 2003.

———. "The Babatha Archive, the Egyptian Papyri and Their Implications for Study of the Greek New Testament." In *Early Christian Manuscripts: Examples of Applied Method and Approach*, edited by T. J. Kraus and T. Nicklas, 213–37. TENT 5. Leiden: Brill, 2010.

———. "Biblical Hermeneutics and *Theological* Responsibility." In *The Future of Biblical Interpretation: Responsible Plurality in Biblical Hermeneutics*, edited by S. E. Porter and M. R. Malcolm, 29–50. Downers Grove, IL: IVP Academic, 2013.

———. "Buried Linguistic Treasure in the Babatha Archive." In *Proceedings of the 25th International Congress of Papyrology, Ann Arbor, July 29–August 4, 2007*, edited by T. Gagos, 623–32. ASP Special Edition. Ann Arbor: Scholarly Publishing Office, The University of Michigan Library, 2010.

———. "Can Traditional Exegesis Enlighten Literary Analysis of the Fourth Gospel? An Examination of the Old Testament Fulfilment Motif and the Passover Theme." In *The Gospels and the Scriptures of Israel*, edited by C. A. Evans and W. R. Stegner, 396–428. JSNTSup 104; SSEJC 3. Sheffield: Sheffield Academic Press, 1994.

———. "The Case for Case Revisited." *JD* 6 (1996): 13–28.

———. "Commentaries on the Book of Romans." In *On the Writing of New Testament*

Commentaries: Festschrift for Grant R. Osborne on the Occasion of His 70th Birthday, edited by S. E. Porter and E. J. Schnabel, 365–404. TENT 8. Leiden: Brill, 2012.

———. "The Concept of Covenant in Paul." In *The Concept of the Covenant in the Second Temple Period*, edited by S. E. Porter and J. C. R. de Roo, 269–85. JSJSup 71. Leiden: Brill, 2003.

———. *Constantine Tischendorf: The Life and Work of a 19th Century Bible Hunter*. London: Bloomsbury, 2015.

———. "The Contemporary English Version and the Ideology of Translation." In *Translating the Bible: Problems and Prospects*, edited by S. E. Porter and R. S. Hess, 18–45. JSNTSup 173. Sheffield: Sheffield Academic Press, 1999.

———. *The Criteria for Authenticity in Historical-Jesus Research: Previous Discussion and New Proposals*. JSNTSup 191. Sheffield: Sheffield Academic Press, 2000.

———. "The Criterion of Greek Language and Its Context: A Further Response." *JSHJ* 4 (2006): 69–74.

———. "The Date of the Composition of Hebrews and Use of the Present Tense-Form." In *Crossing the Boundaries: Essays on Biblical Interpretation in Honour of Michael D. Goulder*, edited by S. E. Porter, P. Joyce, and D. E. Orton, 313–32. BIS 8. Leiden: Brill, 1994.

———. "Dialect and Register in the Greek of the New Testament: Theory." In *Rethinking Contexts, Rereading Texts: Contributions from the Social Sciences to Biblical Interpretation*, edited by M. D. Carroll R., 190–208. JSOTSup 299. Sheffield: Sheffield Academic Press, 2000.

———. "Did Jesus Ever Teach in Greek?" *TynBul* 44 (1993): 199–235. Revised and reprinted in Porter, *Studies in the Greek New Testament: Theory and Practice*, 139–71. SBG 6. New York: Peter Lang, 1996.

———. "Did Paul Baptize Himself? A Problem of the Greek Voice System." In *Dimensions of Baptism*, edited by S. E. Porter and A. R. Cross, 91–109. JSNTSup 234. Sheffield: Sheffield Academic Press, 2002.

———. "Did Paul Have Opponents in Rome and What Were They Opposing?" In *Paul and His Opponents*, edited by S. E. Porter, 149–68. PAST 2. Leiden: Brill, 2005.

———. "Did Paul Speak Latin?" In *Paul: Jew, Greek, and Roman*, edited by S. E. Porter, 289–308. PAST 5. Leiden: Brill, 2008.

———, ed. *Diglossia and Other Topics in New Testament Linguistics*. JSNTSup 193; SNTG 6. Sheffield: Sheffield Academic Press, 2000.

———. "Discourse Analysis and New Testament Studies: An Introductory Survey." In *Discourse Analysis and Other Topics in Biblical Greek*, edited by S. E. Porter and D. A. Carson, 14–35. JSNTSup 113; SNTG 2. Sheffield: Sheffield Academic Press, 1995.

———. "Early Apocryphal Gospels and the New Testament Text." In *The Early Text of the New Testament*, edited by C. E. Hill and M. J. Kruger, 350–69. Oxford: Oxford University Press, 2012.

———. "The Ending of John's Gospel." In *From Biblical Criticism to Biblical Faith: Essays in Honor of Lee Martin McDonald*, edited by C. A. Evans and W. Brackney, 55–73. Macon, GA: Mercer University Press, 2007.

———. "Eugene Nida and Translation." *BT* 56 (2005): 8–19.

———. "The Functional Distribution of Koine Greek in First-Century Palestine." In *Diglossia and Other Topics in New Testament Linguistics*, edited by S. E. Porter, 53–78. JSNTSup 193; SNTG 6. Sheffield: Sheffield Academic Press, 2000.

———. "A Functional Letter Perspective: Towards a Grammar of Epistolary Form." In *Paul and the Ancient Letter Form*, edited by S. E. Porter and S. A. Adams, 9–31. PAST 6. Leiden: Brill, 2010.

———. "Granville Sharp's Rule: A Response to Dan Wallace, or Why a Critical Book Review Should Be Left Alone." *JETS* 56 (2013): 93–100.

———. "Greek Grammar and Lexicography." In *Dictionary of Biblical Criticism and Interpretation*, edited by S. E. Porter, 136–39. London: Routledge, 2007.

———. "Greek Grammar and Syntax." In *The Face of New Testament Studies: A Survey* of Recent Research, edited by S. McKnight and G. R. Osborne, 76–103. Grand Rapids: Baker Academic, 2004.

———. "Greek Language." In vol. 2 of The New Interpreter's Dictionary of the Bible, edited by K. D. Sakenfeld, 673–81. Nashville: Abingdon, 2007.

———. "Greek Language." In Oxford Bibliographies Online: Biblical Studies, edited by C. Ferraro. New York: Oxford University Press, 2014.

———. "Greek Language and Linguistics (Keeping Up with Recent Studies 17)." ExpTim 103 (1991–92): 202–8. Revised and reprinted in Porter, Studies in the Greek New Testament: Theory and Practice, 7–20. SBG 6. New York: Peter Lang, 1996.

———. "The Greek Language of the New Testament." In Handbook to Exegesis of the New Testament, edited by S. E. Porter, 99–130. NTTS 25. Leiden: Brill, 1997.

———. "Greek Linguistics and Lexicography." In Understanding the Times: New Testament Studies in the 21st Century; Essays in Honor of D. A. Carson on the Occasion of His 65th Birthday, edited by A. J. Köstenberger and R. W. Yarbrough, 19–61. Wheaton, IL: Crossway, 2011.

———. "The Greek of the Gospel of Peter: Implications for Syntax and Discourse Study." In Das Evangelium nach Petrus: Text, Kontexte, Intertexte, edited by T. J. Kraus and T. Nicklas, 77–90. TUGAL 158. Berlin: de Gruyter, 2007.

———. "The Greek of the Jews and Early Christians: The Language of the People from a Historical Sociolinguistic Perspective." In Far from Minimal: Celebrating the Work and Influence of Philip R. Davies, edited by D. Burns and J. W. Rogerson, 350–64. LHBOTS 484. London: T&T Clark, 2012.

———. "Greek of the New Testament." In Dictionary of New Testament Background, edited by C. A. Evans and S. E. Porter, 426–35. Downers Grove, IL: InterVarsity, 2000.

———. "The Greek Papyri of the Judaean Desert and the World of the Roman East." In The Scrolls and the Scriptures: Qumran Fifty Years After, edited by S. E. Porter and

C. A. Evans, 293–316. RILP 3; JSPSup 26. Sheffield: Sheffield Academic Press, 1997.

———, ed. Handbook to Exegesis of the New Testament. NTTS 25. Leiden: Brill, 1997.

———. "Hermeneutics, Biblical Interpretation and Theology: Hunch, Holy Spirit or Hard Work?" In Beyond the Bible: Moving from Scripture to Theology, by I. H. Marshall, with essays by K. Vanhoozer and S. E. Porter, 97–127. Grand Rapids: Baker Academic; Milton Keynes: Paternoster, 2004.

———. "History of Scholarship on the Language of the Septuagint." In Handbuch zur Septuaginta. Vol. 4, Sprache, edited by E. Bons and J. Joosten. Gütersloh: Gütersloher Verlag, forthcoming.

———. "How Do We Know What We Think We Know? Methodological Reflections on Jesus Research." In Jesus Research: New Methodologies and Perceptions, edited by J. H. Charlesworth with B. Rhea in consultation with P. Pokorný, 82–99. Grand Rapids: Eerdmans, 2014.

———. "How Should κολλώμενος in 1 Corinthians 6:16, 17 Be Translated?" ETL 67 (1991): 105–6.

———. How We Got the New Testament: Text, Transmission, Translation. Grand Rapids: Baker Academic, 2013.

———. Idioms of the Greek New Testament. BLG 2. Sheffield: Sheffield Academic Press, 1992. 2nd ed., 1994.

———. "Images of Christ in Paul's Letters." In Images of Christ: Ancient and Modern, edited by S. E. Porter, M. A. Hayes, and D. Tombs, 95–112. RILP 2. Sheffield: Sheffield Academic Press, 1997.

———. "In Defence of Verbal Aspect." In Biblical Greek Language and Linguistics: Open Questions in Current Research, edited by S. E. Porter and D. A. Carson, 26–45. JSNTSup 80; SNTG 1. Sheffield: Sheffield Academic Press, 1993. Revised and reprinted in Porter, Studies in the Greek New Testament: Theory and Practice, 21–38. SBG 6. New York: Peter Lang, 1996.

———. "'In the Vicinity of Jericho': Luke 18:35 in the Light of Its Synoptic Parallels." BBR 2 (1992): 91–104. Revised and reprinted in

Porter, *Studies in the Greek New Testament: Theory and Practice*, 125–38. SBG 6. New York: Peter Lang, 1996.

———. "Introduction: The Greek of the New Testament as a Disputed Area of Research." In *The Language of the New Testament: Classic Essays*, edited by S. E. Porter, 11–38. JSNTSup 60. Sheffield: Sheffield Academic Press, 1991. Revised and reprinted in Porter, *Studies in the Greek New Testament: Theory and Practice*, 75–99. SBG 6. New York: Peter Lang, 1996.

———. "Is ἀμβιτεύειν Really ἐμβατεύειν (*P. Oxy* XVII 2110.15)?" *BASP* 27 (1990): 45–47.

———. "Is Critical Discourse Analysis Critical? An Evaluation Using Philemon as a Test Case." In *Discourse Analysis and the New Testament: Approaches and Results*, edited by S. E. Porter and J. T. Reed, 47–70. JSNTSup 170; SNTG 4. Sheffield: Sheffield Academic Press, 1999.

———. "Is *dipsuchos* (James 1:8; 4:8) a 'Christian' Word?" *Bib* 71 (1990): 469–98.

———. "ἴστε γινώσκοντες in Ephesians 5:5: Does Chiasm Solve a Problem?" *ZNW* 81 (1990): 270–76.

———. "Jesus and the Use of Greek: A Response to Maurice Casey." *BBR* 10 (2000): 71–87.

———. "Jesus and the Use of Greek in Galilee." In *Studying the Historical Jesus: Evaluations of the State of Current Research*, edited by B. Chilton and C. A. Evans, 123–54. NTTS 19. Leiden: Brill, 1994.

———. *John, His Gospel, and Jesus*. Grand Rapids: Eerdmans, forthcoming.

———. "Καταλλάσσω in Ancient Greek Literature and Romans 5: A Study of Pauline Usage." In *Studies in the Greek New Testament: Theory and Practice*, by S. E. Porter, 195–212. SBG 6. New York: Peter Lang, 1996.

———. Καταλλάσσω *in Ancient Greek Literature, with Reference to the Pauline Writings*. EFN 5. Córdoba: Ediciones el Almendro, 1994.

———. "Language and Translation of the New Testament." In *The Oxford Handbook of Biblical Studies*, edited by J. W. Rogerson

and J. M. Lieu, 184–210. Oxford: Oxford University Press, 2006.

———. "Language Criticism." In *Encyclopedia of the Historical Jesus*, edited by C. A. Evans, 361–65. London: Routledge, 2008.

———. "The Language of the Apocalypse in Recent Discussion." *NTS* 35 (1989): 582–603.

———, ed. *The Language of the New Testament: Classic Essays*. JSNTSup 60. Sheffield: JSOT Press, 1991.

———. "The Language(s) Jesus Spoke." In *Handbook for the Study of the Historical Jesus*. Vol. 3, *The Historical Jesus*, edited by T. Holmén and S. E. Porter, 2455–71. Leiden: Brill, 2011.

———. "Languages of the Bible." In *Dictionary of the Bible and Western Culture: A Handbook for Students*, edited by M. A. Beavis and M. J. Gilmour, 286–87. Sheffield: Sheffield Phoenix Press, 2012.

———. "The Languages That Paul Did Not Speak." In *Paul's World*, edited by S. E. Porter, 131–49. PAST 4. Leiden: Brill, 2008.

———. "Latin Language." In *Dictionary of New Testament Background*, edited by C. A. Evans and S. E. Porter, 630–31. Downers Grove, IL: InterVarsity, 2000.

———. "The Legacy of B. F. Westcott and Oral Gospel Tradition." In festschrift, edited by J. Neusner et al. Leiden: Brill, forthcoming.

———. "Lexicons (Theological)." In *Dictionary of Biblical Criticism and Interpretation*, edited by S. E. Porter, 195–96. London: Routledge, 2007.

———. "The Linguistic Competence of New Testament Commentaries." In *On the Writing of New Testament Commentaries: Festschrift for Grant R. Osborne on the Occasion of His 70th Birthday*, edited by S. E. Porter and E. J. Schnabel, 33–56. TENT 8. Leiden: Brill, 2012.

———. "Linguistic Criticism." In *Dictionary of Biblical Criticism and Interpretation*, edited by S. E. Porter, 199–202. London: Routledge, 2007.

———. "Linguistics and Biblical Interpretation." In *Methods of Biblical Interpretation: Excerpted from the Dictionary of Biblical*

Interpretation, 35–40. Nashville: Abingdon, 2004.

———. "Linguistics and Rhetorical Criticism." In *Linguistics and the New Testament: Critical Junctures*, edited by S. E. Porter and D. A. Carson, 63–92. JSNTSup 168; SNTG 5. Sheffield: Sheffield Academic Press, 1999.

———. "Literary Approaches to the New Testament: From Formalism to Deconstruction and Back." In *Approaches to New Testament Study*, edited by S. E. Porter and D. Tombs, 77–128. JSNTSup 120. Sheffield: Sheffield Academic Press, 1995.

———. "Luke 17.11–19 and the Criteria for Authenticity Revisited." *JSHJ* 1 (2003): 201–24.

———. "Mark 1.4, Baptism and Translation." In *Baptism, the New Testament and the Church: Historical and Contemporary Studies in Honour of R. E. O. White*, edited by S. E. Porter and A. R. Cross, 81–98. JSNTSup 171. Sheffield: Sheffield Academic Press, 1999.

———. "Matthew and Mark: The Contribution of Recent Linguistic Thought." In *Mark and Matthew: Comparative Readings. Part 1, Understanding the Earliest Gospels in Their First-Century Settings*, edited by E.-M. Becker and A. Runesson, 97–119. WUNT 271. Tübingen: Mohr Siebeck, 2011.

———. "A Modern Grammar of an Ancient Language: A Critique of the Schmidt Proposal." *Forum* 2 (1999): 201–13.

———. "Modern Translations." In *The Oxford Illustrated History of the Bible*, edited by J. Rogerson, 134–61. Oxford: Oxford University Press, 2001.

———. "New Perspectives on the Exegesis of the New Testament: Anglo-American Insights." In *Herkunft und Zukunft der neutestamentlichen Wissenschaft*, edited by O. Wischmeyer, 63–84. NET 6. Tübingen: Francke, 2003.

———. "New Testament." In vol. 2 of *Encyclopedia of Ancient Greek Language and Linguistics*, edited by G. K. Giannakis, 497–500. Leiden: Brill, 2014.

———. "New Testament Studies and Papyrology: What Can We Learn from Each Other?"

In *Akten des 23. Internationalen Papyrologenkongresses, Wien, 22.–28. Juli 2001*, edited by B. Palme, 559–72. PV 1. Vienna: Verlag der Österreichischen Akademie der Wissenschaften, 2007.

———. "Not Only That (οὐ μόνον), but It Has Been Said Before: A Response to Verlyn Verbrugge, or Why Reading Previous Scholarship Can Avoid Scholarly Misunderstandings." *JETS* 56 (2013): 577–83.

———. "Paul of Tarsus and His Letters." In *Handbook of Classical Rhetoric in the Hellenistic Period: 330 B.C.–A.D. 400*, edited by S. E. Porter, 533–85. Leiden: Brill, 1997.

———. "Penitence and Repentance in the Epistles." In *Repentance in Christian Theology*, edited by M. J. Boda and G. T. Smith, 127–50. Collegeville, MN: Liturgical Press, 2006.

———. "Pericope Markers and the Paragraph: Textual and Linguistic Considerations." In *The Impact of Unit Delimitation on Exegesis*, edited by R. de Hoop, M. C. A. Korpel, and S. E. Porter, 175–95. Pericope 7. Leiden: Brill, 2008.

———. "P.Oxy. 744.4 and Colossians 3:9." *Bib* 73 (1992): 565–67.

———. "Problems in the Language of the Bible: Misunderstandings that Continue to Plague Biblical Interpretation." In *The Nature of Religious Language: A Colloquium*, edited by S. E. Porter, 20–46. RILP 1. Sheffield: Sheffield Academic Press, 1996.

———. "Prolegomena to a Syntax of the Greek Papyri." In *Proceedings of the 24th International Congress of Papyrology, Helsinki, 1st–7th of August 2004*, edited by J. Frösén, T. Purola, and E. Salmenkivi, 921–33. Helsinki: Societas Scientiarum Fennica, 2007.

———. "Prominence: A Theoretical Overview." In *The Linguist as Pedagogue: Trends in the Teaching and Linguistic Analysis of the Greek New Testament*, edited by S. E. Porter and M. B. O'Donnell, 45–74. NTM 11. Sheffield: Sheffield Phoenix Press, 2009.

———. "Reconciliation and 2 Cor 5,18–21." In *The Corinthian Correspondence*, edited by R. Bieringer, 693–705. BETL 125. Leuven: Leuven University Press, 1996.

———. "Register in the Greek of the New Testament: Application with Reference to Mark's Gospel." In *Rethinking Contexts, Rereading Texts: Contributions from the Social Sciences to Biblical Interpretation*, edited by M. D. Carroll R., 209–29. JSOT-Sup 299. Sheffield: Sheffield Academic Press, 2000.

———. Review of *Granville Sharp's Canon and Its Kin: Semantics and Significance*, by Daniel B. Wallace. *JETS* 53 (2010): 828–32.

———. "Rhetorical Analysis and Discourse Analysis of the Pauline Corpus." In *The Rhetorical Analysis of Scripture: Essays from the 1995 London Conference*, edited by S. E. Porter and T. H. Olbricht, 249–74. JSNTSup 146. Sheffield: Sheffield Academic Press, 1997.

———. "The Role of Greek Language Criteria in Historical Jesus Research." In *Handbook for the Study of the Historical Jesus*. Vol. 1, *How to Study the Historical Jesus*, edited by T. Holmén and S. E. Porter, 361–404. Leiden: Brill, 2011.

———. "Romans 13:1–7 as Pauline Political Rhetoric." *FN* 3 (1990): 115–39.

———. "Septuagint." In vol. 3 of *Encyclopedia of Ancient Greek Language and Linguistics*, edited by G. K. Giannakis, 287–90. Leiden: Brill, 2014.

———. "A Single Horizon Hermeneutics: A Proposal for Interpretive Identification." *MJTM* 13 (2011–12): 45–66.

———. "Some Issues in Modern Translation Theory and Study of the Greek New Testament." *CBR* 9 (2001): 350–82.

———. *Studies in the Greek New Testament: Theory and Practice*. SBG 6. New York: Peter Lang, 1996.

———. "Studying Ancient Languages from a Modern Linguistic Perspective: Essential Terms and Terminology." *FN* 2 (1989): 147–72.

———. "Tense Terminology and Greek Language Study: A Linguistic Re-Evaluation." *SWPLL* 3 (1986): 77–86. Revised and reprinted in Porter, *Studies in the Greek New Testament: Theory and Practice*, 39–48. SBG 6. New York: Peter Lang, 1996.

———. "Θαυμάζω in Mark 6:6 and Luke 11:38: A Note on Monosemy." *BAGL* 2 (2013): 75–79.

———. "Time and Order in Participles in Mark and Luke: A Response to Robert Picirilli." *BBR* 17 (2007): 261–67.

———. "Translation, Exegesis, and 1 Thessalonians 2:14–15: Could a Comma Have Changed the Course of History?" *BT* 64 (2013): 82–98.

———. "Translations of the Bible (since the KJV)." In *Dictionary of Biblical Criticism and Interpretation*, edited by S. E. Porter, 362–69. London: Routledge, 2007.

———. "Two Myths: Corporate Personality and Language/Mentality Determinism." *SJT* 43 (1990): 289–307.

———. "Vague Verbs, Periphrastics, and Matthew 16:19." *FN* 1 (1988): 155–73. Revised and reprinted in *Studies in the Greek New Testament: Theory and Practice*, by S. E. Porter, 103–24. SBG 6. New York: Peter Lang, 1996.

———. "Verbal Aspect and Discourse Function in Mark 16:1–8: Three Significant Instances." In *Studies in the Greek Bible: Essays in Honor of Francis T. Gignac, S.J.*, edited by J. Corley and V. Skemp, 123–37. CBQMS 44. Washington, DC: Catholic Biblical Association of America, 2008.

———. "Verbal Aspect as a Prominence Indicator: A Response to Jody Barnard." In *Greeks, Jews, and Christians: Historical, Religious, and Philological Studies in Honor of Jesús Peláez del Rosal*, edited by L. R. Lanzillotta and I. M. Gallarte, 421–48. Córdoba: Ediciones el Almendro, 2013.

———. "Verbal Aspect in NT Greek and Bible Translation: A Review of Research." *TIC Talk* 15 (Spring 1991): 1–3.

———. *Verbal Aspect in the Greek of the New Testament, with Reference to Tense and Mood*. SBG 1. New York: Peter Lang, 1989; 2nd ed., 1993.

———. "What Can We Learn about Greek Grammar from a Mosaic?" In *The Language of the New Testament: Context, History, and Development*, edited by S. E. Porter and

A. W. Pitts, 29–41. ECHC 3; LBS 6. Leiden: Brill, 2013.

———. "What Difference Does Hermeneutics Make? Hermeneutical Theory Applied." *JD* 34 / *PasJ* 27 (July 2010): 1–50.

———. "What Does It Mean to Be 'Saved by Childbirth' (1 Timothy 2:15)?" *JSNT* 49 (1993): 87–102.

———. "What Exactly Is Theological Interpretation of Scripture, and Is It Hermeneutically Robust Enough for the Task to Which It Has Been Appointed?" In *Horizons in Hermeneutics: A Festschrift in Honor of Anthony C. Thiselton*, edited by S. E. Porter and M. R. Malcolm, 234–67. Grand Rapids: Eerdmans, 2013.

———. "Why Hasn't Literary Stylistics Caught On in New Testament Studies?" In *Discourse Studies and Biblical Interpretation: A Festschrift in Honor of Stephen H. Levinsohn*, edited by S. E. Runge, 35–57. Bellingham, WA: Logos Bible Software, 2011.

———. "Wittgenstein's Classes of Utterances and Pauline Ethical Texts." *JETS* 32 (1989): 85–97. Revised and reprinted in Porter, *Studies in the Greek New Testament: Theory and Practice*, 239–54. SBG 6. New York: Peter Lang, 1996.

———. "Word Order and Clause Structure in New Testament Greek: An Unexplored Area of Greek Linguistics Using Philippians as a Test Case." *FN* 6 (1993): 177–206.

Porter, S. E., and D. A. Carson, eds. *Biblical Greek Language and Linguistics: Open Questions in Current Research*. JSNTSup 80; SNTG 1. Sheffield: Sheffield Academic Press, 1993.

———, eds. *Discourse Analysis and Other Topics in Biblical Greek*. JSNTSup 113; SNTG 2. Sheffield: Sheffield Academic Press, 1995.

———, eds. *Linguistics and the New Testament: Critical Junctures*. JSNTSup 368; SNTG 5. Sheffield: Sheffield Academic Press, 1999.

Porter, S. E., and W. V. Cirafesi. "ὑστερέω and πίστις Χριστοῦ in Romans 3:23: A Response to Steven Enderlein." *JSPL* 3 (2013): 1–9.

Porter, S. E., and K. D. Clarke. "What Is Exegesis? An Analysis of Various Definitions." In *Handbook to Exegesis of the New Testament*, edited by S. E. Porter, 3–21. NTTS 25. Leiden: Brill, 1997.

Porter, S. E., and A. K. Gabriel. *Johannine Writings and Apocalyptic: An Annotated Bibliography*. JOST 1. Leiden: Brill, 2013.

Porter, S. E., and N. J. C. Gotteri. "Ambiguity, Vagueness and the Working Systemic Linguist." *SWPLL* 2 (1985): 105–18.

Porter, S. E., and M. B. O'Donnell. "Building and Examining Linguistic Phenomena in a Corpus of Representative Papyri." In *The Language of the Papyri*, edited by T. V. Evans and D. D. Obbink, 287–311. Oxford: Oxford University Press, 2010.

———. "Comparative Discourse Analysis as a Tool in Assessing Translations Using Luke 16:19–31 as a Test Case." In *Translating the New Testament: Text, Translation, Theology*, edited by S. E. Porter and M. J. Boda, 185–99. MNTS. Grand Rapids: Eerdmans, 2009.

———. "Conjunctions, Clines and Levels of Discourse." *FN* 20 (2007): 3–14.

———. "The Greek Verbal Network Viewed from a Probabilistic Standpoint: An Exercise in Hallidayan Linguistics." *FN* 14 (2001): 3–41.

———. "The Implications of Textual Variants for Authenticating the Activities of Jesus." In *Authenticating the Activities of Jesus*, edited by B. Chilton and C. A. Evans, 121–51. NTTS 28.2. Leiden: Brill, 1999.

———. "The Implications of Textual Variants for Authenticating the Words of Jesus." In *Authenticating the Words of Jesus*, edited by B. Chilton and C. A. Evans, 97–133. NTTS 28.1. Leiden: Brill, 1999.

———. "'On the Shoulders of Giants'—The Expansion and Application of the Louw-Nida Lexicon." Paper presented at the annual meeting of the Society of Biblical Literature, Philadelphia, Pennsylvania, November 19–22, 2005.

———. "Semantics and Patterns of Argumentation in the Book of Romans: Definitions, Proposals, Data and Experiments." In *Diglossia and Other Topics in New Testament Linguistics*, edited by S. E. Porter, 154–204.

JSNTSup 193; SNTG 6. Sheffield: Sheffield Academic Press, 2000.

———. "Theoretical Issues for Corpus Linguistics and the Study of Ancient Languages." In *Corpus Linguistics by the Lune: A Festschrift for Geoffrey Leech*, edited by A. Wilson, P. Rayson, and T. McEnery, 119–37. LSL 8. Frankfurt am Main: Peter Lang, 2003.

———. "The Vocative Case in Greek: Addressing the Case at Hand." In *Grammatica intellectio Scripturae: Saggi filologici di Greco biblico in onore di Lino Cignelli OFM*, edited by R. Pierri, 35–48. SBFA 68. Jerusalem: Franciscan Printing Press, 2006.

Porter, S. E., and H. T. Ong. "'Standard of Faith' or 'Measure of a Trusteeship'? A Study in Romans 12:3—A Response." *JGRChJ* 9 (2013): 97–103.

Porter, S. E., and A. W. Pitts. "New Testament Greek Language and Linguistics in Recent Research." *CBR* 6 (2008): 214–55.

———. "Πίστις with a Preposition and Genitive Modifier: Lexical, Semantic, and Syntactic Considerations in the πίστις Χριστοῦ Discussion." In *The Faith of Jesus Christ: Exegetical, Biblical, and Theological Studies*, edited by M. F. Bird and P. M. Sprinkle, 33–53. Peabody, MA: Hendrickson; Carlisle: Paternoster, 2009.

Porter, S. E., and W. J. Porter. "P. Vindob. G 26225: A New Romanos Melodus Papyrus in the Vienna Collection." *JÖB* 52 (2002): 135–48.

Porter, S. E., and J. T. Reed, eds. *Discourse Analysis and the New Testament: Approaches and Results*. JSNTSup 170; SNTG 4. Sheffield: Sheffield Academic Press, 1999.

———. *Fundamentals of New Testament Greek: Workbook*. Grand Rapids: Eerdmans, 2010.

———. "Greek Grammar since BDF: A Retrospective and Prospective Analysis." *FN* 4 (1991): 143–64.

Porter, S. E., J. T. Reed, and M. B. O'Donnell. *Fundamentals of New Testament Greek*. Grand Rapids: Eerdmans, 2010.

Porter, S. E., and J. C. Robinson. *Hermeneutics: An Introduction to Interpretive Theory*. Grand Rapids: Eerdmans, 2011.

Porter, S. E., and B. M. Stovell, eds. *Biblical Hermeneutics: Five Views*. Downers Grove, IL: IVP Academic, 2012.

Porter, S. E., and D. Tombs, eds. *Approaches to New Testament Study*. JSNTSup 120. Sheffield: JSOT Press, 1995.

Powell, M. A. *What Is Narrative Criticism? A New Approach to the Bible*. London: SPCK, 1990.

Preuschen, E. *Vollständiges griechisch-deutsches Handwörterbuch zu den Schriften des Neuen Testaments und der übrigen urchristlichen Literatur*. Gießen: Töpelmann, 1910.

Prince, G. *A Grammar of Stories: An Introduction*. DPLSMi 13. The Hague: Mouton, 1973.

———. *Narratology: The Form and Functioning of Narrative*. JLSMa 108. Berlin: Mouton, 1982.

Propp, V. *The Mythology of the Folk Tale*. Translated by L. Scott. Austin: University of Texas Press, 1968.

Pryke, E. J. *Redactional Style in the Marcan Gospel: A Study of Syntax and Vocabulary as Guides to Redaction in Mark*. SNTSMS 33. Cambridge: Cambridge University Press, 1978.

Quinn, J. D., and W. C. Wacker. *The First and Second Letters to Timothy: A New Translation with Notes and Commentary*. ECC. Grand Rapids: Eerdmans, 2000.

Radney, J. R. "Some Factors That Influence Fronting in Koine Clauses." *OPTT* 2 (1988): 1–79.

Rahner, K. *The Trinity*. Translated by J. Donceel. New York: Seabury, 1974.

Rawlings, H. R., III. *A Semantic Study of Prophasis to 400 BC*. Wiesbaden: F. Steiner, 1975.

Reddish, M. G. *An Introduction to the Gospels*. Nashville: Abingdon, 1997.

Reed, J. T. *A Discourse Analysis of Philippians: Method and Rhetoric in the Debate over Literary Integrity*. JSNTSup 136. Sheffield: Sheffield Academic Press, 1997.

———. "The Infinitive with Two Substantival Accusatives: An Ambiguous Construction?" *NovT* 33 (1991): 1–27.

Reiser, M. *Syntax und Stil des Markusevangeliums im Licht der hellenistischen Volksliteratur.* WUNT 2/11. Tübingen: Mohr Siebeck, 1984.

Resseguie, J. L. *Narrative Criticism of the New Testament: An Introduction.* Grand Rapids: Baker Academic, 2005.

———. *Strange Gospel: Narrative Design and Point of View in John.* BIS 56. Leiden: Brill, 2001.

Rhoads, D. "Narrative Criticism and the Gospel of Mark." *JAAR* 50 (1982): 411–34.

———. *Reading Mark: Engaging the Gospel.* Minneapolis: Fortress, 2004.

Rhoads, D., J. Dewey, and D. Michie. *Mark as Story: An Introduction to the Narrative of a Gospel.* 2nd ed. Minneapolis: Fortress, 1999. 3rd ed., 2012.

Rhoads, D., and D. Michie. *Mark as Story: An Introduction to the Narrative of a Gospel.* Philadelphia: Fortress, 1982.

Richards, I. A. *Practical Criticism: A Study of Literary Judgment.* New York: Harcourt, Brace, 1929.

Richardson, S. *The Homeric Narrator.* Nashville: Vanderbilt University Press, 1990.

Rijksbaron, A. *The Syntax and Semantics of the Verb in Classical Greek: An Introduction.* Amsterdam: Gieben, 1984. 3rd ed., 2002.

Rimmon-Kenan, S. *Narrative Fiction: Contemporary Poetics.* London: Methuen, 1983.

Roberts, C. H. *Manuscript, Society and Belief in Early Christian Egypt.* London: British Academy; Oxford University Press, 1979.

Robertson, A. T. *A Grammar of the Greek New Testament in the Light of Historical Research.* 4th ed. Nashville: Broadman, 1934.

Robins, R. H. "Polysemy and the Lexicographer." In *Studies in Lexicography,* edited by R. Burchfield, 52–75. Oxford: Clarendon, 1987.

Robinson, M. A. "Rule 9, Isolated Variants, and the 'Test-Tube' Nature of the NA[27]/UBS[4] Text: A Byzantine-Priority Perspective." In *Translating the New Testament: Text, Translation, Theology,* edited by S. E. Porter and M. J. Boda, 27–61. Grand Rapids: Eerdmans, 2009.

Rohrbaugh, R., ed. *The Social Sciences and New Testament Interpretation.* Peabody, MA: Hendrickson, 1996.

Roloff, J. *Der erste Brief an Timotheus.* EKK 15. Zurich: Benziger, 1988.

Rudolph, K. *Gnosis: The Nature and History of Gnosticism.* Translated by R. McL. Wilson. New York: HarperCollins, 1984.

Rudolph, M. A. "Beyond Guthrie? Text-Linguistics and New Testament Studies." *FN* 26 (2013): 27–47.

Ruhl, C. *On Monosemy: A Study in Linguistic Semantics.* New York: SUNY Press, 1989.

Ruipérez, M. S. *Estructura del sistema de aspectos y tiempos del verbo griego antigua: Análisis funcional sincrónico.* Salamanca: Colegio Trilingue de la Universidad, 1954.

Runge, S. E. "Contrastive Substitution and the Greek Verb: Reassessing Porter's Argument." *NovT* 56 (2014): 154–73.

———. *Discourse Grammar of the Greek New Testament: A Practical Introduction for Teaching and Exegesis.* Peabody, MA: Hendrickson, 2010.

Russell, B. "Descriptions." In *The Philosophy of Language,* edited by A. P. Martinisch, 212–18. 2nd ed. Oxford: Oxford University Press, 1990.

Salkie, R. *Text and Discourse Analysis.* LW. London: Routledge, 1995.

Sanders, E. P. *The Tendencies of the Synoptic Tradition.* SNTSMS 9. Cambridge: Cambridge University Press, 1969.

Sapir, E. *Language: An Introduction to the Study of Speech.* New York: Harcourt, Brace, 1921.

———. *Selected Writings in Language, Culture, and Personality.* Edited by D. G. Mandelbaum. Berkeley: University of California Press, 1984.

Sauge, A. *Les degrés du verbe: Sens et formation du parfait en grec ancient.* Bern: Peter Lang, 2000.

Saussure, F. de. *Course in General Linguistics.* Translated by W. Baskin. Edited by C. Bally, A. Sechehaye, and A. Reidlinger. London: Fontana, 1959.

Schiffrin, D. *Approaches to Discourse.* Oxford: Blackwell, 1994.

———. *Discourse Markers*. SIS 5. Cambridge: Cambridge University Press, 1987.

Schiffrin, D., D. Tannen, and H. E. Hamilton, eds. *The Handbook of Discourse Analysis*. Oxford: Blackwell, 2001.

Schlesinger, I. M. "The Wax and Wane of Whorfian Views." In *The Influence of Language on Culture and Thought: Essays in Honor of Joshua A. Fishman's Sixty-Fifth Birthday*, edited by R. L. Cooper and B. Spolsky, 7–44. Berlin: de Gruyter, 1991.

Schmithals, W. *Gnosticism in Corinth: An Investigation of the Letters to the Corinthians*. Translated by J. E. Steely. Nashville: Abingdon, 1971.

———. *Paul and the Gnostics*. Translated by J. E. Steely. Nashville: Abingdon, 1972.

Schnabel, E. J. *Early Christian Mission*. 2 vols. Downers Grove, IL: InterVarsity, 2004.

Schnelle, U. *Theology of the New Testament*. Translated by M. E. Boring. Grand Rapids: Baker Academic, 2009.

Schoedel, W. R. *Athenagoras: Legatio; and, De resurrectione*. Oxford: Clarendon, 1972.

Scholes, R., and R. Kellogg. *The Nature of Narrative*. New York: Oxford University Press, 1966.

Schreiner, T. R. *New Testament Theology: Magnifying God in Christ*. Grand Rapids: Baker Academic, 2008.

Schweizer, E. *The Good News according to Matthew*. Translated by D. E. Green. Atlanta: John Knox, 1975.

Schwyzer, E. *Griechische Grammatik auf der Grundlage von Karl Brugmanns "Griechischer Grammatik."* 4 vols. HA 2/1. Munich: Beck, 1939–71.

Scott, E. F. *The Pastoral Epistles*. MNTC. London: Hodder & Stoughton, 1936.

Scott, G. "The Foundation of the Doctrine of the Trinity: The Early Church." In *The Trinity: An Essential for Faith in Our Time*, edited by A. Stirling, 109–38. Nappanee, IN: Evangel, 2000.

Searle, J. "Proper Names." In *Philosophical Logic*, edited by P. F. Strawson, 89–96. ORP. Oxford: Oxford University Press, 1967.

———. "Proper Names and Intentionality." In *The Philosophy of Language*, edited by A. P. Martinisch, 330–46. 2nd ed. Oxford: Oxford University Press, 1990.

Seifrid, M. A. *Justification by Faith: The Origin and Development of a Central Pauline Theme*. NovTSup 68. Leiden: Brill, 1992.

Shepherd, D. "'Do You Love Me?': A Narrative-Critical Reappraisal of ἀγαπάω and φιλέω in John 21:15–17." *JBL* 129 (2010): 777–92.

Shimasaki, K. *Focus Structure in Biblical Hebrew: A Study of Word Order and Information Structure*. Bethesda, MD: CDL Press, 2002.

Short, C. "The Order of Words in Attic Greek Prose: An Essay." In *An English Greek Lexicon: With Many New Articles, an Appendix of Proper Names, and Pillon's "Greek Synonyms,"* by C. D. Yonge, edited by H. Drisler, i–cxv. New York: Harper, 1870.

Sicking, C. M. J., and P. Stork. *Two Studies in the Semantics of the Verb in Classical Greek*. Mnemosyne 160. Leiden: Brill, 1996.

Sievers, J. *Synopsis of the Greek Sources for the Hasmonean Period: 1–2 Maccabees and Josephus, "War" 1 and "Antiquities" 12–14*. SubBi 20. Rome: Pontifical Biblical Institute, 2001.

Sihler, A. L. *New Comparative Grammar of Greek and Latin*. New York: Oxford University Press, 1995.

Silva, M. *Biblical Words and their Meaning: An Introduction to Lexical Semantics*. Rev. ed. Grand Rapid: Zondervan, 1994.

———. "Bilingualism and the Character of Palestinian Greek." *Bib* 61 (1980): 198–219. Reprinted in *The Language of the New Testament: Classic Essays*, edited by S. E. Porter, 205–26. JSNTSup 60. Sheffield: JSOT Press, 1991.

Sim, M. G. *Marking Thought and Talk in New Testament Greek: New Light from Linguistics on the Particles* ἵνα *and* ὅτι. Eugene, OR: Pickwick, 2010.

Sinclair, J., ed. *Collins Cobuild English Grammar*. London: HarperCollins, 1990.

———, ed. *Collins Cobuild English Language Dictionary*. London: HarperCollins, 1987. 2nd ed. 1995.

———. *Corpus, Concordance, Collocation.* Oxford: Oxford University Press, 1991.

———, ed. *Looking Up: An Account of the Cobuild Project in Lexical Computing.* London: HarperCollins, 1987.

Slobin, D. I. "From 'Thought and Language' to 'Thinking for Speaking.'" In *Rethinking Linguistic Relativity*, edited by J. J. Gumperz and S. C. Levinson, 70–96. SSCFL 17. Cambridge: Cambridge University Press, 1996.

Sluiter, I. "Causal ἵνα—Sound Greek." *Glotta* 70 (1992): 39–53.

Smith, R. E. "The Unmarked Order of Pronominal Objects and Indirect Objects." *START* 12 (1984): 24–26.

Smyth, H. W. *Greek Grammar.* Revised by G. Messing. Rev. ed. Cambridge, MA: Harvard University Press, 1956.

Snyder, J. A. *Language and Identity in Ancient Narratives.* WUNT 2/370. Tübingen: Mohr Siebeck, 2014.

Sollors, W., ed. *The Return of Thematic Criticism.* Cambridge, MA: Harvard University Press, 1993.

Song, J. J. *Word Order.* RSL. Cambridge: Cambridge University Press, 2012.

Spencer, A. B. *Paul's Literary Style: A Stylistic and Historical Comparison of II Corinthians 11:16–12:13, Romans 8:9–39, and Philippians 3:2–4:13.* Jackson, MS: Evangelical Theological Society, 1984. Reprint, Lanham, MD: University Press of America, 1998.

Spencer, A., and A. R. Luís. *Clitics: An Introduction.* CTL. Cambridge: Cambridge University Press, 2012.

Spicq, C. *Saint Paul: Les Épîtres pastorales.* ÉBib. Paris: Gabalda, 1947.

Staley, J. L. *The Print's First Kiss: A Rhetorical Investigation of the Implied Reader in the Fourth Gospel.* SBLDS 82. Atlanta: Scholars Press, 1988.

———. *Reading with a Passion: Rhetoric, Autobiography, and the American West in the Gospel of John.* New York: Continuum, 1995.

Stamps, D. L. "Rhetorical and Narratological Criticism." In *Handbook to Exegesis of the New Testament*, edited by S. E. Porter, 219–40. NTTS 25. Leiden: Brill, 1997.

Stauffer, E. *New Testament Theology.* Translated by J. Marsh. London: SCM, 1955.

Stein, R. H. *Studying the Synoptic Gospels: Origin and Interpretation.* 2nd ed. Grand Rapids: Baker Academic, 2001.

Steiner, P. "The Conceptual Basis of Prague Structuralism." In *Sound, Sign, and Meaning: Quinquagenary of the Prague Linguistic Circle*, edited by L. Matejka, 351–85. Ann Arbor: University of Michigan, 1976.

Sternberg, M. *Expositional Modes and Temporal Ordering in Fiction.* Baltimore: Johns Hopkins University Press, 1978.

———. *The Poetics of Biblical Narrative: Ideological Literature and the Drama of Reading.* ISBL. Bloomington: Indiana University Press, 1985.

Stettler, C. "The Opponents at Colossae." In *Paul and His Opponents*, edited by S. E. Porter, 169–200. PAST 2. Leiden: Brill, 2005.

Stevens, G. B. *The Theology of the New Testament.* Edinburgh: T&T Clark, 1911.

Stibbe, M. W. G. *John as Storyteller: Narrative Criticism and the Fourth Gospel.* SNTSMS 73. Cambridge: Cambridge University Press, 1992.

Stirling, A., ed. *The Trinity: An Essential for Faith in Our Time.* Nappanee, IN: Evangel, 2000.

Stovell, B. M. *Mapping Metaphorical Discourse in the Fourth Gospel: John's Eternal King.* LBS 5. Leiden: Brill, 2012.

Strecker, G. *Theology of the New Testament.* Translated by M. E. Boring. Berlin: de Gruyter, 2000.

Stubbs, M. *Discourse Analysis: The Sociolinguistic Analysis of Natural Language.* Oxford: Blackwell, 1983.

———. *Text and Corpus Analysis.* Oxford: Blackwell, 1996.

Stump, G. T. *Inflectional Morphology: A Theory of Paradigm Structure.* CSL 93. Cambridge: Cambridge University Press, 2001.

Sumney, J. L. *Identifying Paul's Opponents: The Question of Method in 2 Corinthians.* JSNTSup 40. Sheffield: JSOT Press, 1990.

———. "Servants of Satan," "False Brothers" and Other Opponents of Paul. JSNTSup 188. Sheffield: Sheffield Academic Press, 1999.

———. "Studying Paul's Opponents: Advances and Challenges." In Paul and His Opponents, edited by S. E. Porter, 7–58. PAST 2. Leiden: Brill, 2005.

Sundwall, J. "Die Zusammensetzung des Markusevangeliums." AAAH 9 (1934): 1–86.

Swart, G. J. "Non-past Referring Imperfects in the New Testament: A Test Case for an Anti-anti-anti-Porter Position." HvTSt 61 (2005): 1085–99.

Tannehill, R. The Narrative Unity of Luke-Acts: A Literary Interpretation. 2 vols. Minneapolis: Fortress, 1986–90.

Taylor, A. "The Change from SOV to SVO in Ancient Greek." LVC 6 (1994): 1–37.

———. "The Distribution of Object Clitics in Koine Greek." In Indo-European Perspectives, edited by M. R. V. Southern, 285–315. Washington, DC: Institute for the Study of Man, 2002.

———. "A Prosodic Account of Clitic Position in Ancient Greek." In Approaching Second: Second Position Clitics and Related Phenomena, edited by A. Halpern and A. Zwicky, 477–503. Stanford, CA: CSLI Publications, 1996.

Taylor, N. H. "Palestinian Christianity and the Caligula Crisis, Part II: The Markan Eschatological Discourse." JSNT 62 (1996): 13–41.

Taylor, V. The Gospel according to St. Mark. London: Macmillan, 1959.

Teeple, H. M. "The Greek Article with Personal Names in the Synoptic Gospels." NTS 19 (1972–73): 302–17.

Thackeray, H. St. J. A Grammar of the Old Testament in Greek: According to the Septuagint. Cambridge: Cambridge University Press, 1909.

Thatcher, T., and S. D. Moore, eds. Anatomies of Narrative Criticism: The Past, Present, and Futures of the Fourth Gospel as Literature. SBLRBS 55. Atlanta: Society of Biblical Literature, 2008.

Thayer, J. H. A Greek-English Lexicon of the New Testament. New York: American Book Company, 1886. 2nd ed., 1889.

Thibault, P. J. Re-Reading Saussure: The Dynamics of Signs in Social Life. London: Routledge, 1997.

Thielman, F. Theology of the New Testament: A Canonical and Synthetic Approach. Grand Rapids: Zondervan, 2005.

Thiselton, A. C. The First Epistle to the Corinthians. NIGTC. Grand Rapids: Eerdmans, 2000.

Thompson, G. "On the Order of Words in Plato and Saint Matthew." Link 2 (1939): 7–17.

———. "The Postponement of Interrogatives in Attic Drama." CQ 33 (1939): 147–52.

Thrall, M. E. Greek Particles in the New Testament: Linguistic and Exegetical Studies. NTTS 3. Leiden: Brill, 1962.

Tice, T. Schleiermacher. Nashville: Abingdon, 2006.

Todorov, T. The Poetics of Prose. Translated by R. Howard. Oxford: Blackwell, 1977.

Tolbert, M. A. Sowing the Gospel: Mark's World in Literary-Historical Perspective. Minneapolis: Fortress, 1989.

Tolmie, D. F. Jesus' Farewell to the Disciples: John 13:1–17:6 in Narratological Perspective. BIS 12. Leiden: Brill, 1995.

Torremans, P. L. C. "Choice of Law regarding Copyright and the Dead Sea Scrolls: The Basic Principles." In On Scrolls, Artefacts and Intellectual Property, edited by T. H. Lim, H. L. MacQueen, and C. M. Carmichael, 116–27. JSPSup 38. Sheffield: Sheffield Academic Press, 2001.

Tovey, D. Narrative Art and Act in the Fourth Gospel. JSNTSup 151. Sheffield: Sheffield Academic Press, 1997.

Towner, P. H. The Letters to Timothy and Titus. NICNT. Grand Rapids: Eerdmans, 2006.

Traube, L. Nomina sacra: Versuch einer Geschichte der christlichen Kürzung. QULPM 2. Darmstadt: Wissenschaftliche Buchgesellschaft, 1967.

Treier, D. J. Introducing Theological Interpretation of Scripture: Recovering a Christian Practice. Grand Rapids: Baker Academic, 2008.

Trenkner, S. *Le style kai dans le récital attique oral*. Brussels: Éditions de l'Institut d'Études Polonaises en Belgique, 1948.

Tuckett, C. M. "'Nomina Sacra': Yes and No." In *The Biblical Canons*, edited by J.-M. Auwers and H. J. de Jonge, 431–58. BETL 163. Leuven: Peeters, 2003.

———. *The Revival of the Griesbach Hypothesis: An Analysis and Appraisal*. SNTSMS 44. Cambridge: Cambridge University Press, 1983.

Turner, C. H. "Marcan Usage: Notes, Critical and Exegetical, on the Second Gospel [3]." *JTS* 26 (1924–25): 145–56.

———. "Marcan Usage: Notes, Critical and Exegetical, on the Second Gospel [7]." *JTS* 28 (1926–27): 9–30.

Turner, N. *A Grammar of New Testament Greek*. Vol. 3, *Syntax*. Edinburgh: T&T Clark, 1963.

Ullmann, S. *The Principles of Semantics*. 2nd ed. Oxford: Blackwell, 1957.

Uspensky, B. *A Poetics of Composition: The Structure of the Artistic Text and Typology of a Compositional Form*. Translated by V. Zavarin and S. Wittig. Berkeley: University of California Press, 1973.

Vachek, J. *The Linguistic School of Prague: An Introduction to Its Theory and Practice*. Bloomington: Indiana University Press, 1966.

———, ed. *A Prague School Reader in Linguistics*. Bloomington: Indiana University Press, 1964.

van der Merwe, C. H. J., J. A. Naudé, and J. H. Kroze. *A Biblical Hebrew Reference Grammar*. BLH 3. Sheffield: Sheffield Academic Press, 1999.

van Dijk, T. A., ed. *Discourse as Structure and Process*. DS 1. London: Sage, 1997.

———, ed. *Discourse Studies: A Multidisciplinary Introduction*. London: Sage, 2011.

———. *Text and Context: Explorations in the Semantics and Pragmatics of Discourse*. LLL. London: Longman, 1977.

Vassiliadis, P. ΛΟΓΟΙ ΙΗΣΟΥ: *Studies in Q*. USFISFCJ 8. Atlanta: Scholars Press, 1999.

Vendler, Z. "Verbs and Times." *PR* 66 (1957): 43–60. Reprinted in Vendler, *Linguistics in Philosophy*, 97–121. Ithaca, NY: Cornell University Press, 1967.

Vergote, J. "Grecque biblique." In *Dictionnaire de la Bible, Supplément 3*, edited by L. Pirot, cols. 1321–69. Paris: Librarie Letouzey et Ane, 1938.

Verkuyl, H. J. *A Theory of Aspectuality: The Interaction between Temporal and Atemporal Structure*. CSL 64. Cambridge: Cambridge University Press, 1993.

Voitila, A. *Présent et imparfait de l'indicatif dans le pentateuque grec: Une étude sur la syntaxe de traduction*. PFES 79. Helsinki: Sociéte d'Exégèse de Finlande; Göttingen: Vandenhoeck & Ruprecht, 2001.

Vorster, W. S. "Literary Reflections on Mark 13:5–37: A Narrated Speech of Jesus." In *Speaking of Jesus: Essays on Biblical Language, Gospel Narrative and the Historical Jesus*, edited by J. E. Botha, 203–22. NovTSup 92. Leiden: Brill, 1999.

Vos, G. *Biblical Theology: Old and New Testaments*. Grand Rapids: Eerdmans, 1948.

Wackernagel, J. *Vorlesungen über Syntax mit besonderer Berücksichtigung von Griechisch, Lateinisch und Deutsch*. 2 vols. Basel: Birkhäuser, 1926–28. ET, *Lectures on Syntax, with Special Reference to Greek, Latin, and Germanic*. Translated by D. Langslow. Oxford: Oxford University Press, 2009.

Wainwright, A. W. *The Trinity in the New Testament*. London: SPCK, 1962.

Wainwright, G. "The Doctrine of the Trinity: Where the Church Stands or Falls." *Int* 45 (1991): 117–32.

Waismann, F. *The Principles of Linguistic Philosophy*. Edited by R. Harré. London: Macmillan, 1965.

Wakker, G. C. "Purpose Clauses in Ancient Greek." In *Getting One's Words into Line: On Word Order and Functional Grammar*, edited by J. Nuyts and G. de Schutter, 89–101. FGS 5. Dordrecht: Foris, 1987.

Wall, R. W., and E. E. Lemcio. *The New Testament as Canon: A Reader in Canonical Criticism*. JSNTSup 76. Sheffield: JSOT Press, 1992.

Wallace, D. B. *Granville Sharp's Canon and Its Kin: Semantics and Significance.* SBG 14. New York: Peter Lang, 2009.

———. "Granville Sharp's Rule: A Rejoinder to Stan Porter." *JETS* 56 (2013): 101–6.

———. *Greek Grammar beyond the Basics: An Exegetical Syntax of the New Testament.* Grand Rapids: Zondervan, 1996.

———. "The Relation of Adjective to Noun in Anarthrous Constructions in the New Testament." *NovT* 26 (1984): 128–67.

———. "The Semantic Range of the Article-Noun-Kai-Noun Plural Construction in the New Testament." *GTJ* 4 (1983): 59–84.

———. "The Semantics and Exegetical Significance of the Object-Complement Construction in the New Testament." *GTJ* 6 (1985): 91–112.

———. "Sharp's Rule Revisited: A Response to Stanley Porter." *JETS* 56 (2013): 79–92.

Wardhaugh, R. *An Introduction to Sociolinguistics.* 5th ed. Oxford: Blackwell, 2006.

Watson, D. F. "A Rhetorical Analysis of Philippians and Its Implications for the Unity Question." *NovT* 30 (1988): 57–88.

Watt, J. M. *Code-Switching in Luke and Acts.* BILS 31. New York: Peter Lang, 1997.

———. "Current Landscape of Diglossia Studies: The Diglossic Continuum in First-Century Palestine." In *Diglossia and Other Topics in New Testament Linguistics,* edited by S. E. Porter, 18–36. JSNTSup 193; SNTG 6. Sheffield: Sheffield Academic Press, 2000.

———. "Of Gutterals and Galileans: The Two Slurs of Matthew 26.73." In *Diglossia and Other Topics in New Testament Linguistics,* edited by S. E. Porter, 107–20. JSNTSup 193; SNTG 6. Sheffield: Sheffield Academic Press, 2000.

———. "Some Implications of Bilingualism." In *The Language of the New Testament: Context, History, and Development,* edited by S. E. Porter and A. W. Pitts, 9–27. ECHC 3; LBS 6. Leiden: Brill, 2013.

Wedderburn A. J. M. *The Reasons for Romans.* SNTW. Edinburgh: T&T Clark, 1988.

Weiner, A. B. *The Trobrianders of Papua New Guinea.* Fort Worth: Harcourt Brace Jovanovich College, 1988.

Weinreich, U. "On the Semantic Structure of Language." In *Universals of Language,* edited by J. Greenberg, 142–216. 2nd ed. Cambridge, MA: MIT Press, 1966.

Weiss, B. *Die Briefe Pauli an Timotheus und Titus.* 7th ed. KEK 11. Göttingen: Vandenhoeck & Ruprecht, 1902.

———. "Der Gebrauch des Artikels bei den Eigennamen." *TSK* 86 (1913): 352–55.

Wellek, R., and A. Warren. *Theory of Literature.* 3rd ed. New York: Harcourt, Brace & World, 1956.

Wenham, D. *The Rediscovery of Jesus' Eschatological Discourse.* GP 4. Sheffield: JSOT Press, 1984.

Westfall, C. L. *A Discourse Analysis of the Letter to the Hebrews: The Relationship between Form and Meaning.* LNTS 297. London: T&T Clark, 2005.

Wetherell, M., S. Taylor, and S. J. Yates, eds. *Discourse Theory and Practice: A Reader.* London: Sage, 2001.

White, N. J. D. "The First and Second Epistles to Timothy and the Epistle to Titus." In vol. 4 of *The Expositor's Greek Testament,* ed. W. R. Nicoll, 55–202. London: Hodder & Stoughton, 1912. Reprint, Grand Rapids: Eerdmans, 1980.

Whorf, B. L. *Language, Thought, and Reality: Selected Writings of Benjamin Lee Whorf.* Edited by J. B. Carroll. Cambridge, MA: MIT Press, 1956.

Widdowson, H. G. *Text, Context, Pretext: Critical Issues in Discourse Analysis.* Oxford: Blackwell, 2004.

Wierzbicka, A. *Understanding Cultures through Their Key Words: English, Russian, Polish, German, and Japanese.* New York: Oxford University Press, 1997.

Wifstrand, A. *Epochs and Styles: Selected Writings on the New Testament, Greek Language and Greek Culture in the Post-Classical Era.* Edited by L. Rydbeck and S. E. Porter. Translated by D. Searby. WUNT 179. Tübingen: Mohr Siebeck, 2005.

Wilke, C. G. *Clavis Novi Testamenti philologica.* 2 vols. Leipzig: Arnold, 1841. 2nd ed., 1851. Revised ed. by C. L. W. Grimm, 1862–68. 2nd ed., 1879. 3rd ed., 1886.

Willi, A. *The Languages of Aristophanes: Aspects of Linguistic Variation in Classical Attic Greek.* Oxford: Oxford University Press, 2003.

Williams, G. *Sociolinguistics: A Sociological Critique.* London: Routledge, 1992.

Wills, J. "Homeric Particle Order." *HS* 106 (1993): 61–81.

Wilshire, L. E. "1 Timothy 2:12 Revisited: A Reply to Paul W. Barnett and Timothy J. Harris." *EvQ* 65 (1993): 43–55.

Winer, G. B. *A Grammar of the Idiom of the New Testament.* Translated by J. H. Thayer. Andover, MA: Draper, 1869.

———. *A Grammar of the New Testament Diction.* Translated by E. Masson. Edinburgh: T&T Clark, 1859.

———. *Grammatik des neutestamentlichen Sprachidioms.* Leipzig: Vogel, 1822. 6th ed., 1855. 8th ed., revised by P. W. Schmiedel. Göttingen: Vandenhoeck & Ruprecht, 1894–98.

———. *A Treatise on the Grammar of New Testament Greek, Regarded as a Sure Basis for New Testament Exegesis.* Translated by W. F. Moulton. 3rd ed. Edinburgh: T&T Clark, 1882.

Witherington, B., III. *Letters and Homilies for Hellenized Christians.* Vol. 1, *A Socio-Rhetorical Commentary on Titus, 1–2 Timothy, and 1–3 John.* Downers Grove, IL: InterVarsity; Nottingham: Apollos, 2001.

Wohlenberg, D. G. *Die Pastoralbriefe.* 3rd ed. KNT 13. Leipzig: Deichertsche, 1923.

Wolters, A. "A Semantic Study of αὐθέντης and Its Derivatives." *JGRChJ* 1 (2000): 145–75.

Wong, S. S. M. *A Classification of Semantic Case-Relations in the Pauline Epistles.* SBG 9. New York: Peter Lang, 1997.

———. "What Case Is This Case? An Application of Semantic Case in Biblical Exegesis." *JD* 1 (1994): 49–73.

Woodard, B. "Literature." In *Opening the American Mind: The Integration of Biblical Truth in the Curriculum of the University,* edited by W. D. Beck, 67–87. Grand Rapids: Baker Books, 1991.

Zerhusen, B. "An Overlooked Judean *Diglossia* in Acts 2?" *BTB* 25 (1995): 118–30.

Zerwick, M. *Untersuchungen zum Markus-Stil: Ein Beitrag zur Durcharbeitung des Neuen Testamentes.* SPIB. Rome: Pontifical Biblical Institute, 1937.

Index of Ancient Sources

Index of Modern Authors

Printed and bound by CPI Group (UK) Ltd, Croydon, CR0 4YY

10/06/2025

14686721-0001